ON THE EDGE

ON THE EDGE

A New History of 20th-Century America

DAVID A. HOROWITZ
Portland State University

PETER N. CARROLL
Stanford University

DAVID D. LEE
Western Kentucky University

WEST PUBLISHING COMPANY
ST. PAUL • NEW YORK • LOS ANGELES • SAN FRANCISCO

Copyediting: Cheryl Drivdahl
Composition: Carlisle Graphics, Rolin Graphics, Type House
Artwork: Rolin Graphics

COPYRIGHT © 1990 by   WEST PUBLISHING COMPANY
                           610 Opperman Drive
                           P.O. Box 64526
                           St. Paul, MN 55164–0526

Printed in the United States of America

97 96 95 94 93   8 7 6 5 4 3 2 1

Library of Congress Cataloging-in-Publication Data

Horowitz, David A.
  On the edge. A new history of twentieth-century America / David A.
Horowitz, Peter N. Carroll, David D. Lee.
    p. cm.
  Includes bibliographical references.
  ISBN 0-314-58086-7
  1. United States—History—20th century. 2. United States— History—1865–1921. I. Carroll, Peter N.
II. Lee, David D., 1948–   III. Title.
E741.H69 1990   89-38285
973.9—dc20   CIP

Photo Credits: Cover National Archives; **i** Culver Pictures; **1** Library of Congress; **4** Chicago Historical Society; **6** Chicago Historical Society; **11** Seaver Center for Western History Research; **13** Library of Congress; **16** Library of Congress; **18** Historical Pictures Service, Chicago; **23** Museum of Fine Arts, Boston; **28** Wide World Photos; **30** Library of Congress; **33** Library of Congress; **34** Culver Pictures; **37** Library of Congress; **38** Library of Congress; **45** Library of Congress; **48** Library of Congress; **49** Brown Brothers; **52** Brown Brothers; **55** Library of Congress; **58** Brown Brothers; **61** Library of Congress; **62** Library of Congress; **63** Library of Congress; **66** Library of Congress; **76** Brown Brothers; **78** Library of Congress; **80** U.S. Army; **89** Library of Congress; **91** Library of Congress; **94** Wide World Photos; **98** Brown Brothers; **101** National Archives; **108** National Archives; **110** Historical Pictures Service, Chicago; **112** National Archives; **113** Library of Congress; **115** State Historical Society of Wisconsin; **118** National Archives; **119** National Archives; **122** Culver Pictures; **124** Historical Pictures Service, Chicago; **131** Library of Congress; **135** Library of Congress; **138** Bettmann Archive; **144** Princeton University Library; **147** Culver Pictures; **150** Historical Pictures Service, Chicago; **152** Bettmann Archive; **157** Brown Brothers; **161** Library of Congress; **164** The Granger Collection; **168** Culver Pictures; **170** Museum of the City of New York; **175** Herbert Hoover Library; **177** Minnesota Historical Society; **180** Oregon Historical Society; **182** Historical Pictures Service, Chicago; **185** Museum of Modern Art; **189** The Archives of Labor and Urban Affairs, Wayne State University; **190** Bettmann Archive; **194** Bettmann Archive; **201** National Archives; **207** Bettmann Archive; **208** Historical Pictures Service, Chicago; **210** Historical Pictures Service, Chicago; **212** Wide World Photos; **217** Bettmann Archive; **221** Library of Congress; **225** Bettmann Archive; **230** Bettmann Archive; **231** Bettmann Archive; **235** Bettmann Archive; **241** Bettmann Archive; **247** Franklin Delano Roosevelt Library; **249** Library of Congress; **254** Bettmann Archive; **256** Bettmann Archive; **260** Historical Pictures Service, Chicago; **262** Library of Congress; **263** Culver Pictures; **264** Culver Pictures; **271** U.S. Navy; **278** Historical Pictures Service, Chicago; **282** Henrik Shipstead Papers, Minnesota Historical Society; **288** Historical Pictures Service, Chicago; **290** Wide World Photos; **292** Franklin Delano Roosevelt Library; **296** Historical Pictures Service, Chicago; **300** Franklin Delano Roosevelt Library; **302** Library of Congress; **305** Wide World Photos (*cont.*)

for David W. Noble
and to the memory of Lois Noble

CONTENTS

PREFACE

On the Edge: A New History of Twentieth-Century America is an interpretive synthesis that follows two major themes. First, it traces the development of the corporate state and the consolidation of government power through World War II and over forty years of Cold War, a period American leaders have defined as one of risk and global instability. Second, it sets these developments within the context of emerging economic patterns, demographic trends, and social values at home. Both the challenges and dilemmas of the years since the 1890s have placed American society on the edge of both possibility and disaster. Our text chronicles this confrontation.

We have taken pains to integrate the history of domestic events and foreign policy, economic developments and cultural attitudes, political behavior and social structure. But On the Edge goes beyond the history of conflict among powerful institutional leaders to portray the significant historical roles played by nominally powerless people—the working class and poor as well as women and the nation's racial, ethnic, and cultural minorities. Indeed, the tension between the powerful and powerless comprises a major thread in the drama that defines American society since the 1890s.

Our intention is to stimulate students to a critical approach to twentieth century American history. Although chapters follow a general chronological outline, they are divided into thematic sections to encourage conceptualization and provocative discussion. Four chapters focus primarily on cultural and social developments. Each chapter also includes two or three biographical sketches which use the lives of individuals to illuminate important themes of the period. Chapter reading lists concentrate on recent hardcover editions found in most college libraries. We have simplified graphs, charts, and tables for quick reference and easy comprehension. The material in this book also appears in two separate volumes, On The Edge: A History of America From 1890 to 1945 and On the Edge: A History of America Since World War II, both available from this publisher.

David Horowitz wishes to extend thanks to Gloria E. Myers and to the Department of History at Portland State University, which provided the steady clerical services of Diane Gould, Diane Lynch, and Lee Ellington. Peter Carroll acknowledges the counsel and support of Jeannette Ferrary. David Lee thanks his fellow historians at Western Kentucky University. Their commitment to fine teaching and sound scholarship creates a truly nurturing environment for the serious study of history. The authors would further like to acknowledge the support and assistance of Acquiring Editor Clark G. Baxter and Production Editor Jeffrey T. Carpenter. Finally, we would like to thank our reviewers: Selma Berrol, Lloyd J. Graybar, Athan Theoharis, Neil R. Stout, James P. Johnson, William M. Leary, Leo P. Ribuffo, Joseph S. Uris, William Tanner, Ronald Lora, Joseph A. Dowling, Kenneth O'Brien, and Eckard V. Toy, Jr.

—David A. Horowitz, Peter N. Carroll, David D. Lee

1

THE NEW CENTURY

I n dry, bureaucratic phrases, the 1890 United States census made a startling
declaration. "Up to and including 1880," the census takers reported, "the
country had a frontier of settlement, but at present the unsettled area has
been so broken into by isolated bodies of settlement that there can hardly be
said to be a frontier line." The closing of the western frontier roughly
coincided with the opening of a vibrant new urban-industrial frontier marked
by many of the same characteristics associated with the westward movement:
an apparent social mobility, the clash of opposing cultures, high levels of
violence, the harsh exploitation of physical and human resources. As the
twentieth century dawned, the city and the corporation began to shape a new
society in the forge of industrialism. The central values of agrarian society—
individualism, competition, and localism—faced challenges by the forces of
bureaucracy, consolidation, and nationalism. Organizations replaced individuals as the building blocks of modern life, and people and institutions
adjusted uneasily to a new era.

THE TECHNOLOGICAL METROPOLIS

"The city has become the central feature of modern civilization," wrote
reformer and social scientist Frederic Howe in 1906. "Man has entered on an
urban age." The twentieth-century industrial city differed greatly from the
mercantile cities that had dotted the land a few decades earlier. The first
national census taken in 1790 found that only one person in twenty lived in

Exhibit 1–1. United States Population, 1880–1920
(in rounded millions based on decennial census)

Year	Population
1880	50.2 m
1890	62.9 m
1900	76.0 m
1910	92.0 m
1920	105.7 m

Source: *Historical Statistics of the United States, Colonial Times to 1970* (U.S. Department of Commerce, 1975).

Exhibit 1–2. Urban* Population as a
Percentage of Total Population, 1880–1920

Year	Percentage
1880	28
1890	35
1900	40
1910	46
1920	51

*According to the Census Bureau, an urban area is one with a population of at least 2500.
Source: *Historical Statistics of the United States, Colonial Times to 1970* (U.S. Department of Commerce, 1975).

an urban area; a century later one in three was an urbanite, and by 1920 one in two lived in a city. Between 1890 and 1920, the urban population grew 300 percent—ten times the rate of the rural population. Some urbanization occurred in the South and on the West Coast, while the cities of the Northeastern Seaboard and the Upper Midwest grew with amazing speed. Chicago symbolized the new urban-industrial frontier: a city of one-half million in 1880, it doubled in size during the next decade and then almost doubled again to reach a population of nearly two million by 1900. In 1910, 70 percent of the nation's total urban population lived in the Northeast and 65 percent of that region's population lived in urban areas.

This spectacular growth coincided with a series of technological innovations that contributed to the changing nature of American cities. R building in the aftermath of the Great Fire of 1871, Chicago developed one emblem of the American metropolis, the skyscraper. In the mid-1880s, William Le Baron Jenney used a steel skeleton as a frame for the Home Insurance Building, a ten-story building without supporting walls for the upper part of the structure. (Jenney supposedly got the idea after casually laying a book on his wife's wire bird cage.) Drawing on Jenney's innovation, the Chicago school of architecture led by Louis Sullivan launched a new era in urban construction. The skyscraper, Sullivan declared, "must be every inch a proud and soaring thing, rising in exultation that from bottom to top it is a unit without a single dissenting line."

In 1896, the New York Chamber of Commerce denounced skyscrapers as "not consistent with public health," and the *New York Times* endorsed a limit on the height of buildings. Even Sullivan, known as the father of the skyscraper, feared that the new architectural style was "profoundly antisocial." Nevertheless, like great cities, skyscrapers reflected a new emphasis on the concentration of economic activity. Commercial and industrial consolidation, in turn, made property in downtown areas scarcer and more expensive. To maximize available space, cities began to build upward. Thus skyscrapers became status symbols and a source of competition among rival cities. Between 1885 and 1913, skyscrapers stretched from Jenney's ten-story pioneer in Chicago to the fifty-five–story Woolworth Building in Manhattan.

Elegant skyscrapers depended on the relatively mundane elevator. In 1853, Vermont inventor Elisha G. Otis demonstrated a device to protect passengers from injury in the event a cable broke while hoisting a platform. Four years later, Otis installed his first elevator in an existing building, a New York department store. The advent of electric power in the 1880s made elevators much faster and more efficient. "In the tall buildings are the most modern and rapid elevators," wrote a Chicago visitor, "machines that fly through the towers like glass balls from a trap at a shooting contest." In the spirit of the times, Otis built a company around his idea and made a fortune.

The elevator offered one dramatic illustration of the widespread impact of electricity. Another was provided by the telephone, exhibited by inventor Alexander Graham Bell at the Centennial Exposition in Philadelphia in 1876. At the turn of the century, only one person in a hundred owned such a device, but by 1912 one person in ten had a telephone. "What startles and frightens backward Europeans," an English visitor commented, "is the

The first skyscraper, Chicago's ten-story Home Insurance Building, used a wrought- and cast-iron internal skeleton for the first six stories and steel beams for the next four. Jenney purposely disguised the innovative frame to make the structure resemble a conventional building.

efficiency and fearful universality of the telephone." Electric lighting, first successfully demonstrated by Thomas Edison in 1879, also spread rapidly in the early twentieth century. A skilled publicist as well as inventor, Edison decorated his laboratory with forty incandescent bulbs during the 1879 Christmas season. The shrewd Edison established a highly successful research laboratory expressly for the purpose of developing new and marketable uses for electric power. His most notable successes included the motion

Exhibit 1–3. Telephones per Thousand of Population

1880	1.1
1890	3.7
1900	17.6
1910	82.0
1920	123.4

Source: *Historical Statistics of the United States, Colonial Times to 1970* (U.S. Department of Commerce, 1975).

picture projector and the phonograph. Simultaneously, other inventors received patents on such electric-powered consumer goods as irons, fans, stoves, and sewing machines.

Technological developments in transportation also dramatically influenced the emerging American metropolis. The "walking city" of the mid–nineteenth century had blended home and work, rich and poor, all in fairly close proximity; most pedestrians could reach nearly any spot in a typical city in thirty minutes. The opening of the Brooklyn Bridge in 1883 symbolized the growing distinction between downtown and surrounding communities. Charles Dickens had called Brooklyn "a kind of sleeping place for New York," but no reliable transportation linked the two across the East River until John Augustus Roebling and his son Washington completed their famous bridge, a structure hailed by an architectural critic as "one of the great and most honorable works of engineering." The appearance of the electric street car or trolley around 1890 substantially increased the distance a commuter could easily travel in a day and made suburbs a characteristic of virtually all major American cities. Within a decade, the development of electric-powered railroad cars made underground railways or subways a reality, and in 1900 New York City began construction of what would ultimately be the nation's largest subway system. Opened in 1904, this subway connected lower Manhattan to the borough of Brooklyn.

Better transportation lessened the importance of living close to places of employment and made it possible for prosperous people to escape the dirt and congestion of the central city by moving to more pastoral locations on the outskirts. By the early 1900s, a new form of transportation, the automobile, began to revolutionize American industry. The first cars appeared almost literally as horseless carriages—some even had sockets for whips—but steadily the general outline of the standard American automobile took shape. By 1910, the tiller steering device had given way to a steering wheel placed on the left side of the vehicle, and most cars had gasoline-powered, water-cooled, four-cylinder engines. In 1908, Henry Ford, a Michigan farm boy who had moved to Detroit, unveiled his famous Model-T, an inexpensive automobile that the owner could easily drive and repair. By 1916, Ford was selling a half million Model-Ts annually at a price of $360 and was on the way to making the automobile a basic feature of American life.

Other car manufacturers, most notably General Motors, soon flourished in the Detroit area, and by 1920, more than nine million motor vehicles traveled the nation's highways. Recognizing the growing importance of the automobile, Congress passed the Federal Highway Act of 1916, which required that

People, horses, trolleys, and motor vehicles choke the intersection of Dearborn and Randolph Streets in downtown Chicago, 1910.

states, rather than counties, plan, construct, and maintain highways. This law marked an important step toward creating a national system of two-lane, all-weather, intercity roads.

LIFE IN THE METROPOLIS

The interaction of a growing population with developing technology rapidly altered the structure of urban life. The blended city of the nineteenth century

Exhibit 1–4. Passenger Car Registrations, 1900–1920
(in rounded thousands)

1900	8
1905	77
1910	458
1915	2332
1920	8132

Source: *Historical Statistics of the United States, Colonial Times to 1970* (U.S. Department of Commerce, 1975).

gave way to the specialized and segmented city of the twentieth. Corporate skyscrapers, retail outlets, entertainment facilities, and professional and financial offices dominated the downtown core, which was also the terminus for mass transit systems. Beyond this area lay manufacturing plants served by the railroads and other major transportation links. The next ring consisted of housing for the working class and poor. After that came the "zone of emergence," inhabited by people who had made a relatively successful adjustment to urban-industrial life but had not yet achieved social or economic security. Families in the zone of emergence frequently sought to purchase their own homes, but economic downturns often threatened their jobs. The last ring consisted of the comfortable middle-class housing of the suburbs. These enclaves featured clusters of stores, schools, churches, and professional services distant from the harsh world of industrial production.

"The city," wrote reformer Josiah Strong, "has been called 'the grave of the physique of our race.' " As technology expedited the growth of cities, urban expansion created overwhelming difficulties. Sanitation presented a particularly serious problem, especially as central city areas became more densely populated. In 1916, New York City dumped 500 million gallons of raw sewage into its rivers every day. Chicago pumped sewage far out into Lake Michigan to minimize contamination of the drinking water it drew closer to shore. Many of the new city dwellers, both immigrants and native-born Americans, came from a rural heritage and brought country solutions such as wells and privies to the problems of water supply and sewage disposal. Barely half the residents of Rochester and Pittsburgh had sewers, and Baltimore and New Orleans had no sewage system at all. A 1901 survey of tenement conditions in Chicago turned up one city block that contained eighty-two privies used by 637 people. Animal waste, particularly from horses, compounded the situation. In 1907, Milwaukee's 12,500 horses produced 133 tons of manure daily, or roughly three-quarters of a pound for each citizen. Remains of dead horses littered the streets, further complicating the problem. With good reason, some hailed the automobile as the technological breakthrough that would rescue cities from the pollution of animal waste.

Intense overcrowding and deplorable housing conditions dominated the urban landscape, particularly for the poor who found themselves packed together in sprawling slums and ghettos. In cities such as Baltimore and Philadelphia, the working class lived in seemingly endless blocks of row houses. The "dumbbell" tenement became the customary form of inner-city residential construction in New York. These structures rose some five stories with each floor containing fourteen rooms divided into four apartments and two bathrooms. Two apartments and a bathroom bulged out on each side from a narrow central staircase, giving the structure its characteristic dumbbell appearance.

In the tenements, wrote journalist Jacob Riis, "all the influences make for evil." Many apartments lacked running water. One section of Manhattan had a population density of 986 persons per acre compared with 760 per acre in Bombay, India. An observer noted that even the architecture "seemed to sweat humanity at every window and door." Manhattan's Lower East Side had one of the highest mortality rates in the world. Surveying Hell's Kitchen, one especially notorious New York slum, cleric and reformer Walter Rauschenbusch commented that "one could hear human virtue cracking and crashing all around."

Not surprisingly, these conditions bred crime, disease, and fire. Between 1870 and 1906, fire extensively damaged four major cities and killed as many as seven thousand people annually. The crime rate rose even faster than the population. In 1893, Chicago averaged one arrest per eleven residents and had eight times as many murders as Paris. Tuberculosis cases were common. Disease, overcrowding, and poor sanitation produced a life expectancy of forty-eight years for whites born in 1900 and a startling thirty-three years for nonwhites. The infant mortality rate was one in one hundred live births. Among industrialized nations, the United States ranked first in productivity and last in public health.

Migrants, Immigrants, and Nativists

Rural migrants and immigrants from Europe contributed heavily to the dramatic urban growth of the late nineteenth and early twentieth centuries. The harshness and drudgery of rural life, especially in the midst of the declining farm economy of the 1890s, contrasted sharply with the seeming glamour and apparent economic vitality of urban life. As a result, thousands of Americans abandoned the farm for the city. Approximately 40 percent of all townships lost population, but the shift was especially pronounced in the Northeast and Midwest. During the 1880s, Chicago doubled in size, and more than half the townships in Iowa and Illinois lost population. Rural New England saw the abandonment of thousands of farms, including 3,300 in Maine, 1,500 in Massachusetts, 1,300 in New Hampshire, and 1,000 in Vermont. By 1910, American natives of rural origins composed roughly one-third of the nation's urban population.

The arrival of millions of immigrants was even more dramatic. Many Chinese and Japanese settled on the West Coast. Europeans constituted the great majority of the new arrivals, 80 percent of whom congregated in the northeastern quadrant of the country. Over twenty-five million foreigners entered the United States during the half century between the Civil War and World War I, fifteen million between 1900 and 1915. Roughly 60 percent of the

Exhibit 1–5. Total Immigration from Eastern and Southern Europe, 1890–1910 (in rounded thousands)

	1890	1900	1910
Eastern	36	98	212
Southern	56	108	253

Source: *Historical Statistics of the United States, Colonial Times to 1970* (U.S. Department of Commerce, 1975).

Exhibit 1–6. Immigration from Eastern and Southern Europe as a Percentage of Total Immigration, 1890–1910

	1890	1900	1910
Eastern	8	21.7	20.3
Southern	12.2	24.1	24.3

Source: *Historical Statistics of the United States, Colonial Times to 1970* (U.S. Department of Commerce, 1975).

population of the twelve largest cities were foreign-born or the children of foreign-born parents. Before 1880, only about two hundred thousand southern and eastern Europeans had immigrated to the United States; in the next twenty years, 8.4 million came to American shores. Ethnically distinct from the "old" immigrants who originated primarily from Great Britain, Germany, and Scandinavia, these "new" immigrants were mostly people of Roman Catholic, Eastern Orthodox, and Jewish faiths who came from impoverished and politically repressive areas with little experience in participatory political processes. They arrived, as social worker Jane Addams put it, "densely ignorant of civic duties."

Even in the New World, immigrants' nationalities continued to shape basic elements of their lives. Czech immigrants tended to be skilled workers and frequently found work as artisans, but unskilled arrivals from Slovak and Polish backgrounds usually went to work in heavy industry. Pursuing trades they had learned in Europe, many Portuguese became fishermen and many Greeks opened breweries. In similar fashion, members of national groups tended to cluster together in neighborhoods, which preserved the outlines of native cultures through language, food, religion, and music. These immigrant neighborhoods in cities such as New York, Chicago, and Boston played a crucial role in absorbing the newcomers into the flow of urban life. Larger communities developed their own institutions such as stores and banks, which provided education, employment, and capital for residents.

Many immigrants had never planned to sever the link with their native countries. Some came with entire families to escape persecution or brought over relatives as they could afford to do so, but many intended to return to Europe and still others eventually found life in the United States to be unsatisfying. Between 1890 and the outbreak of World War I in 1914, almost 50 percent of Italian and Slavic immigrants left the United States. Among these groups, new arrivals tended to be males who planned to make some money and then go back home; consequently, women constituted only one-third of the Catholic immigrants from southern and eastern Europe. Between 1870 and 1900, emigration equaled nearly one fourth immigration, a proportion that grew to two-fifths between 1900 and the summer of 1914.

Persecution in eastern Europe and Russia precipitated a large Jewish migration to the United States. Unlike some Italian and Slavic immigrants who planned to return to Europe, most Jews intended to stay in America; consequently, their ranks included as many women as men. Although poorer than the nearly two hundred thousand Jews of German origin who had arrived in the nineteenth century, the eastern European Jews brought extensive mercantile and trading skills as well as a commitment to scholarship. With a strong tradition of family solidarity in the face of outside hostility, these Jews quickly established themselves as small merchants and manufacturers in eastern and midwestern cities. More than half of all Jewish immigrants settled in New York City, where many used skills learned in eastern Europe to succeed as workers and entrepreneurs in the expanding garment trades. German and eastern European Jews experienced more upward mobility than any other immigrant group, and by 1914 sent a higher proportion of their children to college.

Jews achieved economic success even though the Anglo-Protestant elite excluded them from important positions in major corporations and banks. Barred from practicing corporation law, Jewish attorneys specialized in criminal and real estate cases. Jewish businessmen participated in the development of new entertainment enterprises such as vaudeville, motion pictures, and popular music, although prejudice from the Anglo-American elite denied them entry into exclusive residential neighborhoods, country clubs, and elite business circles. Jewish children were usually excluded from private schools, and Ivy League colleges imposed quotas on Jewish enrollments.

Yiddish culture blossomed freely on the Lower East Side of Manhattan. A German-based language spoken in the ghettos of eastern Europe, Yiddish lent itself to the outpouring of poetry, song, theater, and socialist writing that accompanied the Jewish migration to the United States. Immigration also revitalized the synagogue as a center of Jewish life and reinforced religious and political traditions of zionism. Zionism thrived particularly among Russian and Polish Jews who believed that only a national state in Palestine could offer protection from anti-Semitism. Representatives of the Jewish community, including attorney Louis Brandeis, asked President Woodrow Wilson to press for the creation of this homeland during World War I, but other Jews insisted that religious freedom made the United States the promised land. Nevertheless, the development of Jewish hospitals, cemeteries, and mutual aid societies reflected the strength of American Jewish culture, as did the growth of predominantly Jewish trade unions such as the International Ladies Garment Workers Union (ILGWU) and the Amalgamated Clothing Workers (ACW).

Roman Catholic leaders also worked to preserve their culture. Catholics established fraternal organizations, hospitals, and cemeteries and reacted to Protestant domination of the public schools by creating a separate parochial school system. Beginning in the 1880s, these institutions provided education from kindergarten to the university level in every major city. The church also established a widespread network of bookstores that sold reading matter and children's games to strengthen Catholic identity. On the other hand, most American bishops came from Irish backgrounds and insisted that all teaching be done in English. This practice denied German, Polish, and Italian Catholics the use of their own languages and also failed to engage many low-income Catholics who did not speak English. Italian immigrants felt especially hostile to church leadership and did not attend mass with the regularity of the Irish.

Its curbs lined with food peddlers, Hester Street on Manhattan's Lower East Side lay at the heart of a thriving community of Russian Jewish immigrants.

Irish domination persisted even in the Southwest, where the church showed little respect for the culture of Spanish-speaking Catholics.

The presence of a large immigrant population provoked a strong nativist reaction. Fear of the new immigration fostered the spread of a pseudoscientific ideology that purported to demonstrate the existence of national and racial hierarchies. In *The Passing of the Great Race* (1916), nativist Madison Grant, then president of the New York Zoological Society, warned that the influx of southern and eastern Europeans threatened the older American stock with "mongrelization." Grant claimed that immigrants "adopt the language of the native American, they wear his clothes, they steal his name and they are beginning to take his women, but they seldom adopt his religion or his ideals." Theodore Roosevelt worried about the "grave signs of deterioration in the English-speaking peoples," fearing that the "higher races" would lose the "warfare of the cradle" and commit "race suicide." The "greatest problem of civilization," Roosevelt asserted, "is to be found in the fact that well-to-do families tend to die out."

Such concerns fostered a strong push to restrict immigration. The first successful efforts in this regard targeted the West Coast Chinese. Before 1850,

**Exhibit 1–7. Average Hourly Earning of Industrial Workers,
1890–1914**

1890	14.4¢
1900	15.1¢
1910	19.8¢
1914	22.0¢

Source: *Historical Statistics of the United States, Colonial Times to 1970* (U.S. Department of Commerce, 1975).

only 775 Chinese lived in California, but Chinese immigration increased sharply during the following decade. Many of the new arrivals found work on railroad gangs; others entered a variety of service occupations. Experts in fruit production, Chinese immigrants played a crucial role in developing California agriculture. Determined to preserve their culture, the Chinese resisted Anglo pressure for cultural conformity and openly expressed their intention to make money and then return to China. Roughly two-thirds of those who immigrated before 1880 subsequently returned to their homeland.

The economic downturn of the 1870s inflamed latent anti-Chinese sentiment, especially among those who feared economic competition from Chinese workers. Amid a rising tide of violence, mobs of whites in Los Angeles lynched eighteen Chinese people, and the Workingmen's party of California forged a political coalition around the issue of Chinese exclusion. Party leader Denis Kearny began and ended his speeches with the demand, "The Chinese must go! They are stealing our jobs," a cry widely echoed by other labor leaders. In 1882, Congress capitulated to racist sentiment and voted to prohibit Chinese immigration for ten years, placing the first restriction of any kind on those who wished to enter the United States. Congress renewed the prohibition ten years later and then made it permanent in 1902.

The arrival of thousands of Japanese immigrants prompted westerners to make a similar demand for exclusion. Indeed, the harsh treatment Japanese received in the United States strained diplomatic relations between the two nations. The Gentlemen's Agreement of 1907 between the American and Japanese governments led to almost complete exclusion of Japanese immigrants (see chapter 2).

Almost simultaneously, the United States began refusing admittance to the poor, the sick, convicts, polygamists, prostitutes, contract laborers, and anarchists. Still not satisfied, exclusionists campaigned hard for a literacy test for all immigrants. Three presidents of both political parties—Grover Cleveland, William Howard Taft, and Woodrow Wilson—successfully vetoed such legislation before Congress finally overrode another Wilson veto in 1917.

LABOR CONFLICT AND RADICALISM

Millions of Americans found that existence in the industrial age depended upon employment in factories, mills, and mines, a life many found to be dangerous, debilitating, and a radical departure from the routines of agricul-

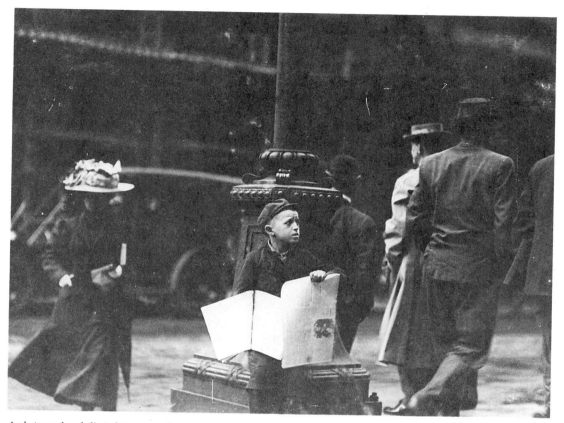

A photographer dedicated to progressive causes, Lewis Hine used his camera to document the evils of child labor. Newsboys as young as six and eight bought papers from dealers to hawk on city streets. The children lost money on all papers they did not sell.

tural societies. Factory work required that repetitious tasks be performed on a strict schedule, a regimen that workers often found monotonous, impersonal, and demeaning. American values of independence and autonomy did not prepare workers to be part of a permanent factory class. Moreover, society offered employees virtually no protection from the vicissitudes of industrial life. As the business cycle of the late nineteenth century ran its course, wage cuts and layoffs victimized the work force. Moreover, health and safety regulations were minimal. By the turn of the century, roughly thirty-five thousand workers died each year in industrial accidents and another five hundred thousand suffered serious injury. Workmen's compensation, unemployment benefits, and reliable retirement plans were virtually unavailable. Meanwhile, workers toiled an average of fifty-nine hours a week for less than ten dollars in earnings. One economist estimated that 60 percent of all adult males did not earn enough to maintain a family.

Child labor constituted an especially striking aspect of this picture. In 1900, approximately 10 percent of all girls between the ages of ten and fifteen and 20 percent of all boys in that age group held jobs, and the figures rose steadily. Coca-Cola founder Asa Candler declared, "The most beautiful sight we see is

**Exhibit 1–8. Children Aged 10–15 in the Work Force,
1890–1910
(in rounded millions)**

1890	1.5 m
1900	1.8 m
1910	1.6 m

Source: *Historical Statistics of the United States, Colonial Times to 1970* (U.S. Department of Commerce, 1975).

the child at labor; as early as he may get at labor the more beautiful, the more useful does his life get to be." By 1913, roughly one-fifth of all American children earned their own livings. One boy, asked why he did not play more, replied, "I don't know how." Public pressure prompted some states to adopt laws regulating child labor, but typically even these reforms permitted children of twelve to work ten hours a day. (See chapter 2 for federal child labor laws.)

No event publicized the horrors of factory life more vividly than the 1911 fire at the Triangle Shirtwaist Company in New York City. The blaze began on the top floor of a ten-story building one Saturday afternoon as the workers— several hundred Italian and Jewish immigrant women—prepared to leave. The women jammed against the exits, but management had locked the doors to keep workers from stealing fabric. When the elevators filled, some people leaped into the shafts, where their bodies jammed the machinery and stopped the cars. Dozens more climbed to the roof and, holding hands, jumped to their death. The tragedy claimed the lives of nearly 150 young women. A few days later, eighty thousand people ignored a steady rain to march in a somber funeral procession. A subsequent investigation blamed company management as well as the building and fire departments, but no one faced criminal charges. The report of the New York State investigating commission did, however, secure passage of some fifty laws designed to improve factory safety.

Labor violence flared frequently along the urban-industrial frontier, especially during times of economic depression. In 1892, Henry Clay Frick, the partner of steel magnate and philanthropist Andrew Carnegie, ordered a 20 percent pay cut at the Homestead Mill in Pennsylvania. When workers protested, Frick fired them and hired strikebreakers along with a private army of Pinkerton detectives to protect the new workers. His actions sparked a pitched battle that left approximately a dozen people dead. In retaliation, anarchist Alexander Berkman shot and wounded Frick while the latter sat in his office. Two years later, a strike at the Pullman Palace Car Works also turned violent. Employment at the plant fell drastically during the depression of the mid-1890s, and management cut the wages of remaining employees five times within a year. Rent for housing in the company town remained unchanged, however, and the company paid a handsome dividend to its stockholders. Finally the Pullman workers walked off the job, igniting a strike that quickly spread to other railway workers when the members of the American Railway Union refused to handle Pullman cars. Responding to pressure from the railroads, the Cleveland administration sent federal troops to break the strike under the guise of restoring disrupted mail service. Ensuing violence left twenty people dead.

Amid the unrest, labor organizers faced discouraging obstacles. The string of violent confrontations alarmed the middle and upper classes, making them even less willing than they might have been to support unions. Furthermore, a sense of solidarity and class consciousness developed slowly in American workers. The attitudes of these groups reflected a prevailing value system that stressed individualism, self-reliance, and the promise of upward social mobility. Unions, on the other hand, posed collectivist strategies for solving the problems of workers, and their very existence seemed to imply the permanence of a worker's status in the factory. Finally, the ethnic diversity of the working class made organizing a nightmare for unionizers, and social tensions frequently overrode economic issues that might have bridged those differences.

Socialists and other leftists formed a significant part of the American labor movement in the early twentieth century. A creative and diverse group, socialists drew support from industrial workers, members of ethnic groups, agrarian radicals, and intellectuals. From the first, American socialists divided over issues of goals and tactics, as the opportunists seeking immediate goals by political means clashed with those who sought a more revolutionary platform. Socialism reached its peak in the two decades before World War I under the leadership of the moderate Eugene V. Debs. The leader of the American Railway Union, Debs went to jail for his part in the 1894 Pullman strike. He spent his time reading Karl Marx and emerged to become a founder of the Socialist party, running five times as its candidate for president. Always small in numbers, the Socialists exercised a disproportionate influence on the political process. At their peak in 1912, they elected two congressmen, fifty-six mayors, thirty-three state legislators, and hundreds of city councilmen—and Debs received nearly one million votes as a presidential candidate.

A more radical wing of American socialism grew out of violent labor conflicts in the West. When the Western Federation of Miners (WFM) struck the Colorado coal fields in 1903, the Mine Owners' Association launched a campaign of terror against the workers. Once the governor declared martial law and practically ordered the militia to destroy the WFM, the conflict escalated into a civil war. In the aftermath of this bloody strike, "Big Bill" Haywood, a charismatic former miner, joined other socialists in organizing the Industrial Workers of the World (IWW), or Wobblies. Bluntly declaring that "the working class and the employing class have nothing in common," the IWW rejected the political action of more moderate socialists. Charismatic organizers like Haywood and Joe Hill pursued an all-embracing union of workers in a classless society, and advocated direct action, including violence, to achieve its goals. Under Haywood's leadership, the Wobblies organized miners, lumberjacks, and migrant workers in the West and used songbooks and hymns to create worker solidarity. Within a few years, the IWW spread into the East, where it won an extended battle to unionize textile mills in Lawrence, Massachusetts, in 1912. Violent confrontations marked the Lawrence campaign and a subsequent, unsuccessful textile strike at Paterson, New Jersey. These tactics stirred considerable fear among middle-class Americans; they also made the union vulnerable to the suppression of leftist groups during World War I, when Haywood felt compelled to leave the United States and abandon the shattered IWW.

Flag waving strikers confront the state militia at Lawrence, Massachusetts, during the struggle to unionize textile workers. One woman died in clashes between authorities and strikers.

The conservative American Federation of Labor (AFL), founded in 1886 and led by Samuel Gompers, was the most enduring union movement of the new century. A cigar maker by trade, Gompers focused unionizing efforts on skilled workers, ignoring the unskilled people who ran the assembly lines in most large plants. This strategy inevitably led to an emphasis on earlier immigrants from northern Europe and the neglect of late immigrants who were more apt to be on the bottom of the employment hierarchy. Skeptical of socialism, Gompers rejected the principle of employee control and believed that workers should stay within the capitalist system to achieve a fairer distribution of industrial wealth. Gompers doubted that the government would defy corporations to provide meaningful assistance to the working

Exhibit 1–9. Labor Union Membership, 1900–1920
(in rounded millions based on Bureau of Labor Statistics)

1900	.8 m
1905	1.9 m
1910	2.1 m
1915	2.6 m
1920	5.0 m

Source: *Historical Statistics of the United States, Colonial Times to 1970* (U.S. Department of Commerce, 1975).

class, and he generally avoided endorsing political candidates. Opposed to violence and reluctant to strike, Gompers sought to protect the interests of a relatively small part of the working class. His approach won the grudging approval of national elites but severely stunted the growth of the American labor movement. Not until the 1930s did the new Congress of Industrial Organization make significant progress in unionizing the mass production industries.

A CORPORATE CULTURE

In 1889, economist David Wells summarized the changes of the preceding twenty years when he wrote, "An almost total revolution has taken place, and is yet in progress, in every branch and in every relation of the world's industrial and commercial system." Military spending during the Civil War era had demonstrated the potential of mass production for a mass market, but enterprises organized on a national scale required enormous amounts of capital and a superbly managed organization. By establishing a corporation, entrepreneurs could raise capital through sales of stock to investors, who in turn would share in future profits. Railroad corporations first exploited such structures during the decades after the Civil War. Many railroad managers had acquired administrative experience while serving in the Union army, and they smoothly transferred those techniques to peacetime corporate administration. Unlike agrarian society, which honored traditional individualism and localism, corporate culture emphasized bureaucratic approaches that sought coordination and integration on a national level. At the end of the Civil War, for example, a diversity of local railroad lines lacked a standard gauge, interchangeable equipment, or a common timetable. By 1890, a complex, well-integrated rail network bound the nation together, delivering people and commodities over great distances with considerable precision.

Techniques of scientific management spread rapidly to the mass production industries. Engineer Frederick Winslow Taylor developed a carbon steel high-speed cutting edge that greatly increased the pace at which a factory could turn out machine tools. With his machinery operating more efficiently, Taylor insisted that his work force also be more efficient. "The man has been first; in the future the system must be first," declared Taylor. Taylorism influenced Henry Ford's decision to bring the moving assembly line to his automobile plant in 1914. By doing so, he cut the assembly time for an automobile from 12.5 hours to ninety minutes. Simultaneously he instituted the five-dollar day at a time when industrial workers made about half that. With these changes, Ford cut the average price of his automobiles from $950 to about $300 and launched an industrial empire. Between 1899 and 1914, nationwide manufacturing productivity rose 76 percent, while the work force grew only 36 percent and physical plants only 13 percent.

The clock provided a prime symbol of the new emphasis on coordination and precision. Railroads took the lead in emphasizing exact measures of time for coordinating arrivals and departures over vast areas, and a large pocket watch became the badge of office for a train station agent. In 1883, the federal

FREDERICK WINSLOW TAYLOR
1856–1915

Folk myth held that Frederick Winslow Taylor, the creator of "scientific management," died with a stopwatch in his hand. Taylor saw himself as a reformer striving to use professional skills to improve the lot of labor and the American consumer. The son of an established eastern family from Germantown, Pennsylvania, Taylor turned to factory work when weak eyesight curbed his formal schooling. He rose quickly from common laborer to the new profession of engineering by taking night classes at the Stevens Institute of Technology. Taylor received approximately a hundred patents during his career, and his work led to a heat treatment for tools that increased the cutting capacity of steel by 200 to 300 percent.

As machines became more rational and efficient, Taylor grew interested in improving the efficiency of workers as well. Armed with a stopwatch, he kept precise records of the time workers needed to accomplish each task and kept track of every motion made during the process. Using such data to identify the elementary operations and design the most efficient procedures for specific jobs, Taylor sought the "substitution of science for the rule of thumb." In a famous demonstration of his methods, the engineer quadrupled the amount of pig iron a worker could carry in a day.

These "time-and-motion" studies formed the basis of Taylor's theory of scientific management. In the 1890s, Taylor started a management consulting business in Philadelphia, distributing a card that read, "Systematizing Shop Management and Manufacturing Costs a Speciality." Bethlehem Steel became his first major client. The founding scientific management consultant in the world, Taylor eventually codified his expertise in *Principles of Scientific Management* (1911).

Taylor's ideas were understandably unpopular with workers. Many believed that Taylorism reduced them to the status of machines and made their tasks unbear- *(cont.)*

government divided the nation into four standard time zones to meet railroad scheduling demands. This emphasis on time had significant implications for workers as well as machinery. In an increasingly structured society, the punctuality of the work force was vastly more important than in a rural economy. Many laborers of this period came from rural cultures that had not prepared them for the discipline of industrial society. Accustomed to work schedules defined by the sun, religious traditions, and their own inclinations, employees often exasperated supervisors concerned with efficiency. Consequently, the clock served not simply as a timepiece, but as a bond shackling the worker to new habits. Industrial America expected workers to be on time, to clock in, and to coordinate like clockwork. "The tick of the clock is the boss in his anger," wrote Yiddish poet Morris Rosenfeld. "The face of the clock has the eyes of the foe."

Industrialization also involved a desperate search for economic order. Through most of the late nineteenth century, American opinion makers clung ably monotonous. Others feared that a streamlined manufacturing process would precipitate layoffs. "The disciplinary relations within the manufacturing organization must be definite and strict," admitted Taylor, but he insisted that his system would actually improve the lot of labor. Greater efficiency meant greater productivity, he argued, thereby making possible shorter hours, higher wages, and lower prices. Smoother procedures also might reduce workers' grievances and improve the relationship between labor and management. Even though Taylor volunteered his services after 1900, workers remained critical of his motives. Their suspicion deepened when industrialists used Taylor's methods to effect work speedups and the elimination of jobs.

Taylor embodied the growing significance of the professional ethic among middle-class graduates of the nation's universities. Optimistic about their ability to manage problems successfully, the new professional class prized order, efficiency, and rationality. These ideas were especially strong among engineers who shared Taylor's view that scientific concepts could solve social as well as mechanical problems. "The shop (indeed, the whole works) should be managed by the planning department," Taylor insisted. Thus social control and manipulation, rather than conscience, should be the real basis for reform. "If a man won't do what is right," Taylor said, "*make* him."

Taylorism transformed the sentiment for social control into a concept of planning. Among the first engineers to apply the principles of his profession to society, Taylor prepared the way for other civic-minded engineers such as Herber Hoover. Like the workers, however, the engineer had no control over how corporate managers might apply his or her techniques. "I have found," Taylor wrote in a paper read before the American Society of Mechanical Engineers in 1909, "that any improvement is not only opposed but aggressively and bitterly opposed by the majority of men."

Taylor died one year after Henry Ford adopted the principles of scientific management to the mass production of automobiles. ■

to the idea of the self-regulating market. Government might support business enterprises, but it rarely if ever regulated them. These assumptions persisted into the early twentieth century, even though industrialization was a disruptive, chaotic, even violent process. Eager to bring structure to their tumultuous surroundings, businesspeople took the initiative in trying to stabilize the economy by minimizing competition through corporate consolidation.

During the late nineteenth century, large parts of the economy fell under the domination of industrial titans. Small, locally owned firms found themselves overwhelmed by enormous national and international concerns with tremendous amounts of capital at their disposal. Standard Oil, for example, consolidated the petroleum refining industry and became the nation's first monopoly corporation. Meanwhile, corporate management grew increasingly professionalized and divorced itself from control by stockholders.

Traumatized by the severe depression of 1893–97, corporate leaders turned to merger and consolidation for survival. Once prosperity returned in 1897,

Exhibit 1–10. Recorded Mergers in Manufacturing and Mining, 1896–1906

1896	26
1897	69
1898	303
1899	1208
1900	340
1901	423
1902	379
1903	142
1904	79
1905	226
1906	128

Source: *Historical Statistics of the United States, Colonial Times to 1970* (U.S. Department of Commerce, 1975).

company officials sought to further rationalize the marketplace. Between 1897 and 1904, corporate directors engineered the merger of some three thousand firms into three hundred supercorporations. These top three hundred companies assumed control of 40 percent of the nation's industrial wealth. Financier J. P. Morgan played a major role in this consolidation. His United States Steel, formed in 1901, became the world's first billion-dollar industrial entity and took control of 60 percent of American steel production. The giant conglomerate took in more income than the United States Treasury. "I like a little competition," the financier told a congressional investigation committee. "I would rather have combination."

Morgan's activities reflected the increased importance of corporate capitalism. The new corporate managers gradually replaced individualistic entrepreneurs like steel magnate Andrew Carnegie and oil baron John D. Rockefeller. Emphasizing such managerial values as cooperation and continuity, corporate administrators organized oligarchies in which industrial leaders set prices and competitors followed. The new competition abandoned ruthless price cutting and increasingly focused on advertising, management, technology, and innovation. Despite its dominant position, United States Steel saw its share of the market drop from 62 percent to 40 percent between 1901 and 1920 because it lagged behind rivals in embracing new technology. Similarly, Standard Oil trailed new companies like Gulf in developing newly discovered petroleum fields in Texas and California; consequently, its share of the market declined from 90 percent in 1899 to 50 percent in 1920.

Investment bankers were crucial to the emergence of the supercorporation. Primarily located in East Coast financial centers, men like J. P. Morgan assembled enormous amounts of money to capitalize corporate mergers. In 1913, the Pujo Investigating Committee of Congress found that a money trust largely underwritten by the Morgan and Rockefeller interests held 341 interlocking directorates in 112 banks, railroads, utilities, and insurance companies. The collective resources of this financial syndicate totaled $22 billion, a figure equal to half the gross national product.

Concentrated economic power brought enormous personal fortunes to a few Americans. In 1900, Andrew Carnegie's annual income amounted to $20 million while the average American worker earned $500 a year. The richest 2 percent of the population owned 60 percent of the nation's wealth at the turn of the century. A decade later, the seventy richest Americans each had a fortune of at least $35 million and collectively held one-sixteenth of the nation's wealth.

Some of the plutocrats embraced what Carnegie labeled the Gospel of Wealth and retired from the business world to pursue philanthropy. Of his personal fortune totaling roughly $400 million, Carnegie gave away $350 million, most notably for three thousand public libraries and seven thousand church organs, and used another $20 million to create the Carnegie Endowment for International Peace. "The man who dies rich dies thus disgraced," he said. "I would as soon leave my son a curse as the Almighty Dollar."

The new American ruling class also invested their accumulated riches in ostentation and snobbery. Callers at the mansion of Mrs. William Astor presented a card, which passed through twenty-seven hands before reaching the lady of the house. The social elite of New York numbered four hundred because that was the capacity of Mrs. Astor's ballroom. Carnegie dispensed his philanthropies from a castle on a lavish estate in the eastern highlands of his native Scotland while striking the pose of a feudal noble. A wag described the luxuriously landscaped Rockefeller estate in Tarrytown, New York, as what God would have done if only He had the money. J. P. Morgan owned homes and estates on both sides of the Atlantic and traveled by special train with the tracks cleared for his approach.

By the late nineteenth century, the social aristocracy had begun to establish a summer colony in Newport, Rhode Island, where for seven weeks they gathered to flaunt their riches. A visiting member of the royal family of Russia declared that he had never even imagined such luxury. The Vanderbilt "cottage," for example, was a $2 million Renaissance palace containing $9 million worth of furnishing. Thorstein Veblen, a leading economist and social critic, coined the phrase "conspicuous consumption" to denounce a life-style typified by gold plumbing fixtures, monogrammed linen bedding for horses, and diamond-studded dog collars.

Exhibit 1–11. Distribution of Wealth and Income in 1890

Estates (by Annual Income)	Number of Families	Aggregate Wealth	Average Wealth per Family
Wealthy classes ($50,000 and over)	125,000	$33,000,000,000	$264,000
Well-to-do classes ($5,000 to $50,000)	1,375,000	23,000,000,000	16,000
Middle classes ($500 to $5,000)	5,500,000	8,200,000,000	1,500
Poorer classes (under $500)	5,500,000	800,000,000	150
	12,500,000	$65,000,000,000	$5,200

Source: Nell Irvin Painter, *Standing at Armageddon: The United States, 1877–1919* (W. W. Norton, New York: 1987), page xix.

THE NEW ADOLESCENCE

"The guardians of the young . . . ," wrote psychologist G. Stanley Hall, should seek the "prolongation of human infancy, and the no whit less important prolongation of adolescence." This extended period of youthful development received its name from the title of Hall's bulky two-volume work *Adolescence* (1904). In the industrial era, according to Hall, young people had to undergo disciplined physical development and postpone sexuality until they were fully prepared for economic self-sufficiency. Hall's pioneering work helped to spark the Child Study movement, which focused serious attention on child development. Urbanization and industrialization precipitated important changes in family life, especially for middle- and upper-class Anglo-Protestants. Most notably, the role of children changed as children became less important to the economic well-being of their parents. As many Americans moved from the farm to the factory, the length of time between physical maturity and economic independence lengthened considerably. A successful career in high-status white-collar jobs depended on a good education. Accordingly, between 1898 and 1914, elementary school enrollments grew steadily while high school and college enrollments more than doubled.

Popular guides to the new adolescence stressed careerism and warned young men about the hazards of sexual relationships. Adolescents should avoid the temptations of drink and fallen women and marry partners with the character of their mothers. Such women would help careers and provide homes that protected husbands from the evils that abounded in the city. These self-help books, often written by doctors, also revealed a fear of all women. Their authors considered women to be more spiritual than men. But in contradictory fashion they also argued that bodily appetites, not intellect, controlled the behavior of women. This concept justified the exclusion of women from politics, because women supposedly could not think as rationally as men. Furthermore, since women could quickly change from individuals of angelic spirituality into creatures of frightening bodily appetites, a young man should not allow his wife to become interested in sexual pleasure because she might become "a drag on the energy, spirit, and resolution of her partner." Young married men, according to this view, needed all their energy to pursue careers and could not afford to spend any in unnecessary sexual activities.

This postponement of economic and sexual independence for young men gradually extended to lower income groups as attendance in public high schools became compulsory after 1900. By 1917, thirty-eight states had enacted laws requiring young people to remain in school until age sixteen. Disciplined and competitive sports, played in uniforms under the direction of adults, first developed in the private schools and universities of the Northeast, became the most prestigious activity for high school boys from lower-income families in all regions of the nation.

NEW ART AND PHILOSOPHY

As Americans began to acknowledge the tensions and dislocations of urban-industrial society, the literary and artistic conventions of the Victorian era

A street fighter and cartoonist as well as a serious artist, George Luks exhibited this portrait of two wrestlers at the 1913 New York Armory show. His work typifies the urban realism of the Ashcan school.

began to fade. Sentimental, romantic, and moralistic art, especially with historical settings, remained popular with middle-class patrons. Yet by 1900, young writers and artists increasingly found nineteenth-century optimism out of place and given to sterile formulations. In literature, a "Little Renaissance" emerged around a cluster of younger writers influenced by the realism and naturalism of European novelists like Emile Zola. Zola had declared that a writer should study human nature with the detachment of a natural scientist and resist the temptation to feel compassion or to apply moral criteria.

Naturalism found expression in the United States through the work of Theodore Dreiser, the son of a German immigrant. Dreiser's *Sister Carrie* (1900) exploded the confines of the Victorian novel by realistically portraying a young woman's corruption by city life. The book's pessimistic tone and frank depiction of sexual themes alarmed Dreiser's publisher, Doubleday, which printed only one thousand copies, and both sales and critical reception disappointed the author. Dreiser portrayed people as animals who abandoned culture and civilization when they pursued their private needs, themes he continued to develop in such later works as *The Financier* (1912) and *The Titan* (1914). Other naturalists included Stephen Crane and Frank Norris, both of whom died early in their careers, and Willa Cather and Ellen Glasgow, both of whom wrote pointed and uncompromising portraits of the harshness of American life. Asked why she did not write an optimistic novel about the

West, Glasgow, a native Virginian, responded, "If there is anything I know less about than the West, it is optimism."

A similar shift took place in American poetry. As the century opened, William Vaughn Moody and Edwin Arlington Robinson, interpreters of the Victorian genteel tradition, ranked as the major figures in American poetry. The 1910s saw the emergence of poets eager to experiment with new methods and more contemporary themes. In 1912, Harriet Monroe founded the influential journal *Poetry* just as a new generation of poets began to publish. Robert Frost, Edgar Lee Masters, e. e. cummings, and Carl Sandburg all published their first works shortly before America entered World War I, as did Amy Lowell, Edna St. Vincent Millay, and Georgia Douglas Johnson. Although quite different in their perspectives, these poets all drew their material from the lives and experiences of the common people. Simultaneously, two Americans who spent their careers largely in Europe, T. S. Eliot and Ezra Pound, developed fresh idioms for poetry, using new rhythms and common speech.

Modern art also shattered Victorian sensibilities on the eve of World War I. Painters like John Sloan and George Bellows depicted the harshness and violence of the contemporary world so forcefully and relentlessly that critics named their style the Ashcan school. "Forget about art," realist Robert Henri told his students, "and paint pictures of what interests you in life." One Ashcan painter, George Luks, claimed to be the best barroom fighter in America and denounced establishment painters as "those pink and white idiots." Ashcan painters often exhibited their work in photographer Alfred Stieglitz's studio at 291 Fifth Avenue, New York. In 1913, these dissident artists organized their own show at New York's Sixty-ninth Regiment Armory. The exhibition included work by Europeans Marcel Duchamp, Henri Matisse, and Pablo Picasso, and introduced such modern art forms as cubism and expressionism to the American public. Theodore Roosevelt spoke for many when he sneeringly compared parts of the show to the "later work of paleolithic artists of the French and Spanish caves." More than any other single cultural event of the time, the New York armory show dramatized the break with nineteenth-century formalism and heralded the artist's new demand for total freedom to explore the internal and external dimensions of the urban-industrial world.

A similar rejection of nineteenth-century certainties contributed to the development of a distinctively American philosophy: pragmatism. As expressed by its chief proponent, Harvard psychologist and philosopher William James, pragmatism rejected the validity of absolutes and fixed principles. James argued that ideas should be tested by their workability and benefit to the greatest number of people. He insisted that an idea contained meaning only in terms of the consequences precipitated by believing the proposition. "What in short," James asked, "is the truth's cash value in experiential terms?"

Pragmatism found an effective advocate in Columbia University educator John Dewey, who applied its tenets to group activity and the creation of social action. Fashioning himself as an "instrumentalist," Dewey considered authoritarian teaching methods such as rote memorization, strict routine, and the mastery of a sharply defined body of knowledge inappropriate to the learning experience. He denounced beliefs in absolute truth as "the ultimate refuge of the stand patter." Instead, Dewey suggested that schools be democratically organized and rooted in direct experience, serving as agents of social reform as well as vehicles for transmitting culture. Such ideas reflected a growing faith among urban professionals that public education could help to stabilize the social order. "Education will solve every problem of our national life," affirmed one New York principal.

POPULAR CULTURE

As the average work week declined from fifty-six to forty-one hours between 1900 and 1920, urban dwellers became a huge market for affordable entertainment. Municipalities provided some leisure activities by building parks and zoos, and trains and automobiles facilitated short excursions into the countryside. Spectator sports such as baseball also attracted vast audiences. A popular game nationwide since the mid–nineteenth century, baseball saw its first professional team established in Cincinnati in 1869. Other cities also established teams, and by 1903, two professional leagues, the National and American, competed for World Series championships. Both leagues rigidly excluded black players, who formed their own professional teams and who received neither the publicity nor the salaries of their white counterparts.

Although its advocates touted the sport as a bastion of wholesome, even naive values, the business of baseball quickly organized itself according to the principles of corporate America. A Supreme Court decision exempted the sport from the antitrust laws, permitting owners to establish monopolies within their markets and perpetual control over players they signed to contracts. Known as the reserve clause, this last arrangement made it impossible for a player to ever negotiate with another owner. This device remained a central feature of the sport until the Court reversed itself in the mid-1970s and recognized the right of players to become free agents.

Organized baseball received a serious blow in 1919 with allegations that gamblers had bribed members of the highly favored Chicago White Sox to throw the World Series to the Cincinnati Reds. The underdog Reds triumphed five games to three. Authorities subsequently indicted White Sox outfielder "Shoeless" Joe Jackson and several other team members, but a jury acquitted them. Hoping to restore baseball's credibility, team owners hired Federal Judge Kenesaw Mountain Landis as the first commissioner of the sport. Landis had recently attracted public notice for imposing severe sentences on radical labor leaders. Ignoring the court verdict, the public relations–conscious Landis promptly banned eight "Black Sox" from baseball for life and then presided over the game with an iron hand until his death in 1944.

Another team sport, football, took on new significance in the education of young people, especially those who attended college. The shift from baseball, which focused on the individual, to football, with its emphasis on teamwork, reflected the new values of a corporate economy. In 1850, Americans had viewed individual enterprise as the key to the growth of the marketplace. But football channeled aggressive characteristics into team cooperation rather than individual competition. And the football team, like the corporation or army unit, could defeat adversaries only through the strong discipline of its members. "I have no sympathy whatever with the over-wrought sentimentality that would keep a young man in cotton wool," declared Theodore Roosevelt. "I have a hearty contempt for him if he counts a broken-arm or collarbone as of any serious consequences when balanced against the chance of showing that he possesses hardihood, physical prowess, and courage." The *New York Times* agreed, saying football "educated boys in those characteristics that had made the Anglo-Saxon race preeminent in history." The twenty-three football-related deaths in 1905 startled even Roosevelt, however, and the president intervened personally to encourage new rules to safeguard participants.

The influence of blacks and immigrants brought spectacular changes in popular culture. Increasingly dissatisfied with the conventions of urban-industrial society and the confinement of Victorian gentility, the middle class turned to new forms of amusement and leisure. Urban nightlife centered on vaudeville, which often featured performers from black or ethnic backgrounds, and cabarets with their risqué entertainment and jazz dancing. Ragtime, first played in southern brothels and then popularized by black composer Scott Joplin, introduced syncopation to the middle class and quickened the pace of popular music. Blues, another form of Afro-American music interpreted by the black composer W. C. Handy, also received widespread exposure in the pulsating environment of the 1910s. While critics derided the emerging culture as vulgar and unrestrained, young ethnics and Anglo-Protestants reveled in its emphasis on self-gratification and self-expression. The new nightlife and popular music relaxed the social and personal boundaries between men and women and encouraged spontaneous behavior and feeling.

Technology had a major impact on mass entertainment. For example, after Thomas Edison's invention of the phonograph in the 1890s, music reached new audiences. Throughout the pre–World War I period, light entertainment and vaudeville were popular with theater audiences and helped to launch the careers of showman George Cohan and comedians Fanny Brice, Eddie Cantor, and Will Rogers. New York's Tin Pan Alley began producing thousands of rather simple songs, which such performers popularized and which publishers made available in sheet music for home performances. By 1920, as the phonograph found wide use, the music business stood on the threshold of a new era.

Technology also changed the face of American journalism by making possible the sensational mass circulation dailies, which provided entertainment as well as information for their readers. High-speed rotary presses, linotype machines, and the photoengraving process reduced printing costs and changed the appearance of publications. Staid, dignified, and politically conservative newspapers and magazines found themselves overwhelmed by their splashy and sensational competitors featuring racy stories about vice and crime. The New York *World*, published by German immigrant Joseph Pulitzer, and later the New York *Journal*, published by his bitter rival William

Randolph Hearst, led the way in pioneering the new journalism. One Sunday cartoon series, "The Kid of Hogan's Alley," printed in yellow, attracted so many readers to Pulitzer's paper that Hearst finally hired the cartoonist away. Undeterred, Pulitzer then engaged George Luks, a prominent artist of the Ashcan school, to continue the series for the *World*. The feature subsequently ran in both papers—and the struggle over the "yellow kid" gave the name yellow journalism to such sensational circulation-boosting tactics.

Technology produced an entirely new entertainment medium, the motion picture. The first truly national medium, movies grew out of the turn-of-the-century culture of the cities, where immigrant Jewish entrepreneurs such as Samuel Goldwyn and Adolph Zukor shaped their early development. Thomas Edison played a major role in developing a practical motion picture projector, which he initially paired with another of his inventions, the phonograph, to create short "vitascopes" for penny arcades. But Edison saw the vitascope as merely a toy and was "very doubtful if there [was] any commercial feature in it." For Edison, the "commercial feature" was the supreme test. "I measure everything by the size of the silver dollar," he said. "If it don't come up to that standard then I know it's no good." Others, however, quickly realized the potential of moving pictures. In 1903, E. S. Porter produced *The Great Train Robbery*, generally acknowledged as the first film to tell a story. By 1910, directors such as D. W. Griffith and performers like Charlie Chaplin and Mary Pickford were attracting weekly audiences of ten million people to the nation's ten thousand movie theaters.

Seeking better weather for extensive outdoor shooting and lower real estate prices, New York and New Jersey filmmakers relocated in Hollywood, California, during the 1910s. By 1916, movie stars such as Chaplin and Pickford made million-dollar salaries. Social workers like Jane Addams believed that movies could bring culture and Anglo-Protestant values to the lower classes. But silent films transcended class barriers and introduced portraits of human passion that often challenged local standards of Victorian propriety. And leaders of the industry, many of them fresh from the immigrant experience, sought mainly to attract audiences through appealing entertainment. "Great successes," explained one entertainment mogul, "are those that take hold of the masses, not the classes."

Appealing for working-class support among city immigrants, early film producers often catered to their audience's fascination with crime, sex, and rebellion against Anglo-Protestant authority. As early as 1903, movies featured such titles as *The Corset Model*, *The Pajama Girls*, and *The Physical Culture Girl*. Consequently, New York City, Chicago, and other communities began to limit youth audiences through review boards and censorships. In 1910, for example, San Francisco censors rejected thirty-two films—including *Saved by a Sailor*, *In Hot Pursuit*, *The Black Viper*, and *Maggie the Dock Rat*—as "unfit for public exhibition." Such agitation led producers to cooperate with the National Board of Review, a voluntary citizens committee organized by New York City reformers in 1908. Community attempts to thwart the rise of a national mass culture met only limited success, however. By 1920, the motion picture industry had firmly established itself as a main influence on popular tastes and values.

DAVID WARK GRIFFITH
1875–1948

"The task I am trying to achieve," D. W. Griffith once explained, "is above all to make you see." The founding genius of American silent cinema was born in Oldham County, Kentucky, the son of a Confederate cavalry officer. After creditors confiscated the family estate, Griffith drifted through a series of odd jobs before entering the entertainment business. Eventually he signed with Biograph and became a motion picture director.

Griffith liberated the movies from the conventions of stagecraft and created a fresh idiom of filmic expression. Working with cameraman Billy Bitzer, he developed the visual syntax of motion pictures by drawing on such techniques as close-up and long shots; the *switch-back*, or parallel montage; and the fade-out. The talented southerner realized that film embodied more intimacy than the stage and encouraged a style of performance that emphasized restraint and subtlety. "I learned more about acting under Griffith's guidance," Mary Pickford confessed, "than I did in all my years in the theatre."

Griffith established the director as the principal artistic force in motion pictures. Convinced that the emotional language of film could elevate reason above animality, he used cinematic technique to highlight youthful idealism, saintly women, virtuous producers, and Victorian family values. Once he left Biograph to become an independent in 1913, Griffith bought the rights to Thomas Dixon's *The Clansman* (1905), a popular novel that romanticized the creation of the first Ku Klux Klan. "As I studied the book," he later recalled, "stronger and stronger came to work the traditions that I had learned as a child, all that my father had told me." The "story of the South," he declared, "had been absorbed into the very fiber of my being."

Ultimately titled *The Birth of a Nation* (1915), the twelve-reel film became Griffith's masterpiece and the most popular movie of the era. Dixon even arranged a White House showing for President Woodrow Wilson, a southern historian sympathetic to the drama's hostile views of Reconstruction. *(cont.)*

THE DISFRANCHISED:
NATIVE AMERICANS AND HISPANICS

Despite the hardships faced by immigrants, their labor and their votes contributed to the political economy of the urban-industrial world, and the Anglo-Protestant establishment could not ignore them. In contrast, Native Americans found themselves so powerless by 1900 that mass society threatened to completely destroy their culture. During the late nineteenth century, railroads, mining, and commercial ranching devastated the Indian way of life on the Great Plains and Rocky Mountains, while white hunters and the army depleted the buffalo and other game that Native Americans used for food and skins. Following military defeat in the 1870s and 1880s, Indian survivors found themselves restricted to reservations organized by the federal government.

Birth of a Nation mirrored southern stereotypes of blacks as rowdy and untrustworthy sensualists easily exploited by harsh northerners. Accordingly, it aroused the ire of the National Association for the Advancement of Colored People and induced editing by the National Board of Review, a voluntary censor created by the film industry. Yet Griffith perceived himself as a Progressive and a reform Democrat and insisted that the story pitted the innocence of agrarian virtue against the machinations of Yankee greed and lust. He had intended only to show the plight of small farmers who allowed monopolists to strip them of their land and corrupt the political process.

Determined to strike back at critics and inspire the common people, Griffith used all his profits to produce *Intolerance* (1916), a four-hour, four-part extravanganza shot on 125 miles of celluloid over a twenty-two–month schedule. Relying on "mental notes" instead of a script, Griffith used the film to depict a pattern of autocracy from ancient Babylon to industrial America. The director clearly sided with virtuous workers against greedy exploiters. The affluent audiences then attending films had little patience with moralistic denunciations of the rich, however, and the movie failed at the box office.

By the end of World War I, the film industry had become a corporate enterprise increasingly under the control of large studios closely linked to investment bankers. Determined to maintain independence, Griffith built his own facilities in Mamaroneck, New York, but the expense proved too great and he returned to Hollywood in 1925. There, Griffith's creative liberties did not mesh with the corporate procedures demanded by the studios. Demoralized by both working conditions and the waning of the Progressive reform spirit, the outmoded director lost his talent for making successful films.

The architect of the full-length feature and the man responsible for enticing middle-class viewers into movie theaters, D. W. Griffith abandoned the industry in 1931. Deprived of the nineteenth-century folk tradition that gave his work vitality, the great evangelist of the screen found himself without a congregation. ◼

Demoralized and impoverished, many Native Americans of the 1890s looked to such prophets as the Paiute Wovoka who promised miraculous salvation from white power. Wovoka prophesied that God would cover the world with a new layer of earth that would bury all white people while Native Americans were elevated by a Ghost Dance revealed to him. Although Wovoka himself lived in Nevada, his teachings spread rapidly among the Sioux on the Northern Plains. To eliminate the Ghost Dance, white reservation authorities arrested several leaders of the Sioux nation.

When Chief Sitting Bull was killed by reservation police, his band sought refuge with Chief Big Foot. The Seventh Cavalry caught the Indians at Wounded Knee Creek in South Dakota and Big Foot surrendered in December 1890. While the troops disarmed the braves, someone fired a shot. Soldiers began shooting, killing 300 of the 350 Sioux men, women, and children. Black Elk, a young survivor of the massacre, later interpreted the event as the end of the Native American way of life.

A Sioux encampment reflects their nomadic, communal way of life based on following the buffalo herds. On the reservations, however, shacks and dugouts gradually replaced the tepees.

Determined to destroy the communal life-style of the Indians, the government imposed white values of private property. The Dawes Act of 1887 divided reservation land into 160-acre units allotted to adult males expected to become independent farmers. The soil was generally poor, however, and white speculators cheated many Native Americans out of their land. The government also did not permit effective self-rule by Indians. For example, Creeks, Cherokees, Choctaws, Chickasaws, and Seminoles who had been driven out of the Southeast in the 1830s learned that they could not continue their traditional political and educational systems. Given the extensive power of government agents, reservation politics consisted primarily of personal rivalry among Indians currying favor with officials. Indian groups tended to split into "mixed bloods," who wanted to cooperate with whites, and "full bloods," who were determined to retain their traditions. Whites also used church-related institutions and reservation public schools to teach Anglo-Protestant values. Even after being removed from their tribes and sent to boarding schools, however, many Native American children rejected their teachers and "returned to the blanket."

Mass society also threatened the culture of Americans of Mexican descent, many of whom shared Indian ancestry. Although Mexican Catholicism incorporated few specific tribal ceremonies, it remained strongly influenced by Native American tradition. After the United States claimed the Southwest at the conclusion of the Mexican War in 1848, Anglo-Protestant culture nearly overwhelmed the Spanish-American heritage in the region. But in New Mexico, which did not become a state until 1912, a resistant cultural group of sixty thousand Nuevo Mexicanos thwarted Anglo dominance. Underground groups such as La Mano Negra and Las Corras Blancas used violence to try to stop the territorial government's transfer of lands to Anglo-controlled mining and ranching interests. Congress appointed a Court of Private Land Claims in 1891 to determine the legal title of lands over which Spanish-Americans had asserted sovereignty since the sixteenth and seventeenth centuries. By World War I, this court had upheld Anglo claims in 80 percent of the cases, and Nuevo Mexicano landholding fell sharply. Yet the community still had enough strength in 1912 to force the state constitution to recognize the legal equality of the Spanish and English languages and to authorize the training of teachers in both tongues. Once New Mexico entered the union, however, the dominant Anglos disregarded these provisions and the public schools taught only English.

In the early twentieth century, the federal government initiated dam-building projects throughout the Southwest to irrigate more than a million acres of agricultural land. Anglo commercial interests hoped to use lands in Texas, Arizona, and southern California for the cultivation of cotton and vegetables that could be shipped on newly developed refrigerator cars. Looking for inexpensive labor to develop these crops, farmers with large-scale operations eagerly attracted workers from across the border in Mexico. There, social and economic changes stimulated violent political revolution and a mass exodus of refugees in the 1910s. The number of permanent Mexican immigrants to the United States jumped from one hundred thousand in 1900 to five hundred thousand by 1920. Consequently, Anglos no longer dominated the major population flow into the Southwest. The new Mexican-Americans, or Chicanos, became a permanent, migrant labor force that traveled across the country cultivating and picking agricultural crops as they ripened. Landowners paid the lowest possible wages and housed these workers in shacks with their children who worked with them in the fields. To keep wages low, in 1917, agricultural corporations persuaded Congress to waive immigration restrictions on farm labor. As a result, employers could import new workers from Mexico to displace farm workers striking for better pay and living conditions.

Lacking property, speaking Spanish, and moving constantly, Chicanos found themselves stereotyped by Anglos as a dirty and inferior race, comparable to blacks. But Mexican-Americans established strong cultural centers with vigorous newspapers in cities such as San Antonio and Los Angeles, and even formed cohesive communities in distant places like Chicago and St. Paul. Yet Chicanos did not develop significant political and economic power until the 1960s.

THE CHANGING ROLE OF WOMEN

Writing in 1904, psychologist G. Stanley Hall assessed the status of women in American life: "The long battle of woman and her friends for equal education and other opportunities is essentially won all along the line." Hall's prema-

Exhibit 1–12. Birth Rate, 1900–1920
(estimated live births per thousand of population)

1900	32.3
1910	30.1
1920	27.7

Source: *Historical Statistics of the United States, Colonial Times to 1970* (U.S. Department of Commerce, 1975).

ture optimism reflected the important changes taking place in the lives of women as the urban-industrial world eroded the values of agrarian America. A declining emphasis on large families among middle-class urban dwellers freed women to assume different responsibilities. This trend ultimately fostered a movement for reproductive freedom. Between 1860 and 1920, the national birthrate declined from 44.3 per thousand of population to 27.7. By 1900, the average total time of all pregnancies for a woman sank from 17 years to 9.7 years. Emma Goldman, a Jewish anarchist who had immigrated from Russia in 1885, pioneered such reform with her advocacy of birth control and free love. Completely rejecting marriage as an assertion of husbands' property rights over wives, Goldman declared that women "must no longer keep their mouths shut and their wombs open."

Although Goldman's radicalism limited her appeal, nurse Margaret Sanger gradually won considerable support for her efforts to educate American women about birth control. A variety of concerns motivated Sanger and her followers. Public health and social workers worried about the impact of repeated pregnancies on the health of a woman. Feminists such as Goldman stressed birth control as a way of giving women more control over their lives. Still others responded to nativist rhetoric about allegedly high birthrates among immigrants at a time when Anglo-Protestant families were declining in size. Despite these differences, all birth control advocates encountered a storm of opposition from cultural conservatives. Sanger faced indictment on obscenity charges, and authorities closed her first birth control clinic. In 1918, a Supreme Court ruling permitted doctors to distribute birth control information, but state laws still prohibited the sale of contraceptives.

As birth control and smaller families increasingly brought changes to the urban middle class, rising divorce rates gave women more opportunities to escape from bad marriages. The divorce rate climbed steadily from less than 5 percent in 1880 to over 10 percent nearly four decades later. Enhanced personal freedom for women translated into a greater participation in education; by 1920, 47.3 percent of all college students were females. Women also achieved greater economic freedom as the total number working outside the home grew from five million in 1900 to seven million in 1910. By that time, women constituted twenty percent of the gainfully employed work force.

Women still faced major obstacles in the work place. Social restraints prohibited married women, especially from the middle and upper classes, from entering the marketplace. Consequently, most women who worked outside the home were either single or lacked any other support. Typically, female workers found themselves restricted to low-paying jobs. As of 1900, 40 percent of the women in the work force were employed as domestics. Aside

With the rise of mass production techniques, many women found employment in factories. These women worked for National Cash Register in Dayton, Ohio, 1902.

from teaching and nursing, the professions remained generally closed to women. The 1890 census counted only two hundred female lawyers in the entire country, for example.

Charlotte Perkins Gilman was the most prophetic advocate of greater freedom for women. In *Women and Economics* (1898) and *The Man-Made World* (1911), Gilman expressed deep frustration with the traditional housekeeping role assigned to women, calling it the "smallest, lowest, oldest" work in the world. She described women as "the highest human type" and asserted that they could find real fulfillment only in the work place. She advocated the creation of communal entities staffed by professionals to supervise children, prepare meals, and provide cleaning services.

Exhibit 1–13. Women in the Labor Force, 1890–1910
(in rounded millions)

1890	4.0 m
1900	5.3 m
1910	7.4 m

Source: *Historical Statistics of the United States, Colonial Times to 1970* (U.S. Department of Commerce, 1975).

MARGARET HIGGINS SANGER
1883–1966

Feminist and birth control advocate Margaret Higgins was the sixth of eleven children born to an Irish-Catholic family in the factory town of Corning, New York. Precluded by financial and social pressures from attending medical school, she became a nurse and then married shortly after graduation despite her assertion that "marriage was akin to suicide."

As an obstetrical nurse, Sanger saw numerous cases of self-inflicted abortion among patients on the poverty-stricken Lower East Side of Manhattan. One woman she nursed to recovery begged her doctor for contraceptive information, only to be told, "Tell Jake to sleep on the roof." When the patient died six months later during a second abortion attempt, Sanger said, "[I] came to a sudden realization that my work as a nurse and my activities in social science were entirely palliative and consequently futile and useless to relieve the misery I saw all about me."

"No woman can call herself free who does not own or control her body," wrote Sanger. Convinced that women could take control of their own lives only by first achieving reproductive freedom, she dedicated herself to the cause of "birth control," a term she coined. Sanger spent a year studying contraception, and then in 1914 began publication of *Woman Rebel*, a journal whose masthead read, "No Gods; No Masters." In its first issue, Sanger asserted that a woman would secure "life, liberty and the pursuit of happiness" when she became "absolute mistress of her own body." Only then could the "new woman" gain "the highest possible fulfillment of her desires on the highest possible plane."

Sanger advocated the diaphragm because it gave women control of reproduction. Her efforts attracted the attention of *(cont.)*

The drive for woman suffrage formed the core of the women's movement in the early twentieth century. Suffrage stirrings began before the Civil War and later achieved victories in Wyoming, Utah, and other western states. The Purity Crusade of the late nineteenth century (see chapter 2) provided suffragists with an immediacy that propelled their movement to the forefront of American society. Believing that women would be better able to achieve social and moral reform if they possessed the right to vote, feminists increased the strength of the National American Women's Suffrage Association (NAWSA) from seventeen thousand members in 1905 to seventy-five

Exhibit 1–14. Women as a Percentage of the Labor Force, 1890–1910

1890	17.2
1900	18.3
1910	19.9

Source: *Historical Statistics of the United States, Colonial Times to 1970* (U.S. Department of Commerce, 1975).

Anglo-Protestant women eager to limit the size of their own families and anxious to control the growing immigrant population of the cities. Indeed, despite her early radicalism, Sanger consistently received a more sympathetic hearing from the middle class than from the working class. But birth control provoked intense opposition from conservative moralists, the Roman Catholic Church, and a great many men. "If the women flinch from bleeding," Theodore Roosevelt warned, "the deserved death of the race takes place even quicker." Sanger's use of specific terms such as gonorrhea and syphilis made her early publications even more controversial.

The male-dominated federal legal structure acted quickly to suppress Sanger's work, indicting her on nine counts of sending birth control information through the mail. Those charges carried potential prison terms of forty-five years. Defying feminist purity crusaders by asserting reproductive rights, Sanger fled to Europe, where she met English psychologist Havelock Ellis and inspected birth control clinics in Holland. The federal government dropped the charges against Sanger when she returned home in 1916, but almost immediately she provoked authorities again by opening the first American birth control clinic in Brooklyn. Although Sanger went to jail for thirty days, her case helped to lay the groundwork for future court rulings permitting contraceptive advice "for the prevention and cure of disease."

Because most states still prohibited the sale of contraceptives, Sanger established the American Birth Control League in 1921 to encourage physicians and social workers to press judges to permit the distribution of information on contraceptives. The struggle to disseminate birth control knowledge consumed the next two decades of Margaret Sanger's life. Not until 1965, however, did a Supreme Court decision definitively strike down all laws restricting the use of contraceptive devices. By then, the American pioneer of birth control had become an early advocate of the contraceptive pill. ∎

thousand by 1910. In 1915, Carrie Chapman Catt assumed leadership of the NAWSA. A shrewd and skillful politician, Catt steered the movement away from civil disobedience and confrontive protests by stressing the contributions that women already made to good citizenship. Within two years, NAWSA membership leaped from one hundred thousand to two million.

Congress approved the proposed Nineteenth Amendment to the Constitution in 1919. Although much of the opposition to women's voting came from the traditional South, the assent of Tennessee, a southern state, provided the three-fourths approval needed for ratification in 1920. A major addition to American democracy, women's suffrage nevertheless rested upon arguments that appealed to nativist fears of ethnic and working-class power. "This government is menaced with great danger," Catt explained. "There is but one way to avert the danger—cut off the vote of the slums and give it to women." By appealing to the middle-class interests of Anglo-Protestant men and women, political leaders hoped to unify the response of American society to instability from below.

Blacks and the Struggle against Racism

Blacks faced a rising tide of discrimination and violence in the early twentieth century. The 1910 census found that 80 percent of black Americans lived in the South, where three-quarters of them worked as tenant farmers or sharecroppers on the region's declining cotton farms. Landowners held many of these people in virtual peonage, prompting an anonymous Florida citizen to comment that "slavery is just as much an 'institution' now as it was before the war." To maintain this system, white elites increasingly relied on vigilantism and segregation as the basic tools of white supremacy. Between 1884 and 1914, white vigilantes and mobs lynched some 3,600 blacks, many in gruesome and public rituals that became a perverted form of entertainment. This surge of violence fostered the rebirth of the white supremacist Ku Klux Klan in 1915. Klan promoters staged the group's revival to coincide with the Atlanta premiere of *Birth of a Nation*, a film by southern director D. W. Griffith that romanticized Klan violence during the Reconstruction period. Klan intimidation and terror supplemented a pervasive system of "Jim Crow" laws, which imposed segregation in educational institutions and transportation facilities. The Supreme Court upheld the constitutionality of such laws in the momentous *Plessy v. Ferguson* decision (1896), which expressed the doctrine of "separate but equal." The court ruled that the Constitution required only that facilities be equal for both races, not that blacks had a right to use the same facilities as whites. In the aftermath of this decision, most southern states adopted a thoroughgoing system of racial segregation in virtually all public areas including drinking fountains and rest rooms.

The South also eliminated most blacks from the voting rolls through a series of contrivances that disfranchised many lower-class whites as well. Frustrated agrarians like Populist leader Tom Watson, convinced by their defeat at the polls that whites could not divide politically until black political influence vanished, led the move to disfranchisement and race baiting (see chapter 2). Their arsenal included the poll tax, which effectively kept the right to vote from impoverished blacks and whites unaccustomed to meeting the payment schedule or keeping the records those laws often required. Literacy tests or understanding clauses—which required the ability to understand a portion of the state constitution read aloud by a clerk—were also effective disfranchising devices. Poor whites occasionally avoided the effects of these measures through grandfather clauses that suspended the requirements for those whose ancestors were able to vote before the beginning of Radical Reconstruction.

Progressive successors to the Populists of the 1890s linked reform and racism in their campaigns. For example, Governor James Vardaman of Mississippi won election through vicious race baiting that forged rural resentment of the middle-class elite with hatred of blacks. Dressed in a white suit, Vardaman rode to his rallies on a white lumber wagon pulled by a team of white oxen. Denouncing the black as "a lazy, lying, lustful animal which no conceivable amount of training can transform into a tolerable citizen," he

Since slavery times, whites had used violence freely as a means of controlling blacks. Whites widely approved such violence, and this 1893 Texas lynching drew several thousand onlookers. The authorities frequently acquiesced in lynchings and sometimes participated in them.

praised vigilantism. "We would be justified in slaughtering every Ethiop on the earth," Vardaman shouted, "to preserve unsullied the honor of one Caucasian home." As governor, the racial demagogue sought increased funding for education, regulation of railroads and banks, and child labor laws. Vardaman intended his reforms for whites only; educating a black person, he explained, only spoiled a good field hand.

The turn of the century brought increased oppression for blacks in other parts of America. A pervasive pseudoscientific racism seemed to offer ample justification for racial inequality. Northern blacks generally escaped the codified segregation characteristic of the South, but they regularly encountered discrimination in housing, education, hiring, and public accommodations. They also faced the danger of spontaneous attacks by whites. Major race riots shook New York City in 1900 and Springfield, Illinois, in 1908. Responding in kind also had its risks. In 1906, a dozen black soldiers stationed in Brownsville, Texas, reacted violently to racial slurs and harassment. When authorities failed to identify the participants, President Theodore Roosevelt arbitrarily gave dishonorable discharges to the members of three companies of the all-black Twenty-fifth Regiment. "The only reason I didn't have them all hung," Roosevelt declared, "was because I couldn't find out which ones . . . did the shooting." Six of those discharged had won the Medal of Honor. The Wilson administration carried such discriminatory attitudes a step further by mandating the segregation of federal facilities (see chapter 3).

The leadership of the troubled black community focused on Booker T. Washington between 1890 and 1915. Born into slavery in Virginia shortly

By 1900, Tuskegee Institute educated 1200 students in forty-two buildings on two thousand acres of land. Washington preached cleanliness and etiquette with such fervor that students chuckled about his "gospel of the toothbrush."

before the Civil War—he did not know the exact date—Washington received his freedom when the Confederacy collapsed. Washington subsequently enrolled at Hampton Institute, a school for blacks that stressed industrial education, training in crafts, agricultural methods, and child-raising practices. While still a young man, he became president of impoverished Tuskegee Institute in Alabama and rescued the school from near-collapse. Stressing such middle-class values as hard work, frugality, good manners, and personal cleanliness, Washington urged blacks to accept a separate status, even with its inherent degradation, and to concentrate on self-improvement. Blacks were to avoid politics and prepare themselves for careers as artisans or farmers. An agrarian in the tradition of former slaveholder and fellow Virginian Thomas Jefferson, Washington believed that the lives of blacks would be better on southern farms than in northern cities. He established himself as a national figure with a speech before the 1895 Atlanta Cotton Exhibition summarizing his views on race relations. "In all things purely social," Washington declared in a vivid metaphor, "we can be as separate as the fingers, yet one as the hand in all things essential to mutual progress."

Washington became an enormously influential figure, although his role as a black representative to the white power structure violated his own notions about black deference and the temporary acceptance of menial positions. Critics like W.E.B. DuBois charged that Washington's strategy ignored the economic realities of urban industrialism and that his accommodationist philosophy deprived blacks of self-esteem. Born a free man in Massachusetts, DuBois had become the first black to earn a Ph.D. from Harvard. "Are you training the Negro for his own benefit or for the benefit of somebody else?" DuBois asked Washington. Accordingly, the northerner rejected acquiescence to segregation and demanded assertive black leadership. He then proposed a strategy to challenge racial discrimination under the leadership of a college-educated black elite that he called "the Talented Tenth."

DuBois took an important step toward implementing his ideas in 1905 when he helped to found the Niagara movement at a hotel in Niagara Falls, Ontario. The movement reorganized itself as the National Association for the Advancement of Colored People (NAACP) four years later. An interracial group of moderate reformers, the NAACP assigned its most visible offices to whites, despite the prominence of DuBois. As a middle-class movement that reflected the leadership of the "Talented Tenth," the NAACP stressed political rather than economic issues and adopted a strategy of testing discriminatory laws in court. In 1915, the organization won a Supreme Court ruling that struck down an Oklahoma version of the grandfather clause, a legal device that denied the vote to anyone whose ancestors lacked the franchise in 1860. Two years later, the NAACP won an even more important victory when *Buchanan v. Worley* overturned a Louisville, Kentucky, law requiring residential segregation. These cases pioneered an approach that the NAACP used with increasing success in the decades to come, leading ultimately to the *Brown v. Board of Education* decision in 1954, which reversed *Plessy v. Ferguson* and overturned the doctrine of separate but equal.

Early twentieth-century Americans sought to create order and stability in a society experiencing explosive social tensions and contradictions. Urbanization and industrialization created greater wealth and greater poverty than the nation had ever known. As Americans endured painful economic and social changes, Anglo-Protestant corporate and cultural elites struggled to impose their values on others, while immigrant and racial groups resisted the pressure for conformity. Some feminists, socialists, and anarchists argued for a pluralist society that recognized cultural diversity and challenged corporate values. Meanwhile, ethnics and blacks laid the foundation for a flourishing popular culture. Inevitably, these social clashes spilled into the political arena, launching new movements bent on using government power to resolve the nation's ills and to prepare the nation for further greatness.

SUGGESTED READINGS

John Garraty, *The New Commonwealth, 1877–1890* (1968) offers a valuable introduction to turn-of-the-century America, as does Ray Ginger, *The Age of Excess* (1965). The work of Robert Wiebe, *The Search for Order, 1877–1920* (1968) and of Samuel Hays, *The Response to Industrialism, 1885–1914* (1957) pioneered the influential application of modernization theory to the period. Howard Mumford Jones, *The Age of Energy: Varieties of American Experience, 1865–1915* (1970) provides an excellent social history of the half century before World War I.

Among innovative urban historians, Stephan Thernstrom, *The Other Bostonians: Poverty and Progress in the American Metropolis, 1880–1970* (1973) and Sam Bass Warner, *Streetcar Suburbs: The Process of Growth in Boston, 1870–1900* (1971) discuss social and geographic movement in the city. Howard Chudacoff, *The Evolution of American Urban Society* (1975) offers an excellent overview of urbanization, as does Zane Miller, *Urbanization of America* (1973). Jacob Riis, *How the Other Half Lives* (1890) documents in words and photographs the plight of the urban poor. On the interaction between urban growth and architecture, see Leland Roth, *A Concise History of American Architecture* (1979).

Urban entertainment is the subject of several works, including Orrin Klapp, *The Collective Search for Identity* (1969); Michael Novak, *The Joy of Sports* (1976); David Voight, *America through Baseball* (1976); Gregory Stone, *Games, Sports, and Power* (1972); Albert McLean, Jr., *American Vaudeville as Ritual* (1965); and Lewis Erenberg, *Steppin' Out: New York Nightlife and the Transformation of American Culture, 1890–1930* (1981). Donald Gropman, *Say It Ain't So, Joe: The Story of Shoeless Joe Jackson* (1979) looks at the 1919 World Series scandal. Robert Sklar, *Movie-Made America: A Social History of the American Movies* (1975) examines the early history of motion pictures, as do Lary May, *Screening Out the Past: The Birth of Mass Culture and the Motion Picture Industry* (1980); Anthony Slide, *Early American Cinema* (1970); George Pratt, *Spellbound in the Dark* (rev. ed., 1973); and Richard Griffith and Arthur Mayer, *The Movies* (1978). For D. W. Griffith, see Richard Schikel, *D. W. Griffith: An American Life* (1984).

Oscar Handlin, *The Uprooted* (2d ed., 1973) is the standard study of the immigration process, but see also Leonard Dinnerstein and David Reimers, *Ethnic Americans: A History of Immigration and Assimilation* (1975). Philip Taylor, *The Distant Magnet: European Emigration to the U.S.A.* (1971) stresses the European background. Moses Rischin, *The Promised City: New York's Jews, 1870–1914* (1970) and Irving Howe, *World of Our Fathers: The Journey of the East European Jews to America and the Life They Found and Made* (1976) discuss assimilation and ethnic identity. Paul Messbarger, *Fiction with a Parochial Purpose: Social Use of American Catholic Literature, 1884–1900* (1970) examines the Catholic community and the role of Irish-Americans. For the West Coast experience, see Sucheng Chan, *This Bittersweet Soil: The Chinese in California Agriculture, 1869–1910* (1987) and Robert A. Wilson and Bill Hosokawa, *East to America: A History of the Japanese in the United States* (1980). Important studies of nativist reaction are John Higham, *Strangers in the Land: Patterns of American Nativism* (1955) and Barbara Solomon, *Ancestors and Immigrants* (1956). *The Protestant Establishment: Aristocracy and Caste in America* (1964) by E. Digby Baltzell examines the white Protestant elite and its fear of Jewish immigration.

Walter Hagan, *American Indians* (1961) is an important starting point for Native American history. Dee Brown, *Bury My Heart at Wounded Knee* (1977) and Francis Paul Prucha, *The Great Father: The United States Government and the American Indian* (1984) vividly depict the Native American experience in the late nineteenth century. H. Craig Miner, *The Corporation and the Indian 1865–1907* (1976) discusses the displacement of Indians. Joan Moore and Alfredo Cuellar, *Mexican Americans* (1970) and Leo Grebler, Moore, and Ralph Guzman, *The Mexican-American People* (1970) provide an excellent perspective on Chicano history.

The Progressive women's movement is portrayed in the relevant sections of Lois Banner, *Women in Modern America* (1974); Peter Filene, *Him Herself: Sex Roles in Modern America* (1974); and William Chafe, *Women and Equality* (1977). Joseph Kett, *Rites of Passage* (1977) describes the new concept of adolescence. See particularly Aileen Kraditor, *The Ideas of the Women's Suffrage Movement, 1890–1900* (1965) and William O'Neill, *Everyone Was Brave: The Rise and Fall of Feminism in America* (1967). For the relationship between family and sexuality, see the relevant chapters of John D'Emilio and Estelle B. Freedman, *Intimate Matters: A History of Sexuality in America* (1988). David Kennedy, *Birth Control in America: The Career of Margaret Sanger* (1970) discusses the work of a major feminist leader. Elaine Tyler May, *Great Expectations: Marriage and Divorce in Post-Victorian America* (1980) and O'Neill, *Divorce in the Progressive Era* (1967) look at the changing status of women.

For accounts of corporate America, see Wiebe, Hays, and Alfred Chandler, *Strategy and Structure: Chapters in the History of American Industrial Enterprise* (1966) and *The Visible Hand: The Managerial Revolution in American Business* (1977). Other important studies are Glenn Porter, *The Rise of Big Business, 1860–1910* (1973) and Thomas Cochran, *Business in American Life* (1972). Also useful in discussing the rise of corporate power is David F. Noble, *America by Design: Science Technology and the Rise of Corporate Capitalism* (1977). Samuel Haber discusses the ideas of Frederick Taylor in *Efficiency and Uplift: Scientific Management in the Progressive Era, 1890–1920* (1964), as does Daniel Nelson in *Frederick W. Taylor and the Rise of Scientific Management* (1980). See also David Nye, *Henry Ford: Ignorant Idealist* (1979). Invaluable on industrialization and cultural change are Jackson Lears, *No Place of Grace: Antimodernism and the Transformation of American Culture* (1981) and Alan Trachtenberg, *The Incorporation of America: Culture and Society in the Gilded Age* (1982).

Provocative essays on working-class culture are available in Herbert Gutman, *Work Culture and Society in Industrializing America* (1976); Melvyn Dubofsky, *Industrialism and the American Worker* (1975); and David Montgomery, *Workers Control in America* (1979). Daniel Rogers, *The Work Ethic in Industrial America, 1850–1920* (1975) examines how industrialization influenced attitudes toward work, and M. A. McLaurin, *Paternalism and Protest: Southern Cotton Mill Workers and Organized Labor, 1875–1905* (1971) portrays the lives of southern textile workers. On the American Federation of Labor, see Harold Livesay, *Samuel Gompers and Organized Labor in America* (1978). Dubofsky, *We Shall Be All: A History of the Industrial Workers of the World* (1969) is an excellent account of the radical Wobblies. On socialism and radicalism, see James Weinstein, *The Decline of Socialism in America* (1967); John Diggins, *The American Left in the Twentieth Century* (1973); Christopher Lasch, *The New Radicalism in America, 1889–1963* (1965); and L. Glen Seretan, *Daniel De Leon: The Odyssey of an American Marxist* (1979).

The classic synthesis of southern history in this period is C. Vann Woodward, *The Origins of the New South, 1877–1913* (1951). On race relations, see Woodward's *Strange Career of Jim Crow* (3d ed., 1974). Jack Temple Kirby, *Darkness at the Dawning: Race and Reform in the Progressive South* (1972) is an excellent supplement. August Meier, *Negro Thought in America, 1880–1915* (1963) probes a critical period in black history. Louis Harlan, *Booker T. Washington* (1972) is the definitive biography of the most influential black man of his time; Elliot M. Rudwick, *W.E.B. DuBois: Propagandist of the Negro Protest* (1969) illuminates Washington's most important critic.

For a discussion of trends in the arts, see Lewis Mumford, *The Brown Decades: A Study of the Arts in America, 1865–1895* (1931) and Milton Brown, *The Story of the Armory Show* (1963). On literature, see Larzer Ziff, *The American 1890s: Life and Times of a Lost Generation* (1966) and Jay Martin, *Harvests of Change: American Literature, 1865–1914* (1967).

Opposite Page:
A dynamic speaker who ''seems to throw the word into the air,'' Theodore Roosevelt addresses a crowd in Brattleboro, Vermont, 1903.

2

THE POLITICS OF PROGRESSIVISM, 1892-1912

The growth of a corporate economy and an ethnically diverse working force in the cities had profound consequences for American politics. Concentration of economic power, class polarization, and regional specialization produced major tensions within the prevailing democratic ideology of nineteenth-century America. As the Anglo-Protestant elite attempted to consolidate its power through reforms in city, state, and federal government, independent farmers and middle-class professionals pursued parallel lines of reform to enhance their own interests and values. At the same time, purity crusaders attempted to cleanse the evolving social order of exploitation, self-indulgence, and moral laxity. The result was Progressive reform, a movement of energy and intensity, but also of complexity and contradiction.

THE DEMOCRATIC IDEOLOGY IN CRISIS

Americans of diverse political viewpoints adhered to a democratic ideology in the late nineteenth century. Most assumed that the nation's presidents represented a genuine majority and spoke for the will of the people. They also believed that the exceptional circumstances of the agricultural frontier enabled all white men to become independent producers and that relative equality prevailed in this producers' democracy. Adhering to classical economic liberalism, most Americans saw freedom as a function of individual property ownership and the ability to enter into contracts. Laws of nature ensured that these personal rights would result in the general good of society. Consequently, small retailers and producers expected government to permit them to compete equally in the economy and control their own businesses.

By the 1890s, however, the rise of corporate industrialism had created enormous concentrations of economic power that threatened the basic tenets of egalitarian ideology. This centralized ownership challenged middle-class concepts of independence, individual ownership, and equality. Americans now confronted an enormous gap between the wealth and power of those on the top of the economic hierarchy and the poverty and powerlessness of those on the bottom. For many, especially in rural areas, government policies on tariffs and the money supply provided prime illustrations of the power of the interests. Many farm leaders argued that the tariff artificially inflated the price of domestic goods while leaving producers to fend for themselves in the highly competitive world agricultural economy. The federal government's commitment to tight money was also unpopular with farmers. Many in the South and the West faced demoralizing debt during a period of severe deflation. Consequently, banks forced them to repay loans with dollars that were becoming scarcer and more valuable over time.

These tensions deepened with the onset of the most severe depression the nation experienced before the 1930s. A stock market panic in May 1893 precipitated the downturn, and the economy fell rapidly for the next several months in a decline marked by eight thousand business failures, four hundred bank closings, and a 20 percent unemployment rate. The collapse

Exhibit 2–1. Unemployment Rates, 1892–1899
(percentage of civilian labor force)

1892	3.0
1893	11.7
1894	18.4
1895	13.7
1896	14.4
1897	14.5
1898	12.4
1899	6.5

Source: *Historical Statistics of the United States, Colonial Times to 1970* (U.S. Department of Commerce, 1975).

sparked bitter strikes at the Homestead and Pullman works, two of the most violent labor incidents in American history (see chapter 1). In addition, Jacob Coxey led a protest march of jobless workers to Washington, proposing that the government loan paper money to local communities for use in hiring the unemployed for public works projects. "General" Coxey's army of some three hundred unemployed set out from Massillon, Ohio, to deliver its "petition in boots" and reached the apprehensive capital on May 1, 1894, where police clubbed and arrested its leader for trespassing.

The major protest movement of the 1890s came not from the cities, however, but from the farms. Although industrialization and the westward movement revolutionized American agriculture in the decades after the Civil War, farmers felt themselves to be the victims rather than the beneficiaries of the industrial age. Between 1860 and 1890, the number of farms grew substantially, as did the size of the rural population (although not so rapidly as that of the urban population) and the productivity of American agriculture. By 1880, machines harvested 80 percent of American wheat. The total amount of improved land leaped from 189 million acres to 414 million in the next twenty years. As railroads spread and cities grew, American farmers began to produce for a national and international market, especially after the advent of the refrigerated railroad car facilitated the shipment of foodstuffs over great distances.

Unlike late-nineteenth-century corporate and financial interests, small and independent producers remained extremely vulnerable to market forces. The rise in wheat and cotton production, for example, coincided with the opening of new farming enterprises in western Canada, South America, and Australia, which resulted in a worldwide surge in the production of basic staples, choking the market and driving prices down. Wheat, which had sold for $1.19 a bushel in 1881, slumped to $0.49 a bushel in 1894, and cotton fell from $0.30 to less than $0.06 a pound in the same period.

The shift to commercial farming undercut the independence and self-sufficiency that, according to cherished American myth, had characterized the yeoman farmer in the preindustrial period. New machinery dramatically increased farm production, and equipment costs forced farmers deeper into unprecedented debt. Farm prosperity consequently depended on the willing-

Stick in hand, "General" Coxey leads his "army" toward Washington.

ness of bankers to extend affordable loans to independent growers. In similar fashion, farmers relied on the railroads as their link with the urban market, making freight rates crucial to the economic viability of the individual farmer.

Farmers also faced a steady decline in status and prestige. The growth of cities and urban culture undermined rural values and brought farm life into disrepute. Agrarian existence was extremely taxing without the electricity, roads, and schools that increasingly defined urban life. As sociologist Frank Giddings put it in 1896, "[Farmers] are no longer ignorant of the luxuries of the towns and the simple manner of life no longer satisfied them." Hamlin Garland provided vivid portraits of the harshness of farm life in the Middle West in his widely read books *A Son of the Middle Border* and *Main-Travelled Roads*. Moreover, the prestige of the farmer declined as city life became the national model. The urbanite represented success and sophistication, while such terms as "rube" and "hick" increasingly described rural dwellers.

Economic hardship and loss of status particularly characterized the rural South, a region still reeling from the devastating effects of the Civil War. Small producers drifted into peonage, in the words of agrarian leader Thomas

Watson, "like victims of some horrid nightmare . . . powerless-oppressed-shocked." Defeat and the end of slavery disrupted the large cotton plantations and forced southern agriculture to establish new arrangements for securing labor and capital. Tenant farming and sharecropping became common for both black and white farmers forced to depend on a crop lien system to finance their planting. The lien system's terms made the South, in the words of one historian, "a giant pawn shop." Under this arrangement, cash-poor farmers traded a portion of their future crop for necessities, which they received on credit from local storekeepers. The merchants usually insisted on the cultivation of cotton—"No cotton, no credit"—because of its ready convertibility to cash. Bloated world supplies drove the price of American cotton to a mere six cents a pound in the 1890s while interest rates and the cost of machinery and fertilizer increased the debt for most producers. Southern farmers grew desperate as the price of cotton fell below the cost of production by 1893.

The southern political structure offered little remedy for this crisis. As the farm economy collapsed, a small minority of upper-middle-class businessmen and lawyers proposed a New South based on northern patterns of industrialization and urbanization. The chief advocate of the New South, Atlanta *Constitution* editor Henry Grady, boasted, "We have sown towns and cities in the place of theories and put business above politics." Grady and other proponents of the New South usually controlled the dominant Democratic parties of the region. Their programs of low taxes for industry left much of the tax burden on farmers.

National political leaders were also indifferent to agrarian complaints. Southern farmers asserted that the federal government was dominated by politicians who supported the interests of northern industry by enacting

By manipulating the crop lien system, white landowners and merchants trapped blacks in a state of near-peonage. The relentless production of cotton depleted the land and ruined prices.

protective tariffs. While southerners sold cotton on an unprotected world market, they bought steel machinery and other supplies in a protected national market. Farmers in the West also joined southerners in resenting government policy that limited the amount of money in circulation to the quantity of gold and silver in the national treasury. This conservative economic policy reflected the political strength of the large bankers of the Northeast. Because the currency supply failed to grow as fast as the economy, the resulting shortage of money kept interest rates high. Consequently, expanding industrialists and farmers bid against each other to borrow money. Yet currency deflation kept prices stable except where tariffs raised them artificially.

POPULIST REFORMERS

Like the business entrepreneurs of the late nineteenth century, independent farmers sought to minimize competition through organization and to exert control over market forces. The Farmers Alliance, begun by Charles Macune in Texas during the 1880s, spread rapidly, becoming especially strong in the South. Organized at a grass roots level, the movement supported thousands of newspapers and speakers who tried to educate producers on the need to develop farmer-owned cooperatives to break the credit monopoly of banking and merchant elites. Such cooperatives enabled members to purchase supplies and market crops without becoming indebted at high interest rates to storekeepers.

By 1890, the agrarian movement had crystallized into three major elements: The Northern Alliance, the Southern Alliance, and the Colored Alliance. But farmers faced major obstacles to building an effective coalition when they tried to appeal to urban labor and discovered serious differences over currency deflation and the price of foodstuffs. More frustrating were the divisions separating western and southern farmers. In a period still defined by the hatreds of the Civil War, the political heritage of the West remained largely Republican and unionist, while that of the South remained Democratic and secessionist.

Southern farmers also confronted a deep chasm caused by the separation of black and white producers. Racial antagonism threatened the effort to build a genuine agrarian movement in which economic issues took precedence. Bold farm leaders such as Thomas Watson of Georgia challenged the system of white solidarity and white supremacy with a direct appeal for black votes. "You are kept apart that you may be separately fleeced of your earnings," Watson shouted at his integrated audiences. "Race antagonism perpetuates a monetary system which beggars both," he charged. Some blacks responded to Watson's appeal, although at considerable personal risk from angry whites; on at least one occasion Watson rallied two thousand white supporters to stand guard over a black minister who had become the target of repeated threats.

By the 1890s, the Alliance realized that its goal of a cooperative, decentralized economy could be achieved only through local and national political action. Centralized control of the money supply made it difficult for Alliance cooperatives to obtain enough capital to construct an effective alternative purchasing and marketing structure to challenge storekeepers. Movement leaders therefore urged the federal government to establish a subtreasury plan. Under this arrangement, farmers could store their crops in government warehouses instead of placing them on the market when prices were low. While waiting for prices to improve, the government would accept those crops as collateral for farm loans. This credit would not only free rural producers from high interest rates, but would also increase the money supply and thus stimulate the inflation of agricultural prices that farmers desired.

In 1890, the Southern Alliance elected four governors, three United States senators, and forty-four representatives while claiming control of eight state legislatures. Among the winners was the fiery Tom Watson, elected to Congress from Georgia. Disappointed in the responsiveness of these newly elected officials, the Alliance decided to pursue a new strategy in 1892. Since neither the Republicans or the Democrats would agree to government assistance for low-income producers, Alliance leaders proceeded to build a new political party: the People's party, or the Populists. On July 4, 1892, 1,300 delegates met in Omaha to nominate General James Weaver, a former Union army officer, for the presidency. To balance the ticket, the convention chose General James G. Field, a disabled Confederate veteran, as his running mate.

Trying to make the People's party a national rather than a purely agrarian movement, party leaders went beyond support of the subtreasury plan to endorse proposals for using government power to assist both farmers and workers. Convention delegates called for government ownership of railroads, telephones, and telegraphs. They proposed a graduated income tax as a way of shifting the tax burden to the prosperous classes, and they demanded a flexible currency to permit the expansion of credit and the money supply. The Populists also tried to attract urban workers with a platform endorsing shorter hours for laborers, immigration restriction, and denunciation of the use of private security forces to break strikes.

The Populists pushed for reforms in the political process to make government institutions more responsive to the public. They demanded that United States senators no longer be chosen by state legislatures but by direct popular vote. They supported voting reforms such as the adoption of the Australian or secret ballot. The People's party also advocated use of the initiative (allowing voters to enact laws independent of state legislature) and the referendum (permitting voters to nullify or revise actions of state legislatures).

Weaver won over one million popular votes (8.5 percent) and twenty-two electoral votes in the 1892 campaign. Populist candidates also took a dozen House and Senate seats. The new occupant of the White House was, however, a Democrat—a burly former sheriff from Buffalo, Grover Cleveland. Although he had defeated the incumbent Republican Benjamin Harrison, Cleveland remained a rigid conservative whose principles clashed with Populist concerns.

TOM EDWARD WATSON
1856–1922

Georgia's Tom Watson, a dynamic political organizer, embodied the dreams and bitterness of agrarian America. As a boy, Watson idolized his grandfather, a plantation owner who worked forty-five slaves on a sizable estate. But the Civil War destroyed the family's wealth, leaving the patriarch dead and Watson's father destitute. The young heir reversed these fortunes and restored the family name through a brilliant career as a criminal lawyer.

A successful man, Watson sought the role of avenger. He directed his wrath toward conservative advocates of a New South who pursued alliances with northern business at the expense of southern dirt farmers. Accusing such interests of plots to "betray the South with a Judas kiss," Watson championed small agriculture and proclaimed himself a Populist after election to Congress in 1890.

Still dissatisfied, the irrepressible Watson single-handedly overturned the foundations of southern politics and race relations. First he broke with the Democratic party of Thomas Jefferson, his spiritual forefather. Then he dared to challenge white solidarity by appealing to white and black farmers to put aside racial differences and vote their common interests. "You are kept apart," Watson told the astonished producers of the South, "that you may be separately fleeced of your earnings." The defiant Populist even denounced lynching and once summoned two thousand poor whites to protect the home of a threatened black supporter.

The aroused political establishment responded ruthlessly to Watson's agenda. To thwart his 1892 reelection plans, conservative Democrats redrew the agitator's congressional district. The strategy worked, and the fiery Populist lost an ugly race marred by violence and fraud. Similar tactics defeated him again two years later. Yet Watson's courage brought national prominence. In 1896, the Populist party nominated the Georgian as its vice-presidential running mate for William Jennings Bryan. A vigorous opponent of fusion with the Democrats, Watson clung to the dream of a successful third party even as Populism evaporated around him. "The sentiment is still there," he mourned shortly after the campaign, "but confidence is gone." A Republican victory in 1896 and two poor showings as Populist presidential candidate in 1904 and 1908 sent Watson into political eclipse.

Embittered by the desertion of allies and his belief that rich whites controlled *(cont.)*

POPULISTS, DEMOCRATS, AND REPUBLICANS: 1896

The Cleveland administration coincided with the Panic of 1893, and its policies greatly inflamed the farmer revolt. As businesses and banks failed, panicked citizens brought their bank notes (paper money) to be redeemed in precious metal. Although it was legal for the Treasury to insist that the public the black vote to destroy southern democracy, Watson increasingly turned to racism and nativism after 1896. By the 1910s, his self-published *Tom Watson's Magazine, Weekly Jeffersonian,* and *Watson's Jeffersonian Magazine* featured vicious diatribes against blacks, Catholics, Jews, and radicals. Leo Frank, a Jewish factory manager unfairly accused of murdering a young Atlanta girl in 1913, found himself the special target of Watson's vituperation. Denouncing Frank as "the typical young libertine Jew" and a "lascivious pervert," Watson used editorial power to inflame the mob that lynched Frank after the governor of Georgia commuted his death sentence.

Watson's campaign against the "sinister wonders" of Catholicism attracted support from other Georgia newspapers and played a major role in the Atlanta founding of the "second" Ku Klux Klan in 1915. Ironically, Watson had once sent his own daughter to a Catholic school. Nevertheless, anti-Catholic bromides and demands for racial segregation and disfranchisement linked neatly to the Progressive movement's obsession with Anglo-Protestant purity. By combining nativist and racist anxieties with grass roots suspicion of northern corporations, Watson gradually established a new power base among the small farmers he had once rallied to reform. By 1917, the Populist leader had

refashioned himself into the most important political force in Georgia.

World War I brought still another twist to Watson's tortured odyssey. Siding with anticorporate critics of Wilson's policy, the Georgia editor joined Mississippi racist Senator James Vardaman to denounce American military intervention in Europe. He now returned to the language of the Populist years and harshly condemned wartime regimentation and centralization as "universal goose-stepping." Watson's scathing attacks on conscription prompted the postmaster general to ban his publications from the mail. The postwar Red Scare, he thundered in 1919, constituted a "deceitful, damnable scheme . . . to convert this republic into a plutocracy."

After losing another race for Congress in 1918, Watson ran for the Senate in 1920. This time he returned to Washington with an overwhelming victory. His triumphant campaign, supported by the Klan, incorporated opposition to the League of Nations with pledges to restore American civil liberties.

Barely a year after taking his Senate seat and calling for recognition of the Soviet Union, Tom Watson died. More than any other figure in the South's passionate history, the cantankerous Populist illustrated the tragedy of lost opportunities and squandered energies. ■

accept silver in exchange for the paper, Cleveland demanded that the government maintain a gold standard, ordering that only gold be exchanged for paper money. By preventing the circulation of silver, Cleveland's policy restricted the total money supply, caused further deflation, and intensified business cutbacks. Meanwhile, the government bought gold to meet public demand for hard metal and New York bankers like J. P. Morgan made huge profits as they imported the precious metal from Europe. Thus many Americans pictured a financial conspiracy between the Cleveland administration and banking interests at the expense of ordinary producers.

Populists felt a further sense of betrayal with the passage of the Wilson-Gorman Tariff Act of 1894. As a Democrat, Cleveland had campaigned against the high McKinley tariff passed in 1890, but the new law retained the same levels of protection enacted by the Republicans. Although Cleveland denounced the measure as an example of "party perfidy and party dishonor," he did not veto it and permitted the bill to become law without his signature. Gleeful Republicans eagerly anticipated the political fallout. "The Democratic mortality will be so great next fall," predicted one Republican congressman, "that their dead will be buried in trenches and marked unknown." Indeed many Democrats did desert their party in the congressional elections of 1894, precipitating the most dramatic realignment of party membership in the history of the House of Representatives.

Populist discontent also fed on some unpopular decisions by the nation's fledgling regulatory agencies and by the judiciary system. Much of this dissatisfaction centered on the Interstate Commerce Commission (ICC) created by Congress in 1887 to regulate railroad rates. The agency remained friendly to the powerful rail corporations, and the courts undercut its weak attempts at regulation. During its first decade, the ICC lost 90 percent of the cases it litigated. In 1897, the Supreme Court ruled in the Maximum Rate case that while the commission could overturn unjust rates it did not have the authority to establish fairer ones.

Populist criticism of the judiciary focused on the Supreme Court's narrow interpretation of the Sherman Anti-Trust Act of 1890. Passed in response to widespread fear of the power of large corporations, this mild law prohibited "conspiracy in restraint of trade" and encouraged business competition. However, the Court ruled in *United States v. E. C. Knight* (1895) that even though a single company controlled 98 percent of all sugar production, competitors were not necessary victimized by a conspiratorial restraint of trade. Moreover, the Court also held that the Sherman Act applied to interstate commerce, not to manufacturing, an opinion that effectively gutted the law.

The economic issues of the 1890s left the Democratic party deeply divided between its eastern wing, which supported the conservative policies of Cleveland, and the angry insurgents from the West and South determined to control the 1896 convention and nominate their own candidate. For many Democrats, the complex issues of the time focused on the simple slogan Free Silver, or the demand for the free and unlimited coinage of silver with sixteen ounces of silver equaling the value of one ounce of gold. Rallying around this issue, agrarian Democrats sought fusion with the Populists to defeat the eastern conservatives.

The burgeoning debate over free silver launched one of the most spectacular careers in American political history. At the end of the Democratic party's tumultuous debate over the question at its Chicago convention, thirty-six-year-old William Jennings Bryan galvanized the assembly with a powerful and vivid denunciation of economic privilege. "You shall not press down upon the brow of labor this crown of thorns," Bryan thundered, "you shall not crucify mankind upon a cross of gold." A former two-term congressman and newspaper editor from Nebraska, Bryan enjoyed some regional promi-

The greatest orator of his time, the charismatic William Jennings Bryan rarely held public office, but he built a political career around his ability to express the ideals and frustrations of agrarian America.

nence as an orator, but his spellbinding address to the convention made him a national figure almost overnight. The next day the party nominated him for the presidency. The youngest major party nominee in history, he barely met the constitutional requirement that presidents be at least thirty-five.

Bryan's nomination by the Democrats brought the culmination of a long-brewing crisis for the Populist party. Although its 1894 popular vote had increased 50 percent over its 1892 total, the party remained underfinanced and poorly organized. Western Populists argued that fusion with the Democrats would advance the party agenda. But Watson expressed southern hostility to state Democratic parties dominated by conservatives. After a bitter debate, the Populists acquiesced to fusion by nominating Bryan for president, but they sought a vestige of independence by nominating the colorful Watson instead of Democratic nominee Arthur Sewall for vice-president.

The more sedate Republican convention chose veteran Ohio politician William McKinley as its first ballot nominee. McKinley, wrote Kansas journalist William Allen White, appeared "on the whole decent, on the whole dumb." House Speaker Joseph Cannon sneered that McKinley kept his ear so close to the ground that he got it full of grasshoppers. A well-known advocate of high tariffs but a moderate on the currency issue, McKinley firmly embraced the Republican demand for maintenance of a strict gold standard. An adroit politician who preferred to compromise issues rather than define them, the staid candidate provided an effective counterpoint to the fervor and frenzy of his opponent Bryan.

A pivotal election in American history, the 1896 contest helped to establish active campaigning as a feature of presidential balloting. Bryan barnstormed eighteen thousand miles by train and delivered more than six hundred speeches to an estimated three million people. By contrast, McKinley and his manager Mark Hanna relied on heavy spending and publicity, pioneering the application of corporate organizational techniques to politics. McKinley himself stayed at home in Canton, Ohio, while Hanna brought the crowds to him. Three-quarters of a million people from a variety of special interests received free trips to Canton, where they listened to the candidate deliver homilies from his front porch. Simultaneously, the Republicans published and distributed an enormous amount of campaign material, much of it playing on fears of Bryan's alleged radicalism. Hanna raised about $3.5 million for the campaign largely through appeals to major corporations, which dreaded the possible consequences of a Bryan victory.

The 1896 election resulted in a watershed victory for McKinley and the Republicans and helped to set the political tone of the country until the realignment precipitated by the Great Depression of the 1930s. Emerging from the contest with a solid majority coalition, the Republicans lost only two presidential elections (in 1912 and 1916) between 1896 and 1932. The party succeeded by reaching beyond its nineteenth-century Anglo-Protestant base and its strong constituencies in the evangelical churches associated with the Methodists and the Baptists. The Democrats, by contrast, failed to capitalize upon their strength among the new immigrants, Roman Catholics, and other voters from "liturgical" and "ritualistic" churches. Offended by the pietistic

**Exhibit 2–2. Voter Participation in Presidential Elections, 1896–1920
(percentage of eligible voters)**

1896	79.3
1900	73.2
1904	65.2
1908	65.4
1912	58.8
1916	61.6
1920	49.2

Source: *Historical Statistics of the United States, Colonial Times to 1970* (U.S. Department of Commerce, 1975).

tone of Bryan's revivalistic rhetoric and its rural symbolism, many traditional Democrats switched parties in 1896. Consequently, the Republicans took healthy majorities in the nation's twelve largest cities.

Republicans were also successful in convincing working-class voters that conservative economic policies would ensure "a full dinner pail." Business managers joined with party propagandists in persuading those voters that their jobs depended on McKinley's victory and that a high tariff protected them from the competition of poorly paid foreign labor. As a result, McKinley

Exhibit 2–3. Election of 1896

	Electoral vote	Popular vote
McKinley (Republican)	271	7,036,000
Bryan (Democrat)	176	6,468,000

MARCUS ALONZO HANNA
1837–1904

Ohio industrialist, corporate progressive, and Republican party stalwart, Marcus Alonzo Hanna belonged to the party of Lincoln almost from its founding. His mildly reformist Quaker family opposed slavery and supported Republican policies favorable to business. After brief service in the Civil War, Hanna entered the coal and iron business in Cleveland and accumulated extraordinary wealth. The young man's financial dealings increasingly pushed him toward politics. Recognizing the value of close links between industry and politics, Hanna considered personal profits and community profits to be indistinguishable, and he used government power to advance his own financial interests. Accordingly, he campaigned against Cleveland's political bosses to protect his holdings in the city's street railway system. A born politician, Hanna later accepted the bosses as allies to ensure their support in future battles.

Eager for greater influence, Hanna actively sought the role of president maker. He chose Ohio congressional representative William McKinley as his protégé in the 1880s. McKinley's scruples and faintly idealistic political style fascinated the cynical and amoral Hanna, comfortable in his acceptance of the shabby public ethics of his time. The congressman's support for high tariffs and malleable views on the currency question added to his appeal. Hanna approached McKinley, one observer noted, with the deference "of a big, bashful boy toward the girl he loves." Usually a dynamic figure, Hanna became "just a shade obsequious in McKinley's presence." McKinley gave the orders, a mutual associate noted, and Hanna obeyed without question. He managed McKinley's successful drive to the White House in 1896, contributing vast sums of his own money and raising millions more from his fellow corporate leaders. *(cont.)*

squeaked out a tight victory, gathering 7.1 million popular votes (51.1 percent) to Bryan's nearly 6.5 million (47.7 percent). In the Electoral College, the tally was a close 271 to 176.

The Democratic defeat in 1896 represented the failure of nineteenth-century agrarian radicals to reform American society in the wake of the industrial revolution. Despite the widespread labor unrest of the 1890s, Bryan won virtually no support among workers, nor did he do well among the more prosperous farmers in the older states of the Middle West. The Republicans, by contrast, did well with both groups and the urban middle class. As agrarian protest waned, the professional and business classes of the cities stepped forward to present their own agenda for reform.

IMPERIAL CHOICES

Amid the domestic disorder of the 1890s, American society paid increasing attention to events abroad. Nineteenth-century Americans had shown little

Although Hanna remained a staunch McKinley backer, he now turned to his own ambitions for elective office, winning a narrow victory in the 1897 Ohio senatorial contest. He also took an active role in founding the influential National Civic Federation as a forum for corporate progressivism. Eager to avoid price competition and contain the cycle of boom and bust, the NCF pledged to end the conflict between capital and labor and to achieve the "normal sense of social solidarity which is the foundation stone of democracy." Hanna saw the NCF as a vehicle for spreading the philosophy of corporate capitalism throughout the Republican party, but the organization also legitimized reforms like trust regulation and workmen's compensation among corporate managers.

In the aftermath of McKinley's death, business interests touted Hanna as the logical nominee in 1904, but the ambitious Theodore Roosevelt blocked his path. During the anthracite coal strike of 1902, the president emerged as the spokesman for corporate capitalism, a role the NCF had expected business leaders to assume. Hanna, by contrast, failed to influence events. Facing a reelection battle in Ohio, the embattled senator asked J. P. Morgan to pressure the owners to settle. "There are several important places where U.S. Steel could do me lots of good," Hanna pleaded. "I am bleeding at every pore already and can't bear the burden." Morgan initially refused, however, and Roosevelt ultimately stepped forward to take credit for resolving the conflict, demonstrating his primacy in the party.

Hanna died in Washington in 1904. His greatest legacy was not his fortune or the McKinley presidency but the Progressive agenda of the National Civic Federation. In the name of self-interest, Mark Hanna had helped to move America's corporations toward stability and reform. ∎

desire for an overseas empire, especially since the western frontier and displacement of Native Americans afforded ample opportunities for military glory and geographic expansion. But the industrial revolution brought the nation a productive capacity that far exceeded the domestic market. Reformers such as single-tax advocate Henry George suggested that a redistribution of wealth might increase the purchasing power of more Americans. But business and political elites looked to overseas opportunities as a source of raw materials, an arena for investments, and a stimulus to foreign trade and the cultivation of new markets.

Pressure for a more assertive foreign policy also came from political, military, and intellectual leaders eager to see America assume a role as a world power. Captain Alfred Thayer Mahan, a naval officer and author of *The Influence of Sea Power upon History* (1890), saw the world as a place of struggle in which the United States must prepare to defend its interests against rival powers. Mahan called for an expansionist foreign policy to secure strategic sea-lanes and overseas markets while ensuring unity at home. "Americans must now begin to look outward," wrote Mahan. "The growing production of the country demands it." These ideas were enormously influential among powerful upper-class leaders such as Theodore Roosevelt, Henry Cabot Lodge, and John Hay, who viewed imperialism as a stimulus to both national vitality and the reinvigoration of their own class.

"I should welcome almost any war," declared Roosevelt, "for I think this country needs one." Roosevelt and his colleagues focused increasingly on the faltering Spanish empire in the Caribbean and the Pacific as an opportunity for American expansion. Between the 1860s and the 1890s, Americans repeatedly expressed popular support for Cuba's revolt against Spanish colonialism. As the fighting on the island raged, the yellow journalism of William Randolph Hearst and Joseph Pulitzer greatly influenced attitudes toward the conflict (see chapter 1). Locked in a bitter circulation war, Hearst and Pulitzer used sensationalist coverage of alleged Spanish atrocities to boost sales. When artist Frederic Remington cabled Hearst from Havana that there would be no war, the publisher responded, "You furnish the pictures and I'll furnish the war."

By 1898, the corporate and banking community embraced the idea of war with Spain. Worried about the security of the $50 million worth of American investments in Cuba, business leaders feared the uncertainty produced by the Cuban Revolution and Spain's inability to deal effectively with the uprising. Instability in the Caribbean also cast a shadow over the construction of a Central American canal to tie the Atlantic seaports to the markets of the Pacific and Asia. Moreover, the State Department and the military warned that expansion-minded Germany might fill the vacuum left behind if the Spanish retreated from Cuba.

These concerns prompted McKinley to sent the battleship *Maine* to Havana harbor in 1898 as a symbol of American power. Two weeks after its arrival, the ship mysteriously exploded and sank, with the loss of 250 American lives. A naval investigation hinted at an internal explosion but could offer no satisfactory explanation of the tragedy. Even without clear evidence, the yellow journalists and other advocates of American intervention denounced the blast as yet another Spanish atrocity and demanded reprisals. Two months later, unable to foresee a peaceful resolution of the situation in Cuba, McKinley asked for a declaration of war, and Congress responded enthusiastically.

Secretary of State John Hay characterized the Spanish-American conflict as a "splendid little war." The United States Navy quickly took the strategic initiative when Commodore George Dewey engineered the defeat of the enemy fleet in the Philippines. After less than three months of ineffective and poorly organized fighting, Spanish troops surrendered in Cuba, Puerto Rico, and the Philippines. In Cuba, American volunteers under the command of Colonel Leonard Wood and Lieutenant Colonel Theodore Roosevelt stormed the heights around the port of Santiago, where Spanish cruisers and destroyers sank before the onslaught of four United States battleships. American war casualties amounted to a mere 379, but more than five thousand American soldiers died from tropical diseases and the consequences of inadequate sanitation and rotten meat. Yet the popular war stimulated American nationalism, unity, and overseas empire.

By the Paris Peace Treaty of 1898, Spain relinquished control of Cuba and ceded the Philippines, Guam, and Puerto Rico to the United States. Since McKinley had convinced Congress to annex the Hawaiian Islands earlier in the year, the United States now stood on the brink of a territorial empire. But nineteenth-century traditions of noninterventionism and self-determination clashed with the imperialist aspirations of the McKinley administration. The Anti-Imperialist League, organized in 1898, opposed Senate ratification of the Paris Peace Treaty and attempted to build a broad-based coalition opposed to the annexation of overseas territory. Led by William Jennings Bryan, former presidents Benjamin Harrison and Grover Cleveland, industrialist Andrew Carnegie, labor leader Samuel Gompers, and intellectuals such as William James, William Graham Sumner, and Mark Twain, the league denounced the building of an empire as a violation of the nation's most fundamental values.

Anti- imperialists feared that a nation with colonial commitments could not preserve liberty at home. Many southern Democrats also objected to the annexation of colonies whose "colored" population might corrupt the purity of the white race. Finally, opponents of territorial expansion argued that American trade could be extended without the acquisition of colonies or the use of military force. But imperialists insisted that only annexation could

A sensational contemporary lithograph graphically depicts the sinking of the "Maine" in Havana harbor.

A swaggering Roosevelt poses with the Rough Riders atop San Juan Hill in Cuba.

provide the military security necessary to pursue trade opportunities against competing nations in the Caribbean, Pacific, and East Asia. The resulting 57–27 vote in favor of accepting the Paris treaty barely met the two-thirds requirement for Senate ratification, but steered the nation toward a new emphasis on foreign expansion.

In 1898, the Paris Peace Treaty gave Cuba nominal independence. Three years later, the United States forced the Cubans to accept the Platt Amendment to their constitution. This proviso gave Washington broad authority over Cuban domestic affairs, allowed the United States to establish a

Exhibit 2–4. Military Personnel on Active Duty, 1896–1900

1896	41,680
1897	43,656
1898	235,785
1899	100,166
1900	125,923

Source: *Historical Statistics of the United States, Colonial Times to 1970* (U.S. Department of Commerce, 1975).

Four thousand American soldiers died in the four-year struggle to "pacify" the Philippines, a Pacific archipelago McKinley had once dismissed as "those darned islands."

permanent naval base at Guantanamo Bay, and permitted American military intervention at will. Simultaneously, Philippine insurgents led by Emilio Aguinaldo turned their struggle against foreign domination against the United States. American troops responded with pacification programs, which placed peasants in concentration camps and destroyed their villages and crops. Using the same techniques that the United States once condemned in Spanish-occupied Cuba, the American army employed torture to break the morale of rebel leaders and ultimately killed over two hundred thousand Filipinos before crushing the persistent uprising.

With the Caribbean pacified and American outposts established in Hawaii, Guam, and the Philippines, the United States acted to assert its influence in East Asia. In China, European colonizers and the newly powerful Japanese strove to create geographic spheres of influence in order to exclude potential competitors. American missionaries and business leaders objected to this denial of access to the huge Chinese population and its lucrative market. Accordingly, in 1899 and 1900, Secretary of State John Hay circulated two diplomatic notes that proclaimed an Open Door policy. Hay stated that the United States sought to maintain the territorial integrity of China and to keep spheres of influence open to trade with all nations. Europe and Japan acquiesced to the Open Door, realizing that a scramble to divide China could lead to a world war. But the United States lacked the naval power to enforce its will and emerged from the affair with an exaggerated sense of its ability to influence events in Asia and the western Pacific. The Open Door policy

Exhibit 2–5. America's Pacific Empire

Exhibit 2–6. Imports and Exports of Goods and Services, 1895–1920
(in rounded billions of dollars)

	Imports	Exports	Trade Surplus
1895	$1.0 b	.9	$ −0.1 b
1900	$1.2 b	$ 1.7 b	$ .5 b
1905	$1.6 b	$ 1.9 b	$ .3 b
1910	$2.1 b	$ 2.2 b	$ .1 b
1915	$2.2 b	$ 4.0 b	$ 1.8 b
1920	$6.7 b	$10.3 b	$ 3.6 b

Source: *Historical Statistics of the United States, Colonial Times to 1970* (U.S. Department of Commerce, 1975).

reflected American hostility to territorial colonialism, but it also embodied Hay's understanding that the expanding American industrial system would benefit most from "equality of opportunity" in foreign markets.

Urban Progressives
and State Reformers

As the United States moved toward the new century, some short-term causes of the unrest of the 1890s began to recede. In 1897, the European wheat crop collapsed, causing the price of wheat to rise and inaugurating an era of economic recovery for American agriculture on the Great Plains. The opening of new mines and the development of better techniques for extracting metal from ore brought a dramatic increase in the world supply of gold. Consequently, the gold-based money supply expanded, bringing the currency inflation that the Populists had so ardently sought. This influx of new money also stimulated industrial expansion, which ended the depression and began a new period of prosperity.

Populist concerns over the power of corporations and the vitality of democratic institutions continued to trouble many Americans. As agrarianism waned, the reform impulse passed to the business and professional elites of the urban middle class, a diverse group who called themselves Progressives. Progressives like Theodore Roosevelt and Jane Addams rejected the nineteenth-century assumption that society benefited when self-interested individuals competed freely in the self-regulating and apolitical marketplace. They viewed such ideas as inappropriate to a structured, complex, and interdependent social order. Increasingly, Progressives stressed the "public interest" as a guide to the behavior of organizations and individuals, believing that government and private agencies should intervene in the affairs of society to protect the larger good. Reformers such as Robert LaFollette of Wisconsin and activist Joseph Folk of St. Louis placed particular faith in the ability of government to bring about social justice.

Progressives appeared optimistic about the future, comfortable with America's basic institutions, and confident of their ability to identify and correct social ills. Since many served as managers in the growing industrial and service sectors, they tended to offer bureaucratic strategies for achieving reform. Progressives stressed efficiency, planning, and the role of experts as central to resolving political and social dilemmas. These reformers sought four basic goals. First, large corporations must acknowledge a social responsibility beyond that of profit making and submit to regulation in the public interest. Second, political reforms should guarantee that government be responsive to those who recognized the public interest and not those who controlled great wealth. Third, government should act to secure social justice for victims of the economic order. Finally, Progressives sought to impose social controls designed to make America a more homogeneous society conforming to the values of the Anglo-Protestant middle class.

Progressives made their initial impact in the nation's cities during the 1890s when they challenged the dominance of the urban political machines by powerful bosses. Political bosses had replaced the traditional Anglo-Protestant elite in city government in the years following the Civil War. As the old leaders moved into new opportunities in corporate and national political life, Irish-American politicians used a highly personal kind of leadership to win the loyalty of ethnic and working-class voters in the cities of the East and Middle West. Their efforts contrasted with the condescending approach of many Anglo-Protestant charity workers; they appealed to Catholic and Jewish beneficiaries of the boss welfare system, who came from European cultures that did not relate to Protestant individualism and that preferred to emphasize collective charity and group support.

Since few public or private programs existed to protect workers against illness, accident, unemployment, or disasters like fires, local bosses such as New York's George Washington Plunkitt regularly intervened to offer needed assistance. Tammany Hall, the headquarters of New York City's political machine, controlled a payroll of $12 million and had more jobs to fill than did Carnegie Steel. In Chicago, social worker Jane Addams guessed that 20 percent of all voters in her district depended upon the goodwill of the ward alderman for their employment. Ethnic bosses also distributed food baskets, sponsored picnics on holidays, and provided recreational opportunities like music and sports clubs for children. By creating networks of social services, urban power brokers met the needs of a large and ethnically divided population in the increasingly depersonalized city.

Despite these achievements, boss rule systemized graft and corruption and was an inefficient and expensive way of providing municipal services. The sale of city franchises for public transportation lines, road construction, and the provision of public utilities, for example, caused the costs of those projects to mushroom and placed additional burdens on the municipal treasury. Plunkitt defended this activity as "honest graft," explaining that "I seen my opportunities and I took 'em." But Progressive reformers agreed with British ambassador Viscount James Bryce, who commented that "the governing of cities is the one conspicuous failure of the United States." Progressives also feared that corrupt political machines appealed to the narrow loyalties of ethnicity and social class instead of to the ideals of civic virtue and responsibility.

Three large-girthed Democratic bosses—George N. Lewis, John S. Kelly, and John J. Mahon—enjoy a mug of beer. Many Progressives linked machine politics and saloons.

Progressive urban reform began with Republican mugwumps (individuals who left the party in 1884) who sought to regain political control of the city in the 1880s. One such reformer, Theodore Roosevelt, ran for mayor of New York City in an unsuccessful campaign in 1886. Nine years later, outrage at machine corruption propelled Roosevelt to the presidency of the City Board of Police Commissioners. In Galveston, Texas, the inability of machine politicians to deal with a devastating tidal wave led to the election of a reform ticket and restructuring of the city charter in 1900. The Galveston Plan introduced the city commission form of government. Under this model, voters selected at-large commissioners, each of whom administered a different part of the city bureaucracy. Urban progressives adopted the Galveston Plan because it professionalized the administration of municipal government and provided leaders with a citywide perspective. But at-large elections also diluted the voting impact of immigrant and working-class districts. Civil service examinations, another progressive reform, further professionalized city management by placing hiring power in government bureaucracies instead of in the corrupt ward syndicates. But the examinations often incorporated the standards and values of the Anglo-Protestant middle class and tended to put Americans from different ethnic or class backgrounds at a disadvantage.

Nonpartisan elections and the growth of city manager systems further depersonalized urban politics. Consequently, loss of interest combined with tighter registration and residency requirements to reduce the level of voter participation in city elections about 20 percent between 1890 and 1920. While ethnic and working-class interests found themselves on the defensive, magazine journalists such as Lincoln Steffens exposed urban political corruption and added to the momentum for reform. Steffens's *The Shame of the Cities* (1904) brought together years of reporting in a patterned chronicle of organized graft in America's leading cities. Such publicity helped to elect turn-of-the-century reform mayors like Seth Low of New York City, Joseph Folk of St. Louis, James D. Phelan of San Francisco, and Mark Fagan of Jersey City. Others like Detroit's Hazen S. Pingree, Toledo's Samuel M. Jones, and Cleveland's Thomas L. Johnson focused on lowering rates for public utilities and transportation. By 1915, municipal governments owned and operated two-thirds of the nation's city waterworks.

Most of the Progressive reform movement's concerns reached far beyond the resources and authority of local political jurisdictions. Moreover, rural-dominated state legislatures retained considerable authority over urban affairs, and any meaningful attempt to reform municipalities led inevitably to the state capital. For these reasons, Progressive reform quickly spread to the state level, where Progressives often found government to be as corrupt and inefficient as at the city level.

Republican Robert LaFollette of Wisconsin best symbolized progressivism at the state level. Elected governor in 1900, LaFollette turned the state into a "laboratory of progressivism" by using university-trained experts to design and administer his programs. The Wisconsin Idea incorporated a "new citizenship" concerned with domination of the "public interest" over corrupt influences. "The will of the people," proclaimed LaFollette, "shall be the law of the land." Accordingly, LaFollette secured passage of the direct primary, thereby taking the nomination of candidates away from the deliberations of boss-dominated conventions. The reform governor also secured two goals of the Populist movement, the initiative and the referendum. Beyond his political reforms, LaFollette created regulatory agencies for railroads and utilities staffed by experts drawn from the state university. He also increased taxes on corporations, imposed graduated taxes on inherited wealth, and created a program of workmen's compensation. Republican insurgents Albert B. Cummins and Albert J. Beveridge emulated LaFollette by riding reform waves to the governors' chairs in Iowa and Indiana, while Charles Evans Hughes and Hiram W. Johnson attempted to address the public interest in New York and California.

As the achievements of the Progressives demonstrate, the most creative political movements in American history often grow from grass roots. However, the Progressives, like the Populists before them, realized that federal power was crucial to achieving their agenda of building a rational order and expanding social justice. Consequently, Progressives increasingly looked to Washington after 1900. As Progressive governors like LaFollette, Johnson, Cummins, and Beveridge moved to the United States Senate, they contributed to the nationalizing of the reform impulse, but the White House fell to the dynamic New York Progressive Theodore Roosevelt.

SOCIAL JUSTICE AND THE PURITY CRUSADE

"Jesus Christ knew a great deal . . . about organizing society . . . ," reform-minded minister Washington Gladden observed wryly, "and the application of his law to industrial society will be found to work surprisingly well." Progressive reform incorporated a humanitarian concern for social justice, a sentiment often motivated by strong religious ideals. By the late nineteenth century, the dominant Protestant denominations usually upheld the values of individual piety and evangelical revivalism. But during the 1890s, a vibrant Social Gospel movement emerged among liberal Protestants, leading ministers such as Gladden and Walter Rauschenbusch to seek a program of social reform rooted in New Testament theology. In *Christianity and the Social Crisis* (1907), Rauschenbusch argued that the social environment shaped a person's character. Consequently, the church must assume a activist ministry among the urban poor. Many Roman Catholics also embraced the Social Gospel as an extension of Pope Leo XIII's 1893 encyclical *Rerum Novarum*, which declared that "a smaller number of very rich men have been able to lay upon the masses of the poor a yoke little better than slavery itself."

Middle-class women played an increasingly important role in the new urban social justice movement. Smaller families and increased leisure time gave city women more personal freedom. Since men monopolized leadership in the political, economic, and professional arenas, women tended to take the initiative in matters involving social justice and public virtue. Perceiving a crisis of morality in industrial America, many middle-class women rejected the philosophy of the self-made man and stressed family values holding that good character depended upon a wholesome social environment. Concluding that the marketplace celebrated only private values, these purity crusaders argued that the public interest had to be advanced by people like themselves.

Progressive women emulated men by forming organizations to work for the restoration of morality in public life. The General Federation of Women's Clubs, one example, grew from a membership of fifty thousand in 1898 to over one million by 1914. Federation president Sarah Platt Decker directed the organization toward improved working conditions for women and children. Other women sought to publicize the plight of the poor. Jane Addams, a restless college graduate, established Hull House, one of the first settlement houses in America, in 1889. Addams's Chicago center modeled itself after London's Toynbee Hall and provided neighbors with a variety of services, including child care facilities, a library, meeting rooms, and classes in housekeeping, cooking, music, and art.

Hull House and other settlement houses became incubators of reform. The middle-class women who staffed these agencies believed that industrial prosperity had made poverty unacceptable. They often went on to work for other causes such as the abolition of child labor. Settlement house leaders formed a National Child Labor Committee to lobby state governments to prohibit children under fourteen from working in factories and to keep children under sixteen out of mines. The committee also hoped to protect child laborers from night work and shifts of more than eight hours a day, a particular problem in southern textile mills where child labor had increased 130 percent during the 1890s. The reformers won partial victories in many states, and in 1912 secured the formation of a Children's Bureau in the Department of Commerce and Labor. By 1914, they had persuaded twenty states to establish programs paying child support pensions to widows or abandoned wives. In 1916, Congress passed the Keating-Owen Child Labor Act, which banned the products of child labor from interstate commerce, but the Supreme Court struck down the measure two years later. The Court also invalidated a 1919 measure taxing items produced by children.

The Progressive concern with child labor contributed to a growing concern about the welfare of children generally. A successful career in high-status white-collar jobs depended on a good education. Accordingly, between 1898 and 1914, elementary school enrollments more than doubled. By 1917, thirty-eight states had enacted laws requiring young people to remain in school until age sixteen. "The children are our to-morrow," wrote journalist Jacob Riis, "and as we mould them today so will they deal with us then."

Progressive women also played a major role in the struggle against prostitution. Red-light districts existed openly in American cities between the Civil War and World War I. Many young female migrants and immigrants found themselves either coerced or enticed into prostitution, which brought several times the earnings of the inadequate wages available in factories, mills, and domestic service. In 1900, a woman holding an unskilled job typically earned from $5 to $7 weekly, while a prostitute could earn $30 to $40 a week. Nevertheless, most prostitutes saw their work as a temporary remedy until they found greater security in a better job or a marriage.

Reformers such as Elizabeth Blackwell and Caroline Wilson, two of the first women physicians, and Antoinette Blackwell, the first woman ordained as a Protestant minister, established organizations to serve as surrogate families for young women who found themselves alone in cities. Activists also campaigned against the double standard that allowed affluent married men to have promiscuous sexual relations with prostitutes. By abolishing white slavery, as they called prostitution, the reformers hoped to destroy the sexual marketplace and force men to accept the same monogamous standard as did middle-class women. As in the antislavery movement before the Civil War, American reformers maintained close contacts with English activists. Consequently, American women followed the English model by creating organizations such as traveler's aid societies in railroad stations to provide safety for rural migrants to the city. By 1900, purity reformers succeeded in establishing vice commissions in virtually every major American city. Their work led to the Mann Act of 1910, which made it a federal crime to transport a woman to another state for immoral purposes.

Many Progressive women also crusaded against the dangers of substance abuse. The use of narcotics such as opium, morphine, and cocaine had grown steadily through the nineteenth century. Physicians often prescribed diluted opium, a substance readily available through patent medicines, and the popular soft drink Coca-Cola contained small amounts of cocaine until 1903. By the turn of the century, the United States had approximately one-quarter of a million narcotics addicts. In addition, public opinion linked drug use with the Chinese and black communities, two groups that dominant white elites were eager to suppress.

The rapidly developing health care professions supported the move to regulate narcotics. Eager to establish professional standards of practice, doctors and pharmacists embraced the idea that widespread drug use was socially harmful. The American Medical Association (AMA) and the American Pharmaceutical Association (APA) insisted that only professionals with the appropriate credentials could dispense drugs. Other groups eager to impose middle-class behavior standards on immigrant and racial groups joined the crusade. Responding to this pressure, Congress passed the Pure Food and Drug Act in 1906 and started the first federal regulation of the pharmaceutical industry. Three years later, the United States prohibited the importation of smoking opium. In 1914, the Harrison Narcotics Act restricted the use of narcotics to medical purposes and required federal registration of all drug producers, a record of all sales, and a doctor's prescription for all drugs.

Alcohol became the main target of the women's Purity Crusade. The predominantly Protestant Anti-Saloon League, founded in 1895, sought the prohibition of the sale and manufacture of alcoholic beverages and depicted alcohol as a socially destructive drug that must be outlawed. Prohibitionists also sought to impose a measure of social control over the new immigrants, many of whom came from cultures that took a tolerant attitude toward alcohol. Urban middle-class reformers saw Prohibition as a way of elevating civic politics by disrupting the immigrant-based political machines. Their crusade attacked the saloons that fostered immigrant culture and served as organizing centers for ward politicians and labor unions.

Prohibition became the rallying cry in a broad effort to replace ethnic and working-class culture with Anglo-Protestant middle-class values. Eager to introduce rationality and efficiency to bureaucratic and economic life, reformers endeavored to undermine the ethnic cultures that they saw as irrational and inefficient. The large number of church holidays characteristic of southern and eastern European communities, for example, hampered the pursuit of a standard workweek with predictable production schedules. The National Safety Council, founded by corporate interests in 1912, emphasized the connection between alcohol consumption and industrial accidents. Physicians seemed to provide scientific evidence for all these concerns. Medical authorities argued that "every function of the normal human body is injured by the use of alcohol—even the moderate use; and that injury is both serious and permanent."

The Prohibition movement received particularly strong support from evangelical white southerners whose religion had denounced alcohol for decades. Most of the early successes of the Purity Crusade came in the South, where Prohibition also served as a tool of social control over blacks and lower-class whites. Using thousands of Baptist and Methodist congregations as a base, prohibitionists persuaded two-thirds of southern counties to "vote dry" by 1907, and won Prohibition laws in six states by 1909. The Webb-Kenyon Act of 1913 permitted these states to interdict the transportation of liquor across their boundaries. Despite these successes, however, an underground economy of moonshiners and bootleggers continued to supply alcohol to customers across the region.

Roosevelt and Corporate Progessivism

Returning prosperity and the successful war against Spain brought President McKinley a 52 percent to 45 percent plurality over William Jennings Bryan in the election of 1900. Bryan tried to make the contest a referendum on imperialism, but most voters believed the Senate settled the issue when it approved annexation of the Philippines.

Six months after his inauguration, McKinley was shot twice at point- blank range by anarchist Leon Czolgosz, while attending the Pan-American Exposition in Buffalo. The president died a few days later. Vice-President Theodore Roosevelt, an urban reformer and charismatic hero of the Spanish-American War, stepped into the presidency in September 1901. "Now look," exclaimed grief-stricken Mark Hanna, "that damned cowboy is president of the United States!"

Theodore Roosevelt brought to the White House a vigor and imagination not seen since the administration of Abraham Lincoln. The son of a wealthy, established New York family, Roosevelt was born to comfort and poor health. He shook off the sickliness of his youth with a vigorous commitment to the strenuous life and grew to adulthood with a conviction that violence and struggle remained the basic ingredients of the human condition. The purpose of a man, Roosevelt declared, was to "work, fight, and breed." Suspicious of the materialism of his era, he welcomed war as "something to think about which isn't material gain," and he bragged to reporters about the "damned Spanish dead" the Rough Riders left behind on San Juan Hill. In addition to winning renown as a soldier, cowboy, and big-game hunter, Roosevelt also wrote several notable historical works, including a study of westward expansion and a distinguished naval history of the War of 1812.

Roosevelt brought the same emphasis on manly action to the world of politics. "Roosevelt, more than any other man living . . . was pure act," exclaimed his contemporary, historian Henry Adams. At a time when most patricians of the upper class shunned politics, the energetic New Yorker saw the pursuit of public office as a social responsibility and zestfully embraced his task. He served a term in the New York State assembly and sat on the United States Civil Service Commission. As the head of the New York City Board of Police Commissioners, Roosevelt prowled the city streets at night to observe the police at work and enforce the city's blue laws regulating private morality. After returning from the Spanish-American War, the popular Roosevelt won election as governor of New York. Republican party bosses, fearful of the governor's energy and Progressive leanings, persuaded McKinley to remove Roosevelt from the state by placing him on the 1900 ticket as the president's running mate. McKinley's assassination made the forty-two-year-old Roosevelt the youngest president in American history.

The new incumbent saw the presidency as the focal point of the political process and a national symbol. "There adheres in the presidency," he proclaimed, "more power than in any other office in any great republic or constitutional monarchy of modern times." Roosevelt took the initiative in dealing with Congress by sending drafts of proposed legislation to Capitol Hill and then lobbying vigorously for their passage. "I did not usurp power," Roosevelt explained later, "but I did greatly broaden the use of executive power." He also saw the presidency as the "bully pulpit" from which he could set the national agenda, define the public interest, and mold public opinion. Roosevelt realized that a popular and public relations–minded president could skillfully use the press to build new kinds of political support not available to his predecessors. Deliberately personalizing the office, he presented himself as the tribune of the people, ready to act decisively in their behalf.

Roosevelt used the presidency to advance a "corporate progressivism" that accepted the existence of big business but used the state to regulate it in the public interest. "Our aim is not to do away with corporations," he told Congress in 1902. "On the contrary, these big aggregations are the inevitable development of modern industrialism, and the effort to destroy them would be futile." Roosevelt feared that irresponsible management would encourage social unrest and radical politics. "One of the chief things I have tried to preach to the American politician and the American businessman," he said, "is not to grasp at money." Accordingly, the president decided to revitalize the Sherman Anti-Trust Act. In particular he targeted the Northern Securities Company, a huge holding company created as a result of a bitter stock fight involving the Rockefeller interests, J. P. Morgan, and railroad barons James J. Hill and E. H. Harriman. Roosevelt denounced the resulting monopoly of western rail lines as precisely the sort of behavior that big business should avoid. He ordered government attorneys to use the Sherman Act to file suit against Northern Securities for restraint of trade.

Despite protests by Morgan, the administration pursued the antitrust action and won its case before the Supreme Court in 1904. The decision in the Northern Securities case modified the Court's ruling in the Knight case and gave new vitality to the Sherman Act. Roosevelt subsequently initiated forty other antitrust actions, earning the reputation of a presidential "trust buster." However, he preferred to deal with the trusts through negotiation rather than legal action. In 1903, the president secured legislation that established the Department of Commerce and Labor, including a Bureau of Corporations. Roosevelt directed the bureau to regulate large corporations instead of breaking them up through antitrust litigation. And he personally asked the chief executives of United States Steel and the International Harvester Company to cooperate with the new agency. Through "gentlemen's agreements," the firms allowed the bureau to investigate their procedures and make recommendations for more responsible business practices. Those who refused to comply faced the threat of antitrust action. When Standard Oil executives declined to cooperate with the Bureau of Corporations, Roosevelt turned to the Sherman Act, and the Supreme Court broke the oil giant into several smaller companies in 1911.

Roosevelt hoped to preserve corporate stability and discourage a strong socialist movement by urging business leaders to accept labor unions that worked within the capitalist system. His approach paralleled that of the influential National Civic Federation (NCF). Founded by Mark Hanna in 1900, the NCF sought harmony between labor and management and urged corporations to recognize social responsibilities by promoting trust regulations, workmen's compensation, and company welfare programs. In an effort to win the support of organized labor, Hanna invited Samuel Gompers of the AFL to serve as NCF vice-president.

These perspectives shaped Roosevelt's reaction to the anthracite coal strike of 1902. Under the leadership of John Mitchell and the United Mine Workers (UMW), workers walked off the job demanding a 10 to 20 percent wage increase, an eight-hour day, and management's recognition of the union. But mine owners refused to bargain with Mitchell and tried to smash the union

Exhibit 2–7. Gross National Product, 1890–1910 (in rounded billions of dollars at current prices)

1890	$13 b
1895	$14 b
1900	$19 b
1905	$25 b
1910	$35 b

Source: *Historical Statistics of the United States, Colonial Times to 1970* (U.S. Department of Commerce, 1975).

with strikebreakers and private security forces. Public opinion tilted toward the workers, especially after owner George Baer proclaimed publicly that "God in His Infinite Wisdom has given control of the property interests" to mining entrepreneurs. As the dispute dragged into the fall, the strike threatened coal supplies for the coming winter. Roosevelt stepped in to resolve the matter by summoning both sides to a conference at the White House, an invitation that delighted Mitchell. The owners, however, refused to accept mediation. This outraged Roosevelt, who threatened to seize the mines and use the army to mine coal. That warning prompted conservatives such as banker J. P. Morgan to pressure the owners to compromise. Ultimately, the miners received a 10 percent raise and a nine-hour day, but the agreement permitted the owners to raise prices by 10 percent and shun union recognition.

Roosevelt insisted that he had given both labor and management a "square deal" while protecting the public interest. In a marked departure from government policy in previous industrial disputes, the president had accepted the legitimacy of labor demands and forced the leaders of a major industry to recognize those claims. Nevertheless, Roosevelt did not champion unions, and his involvement in the crisis amounted to an extension of conservative, rather than liberal, impulses. "The friends of property must realize that the surest way to provoke an explosion of wrong and injustice is to be shortsighted, narrow-minded, greedy, and arrogant," he told Attorney General Philander C. Knox.

Roosevelt's most consistent use of executive power came in the area of natural resources. Emphasizing the efficient use of resources rather than the preservation of virgin wilderness, the president sought to withdraw most federally owned forestlands from unplanned economic exploitation by private interests. Western congressional representatives opposed this scheme because it threatened to slow the rate of economic growth. To reconcile these politicians to his policy, Roosevelt promised that the government would build dams and irrigation systems throughout the West. Accordingly, the New-lands Reclamation Act of 1902 opened millions of acres of desert land to farming.

Roosevelt also transferred public forestlands from the Department of the Interior to the Department of Agriculture, where his friend Gifford Pinchot headed the Bureau of Forestry. Like Roosevelt, Pinchot believed that the free enterprise system needed overall planning and control by government professionals who had a broader view of national economic problems than did private interests. Pinchot applied the techniques of scientific management to American forests, expecting government experts to plan for the multiple use of forests by lumberers, ranchers, and vacationers.

More confident after being elected by a 57 percent plurality in his own right in 1904, Roosevelt expanded the federal bureaucracy and the power of the presidency. A prime achievement came in the complex area of railroad regulation, where both agrarian radicals and middle-class reformers had long sought effective control of rates. Even in his more cautious first term, Roosevelt had supported the Elkins Act of 1903, which outlawed rebates from railroads to large shippers. However, the president preferred to base industry regulation on bureaucratic review rather than on specific legislation. Consequently, he secured passage of the Hepburn Act in 1906, increasing the jurisdiction of the Interstate Commerce Commission and providing the commission greater authority to set transportation rates. Many railroad executives supported railroad regulation as a step toward greater economic stability. Rates administered by the federal government limited price competition among lines and freed a national industry from inconsistent regulation by the states. Reforms such as the Hepburn Act typified the pursuit of an ordered society by corporate progressives and their allies.

Responding to an enormous public outcry about unsanitary and unsafe conditions in consumer industries, the Roosevelt administration backed other types of regulatory legislation. These laws grew out of the effort of government bureaucrats, consumer organizations, business groups, and the investigative reporters whom Roosevelt labeled muckrakers. One example of this effort, Upton Sinclair's novel *The Jungle* (1906), graphically described the filth that regularly went into meat products as well as the plight of the meat-packing workers. The movement for congressional action also received support from Harvey Wiley of the Department of Agriculture, the government's chief chemist. This agitation produced the Pure Food and Drug Act of 1906, which prohibited the production and sale of adulterated goods and outlawed false labeling of food and drug items. The Meat Inspection Act of 1906 established federal inspection to ensure that packers met sanitation standards set by the government. Large meat-packing and drug companies accepted the new legislation because it imposed standards of production that they could meet more easily than could smaller competitors. Well-established concerns also hoped to reduce competition from specious patent medicine companies and thereby improve consumer confidence in their products.

As a corporate progressive, Roosevelt understood the growing enthusiasm in both major political parties for reform within the capitalist system. At the height of the coal strike, the president said of the operators: "Do they not realize they are putting a very heavy burden on us who stand against socialists; against anarchic disorder?" As one British observer put it, Roosevelt opposed "government by a plutocracy and . . . by a mob."

By 1908, the president's desire to check both irresponsible profiteering and the vitality of a growing Socialist party had led him to espouse income and inheritance taxes to keep the rich from monopolizing national wealth. Roosevelt criticized the courts for their hostility toward labor unions, state workmen's compensation laws, and state regulation of working conditions for women. The president tried to persuade Americans to give up the idealized nineteenth-century marketplace of small farmers and independent businessmen. He urged them to instead accept large corporations and labor unions and to support a national bureaucracy that could regulate the activities of both. Only energized governments, he believed, could fulfill the nation's destiny for greatness.

Ida Minerva Tarbell
1857–1944

At a time when social conventions usually bound women to traditional roles, Ida Tarbell rejected domestic life to become a journalist. Fascinated by science from girlhood, she entered Allegheny College as a biology student in 1876 determined to pursue a career, but she soon discovered that in science "there was almost nothing . . . open to women." Upon graduation Tarbell became a teacher, entering a profession more accessible to women, but she fled the classroom and its "killing schedule" after two years. She then took a job in a magazine office and began to write. In 1891, Tarbell broke with her comfortable but mundane surroundings and went to Paris, where she met S. S. McClure of *McClure's Magazine,* a successful popular periodical with a large middle-class readership. Through the 1890s, she published occasional pieces for *McClure;s* and worked on anecdotal biographies of Napoleon Bonaparte and Abraham Lincoln.

Tarbell's combination of patient study, objective observation, and fair-minded ethics made her a leading muckraker of the early twentieth century. Prodded by the shrewd McClure, she spent five years doing research and interviews for a story about Standard Oil, the "mother" of trusts. The resulting nineteen articles for *McClure's* and the two-volume *History of the Standard Oil Company* (1904) portrayed a pattern of corporate bribery, fraud, coercion, double-dealing, and outright violence that constituted a searing indictment of the morality of the trusts. Tarbell saw herself as a reporter who gathered facts that spoke for themselves. Uncomfortable with characterizations as the "Joan of Arc of the oil industry," she took little interest when the federal government began an antitrust suit against Standard Oil in 1907. As she later remembered in her autobiography, Tarbell found herself "fifty, fagged, wanting to be let alone while I collect trustworthy information for my articles."

The series in *McClure's* brought discussion of trust regulation into the homes of *(cont.)*

ROOSEVELT AND WORLD POWER

Roosevelt came to the presidency with strong ideas about the importance of using American power in the world arena. He hoped to consolidate the gains of the Spanish-American War by building an interocean canal through Central America, thereby providing Atlantic ports with easy access to the markets and naval bases of East Asia and the Pacific. Roosevelt invited British cooperation in the matter, and finally, after a half century of wrangling over an isthmian canal, the United States and Britain signed the Hay-Pauncefote Treaty in November 1901, just two months after Roosevelt assumed the presidency. Eager to court the United States as a possible ally against an increasingly restless Germany, Britain renounced its interest in the Central American project and permitted the United States to build and fortify the canal.

middle-class America. But Tarbell remained a conservative in many areas. Despite her own experience with gender discrimination, she gave only tepid support to women's issues and criticized assertive feminist leaders for their alleged insensitivity to the importance of home and family. In a 1912 article entitled "Making a Man of Herself," Tarbell warned young women of "the essential barrenness of the achieving woman's triumph, its lack of the savor and tang of life, the multitude of makeshifts she must practice to recompense her for the lack of the great adventure of natural living." Such comments from a woman of her accomplishments sparked angry outcries from women activists. Helen Keller, a young writer who had achieved fame by triumphing over multiple handicaps, denounced Tarbell as too old to understand the changing world.

Stung by such criticism, Tarbell again shifted her interests. Influenced by automobile magnate Henry Ford, she began a new study of American business in the 1910s, this time focusing on factory conditions. As she described Ford's mass production methods, wage policies, and treatment of workers, Tarbell became a staunch champion of welfare capitalism. She also praised the scientific management of Frederick W. Taylor as the key to industrial peace. Tarbell released *New Ideals in Business* in 1916.

Turning again to biography in the 1920s, Tarbell portrayed United States Steel's Elbert H. Gary as an industrial statesman committed to ethical capitalism. A subsequent work treated General Electric chairman Owen D. Young in similar terms.

Some critics like the reformist New York *World* spoke of the "taming of Ida Tarbell," but it was a commitment to the nineteenth-century concepts of individualism and morality that molded the journalist's conclusions. Tarbell remained suspicious of what she called "the most dangerous fallacy of our times—and that is that we can be saved . . . by laws and systems." A classic Progressive, Ida Tarbell never abandoned her skepticism of interest group politics and collective militance. Believing in personal accountability, she preferred to trust the "fair play" of the great men she described in her biographies. ∎

Encouraged by the British attitude, Roosevelt signed the Hay-Herran Treaty with Colombia in 1903, thereby securing permanent rights to a canal zone through the middle of Panama, a province of Colombia. The Colombian senate rejected the agreement, however, because it considered the price too low for those rights. Roosevelt expressed outrage. "You could no more make an agreement with the Colombia rulers," he roared, "than you could nail currant jelly to the wall." The former Rough Rider promptly sent the navy to support a Panamanian rebellion against Colombia and then signed the Hay-Buneau-Varilla Treaty with the fledgling government of Panama, providing the same terms originally offered to Colombia. Congress ratified the treaty in 1904, and the Panama Canal opened to traffic in 1914. "I took the Canal Zone and let Congress debate," Roosevelt later boasted. But in 1921, the United States felt obligated to compensate Colombia with $25 million for the American role in the Panamanian revolution.

Theodore Roosevelt eagerly climbed aboard a steam shovel during a 1906 visit to the Panama Canal Zone.

The president nourished American assertiveness in the Western Hemisphere with his 1904 announcement of the Roosevelt Corollary to the Monroe Doctrine. Alarmed by the intervention of European nations in Latin America to collect debts and advance their own business interests, Roosevelt broadened the Monroe Doctrine from a statement opposing further European colonization in the hemisphere to a sweeping assertion of America's right to intervene in the internal affairs of its neighbors. "If we intend to say 'Hands off' to the powers of Europe," the president proclaimed, "then sooner or later we must keep order ourselves." Roosevelt applied the corollary for the first time in 1905, when he sent troops to Santo Domingo to forestall a revolution that stood to benefit German shipping interests.

The president's attempts to project American power into conflicts in Asia and Europe were less successful than his efforts to build an American sphere of influence in Latin America. Concerned with guaranteeing the Open Door

Exhibit 2–8. U.S. Involvement in the Caribbean

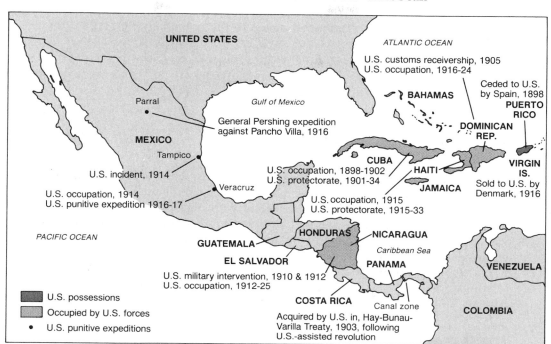

in China and other parts of Asia, Roosevelt feared that the Russo-Japanese War might establish Japan as the dominant power in the Pacific. Consequently, he eagerly grasped the opportunity to mediate the conflict. His role in negotiating the Treaty of Portsmouth won him the Nobel Peace Prize in 1906. Yet his work proved futile. The collapse of the Chinese empire and the swift emergence of Japan subsequently altered the balance of power in the region and threatened the commercial interests that the United States sought to protect.

Japanese-American relations deteriorated with the rise of anti-Asian racism on the West Coast. While newspapers shrieked warnings about the "yellow peril," riots against Asians broke out across California. In 1906, the San Francisco school board voted to place Asian children in segregated schools. Roosevelt responded by persuading the board to rescind its vote in exchange for a Gentlemen's Agreement with Japan to limit the influx of immigrants to the United States. Simultaneously, the president sent sixteen battleships on a forty-five-thousand-mile voyage around the world, including a stop in Yokohama, Japan. Although the Root-Takahira Treaty of 1908 compelled the United States to accept Japanese restrictions on the Open Door in Manchuria, Japan agreed to respect the policy in the rest of China.

The president also sought to uphold an existing balance of power in Europe by restraining the growing power of Germany and supporting British and French interests. Roosevelt successfully mediated an imperial conflict between Germany and France over North Africa by supporting British and

French demands at the Algeciras Conference of 1906. The resulting agreement not only strengthened the informal alliance among the United States, Britain, and France, but guaranteed access to the potentially rich region for American business interests. The search for a stabilized world balance of power and an open door for American business characterized Roosevelt's foreign policy.

TAFT VERSUS THE PROGRESSIVE MOVEMENT

When Roosevelt left the White House in 1909, he handed control of the Republican party and the Progressive movement to William Howard Taft, a talented administrator and lawyer. Taft had won high praise for his performance as governor-general of the Philippines and had served as secretary of war and presidential confidant during the Roosevelt administration. With the enthusiastic backing of his friend, Taft handily won the Republican nomination and rolled to an easy 52 percent to 43 percent victory over William Jennings Bryan in the fall election. Roosevelt promptly vanished on a lengthy African safari, where the famous conservationist took dozens of trophies.

The unlikely looking viceroy of America's Pacific empire, William Howard Taft sits ponderously astride a water buffalo during his tenure as governor-general of the Philippines, 1900–1904.

"Everytime Mr. Roosevelt gets near the heart of a wild thing," one environmentalist commented, "he invariably puts a bullet through it."

Unlike the physically fit Roosevelt, Taft weighed over three hundred pounds and was given to nothing more strenuous than golf, a sport not yet popular with the general public. Taft also lacked Roosevelt's gift for public relations and self-promotion. Nor could he stir a crowd or charm the press. The new president had campaigned on a promise to continue Roosevelt's reform programs and to administer them with efficiency. He preferred to consolidate existing gains rather than to press new initiatives. "The lesson must be learned," he declared, "that there is only a limited zone within which legislation and governments can accomplish good."

Taft also faced a growing split between the old guard and the progressive wings of the Republican party. For all his administrative skills, the president lacked the temperament to deal with such political problems and ultimately alienated both conservatives and progressives. Consequently, at a time when the Progressive movement surged nationally, Taft offered the country confused and unproductive leadership that finally destroyed his presidency. For example, the chief executive's courageous effort to achieve tariff reform not only failed but also resulted in higher rates. Calling Congress into special session in 1909, the president requested a moderate reduction in the high levels of the Dingley Tariff of 1897. But Taft outraged Republican progressives from the Plains states when he accepted the Payne-Aldrich Tariff, which actually raised rates and threatened overseas crop sales. Taft further offended progressives by replacing Roosevelt's conservation-minded secretary of the interior James R. Garfield and then dismissing Gifford Pinchot, a reformer who had gained fame as Roosevelt's director of national forests. The new interior secretary, corporate attorney Richard Ballinger, argued that free enterprise should develop the resources on national lands.

The split between the president and the progressives deepened as a consequence of Taft's intervention in an attempt by insurgents to weaken the power of dictatorial House Speaker Joe Cannon, a staunch conservative. Taft initially supported the congressional revolt, calling Cannon "dirty and vulgar." But later he repudiated the insurgents because he feared that Cannon would crush the president's attempt at tariff reform. In 1910, progressive insurgents once again challenged Cannon under the leadership of Nebraska representative George W. Norris and successfully stripped the Speaker of his power to make committee assignments. To the chagrin of Norris and his associates, Taft again refused to support the reform cause, testily dismissing them as "yelping and snarling" and "rather forward."

Taft's political strength had seriously eroded by the middle of his term. In 1910, Republicans lost control of the House of Representatives for the first time in eighteen years. The Democrats also gained ten seats in the Senate and propelled several attractive candidates to national prominence, among them the newly elected governor of New Jersey, Woodrow Wilson. At this point, Taft faced the return of his now estranged friend Roosevelt from the African jungles. Roosevelt associates like Pinchot readily convinced the former president that Taft had betrayed the Progressive cause. Moreover, Roosevelt sought a stronger brand of progressivism by stressing the need for enhanced democracy. He attracted national publicity with a speech at Osawatomie, Kansas, that sounded the call for a New Nationalism. The speech stressed the need for national political leaders to establish regulatory policies that would direct capitalists, workers, and farmers away from selfish concerns toward a unified national interest. "Our country means nothing," declared Roosevelt, "unless it means the triumph of a real democracy."

The final break between Roosevelt and Taft came over the president's decision to initiate antitrust proceedings against United States Steel. During a sharp economic downturn in 1907, Roosevelt had persuaded J. P. Morgan to release money into the economy to halt the slide. In exchange for his cooperation, Morgan won Roosevelt's promise not to prosecute the steel giant, which Morgan had created. Roosevelt justified his action by saying that United States Steel had already agreed to supervision by the Bureau of Corporations. Taft's action not only reversed the promise made by his predecessor, but also made Roosevelt appear to be a tool of Wall Street rather than a committed Progressive. The enraged Roosevelt decided to challenge Taft for the Republican nomination. On Lincoln's Birthday in 1912, he added a new phrase to America's political lexicon when he announced, "My hat is in the ring."

THE ELECTION OF 1912

The presidential election of 1912 incorporated a spirited debate over America's future by three mainstream candidates who compelled voters to focus on personalities and issues instead of party affiliation. In the Republican party, Taft and Roosevelt waged a bitter battle that left the party machinery in the hands of conservatives despite Roosevelt's enormous popularity with the rank and file. In the thirteen states that conducted presidential primaries, including the president's home state of Ohio, Roosevelt repeatedly defeated Taft at the polls. At the Chicago convention, however, control rested with the party leadership, most of whom supported the incumbent Taft. When the convention ruled in favor of Taft delegates in a major credentials challenge, Roosevelt and his backers marched defiantly from the hall, and Taft won the nomination on the first ballot.

Refusing to accept defeat, Roosevelt broke with the Republican party and summoned party dissidents and progressives from business and professional backgrounds to launch a new party, the Progressives. Insisting that he was eager for the contest, Roosevelt gave the fledgling party a permanent nickname when he declared himself to be as "strong as a bull moose." In near-religious fervor, the delegates roared their unanimous approval of his nomination. "We stand at Armageddon," Roosevelt thundered, "and we battle for the Lord."

The Democrats nominated New Jersey reform governor Woodrow Wilson. The Virginia-born son of a Presbyterian minister, Wilson followed many talented young southerners of his generation to make a career in the North. Completing a Ph.D. in government at Johns Hopkins University, he began an academic career that led him to the presidency of Princeton University in 1902. Wilson resigned eight years later, embittered by a long struggle over the future of the graduate school, and ran for governor of New Jersey. The candidate of state bosses who saw him as a respectable front man, the governor was also a vigorous Progressive. In a state already notorious for its corrupt politics, Wilson built a strong record of reform and established himself as a legitimate contender for national office. At the Democratic convention, the new candidate prevailed on the forty-sixth ballot when Bryan led party elders in supporting him.

The 1912 campaign evolved into a confrontation between Roosevelt and Wilson. Expanding the New Nationalism, Roosevelt preached the virtues of economic development, cultural unity, and social justice. Concerned as always with national strength and vitality, he called for the acceptance of large corporations if they were regulated in the public interest. Roosevelt's platform envisioned federal regulatory agencies, the prohibition of child labor, the eight-hour day, and such democratic reforms as women's suffrage and the direct election of senators. Wilson expressed an alternative vision of American society under the label of the New Freedom. The Democrat differed with Roosevelt by portraying economic concentration as unfair and inefficient. Far from serving as a coordinator of such units, Wilson believed that government should act to dismantle trusts and restore competition. "If America is not to have free enterprise," he proclaimed, "then she can have freedom of no sort whatever." While Roosevelt pursued strength through concentration and

Exhibit 2–9. Election of 1912

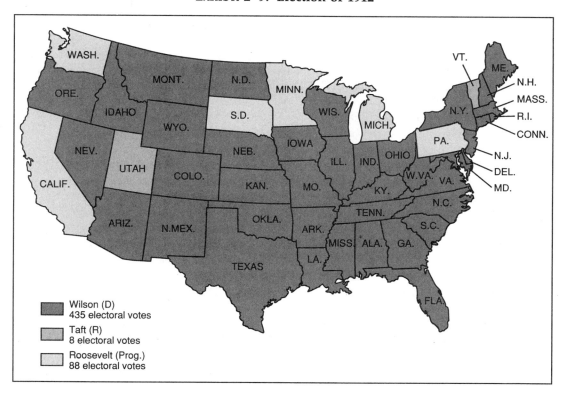

Wilson (D)
435 electoral votes

Taft (R)
8 electoral votes

Roosevelt (Prog.)
88 electoral votes

unity, Wilson appealed to the sentiments of the small producer and supported lower tariffs.

Republican Taft had little impact on the 1912 campaign, finishing third with a mere 23 percent of the vote. A fourth candidate, Socialist Eugene Debs, compiled over nine hundred thousand votes, 6 percent of the total. Debs called for government ownership of basic enterprises such as railroads, grain elevators, mines, and banks; demanded unemployment insurance and pensions for the elderly; and supported a variety of democratic reforms including elimination of the United States Senate, institution of a single-term presidency, and removal of the Supreme Court's power of judicial review.

The split in the Republican party put Woodrow Wilson in the White House. Although Roosevelt won 27 percent of the popular vote, he failed to bring a significant number of Democratic progressives into his third party effort. Consequently, Wilson prevailed with less than 42 percent of the popular vote, although his Electoral College tally amounted to a resounding 435–88 margin. President Taft carried only two states and eight electoral votes. The dominance of the two progressive candidates indicated that the political strength of the reform movement had reached its crest. Woodrow Wilson now faced the challenge of translating that impulse into meaningful legislation and policy.

Suggested Readings

Indispensible to understanding the Populists is Lawrence Godwyn, *Democratic Promise: The Populist Movement in America* (1976). John Hicks, *The Populist Revolt* (1931) and Theodore Saloutos, *Farmer Movements in the South, 1865–1933* (1960) generally describe agricultural issues and Populism. A more specialized study is Robert C. McMath, Jr., *Populist Vanguard: A History of the Southern Farm Alliance* (1975). Still valuable is C. Vann Woodward, *Tom Watson: Agrarian Rebel* (1938, 1955). Bruce Palmer, *Man over Money* (1980) looks at Populist ideology. See also Lewis Gould, *The Presidency of William McKinley* (1980); Paolo Coletta, *William Jennings Bryan, Political Evangelist, 1860–1908* (1964); and Louis Koenig, *Bryan* (1971).

Excellent general introductions to the foreign policy issues of the 1890s are Charles S. Campbell, *The Transformation of American Foreign Relations, 1865–1900* (1976) and Robert L. Beisner, *From the Old Diplomacy to the New, 1865–1900* (1975). William Appleman Williams fused an economic and ideological analysis of American imperialism with *The Tragedy of American Diplomacy* (rev. ed., 1972). See also the pertinent sections of Robert Dallek, *The American Style of Foreign Policy: Culture, Politics, and Foreign Policy* (1983). Philip Foner, *The Spanish-Cuban-American War and the Birth of American Imperialism* (1972) discusses the growing conflict with Spain, as does David Trask, *The War with Spain in 1898* (1981). Robert Beisner, *The Anti-Imperialists, 1898–1900* (1968) and E. Berkeley Tompkins, *Anti-Imperialism in the United States: The Great Debate, 1890–1920* (1970) cover the debate on overseas expansion. See also Stuart Creighton Miller, *"Benevolent Assimilation": The American Conquest of the Philippines, 1899–1903* (1982); Glenn May, *Social Engineering in the*

Philippines: The Aims, Execution and Impact of American Colonial Policy, 1900–1913 (1980); and Peter W. Stanley and John Curtis Perry, *Sentimental Imperialists: The American Experience in East Asia* (1981).

On the Progressive movement, Samuel Hays, *The Response to Industrialism, 1885–1914* (1957) and Robert Wiebe, *The Search for Order, 1877–1920* (1968) view the Progressives as members of a confident middle class intent on applying rationalization and bureaucracy to the nation's ills. Arthur Link and Richard L. McCormick, *Progressivism* (1983) and Dewey Grantham, *Southern Progressivism: The Reconciliation of Progress and Tradition* (1983) are also important. Gabriel Kolko, *The Triumph of Conservatism* (1963) argues that Progressivism was a tool of corporate business bent on rationalizing production and distribution. Also valuable are R. Jeffrey Lustig, *Corporate Liberalism: The Origin of Modern American Political Theory, 1890–1920* (1982) and James Weinstein, *The Corporate Ideal in the Liberal State, 1900–1918* (1969).

Excellent general studies of urban reform are Michael H. Ebner and Eugene M. Tobin, eds., *The Age of Urban Reform: New Perspectives on the Progressive Era* (1977); John Allswang, *Bosses, Machines, and Urban Voters: An American Symbiosis* (1977); and Michael McGerr, *The Decline of Popular Politics: The American North, 1865–1928* (1986). The classic study of muckraking journalists is Louis Filler, *The Muckrakers* (rev. ed., 1976). On social conditions that so alarmed many Progressives, see James Patterson, *America's Struggle against Poverty* (1980). On Jane Addams, consult Allen Davis, *American Heroine: The Life and Legend of Jane Addams* (1973). See also Paul Boyer, *Urban Masses and Moral Order, 1820–1920* (1978).

For discussion of social and political thought, see David W. Noble, *The Progressive Mind, 1890–1917* (1970) and Arthur Ekirch, *Progressivism in America* (1974). Charles Forcey, *The Crossroads of Liberalism: Croly, Weyl, Lippmann and the Progressive Era, 1900–1925* (1961) provides an excellent analysis of some leading progressive thinkers. Especially valuable on the coalescence of the Progressive movement is David P. Thelen, *The New Citizenship: Origins of Progressivism in Wisconsin, 1885–1900* (1972). Also important is Thelen, *Robert LaFollette and the Insurgent Spirit* (1976).

Women in the Progressive years are portrayed in Lois Banner, *Women in Modern America* (1974) and William L. O'Neill, *Everyone Was Brave* (1969). O'Neill, *Divorce in the Progressive Era* (1967) and David Kennedy, *Birth Control in America: The Career of Margaret Sanger* (1970) examine the changing roles of women. Also valuable are Rosalind Rosenberg, *Beyond Separate Spheres: Intellectual Roots of Modern Feminism* (1982) and Barbara Hilkert Andolsen, *"Daughters of Jefferson, Daughters of Bootblacks": Racism and American Feminism* (1986).

On progressivism and the Purity Crusade, see Joseph Gusfield, *Symbolic Crusade: Status Politics and the American Temperance Movement* (1963); James Timberlake, *Prohibition and the Progressive Movement, 1900–1920* (1970); and Lewis Gould, *Progressives and Prohibitionists: Texas Democrats and the Wilson Era* (1973). Donald J. Pivar, *Purity Crusade: Sexual Morality and Social Control, 1868–1900* (1973) focuses on the role of middle-class women. David Musto studies the roots of national attitudes toward narcotics in *The American Disease: Origins of Narcotic Control* (1973). Ruth Rosen, *The Lost Sisterhood: Prostitution in*

America, 1900–1918 (1982) and Thomas Connelly, *The Response to Prostitution in the Progressive Era* (1980) discuss prostitution. Robert Crunden, *Ministers of Reform: The Progressives' Achievement in American Civilization, 1889–1920* (1982) and George Marsden, *Fundamentalism and American Culture: The Shaping of Twentieth-Century Evangelicalism, 1870–1925* (1980) examine religion and reform.

The literature on the Roosevelt presidency is substantial. Edmund Morris, *The Rise of Theodore Roosevelt* (1979) and David McCullough, *Mornings on Horseback* (1981) provide readable introductions to Theodore Roosevelt. John Milton Cooper, Jr., *The Warrior and the Priest: Woodrow Wilson and Theodore Roosevelt* (1983) is a joint biography of the two rivals. An illuminating interpretation of Roosevelt policies is found in Lewis Gould, *Reform and Regulation: American Politics, 1900–1916* (1978) and Steven Piott, *The Anti-Monopoly Persuasion: Popular Resistance to the Rise of Big Business in the Midwest* (1985). On Roosevelt's foreign policy, consult Frederick W. Marks, *Velvet on Iron: The Diplomacy of Theodore Roosevelt* (1982) and Raymond Esthus, *Theodore Roosevelt and the International Rivalries* (1970). Paolo Coletta, *The Presidency of William Howard Taft* (1973) offers the best defense of Taft as chief executive.

The military role in foreign policy can be found in Richard Challener, *Admirals, Generals, and American Foreign Policy, 1898–1914* (1973). For American involvement in Asia see Akira Iriye, *Pacific Estrangement: Japanese and American Expansion, 1897–1911* (1972) and Jerry Israel, *Progressivism and the Open Door: America and China, 1905–1921* (1971). Dana Munro, *Intervention and Dollar Diplomacy in the Caribbean, 1900–1921* (1964) looks at the motives behind American policy in Latin America, and David McCullough, *The Path between the Seas* (1977) gives a lively account of the building of the Panama Canal.

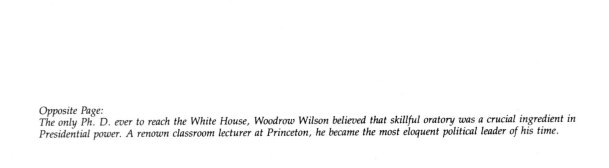

Opposite Page:
The only Ph. D. ever to reach the White House, Woodrow Wilson believed that skillful oratory was a crucial ingredient in Presidential power. A renown classroom lecturer at Princeton, he became the most eloquent political leader of his time.

3

WOODROW WILSON AND THE CORPORATE ORDER, 1912-1920

P rogressive reform culminated in the presidency of Woodrow Wilson. With the creation of the regulatory state, government assumed greater responsibility for social welfare and economic prosperity. But the most significant aspect of increased federal power was the enhanced role for the United States in global affairs. Building on the Open Door policy of the late 1890s, Wilson blended liberal political ideology and economic imperatives into a quest for international order. Although his dream of collective security remained unfulfilled in his lifetime, this visionary president established the major patterns of American foreign policy in the twentieth century. By doing so, he dramatized both the opportunities and the consequences of an American world presence.

WILSON AND THE NEW FREEDOM

Like his arch rival Theodore Roosevelt, Woodrow Wilson came to the White House with strong ideas about the use of presidential power. A staunch admirer of the British parliamentary system, he believed that the president, like the prime minister, should take a vigorous role in leading his party and securing legislation. The first president since John Adams to address Congress in person, Wilson devised his own legislative program and lobbied aggressively for its passage. He installed a private telephone line linking the White House with the Capitol and dispatched lobbyists to line up support for administration measures. Wilson stated his intention to demonstrate "that the President of the United States is a person, not a mere department of the Government hailing Congress from some isolated island of jealous power." Despite his reputation as an idealist, the new president willingly used the spoils of office to reward backers and punish opponents. The running of the government compared to child's play for anyone who had managed the faculty of a university, chuckled the former president of Princeton.

While Wilson proved himself to be a shrewd manipulator of the levers of institutional power, he portrayed the president as the chief advocate for the Progressive concept of the public interest. "The nation as a whole has chosen him, and is conscious that it has no other political spokesman," he explained. "His is the only voice in national affairs." Wilson realized that public opinion could be an important source of power for the chief executive. "Let him once win the admiration and confidence of the country," he wrote of the president in 1907, "and no other single force can withstand him, no combination of forces will easily overpower him." Recognizing that the press constituted a crucial link between the people and the president, Wilson began the practice of holding news conferences and often appealed to public opinion to pressure recalcitrant legislators.

The president put his theories to work in support of an extensive program of domestic reform that he called the New Freedom. Theodore Roosevelt's Progressive platform had described the concentration of economic activity in corporations as "both inevitable and necessary for

Determined to lead the legislative branch, Wilson presented his agenda in person to joint meetings of the House and Senate.

national and international business efficiency." Wilson, by contrast, tapped the resentment many farmers and small business interests felt toward the corporate elite. "What this country needs above everything else," he declared, "is a body of laws which will look after the men who are on the make rather than the men who are already made." Seeming to echo the Populist demands for a producers' democracy, Wilson warned, "If America is not to have freedom of enterprise, then she can have freedom of no sort whatever."

The new president boldly summoned Congress into special session on his first day in office to consider the persistent question of tariff reform, the issue that had begun the unraveling of the Taft administration. Appearing before a joint session to deliver an address clearly aimed more at the public than at the lawmakers, Wilson called for a downward revision of import duties. His fellow southerner and former rival for the Democratic nomination Congressman Oscar Underwood promptly introduced such a bill. The controversial proposal attracted immediate support from farmers and consumers who had long sought tariff reduction and from some industralists who wanted lower rates for imported raw materials. Exporters and shippers also hoped that reductions in American rates would lead to reciprocal decreases abroad, thereby stimulating foreign trade. Wilson's forceful leadership marshaled a

Exhibit 3–1. Number of Individual Income Tax Returns filed, 1916–1919 (in rounded millions)

1915	.3 m
1916	.4 m
1917	3.5 m
1918	4.4 m
1919	5.3 m

Source: *Historical Statistics of the United States, Colonial Times to 1970* (U.S. Department of Commerce, 1975).

solid Democratic majority behind the measure and secured its passage. The Underwood-Simmons Act of 1913 thus brought the first significant tariff reduction since the pre–Civil War era.

The new tariff played a key role in changing the revenue base of the federal government. Throughout the nineteenth century, federal revenues came principally from public lands and import duties. But only weeks before Wilson took office in 1913, the states completed the process of ratifying the Sixteenth Amendment to the Constitution, thereby permitting the enactment of income tax laws. Democratic representative Cordell Hull of Tennessee now proposed, as a companion piece to tariff reform, an income tax to replace revenue lost through tariff reductions. The law imposed a 1 percent tax on individuals and corporations earning over $4,000 annually with rates ranging to 7 percent for incomes over $500,000. The new tax law gave the federal government access to unprecedented sources of wealth and prepared the way for its expanded social and military role in the years ahead.

Eager to sustain the momentum of his program, Wilson kept Congress in session through a humid Washington summer to consider reform of the nation's banking system. Like the tariff, banking had been a national issue since the early days of the republic when Alexander Hamilton and Thomas Jefferson had debated the merits of a central bank. In the 1830s, Andrew Jackson settled the issue for decades when he destroyed the Second National Bank, making the United States the only major western nation without a central banking authority. But the rise of powerful investment bankers such as J. P. Morgan intensified the controversy over banking issues in the late nineteenth century. Wilson spoke for many when he proclaimed in 1911, "The great monopoly in our country is the money monopoly." In 1912, the Pujo Committee of the House launched a highly publicized investigation of the "money trust." A series of articles by Progressive attorney Louis Brandeis, published under the title *Other People's Money and How the Bankers Use It* (1914), spoke to the same anxieties.

Anticorporate progressives such as William Jennings Bryan and Minnesota representative Charles A. Lindbergh bitterly denounced domination of banking by the Morgan and Rockefeller interests and sought complete government control. In contrast, corporate progressives such as Virginia senator Carter Glass hoped to decentralize and rationalize the banking system while still leaving authority in the hands of bankers themselves. Brandeis acknowledged that most local banks lacked the resources to provide adequate credit to farmers and sustain themselves in the midst of economic depression. Accordingly, the attorney worked with Wilson in devising a regulatory structure that blended federal supervision of the whole financial system with banker control of boards at the regional level.

With the White House deeply involved in the debate, Congress passed the Federal Reserve Act of 1913, the most important domestic legislation of the Wilson presidency. The new system included twelve Federal Reserve banks, which represented the nation's geographic regions. All banks that operated nationally were required to invest part of their capital in the Federal Reserve bank in their district, and state banks could do the same. A Federal Reserve Board, appointed by the president, decided on the rate of interest to be paid to the regional Federal Reserve by investor banks. If the board wanted to encourage expansion, it lowered the interest rate, making it easier to borrow money; if it wanted to curb inflation, it raised interest rates. The Federal Reserve system also provided reserves to cover local financial crises and established the nation's first coordinated check clearance procedures.

Wilson turned to the explosive issue of the trusts in 1914. By then he had begun to shift his view of supercorporations, replacing the small-business ethic of the New Freedom with the corporate progressivism of the New Nationalism. Again influenced by Louis Brandeis, who was making a similar conversion, Wilson developed two strategies. First he pushed for passage of the Clayton Anti-Trust Act, which attempted to close legal loopholes in existing legislation by barring interlocking directorates, price discrimination, and holding companies among competing firms. The Clayton Act fulfilled the New Freedom promise to discipline monopolistic corporations, but it also demonstrated Wilson's commitment to corporate progressivism. Supported by the National Civic Federation and the Chamber of Commerce, the law targeted the "destructive competition" that prevented corporate planning. To the relief of corporations operating under uncertain state and judicial guidelines, the Clayton Act clarified the limits of corporate competition by specifying "unfair practices." Yet even its advocates found the law cumbersome and unwieldly, particularly since it required prosecutors to prove that prohibited acts constituted the creation of a monopoly.

Wilson's second strategy focused on the creation of a regulatory agency for trusts modeled on the Interstate Commerce Commission. The president's rhetoric reflected his new perspective. "Nobody can fail to see that modern business is going to be done by corporations," he declared. Emphasizing that "the old time of individual competition is gone by," Wilson drew a distinction between big business and monopoly. "A trust is an arrangement to get rid of competition," he explained, "and a big business is a business that has survived competition by conquering in the field of intelligence and economy."

In 1914, Congress passed the Federal Trade Commission Act, which empowered a new regulatory agency to conduct investigations and issue restraining orders to prevent "unfair trade practices." By stressing administrative regulation over antitrust prosecution, the Wilson administration had rejected its earlier commitment to restoring competition. Instead it embraced the Progressive concept of regulation in the public interest through scientific review of data by experts in the field. Moreover, Wilson generally appointed

Louis Dembitz Brandeis
1856–1941

"A lawyer who has not studied economics and sociology is very apt to become a public enemy," declared Louis Brandeis. Born in Louisville, Kentucky, the son of German-Jewish immigrants, Brandeis reshaped twentieth-century jurisprudence by defending the interests of working people against corporate power. A successful private law practice made him a millionaire by the age of fifty and freed him to devote time to public issues. The bloody Homestead steel strike of 1892 marked a crucial turning point in his life and career. Concluding that "organized capital hired a private army to shoot at organized labor for resisting an arbitrary cut in wages," Brandeis committed himself to assisting the working class.

His most important contribution came in his appearance before the Supreme Court in *Muller v. Oregon* (1908). Representing the state of Oregon in a suit challenging the constitutionality of a law setting a maximum workday of ten hours for women, Brandeis brushed aside legal principles with a cursory three-page summary. "There is no logic that is properly applicable to these laws except the logic of facts," he argued. He used one hundred pages to document expert opinion concerning the adverse impact of excessive hours on the health of women. The Brandeis brief marked the first use of sociological data in a Supreme Court case and revolutionized legal argument. "My, how I detest that man's ideas," wrote conservative Justice George Sutherland of Brandeis. "But he is one of the greatest technical lawyers I have ever known."

Politically independent, the progressive Brandeis supported both Republicans and Democrats for national office. In 1912, he initially endorsed Robert LaFollette for the Republican nomination but later supported Woodrow Wilson when the Republican party divided. He subsequently be- *(cont.)*

members of the business community to the Federal Trade Commission, making it an agency for economic rationalization that established predictable ground rules for corporate competition. Not surprisingly, the administration initiated very few antitrust suits and generally encouraged negotiated settlements between corporations and the Department of Justice. Corporate progressives and future advocates of government regulation continued to base their proposals on the Wilsonian model of administrative government.

With the creation of the Federal Trade Commission (FTC), Wilson considered his legislative tasks complete, but political pressures forced him to take further reform initiatives. At first the president backed away from proposals that appeared to benefit only special interests as opposed to broader, national concerns. But the opposition Republicans fared well in the congressional elections of 1914, and Wilson began to change his position as the 1916 presidential contest approached. The leader of a minority party, he recognized the importance of building a coalition and threw the power of the presidency into that effort. Wilson also saw the presidency as a neutral broker came a close adviser to Wilson and a prime architect of the New Freedom. Brandeis played a major role in shaping the Federal Reserve Act of 1913, insisting that the system must ultimately be placed under control of the federal government, instead of the banking community. He also took a significant part in developing the administration's antitrust policy by drafting the Federal Trade Commission Act of 1914.

Wilson risked controversy to nominate Brandeis to a seat on the Supreme Court in 1916. Unlike most justices, Brandeis had held no previous public office, and his legal work on behalf of social causes had given him a reputation as a radical. As the Senate Judiciary Committee spent four months reviewing the nomination, conservative business and political interests strongly opposed confirmation. Seven past presidents of the American Bar Association, including former cabinet officer Elihu Root and former president William Howard Taft, testified in opposition, arguing that Brandeis's career as an advocate proved his lack of judicial temperament. Ultimately, however, the Senate confirmed the nomination and Brandeis served on the bench for twenty-three years.

The new justice joined the Court in the midst of one of its most conservative periods. He frequently joined Oliver Wendell Holmes in dissenting from the prevailing majority. Brandeis shared the Progressive faith that government could solve social and economic problems, and he generally affirmed regulatory and social justice legislation. He considered such laws part of a healthy and desirable process of experimentation in the social sciences. Devoted to the Court, Brandeis labored extensively over his richly detailed opinions, drafting everything in longhand without the aid of a secretary.

When the new Supreme Court building opened in 1935, Justice Brandeis refused to assume his new quarters, contending that the authority of the Court should rest on the persuasiveness of its opinions instead of on the trappings of institutional power. Brandeis retired in 1939, replaced on the Court by William Douglas. ◼

among the economy's organized interests. Accordingly, the Clayton Act specifically exempted labor unions and agricultural organizations from antitrust prosecution and restricted the use of court injunctions against union activities. Wilson built upon this legacy in 1916 by signing laws to improve the conditions of merchant seamen, to regulate child labor, and to provide workmen's compensation for federal employees. He also reluctantly approved the Adamson Act, which reduced the workday to eight hours for railroad employees. Moreover, the president appealed for support from farm organizations by authorizing the creation of an agricultural extension service and federal land banks to provide rural credits. A federal highway planning measure added to the impressive legislative package.

Wilson's commitment to a Progressive leadership of professional experts had enabled him to reverse the Democratic party's historic aversion to government centralization. In keeping with this faith, Wilson stunned the nation in 1916 by appointing Brandeis as the first Jew to sit on the Supreme Court. Brandeis had appeared before the Court in 1908 to plead for the constitutionality of a state law setting maximum working hours for women. In *Muller v. Oregon*, the Court had sustained the Brandeis brief, concluding that social policy concerns could override constitutional precedent. Both Brandeis and the president rejected nineteenth-century principles of a free marketplace and strict constitutional limits, and the Democratic administration now openly courted the labor vote in the coming election. By 1916, Woodrow Wilson had presided over an unprecedented program for the regulation of labor, agriculture, and business by government experts. The president's political skill had helped to rationalize the corporate economy, soften its consequences, and make it more acceptable to the American people.

Reform and Imperialism in Latin America

Shortly before assuming the presidency, Wilson commented on the potential irony that his administration might be forced to devote most of its attention to foreign affairs. By 1916, turmoil in Latin America and cataclysm in Europe appeared to be making the president's comment a prophetic one. Despite the expansion of American foreign policy under Theodore Roosevelt, most voters continued to ignore overseas affairs and assume that the oceans protected the United States from danger. Consequently, few Americans showed any awareness of their leaders' attempts to reshape the armed services to support the nation's growing role in the Caribbean and the Pacific. Reflecting the organizational and managerial changes characteristic of the corporate order, the Army and the Navy developed comprehensive staff systems to centralize control of military policy. Both services also established war colleges to professionalize the military and to devise American strategy from a global perspective. The Dick Act of 1903 furthered military centralization by placing state militias, renamed the National Guard, under the control of the federal government for the first time.

As American corporate investment overseas tripled from $1 billion to $3 billion between 1900 and 1910, three consecutive presidents—William McKinley, Theodore Roosevelt, and William Howard Taft—firmly supported maintenance of the Open Door policy. Indeed, Taft so willingly placed the resources of the State, War, and Navy Departments at the disposal of investors that his foreign policy became known as Dollar Diplomacy. He and Secretary of State Philander C. Knox encouraged American investment in Latin America as a way of minimizing European influence in the region. When domestic conditions seemed to threaten the security of American profits, the president sent troops to Nicaragua, Guatemala, Honduras, and Haiti. Taft advocated "active intervention to secure for our merchandise and our capitalists opportunity for profitable investment." Yet, like his predecessors, he found that efforts in Asia fell short. The Japanese, for example, easily thwarted administration plans to involve American capital in major railroad projects in China and Manchuria.

Woodrow Wilson inherited two decades of presidential willingness to use military force to expand American economic interests overseas. As a historian

**Exhibit 3–2. US Investment Abroad versus
Foreign Investment in the US, 1897–1919
(in billions of dollars)**

	US Investment Abroad	*Foreign Investment in US*
1897	$ .7 b	$3.4 b
1908	$2.5 b	$6.4 b
1914	$5.0 b	$7.2 b
1919	$9.7 b	$3.3 b

Source: *Historical Statistics of the United States, Colonial Times to 1970* (U.S. Department of Commerce, 1975).

who shared Frederick Jackson Turner's theories concerning the importance of expanding frontiers of opportunity, Wilson believed that the preservation of American democracy and prosperity depended upon active participation in world trade. But he also realized that access to markets, raw materials, and investments depended upon political stability and reliability in host nations. Accordingly, Wilson looked to encourage the development of democracy and American institutions among the "lower peoples" of Latin America, the nation's historic sphere of influence. Although the president and Secretary of State William Jennings Bryan repudiated Dollar Diplomacy, the Wilson administration actually escalated military intervention in the Caribbean and Central America, sending troops to occupy Nicaragua, Cuba, and Santo Domingo. In Haiti, Wilson dispatched the military to pressure the government into signing a treaty that ensured American control of the country's finances, public works, army, and foreign relations. Concerned also with the security of the Caribbean as European war tensions mounted in 1916, the president instructed Denmark to sell the Virgin Islands to the United States or face their forcible seizure by American forces.

Wilson's grandest scheme for forcing Latin American progress focused on Mexico. Democratic forces had started a revolution there in 1911, but two years later General Victoriano Huerta led a successful counterrevolution. Wilson refused to recognize the Huerta dictatorship on the grounds that it lacked popular support, and he gave the general an ultimatum to relinquish power. "I will not recognize a government of butchers," the president insisted. By his refusal to recognize the Huerta regime, Wilson introduced a new diplomatic ploy. Never before had the United States refused to recognize an existing government. "I am going to teach the South American governments to elect good men," the president explained to a British diplomat. He then threw American support behind General Venustiano Carranza and ordered the Navy to seize the Mexican port of Vera Cruz to prevent a German steamer from landing arms for Huerta. Carranza's army captured Mexico City but failed to control the chaotic fighting that raged throughout the country.

Convinced that Carranza lacked the strength to restore order, Wilson then turned to General Francisco (Pancho) Villa, a charismatic bandit and revolutionary who was considered a potential reformer. Americans received first-hand accounts of Villa's romantic dreams and exploits through John Reed's dispatches in news publications owned by William Randolph Hearst.

When Carranza regrouped and pushed Villa into the mountains of northern Mexico, Wilson again switched sides and recognized the Carranza government in 1915. Villa then further confused the situation by shrewdly playing on Mexican resentment of American meddling. In a deliberate act of provocation, he crossed the Mexico–United States border in 1916 and burned the town of Columbus, New Mexico, killing nineteen Americans. Outraged, Wilson placed General John J. Pershing in command of a punitive expedition and ordered it to pursue Villa into Mexico. Pershing led some seven thousand American soldiers three hundred miles into Mexico. As Villa had anticipated, most Mexicans resented this American intrusion on their sovereignty, and President Carranza ordered the United States to withdraw. The expedition never captured Villa, and it served as a major irritant to Mexican relations until Wilson finally recalled the soldiers early in 1917.

NEUTRALITY IN EUROPE

In June 1914, Slav nationalists murdered Hapsburg archduke Francis Ferdinand and his wife Sophie in the dusty Balkan town of Sarajevo. These murders constituted the first in a rapid series of events that, before the end of summer, plunged Europe into the first general war on the continent since the fall of Napoleon. The conflict arrayed the Allies (Great Britain, France, and Russia) against the Central Powers (Germany and the Hapsburg Empire).

General Pershing's troops wind through the Mexican desert in their futile pursuit of Pancho Villa.

Exhibit 3–3. Value of US Merchandise Exports to Britain and Germany, 1914–1916 (in rounded millions of dollars)

	Britain	Germany
1914$	$ 594 m	$345 m
1915	$ 912 m	$ 29 m
1916	$1887 m	$ 2 m

Source: *Historical Statistics of the United States, Colonial Times to 1970* (U.S. Department of Commerce, 1975).

Wilson promptly proclaimed a policy of neutrality, calling the clash "a war with which we have nothing to do, whose causes cannot touch us." He asked the American people to be "neutral in fact as well as in name" and "impartial in thought as well as in action."

The president's public insistence that the United States had no stake in the European war was far from accurate. Since the 1890s, foreign policy leaders had generally seen Germany rather than Britain as the greatest potential threat to American security. Indeed, until the turn of the century, the British fleet served Washington's interests by limiting European involvement in Latin America. Consequently, Theodore Roosevelt and many others expressed alarm at the prospect of a German victory. Strong cultural ties also linked the former North American colonies with the mother country, particularly among the predominantly Anglo-Protestant officials of the State Department. Wilson himself greatly admired the British people and their institutions. Not surprisingly, within months of the outbreak of hostilities, the president privately admitted that the United States might have to take an active part in the fighting if Germany appeared likely to win.

Economic issues increasingly drew the United States into the Allied camp. War disrupted the productive capacity of Europe while simultaneously creating an enormous demand for industrial goods and agricultural products. Consequently, American trade with the Allies increased from $825 million in 1914 to $3.2 billion in 1916 and stimulated an economic boom in the United States. When the Allies began to run short of money in 1915, American financiers invested heavily in the war effort through huge loans to the governments of Britain and France. Believing in the importance of foreign trade as a stimulant to the economy and world order, Wilson permitted the Federal Reserve banks to guarantee these obligations. By 1917, American bankers had loaned the two nations $2.5 billion. Secretary of State Bryan vigorously opposed these loans, declaring, "Money is the worst of contrabands—it commands all other things." The secretary's influence rapidly waned, however. "Our firm had never for one minute been neutral," a House of Morgan banker later explained. "From the start we did everything we could to contribute to the cause of the Allies." By contrast, American trade with the Central Powers nearly disappeared and loans to Germany totaled only $300 million.

Roosevelt and many Republican leaders pressed the Wilson administration to adopt an assertive neutral rights policy and initiate a program of military preparedness. But the president hoped that a neutral United States might be in a position to shape the peace. Wilson's approach to foreign policy fused idealism with the imperatives of economic expansion. The president saw the war as an opportunity to end European empires and open the world to free trade. He hoped that the terrible costs of the war would teach Europe the necessity of ending imperial competition and believed that the United States could provide leadership for a peace settlement based on an international Open Door. "We are the mediating nation of the world," Wilson declared. "We are compounded of all the nations of the world. We are, therefore, able to understand all nations."

While Wilson awaited the opportunity to initiate a new international community, the actions of the belligerents buffeted American neutrality. Once hostilities broke out, Britain and Germany each tried to impose blockades on the other's ports. Just as Britain became an important market for American goods and capital, the Royal Navy mined the entrance to the North Sea and seriously curbed neutral trade with Germany. Consequently, the United States acquiesced in the British blockade even while Wilson denounced the Germans for violating the rights of neutrals.

Germany's growing reliance on submarine warfare provided the most serious irritant to its relations with the United States. The British blockade mainly relied on surface vessels that employed traditional methods of naval warfare and seldom claimed civilian casualties. Unable to meet the British challenge on the open sea, the Germans turned to a new type of warfare employing the U-boat, or submarine. As deadly as it could be to surface vessels, the submarine was itself extremely vulnerable to attack, especially when it surfaced. Even when it submerged, a skillful sharpshooter could render a submarine helpless by shooting out its periscope. The U-boat, therefore, became a weapon of stealth, and Germany's strategy of submarine warfare resulted in considerable loss of property and numerous civilian casualties.

Germany's desperate effort to cut supply lines to the British Isles played into the hands of Allied propagandists. Since Britain controlled the only trans-Atlantic cable, it dominated the flow of war news to the United States. The American media readily accepted British interpretation of events and printed numerous stories of alleged German atrocities, all of which confirmed the image of Germany as an outlaw nation. British propaganda portrayed the Germans as "Huns," a barbaric and savage people who severed the hands of Belgian babies and raped women. Consequently, stories relating the loss of innocent lives to the attacks of German submarines outraged American public opinion.

Wilson's neutrality policy rested on ambiguous and unrealistic assumptions. The president placed different importance upon British and German offenses. Moreover, he demanded that American merchants have the unimpeded right to turn profits in the midst of a war zone while assuming no risks for their actions. The fate of the *Lusitania* illustrated the difficulties of American policy. In May 1915, a German submarine sank the British passenger liner within sight of the Irish coast, causing the deaths of 1,198 passengers including 128 Americans. Theodore Roosevelt denounced the sinking as an "act of piracy," although the *Lusitania* almost certainly used its passengers as a shield for the munitions it carried to the British war effort.

Wilson responded to the sinking by sending a strongly worded note to the German government. Secretary of State Bryan, an adamant neutralist, resigned to protest the president's unwillingness to mount equal criticism of British offenses. The departing secretary criticized the idea that "ammunition intended for one of the belligerents should be safeguarded in transit by the lives of American citizens." Many congressional representatives supported the McLemore Resolution, which warned Americans not to travel to Europe, but Wilson refused to accept any limitations on neutral rights. By rejecting such restrictions, the president placed himself in a position that required defense of those rights.

In 1915, the Germans acceded to Wilson's demands and promised not to challenge passenger liners, but they increased strikes on merchant vessels. The issue came to a head again in early 1916 when the Allies began to arm merchant ships and send them against submarines. Germany countered that it would fire on those vessels without warning. A few weeks later, it attacked an unarmed French steamer, the *Sussex*, and injured several Americans. When Wilson delivered an ultimatum that called for Germany to either stop sinking merchant and passenger ships or risk intervention by the United States, Berlin responded with the Sussex Pledge accepting American demands. Yet the president realized how precarious the balance between peace and war had become. "Any little German lieutenant can put us into war at any time by some calculated outrage," he fretted.

Although Wilson publicly spoke of ending the use of military power in foreign affairs, he simultaneously urged an increase in the size of the American military. Claiming that mobilization would encourage belligerents to respect American rights, he told an aide, "Let us build a navy bigger [than Great Britain's] and do what we please." Plagued by anti-interventionist sentiment in Congress, he toured the country to win support for his program, the National Defense Act of 1916, plus a naval appropriations bill. The half-billion-dollar preparedness program raised sensitive questions of financing. Conservative Republicans hoped to fund mobilization through bonds, but preparedness adversaries from both parties charged that corporate interests sought a military buildup to protect their overseas holdings. Led by Claude Kitchins, Democratic chair of the House Ways and Means Committee, Congress passed the Revenue Act of 1916, the first major income and inheritance tax in American history.

By 1916, a coalition of British sympathizers, recipients of wartime prosperity, members of the eastern defense and foreign policy establishment, and belligerent nationalists pressed Wilson toward intervention. But many Americans wanted the United States to remain at peace. German-American who were sympathetic to their homeland and Irish-Americans who despised British colonialism constituted the most bitter foes of American involvement. Social justice Progressives like Jane Addams and Amos Pinchot also opposed intervention because they feared its effects on the nation's strides toward reform and the peaceful settlement of international disputes. Organizations such as the Carnegie Endowment for International Peace had successfully urged presidents Roosevelt, Taft, and Wilson to sign arbitration treaties with the major powers, resulting in agreements with all except Germany. The largest group of war opponents consisted of midwestern and western farmers and business people who saw the conflict as a plutocratic struggle of no significance to small producers. Cut off from European trade and financial ties, these Americans also lacked the association with British culture and ethnicity that more prominently characterized people of the South and the upper class of the East.

Questions of war and peace dominated the presidential contest of 1916. The Republicans nominated Progressive Charles Evans Hughes, a Supreme Court justice and former governor of New York. A reunited Republican party posed a serious threat to Wilson's reelection, but the president carefully established himself as the "peace candidate." As Wilsonians adopted the slogan "He kept us out of war," Theodore Roosevelt's bellicose pronouncements unintentionally validated the Democratic claim to be the party of peace. As a result, Wilson and Vice-President Thomas R. Marshall won a close victory, taking 49.4 percent of the vote to 46.2 percent for the Republicans. In the Electoral College, the Democratic ticket prevailed by 277–254, the smallest victory margin since 1876. Wilson's coalition of southerners, westerners, urban ethnics, antiwar Republicans, and reform-minded Progressives and Socialists barely enabled him to retain the White House.

Exhibit 3–4. Election of 1916

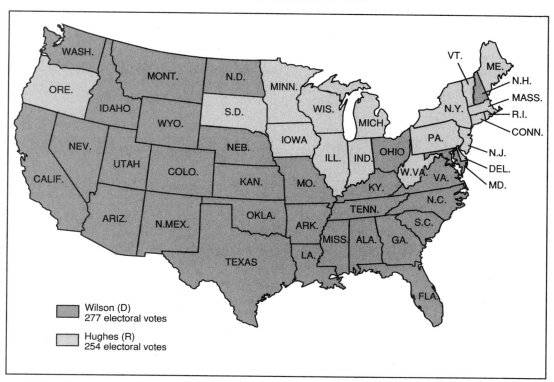

Wilson (D)
277 electoral votes

Hughes (R)
254 electoral votes

THE COMING OF WAR

Safely reelected, Wilson decided to make another major effort to mediate the war. The president had pursued such a course almost since the fighting began. "I have tried to look at this war ten years ahead," he told journalist Ida Tarbell, "to be a historian at the same time I was an actor." Early in the war, he twice sent his personal representative Colonel Edward House to Europe, but to no avail. The Germans resented the pro-Allied bias of the American position, and the British and French believed they would win the war. By 1915, the cost of the conflict had risen so high that neither side would consider a negotiated peace. In late 1916, Wilson tried again by inviting the belligerents to state their terms for peace. Germany made no public response although it wanted Lithuania, Poland, Belgium, and the Belgian Congo. The Allies insisted upon German withdrawal from Belgium, the return of Alsace-Lorraine to France, substantial indemnity payments, an end to Germany's overseas colonialism, and the division of the Hapsburg Empire.

Frustrated and impatient, Wilson then seized the moment to propose a peace rooted in the ideals and economic imperatives of the Open Door. In an address to Congress in January 1917, the president called for a "peace without victory" to preserve a world marketplace guaranteed by freedom of the seas, not huge navies or armies. Although the proposal demonstrated visionary eloquence and enhanced Wilson's global stature, it failed to break the European stalemate, and peace prospects rapidly deteriorated. With the land war deadlocked on the western front and the British blockade creating severe shortages, German leaders met with Kaiser Wilhelm and voted to revoke the *Sussex* Pledge and resume unrestricted submarine warfare. U-boats now would attack the ships of neutral nations as well as those of their adversaries. Germany recognized that this escalation would seriously jeopardize relations with the United States, but it hoped to win the war before the Americans could establish a military presence in Europe.

Convinced that American democracy and prosperity depended upon global freedom of action, and sensitive to issues of national honor, Wilson promptly severed diplomatic relations with Germany. Aware of the enormous quantities of goods awaiting shipment to Europe, the president asked Congress for authority to arm American merchant ships. Seeking to build public support for his case, Wilson released the Zimmermann note, a secret German dispatch recently intercepted by the British. This message, sent from Berlin's foreign secretary to its ambassador in Mexico, directed the ambassador to encourage Mexico to attack the United States in the event America entered the European war. In exchange, Germany would help Mexico to recover its "lost provinces" of Texas, New Mexico, and Arizona. One day after the publication of the Zimmermann note, the House overwhelmingly approved the Armed Ship bill. In the Senate, Republican insurgents Robert LaFollette and George Norris organized a filibuster just before the congressional term expired. Infuriated at this temporary obstacle to military preparedness and executive prerogative, Wilson announced that "a little group of willful men representing no opinion but their own have rendered the great government of the United States helpless and contemptible." Acting on the advice of Secretary of State Robert Lansing, the president armed the merchant vessels by executive order.

Events now proceeded rapidly. In Russia, the March revolution of 1917 toppled the tsarist government and ended three hundred years of rule by the Romanov family. As a republican form of government assumed power, the United States found itself relieved of the embarrassment of tying itself to a despotic ally. In mid-March, German submarines sank three American merchant ships in a single day, killing two dozen people. Less than three weeks later, on a rainy April evening, Wilson and a cavalry escort rode down Pennsylvania Avenue to ask Congress for a declaration of war. In a powerful speech, the president told his country that "the right is more precious than the peace." "The world," he said, "must be made safe for democracy."

Wilson left the chamber to a roaring ovation, but a scattering of antimilitarists in the South joined midwestern and western noninterventionists to resist American involvement. Denouncing the war as a conflict to secure the interests of American bankers and munitions makers, George Norris told the Senate, "We are going to war upon the command of gold." Robert LaFollette defined "patriots" as "those who are back of the thirty-eight corporations most benefitted by the war effort." The angry debate raged for four days, but

**Exhibit 3–5. Public Debt of the Federal Government, 1916–1919
(in rounded billions)**

1916	$ 1.2 b
1917	$ 3.0 b
1918	$12.5 b
1919	$25.5 b

Source: *Historical Statistics of the United States, Colonial Times to 1970* (U.S. Department of Commerce, 1975).

by April 6 the declaration had passed both chambers with six senators and fifty representatives voting no. Wilson reflected the anguish of the moment. As he finished his speech, the president asked an aide why anyone would cheer a message that would result in the death of thousands of people. According to his secretary, Woodrow Wilson wept after he returned to the White House.

ORGANIZING FOR VICTORY

American involvement came at a crucial time in the Great War. The fighting on the western front had been a bloody stalemate for over two years, its casualty rates sapping the vitality of a generation of Europeans. Political unrest in Russia seemed likely to diminish the ability of the Russian army to sustain the eastern front, freeing the Central Powers to divert more of their forces to the war against the nearly depleted British and French troops. The success of unrestricted submarine warfare compounded Allied problems. In April 1917, Britain had only a six-week supply of food, and the U-boats were sinking nine hundred thousand tons of shipping each month.

Almost immediately, the American government faced the task of deciding how to finance a war that would ultimately cost $32 billion. With great fanfare blending modern public relations techniques, prominent entertainment figures, and old-fashioned patriotism, the government launched a series of Liberty Bond drives, which netted $23 billion in loans from individual subscribers. This reliance on bonds also limited consumer spending, thus curtailing demand for commodities and thereby cooling inflation. Under pressure from LaFollette and other insurgents, Congress raised billions of additional revenue with new taxes on "excess profits," high incomes, and luxuries.

The Wilson administration sought a working partnership between government and the private sector in organizing the national war effort. Accordingly, mobilization provided corporate progressives with the chance to create a rationalized economy without the unpredictable element of price competition. The War Industries Board (WIB) headed by financier Bernard Baruch set production goals for corporations in war industries and controlled the flow of raw materials so war output would have top priority. The board promoted what Wilson called the "new competition," in which the government sanctioned price fixing and collusive bidding. As Baruch's biographer noted, the government became party to a "conspiracy in restraint of trade for reasons of national security." Since most government contracts went to the largest corporations without competitive bidding, firms that cooperated with the WIB received guaranteed profits. Under Baruch's leadership, the WIB dealt mostly with the largest corporations and encouraged the trend toward economic consolidation. In blurring the line between government and industry, Baruch created an American version of corporatism. A concept more popular in Europe than in the United States, corporatism linked political and economic elites in a commitment to a sense of community and social responsibility. Accordingly, the state served as partner and facilitator rather than regulator, a role similar to the one assumed by the War Industries Board.

Under Herbert Hoover, a mining engineer turned public servant, the Food Administration took control of the production and distribution of agricultural products. This agency set high prices for commodities to encourage production and then purchased the entire crop. As large harvests of midwestern wheat and southern cotton fed and clothed American and Allied troops, agricultural income jumped 30 percent. Anxious to avoid a system of excessive bureaucratic regulation, Hoover employed mechanisms that encouraged the voluntary cooperation of private citizens with a federal agency. Through an elaborate public relations effort, the Food Administration persuaded millions to adopt voluntary solutions to the problems of agricultural distribution by observing weekly days on which they ate no meat or wheat products. The success of this campaign enabled the agency to supply domestic, military, and foreign consumers without resorting to compulsory rationing.

Similar forms of centralized planning were applied to the Fuel Administration, which distributed coal to both citizens and defense plants, and to the Railroad Administration, which provided central management for a private system owned by several companies. Wilson also signed the Webb-Pomerene Act of 1918 authorizing American corporations to coordinate price and marketing policies in overseas trade. The Edge Act of 1919 allowed bankers to cooperate to control investments abroad. All this seemed to confirm the Progressive faith in government planning based on expert leadership.

Progressives also used the war emergency to establish a working relationship with the American Federation of Labor. Led by Samuel Gompers, the AFL had supported Wilson's preparedness program, hoping that military spending would revive the economy. Once Congress declared war, the federation saw the opportunity for lower unemployment, increased union membership, high wages, shorter hours, and a voice in shaping government policy. Gompers achieved most of these goals through the War Labor Board (WLB), a national planning body that encouraged the formation of unions and collective bargaining arrangements in return for labor's cooperation in the war effort. At the recommendation of the WLB, Wilson created the United States Employment Service, which placed nearly four million workers in war work. Government support of organized labor helped to double union membership to five million during the war years. As the annual gross national

Exhibit 3–6. Gross National Product, 1916–1920
(in rounded billions at current prices)

1916	$48.3 b
1917	$60.4 b
1918	$76.4 b
1919	$84.0 b
1920	$91.5 b

Source: *Historical Statistics of the United States, Colonial Times to 1970* (U.S. Department of Commerce, 1975).

product grew from $48.3 billion to $91.5 billion between 1916 and 1920, the average annual wage of workers rose from $600 to $1,400. Bolstered by labor representation, the WLB prodded corporations to move toward an eight-hour day and comparable pay for women. Despite the implementation of Progressive social policy in war agencies, however, proposals for federal pensions for the elderly and unemployment insurance died because opponents linked them with German welfare policies. Moreover, the doubling of cost-of-living indexes between 1915 and 1920 largely negated the wage increases of the war years.

THE WAR AGAINST DISSENT

As participants in a movement substantially based on Anglo-Protestant assumptions, many Progressives feared the growing heterogeneity of twentieth-century American society. Alarmed by the enormous influx of immigrants after 1890, Progressives often pushed for social conformity as well as economic rationalization. The war only heightened this concern. In the quarter century before 1917, the United States had absorbed eighteen million immigrants, and by 1917, one American in three was either an immigrant or the child of an immigrant. Since administration leaders linked unified public support for the war with victory, the presence of a large immigrant population, much of it drawn from the nations of the Central Powers, seemed to pose a real threat to national resolve. All this could conveniently justify a thoroughgoing effort to mobilize public opinion and to crush dissent.

The Wilson administration created an enormous propaganda bureaucracy designed to rally popular opinion behind the war. Under the leadership of Progressive journalist George Creel, the Committee on Public Information (CPI) employed 150,000 people and distributed seventy-five million pieces of printed material presenting a prowar point of view. Creel persuaded many of his fellow journalists to engage in self-censorship of war-related reporting and mounted an extensive campaign to sell government bonds. The passions stirred by the CPI soon began to consume the organization, and denunciations of the enemy became increasingly harsh and xenophobic. Creel's agency encouraged people to inform on their neighbors and helped to create the vicious climate that sparked the postwar Red Scare.

Government propaganda used such advertising techniques as sexual themes and innuendo to rally popular support for the war.

Despite such efforts, many Americans continued to criticize the nation's involvement in the European war. Socialist party leader Eugene Debs joined anticorporate progressives like Robert LaFollette and George Norris in portraying the conflict as a crusade to defend the interests of a trans-Atlantic elite. After the Socialists labeled the war a "crime against humanity" in 1917, they took 30 percent or more of the vote in municipal elections in working-class cities such as Chicago, Dayton, Toledo, and Buffalo. Meanwhile, LaFollette, Idaho senator William E. Borah, and a group of southern representatives invoked republican and constitutional tradition to bitterly oppose compulsory military service, approved by Congress in June 1917. The Wisconsin senator also joined Bryan in demanding heavy taxation of war profits to conscript capital instead of the labor of draftees. Both men called for future referenda of the electorate before Congress declared war. Accused of giving aid and comfort to the enemy, LaFollette received the condemnation of the faculty of the University of Wisconsin in his home state. He also faced charges for removal from the Senate, which were eventually dismissed by a 51–21 vote of the full body.

"War is the health of the state," wrote radical essayist Randolph Bourne in his controversial book *The State* (1918). Accordingly, the Wilson administration responded to dissent with repressive legislation. Tighter immigration laws passed in 1917 and 1918 permitted authorities to deport aliens who called for the destruction of private property or who belonged to organizations working for revolution. As bureaucratic procedures, such deportations did not require trials. The Espionage Act of 1917 prohibited any action that might be construed as aiding the enemy or discouraging military service. The law also authorized the postmaster general to prohibit "treasonable" publications from using the mail. Under these provisions, the government imprisoned Debs and excluded the Socialist party's periodicals from the mail. Movie producer Robert Goldstein received a ten-year prison sentence because his film *The Spirit of '76* showed British soldiers attacking American civilians during the revolutionary war.

In 1918, Congress passed the Sedition Act making it a crime to "utter, print, write, or publish any disloyal, profane, scurrilous, or abusive language" about the armed forces. The government rarely enforced this law, although Wilson did send federal troops to Oklahoma, the state with the highest proportion of Socialist party members, to extinguish the Green Corn Rebellion of farmers protesting American involvement in the war. Also in 1918, federal officials targeted the Socialist party for indictments and arrested more than fifteen hundred people for criticizing the government.

Radicals and pacifists became special targets of government persecution. Under the leadership of "Big Bill" Haywood, the Industrial Workers of the World rejected both the American Federation of Labor's craft unionism and the Socialist party's commitment to gradual political reform. Woodrow Wilson commented privately that IWW leaders "certainly are worthy of being suppressed," and the government dispatched troops to break Wobbly-led strikes in Washington and Montana. Approximately 165 IWW leaders faced arrest, and Haywood himself avoided imprisonment only by escaping to Russia. Government repression also led to the imprisonment of four hundred conscientious objectors to military service; the administration recognized only members of pacifist churches such as the Quakers and Mennonites as legitimate claimants to conscientious objector status.

GEORGE CREEL
1876–1953

As the United States entered World War I, Woodrow Wilson asked George Creel to chair the Committee on Public Information. Recognizing that the conflict was unpopular, Wilson hoped the CPI, under Creel's leadership, could use new techniques of public relations and advertising to build a prowar consensus in American society. By doing so, the president authorized the first government propaganda agency in American history.

The son of a former Confederate army officer, George Creel struggled through an early career as a journalist until he founded a Kansas City newspaper early in the century. A staunch Progressive, he threw himself into the muckraking tradition, denouncing the city's political machine and demanding a variety of reforms to improve public services, protect workers, and make the political process more responsive to middle-class interests. Creel was an admirer of Woodrow Wilson, and he supported the president's reelection bid in 1916 by writing some effective political tracts. Impressed by Creel's Progressive credentials and persuasive powers, Wilson assigned him the task of interpreting America's war aims for audiences at home and abroad.

Creel immediately recruited a core of new public relations professionals and set in motion a campaign of "moral publicity." The Committee on Public Information distributed seventy-five million pamphlets, six thousand press releases, and fourteen thousand drawings. It assembled a speakers bureau of seventy-five thousand participants and even arranged for four thousand historians to check the accuracy of their texts.

Creel also exercised tremendous authority over the export of films and publications, manipulating these cultural exports to ensure that the "wholesome life of America" found exposure before the world. Creel and his associates painted Americans as virtuous and Germans as villains in films like *(cont.)*

The Supreme Court upheld the Wilson administration's attempts to build wartime unity by repressing dissent. In *Schenck v. U.S.* (1919), the Court ruled that constitutional protection of free speech did not apply during wartime. This decision sustained the conviction of a Socialist party official who had mailed to draft-age men circulars that questioned the constitutionality of conscription. As Justice Oliver Wendall Holmes argued in a unanimous opinion, "The most stringent protection of free speech would not protect a man falsely shouting fire in a crowded theater and causing a panic." Holmes stated that the Court could deny free speech when a "clear and present danger" existed to public safety and national security. The high court also upheld the Espionage Act conviction of Eugene Debs, sentenced to ten years in prison for telling an audience that the "master" class made wars and the "subject" class fought them.

Institutional efforts to suppress dissent ultimately encouraged private citizens to attack critics of the government and the war effort. In Indiana, a

The Prussian Cur and *The Kaiser: The Beast of Berlin.* Through advertisements in such popular magazines as the *Saturday Evening Post,* the CPI encouraged citizens to report anyone who "spreads pessimistic stories, cries for peace, or belittles our efforts to win this war." Creel also persuaded the press to engage in voluntary censorship. Meanwhile, the foreign section of the CPI worked to influence European public opinion by portraying Wilson as a hero who would bring political redemption to the world. As part of this effort, the CPI bribed European newspaper editors, subsidized European publishers, and provided free copies of American propaganda.

Creel turned the CPI into a vehicle for imposing cultural conformity as well as political unity. Like other Anglo-Protestants, Creel feared the cultural pluralism practiced by many European immigrants who tried to keep their own languages. The CPI made it clear that the use of any tongue other than English was unpatriotic. "When I think of the many voices that were heard before the war," Creel declared, "interpreting America from a class or sectional or selfish standpoint, I am not sure that, if the war had to come, it did not come at the right time for the preservation and reinterpretation of American Ideals." Indeed, Creel's memoir, *How We Advertised America* (1920), celebrated the new professions of advertising and public relations, and their ability to create a mass society where all individuals shared a uniform set of values.

Such concerns for national unity and cultural conformity marked Creel's reaction to the Second World War and the second Red Scare. Demanding a harsh peace, he spoke of the "blood guilt" of the German and Japanese people, the kind of vicious characterization of enemy civilians that the CPI usually avoided a generation earlier. He also embraced the conspiracy theories of the Republican right wing, charging that a generation of liberal politicians had forged a plot that climaxed in Roosevelt's alleged capitulation to the Soviets at the Yalta conference in 1945. He continued to crusade against dissidents of all types until his death in 1953. ■

jury promptly dismissed charges against a man who had shot someone for yelling "To hell with the United States." Occasionally such vigilantism had semiofficial sanction. For example, the government issued to the quarter million members of the American Protective League (APL) cards that identified them as agents of the Justice Department. These "agents" spied on neighbors and harassed nonconformists. Not surprisingly, German-Americans became special targets of these excesses. War hysteria translated German measles into liberty measles, dachshunds into liberty pups, and sauerkraut into liberty cabbage. More ominous forms of repression included the suspension of German-language publications, the prohibition of the teaching of German, and physical attacks on German speakers. A Congregational minister denounced the Lutheran Church as "not the bride of Christ but the paramour of kaiserism." Some employers dismissed German-Americans from their jobs, and vigilante mobs in Minnesota and Wisconsin sometimes beat suspected "Huns" and intimidated them into purchasing war bonds.

Head bowed, musician Ernst Kunwald, former conductor of the Cincinnati Symphony Orchestra, is taken into custody as an enemy alien.

WOMEN AND BLACKS IN WARTIME

Despite the pacifism of antiwar activists such as Jane Addams and Montana representative Jeanette Rankin, middle-class women embraced Wilson's promise concerning the "war to end all wars" and firmly supported the military effort. Many served in the Army Nurses Corps or the Red Cross; others contributed to the voluntary rationing plan organized by the Food Administration or made bandages and clothing for those in the service. Before the war, Wilson had ordered the arrest of the leaders of the Woman's party who picketed the White House. Led by Alice Paul, these feminists contended that no war could be a struggle for democracy as long as women did not have the vote. Officials treated such dissenters roughly and force-fed them in jail when they went on hunger strikes. After the war began, activists Carrie Chapman Catt and Anna Howard Shaw rejected radicalism to become leaders of the administration's Women's Committee of the Council of National Defense.

The war also stimulated women's participation in the labor force. By interrupting immigration from Europe at the same time that it boosted economic production, the conflict created a shortage of labor, which was intensified by the conscription of several million young men. Some 1.5 million women consequently entered the labor force as factory workers, although

Women defense workers inspect .45 automatic pistol components at Colt's Patent Firearms Plant in Hartford, Connecticut.

most later relinquished their jobs to returning male veterans. As working women supported the wartime economy, the Wilson administration endorsed women's suffrage and the states ratified the Nineteenth Amendment in 1920.

World War I provided the perfect context for the fulfillment of the women's Purity Crusade. The Eighteenth Amendment, which ended the sale of alcoholic beverages, received congressional approval in 1917 and became law in 1920. Wartime shortages made it appear frivolous to use vital grains for beer and whiskey, while economic mobilization underscored the need for productive efficiency by a sober and healthy work force. In addition, the war intensified the desire to "Americanize" new immigrants by imposing Anglo-Protestant values of sobriety, particularly since German-Americans ran most of the large breweries. To ensure that the war reflected the ideals of the Purity Crusade, female leaders of the American Social Hygiene Association helped to establish the Commission on Training Camp Activities. This government agency worked to keep prostitutes from gathering around army camps and provided soldiers with regular medical exams and information about venereal disease. Wartime tensions and pressures nevertheless accelerated the collapse of chaperoning and encouraged more liberal sexual relationships as middle-class women began to challenge the double standard that permitted only men

Exhibit 3–7. Woman Suffrage Before the 19th Amendment

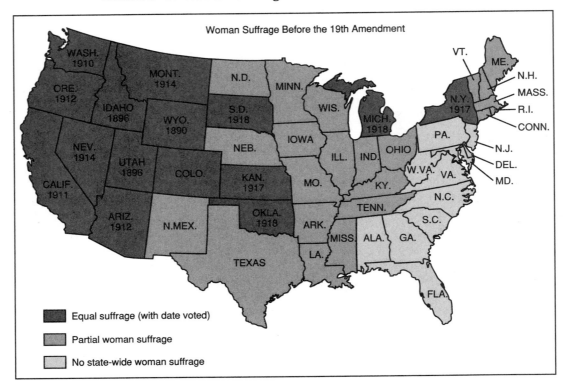

Woman Suffrage Before the 19th Amendment

Legend:
- Equal suffrage (with date voted)
- Partial woman suffrage
- No state-wide woman suffrage

to enjoy premarital sex. World War I, therefore, aroused moral anxieties about sexual propriety and the traditional role of middle-class women.

The onset of World War I also brought new roles for black people. Wilson had appealed for black votes in 1912 and even won W.E.B. DuBois's endorsement, but most administration officials shared the president's southern heritage and made the South's racial mores a part of federal policy. In this spirit, Wilson had permitted the dismissal of black government employees on the basis of race and sanctioned the systematic segregation of the federal civil service. When newspaper editor and black activist William Monroe Trotter called at the White House to protest these unprecedented policies, the president quickly ordered him to leave.

Just as World War I established economic opportunities for women, it also created jobs for blacks in the northern centers of steel production, meat packing, and other industries. As a result, even before America entered the war, the Great Migration of blacks had begun. A momentous event in the history of black America, the Great Migration shifted nearly half the black population of the United States from southern farms to northern cities before it ended some fifty years later. The black population of Chicago, for example, doubled in only four years.

Once America joined the fighting and the need for workers further increased, the Wilson administration reaffirmed the citizenship of blacks by conscripting them. Black leaders hoped that military service would improve the position of blacks. DuBois advised followers to "close our ranks shoulder to shoulder with our own white fellow citizens and the allied nations that are fighting for democracy." But racial traditions persisted in the military. The Marines accepted no black recruits, and the Navy enlisted them only as mess personnel. The Army originally intended to use blacks only as laborers, but the National Association for the Advancement of Colored People successfully pressured the service into organizing black combat units and establishing a black officer's training camp. However, no black officer ever commanded a white soldier even though more than four hundred thousand black soldiers served in World War I. The first black regiments sent to Europe were compelled to fight as part of the French Army. Although many black soldiers were decorated by the French, none earned the Medal of Honor from their own government.

The war years nevertheless inaugurated a new era in the black experience in the United States. Blacks in northern cities were free of the more stifling aspects of southern legal segregation. Like other new arrivals in American cities, they used the franchise to influence local politics in ways that were not possible in the South. More dramatically, the war offered liberation from domestic segregation for black soldiers, some of whom were accepted as social and sexual equals in France, an experience almost unknown for blacks in the United States. In turn, black military bandsmen gave Europeans their first taste of a distinctive American art form: jazz.

Black infantrymen test their gas masks shortly after arriving in France.

Exhibit 3–8. Death Rates by Race, 1900–1920
(per 1000 of population)

	Black	White
1900	25.0	17.0
1905	25.5	15.7
1910	21.7	14.5
1915	20.2	12.9
1920	17.7	12.6

Source: *Historical Statistics of the United States, Colonial Times to 1970* (U.S. Department of Commerce, 1975).

Exhibit 3–9. Life Expectancy by Race, 1900–1920

	Black	White
1900	33.0	47.6
1910	35.6	50.3
1920	45.3	54.9

Source: *Historical Statistics of the United States, Colonial Times to 1970* (U.S. Department of Commerce, 1975).

These changes fostered a growing assertiveness in the black community, which unnerved whites committed to maintaining racial dominance. When race riots erupted in twenty-five cities during the bloody summer of 1919, blacks fought back against white aggression and seventy-eight black Americans died. In the North, these explosions stemmed from fears by lower-income whites that blacks were taking scarce jobs and that the expansion of black ghettos would destroy white neighborhoods. In the South, whites continued to react with savage violence to any perceived threat to white supremacy. Southerners particularly feared the sense of pride that marked many returning black veterans, and some returning soldiers were lynched while still in uniform. Blacks, in turn, resented white efforts to deprive the black community of jobs and housing. By the 1920s, these conditions produced mass movements of racial pride and separatism among working-class blacks in the cities.

THE DOUGHBOYS
AND MILITARY VICTORY

The American entry into World War I presented the question of how to raise a military force. Theodore Roosevelt offered to recruit a volunteer outfit and lead it overseas immediately, just as he had done twenty years earlier in the Spanish-American War. Like many others, he felt assured that the zeal of volunteer fighting men would more than compensate for their lack of

Exhibit 3–10. American Troops on the Western Front, 1918

training. Wilson, however, insisted on a selective service system that would permit the government to organize human resources for a variety of needs and ensure that the fighting forces would be representative of American society, not simply drawn from the less privileged classes. Despite the comment by Democratic House Speaker Champ Clark that there was "precious little difference between a conscript and a convict," the Selective Service Act allowed the army to draft three million doughboys before the armistice. Another two million volunteered for service.

In selecting the commander for the American Expeditionary Force (AEF), Wilson bypassed General Leonard Wood, an associate of Theodore Roosevelt, and turned instead to General John J. Pershing, a highly respected career officer who had recently returned from leading the unsuccessful Punitive Expedition in pursuit of Pancho Villa. A consummate professional soldier, Pershing refused to commit troops to combat until they had completed their

Exhibit 3–11. Military Personnel on Active Duty, 1916–1920

1916	179,376
1917	643,833
1918	2,897,167
1919	1,172,602
1920	343,302

Source: *Historical Statistics of the United States, Colonial Times to 1970* (U.S. Department of Commerce, 1975).

Mass armies using animal power and machines posed staggering logistical problems for military planners. Men, mules, and machines jam a country road as the Meuse-Argonne offensive begins.

training, declaring that, "the standards of the American Army will be those of West Point." His policy caused friction with the war-weary Allies, who also resented Pershing's insistence on a separate military command. Pershing adamantly refused to use American troops as replacements for depleted British and French units. Consequently, the AEF did not begin to arrive in France until late 1917 and did not constitute a significant army until the spring of 1918, virtually a full year after America entered the war. A token force landed on July 4, 1917, however, with an American officer exclaiming, "Lafayette, we are here!"

The AEF arrived at a crucial point in the fighting, reaching France in time to help blunt the 1918 German spring offensive designed to break through the Allied lines and end the war. The midsummer Allied counterattack included a significant role for American units. In September, the American First Army pushed the Germans out of the St. Mihiel salient and then joined a huge drive through the Argonne Forest. The attack committed one million Americans to an assault along a two-hundred-mile front over forty-seven days, the largest battle in the history of the United States Army to that time. Forced back to their own national boundaries, the Germans asked for a cease-fire as the imperial government dissolved. The fighting ended at 11:00 A.M. on November 11, 1918.

"We've paid our debt to Lafayette," proclaimed the doughboys; "who the hell do we owe now?" Most Americans believed that the military power of the

A machine gun crew fires on German positions in Belleau Wood. Capable of spewing 450 rounds a minute, the machine gun symbolized the mass killing characteristic of war in the industrial age.

United States had won the war. The United States had contributed to the defeat of Germany by securing the North Atlantic sea-lanes against the submarine threat and permitting the shipment of men and supplies to the Allies. Moreover, the timely arrival of American soldiers had tipped the balance of power and finally made possible a successful offensive against the Central Powers after years of debilitating trench warfare. But although American involvement was crucial, perhaps decisive, the British and French bore the brunt of the fighting. The United States suffered 112,432 deaths in the war, half of them from disease; the French lost 1,380,000, the Russians 1,700,000, and the British Empire 947,000. In one horrifying half hour at the Battle of the Somme 40,000 British soldiers lost their lives to German machine guns. Among the Central Powers, Germany lost 1,800,000 people and the Hapsburg Empire lost 1,200,000. An additional 20,000,000 Europeans were wounded.

THE RED SCARE

The fighting ended abruptly in November 1918, but the passions stirred by the conflict continued to gather momentum. In 1919 and 1920, American

Exhibit 3–12. Unemployment Rates, 1914–1920
(per cent of civilian labor force)

1914	7.9
1915	8.5
1916	5.1
1917	4.6
1918	1.4
1919	1.4
1920	5.2

Source: *Historical Statistics of the United States, Colonial Times to 1970* (U.S. Department of Commerce, 1975).

society found itself gripped by social unrest that sent a spasm of fear throughout the country. Concerned that inflation threatened to outstrip wage increases, more than four million workers took part in 3,600 strikes. Early in 1919, the most ambitious general strike in American history gripped Seattle, prompting middle-class fears that European methods of class conflict had returned with the doughboys. That fall, coal miners defied the leadership of the United Mine Workers and successfully struck for better wages. Meanwhile, the AFL organized all aspects of steel production and led 375,000 workers in the industry's first strike since 1892. Union organizers focused on better wages, an eight-hour day, and improved working conditions; companies such as United States Steel portrayed the conflict as radically inspired and used violence and strikebreakers to end the walkout. In Boston, police officers responded to the firing of nineteen AFL union members by walking off the job. Refusing to arbitrate, Republican Massachusetts governor Calvin Coolidge voiced the anxiety of the middle class by stating, "There is no right to strike against the public safety by anybody, anywhere, anytime."

A series of terrorist incidents and threats coincided with the labor unrest of 1919. In the spring, postal officials discovered several mail bombs addressed to John D. Rockefeller, Supreme Court justice Holmes, and other powerful political and corporate leaders. Those packages, which were intended for delivery on May Day, came to the attention of authorities because they lacked sufficient postage. The following month, bombs exploded within minutes of each other in eight cities. One of these explosions shook the home of Attorney General A. Mitchell Palmer and startled his neighbor, Assistant Secretary of the Navy Franklin D. Roosevelt. Despite a lack of evidence, most members of the middle class associated such anarchy with the union movement.

Labor unrest and threats of terrorism combined with fears arising from Russia's Bolshevik revolution of 1917 to bring about the first American Red Scare. In 1918, two small Communist parties emerged in the United States. Suspecting that Soviet doctrines might find fertile ground among the European ethnics of America's industrial cities, the Wilson administration organized to fight the "red" threat. Accordingly, Attorney General Palmer named an obscure government lawyer, J. Edgar Hoover, to head an antiradical division of the Department of Justice, and began rounding up labor leaders, peace activists, socialists, communists, and alien dissenters. On a single evening in January 1920, Palmer's agents detained six thousand alleged communists and radicals, holding many without charge and subjecting some to police brutality. Permitting radical aliens to see an attorney "defeats the ends of justice," explained Hoover. People who inquired about arrested friends and relatives often found themselves detained. Far from uncovering the arsenals its organizers had predicted, the raid netted three pistols and no explosives. Although the government released most of the arrested activists, it deported some five hundred aliens. As thousands of New Yorkers cheered from the docks, the U.S.S. *Buford,* the so-called Soviet Ark, sailed for Finland with 249 aliens, among them activist Emma Goldman and Alexander Berkman, the man who had tried to kill steel executive Henry Clay Frick in 1892.

Palmer's actions were part of a nationwide persecution of radicals that sought to revive central cultural beliefs and attitudes by eliminating "alien" influences and ideologies. Democratic Tennessee senator Kenneth McKellar urged that American citizens with radical ideas be sent to a penal colony in Guam. The New York state legislature expelled five Socialists. The House of Representatives twice refused to seat Milwaukee Socialist Victor Berger. Referring to the raging influenza epidemic, Berger said that all the American people had gotten from the war was flu and inflation. Twenty-eight states enacted sedition laws, which resulted in the arrest of fourteen hundred people and the conviction of three hundred. Some states required public school teachers to sign loyalty oaths, and local communities banned politically controversial books from their libraries. In some cases, radicals became the target of vigilante violence. Chicago jail inmates rioted when authorities incarcerated "reds" in their cells. A mob in Centralia, Washington, castrated IWW organizer Wesley Everest and lynched him from a railroad bridge after a shoot-out between union loyalists and the American Legion resulted in the death of two vigilantes and six Wobblies. The coroner's report found that Everest had "jumped off with a rope around his neck and shot himself full of holes."

Despite such antiradical fervor, the Red Scare ran its course by mid-1920. Palmer appeared ridiculous after his warnings of a May 1 uprising of revolutionaries proved to be unfounded and he mistakenly identified a design for an improved phonograph as a plan for explosives. With labor unrest quieted, the radical left in disarray, and the Soviet threat no longer perceived as immediate, middle-class Americans felt more secure than at any time since 1917. Even the unexplained explosion of a wagonload of bombs on Wall Street in September 1920, killing thirty-three and injuring two hundred, did not shake the new sense of security, and stock prices continued their rise the following day. The xenophobic fear of European ideologies and class conflict carried into the new decade, however, and a second, more pervasive Red Scare awaited Americans after the next world war.

JOHN REED
1887–1920

A rich man's son from Portland, Oregon, John Reed was one of two Americans to be buried inside the Kremlin Wall in Soviet Russia. "This proletarian revolution will last . . . in history," he proclaimed of the 1917 upheaval that created the Soviet Union, "a pillar of fire for mankind forever."

The strange odyssey of John Reed began at Harvard University, where the ambitious westerner donned a cheerleader's uniform and exulted in the "supreme blissful sensation of swaying two thousand voices in great crashing choruses." A prolific writer, he drifted to Europe after graduation and later settled in New York City, where he embraced the bohemian lifestyle of Greenwich Village. Influenced by Progressive-minded parents who ardently supported the political career of Theodore Roosevelt and by muckraking journalists like Lincoln Steffens and Ida Tarbell, Reed grew increasingly committed to social causes. As Reed wrote, the radical intellectuals he met in the Village taught him that "my happiness is built on the misery of others." Moving steadily toward political activism and socialism, he joined the staff of Max Eastman's radical journal *The Masses* in 1913. Covering the IWW strike in Paterson, New Jersey, he was jailed with protesting workers. The experience committed him to organizing artists to help stage the giant Madison Square Garden Pageant for the benefit of the union.

Reed first attracted national attention as a war correspondent for the Hearst publications. He was sent to Mexico to report on the major social revolution of the era. There he spent four months in the desert with Pancho Villa and became known for his ability to match the general's drinking and dancing exploits. Reed sent back a series of brilliant dispatches that captured the tedium and the horror of combat. His book *Insurgent Mexico* (1914) established him as the foremost war journalist of his time.

When World War I erupted, Reed immediately left for Europe to report on the western front and returned a second time *(cont.)*

THE LEAGUE AND A PROGRESSIVE WORLD ORDER

While the war raged, Wilson developed a plan for peace, which he outlined to Congress in January 1918. As the basis for the postwar order, he proposed Fourteen Points including disarmament, freedom of the seas, and self-determination for colonized nations and the people of Europe. Most important to Wilson was the creation of a League of Nations to enforce this new world order. In a dramatic gesture, the president decided to lead the American delegation to the peace conference himself. Before that time, the only chief executive to have left the country while in office was Theodore Roosevelt, who had traveled to the American-held Canal Zone in Panama. In to visit the eastern war zone. His writing portrayed the bloody conflict as a capitalist civil war.

Reed came home to the United States more committed than ever to the revolutionary struggle. In 1916, he met and subsequently married writer Louise Bryant. The next year, the couple sailed for Russia, arriving in Petrograd on the eve of the November revolution, which brought Lenin and the Bolsheviks to power. Reed cultivated a close friendship with the Russian leader and threw himself into the revolutionary process. His classic *Ten Days That Shook the World* (1919), a journalistic diary of those tumultuous events, provided a stirring and optimistic account of the Communist revolution.

Back in the United States, Reed's radicalism alarmed government officials, and he returned to a nation systematically suppressing dissent. His articles in *The Masses*, especially one under the headline "Knit a Straight-Jacket for Your Soldier Boy," precipitated an indictment against the magazine for sedition. Two juries failed to return verdicts in the case, but authorities in New York and Philadelphia indicted Reed for "incendiary speeches." Unintimidated, Reed and Bryant insisted on testifying before a Senate committee. While claiming that he "did not know how it was to be attained," he bluntly told his interrogators, "I have always advocated a Revolution for the United States."

Reed worked arduously to build a Communist movement in the United States. In mid-1919, however, the National Socialist Convention expelled the journalist and other pro-Bolsheviks. The exiles quickly divided into two factions, the Communist party and Reed's Communist Labor party. The novice organizer hoped to build a revolutionary movement of American workers outside the mainstream labor organizations, but he now faced indictment for sedition. He fled the United States on a forged passport, only to be deprived of his papers and jailed for three months in Finland. Released as part of a prisoner exchange, Reed finally reached Moscow, where he soon grew impatient with the rigid and remote bureaucracy dominating the revolutionary movement. When he died of typhus in 1920, the Bolsheviks buried Reed in the Kremlin as a hero of their revolution. ■

the Progressive tradition, the American Peace Commission, which sailed with Wilson, included numerous experts on a variety of world problems, all eager to lend their talents to the constructing of an enduring settlement.

Wilson arrived in Europe amid enormous popular acclaim, and the tumultuous reception only reinforced his conviction that he should play a special role at the Versailles Peace Conference. European leaders greeted the American president more coolly than did their constituents, however. British prime minister David Lloyd George remarked that talking to Wilson was like talking to Jesus Christ. Georges Clemenceau of France speculated sourly that nations were as likely to ignore the Fourteen Points as they had the Ten Commandments. Wilsonian idealism meant little to Lloyd George and Clemenceau. Traumatized by the horrible suffering of the past four years, Britain and France thought instead in terms of traditional Great Power concerns, namely national security and economic compensation. Wilson's

The Big Four, Vittorio Orlando of Italy, David Lloyd George of Great Britain, Georges Clemenceau of France, and Woodrow Wilson, pose for photographers during the deliberations at Versailles.

only bargaining chip remained his personal appeal to the war-weary people of Europe, a tactic similar to the one he had used with great success in dealings with Congress. But the Allied political leaders did not respond easily to popular pressure.

Wilson did share the Allied fear concerning the spread of communism. He saw Soviet Russia as an outlaw state that, like Germany, had no place at the peace conference. V. I. Lenin, the Bolshevik leader, had declared that the future of the industrial world belonged to communism. According to this analysis, capitalist nations would continue to fight wars among themselves as they competed for overseas markets and raw materials, until the working class took control and instituted a cooperative global system. This vision of a Communist world order challenged Wilson's vision of a peaceful capitalist system, the very goal that had led him into involvement in the European war. As Communist uprisings threatened to spread throughout eastern and central Europe, the president hoped to contain revolution within Russia and prevent it from spreading west. During the summer of 1918, Wilson had sent American troops into Russia, ostensibly to keep supplies from falling into German hands. American troops remained in northern Russia and Siberia until June 1919, and in Manchuria until April 1920. Although Americans took no part in the Russian civil war, Wilson clearly hoped that their presence, along with troops from France, Britain, and Japan, would influence the outcome. The president's overriding concern with communism forced him to seek solidarity with the Allies despite their rejection of the American peace plan.

In light of Wilsonian rhetoric, the resulting Treaty of Versailles was a distinct disappointment that deeply compromised the spirit and the substance of the Fourteen Points. A peace negotiated in secret by the victors, it ignored the idea of freedom of the seas and violated the principle of self-determination. Far from supporting a "peace without victory," the treaty imposed harsh penalties on the defeated Germans. Britain and France demanded that Germany accept guilt for causing the war, pay $35 billion in war reparations to the Allies, and limit the size of its armed forces. Britain, France, and Japan divided Germany's colonies among themselves and refused to consider dissolving their own empires. While Germany and Austria lost sovereignty over non-German peoples of Europe, the settlement placed many German-speaking people in the newly formed nations of Central Europe and in Italy. The Supreme Allied Commander, Marshal Ferdinand Foch, suggested that the treaty provided for not peace but rather armistice for the next twenty years.

Wilson accepted these compromises because the peace treaty included his cherished proposal for a League of Nations. Defining the nation's freedom and welfare in global terms, Woodrow Wilson had used American military power to ensure the observance of essential principles of international law and commerce. The president now hoped to use the peace to create a stable world order in which disputes between nations might be resolved without violence. In a dangerous and revolutionary political environment, Wilson

Exhibit 3–13. American Intervention in Russia

insisted that no international peace mechanism could work if it did not contain a system of collective security. Accordingly, Article X of the League Covenant required member nations to preserve the territorial integrity and political independence of all participants against external aggression.

Wilson returned to the United States well aware that he faced a difficult struggle to secure Senate ratification of the Versailles treaty. Having chosen to lead the American delegation to France and remain there for the full term of the negotiations, the president had left no political buffer between himself and the work of the conference. Moreover, because he had failed to appoint prominent Republicans to the delegation, the treaty appeared to be a partisan document. And since the Republicans had exploited war restlessness and discomfort with internationalism to sweep to power in both houses of Congress in 1918, Wilson faced a hostile Senate leadership. The treaty also offended several ethnic groups important to the Democratic party. Irish-Americans, who resented the alliance with the hated British, wanted the treaty to create an independent, united Ireland. Italian-Americans, in turn, wanted larger territorial concessions for Italy.

Three groups of senators impeded the president's quest for League membership. First, eastern Republicans such as Majority Leader Henry Cabot Lodge, a personal adversary, opposed ratification for political and tactical reasons. Second, a coalition of sixteen "irreconcilable" eastern Republicans and western progressives refused to endorse the League under any circumstances. Led by LaFollette, Borah, and California's Hiram Johnson, the Republican Progressives feared the use of American troops to bolster the "tottering" governments of imperial Europe. "Shall American boys police the world?" asked Johnson in a widely acclaimed Senate speech in 1919. Third, thirty-five Republican "reservationists" hoped to approve membership in the league without Article X. This group maintained that collective security might weaken the United States by tying it to a European status quo when the nation should focus on economic internationalism.

Because public opinion appeared to support Wilson, Lodge offered to recommend League membership with reservations affirming American autonomy. But instead of negotiating, Wilson mounted a long and exhausting speaking tour during September 1919 to build public enthusiasm for an unamended treaty. Midway through his trip, the president collapsed. Rushed back to Washington, he suffered a paralyzing stroke. With the president unable to assume his responsibilities for two months, First Lady Edith Galt Wilson and White House physician Cary Grayson became the only links between the Oval Office and the outside world. Wilson's physical collapse destroyed the slim chance of compromise with the reservationists. When the Senate considered a resolution to pass the treaty with the Lodge reservations in November 1919, Wilson ordered Democrats to invoke customary party loyalty and defeat it. The following March, the Senate adopted the Lodge reservations but a bipartisan coalition of Wilson loyalists and irreconcilables prevented ratification by the necessary two-thirds majority. Two years later, the United States signed a separate peace with Germany.

As the nation retreated from Wilsonian internationalism, the president's administration and party lay in tatters. A high-minded Progressive of visionary rhetoric and energy, Wilson had redefined political liberalism by using the state to institutionalize basic regulatory and social welfare functions. Perceiving the same need for order in the international arena, the president led the nation into unprecedented involvement in Europe. But just at the moment of triumph, Woodrow Wilson suffered profound personal and political defeat. Having used great political skill to expand the power and prestige of the presidency, Wilson destroyed all that he created.

The president believed that collective security would ensure a stable world for both democracy and American corporate capitalism. But the burden appeared too much for a generation overwhelmed by the sacrifices of war and the social change that accompanied it. As Americans prepared to vote for leaders for the coming decade, a majority shied away from assertive executives, emotional rhetoric, and international commitments.

SUGGESTED READINGS

The work of Arthur Link is central to any understanding of Woodrow Wilson. Editor of the Woodrow Wilson papers and author of a multivolume biography, *Woodrow Wilson* (1947–1965), Link offers a sympathetic yet insightful portrait of this significant president. Two of his briefer books, *Woodrow Wilson and the Progressive Era, 1910–1917* (1954) and *Woodrow Wilson: Revolution, War, and Peace* (1979), concisely introduce Link's interpretations of Wilson's programs. John Milton Cooper, Jr., *The Warrior and the Priest* (1983) provides a fascinating comparison between Wilson and Theodore Roosevelt.

American foreign policy during the Wilson years stirs considerable controversy among historians. Kendrick A. Clements, *William Jennings Bryan: Missionary Isolationist* (1982) looks at Bryan and foreign policy. On policy toward Latin America, see Dana G. Munro, *Intervention and Dollar Diplomacy in the Caribbean, 1900–1921* (1964) for a critique by a former State Department official; Daniel F. Smith, *The U.S. and Revolutionary Nationalism in Mexico, 1916–1932* (1972) stresses economic influences on Wilsonian interventionism. Robert E. Quick, *An Affair of Honor: Woodrow Wilson and the Occupation of Veracruz* (1962) criticizes Wilson for his actions in that crisis. P. Edward Haley, *Revolution and Interventionism: The Diplomacy of Taft and Wilson with Mexico, 1910–1917* (1970) is a balanced and valuable study. The most thorough examination of Wilson's policy toward Asia is Roy W. Curry, *Woodrow Wilson and Far Eastern Policy, 1913–1921* (1968).

Wilson's policy regarding the war in Europe has provoked a tremendous outpouring of historical literature. Ross Gregory, *The Origins of American Intervention in the First World War* (1971) and Patrick Devlin, *Too Proud to Fight: Woodrow Wilson's Neutrality* (1975) generally support the president's actions. Two early revisionist works are Walter Mills, *The Road to War* (1935) and Charles C. Tansill, *America Goes to War* (1938). Otis Graham, *The Great Campaigns: Reform and War in America, 1900–1928* (1971) argues that Wilson could have pursued a more conciliatory policy toward Germany. Also useful is Manfred Jonas, *The United States and Germany* (1984). On preparedness, see

Michael Pearlman, *To Make Democracy for America: Patricians and Preparedness in the Progressive Era* (1984). John M. Cooper, Jr., *The Vanity of Power: American Isolationism and the First World War, 1914–1917* (1969) describes the domestic opposition.

Three general accounts of military affairs are Edward M. Coffman, *The War to End All Wars* (1969); Russell Weigley, *The American Way of War* (1973); and Henry De Weerd, *President Wilson Fights His War* (1968). Laurence Stallings, *The Doughboys* (1963) is a colorful and anecdotal account of army life. A. E. Barbeau and Florette Henri, *The Unknown Soldiers: Black American Troops in World War I* (1974) describes the impact of the war in the black community. Charles Chatfield, *For Peace and Justice* (1971) discusses pacifist opposition to the fighting.

By far the best general account of the home front is David Kennedy, *Over Here* (1980), a thorough yet readable examination of how the war changed American society. On women in wartime, see Maurine W. Greenwald, *Women, War, and Work: The Impact of World War I on Women Workers in the United States* (1980) and Barbara Steinson, *American Women's Activism in World War I* (1982). Robert D. Cuff, *The War Industries Board: Business-Government Relations during World War I* (1973) is an excellent study of industrial mobilization that can be supplemented by *The Speculator* (1981), a biography of WIB chairman Bernard Baruch by Jordan Schwarz. Stephen Vaughn, *Holding Fast the Inner Lines: Democracy, Nationalism, and the Committee on Public Information* (1980); William Preston, *Aliens and Dissenters: Federal Suppression of Radicals, 1903–1933* (1963); and Paul L. Murphy, *The Meaning of Free Speech: First Amendment Freedoms from Wilson to FDR* (1972) examine civil liberties and domestic propaganda. Frederick Luebke, *Bonds of Loyalty* (1974) assesses the plight of German-Americans during the war years. George Blakey, *Historians on the Homefront* (1970) and Stephen Vaughn, *Holding Fast the Inner Lines* (1980) look at efforts to manipulate public opinion.

On the peace process, see Robert H. Ferrell, *Woodrow Wilson and World War I* (1985) and Inga Floto, *Colonel House at Paris* (1980). William Widenor, *Henry Cabot Lodge and the Search for an American Foreign Policy* (1980) describes the opposition to the president. See also Lloyd Gardner, *Safe for Democracy: The Anglo-American Response to Revolution, 1913–1923* (1984). Robert Murray, *The Red Scare* (1955) discusses fear of radicalism, and Burl Noggle, *Into the Twenties* (1974) discusses economic unrest. William Tuttle, *Race Riot* (1970) and Robert Haynes, *A Night of Violence: The Houston Riot of 1917* (1976) describe urban racial violence.

Opposite Page:
A cherished consumer item available on the installment plan, the automobile helped to spark social and cultural change. As a result, moral traditionalists associated the "flivver" with the "flapper" and the "flask."

4

THE CONFLICT OF
CULTURE IN THE 1920s

A mericans of the 1920s found themselves bitterly divided over wrenching cultural issues. These divisions pitted disaffected Anglo-Protestants and traditional rural dwellers against more cosmopolitan urbanites from a diversity of ethnic groups and cultural backgrounds. While many city dwellers were embracing new technology, social pluralism, and modern cultural values, a revised Purity Crusade attempted to rid society of "alien" ideologies, behaviors, and groups. Beneath these purges lay fears of the secularizing influences of consumerism. Beyond the dissolution of community and the erosion of traditional morality, cultural conservatives faced an alarming increase of urban newcomers, women, and rebellious youth who seemed eager to defy the core values of American society. In effect, consumer hedonism, moral ferment, and a fascinating popular culture competed with nostalgia for a religiously and ethnically homogeneous society.

CITIES, SUBURBS, AND THE AUTOMOBILE CULTURE

Workers in New York City finished the 1,250-foot-tall Empire State Building in 1930. The world's tallest structure symbolized the central importance of cities in the twentieth century. The federal census of 1920 had found that more than half the American people lived in urban communities of at least twenty-five hundred persons. Thus, thirty years after the Census Bureau had proclaimed the end of the frontier, it announced the dawning of the urban age.

As six million farmers deserted failing agriculture in the 1920s, multitudes sought opportunity in expanding cities such as Pittsburgh, Detroit, Chicago, Denver, and Los Angeles. In the South, the nation's most rapidly urbanizing region, Memphis, Atlanta, and Chattanooga took on new life. Automobile manufacturing and oil refining gave added vitality to industrial centers such as Cleveland, Akron, Houston, and Tulsa. Meanwhile, the emerging commercial and service economy created booming regional centers in Atlanta, Nashville, Indianapolis, Kansas City, Minneapolis, Portland, and Seattle. Resort havens in San Diego, Tampa, and Miami doubled and tripled their populations. By 1929, each of ninety-three American cities held over one-hundred thousand people.

Market forces responded dramatically to urban vitality. Land values in cities with over three-hundred thousand people doubled to $50 billion in the

Exhibit 4–1. Urban and Rural Population, 1920–1930*
(in rounded millions)

	Urban	Rural
1920	54.2m	51.5m
1930	68.9m	53.8m

Source: *Historical Statistics of the United States, Colonial Times to 1970* (1975) (*urban = population centers over 2500 people)

first five years of the decade. The need to conserve expensive ground space and the centralization of corporate administration led developers to make the skyscraper one of the most dramatic symbols of technical progress and economic power in the New Era of postwar development. By 1930, the nation boasted 377 buildings at least twenty floors high, including Chicago's 36-story Tribune Tower, Cleveland's 52-level Terminal Tower, and the 102-story Empire State Building.

Over 70 percent of the nation's postwar population growth occurred in metropolitan areas. By 1930, for example, Greater Los Angeles had swollen to 2.3 million inhabitants, nearly twice as many as in the city proper. Widely dispersed metropolises such as Los Angeles, Dallas, Detroit, and Kansas City represented the new "automobile cities" that characterized urban development.

The suburbs experienced even greater growth. Automobile accessibility, lower tax and property rates, and the widespread availability of electrical power promoted industrial relocation and the quadrupling of suburban residential population in the decade. In 1925, Kansas City housing developer Jesse C. Nichols, a Harvard graduate, opened the nation's first suburban shopping center. Sears Roebuck and other retailers soon followed with plush stores in outlying areas that featured free parking and abundant floor space.

Predominantly middle-class suburbanites sought pastoral living, nearness to city services, and escape from urban social evils such as crime and visible poverty. Since hard-surfaced roads and automobiles eased commuting downtown, fringe settlements frequently evolved into bedroom communities characterized by similarities of class, age, race, ethnicity, and culture. Restrictive covenants, or agreements, often enabled homeowners to exclude undesirable groups such as Jews and blacks, and strict regulation of property use gave secure suburban asylums a uniform character. Meanwhile, urban planning commissions in the established cities used zoning regulations and municipal ordinances to reinforce their own codes of racial segregation and social exclusivity.

Older municipalities paid a heavy price for suburbanization. Compelled to maintain roads and services for commuters, urban jurisdictions lost retail revenues to outlying areas while their tax base declined. City housing stock also deteriorated when exploitive landlords raised rents without updating their properties. By 1930, the federal census reported that one-fourth of the urban homes in the United States did not meet minimum government living standards. For example, two-thirds of the housing units in Indianapolis and nine-tenths of those in Atlanta lacked running water.

Postwar urban critic Lewis Mumford pleaded with Americans to "forget the damned motor car and build cities for lovers and friends." But automobile registration leaped from 6.7 million to over twenty-three million in the 1920s and led to the growth of suburbs and new urban centers. Car ownership created a sense of liberation and exhilaration and increased options for personal choice. It allowed mobility to affluent women, customarily restrained from adventure outside the home, and to southern blacks, now free to move beyond white-dominated communities. It gave ordinary people a sense of identity, becoming as much a symbol of material success and accomplishment as was ownership of a home. Yet the automobile placed new

Exhibit 4–2. Passenger Car Registration, 1920–1928
(in rounded millions)

1920	8.2m
1922	10.9m
1924	15.5m
1926	19.2m
1928	21.6m

Source: *Recent Economic Changes* (1929)

burdens on society. Gasoline taxes soon constituted the major financial source of road construction, but cities still spent some $400 million a year on urban improvements to accommodate traffic. States spent even more. In the South, a jump of 157 percent in highway expenditures led to greatly expanded state government activity in the postwar decade.

The mania for street and highway construction stemmed from a coalition of automobile industry groups, road builders, and land developers. These interests argued that the automobile would create new channels of commerce, open surrounding areas to development, and reduce congestion in central cities. The effect proved to be quite the opposite, however. Older homes were torn down for new roads, and the vital thoroughfares of cohesive neighborhoods became mere arterials for the movement of traffic. As filling stations, dealerships, garages, and parking lots began to dominate city outskirts and suburbs, traffic congestion, exhaust, noise, and a lack of adequate parking plagued the central city and disrupted urban planning.

Automobile culture also destroyed public transit. National ridership on electric streetcars peaked at 15.7 billion in 1923, but trolleys and interurban electric rail lines could not compete with the rising popularity of the internal combustion engine. Gasoline-driven buses joined cars as a replacement for trolleys on the outskirts of major cities by 1925. Meanwhile, taxpayers refused to subsidize public transportation because they viewed it as a private business not worthy of aid. General Motors took advantage of these conditions to buy up bankrupt mass transit lines and convert them to the use of rubber-tire vehicles. Although steam commuter railroads continued to prosper through the decade, cars, trucks, and buses helped reduce overall rail passenger traffic by one-third and contributed to the stagnation of the railroad freight industry. A technological wonder that contained no system for coordinating its movements with others, the automobile remained a perfect symbol of the dual nature of progress.

Automobile advertisements, budgeted at $10 million a year by 1929, told Americans that cars would "bring the family together." Yet the recreational aspects of "automobility" stressed pleasure and individual whim, not family or social solidarity. In the insular communities of the nation's small towns, neighborly celebrations lost importance when residents used weekends and traditional holidays for out-of-town automobile trips.

Cars also enabled young Americans to conduct unchaperoned relations with the opposite sex, providing an independence that disturbed moral

Suzette Dewey, daughter of assistant treasury secretary Charles Dewey, poses beside her roadster in 1927. The automobile provided new mobility for working-class, black, young, and female Americans and became one of the leading symbols of 1920s culture.

critics. One lecturer noted that the once-sacred family had degenerated into "a physical service station." Ministers linked the automobile to rising crime rates and blamed cars for altering sexual mores, shattering bonds of family life, and undermining community standards of decency. Joyriding on the Sabbath, for example, deeply disturbed religious traditionalists. In the South, where the Progressive Purity Crusade still maintained fire, cultural authorities muted the economic optimism associated with the automobile by expressing deep social misgivings. Nashville's Salvation Army, for instance, attributed the misfortunes of most of the unwed mothers in its maternity homes to "the predatory drivers of automobiles."

Hollywood and
the Consumer Ethic

More Americans attended Sunday movies by 1920 than attended church. Capitalized at over $1 billion, the burgeoning motion picture industry attracted more than seventy-seven million weekly admissions by the end of the decade. Surveys showed that young women attended movies an average forty-six times a year, while American youth most often chose movie idols such as Douglas Fairbanks and Mary Pickford as favorite role models. Enhanced by a glamorous star system, alluring theater palaces, and deeply affecting imagery, the motion picture industry profoundly affected social values and consumer styles. Silent movies became the secular religion of the New Era and Hollywood its mecca.

Before World War I, Jewish entrepreneurs and other independents produced most American films, targeting the urban working class as their prime audience. After 1918, directors like Mack Sennett continued to use comic figures such as Charlie Chaplin and Fatty Arbuckle to mock state bureaucracy, police, routinized labor, and genteel hypocrisy. Other silent-film comedies featured Harold Lloyd, Harry Langdon, and Buster Keaton, and satirized clumsy aspirations toward middle-class respectability.

By 1920, the industry had received financial backing from major banks and organized itself into an oligarchy of eight major studios. The Big Eight produced, distributed, and exhibited nearly all of the nation's films. Looking to expand their market to the affluent middle class, the studios sought out sexual and romantic themes reflective of the experience of urban cosmopolities. Moviemakers thereby came to play a major role in redefining middle-class ideals to fit the more relaxed mores of the consumer age.

The most influential postwar romances featured European stars such as Rudolph Valentino (*The Sheik*, 1920), Erich von Stroheim (*Foolish Wives*, 1922), and Greta Garbo (*The Temptress*, 1926). The sensual eroticism of these mysterious foreigners posed no threat to American notions of innocence. At the same time, Cecil B. De Mille and other filmmakers worked with American actresses like Clara Bow, Joan Crawford, and Gloria Swanson to express the redefined sexuality of the "flapper", a central character in American film during the 1920s.

As early as 1915, journalist H. L. Mencken had used the term flapper to describe brazen and volatile young women who sought sexual satisfaction, social equality, and freedom of choice. Flappers of the postwar era wore bobbed hair that concealed the forehead, and exposed youthful legs with knee-high skirts or dresses. Abbreviated hemlines, flattened chests, hidden waists, and narrowed hips conveyed the impression of boyish women in energetic motion. To prove their emancipation from Victorian codes of feminine modesty, flappers not only drove cars but frequently wore rouge and lipstick, used slang, smoked cigarettes in public, and joined men in illegal speakeasies, jazz clubs, and dance halls. On the screen, they appeared as "modern" and independent women of confident gait and unrestrained energy. Joan Crawford provided a memorable portrait of this role with her frantic version of the Charleston in *Our Dancing Daughters* (1928).

Sociologist Edward A. Ross declared in 1928 that the silver screen had made young people "sex-wise, sex-excited, and sex absorbed." As motion pictures instructed adolescents in techniques of kissing, eye movement, and appealing flirtation, they offered a form of rudimentary sex education. Advertisements for films such as *Sinners in Silk* (1924) and *Alimony* (1924) raved about "beautiful jazz babies, champagne baths, midnight revels, petting parties in the purple dawn." Yet Hollywood trod a thin line between sexual sensationalism and moral convention. In 1922, the Big Eight responded to a series of moral scandals involving performers such as Fatty Arbuckle by turning to Will H. Hays, a Republican fund raiser and postmaster general. As the first head of the Motion Picture Producers and Distributors Association, Hays coordinated industry censorship by reviewing films and scripts and scrutinizing performers to avoid further scandal. These public relations efforts succeeded in discouraging demands for state and federal censorship by religious and civic groups.

Hoping to pad box office receipts by titillating audiences without offending moralists, filmmakers perfected skillful compromises. Actresses Gloria Swanson and Joan Crawford frequently played assertive women who used their toughness to protect purity instead of dispensing with it. De Mille productions such as *The Ten Commandments* (1923) and *The Godless Girl* (1929) portrayed immorality but sermonized against promiscuity and youthful sex. Movies like the sensational *It* (1927), starring Clara Bow, depicted the quest of working women for loving husbands, not sexual dalliance. Even provocative features such as De Mille's *The Affairs of Anatol* (1921) brought husband and wife back together at the final reel. De Mille and others repeatedly used these films to emphasize that successful marriages depended upon mutual recognition of sexual and emotional needs.

"They are what people would like to be," commented film actor Stephan Stills on the popularity of 1920s movie stars. Hollywood provided audiences with positive role models for the consumer economy. Both on screen and off, performers such as Douglas Fairbanks, Mary Pickford, and Gloria Swanson personified the promise of freedom in the realm of leisure. They demonstrated that status now came from styles of consumption, not from productivity. And their films suggested that discomfort with bureaucratic work routines and loss of autonomy could be alleviated through the adoption of exciting life-styles. Moviegoers learned to associate sexiness with apparel, makeup, and perfume as adjuncts to the body. While Fairbanks promoted lines of sports clothes for men of leisure, Swanson endorsed cosmetic and beauty aids for women.

In an age of increasing use of birth control devices, De Mille and other filmmakers suggested a new marital ethic: men were to leave their obsession with work if women abandoned their preoccupation with purity. Redefining success as the means to the good life, Hollywood legitimized the consumer-age family as an avenue to romantic love and personal happiness. Although Swanson married four times during the 1920s, the silver screen taught that

Clara Bow, the "It" girl. Her direct and frank sexuality attracted middle-class urbanites to the movies in the 1920s. Motion pictures forged a new consensus over playful marriage and self-indulgent consumerism.

relations between husbands and wives could be stabilized by an infusion of dynamic personality, cosmopolitan fun, and healthy beauty and sex.

Movies placed new emphasis on youth and innovation instead of age and experience. Old producer virtues such as thrift and frugality could not compete with the new attractions of self-expression, liberation, and fulfillment within the confines of marriage and required work. And film stars embodied the grooming, poise, and charm needed to succeed as a personality in the leisure culture of romance and adventure

THE JAZZ AGE AND THE NEW MORALITY

In 1925, New York City's ballrooms and dance halls took in six million admissions. A thriving Manhattan nightlife had attracted affluent urbanites and visitors since the 1890s. For the first twenty years of the new century, the city's cabarets provided ragtime music and dance floors for fashionable practitioners of the tango, fox-trot, and turkey trot. After World War I, the rag styles of music popularized by black orchestra leader James Reese Europe blended into more carefree and rhythmic jazz forms. Cabaret patrons could trek to Harlem to hear black stride pianists such as James P. Johnson and Thomas ("Fats") Waller, or listen to improvised jazz by small combos at clubs such as Ed Small's Paradise. New York's network radio and recording industries also attracted the nation's leading jazz bands. Harlem dance clubs featured innovators such as the Chick Webb Band and Duke Ellington's Washingtonians, the house band at the Cotton Club after 1927. At Broadway's popular Roseland Ballroom, dancers swayed to the beat of the Fletcher Henderson Band, an all-black ensemble that featured New Orleans cornetist Louis Armstrong and developed the swing style popularized by white imitators in the late 1930s. Less adventurous admirers of jazz could attend the concert performances of the Paul Whiteman Orchestra, which featured soloists such as Indiana cornetist Bix Beiderbecke and vocalist Bing Crosby.

Like the movies, cabarets and nightclubs freed patrons from the restraints of work and home. They established a friendly environment in which informality, humor, and comradery prevailed, conveying an atmosphere of public sociability instead of social respectability. Ethnic entertainers like Sophie Tucker, Eddie Cantor, and Jimmy Durante broke further barriers by sharing their vitality and spontaneity with patrons during and after performances. Self-expression and public displays of private impulses characterized both performers and audiences in the cabaret setting. The consumption of liquor also erased customary inhibitions and helped create a sense of excitement for a generation rejecting formal styles of public behavior. Socially active college students frequently sought out illegal speakeasies in order to drink bootleg liquor, rub elbows with gangsters, dance to "hot" jazz combos, and pursue sexual adventure. Such temptation helped loosen the hold of the Progressive Purity Crusade and imbued the 1920s with their memorable label, the Jazz Age.

Much of New York's popular music found its way to national radio audiences. Black performers like Louis Armstrong and Fletcher Henderson provided the inspiration for many performances and recordings, but middle-class listeners set the prevailing tastes and white performers like crooner Rudy Vallee captured the limelight. A substantial number of the era's popular hits, including "Yes, We Have No Bananas" (1923), "Somebody Stole My Gal" (1923), and "Yes, Sir, That's My Baby" (1924), contained lighthearted novelty and dance themes conducive to a casual quest for physical pleasure. But a few commercial songwriters like Ira and George Gershwin artfully fused sentiments of spiritual and sexual love by combining blues influences with reflective lyrics. Songs like the Gershwins' "The Man I Love" (1924) and "Someone to Watch Over Me" (1926), often sung by throaty torch singers such as Helen Morgan, appealed to working-class women who lived apart from families. Such music also won favor with middle-class college students, whose peer culture sought independence from family influence and traditional mores. Both blues themes and dance rhythms could be found in Eddie Cantor's "Makin' Whoopee" (1928), an irreverent reflection upon divorce and alimony that became the unofficial anthem of the speakeasies and whose title became a common phrase for having sex.

"The only subjects that are getting any attention from the 'political minded,'" "are Prohibition, Birth Control, and the Bible Issue," observed a University of California, Los Angeles (UCLA), college newspaper editor in 1926. As radio, the movies, and national magazines popularized new role models and the consumer ethic, postwar Americans revised standards of sexual propriety. Divorce doubled between 1914 and 1929; its frequency approached one-sixth that of marriage by the end of the 1920s. More disturbing to moralists, women born after 1900 were twice as likely to engage in premarital sex as those born before the turn of the century. The sexual freedom of the 1920s rested substantially upon the increased availability and effectiveness of condoms, jellies, and the diaphragm. College students expressed huge interest in these birth control techniques. But as the American Birth Control League sought to contain family size and taught that sexual intercourse need not be limited to procreation, married couples became the leading beneficiaries of the revolution in sexual practices.

Family planning reduced the number of offspring and freed women for life outside the home. By minimizing fears of unwanted pregnancy, birth control also reduced the guilt and anxiety previously associated with sexual expression. Although twenty-two states restricted or forbade the dissemination of contraceptive devices, a 1929 study reported that three-fourths of married women in their early thirties used such devices. Two years later, the Federal Council of the Churches of Christ endorsed artificial contraception. By then, family size had declined from 4.6 in 1900 to less than 3.8.

With the collapse of cultural cohesion over purity and sexual propriety, magazine articles of the 1920s increasingly approved of birth control, sexual freedom, and divorce. Such tolerance found expression in Ben Lindsey's controversial book *The Revolt of Modern Youth* (1925). A juvenile court judge in Denver, Lindsey acknowledged the movement toward sexual honesty by calling for companionate marriage based on intimate affection, contraception,

Exhibit 4–3. Marriage and Divorce Rate, 1920–1928
(per 1000 population)

	Marriage Rate	Divorce Rate
1920	12.0	1.6
1928	9.8	1.7

Source: *Historical Statistics of the United States, Colonial Times to 1970* (1975)

**Exhibit 4–4. Public Secondary School Enrollment, 1920–1930
(in rounded millions)**

1920	2.2m
1930	4.4m

Source: *Historical Statistics of the United States, Colonial Times to 1970* (1975)

and divorce by mutual consent for childless couples. Critics associated Lindsey's proposals with the antics of a youth generation gone wild and a civilization without ethical bearings.

The target of anxieties over changes in moral and sexual codes, youth assumed the status of a major social problem in the 1920s. Middle-class families of the cities had used abstinence or birth control to sharply reduce family size since the mid–nineteenth century. Because they rarely ran family businesses needing the labor of children, urban parents could focus more attention on fewer offspring. Consequently, affection and emotional expressiveness replaced more traditional demands for respect and authority as the binding force of many middle-class families. Meanwhile, technology and occupational specialization compelled the extension of education as a preparation for the preferred job market. High school enrollment multiplied six times between 1900 and 1930. And college and university attendance tripled to over one million, although less than 12 percent of college-age youth attended institutions of higher learning at the end of the 1920s. Nevertheless, the small residential student population played an enormous role in setting social fashions and shaping values within affluent society.

Novelist F. Scott Fitzgerald wrote of campus life in the sensational *This Side of Paradise* (1920). "None of the Victorian mothers," he said, "had any idea how casually their daughters were accustomed to be kissed." College youth quickly embraced the casual dress and slang of the Jazz Age. An emerging campus peer culture also accepted the consumption of liquor and cigarettes as marks of adulthood. Young people embraced Hollywood's portrait of love as erotic and redefined the relationship between maturing men and women. Freed from the constraints of family and community, unchaperoned couples explored the new freedoms of dating and "petting", and coined the terms "boyfriend" and "girlfriend" to replace the cumbersome "lovers" and "sweethearts".

Collegiate culture did not, however, encourage an abandonment of morality, as critics charged. Instead, peer propriety, expressed through fraternities, sororities, and campus social life, established a clear sense of limits in a series of graded sexual relationships. Petting parties usually confined body touching to socially acceptable boundaries, and peer pressure normally restricted sexual intercourse to couples seriously preparing for marriage. Violation of these norms could result in social ostracism and humiliation. Despite the surface appearances of the Jazz Age, therefore, youthful commitment to family and sexual morality remained strong. Campus youth culture redefined social morality but did not obliterate it.

THE LOST GENERATION

Expatriate writer Gertrude Stein described the American exiles who flocked to postwar Paris as a lost generation. Artists, writers, and intellectuals of the 1920s viewed themselves as the disinherited children of the middle class. The brutality of World War I, which killed some ten million people, presented the intelligentsia with a powerful metaphor of disillusionment. As historian Carl Becker commented in 1920, the war comprised "the most futile, the most desolating and repulsive exhibition of human power and cruelty without compensating advantage that has ever been on earth." Ernest Hemingway's bitter novels *The Sun Also Rises* (1926) and *A Farewell to Arms* (1929) described the lost generation's reaction to the ideological sham and cant of its elders. War "kills the very good and the very gentle and the very brave impartially," Hemingway wrote in terse prose. He confessed to be "always embarassed by the words 'sacred,' 'glorious,' and 'sacrifice.' " Only death was an absolute in a world view devoid of political ideology and meaning.

Writers such as Stein, Hemingway, F. Scott Fitzgerald, John Dos Passos, and Malcolm Cowley drifted to postwar Europe to search for spiritual roots outside the confines of American society. One expatriate described their exile as an "attempt to recover the good life and the traditions of art, to free themselves from organized stupidity." Bohemian enclaves in Paris and New York's Greenwich Village reasserted the artist's alienation from mainstream culture. The dissidents struggled against a standardized America beset by the twin evils of materialism and puritanism. "Everybody was in it for the money," complained essayist Cowley, "everybody was hoping to make a killing and get away."

"I love my country, but I don't like it," novelist Sinclair Lewis once remarked. The first American author to receive the Nobel Prize for literature, Lewis published *Main Street* in 1920. That portrait of a married woman's attempt to overcome the conventions of small-town tribalism sold four-hundred thousand copies within weeks of publication. "It is dullness made God," Lewis wrote of life on the Great Northern Plains. Two years later, his novel *Babbitt* acidly depicted a complacent booster in the monotonous Middle West. Lewis's satire reverberated in *American Mercury* editor H. L. Mencken's merciless attacks on the native "booboisie". Similarly, Fitzgerald's masterpiece, *The Great Gatsby* (1925), stripped the illusions of materialism and the Jazz Age life-styles of the eastern aristocracy.

For Cowley, Lewis, and Fitzgerald, the heartland of the nation no longer appeared as America's garden but as a wasteland of conservatism, piety, and hypocrisy. The new generation of artists and writers viewed the guardians of middle-class culture as hopelessly stupid and comical parodies of human nature, as Philistines unable to separate art from morality. They condemned the middle class for making money into a religion and for assuming that economic success gave it cultural privilege and immunity from criticism. Social critics such as Edmund Wilson, Harold Stearns, Van Wyck Brooks, and Lewis Mumford also questioned postwar technology and objected that the assembly line and skyscraper portended a terrible monotony in American life.

Imagist poets such as Ezra Pound, T. S. Eliot, Hart Crane, and Amy Lowell offered similar indictments of conventional culture.

Literary historian Cowley remembered that 1920s writers felt like "strangers in their own land." Many of the rebels invoked the teachings of Viennese psychoanalyst Sigmund Freud to seek liberation from emotional repression and conformity. Hoping to allow their children to "develop their own personalities" and "blossom freely like flowers," Cowley, Crane, Stearns, and others outlined a bohemian code. Its goals included momentary gratification, individuality and female equality, creative work, and self-expression. Imaginative people would achieve these, Cowley wrote, even if it meant breaking every law, convention, or rule of art. Despite Crane's suicide and Fitzgerald's alcoholism, the lost generation left a rich literary legacy and helped to establish creative artists and writers as cultural critics of American society.

FEMINISTS AND SOCIAL REFORMERS

In a letter to his son in 1921, California Progressive Hiram W. Johnson despaired of "the non-childbearing, smoking, drinking, and neurotic creature who symbolized one of the cracks in the thin veneer of civilization." The life-styles of the postwar flapper and bohemian provided new options for small numbers of affluent women, but their emphasis on female eroticism did not significantly change the nineteenth-century notion that normal fulfillment came only through marriage and motherhood. Young middle-class women of the 1920s rebelled against the sexual repression and self-denial embodied by the Victorian "cult of true womanhood," but they also rejected the demands for sacrifice and social commitment made by older Progressive purity crusaders and suffragists. The new generation viewed the prewar activists as unfeminine and asexual and failed to grasp their predecessors' idea of sisterhood. Instead, women of the postwar era strove for individual satisfactions, hoping to pursue promising careers while maintaining romance and family responsibilities at home. Yet one study revealed that 94 percent of women in eastern Ivy League colleges intended to choose marriage over a career if a conflict arose between the two.

Traditional ideas about women as guardians of the family fit into a corporate economy that touted middle-class wives as "model consumers" and household business managers. As the urban home of the twentieth century developed into a center for buying goods instead of making them, consumption became a central activity for middle-class women. Postwar advertisers primarily targeted housewives, not only promoting mass-produced appliances like vacuum cleaners, but also catering to desires for fashion, beauty, and sex appeal. Psychologists, educators, the clergy, and advertisers told women that their natural place remained in the home, where their first task was motherhood. Not surprisingly, education for women in high schools and colleges stressed home economics and child rearing. Pyschologists such as John B. Watson suggested that child care required particular training and dedication. Despite attempts to professionalize home-making, this unpaid labor continued to be task oriented, not geared to clock

— FRANCIS SCOTT KEY FITZGERALD —
—————— 1896–1940 ——————
—————— ZELDA SAYRE FITZGERALD ——————
—————— 1900–1948 ——————

The fiction of F. Scott Fitzgerald—indeed, Fitzgerald's entire career and marriage with Zelda Sayre—epitomized the cultural turbulence that shook traditional values during the Jazz Age of the 1920s. Catapulted to fame by the publication of his first novel, *This Side of Paradise*, in 1920, Fitzgerald depicted a "a new generation grown up to find all Gods dead, all wars fought, all faiths in man shaken."

Born in St. Paul, Minnesota, Fitzgerald left the wholesome but bland Midwest for the sophistication of the East. First he lived as an undergraduate at Princeton (he quit without graduating in 1917), then as an Army officer, and later as an advertising writer in New York. Captivated by wealth, extravagance, and the wholesale rejection of Victorian morality, the novelist and storywriter celebrated a younger generation preoccupied with booze, sex, jazz, and easy money. His overnight literary success enabled Fitzgerald to fulfill his version of the American Dream, at least for a while.

Fitzgerald met Zelda Sayre, while stationed in her home town, Montgomery, Alabama. Zelda symbolized the rich, beautiful, outrageous flapper that attracted the young military officer. Wild and zany, she held ambitions of escape as a ballet dancer. Together they set off for Paris, where they lived at the core of an expatriate literary community that included Gertrude Stein and Ernest Hemingway and that embodied the repudiation of the producer values of provincial, small-town America.

(cont.)

time, and often unlimited in scope. The work week for mothers in the 1920s averaged fifty-six hours. Although advertisers boasted that technological innovations would liberate women from home chores, labor-saving devices simply raised standards of household care. For many women, homemaking tasks remained long, tedious, and unfulfilling.

Life in the work force was hardly more promising. Although the number of women in the labor market grew by more than one-fourth in the 1920s, women constituted only 21 percent of American workers by 1929 and the proportion of women who worked remained at roughly one in four, a ratio that held constant from 1910 to 1940. As in the prewar years, one-third of female labor worked as servants and another one-fourth in low-paying jobs in factories and mills. However, the growth of white-collar services accelerated the expansion of clerical and stenographic positions. Married women in the middle class began to take advantage of these income opportunities in the

The extravagant life-style haunted Fitzgerald and compromised his work. "I can't reduce our scale of living and I can't stand this financial insecurity," he complained to his editor. Often—too often, he thought—Fitzgerald wrote popular stories for money (over 160 short stories in his brief career), while publishing the novels *The Beautiful and Damned* (1922) and *The Great Gatsby* (1925).

Meanwhile, Fitzgerald's success and dominating presence undermined Zelda's confidence. He envied her talent, and his ambivalence about flappers—"brave, shallow, cynical, impatient, turbulent, and empty" he called them—accentuated her frustration. She suffered a series of emotional breakdowns and required hospitalization. While confined, Zelda completed the novel *Save Me the Waltz* (1932), the Gatsby story told from a woman's perspective. She remained institutionalized for the rest of her life.

The economic downturn of the 1930s further eroded Fitzgerald's confidence. In 1931, he earned over $40,000 a year; eight years later his royalties totaled $33! His novel *Tender Is the Night* (1934) received poor critical responses, and his alcoholism became more acute. Fitzgerald moved to Hollywood in 1937 to write movie scripts, but he continued to drink. He died of alcoholism while writing a novel about Hollywood, *The Last Tycoon*, published posthumously in 1941.

Through their work and life-styles, the Fitzgeralds represented the modern revolt against traditional values while paradoxically lamenting the loss of old certitudes. To the aphorism "You can't repeat the past," Fitzgerald's Gatsby exclaims, "Why of course you can! . . . I'm going to fix everything just the way it was before. . . ." But F. Scott and Zelda, for all their bravado, knew otherwise and suffered a relentless sense of failure. ■

1920s, increasing their participation in the work force from 1.9 million to 3.1 million. Women also increased their share of professional work to one-seventh, but they often found themselves in the "female" professions of nursing, teaching, and social work. Most professions and most civil service exams excluded women altogether, and the proportion of women in medicine declined as medical schools tightened strict quotas on female admissions. Women in all fields averaged less than 60 percent of what men made in the same line of work. Yet the number of female college graduates tripled in the decade, and female professionals organized associations for mutual support in fields such as dentistry, architecture, and journalism.

While the younger generation of women emphasized personal gratification, Progressive Era activists like Jane Addams continued to organize for social issues such as world peace. A pacifist who opposed American entry into World War I, Addams had assumed the presidency of the Women's

Exhibit 4–5. Women Workers, 1920–1930
(in rounded millions)

	Female	Male	Total
1920	8.5m	33.1m	41.6m
1930	10.7m	38.1m	48.8m

Source: *Historical Statistics of the United States, Colonial Times to 1970* (1975)

International League for Peace and Freedom at its inception in 1915. Like Carrie Chapman Catt, who formed the National Conference on the Cause and Cure of War, Addams believed that the horrors of the European conflict had proven the futility of violence, which she saw as an extension of the irrationalities of male behavior. Women's organizations played a major role in the support of disarmament and the international peace conferences of the 1920s. These groups also helped win Senate approval for the Kellogg-Briand Pact of 1928, which renounced the use of war as an instrument of national policy (see chapter 5). Antiwar activism brought Addams the Nobel Prize for peace in 1931.

Progressive feminists like Addams and Catt delighted in the prospects of women's suffrage, enacted in 1920. Hoping to use newly gained electoral-power to elevate the nation's morals and to speed the passage of reform, social feminists organized the nonpartisan League of Women Voters to press for legislation relating to consumers, conservation, municipal government, indigent mothers, and child labor. The Women's Joint Congressional Committee, a coalition embracing nearly every important women's organization in the country, worked with the league as a clearinghouse for social legislation affecting women and children. In the South, female Progressives won new power by helping to institute budget reforms in rapidly growing state governments, creating state commissions to protect children, and agitating for improved working conditions for women in the textile industry.

Social feminists skillfully used congressional fear of the women's vote to win two dramatic victories in 1921. First, they gained passage of the Packers and Stockyards Act, which lowered meat, poultry, and dairy prices by prohibiting discriminatory practices in those industries. Second, they pressed Congress to enact the Sheppard-Towner Maternity and Infancy Protection Act, the first federal venture into social welfare assistance. This law appropriated $1 million to public health centers to teach maternity and infant hygiene; it expired in 1929 as a result of controversy over government interference with family life and states' rights.

Between 1912 and 1923, feminist reformers helped to obtain fifty state minimum wage laws for women and two federal laws severely restricting child labor. Yet the Supreme Court invalidated all such legislation (see chapters 1 and 5). Stunned into action, social welfare activist Florence Kelley used the National Child Labor Committee to win congressional approval of a child labor amendment to the Constitution in 1924. The amendment proposed to give Congress the right to prohibit or regulate the labor of minors.

Clerical work in expanding corporations and government bureaucracies provided new opportunities for women in the 1920s work force. Married women took particular advantage of these openings, increasing their participation in the labor force to 3.1 million by the end of the decade.

It reflected both feminist alliances with organized labor and the conviction of female purity crusaders that the state needed to exercise control of youngsters to improve the moral health of society. As opposition to maternity and infant care had shown, however, many Americans expressed reluctance to give the secular state control over family relations and home affairs. In eastern states with heavy Catholic populations, the church campaigned against the child labor amendment as an invasion of parental discretion. Ratification of the measure failed overwhelmingly, and Congress did not enact similar controls until 1938.

Defeat of the child labor amendment signaled a bitter defeat for social feminists. Reformers also objected to the introduction of a constitutional Equal Rights Amendment (ERA) by the small National Woman's Party headed by Alice Paul, an uncompromising feminist. Brought before Congress every year beginning in 1923, the pioneering proposal sought to extend sexual equality to all areas of law, public policy, and employment. Yet the measure frightened social feminists, who feared that the ERA would eradicate remaining protections for female workers and turn public opinion away from their agenda.

A unified women's vote failed to materialize in the 1920s. American feminism survived the period more as an attitude than as a series of programs or solutions. Social feminists had laid the foundation for a peace movement and government activity in education, labor, health, and social security. But although these efforts created a legacy that would be extended by subsequent reformers and organizers, a major feminist movement would not reappear until the 1960s.

Black Metropolis

When black nationalist Marcus Garvey proclaimed, "Up you mighty Race! You can accomplish what you will!" he reflected both the promise and the adversity of black life in the 1920s. Encouraged by the job opportunities of wartime mobilization and the New Era boom, blacks left the rural South in unprecedented numbers between 1915 and 1928. Altogether, the Great Migration brought 1.2 million newcomers to northern and western cities. By 1930, New York and Chicago contained black subcities of more than 225,000 each, and at least two-fifths of the nation's black people lived in urban centers.

Since blacks numbered among the last migrants to the older neighborhoods of the industrial cities, most of the available jobs involved menial tasks at low pay. Black workers served as sweepers and firemen in the midwestern steel industry. In Detroit, where the black population increased sixfold in the 1920s, Henry Ford pioneered the hiring of blacks on the assembly line. Urbanization produced a black working class adapted to modern industry, but by 1930, black Americans held only 2 percent of the white-collar and skilled jobs in the country.

Racial discrimination often forced black migrants to live in the most dilapidated neighborhoods. Although the Supreme Court outlawed residential segregation ordinances in 1917, white neighborhood associations resorted to restrictive covenants by which property holders agreed not to sell to blacks. Black residents usually found themselves in districts of the city abandoned by immigrant families moving to better neighborhoods. Confined to a racial ghetto, they often confronted unprincipled landlords who charged soaring rents for neglected housing. In New York's Harlem, for example, rents doubled between 1919 and 1927.

A combination of high rents and poor wages compelled black families to share crowded housing space. Unfamiliar with urban health problems, rural migrants frequently tolerated unsanitary conditions. Population density in Harlem approached 336 people an acre, and the district's death rate remained 42 percent above that of the rest of New York. Migration and the struggle for economic survival also disrupted the stability of black families, since black women found jobs as domestics but black men faced the hiring prejudices of employers and unions. Consequently, blacks in migrant neighborhoods experienced higher rates of desertion, divorce, and illegitimacy than did whites. Prostitution, gambling, bootlegging, the numbers racket, and narcotics addiction all became part of the impoverished ghetto environment.

Despite these difficulties, black community leaders and newspaper editors encouraged development of a "black metropolis." Black pride, habit, and the need for mutual protection led to efforts to "advance the race" by promoting economic self-sufficiency through racial clubs, fraternal orders, and mutual aid societies. But only one organization, the Universal Negro Improvement Association (UNIA), managed to create major support from working-class blacks in the northern ghettos. Founded in 1914 by Marcus Garvey, a Jamaican, the UNIA enrolled about one-hundred thousand members at the peak of its appeal, although Garvey claimed as many as two million. The improvement association espoused black pride and inspired poorer followers to dream of racial freedom and economic independence under black leadership.

Describing himself as the provisional president of the African republic, Garvey demanded an "Africa for the Africans." He suggested that a limited number of American blacks might go to Liberia to teach the skills necessary to redeem Africa from European colonialism. Garvey accurately prophesied that a liberated Africa would be an inspiration for black people in the Western Hemisphere. He also preached support of black business in a "buy black" campaign. The UNIA organized grocery chains, restaurants, laundries, a hotel, a doll factory, a printing plant, and a newspaper called *Negro World*. Its Black Star Steamship Line proposed to establish a commercial link between the United States, the West Indies, and Africa.

Although condemned by established black leaders such as W.E.B. DuBois, Garvey's black nationalism brought hope into the lives of a generation embittered by the realities of the urban promised land. By 1922, however, UNIA businesses faltered through mismanagement, and federal prosecutors indicted Garvey for selling fraudulent stock. Garvey insisted that trusted associates had betrayed him, but he alone faced conviction. In 1927, after keeping him in a federal prison for two years, the government deported Garvey as an alien who had committed a felony.

The Universal Negro Improvement Association collapsed, but the fervor of black nationalism never left the ghetto. While Garvey spoke to the deep-seated feeling of urban blacks, the National Association for the Advancement of Colored People (NAACP) and the Urban League continued to struggle for black justice in the white community. Under prodding by the NAACP, the Dyer Anti-Lynching Bill passed the House of Representatives in 1921, but southern Democrats filibustered the bill to death in the Senate. Yet the ability of civil rights groups to mobilize members of black voluntary associations, churches, and mutual benefit societies bore fruit in 1930, when the Senate blocked the Supreme Court nomination of conservative judge John J. Parker, who had publicly commented about the unpreparedness of blacks for the "burdens and responsibilities of government." The defeat of the Parker nomination, also opposed by the AFL, suggested a powerful coalition among forces of urban liberalism, labor, and civil rights.

Black activists vigorously pursued equal rights on the local level. In Springfield and Dayton, Ohio, parents and students mounted classroom boycotts when authorities reintroduced school segregation in 1922. Protesters in Gary, Indiana, objected to the building of an all-black school in 1927. Although these efforts did not succeed, they reflected a social assertiveness enhanced by the postwar migration to the North. In Chicago

Marcus Garvey, the most popular and charismatic black leader of the 1920s. Garvey's Universal Negro Improvement Association preached black pride and economic self-sufficiency. The black nationalist movement attracted over one-hundred thousand working-class followers.

and other large cities, blacks joined white political machines to win jobs and protect community interests. Chicago's First District elected Oscar De Priest as the first black congressman ever to come from the North. By supporting the machine of Republican mayor Bill Thompson, Chicago blacks obtained one-fourth of the postal service jobs in the city by the end of the decade.

In the South, middle-class black college students also demonstrated greater willingness to defend black interests. When the Ku Klux Klan marched on an all-black veterans hospital in Tuskegee, Alabama, in 1923, students at the nearby Tuskegee Institute rushed to defend the institution from potential violence. Students at Nashville's Fisk University mounted campus strikes in 1924 and 1925 to protest administration censorship and the paternalism of the school's white president. This social action pointed to the existence of a new generation of race-conscious students in the South's black colleges.

"I am a Negro—and beautiful," exclaimed Harlem poet Langston Hughes at middecade. Inspired by the potential of the black metropolis, black intellectuals, writers, and artists expressed a new racial pride and militance. The leading lights of the movement spoke of the New Negro and depicted the subsequent outpouring of race-conscious poetry, prose, and art as part of a Harlem Renaissance. Borrowing from the rich oral traditions of Afro-American culture, the stark verses of Hughes, Sterling Brown, and James Weldon Johnson used the rhythms and moods of spirituals, blues, and everyday vernacular. Claude McKay brought these techniques to the novel in *Home to Harlem* (1928), an odyssey of the black working class. Jean Toomer's *Cane* (1923) vividly captured the life of poor southern blacks. The Harlem Renaissance also stimulated young black painters and sculptors to emulate the grace of African forms.

Taking their cue from W.E.B. DuBois, black editor of the NAACP's *Crisis* magazine, progressive whites rushed to praise the new vitality of black culture. In 1925, the reformist *Survey Graphic* asked Alain Locke, the nation's first black Rhodes scholar, to edit a special Harlem issue on the New Negro. Black leaders such as DuBois and James Weldon Johnson hoped that Afro-American cultural creativity would encourage acceptance of blacks by the American people.

The Harlem Renaissance also extended to popular culture. Responding to the growth of a huge market of urban blacks, commercial recording companies released race records performed by outstanding black blues artists such as Bessie Smith, Ethel Waters, Ma Rainey, and Louis Armstrong. Similarly, black and white film companies distributed movies made especially for the new market. Harlem's nightclubs and revues made the district a symbol of the Jazz Age in an era of Prohibition. Advertised in handbills as an erotic utopia "where white people from downtown could be entertained by colored girls," Harlem became America's answer to Paris for white "slumming parties". Whites eagerly sought a "primitive spontaneity" in black life, even when patronizing Harlem establishments, such as the Cotton Club, that served only white customers. Visitors to the district frequently stereotyped blacks as a "singing race", an "expressive" and "erotic" people who could love and laugh freely in a puritan land. Carl Van Vechten's *Nigger Heaven* (1925), a white view of Harlem orgies and seduction, sold one-hundred thousand copies in its first year of publication. While the conditions of the ghetto festered, Jazz Age adventurers enjoyed "a vogue in things Negro."

JAMES WELDON JOHNSON
1871–1938

In *The Autobiography of an Ex-Colored Man* (1912), James Weldon Johnson's tragic protagonist regretted that he had passed up the opportunity "to have taken part in a work so glorious" as building a new black America. Yet the versatile and multitalented Johnson accomplished precisely what his fictional hero failed to do and became a central black role model of the Harlem Renaissance of the 1920s.

Born in Jacksonville, Florida to an immigrant from Nassau and the headwaiter of a hotel, Johnson attended preparatory school and college at all-black Atlanta University. Returning home in 1894, he became principal of the black grade school from which he had graduated and added secondary-level classes to the school's curriculum. Johnson also started a black city newspaper, but the enterprise soon suffered financial failure. Pressed for funds and concerned with the improvement of black living conditions, he studied law with a white attorney and became the first black admitted to the Florida bar by court examination.

Johnson and his musician brother Rosamond began collaborating on black dialect songs and comic operas in 1898. The duo also composed "Lift Every Voice and Sing" for a school assembly dedicated to Abraham Lincoln. By 1915, this stirring song had emerged as the unofficial "Negro National Anthem."

Buoyed by their early success, the Johnson brothers left for New York City in 1902, where they worked with black vaudeville performer Bob Cole. "Under the Bamboo Tree" (1902), a rag-style ditty, became their first hit and sold four-hundred thousand sheet music copies. The trio sought to move beyond the era's popular but demeaning "coon songs" and minstrel shows by introducing what lyricist Johnson called "a higher degree of artistry" to black music. But after completing the words for over two hundred songs and a major musical, the restless songwriter deserted popular culture for new arenas.

Using Republican ties forged through his electoral support of President Theodore Roosevelt in 1904, Johnson won appointments as American consul to multiracial Venezuela and Nicaragua between 1906 and 1913. In his free time, he worked on *The Autobiography of an Ex-Colored Man*, an anonymously published story of a light-skinned black who passed for white and observed the nation's racial foibles with a sense of irony. In 1913, the *New York Times* published Johnson's "Fifty Years," a rhymed tribute to the Emancipation Proclamation. Hoping to support himself by serious writing, Johnson resigned from government service, changed his middle name from William to the literary-sounding Weldon, and returned to New York City. *(cont.)*

THE DIVERSITY OF ETHNIC AMERICA

Anglo reformers in the American Indian Defense Association helped to achieve full citizenship for Native Americans through passage of the Snyder Act of 1924. Yet, despite these efforts, the government's Bureau of Indian

Soon the energetic Johnson joined the *New York Age*, the city's oldest black newspaper, as leading editorial writer. Moved by W.E.B. DuBois's call for social activism, he became field secretary for the fledgling NAACP in 1916 and multiplied the organization's branches fivefold within three years. Johnson investigated lynchings and peonage and helped build southern chapter strength from three to 131. When war tension led to a massacre of blacks in East St. Louis, Illinois, in 1917, the NAACP field secretary organized a silent parade of nearly ten thousand protesters down New York's Fifth Avenue.

Becoming the NAACP's first black executive secretary in 1920, Johnson went to Haiti to report on the killing of three thousand people by United States Marines. He soon demanded military withdrawal from the predominantly black nation. As NAACP strength surpassed one-hundred thousand, Johnson led the campaign to win House passage of the Dyer Anti-Lynching Bill of 1921, although a southern-led filibuster killed the measure in the Senate. Despite the defeat, NAACP lawyers pressed legal strategies and won a dramatic victory when the Supreme Court took a first step in outlawing the "white" primary in 1927.

An integrationist, Johnson nevertheless believed that the blending of the races would be more palatable if society acknowledged the cultural contributions of blacks. He edited an anthology of black poetry in 1922, emphasizing the importance of black folk literature and popular music. Appealing to the growing self-respect among young black artists and intellectuals associated with the Harlem Renaissance, Johnson issued two collections of Negro spirituals in 1925 and 1926.

In 1927, Johnson published his greatest work of poetry, *God's Trombones—Seven Negro Folk Sermons*. Using the free cadence of an old black preacher, he captured the heart of black idiom by avoiding both dialect verse and strict metric form. "Your arm's too short to box with God," one sermon proclaimed. *God's Trombones* helped to revitalize black poetry with the rhythm of speech and stimulated a pride in black identity. In the same year, publishers issued a new edition of *The Autobiography of an Ex-Colored Man* with Johnson's name on the cover. To further his work as a cultural architect, Johnson also released *Black Manhattan* (1930), an informal history that focused on black contributions to the arts.

A poised, dignified man with an ironic sense of humor, Johnson left the NAACP in 1930 to take up a career as professor of literature at Fisk University. When he issued his autobiography, *Along This Way*, in 1933, James Weldon Johnson could point to his role in moving black Americans from the enforced racial accommodation of the early twentieth century to an emerging assertion of prideful culture and militant politics. ■

Affairs (BIA) frequently maintained cooperation with economic interests that infringed on reservation land and resources. For example, Congress defeated an attempt to transfer Pueblo property titles to whites in 1924 and created a special board to compensate members of the tribe for lost lands. But in 1932, Senate investigators revealed that the Pueblo Lands Board had worked with speculators, railroad interests, and cattle companies to assess tribal lands below fair market value. In another example of government mismanagement of Native American interests, the Federal Power Commission permitted Montana power interests to develop a hydroelectric site on the Flathead Indian Reservation in 1930. Between 1887 and 1934, Native American land domain dwindled from 138 million acres to forty-seven million acres.

Government policy in the 1920s concentrated on Americanizing Indians. Over tribal resistance, the commissioner of Indian affairs ordered the prohibition of Native American religious dancing, specifically targeting the Hopi Snake Dance and the Plains Indians Sun Dance. Government authorities contended that the abolition of "pagan" ritual constituted a first step toward the Native American's preparation for participation in American society. Such reasoning led President Herbert Hoover to increase annual aid for Indian education from $3 million to $12 million. Yet government boarding schools taught tribal Americans to despise their heritage, and some resorted to chaining students to their beds to prevent them from returning home. In protest, reformer John Collier led a personal crusade to permit young men to leave the schools for periods of religious rituals. Nevertheless, Native Americans lacked the political power to alter oppressive government policies, and cultural and economic stagnation remained the defining feature of reservation life.

While Anglo economic interests focused on the land and resources of Native Americans, they also looked to the labor of Mexican-Americans in southwestern agriculture, transportation, and mining. In 1925, a bill to restrict immigration from Mexico won support from labor, veterans, and nativist groups, but economic interests in the Southwest insisted upon access to low-cost labor from south of the border. Mexican population in the forty-eight states doubled in the 1920s; by 1930, over 1.5 million people of Mexican descent lived in the United States, six-hundred thousand of them Mexican-born. Ninety percent of Mexican-Americans lived in the southwestern states of Arizona, New Mexico, Texas, Colorado, and California. Los Angeles, the leading mecca for the immigration from the south, held the largest population of Mexicans in the world after Mexico City.

Often hired as migrant field hands, the Mexican work force confronted oppressive exploitation by cost-conscious employers and lack of interest by organizers for established unions. Government officials considered the new immigrants outside the realm of social agencies and schools. Consequently, Mexican-Americans worked long hours at physical labor with little compensation and no regulation of work or living conditions. By 1930, 55 percent of Mexican immigrants still spoke no English and only 5.5 percent of Mexican immigrant adults had become American citizens.

Asian-Americans faced particularly virulent strains of racism in the postwar era. After the Chinese Exclusion Act of 1882 ended immigration from China and reversed patterns of migration, the Chinese population in the United States declined from three-hundred thousand to eighty thousand by 1943. Despite strong cultural biases against their presence, however, the Chinese had family and kinship ties and strong community associations that strengthened their social and economic life in West Coast settlements.

American law did not stop Japanese immigration until 1924, although the Gentlemen's Agreement between the United States and Japan had discouraged arrivals since 1907. By 1925, 275,000 Japanese lived within American borders. Because many Japanese succeeded as West Coast farmers, orchardists, and merchants, prejudice against their presence combined cultural anxieties with fears of economic competition. American farmers and workers objected that Japanese settlers circumvented prohibitions against further immigration by sending for "picture brides" (women who migrated to marry Japanese men who had selected their photographs). California Progressives used such arguments as well as the support of organized labor and in 1913 enacted an alien land law that outlawed Japanese farm ownership. By the early 1920s, nativists in the state had launched a campaign against the kimono as a potential threat to the purity of white women. In Oregon, a Democratic governor signed a 1923 alien land law after vowing to discourage "Mongolian races" from gaining a foothold on state soil. The Supreme Court upheld such legislation in the same year, and the Immigration Act of 1924 declared the Japanese as "aliens ineligible of citizenship." Such policies led to a halving of Japanese agricultural holdings between 1910 and 1940. Yet Japanese entrepreneurs in western cities created a rich community life characterized by credit unions, employment agencies, newspapers, trade guilds, and ethnic benevolent societies.

Many European Americans also maintained ethnic roots. By 1930, 30 percent of the 122 million residents of the United States were immigrants or the children of immigrants. Nearly three-fifths of those living in postwar cities of one-hundred thousand fit the same category. Although World War I and its aftermath substantially reduced immigration rates, recent arrivals from Europe continued to live in the ethnic communities created in the prewar years. By the early 1920s, ten million ethnic Americans read more than one thousand foreign-language newspapers published in the United States. Ethnics like the Poles, Slavs, Hungarians, and Italians of Chicago supported religious, benevolent, and mutual aid societies. Eastern, central, and southern Europeans gravitated to industrial centers such as New York, Philadelphia, Buffalo, and Cleveland. Only the cohesiveness of Jewish ghettos began to decline in the 1920s, as socially mobile Jews moved to newer residential neighborhoods and second-generation offspring loosened ties to religious orthodoxy and Yiddish organizations.

Exhibit 4–6. National Origins of Foreign-Born Americans, 1920–1930 (in rounded millions)

	1920	1930
Northwestern Europe	3.8m	3.7m
Central and Eastern Europe	6.1m	5.9m
Southern Europe	1.9m	2.1m
Latin America	0.6m	0.8m
Canada	1.1m	1.3m
All Foreign-Born	13.9m	14.2m

Source: *Historical Statistics of the United States, Colonial Times to 1970* (1975)

Ever since the 1880s, immigrants had constituted the semiskilled labor pool for American industrial expansion. The vast majority of working-class ethnics remained factory workers or menial service and clerical operators in the industrial East and Midwest; Italian-Americans, for example, dominated the construction trades. But by the 1920s, some immigrant families had raised enough capital to open neighborhood stores. Others saw children move up to skilled and supervisory industrial work, or join the middle class as educated professionals and managers. For a small number of immigrant enterpreneurs, the road out of the working class lay in machine politics and businesses that thrived on friendly political contacts: construction, utilities, local banking, insurance, and garbage collection. Discrimination against Irish-Americans and eastern and southern Europeans forced immigrants and their offspring to rely on acquaintances and family connections. As a result, ethnic networks in the large cities connected politics, labor unions, entertainment, gambling, and organized crime, usually centered in the same districts. Blacks migrating from the South, the Irish, eastern European Jews, and Italians made up the lower rungs of the organized crime trades. All had left regions deeply suspicious of governmental authority and faced massive discrimination in America's cities. Each also made contributions to the era's theater, burlesque, cabaret, and recording industries.

Prohibition accelerated the rise of Italian-Americans in the organized underworld. Following open warfare that took the lives of four hundred gangsters between 1923 and 1926, Al Capone emerged as undisputed leader of Chicago's bootlegging syndicate. Capone consolidated gambling, racketeering, and liquor running and made them into a nationwide industry. "My rackets are run on strictly American lines," he boasted. Infuriated reformers agonized that friendships and ethnic loyalties tied Chicago gangsters to "legitimate" society and the courts, but civic-minded leaders could do little to change the system. Ethnic urbanites often wished to be left alone to enjoy themselves without the interference of the state or society; consequently, they tolerated political machines that protected their right to drink in ethnically owned speakeasies of the Prohibition Era. Black, Polish, German, Czech, and Italian voters demonstrated their loyalties when they returned Chicago Republican Bill Thompson to city hall in 1927. The incumbent Democratic reformers had offended ethnic sensibilities by organizing police searches of homes during a campaign to enforce Prohibition.

The ethnic communities of midwestern and eastern cities focused on the family, parish, and neighborhood and sought to rebuild the protective social environment of Old World cultures. For groups such as the Slavs, Poles, and Italians, ethnicity meant the intimate sharing of communal life, traditions, and rituals. White ethnics continued to associate and live with members of their own nationality in the 1920s. But like the Irish before them, the new immigrants and their families increasingly viewed politics as a tool of survival and collective improvement. When Chicago's Bill Thompson made several disparaging remarks about eastern Europeans before the 1931 elections, his ethnic constituents worked with Democratic reformers to replace him with Bohemian immigrant Anton J. Cermak. By defeating the Irish-American incumbent, Cermak become one of the first eastern Europeans to rise to political power in an American city. This incident was a fitting preview of the

"My rackets are run on strictly American lines," bootlegging syndicate leader Al Capone boasted. Prohibition created a nationwide industry in liquor running and contributed to the growth of organized crime between 1920 and repeal in 1933. The conflict over the consumption of alcohol bitterly divided the American people.

powerful effect of the ethnic vote on the Democratic party and American politics.

THE NATIVIST ASSAULT

Throughout the 1920s, biology lecturer Edward Wiggam toured the small towns of the Middle West with a sobering call to action. An average of one child was born to every three graduates of the nation's leading women's colleges, he explained, but "one low-class, broad-backed, flat-chested, stout-legged, high-necked, stupid, ugly immigrant woman will in the same time produce three." Wiggam's pathological nativism revealed deep currents of anxiety among the nation's dominant Anglo-Protestants. Native-born Americans wondered whether their beloved republic could absorb more immigrants from southern and eastern Europe without the national culture being radically altered.

World War I blunted some of the racial nativism and anti-Catholicism of the Progressive Era. But when the conflict did not appear to advance the Americanization of the country's immigrants, nativist leaders attributed labor militance and domestic radicalism to the dangerous influx of foreigners. The 1917 Bolshevik revolution in Russia furthered these anxieties. By 1920, twenty-four states outlawed membership in the radical Industrial Workers of the World (IWW) and thirty-five enacted criminal syndicalist laws to discourage subversive activity. The Immigration Act of 1920 punished aliens for possessing subversive literature or making financial contributions to organizations that the federal government considered seditious.

The campaign against contaminants of national life constituted a major focus of the American Legion, a patriotic veterans group founded by military leaders in 1919. The legion quickly recruited one-fourth of the nation's war veterans and exercised considerable local control as a guardian against Communist influence and radicalism of all kinds. For example, both the legion and the Daughters of the American Revolution (DAR) circulated the infamous Spider Web Chart, a creation of the War Department that purported to trace the links of women's peace organizations to bolshevik connections. "Patrioteering" provided beleaguered members of the middle class with an opportunity to demonstrate allegiance to a nostalgic ideal of American unity and to restore the country to traditional status arrangements. Thirty ultra-patriotic organizations thrived in the early 1920s, demanding nothing short of "100 percent Americanism."

Italian-Americans became special targets of those who associated "hyphenated Americans" with domestic radicalism. Reacting to the tensions of a coal miners' strike and bank robberies attributed to the Italian Black Hand, a nativist mob invaded the Italian district of West Frankfort, Illinois, in 1920, dragged immigrant families from their homes, and burned rows of houses. When the Italian community retaliated against the invasion, five hundred state troopers needed three days to end the fighting.

The tendency to associate immigrants with crime and radicalism also surfaced in the arrest of Nicola Sacco and Bartolomeo Vanzetti outside Boston in 1920. Self-proclaimed anarchists, the two Italian-Americans pleaded innocent to charges of robbing an armored bank delivery truck and killing a guard. When the court convicted them on scant evidence, Sacco and Vanzetti appealed the case with the aid of the American Civil Liberties Union (ACLU), founded in 1919 to defend victims of the Red Scare. The ACLU protested that the immigrant anarchists' political views had replaced solid evidence in their trial, and argued that the court had dismissed the testimony of eighteen Italian-American witnesses as unreliable. After long appeals and delays, state authorities electrocuted Sacco and Vanzetti in August 1927. Although later scholars suggested that at least one of the men may have been guilty, the Sacco-Vanzetti case helped to politicize a generation of literary radicals like novelist John Dos Passos.

Nativists of the 1920s viewed immigrants as dirty, radical, and vice-inclined lowlifes who rejected American values and customs and so threatened democracy and social order. "Most of the bootleggers . . . appear to be foreigners," announced sociologist Harry Pratt Fairchild in *The Melting Pot Mistake* (1926). Jews inspired somewhat different portraits as intellectual dissidents, unscrupulous materialists, or tasteless producers of Hollywood movies and "skunk cabbage" jazz. In 1921, Henry Ford launched a nationwide crusade by having car dealers circulate copies of the "Protocol of the Elders of Zion," a fraudulent documentaion of an international Jewish conspiracy for world power. Ford's *Dearborn Independent*, distributed through thousands of Ford dealerships, played upon anti-Semitic prejudice by insisting, that international Jewish financiers dominated the American economy. Quotas regulating the entry of Jews into colleges and medical schools, clubs, residential areas, and businesses continued throughout the decade.

By the early 1920s, mechanization had reduced the need for unskilled labor and industrialists sought a more integrated labor force uncontaminated by foreign ideologies such as bolshevism or class consciousness. Business leaders contended that language and inexperience made foreign-born workers vulnerable to accidents and costly labor turnover. These arguments reinforced the fear that further immigration threatened the national character. "We have put all the sand into our cement that it will stand," lectured General Leonard Wood of the American Legion. One of many national groups to support restrictionism, the legion sponsored a 1920 essay contest on why Congress should suspend immigration. Maryland senator William Bruce expressed typical nativist sentiment when he compared immigrants to "indigestible lumps" in the "national stomach" and "insoluble blood-clots in the national circulation."

Anglo-Protestant nativists and labor leaders had faced presidential vetoes of immigrant restriction bills in the years before World War I. Furthermore, Congress had overriden Woodrow Wilson's veto to enact a literacy test for adult immigrants in 1917. In the first successful act of restriction, legislators set a maximum quota of 357,000 immigrants a year in 1921. The emergency statute limited future arrivals from any nation to 3 percent of the foreign-born population of that nationality residing in the United States in 1910. A second law, the National Origins Act of 1924, created a gradual timetable for a ceiling of 150,000 immigrants each year, using a 2 percent quota for each national group. The law stipulated that the quota system would be based on the 1890 census until 1927. After that, national origin apportionment would depend upon the census of 1920.

Exhibit 4–7. Changing Patterns of Immigration, 1921–1929 (in rounded figures)

	1921	1925	1929
Northwestern Europe	132,000	79,000	68,000
Central Europe	179,000	56,000	64,000
Eastern Europe	43,000	4,700	4,500
Southern Europe	299,000	8,400	22,000
Canada	72,000	103,000	66,000
All immigrants	800,000	294,000	279,000

Source: *Historical Statistics of the United States, Colonial Times to 1970* (1975)

The immigration laws of the 1920s froze the ethnic proportions of the American population, discouraging the "new immigration" from southern and eastern Europe (largely Roman Catholic, Eastern Orthodox, and Jewish), and encouraging migration from northern and western Europe (predominantly Protestant). The new legislation also formalized prohibition of Japanese immigration. In contrast, the restrictive quotas did not apply to immigrants from the Western Hemisphere. Accordingly, federal law encouraged the use of Mexican labor in southwest agriculture and migration from Canada. By 1925, 35 percent of the nation's immigrants came from its northern neighbor. Although restriction legislation implemented the major goals of postwar nativism, it removed the urgency from the anti-immigrant crusade. By the 1930s, nativist anxieties concerning the integration of European immigrants, Catholics, and Jews had considerably lessened.

THE KU KLUX KLAN

The Nordic-American, Hiram Wesley Evans complained in 1926, remained "a stranger in large parts of the land his fathers gave him." In his midforties, of middle height and rotund face, the soft-spoken Evans pictured himself as "the most average man in America." But as Imperial Wizard of the Ku Klux Klan (KKK), the Alabama-born dentist of the Disciples Church presided over a mass movement of some two to five million followers. Although Klansmen might be hicks, rubes, and "drivers of second-hand Fords," Evans proclaimed, they insisted on the "inherited right . . . to maintain and develop our racial heritage in our own, Protestant, American way . . ."

Organized in Atlanta in 1915, the secret Ku Klux Klan admitted "native born, white, gentile Americans" who believed in white supremacy and professed national loyalty. Initiates took confidential oaths of allegiance and wore white robes and hoods to fulfill prescribed ritual and maintain anonymity from potential adversaries. Unlike the Klan of the 1860s, the revitalized order did not confine its appeal to the Deep South. On the contrary, its influence spread among lower-middle-class Anglo-Protestants in small towns of the North and in growing cities like Knoxville, Dallas, Indianapolis, and Denver.

The Klan initially built its support by exploiting white supremacy. Responding to the infusion of black migrants in southern cities and the new pride among returning black war veterans, Klansmen paraded through the South on the eve of the 1920 election to discourage minority voting. Black men who "insulted" white women or unduly asserted themselves faced repeated vigilante threats, occasional whippings, and even in some cases branding. Such terrorism led Evans to denounce unlawful violence by Klansmen when he took control of the secret order in 1922.

Beyond a lingering racism, the postwar Klan focused most of its hostility on the institutional power of the Roman Catholic Church, a denomination that encompassed 36 percent of the nation's population. Klansmen claimed that the political and economic power of the church represented "a menace to

The Ku Klux Klan marches through the streets of Washington, D.C. in 1925. The Klan of the 1920s saw itself as a mass political lobby and used its millions of members to campaign for Prohibition enforcement, immigration restriction, and a strong public school system.

the spiritual and moral integrity of America." Klan meetings, or "klonklaves", featured a distinctly Protestant spirit, with "The Old Rugged Cross" the near-official hymn of gatherings. Michigan and Nebraska debated constitutional amendments to ban parochial schools in 1920 and 1921. The following year, Oregon elected a Klan-supported governor, abolished Columbus Day as a state holiday, and passed an initiative requiring children to attend public schools. An Oregon Klan pamphlet proclaimed that schools should be nonsectarian and democratic "for all the children of all the people." The Supreme Court struck down this law in 1925, asserting that the state had no right to "standardize its children." In Illinois, a Klan mob burned a Catholic church to the ground.

Klan activities also focused on foreigners who refused to "melt" into Anglo-Protestant culture. Immigrants maintained primary allegiance to their ethnic group and could never be Americanized, said Klan leader Evans. Only Anglo-Saxons or Nordics had the inherent capacity for American citizenship, as shown by immigrant lawbreaking and alcohol consumption. Moreover, ethnic newcomers adhered to the detested foreign ideology of bolshevism, which the Klan associated with most forms of political dissent. Ironically,

Klansmen and other anti-Semites castigated American Jews as both bankers and bolsheviks. Evans continually reminded followers of the need to preserve the nation's pioneer legacy through immigration restriction, support for the public school system, and purity measures such as Prohibition. Official Klan policy excoriated the "Jew, Jug, and Jesuit." Meanwhile, local "klaverns" (lodges) endorsed "100 percent Americans" and "traditional" values by mounting boycotts against Catholic, Jewish, and foreign merchants.

The postwar Klan thrived in boom towns like Des Moines, Birmingham, Memphis, and Tulsa, cities often threatened by an influx of blacks or immigrants. Uprooted and dislocated, Klansmen adhered to traditional values amid the secularization of city culture and the conversion of upper-middle-class youth to the ways of the Jazz Age. Followers of the Klan saw themselves as knights—guardians of the public virtue in a period of bootleggers, gangsters, and prostitutes. In Birmingham, Klan patrols shined lights on couples in parked cars and ordered the occupants to move on. "Go joyriding with your own wife," read one KKK placard. Objections extended to lurid movies, salacious literature, easy divorce, family disintegration, sexy dancing, Sabbath sports, and corrupt politicians. Evans talked of "a return of power into the hands of the everyday, not highly cultured, not overly intellectualized, but entirely unspoiled and not de-Americanized average citizen of the old stock."

Klan rallies, marches, and picnics sought to build a cohesive culture of Anglo-Protestants. On July 4, 1923, nearly two-hundred thousand people gathered near Kokomo, Indiana, to watch Imperial Wizard Evans descend by airplane to address a gathering throng. Another eighty thousand marched in uniform to Capitol Hill in 1926. In some respects, the two thousand nationwide klaverns reflected the "lodge vogue" shared by the middle-class men of postwar America. Like service clubs such as the Elks, Rotary, and Kiwanis, Klan revivals and meetings brought relief from the sterility of small-town life and provided fraternal cohesion for those in larger cities.

By 1923, Evans's leadership had converted the KKK into a highly effective political machine that rewarded friends and punished enemies of both major parties. Klan-backed candidates went to the Senate from Republican Colorado and Democratic Texas. In 1923, the Klan-dominated legislature of Oklahoma successfully impeached a Democratic governor when he turned against the organization by invoking martial law against Klan-inspired violence. In Indiana, where the secret order boasted nearly one-half million members, Klansmen took over the Republican party, the governorship, and local government and school boards in Indianapolis and Gary. Klans across the nation also elected several congressional representatives.

Despite the organization's dramatic achievements, Klan political power proved temporary. In 1925, an Indiana statehouse secretary poisoned herself after being abducted by the region's grand dragon and placed on a train to Chicago. The sensational scandal produced a second-degree murder conviction and a life sentence for the Klansman, David C. Stephenson. When the Klan-supported governor refused to pardon him, Stephenson produced a "black book" with evidence that sent a congressman, the mayor of Indianapolis, a county sheriff, and other Indiana Klan officials to prison.

Internal dissension in Klan politics and further moral and financial scandals marked the demise of the organization by the late 1920s. Community leaders also realized that less contentious organizations such as the Elks or Rotary could better fulfill Klan patriotic and civic goals. By denying the cultural pluralism of American society and resorting to secret methods, the Ku Klux Klan had become an unwelcome and disruptive force in national life.

THE FUNDAMENTALIST CRUSADE

"One by one," complained Ku Klux Klan leader Evans in 1926, "all our traditional moral standards went by the boards. The sacredness of our Sabbath, of our homes, of chastity, and finally even of our right to teach our children in our own schools fundamental facts and truths were torn from us." By 1920, a massive revival of traditional faith had come to play a major role in American Protestantism. Represented by the World's Christian Fundamentals Association (WCFA), which claimed six million members in 1927, Baptists, Presbyterians, and other evangelicals sought to counter the spread of "modernist" theology in America's churches. In 1920, objecting particularly to efforts to align Christian belief with rationalist philosophy and Darwinian evolution theory, 155 Baptist ministers supported a call for a general conference on fundamentals. Curtis Lee Laws, editor of the Baptist newspaper *The Watchman Examiner*, urged participants "to do royal battle for the Fundamentals" and coined a new term *fundmentalism*.

"Two worlds have crashed, the world of tradition and the world of modernism," announced liberal *Christian Century* editor Charles Clayton Morrison in 1924. Modernists such as Shailer Matthews, dean of the University of Chicago Divinity School, pictured Christianity as a moral and spiritual movement that used a "scientific, historical, and social method" to apply religion to the needs of living persons. But Protestant traditionalists like Princeton's Presbyterian biblical scholar J. Gresham Machen replied that if liberalism controlled the church's preaching, "Christianity would at last have perished from the earth and the gospel would have sounded for the last time."

Fundamentalists insisted that the Bible be read as literal truth, but also condemned the "growing worldliness" and "materialist" outlook of the modern ministry, ridiculing church movies, dancing lessons, bowling alleys, and other seemingly frivolous pursuits. Portraying the battle for the Bible as a struggle to save civilization from wrenching cultural changes, a host of ministers and reformers flocked to the Fundamentalist cause in the 1920s. For example, Presbyterian William ("Billy") Sunday, a former professional baseball player, mixed denunciation of sinners and intellectuals with acrobatic preaching to complete an estimated three-hundred thousand hands-on conversions between 1910 and 1930.

"Monkey Men Means Money Morals," protested Fundmentalists in the early 1920s. Postwar biology textbooks increasingly presented Darwinian theory as scientific fact and offended those who accepted the story of Genesis as the cornerstone of Christian faith. Building upon their victories in the Protestant denominations and church-related colleges, southern Fundamentalists and others began to move against the teaching of evolution in the public schools. Between 1921 and 1929, Fundamentalist organizers introduced forty-one anti-evolution bills before twenty-one statehouses. One measure passed the Tennessee legislature in 1925 as a symbolic gesture to revivalist sentiment. The American Civil Liberties Union, however, objected to the law as an infringement on constitutional rights of free speech and found a high school teacher willing to challenge it by allowing himself to be charged. The ensuing trial of John Scopes became a major media event of the decade when the ACLU hired Clarence Darrow, the nation's most prominent defense attorney, and evangelical reformer William Jennings Bryan answered the WCFA's request to assist the prosecution.

Bryan called the Dayton, Tennessee, trial a "duel to the death" between Christianity and the doctrine of evolution. "It is better to trust the Rock of Ages," he proclaimed, "than to know the age of rocks." Bryan hoped to show that the doctrine of evolution paralyzed social reform because it emphasized struggle and conflict instead of Christian love. Amidst a maddening environment of religious demonstrators, movie cameras, radio hookups, and news reporters, the Scopes trial of 1925 climaxed when Darrow, an agnostic, called Bryan to the stand. Speaking for traditional faith, the Great Commoner testified that he read the Bible literally. But when asked how long it took to create Earth, Bryan interpreted scripture by suggesting six time periods rather

Clarence Darrow (left) and William Jennings Bryan (right), opposing attorneys in the Scopes Trial of 1925. Both men used their legal and oratory skills to mount conflicting arguments over the right to teach evolution in the public schools.

than six days. The close of the sensational "monkey trial" found Scopes guilty, but Bryan had been widely derided and mocked. Led by H. L. Mencken of the *Baltimore Sun*, the national press portrayed the confrontation as a triumph of scientific cosmopolitanism over "old-time religion." Five days later, Bryan died in his sleep.

Although the Tennessee statute remained law until 1966, the Scopes trial isolated the Fundamentalist movement by associating it with village conformity and the suppression of free inquiry. Not until the 1970s would it regain national attention and major influence.

PROHIBITION, PURITY, AND NEW HEROES

William Jennings Bryan believed that Fundamentalism and Prohibition ranked as the two great moral issues of the 1920s. Progressive purity crusaders and Protestant allies had taken advantage of the wartime spirit of sacrifice and discipline to obtain congressional passage of the Eighteenth Amendment in 1917. The long-heralded measure, which outlawed the manufacture, sale, importing, or transportation of "intoxicating liquors", took effect in 1920. Nativist preachers like Billy Sunday viewed Prohibition as a means of unifying American culture around traditional values of hard work and Protestant piety. Prohibitionists sharply attacked the "infidel" saloon, the "breeding place" of ethnic crime, prostitution, machine politics, and labor unions. And industrialists such as Henry Ford insisted that a mechanized production system demanded sober workers.

Despite such passionate endorsements, national Prohibition brought mixed results. Beer drinking dropped dramatically, halving the consumption of alcohol by the working class. Compliance with the Eighteenth Amendment declined by mid-decade, however, and the use of spirits by middle- and upper-class Americans increased, leading to charges that Prohibition constituted class legislation against the poor.

Believing the amendment's blanket condemnation of the liquor trade to be sufficient, the Anti-Saloon League had not pressed Congress for extensive appropriations for enforcement. As a result, the Harding and Coolidge administrations felt no compulsion to implement Prohibition policy rigorously; in fact, Harding maintained a personal bootlegger while serving in the White House. By 1927, only eighteen states had appropriated enforcement funds, and those funds were often inadequate. Furthermore, prosecutors and juries in the larger cities declined to challenge the casual use of beer and wine by ethnic Americans. The emergence of a thriving underworld to meet the demand for bootleg liquor aggravated the threat to lawful order. Open violation demonstrated the futility of Prohibition and encouraged criticism of the "noble experiment."

In 1928, Democratic presidential candidate Al Smith expressed his personal opposition to the Eighteenth Amendment, although he pledged to uphold its provisions. By then, the Association Against the Prohibition Amendment had effectively mobilized the support of wealthy Democrats such as General Motors vice-president John J. Raskob and powerful industrialists like former prohibitionist Pierre S. DuPont. The Wickersham Report, presented to President Herbert Hoover in 1929, added to the controversy by outlining the obstacles to effective enforcement. But Prohibition repeal did not come until a Democratic Congress referred to the states ratification of the Twenty-first Amendment in 1933, although many southern states simply established local option. The demise of Prohibition suggested the waning of Anglo-Protestant dominance and the eclipse of rural nostalgia and pietistic moral standards.

Amid mixed responses to Prohibition, social tradition continued to play a major role in American life. Chautauqua cultural festivals, religious and educational camp meetings first held at western New York's Lake Chautauqua in the 1870s, maintained the nineteenth-century cult of self-improvement in tents and fairgrounds of small towns across the nation. By 1924, one hundred Chautauqua circuits reached thirty million people. Baptist minister Russell Conwell delivered his "Acres of Diamond" parable on success six thousand times to these audiences, and William Jennings Bryan provided three thousand renditions of his inspiratioinal "Prince of Peace" lecture. On the radio, Pentecostal evangelist Aimee Semple McPherson dramatized sermons that condemned the Jazz Age and stressed the gospel of love. The "Grand Ole Opry," a country music variety show that upheld traditional values and rural humor, began nationwide radio broadcasts from Nashville in 1926.

Postwar purity reformers repeatedly condemned urban popular culture and changed roles for youth, women, ethnics, and racial minorities. In Boston, an alliance of the Catholic church and the Protestant social elite maintained strict censorship of books such as Theodore Dreiser's *An American Tragedy* (1925), a realistic portrait of sexuality and amoral ambition in the postwar era. Thirty-two bills for censorship of the movies appeared before state legislatures in 1921. Moral activists also called for the prohibition of Sunday film showings and for a Federal Motion Picture Commission to discourage producers from commercializing vice and exploiting audiences of minors. Several states considered banning Sunday baseball, boxing, and dancing as violations of the Sabbath. Some states, like Illinois, considered bills to make the possession of liquor a crime. In predominantly Mormon Utah, legislators debated a proposal to fix women's skirts three inches above the ankle.

"Does Jazz Put the Sin in Syncopation?" asked Mrs. Marx Obendorfer, national chairwoman of the General Federation of Women's Clubs, in 1921. Promoting a crusade against jazz during that year, the *Ladies Home Journal* castigated "cheap, common tawdry music" that brought "moral ruin." Purity crusaders associated jazz with unruly African rhythms and objected to the sensual appeal of "vulgar" instruments like the "moaning" saxophone. Such agitation led New York State to pass the Cotillo Act of 1922, which established municipal regulation of the performing and dancing of jazz and allowed the city of New York to prohibit both activities on Broadway after midnight. Sixty other municipalities, including Cleveland, Detroit, Kansas City, and Philadelphia, totally banned such music from their public dance halls.

As Americans found themselves a society dominated by corporate institutions and changing moral values, individual athletes and organized sports offered a vicarious sense of accomplishment that was not available through routinized work and ordinary life. Sports accomplishments took on new importance for a generation of men cut off from the physical tasks of rural life. College football, with its tribal ritualism and clockwork precision, dominated campus life in the postwar era and provided fans with mythic heroes such as University of Illinois halfback Harold ("Red") Grange. The same kind of community spirit pervaded rivalries between small-town basketball teams throughout the Midwest. The greatest sports heroes came from the ethnics and poor whites who gravitated to professional boxing and baseball. Jack Dempsey, an Irish-American, thrilled boxing fans with gutsy and ferocious fighting reminiscent of street brawls. And Babe Ruth, raised in a Catholic boys' home in Baltimore, helped make baseball the national pastime by hitting sixty home runs in 1927, more than the total compiled by any team opponent of his famed New York Yankees.

The romanticization of athletic heroes reflected the development of a national sports media in newspapers and the radio. Not surprisingly, both nostalgia and media publicity played key roles in the most celebrated event of the 1920s: Charles A. Lindbergh's solo flight across the Atlantic Ocean in 1927. Lindbergh took off from Long Island's Roosevelt Field and, without instruments, piloted his single-engine *Spirit of St. Louis* nonstop for thirty-three hours and thirty minutes. Two continents were waiting when he landed the tiny aircraft to cheering throngs at an airfield near Paris. President Calvin Coolidge immediately ordered a battleship to return the aviator and his airplane to the United States. Newspapers splashed front pages with celebrations of the accomplishments of the Lone Eagle. Four million people soon turned out to see the twenty-five-year-old Minnesotan parade down Broadway in an unprecedented ticker tape celebration in downtown New York.

Lindbergh's courageous feat stirred the imagination of the media-conscious American people. By combining personal ingenuity with sophisticated machine technology, the youthful adventurer suggested that individuals could still play a role in a highly organized society. In an era defined by the search for moral certainties and reassurance, Lindbergh symbolized the renewal of the lost virtue.

CITY VERSUS COUNTRY: THE CROSS OF CULTURE

"The country must fight her way back to liberty and throw off the incubus of prohibition laws, censorship, William Jennings Bryanism, ignorance, and scriptural dogmatism." This is what poet Edgar Lee Masters, author of the *Spoon River Anthology* (1915), told a Des Moines newspaper in 1925. In response, an Iowa evangelist attacked Masters's adopted home of Chicago and suggested that the poet might find all the modernism he wanted in

AIMEE SEMPLE McPHERSON
1890–1944

When Aimee Semple McPherson opened a Pentecostal temple in Los Angeles on New Year's Day 1923, she demonstrated that Protestant Fundmentalism did not confine itself to the southeastern mountains or the remote countryside. McPherson's church embodied the compassionate side of a creed that attacked evolution theory as promoting a materialistic world ruled by force instead of love.

McPherson fashioned herself as an evangelical faith healer. She had been converted at the age of seventeen by Robert Semple, an itinerate preacher. The two married and left for missionary work in China, but Semple died and the young widow returned home. After an unhappy marriage to a grocery salesman, McPherson decorated her "gospel automobile" with religious slogans and set out for California.

The "foursquare gospel" of Aimee Semple fell within the pietistic tradition of American Protestantism. It appealed to people of little education and small means, worshippers brought up in the revivalist spirit of the evangelical churches. Most of McPherson's followers remained retirees transplanted from the Midwest and elsewhere. They responded enthusiastically to simple sermons of love and faith healing.

McPherson made Los Angeles the headquarters for countless cross-country revival tours, spreading in tents, churches, and public auditoriums the word that the Jazz Age was speeding to hell. Endorsed by the mayor of Denver in 1921, she filled that city's coliseum for a month with twelve thousand people nightly. The following year, McPherson addressed a secret klavern of the Oakland Ku Klux Klan. Once the Pentecostal *(cont.)*

Russia. Such exchanges dramatized bitter divisions between city and country in the 1920s. Small-town ministers, political leaders, and newspaper editors castigated urban conglomerates as "death chambers of civilization." Contending that artificial aspects of city life played havoc with the nervous system and sapped individual vitality, rural idealists warned about the "mad craze for sensation" in forsaken places such as Chicago and New York.

The struggle between "two inimical civilizations" had important implications for social policy and politics. Iowa refused to approve legalized boxing in 1929, with rural legislators condemning the sport as a spectator pastime fostering cheap commercialism, unearned income, and ethnic gambling and crime. Illinois, however, sanctioned boxing and horse race gambling in 1925 and 1927, although only under the strictest regulation. Tax issues also separated rural and urban voters. Midwestern farmers, for example, pursued economic interests by supporting heavy levies on intangible property and incomes. In contrast, city renters and salaried urbanites preferred to maintain taxes on tangible property and land. Protesting that rising taxes disproportionately supported programs that benefited the city instead of the country-temple opened, her religious enterprises expanded to a Bible college, publishing house, branch churches, and overseas missions. In 1924, she purchased Los Angeles's third radio station.

The distinguishing feature of McPherson's gospel remained her belief that a Jazz Age preacher must "fight fire with fire." She became the first woman to deliver a sermon over the radio. In San Diego, she scattered religious tracts and handbills from an open biplane. The Los Angeles temple provided telephone callers with the time of day as a free service.

McPherson merged the magic of Hollywood with religious ecstasy. She dressed in long white gowns, which dramatically offset her cascading blond hair. Temple services used full orchestras, choirs, elaborate costumes, and colorful pageantry to portray Bible stories in spectacular fashion. Preacher McPherson once illustrated a sermon entitled "The Green Light Is On" by riding a motorcycle down the center aisle.

The evangelist's fusion of traditionalism and modernism brought press outrage when she disappeared in 1926, only to be linked to a Mexican abortion and an affair with the temple radio operator. Nevertheless, her following continued to pay homage to "Everybody's Sister."

After surviving several court suits in the mid-1930s, McPherson died in 1944 from an overdose of barbital sedatives complicated by a kidney ailment. But the Pentecostal movement, a response to the secular hedonism of the urban middle class, remained a vital force in American Protestantism. Despite her Jazz Age trappings, Aimee Semple McPherson remained a symbol of Anglo-Protestant nostalgia for the purity of a simpler America. Her pioneering fusion of religion and show business anticipated the television evangelists of a later era and spoke eloquently for grass roots impatience with overintellectualized theology and relativistic moral values. ■

side, rural voters frequently opposed escalating salaries and appropriations for state bureaucracies and schools. And while those outside the big cities fought against paved highways between large population centers, they pressed legislators for more farm-to-market roads.

Urban-rural conflict devastated the Democratic party of the 1920s. Ever since the William Jennings Bryan campaign of 1896, the party had divided between those who identified with the city and the immigrants, and southerners and westerners who emphasized the rural virtues of the Anglo-Protestant heritage. In 1924, these views collided at the Democratic National Convention at New York City's Madison Square Garden. With convention proceedings broadcast for the first time by radio, furious debates raged over Prohibition and the League of Nations. When Bryan convinced the gathering to turn down a resolution to condemn the Ku Klux Klan by name (it failed by one vote out of 1,084 cast), police officials intervened to prevent enraged gallery partisans from attacking the convention floor. In the battle for the presidential nomination, Governor Al Smith of New York, a Roman Catholic and a "wet" opponent of Prohibition, faced William Gibbs McAdoo, heir to the Bryan leadership of the rural "drys." After 102 ballots in the steamy hall, the Democrats finally compromised on Wall Street lawyer John W. Davis, who did little to advance the party's fortunes in the general election (see chapter 5).

Four years later, the Democrats could no longer ignore their growing urban and ethnic constituency. Despite Republican support for Prohibition and immigration restriction, the major cities outside the South had consistently opposed Democratic presidential tickets since 1896. The Democrats tried to reverse their failure to carry the large cities by turning to Al Smith in 1928, but the cultural implications of the Smith candidacy proved too great for a national electorate still dominated by Anglo-Protestants. The Anti-Saloon League argued that the candidate appealed "to the sporty, jazzy, and liberal

New York Governor Al Smith, Democratic candidate for president in 1928. A Catholic and opponent of Prohibition, Smith represented urban and ethnic constituencies in a period of cultural confusion over the nation's identity.

element of our population." Accused of being "New York minded," Smith faced ridicule for his derby hat and vernacular speech. Tennessee editor George Fort Milton suggested that the Democratic nominee represented "aliens who feel that the older America, the America of the Anglo-Saxon stock, is a hateful thing which must be overturned and humiliated." Smith's candidacy, observed the Kansas journalist William Allen White, threatened the "whole Puritan civilization which has built a sturdy, orderly nation."

Al Smith's Catholic and working-class background alienated the majority of voters still coming to terms with the American city and so presented Republican Herbert Hoover with an easy electoral victory (see chapter 5). For the first time since Reconstruction, Republicans split the Democratic South, taking Maryland, Virginia, Kentucky, Tennessee, North Carolina, Florida, and Texas. In Minnesota, the *St. Paul Pioneer Press* rejoiced that America was "not yet dominated by its great cities. . . Main Street is still the principal thoroughfare of the nation." Yet the election brought out an energetic 56.9 percent of eligible voters, the highest rate since the 1916 election. Smith became the first Democrat to tie the national party to first- and second-generation immigrants. Republicans, in contrast, largely ignored the urban and ethnic support they inherited at the start of the decade and lost millions of votes through persistent identification with Prohibition and immigration restriction. The Smith political revolution of 1928 represented a new sensitivity to ethnic concerns and suggested that Catholics, Jews, and city voters would play a far larger role in national politics.

By the close of the 1920s, the main foundations of modern American culture had taken shape. Technological change had brought the national media, the automobile, and consumer advertising—innovations that initially served the secular and ethnically diverse cities. Yet cars, radios, appliances, and movies also enticed ruralists. Consequently, the primary importance of family, home, church, and local community began to recede in national life. Americans now faced the central paradox that acceptance of consumer technology threatened cherished values such as simple living, self-reliance, serenity, and the dominance of religious guidelines. Nevertheless, more of the new life attracted than repelled. By moving toward acceptance of ethnic diversity and the sharing of consumer values, Americans of the 1920s experienced the irreversible transition from traditional to modern society.

Exhibit 4–8. Voter Participation in Presidential Elections, 1916–1928 (percentage of eligible voters)

1916	61.6%
1920	49.2%
1924	48.9%
1928	56.9%

Source: *Historical Statistics of the United States, Colonial Times to 1970* (1975)

SUGGESTED READINGS

Overviews of 1920s cultural history can be found in Paul A. Carter, *Another Part of the Twenties* (1977) and *The Twenties in America* (1975). See also Roderick Nash, *The Nervous Generation: American Thought, 1917–1930* (1969). William E. Leuchtenburg, *Perils of Prosperity, 1914–1932* (1958) and Gilman M. Ostrander, *American Civilization in the First Machine Age, 1890–1940* (1970) both present overriding interpretations that emphasize technology, youth, and moral innovation. Two helpful contemporary studies are Robert S. Lynd and Helen M. Lynd, *Middletown: A Study in American Culture* (1929) and President's Conference on Unemployment, *Recent Social Trends in the United States* (1933).

Relevant sections of Kenneth T. Jackson, *The Crabgrass Frontier: The Suburbanization of the United States* (1985) focus on automobile culture in the suburbs. See also William H. Wilson *Coming of Age: Urban America, 1915–1945* (1974). The influence of the automobile is further explored in Scott Bottles, *Los Angeles and the Automobile: The Making of the Modern City* (1987); Ed Cray, *Chrome Colossus: General Motors and Its Times* (1980); and James J. Flink, *The Car Culture* (1975).

For an account of consumer values and advertising in the 1920s, see Stuart Ewen, *Captains of Consciousness* (1976). Critiques of commercialism and mass production are portrayed in Daniel Horowitz, *The Morality of Spending: Attitudes Toward the Consumer Society in America, 1875–1940* (1985). See also the works by Erenberg and Elaine Tyler May listed in chapter 1. An innovative approach to college youth and changing social mores is Paula Fass, *The Damned and the Beautiful: American Youth in the 1920s* (1977). See also the appropriate sections of Louis Filler, *Vanguards and Followers: Youth in the American Tradition* (1978).

For the social context of Hollywood films, see the relevant chapters of Robert Sklar, *Movie-Made America: A Cultural History of American Movies* (1975). Lary May, *Screening Out the Past: The Birth of Mass Culture and the Motion Picture Industry* (1980) provides a brilliant analysis of the manner in which the movies reinforced consumer ideals and the revolt against Victorian morality. See also Marjorie Rosen, *Popcorn Venus: Women, Movies, and the American Dream* (1973). Evolving sports culture is portrayed in Marshall Smelser, *The Life that Ruth Built: A Biography* (1975) and Randy Roberts, *Jack Dempsey, The Manassa Mauler* (1979).

The most complete account of the postwar literary renaissance is Frederick J. Hoffman, *The Twenties* (1949), which should be supplemented with Malcolm Cowley, *Exile's Return: A Literary Odyssey of the 1920s* (1956) and Max Eastman, *Love and Revolution: My Journey Through an Epoch* (1964).

Recent studies of women in the era include Dorothy M. Brown, *Setting a Course: American Women in the 1920s* (1987); the relevant sections of Sheila Rothman, *Woman's Proper Place: A History of Changing Ideals and Practices, 1870 to the Present* (1978); and Winifred D. Wandersee, *Women's Work and Family Values, 1920–1940* (1981). Women's involvement in social work is described by Clarke A. Chambers, *Seedtime of Reform: American Social Service and Social Action, 1918–1933* (1963). For feminism and postwar political and economic changes, see Stanley J. Lemons, *The Woman Citizen: Social Feminism in the 1920s* (1973) and the initial segment of William H. Chafe, *The American Woman: Her Changing Social, Economic, and Political Role, 1920–1970* (1972). Evolving male roles are portrayed in the appropriate sections of Peter G. Filene, *Him/Her Self: Sex Roles in Modern America* (1986) and Joe Dubbert, *A Man's Place: Masculinity in Transition* (1979).

The rise of the black ghetto can be explored in the insightful Gilbert Osofsky, *Harlem: The Making of a Ghetto* (1966). Relevant sections of August Meier and Elliot Rudwick, *From Plantation to Ghetto* (1976) and June Sochen, *The Unbridgeable Gap: Blacks and Their Quest for the American Dream, 1900–1930* (1972) discuss black protest and the Harlem Renaissance. See Eugene Levy, *James Weldon Johnson: Black Leader, Black Voice* (1973). Immigrant cultures are described in the appropriate segments of Richard Gambino, *Blood of My Blood: The Dilemma of the Italian-Americans* (1975) and Richard Krickus, *Pursuing the American Dream: White Ethnics and the New Populism* (1976).

A detailed account of the immigration restriction crusade can be found in the closing portion of John Higham, *Strangers in the Land: Patterns of American Nativism, 1860–1925* (1955). The roots and influence of the Ku Klux Klan are treated in Charles C. Alexander, *The Ku Klux Klan in the Southwest* (1965): Kenneth T. Jackson, *The Ku Klux Klan in the City, 1915–1930* (1967); and Robert A. Goldberg, *Hooded Empire: The Ku Klux Klan in Colorado* (1981). Prohibition as a reform is explained by Norman H. Clark, *Deliver Us from Evil: An Interpretation of American Prohibition* (1976). For a geographical interpretation of cultural conflict, see Don S. Kirschner, *City and Country: Rural Responses to Urbanization in the 1920s* (1970). The standard work on Fundamentalism in the period is Norman F. Furniss, *The Fundamentalist Controversy, 1918–1933* (1954), but it should be supplemented by the relevant sections of George M. Marsden, *Fundamentalism and American Culture: The Shaping of Twentieth Century Evangelicalism, 1870–1925* (1980).

Ethnocultural conflict in 1920s politics is explored by David Burner, *The Politics of Provincialism: The Democratic Party in Transition, 1918–1932* (1968). For a portrait of Al Smith, see Paula Eldot, *Governor Alfred E. Smith: The Politician as Reformer* (1981). An attempt to use quantitative methods to reassert the importance of religion to the 1928 election can be found in Allan J. Lichtman, *Prejudice and the Old Politics: The Presidential Election of 1928* (1979). For ethnic influence in one city's politics, see the relevant chapters of John M. Allswang, *A House for All Peoples: Ethnic Politics in Chicago, 1890–1936* (1971).

5

FROM THE NEW ERA TO THE GREAT DEPRESSION, 1920-1932

A s a spectacular boom boosted the American economy between 1922 and 1929, confident corporate leaders proclaimed a New Era in human affairs. Economic statistics supported their contentions. Industrial production soared 70 percent between 1922 and 1928 and the gross national product (GNP) rose 40 percent. Meanwhile, national income leaped from $60 billion in 1922 to $87 billion by the end of the decade. A creditor for the first time in its history, the United States saw its foreign investment leap to $12.2 billion by 1927. Business expansion resulted in a 30 percent increase in per capita income between 1922 and 1928 and a corresponding 22 percent jump in real wages. New technologies, merchandising and distribution advances, enthusiastic consumer spending, and innovations in corporate and government administration pointed to permanent prosperity and social stability. But shortsighted speculation and insufficient attention to independent agriculture and decaying industries undermined the sophisticated approach of New Era leaders. Accordingly, the attempt to fuse a corporate consensus met increasing resistance from family farmers, blue-collar workers, independent business interests, and anti-corporate reformers. When New Era prosperity crashed in 1929, political leaders faced the most devastating crisis in American history since the Civil War.

NEW ERA PROGRESS

New Era prosperity drew its vitality from an energetic consumerism. Following the expansion of wartime metal, chemical, and machine industries, American manufacturers stimulated peacetime demand by applying newly acquired technology to a tantalizing array of consumer products. Americans had been "transported to a new world," exulted *Nation's Business*, the United States Chamber of Commerce monthly. In the petroleum industry, which

Exhibit 5–1. Gross National Product, 1922–1928
(in rounded billions of dollars at current prices)

1922	$74.1b
1924	$84.7b
1926	$97.0b
1928	$97.0b

Source: *Historical Statistics of the United States, Colonial Times to 1970* (1975)

Exhibit 5–2. Per Capita Income, 1921–1926
(money income in 1925 dollars)

1921	$500
1923	$616
1926	$659

Source: *Recent Economic Changes* (1929)

The electrical range and stove represented the wonder of modern home appliances. Use of electric power soared in the 1920s and brought an outpouring of corporate rhetoric addressed to an anticipated liberation from household drudgery for women.

generated one billion barrels of crude oil annually by 1929, corporate laboratories turned out synthetic petrochemicals such as acetate and Dacron as well as varied plastics, cosmetics, and synthetic tires. Dupont, a major war contractor, developed rayon (an artificial fiber made by dissolving wood chips in an acetate solution), which became popular in clothing, carpets, and upholstery. Dupont researchers also invented cellophane, used by manufacturers to package many of the mass-produced goods of the 1920s. Meanwhile, the electrical industry made dramatic advances in product technology and marketing, producing a host of office machines such as addressographs and air conditioners. By the close of the decade, the nation also boasted twenty million household and business telephones, up from 1.3 million in 1900. "The telephone is the social cord from which . . . group life depends," proclaimed a Bell System pamphlet in 1926.

"His god was Modern Appliances," Sinclair Lewis wrote of the leading character in *Babbitt* (1922), a satirical novel of small-town life in the consumer era. Indeed, the technological revolution had its greatest impact in the home. After World War I, electricial products manufacturers such as General Electric and Westinghouse shifted emphasis from large-scale industrial equipment to smaller consumer items. Accordingly, their amply funded research laboratories developed mass-produced appliances such as washing machines, refrigerators, electrical irons, toasters, and vacuum cleaners. Business writers such as Mark Sullivan spoke of "the magic genii of electricity" and promised that the new technology would relieve human drudgery and democratize leisure.

Exhibit 5–3. Production of Electric Household Appliances, 1919–1925
(value in rounded millions of dollars)

1919	$38.7m
1925	$75.1m

Source: *Recent Economic Changes* (1929)

Not surprisingly, home use contributed to a surge in electrical power consumption from forty-three billion kilowatt hours in 1917 to 114 billion in 1930.

Fusing postwar vacuum tube technology with financial power, General Electric played a key role in developing a revolutionary form of national communication: the radio. Described as the "the miracle of the ages" by communication executives, radio won widespread recognition when Pittsburgh's KDKA broadcast the 1920 election night results from a two-story garage. By 1929, annual sales of receiver sets reached $842.5 million. Two years later, the NBC and CBS radio networks encompassed 150 affiliates and more than twelve million American families owned radio receivers. Radios were among the first mass-produced goods to be made of plastic. They offered news, drama, humor, entertainment, and personalities, and provided advertisers with an effective method of cultivating a widely dispersed national market. Despite congressional proposals to ban commercial advertising and network reluctance to quote advertising prices on the air, network sponsors spent $7 million a year on radio time by 1927.

Automobile maker Henry Ford, a leading folk and business idol of the age, described machinery as the new messiah of the 1920s. Ford's Model-T, which sold for as little as $295 in 1928, offered the possibility of instant mobility for millions of Americans of modest means. The automobile gave immediate status to all buyers. Car producers sold just under two million vehicles in 1919, but by 1929, the industry marketed over 5.6 million a year. When the decade closed, two of every three households in the nation owned a "flivver." Automobile manufacturing accounted for one-eighth of all industrial activity, making it the New Era's most important commodity stimulus to investment

Exhibit 5–4. Number of Electrical Appliances in Use, 1923–1928
(in rounded millions)

	1923	*1928*
Flatirons	7.0m	15.3m
Washing machines	2.9m	5.0m
Vacuum cleaners	3.8m	6.8m
Fans	3.5m	4.9m
Heaters	1.3m	2.6m
Toasters	1.0m	4.5m
Refrigerators	27,000	0.8m

Source: *Recent Economic Changes* (1929)

**Exhibit 5–5. Increases in Retail Installment Sales, 1923–1926
(in rounded millions of dollars)**

Automobiles	$458m
Radio sets	$115m
Washing machines	$37m
Mechanical refrigerators	$50m
Clothing (to 1925)	$125m
All retail installment sales	$1100m

Source: *Recent Economic Changes* (1929)

and total output. The automobile boom also created millions of jobs in auxiliary industries from steel and rubber to fuel servicing and road construction. The Federal Highway Act of 1921, which created the Bureau of Public Roads to plan a system of national highways, provided the government's first matching grants to states for highway building. By decade's end, expenditures on road construction surpassed $1 billion a year.

"I'll go without food before I'll see us give up the car," a working-class wife in Indiana told researchers in the late 1920s. Since most automobile owners bought on time, the choice was often grounded in reality. Installment purchases accounted for at least half the cars sold by General Motors at mid-decade. Credit sales of automobiles and trucks reached approximately $3 billion during 1925, accounting for more than half of all retail installment sales. Credit purchases, in turn, accounted for some 15 percent of total retail revenues. Buying on time was so popular in 1929, General Motors vice-president John J. Raskob proposed selling stock market certificates on the same basis. "No one can become rich by saving," Raskob informed readers of the *Ladies Home Journal,* thereby expressing the central dynamic of New Era consumerism.

Like the installment plan, advertising sustained the consumer economy. By 1927, advertisers spent $1.5 billion annually to promote American buying habits, a figure that would translate into fifteen dollars per capita by decade's end. A few literary intellectuals such as Matthew Josephson believed that advertising contained a primitive folk poetry that reflected and appealed to the appetites and sentiments of the common people. But most print and radio advertisements incorporated conformist calls for "style consciousness" and psychological inducements such as fear of social isolation or the promotion of family unity. Advertising contributed to the tripling of household expenditures between 1909 and 1929. By the close of the decade, annual personal

**Exhibit 5–6. Expenditures for Magazine Advertising, 1921–1927
(in rounded millions of dollars)**

1921	$95.7m
1927	$176.8m

Source: *Recent Economic Changes* (1929)

Chainstores such as this market in Portland, Oregon played an increasing role in the merchandising strategies of the 1920s. The number of chain outlets jumped over five times between 1918 and 1929.

spending totaled $77.3 billion, a staggering figure triggered by dramatic increases in outlays for amusements, leisure pursuits, clothing, personal appearance, furniture, and automobiles.

"We live in a Fordized America," declared Boston department store entrepreneur Edward A. Filene. The inventor of the "bargain basement" and the employee credit union, Filene attributed New Era prosperity to chain stores that distributed mass-produced items at low prices to a mass market of consumers. During the nineteenth century, the Great Atlantic and Pacific Tea Company revolutionized the grocery industry through the national distribution of foods in A & P chain stores. Between 1918 and 1929, chain syndicates such as J. C. Penney and Woolworth moved into the variety and sundries fields, increasing the number of chain outlets from 30,000 to 160,000. Like Henry Ford, Filene drew the connection between economic prosperity and widely diffused purchasing power, proclaiming that leisure time and high wages enabled workers to pump their earnings back into the system as consumers. "Slowly we are learning that low wages for labor do not necessarily mean high profits for capital," concurred General Electric's Owen D. Young.

In *The Present Economic Revolution in the United States* (1925), Harvard's Thomas Nixon Carver asserted that New Era economic democracy gave consumers the freedom to choose among varied and affordable products. The *Magazine of Business* even boasted that the "average woman" prized the vacuum cleaner and electric iron more than the vote and favorably compared the fruits of corporate democracy with the reforms of William Jennings Bryan and Robert M. LaFollette. Former muckrakers like Lincoln Steffens, Ida

Exhibit 5–7. Price Changes, 1922–1927

Security prices	+9.1%
Wages	+2.8%
Retail food prices	+2.4%
Automobile prices	+0.9%
Rents	0.0%
Transportation costs	−1.5%
Index of general price level	+1.5%

Source: *Recent Economic Changes* (1929)

Tarbell, and Socialist John Spargo agreed that scientific management and mass distribution had revitalized American society. "Today in America we are building a new civilization," concluded American Telephone and Telegraph's (AT&T's) Walter S. Gifford in 1925.

MANAGERIAL PROGRESSIVES

Corporate leaders before World War I, such as Mark Hanna and George Perkins, envisioned a society in which the fruits of capitalism would be widely distributed to uplift the quality of life for all Americans. This democracy of consumers depended upon responsible corporation managers. The Harvard Graduate School of Business Administration, founded in 1908, and other prestigious institutions sought to elevate corporate administration to professional status by focusing upon the importance of cooperation, scientific management, and rational planning. These creeds of corporate responsibility received a severe testing during World War I, when the War Industries Board mobilized a peacetime economy for massive military support. "Our industry came re-born out of the intense experience of the war," WIB chairman Bernard Baruch later recalled. By the 1920s, a "new generation" of business professionals—led by General Electric's Owen Young and Gerard Swope, AT&T's Walter Gifford, General Motors' Alfred P. Sloan, Jr., and paper products entrepreneur and American Management Association founder Henry S. Dennison—rose to the forefront of American corporate officialdom.

New Era business leaders pictured themselves as trustees for the public and employees. Acknowledging their obligations to stockholders and the profit motive, professional managers nevertheless sought to tie ethical standards, social responsibility, and the spirit of service to corporate goals. "Service always pays better than selfishness," Henry Ford insisted in *My Philosophy of Industry* (1929), reiterating a widely held notion that the success of large corporations depended upon the goodwill of the consuming public. As part of the effort to professionalize corporate management and develop useful public relations, 750 business firms subscribed to the United States Chamber of Commerce's national code of ethics by 1925. "Everywhere are new forces touching the conduct of business," declared the new *Business Week* in 1929.

OWEN D. YOUNG
1874–1962

On June 4, 1927, General Electric board chairman Owen D. Young stood before three thousand people to deliver the dedication address for Harvard University's expanded Graduate School of Business Administration. The event symbolized American society's acceptance of business professionalism and marked a personal triumph for Young, whose complete remarks were printed in the forthcoming *Harvard Business Review.*

Born on an eighty-acre farm in upstate New York, Young attended a one-room schoolhouse before graduating from St. Lawrence University in 1894. He hoped to enter Harvard Law School, but settled on Boston University when school officials in Cambridge discouraged his plans to attend classes while working part-time. After graduation, Young joined a Boston law firm and cultivated clients in the burgeoning electrical industry. These contacts led to an offer to join General Electric as general counsel and vice-president in 1913.

As a corporate attorney, Young assumed responsibility for negotiating patent disputes and labor conflicts. During World War I, he settled a strike at General Electric's plant in Lynn, Massachusetts, the last labor trouble the company experienced until the late 1930s. The young vice-president maintained that worker unrest extended beyond wage and hour issues to intangible psychological concerns such as employee powerlessness. His theory influenced the report of the Second Industrial Conference of 1920 and brought Young an appointment to President Harding's Conference on Unemployment. Young soon found himself with full-time commitments to the developing fields of industrial and public relations. In 1922, General Electric's directors selected the skillful attorney as corporate chairman of the board.

By the mid-1920s, Young not only presided over the largest electrical products corporation in the world, but sat on the board of powerful General Motors. He also served as executive committee chairman for Radio Corporation of America (RCA), which he had organized in 1919 by arranging to pool radio technology developed by several major corporations. With the progressive Gerard Swope as president, Young increased General Electric's emphasis on consumer sales of large appliances instead of capital goods for industry. He stressed a "new capitalism" that fostered cooperation with both government and labor and reflected General Electric's need to cultivate the long-range goodwill of the public. *(cont.)*

Proponents of the new management argued that long-range administrative planning and scientific methods ensured the permanent conquest of the business cycle. Large corporations had worked with competitors in the commodity committees of the War Industries Board, where they shared information, divided markets and resources, fixed prices, and established common labor policies. After the war, business leaders in the oil, cotton textile, lumber, construction, and other industries formed trade organizations independent of government involvement. Often dominated by major corpo-

Young endorsed Herbert Hoover's concept of corporate self-regulation under government supervision. And he extended profit sharing, pensions, and life and unemployment insurance to the company's work force. "Business is constantly on the firing line, adopting new methods and exploring new areas," he explained to former muckraker Ida Tarbell. Early in 1927, he appeared on the cover of *System*, the leading management journal in the nation.

"Today and here," Young declared when he spoke at Harvard, "business finally assumes the obligations of a profession." Young noted that 55 percent of Harvard's 1916 graduating class had entered business. Professional business schools would provide the data for enlightened decision making and rational policy in an increasingly complex world, he promised. The "self-imposed rules" of the trade association, Young proclaimed, would thereby shape business morality and enable corporate professionals to honor ideals of service and social responsibility. "Perhaps some day," he told the assembly, corporations might organize cooperative undertakings so that workers could simply buy capital and be entitled to all profits above cost. This would produce a democratic industry without "hired men," Young speculated.

General Electric's chairman saw himself as a trustee for the company's fifty thousand stockholders and one-hundred thousand employees as well as consumers and the general public. He boasted that the large corporations of the New Era had "completely divorced ownership from responsibility." "I can indict the capitalistic system as well as the bolshevist. I know its failures as well as he," Young told students at Bryn Mawr College in 1928. But the resourceful board chairman foresaw "a world of new experiment" that would ensure comfort and economic advancement for consumers as well as a "cultural wage" to permit intellectual development by the working class.

Young represented the idealized corporate professional of the New Era. Although admitting that business "provided satisfactory financial rewards," he insisted that the "widening intellectual horizon" of corporate life stretched minds and stimulated the imagination. Young personally embodied such standards by participating in national industrial conferences and by conducting negotiations for adoption of the Dawes and Young plans for Europe's postwar financial recovery.

By 1932, Young's insistence on domestic economic revitalization brought mention of his name as a possible Democratic candidate for the presidency. More than any single figure of his generation, Owen D. Young personified the consistency between progressive ideals and the imperatives of the American corporate economy. ∎

rations, the nation's four thousand trade associations engaged in industry-wide research and market extension campaigns, strove to improve productive efficiency, and cooperated to frame codes of business ethics.

Trade associations helped promote more effective budgeting techniques, business forecasting, the elimination of waste, and standardization and simplification of parts. This application of scientific management contributed to a 70 percent improvement in worker productivity between 1919 and 1929. Trade organizations also insulated large firms from the competitive tactics of new businesses and the risk of government intervention. To the delight of proponents like Secretary of Commerce Herbert Hoover, they provided an example of how "destructive" competition and economic individualism could be replaced by rational cooperation and planning. Trade associations embodied the New Era hope that harmony, abundance, and progress would prevail over political controversy, social conflict, and class strife. Federal Trade Commission chairman William E. Humphrey even claimed that Washington trade representatives spoke "with the voice of the people" and constituted a "sort of parliament."

PROGRESS AND POVERTY

Despite the optimism of corporate leaders, New Era prosperity proved highly selective. An initial wave of business mergers shook American industry between 1895 and 1903. Then, after twenty-two years of relative stability, entrepreneurs staged nearly six thousand combinations between 1925 and 1931. By the end of the 1920s, three automobile companies—General Motors, Ford, and Chrysler—produced 83 percent of the nation's cars. Monopolies consolidated domination over aluminum, salt, sugar, and tropical fruits. Mergers tightened the control of oligopolies of two to four corporations in petroleum, steel, glass, cement, copper, tobacco, meat packing, milk, and bread. Such consolidation accounted for the extinction of nearly five thousand manufacturing and mining firms during the 1920s. In the retail field, chain stores increased their share of sales from 4 percent in 1921 to 16 percent in 1927. Stimulated by the tripling of profits in consumer and service industries in the decade, Wall Street speculators further accelerated the mania for economic consolidation. By 1930, the two hundred largest corporations in the United States controlled just under half of all nonbanking corporate wealth.

Economic growth centered in white-collar and service industries such as banking, communications, sales, and utilities, where employment jumped by nearly half in the 1920s. Occupations in these sectors constituted nearly one-fourth of the national labor force by the end of the decade. Thus millions of Americans escaped blue-collar drudgery, although salaries often lagged behind increased status. Many of the new positions went to married women, who expanded their participation in the work force from 1.9 million to 3.1 million between 1921 and 1924, and eagerly assumed roles as clerks, saleswomen, and stenographers in the thriving service economy.

While the service industries prospered, factory employment failed to rise. In the depressed textile and shoe industries, job rates slackened severely. Moreover, the replacement of skilled labor with unskilled workers in the new assembly line industries changed the nature of industrial toil. As managers focused on productivity and efficiency, speed replaced experience and judgment as a necessary quality on the assembly line. Consequently, factories began to insist on age limits for hiring. Critics commented that factory workers increasingly resembled dehumanized automatons, endlessly repeating specific tasks and losing all control over work rhythms and routines.

White-collar routine as portrayed in a 1925 film, The Crowd. *Employment in white-collar and service industries jumped by nearly half in the 1920s. Routinization of middle-class labor led to increased emphasis on leisure-time activity.*

Silent-film comedians such as Buster Keaton and Charlie Chaplin portrayed the futility of the "small-man hero" in coping with the dehumanizing power of machinery in mass production.

For the affluent, the New Era economy provided lucrative areas of investment in the stock market, real estate, and the emerging service and consumer industries. The wealthiest 5 percent of American income recipients actually added to their share of total income during the 1920s. While overall wages rose, however, more than two-fifths of the nation's households lived at what the Brookings Institution described as "subsistence-and-poverty" levels in 1929. Another 36 percent enjoyed only a "minimum comfort level." Seventy-one percent of all families earned less than $2500 a year. And the income of the poorest 42 percent of Americans equaled that of the richest 0.1 percent. Despite the visions of New Era enthusiasts, small farmers, agricul-

Exhibit 5–8. White Collar and Manual Employees, 1920–1930 (in rounded millions)

	White Collar	Manual	All Employees
1920	10.5m	17.0m	42.2m
1930	14.3m	19.3m	48.7m

Source: *Historical Statistics of the United States, Colonial Times to 1970* (1975)

Exhibit 5–9. Productivity of Manufacturing Workers, 1920–1927
(1899 = 100) (output per person)

1920	107.9
1923	132.5
1927	149.5

Source: *Recent Economic Changes* (1929)

Exhibit 5–10. Unemployment, 1923–1929
(percentage of civilian labor force)

1923	2.4%
1925	3.2%
1927	3.3%
1929	3.2%

Source: *Historical Statistics of the United States, Colonial Times to 1970* (1975)

tural laborers and tenants, coal and textile workers, blacks, and Native Americans remained in varying stages of poverty (see chapter 4). These inequities jeopardized corporate hopes for permanent prosperity and social peace.

MANAGEMENT AND LABOR

Industrial managers hoped to avoid class antagonism through "welfare capitalism" and a "human approach to industry." World War I had taught business leaders the importance of morale to labor stability and productive efficiency. "People do the best work when they are best cared for," observed John H. Patterson, a pioneer in corporate welfare techniques at National Cash Register. The human approach to industry stressed higher wages, improved working conditions, employee representation, fringe benefits, and profit sharing. Half the nation's large corporations had industrial relations departments in which psychologists applied themselves to problems of worker depersonalization and lack of consistency. Companies like General Motors, Firestone, and Eastman Kodak provided group insurance, private pension plans, and stock ownership through payroll deduction. United States Steel

Exhibit 5–11. Consumer Price Index, 1920–1928
(1967 = 100)

1920	60.0
1922	50.2
1924	51.2
1926	53.0
1928	51.3

Source: *Historical Statistics of the United States, Colonial Times to 1970* (1975)

offered employee medical services, sports clubs, and self-improvement classes. Other firms supplied low-cost cafeterias, locker rooms, showers, libraries, and even employee swimming pools.

To advance worker representation, many corporations devised shop committees and company unions and councils. Although managers promoted these groups as experiments in industrial democracy, company officials rarely delegated responsibility or power and prohibited most unions from dealing with crucial wage and hours issues. *Labor Age* complained in 1927 that General Electric pampered employee committee members with steaks while refusing to discuss issues such as pay increases for workers.

Although employee turnover halved in the 1920s, labor relations were the most difficult challenge for New Era management. Wartime tolerance for trade unions had evaporated during the labor strife of 1919, when industrial leaders feared the effects of international communism on the immigrant working class. Corporate managers who viewed themselves as trustees for the economic order seldom relinquished cherished prerogatives. "I will not permit myself to be in a position of having labor dictate to management," declared Charles Schwab of Bethlehem Steel. Such reasoning found support among corporations that participated in the open-shop campaign against trade unions organized by the National Association of Manufacturers (NAM). Insisting that employment not be contingent upon union membership, the NAM was highly successful in new industries such as automaking, utilities, petrochemicals, and rubber. In growing production centers in Detroit, Seattle, and Los Angeles, the open-shop campaign portrayed collective bargaining as alien to American traditions. Hostility to unionism also surfaced in newly industrialized areas of the South, the mountain states, and the Midwest.

Antiunion activity found a receptive climate in the nation's courts. In *American Steel Foundries v. Tri-City Central Trades Council* (1921), the Supreme Court upheld the use of injunctions against unions for purposes of "equity" and ruled all union picketing illegal when it involved more than one person. The following year, a decision in *United Mine Workers v. Coronado Coal Co.* held unions liable for damages when strikes affected interstate commerce or involved the destruction of property. Despite an $8 million legal effort by the United Mine Workers, federal courts also sustained injunctions enforcing "yellow-dog" contracts in West Virginia coal mines after federal troops squashed a strike in 1921. These contracts prohibited union membership among new workers, and the injunctions enforcing them made union officers liable to contempt of court if they induced miners to strike.

Traditional craft unions compounded their difficulties by a sluggish response to the shift from manual to white-collar work. Since office workers and service personnel saw themselves as new members of the middle class, they tended to rebuff union affiliation, which they associated with manual labor. Mass production also replaced many of the traditional craft workers who once made up the core of organized labor. Assembly line industries such as automobile manufacturing now drew heavily upon semiskilled immigrants and migrants from the rural countryside, workers who were ignored by union activists until the 1930s. Moreover, the conservative craft unions of the American Federation of Labor hesitated to organize blacks or women. Fewer

Exhibit 5–12. Employees Engaged in Manufacturing, 1920–1927 (in millions)

1920	10.7m
1922	9.0m
1925	9.9m
1927	9.7m

Source: *Recent Economic Changes* (1929)

than 3 percent of all working women belonged to unions in 1929, as compared with 11 percent of men. The constitutions or rituals of twenty-four international unions directly excluded black workers, forcing many to seek employment in open-shop industries such as automaking and steel, or to accept work as strikebreakers.

Under the leadership of William Green, who succeeded Samuel Gompers as AFL president in 1924, organized labor strove to recover the respectability that had defined its image before the chaotic strikes of 1919. Green saw the union movement as an auxiliary to business and stressed concord rather than conflict. Committed to New Era goals of increased output and industrial peace, he reiterated Gompers's advocacy of capitalist order and enmity to bolshevism and radicalism. When police and Virginia state militia forcibly crushed a cotton mill strike in the late 1920s, the AFL quickly abandoned its attempt to organize the southern textile industry. Subsequent strikes in the Piedmont mills of North Carolina and Tennessee brought national publicity over vigilante action against unionists, but the Communist party, not the AFL, supported the strikers in these bitter conflicts.

Organized labor also failed to protect workers in declining industries. The garment unions, for example, had no choice but to supervise layoffs in an industry plagued by both the popularity of synthetic fibers and short dresses and the exodus of small clothing producers to nonunion sections of the South and West. The International Ladies Garment Workers Union saw its predominantly female membership plummet from 120,000 in the early 1920s to forty-five thousand by 1932. In the coal industry, the United Mine Workers tried to hold the line against falling wages caused by the increased use of petroleum. A 1922 strike in hard coal resulted in an eight-hour day and collective bargaining rights. But by mid-decade, northern operators in soft coal moved to destroy the union, using both violence and layoffs. By 1930, UMW membership had tumbled from 450,000 to 150,000.

Only in the railroad industry did organized labor survive with any effectiveness. A strike of four-hundred thousand AFL shopcraft workers brought rail transportation to a halt in 1922. This was the largest walkout of the decade and the first railroad strike since the Pullman conflict of 1894. When Attorney General Harry Daugherty won a federal injunction, the strike failed. Yet, four years later, the Watson-Parker Act recognized collective bargaining for railroad workers, although it prohibited strikes during a sixty-day negotiations period. Given organized labor's mood of conciliation and limited objectives, the legislation appeared to be a minor victory.

Pennsylvania coal miners on strike. Despite labor militance, declining employment in the depressed coal industry left the United Mine Workers with one-third of their membership by 1930.

By 1933, hostility to unionism, poor labor strategy, and economic depression had reduced union membership from more than five million in 1920 to less than three million. Not since the 1890s had organized labor experienced such difficulty.

THE HARDING CONSENSUS

"America's present need is not heroics but healing," declared Republican presidential candidate Warren G. Harding in 1920, "not nostrums but normalcy, not revolution but restoration, not agitation but adjustment . . ." Harding was a handsome but undistinguished senator from Ohio, where he had risen to prominence as the owner of a printing establishment in the small town of Marion. He won the presidential nomination when Republican progressives and conservatives settled on a compromise candidate. The nominee pictured himself as a "white-haired progressive" who had adopted the latest techniques in his printing firm. Consequently, Harding had no objection when rank-and-file progressives insisted that Governor Calvin Coolidge of Massachusetts be the party's vice-presidential choice. Coolidge had won popular appeal with an upright tone and successful suppression of the Boston police strike of 1919.

Harding's campaign captured a nostalgia for prewar stability and hometown virtue. Mainstream Republicans sensed that middle-class voters had been overwhelmed by the emotional excesses of World War I, the debate over the League of Nations, and the strains of the Red Scare. "Too much has been said of bolshevism in America," Harding proclaimed. The candidate instead talked about the "Marion Idea" of neighborly cooperation and classless democracy, denounced "executive autocracy" and "government paternalism," and charged that excessive statism would "make us a nation of dependent incompetents."

The Republican candidate hoped that international peace and corporate prosperity would reduce political strife and build a coherent national consensus. Although Harding spoke only fleetingly of issues such as lower taxes and a high tariff, his relaxed confidence and sense of goodwill prevailed at the polls. The Republican ticket took 60.4 percent of the popular vote over Democratic governor James M. Cox of Ohio and his running mate, assistant Navy secretary Franklin D. Roosevelt, Theodore's cousin. Cox's popular tally surpassed Woodrow Wilson's victorious 1916 total, but Harding's sixteen million votes nearly doubled the amount previously won by the Republicans. Carrying every state outside the South, and Tennessee as well, Harding and Coolidge swept to an overwhelming margin of 404–127 in the Electoral College. Meanwhile, Republicans added to their majorities in both houses of Congress and amassed a plurality of 1.6 million votes in the nation's twelve

President Warren G. Harding (left) and Vice-President Calvin Coolidge (right), easy victors in the 1920 race for the White House. Harding and Coolidge hoped to build a political consensus based on business prosperity and good will.

Exhibit 5–13. Election of 1920.

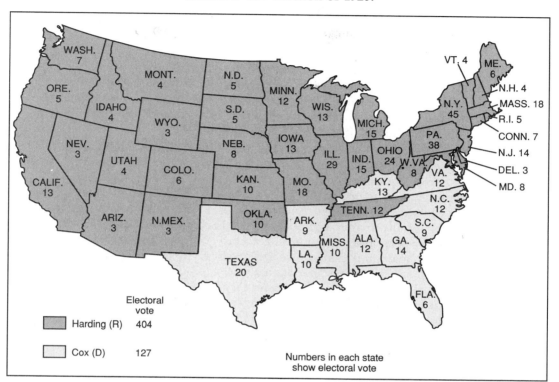

Electoral vote

Harding (R) 404

Cox (D) 127

Numbers in each state show electoral vote

largest cities, sure signs that the Wilsonian coalition of rural southerners, westerners, and urbanites had not survived World War I.

Beginning in 1920, women's suffrage contributed to an increase in ballots cast. Yet voter participation never surpassed 57 percent in presidential elections of the 1920s, a continuation of a trend of low turnouts that dated back to the Progressive years. Voting rates reached their lowest levels in the large industrial cities where working-class ethnics lived. Poor turnout suggested both a pervasive apathy to national political issues and the reluctance of eligible women from immigrant families to cast ballots when patriarchal cultural traditions discouraged such participation.

Harding sought to fulfill his promise of reduced political discord by pardoning Socialist party leader Eugene V. Debs, imprisoned under wartime sedition laws. Despite his incarceration, Debs had received over nine-hundred thousand votes (3.4 percent of the total) as a presidential candidate in the 1920 election. Harding invited Debs to the White House, where the two reportedly chatted and smoked cigars.

The president also acted to honor his commitment to lower taxes by extending a free hand to Secretary of the Treasury Andrew Mellon, a multimillionaire Pittsburgh industrialist and financier. Mellon worked with Budget Director Charles G. Dawes, a Chicago banker, to reduce government

expenses and thereby relieve corporations and wealthy individuals of bur-
donsome taxation. "I have never viewed taxation as a means of rewarding
one class of taxpayers or punishing another," explained Mellon. But the
treasury secretary argued that lower taxes would free affluent individuals and
corporations to invest their capital and create jobs and prosperity. During
1921, Mellon persuaded Congress to repeal the wartime excess-profits tax and
cut maximum income surtaxes to 50 percent, while raising postage rates,
excise taxes, and licensing fees. These regressive tax policies ultimately
impeded the distribution of consumer purchasing power and encouraged
unsound speculation by those with surplus capital.

Even before Mellon's fiscal program took effect, the administration responded to a serious economic depression. As government spending for
wartime necessities ended, industrial output halved between 1920 and 1921
and unemployment soared to 12 percent. "One walked through miles upon
miles of deserted mills," a New York banker later recalled, "wondering what
had become of the many thousand human beings who had tended the
machines." In response, commerce secretary Hoover urged Harding to
convene the Washington Conference on Unemployment in September 1921.
The meeting marked the first time a president had called national attention to
joblessness. As a result, 225 cities created local emergency committees and
voluntary relief groups. Meanwhile, Congress passed the Federal Highway
Act and allotted $450 million for state and local public works. The president's
Conference on Unemployment also commissioned an analysis of business
cycles by the National Bureau of Economics Research, a private council.
Released in 1923, the unprecedented report suggested that economic slumps
resulted from waste, extravagance, speculation, inflation, and inefficiency
developed during booms.

The 1921 depression stimulated Hoover to obtain increased congressional
funds to reorganize the Bureau of Foreign and Domestic Commerce into the

Exhibit 5–14. Unemployment, 1920–1922
(percentage of civilian labor force)

1920	5.2%
1921	11.7%
1922	6.7%

Source: *Historical Statistics of the United States, Colonial Times to 1970* (1975)

Exhibit 5–15. Gross National Product, 1920–1922
(in rounded billions of dollars at current prices)

1920	$91.5b
1921	$69.6b
1922	$74.1b

Source: *Historical Statistics of the United States, Colonial Times to 1970* (1975)

thirty-seven commodity lines most often found in overseas trade. The bureau became a clearinghouse for the collection and dissemination of commercial statistics. Beginning in July 1921, *A Survey of Current Business* published monthly data on current production, prices, and inventories. Hoover also expanded the Bureau of Standards to promote his campaign to standardize industrial weights, measures, sizes, and designs.

"We are passing from a period of extremely individualistic action into a period of associational activities," declared the commerce secretary in *American Individualism* (1922). Speaking of an "American System," Hoover hoped to reconcile the nation's corporate structure and democratic heritage by promoting voluntary organizations. He believed that government could assist trade associations, professional societies, farm marketing organizations, and labor groups to strive for efficiency and cooperation. Hoover's "cooperative" capitalism sought to preserve individual initiative and private enterprise by minimizing the domination of single corporations, powerful cartels, and government bureaucracies. Such "associated" or "tempered" individualism, he argued, would preserve both American liberty and economic success. Under Hoover's leadership, the Department of Commerce organized education conferences to lay the groundwork for regulation of the new radio and commercial aviation industries, and promoted trade associations and agricultural marketing societies. The Capper-Volstead Act of 1922 exempted farm produce organizations from antitrust legislation and permitted them to process and market staples in interstate commerce. The Department of Commerce also authorized $300 million in government loans to agricultural associations between 1921 and 1924.

Hoover's penchant for industrial efficiency brought him into a major controversy over oil pollution in ocean waters. In 1921, the secretary convened a conference of fish commissioners from Atlantic and Gulf Coast states and argued that 90 percent of oil pollution came from coastal shipping. Over resistance from the American Petroleum Institute and Standard Oil, Congress passed the Oil Pollution Act of 1924, but the law merely provided modest fines for polluting coastal waters.

The Harding administration preferred to emphasize the social benefit of corporate values. But cooperation between business and government could easily be exploited for selfish ends. By 1923, Senate hearings revealed outright collusion between government officials and corporate leaders in the domestic oil industry. Secretary of the Interior Albert B. Fall had leased valuable government petroleum reserves, including the Teapot Dome area of Wyoming, to private interests. In return, Fall had received more than $300,000 in bribe payments. A special government prosecution team also discovered multimillion-dollar graft in the newly created Veterans Bureau and kickbacks to Attorney General Daugherty through the office of the alien property custodian. By 1924, the secretary of interior was in prison, the attorney general had resigned in disgrace, the secretary of the Navy had barely escaped conviction, and two other Harding officials had committed suicide. Yet, as the Senate hearings persisted, many Americans seemed to lose interest.

President Warren G. Harding tosses an opening day baseball into play. Harding sought to bring postwar America back to moderation and consensus. He remained a popular figure until his death in 1923.

"I cannot hope to be one of the great presidents," Harding once confided, "but perhaps I may be remembered as one of the best loved." Nevertheless, the president's amiable tolerance for personal cronies led to the Teapot Dome scandals and political embarrassment. Demoralized by early evidence of the betrayal of friends, Harding suffered a stroke while on a West Coast speaking tour in August 1923 and died a few days later in a San Francisco hotel room. Responsibility for facing the mounting administration scandals fell to Calvin Coolidge.

COOLIDGE ECONOMICS

After months of silence on the matter, Coolidge defused the Teapot Dome affair by quietly replacing discredited Attorney General Daugherty with Harlan Fiske Stone, a highly esteemed former dean of Columbia Law School.

Stone fired William J. Burns, the director of the Federal Bureau of Investigation, and ordered newly appointed J. Edgar Hoover to professionalize criminal investigations through the use of new techniques such as finger-printing. Reflecting New Era optimism over political stability, he also directed Hoover to discontinue anti-radical surveillance. Meanwhile, the new president's cool head prevailed during a potentially disruptive anthracite coal strike in Pennsylvania late in 1923. Pressed by northeastern congressional representatives to forcibly end the conflict and ensure fuel supplies for the winter, Coolidge stepped aside and permitted Governor Gifford Pinchot to arrange a settlement on terms favorable to the strikers. The president then let the newly elected progressive governor take the onus for the price increases passed on to consumers. To balance his political support, Coolidge appealed to Republican progressives by publicly embarrassing U. S. Steel into abandoning the twelve-hour day. And as the 1924 Republican convention approached, he courted progressive Idaho senator William E. Borah by offering him the vice-presidential nomination. Although Borah refused and a scattering of Republican progressives sought to bolt the ticket, Coolidge remained in full control of the party by 1924.

A dour, silent, and canny politician, Calvin Coolidge embodied the aura of Yankee austerity and respectability that voters sought in a period of easy money and frenzied speculation. The president's clear and distinct speaking voice, broadcast on monthly radio addresses during the election year, earned him a rating as the fourth most popular radio personality in the nation by mid-decade. Acknowledging that "the chief business of the American people is business," Coolidge selected Budget Director Dawes as his vice-presidential running mate. The Republicans faced little competition from the Democrats' conservative Wall Street nominee John W. Davis and Nebraskan Charles Bryan, chosen in the bitterly divided 1924 convention (see chapter 4). And even a strong third-party effort by progressive Robert M. LaFollette (16.6 percent of the popular vote) failed to prevent a Coolidge landslide. Focusing on LaFollette's alleged radicalism and urging the country to "keep cool with Coolidge," the Republican ticket nearly doubled the Democratic popular vote and dominated the Electoral College with an impressive 382–136–13 margin.

Buoyed by the voters' mandate for conservative economic policies, treasury secretary Mellon proceeded with his program of tax relief for the affluent. Accordingly, the Revenue Act of 1926 wiped out the gift tax, cut estate taxes by half, and trimmed the surtax on incomes to 20 percent. Two years later, Congress reduced taxes by over $220 million and gave Treasury refunds to large corporations. By the end of the decade, government spending had been halved, the national debt reduced by one-third, and taxes on the wealthy and corporations lessened by $350 million a year.

Coolidge's Federal Trade Commission (FTC) further reflected the administration's endorsement of corporate methods and goals. The Supreme Court had ruled in 1920 that U. S. Steel's large size and monopoly status did not violate the "rule of reason" because prosecutors had not proven that the corporation engaged in overt coercion or predatory practices. Once Coolidge appointed corporate attorney and lumber lobbyist William Humphrey as

Exhibit 5–16. Election of 1924.

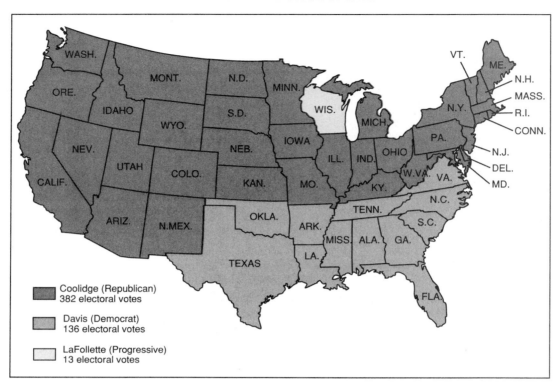

Coolidge (Republican)
382 electoral votes

Davis (Democrat)
136 electoral votes

LaFollette (Progressive)
13 electoral votes

chairman of the FTC in 1925, the regulatory agency narrowed its supervision of unfair methods of competition. With Humphrey at the helm, the bureau investigated only cases in which unfair practices were explicitly detrimental to the public interest, and then settled matters in private sessions with offenders. Frequently it referred these informal agreements, or "stipulations," to trade practice conferences, which left corporations to "self-rule." An FTC summary in 1927 described the agency's task as "helping business to help itself."

Under Chief Justice William Howard Taft, appointed by Harding as a gesture to conservatives in 1921, the Supreme Court grappled with the legal contradictions between corporate cooperation and free competition. At first the Court ruled in *American Column and Lumber Co. v. United States* (1921) that exchange of information by trade associations violated restraint of trade laws. But four years later the majority legitimized cooperation within trade associations in *Maple Flooring Association v. United States*. By supporting commerce secretary Hoover's position, the Court upheld the exchange of statistics in trade associations if no price or production control was involved. Acknowledging the transition from a competitive economy to a corporate system, the Court ruled that traditional concepts of free competition took secondary importance to the circulation of information needed to prevent overproduction and economic crises. Thus, the Court accepted the argument that technology forced individuals to depend on large corporations for the necessities of life and that corporations must be free to engage in cooperative efforts to improve industrial efficiency.

The Taft Court also broadened the use of federal power under the interstate commerce clause of the Constitution. Ruling on the Esch-Cummins Transportation Act of 1920 in two separate cases, it upheld the Interstate Commerce Commission's right to raise *intrastate* railroad rates and to administer a revolving fund to distribute company profits to weaker lines. In *Stafford v. Wallace* (1922), the Court sustained the Packers and Stockyards Act of 1921, a law forbidding interstate meat packers from engaging in unfair market practices. The Court thereby sanctioned congressional regulation of grain exchanges to prevent fraudulent and manipulated prices. Taft's majority opinion stated that Congress had the right to regulate interstate commerce when it was obstructed, and that Congress had the power to determine when that had occurred. Despite this expansion of the commerce clause, however, the Court ruled in *Bailey v. Drexel* (1922) that Congress could not use the tax power to control child labor. The following year, *Adkins v. Children's Hospital* established that minimum wage laws for female workers violated the contractual rights of labor in a free market, although women's wages averaged only 57 percent of men's by decade's end.

In 1927, a great flood of the Mississippi River brought a dramatic opportunity to test commerce secretary Hoover's belief in voluntary solutions to social problems. Hoover immediately created the Special Mississippi Flood Committee to coordinate relief efforts by scores of government agencies and private groups such as the Red Cross. With the river swollen to a fifty-mile width at points, the commerce secretary relied on grass roots voluntarism to construct 150 refugee camps to house 325,000 people. The committee also coordinated fund raising by statewide credit corporations. Hoover, in turn, encouraged local chambers of commerce to invest in the credit corporations, so that $17 million of the $20 million spent by the flood committee stemmed from private sources. The secretary of commerce proclaimed that the successful project demonstrated the combination of organization, "neighborly helpfulness," and individualism that accounted for the superior quality of life in America.

Hoover never forgot the Mississippi disaster's lessons. Although midwesterners continued to settle on the dangerous floodplains, Congress appropriated $300 million for levees, drainage basins, and spillways in the Jones-Reid Act of 1928, an early step toward government management of river ecology. Hoover's popular blend of corporate planning and voluntarism earned him a reputation as the "boy wonder" of the Coolidge cabinet and the Republican party.

BUSINESS INTERNATIONALISM

During 1928, German economist Moritz J. Bonn used the pages of the *Atlantic Monthly* to declare that the United States had carried the Declaration of

Independence "to its logical conclusion . . . it is no longer a European colony in the economic sense." The same theme pervaded Bureau of Foreign and Domestic Commerce director Julius Klein's *Frontiers of Trade* (1929), which stated that the nations' foreign economic activity had stimulated and stabilized the prosperity of the 1920s. As the United States emerged as the leading creditor in the world, American financiers and banks channeled billions into overseas loans and investments in the postwar decade. Americans also became the world's leading sellers of goods, accounting for nearly 16 percent of all global exports by the late 1920s. Foreign commodity sales leaped by nearly 60 percent between 1922 and 1926. At decade's end, overseas customers purchased an annual $541 million of cars and parts from the United States, as well as $561 million of oil products and $601 million of machinery.

Multinational American corporations increased the nation's global economic power by dramatically expanded foreign operations after World War I. Led by International Telephone and Telegraph (organized in 1920), Pan American Airways, General Motors, Ford, General Electric, and Standard Oil, over thirteen hundred wholly American owned or controlled corporations permeated the European economy by 1929. These multinational companies held worldwide assets but derived most of their capital from and sent most of their profits to the United States. Their activity helped account for an $8.5 billion return on American overseas investment between 1920 and 1933.

Since New Era government administrators believed that foreign investment and trade were essential to domestic prosperity and stability, they placed great importance upon providing an appropriate international climate for American corporations and banks. Commerce secretary Hoover and the State Department shared Woodrow Wilson's desire to break down national empires and create an "open door" for American business opportunity. Under Hoover, the Department of Commerce sharply opposed foreign cartels

Exhibit 5–17. American Foreign Investment, 1922–1927
(in rounded billions of dollars)

1922	$8.5b
1925	$10.4b
1927	$12.2b

Source: *Recent Economic Changes* (1929)

Exhibit 5–18. Imports and Exports of Goods and Services, 1922–1928
(in rounded billions of dollars)

	Imports	Exports	Trade Surplus
1922	$4.0b	$5.0b	$1.0b
1924	$4.6b	$5.9b	$1.3b
1926	$5.6b	$6.4b	$0.8b
1928	$5.5b	$6.8b	$1.3b

Source: *Historical Statistics of the United States, Colonial Times to 1970* (1975)

that deprived American manufacturers of easy access to raw materials such as rubber and precious metals. The department also worked with the major oil corporations in gaining refining concessions in Venezuela, the Dutch East Indies, Iraq, and the Persian Gulf states of Bahrain and Kuwait. After 1922, the State Department insisted on approving foreign loans before they could be submitted to subscription by the American public, hoping thereby to direct investment to politically stable areas. Ironically, American bankers then used this certification to suggest the financial attractiveness of their bonds. State Department administrators unabashedly sent bankers such as Charles Dawes and Thomas Lamont on official missions to negotiate government foreign loans.

Despite a broad scope of interests in the 1920s, American diplomatic activity focused primarily on Europe, where it endeavored to protect friendly relations with Britain and France and ensure the reintegration of Germany into the western community. Under the Dawes Plan of 1924, devised by Harding's budget director, the former Allies agreed to a reduced schedule of German war reparations. At the same time, J. P. Morgan and other private bankers agreed to substantial loans to Germany to stimulate economic reconstruction. American banks lent over $1.2 billion to Germany between 1924 and 1930. German reparations then allowed the Allies to repay public war loans owed the United States, although Washington renegotiated the loans so that the $10 billion Allied war debt shrank by some 43 percent. The Young Plan of 1930, a creation of industrialist Owen Young, further reduced German reparations, spread the payments over fifty-eight years, and involved private American banks as sponsors. In essence, American investors exported credits to Germany, where those credits found their way into German reparation payments. Eventually the same capital returned to the United States as part of Allied payment of American war loans. Not only did the United States replace Britain in dominance of international finance and commerce, but American capital now stimulated European purchase of American commodities and farm produce.

Despite such internationalism, high tariffs hurt the long-range interest of the American economy. The Fordney-McCumber Tariff of 1922, for example, provided substantial protection rates for infant industries and agricultural produce. But trade barriers erected for special interest at home conflicted with the nation's creditor status, discouraged repayment of foreign debts, and inhibited expansion of overseas markets. The Hawley-Smoot Tariff of 1930 raised rates even further. Not until Congress passed the Reciprocal Trade Agreement Act of 1934 did the president win discretionary power to lower tariff schedules (see chapter 6).

American rejection of membership in the League of Nations and the World Court did not rule out diplomatic activity. The United States enthusiastically hosted the Washington Armaments Conference of 1921–22, which fixed the number of American, British, and Japanese battleships and battle cruisers at a ratio of 5:5:3 and assigned France and Italy smaller percentages. The conference also drafted the Four-Power Treaty, which replaced an alliance between Britain and Japan and committed signatories to respect each other's Pacific island possessions. A Nine-Power Treaty reaffirmed support for the

Open Door in China and called for maintenance of the status quo in East Asia. The United States anticipated that American economic power would ultimately confine Japanese actions in an area of the world where Washington remained militarily weak. (For the subsequent history of these agreements, see chapter 7.)

Most Americans hoped that the nation's economic empire could be preserved without war or huge armaments. By avoiding entangling diplomatic or military alliances, the United States sought to pursue an independent internationalism and to ensure peaceful access to world markets. Accordingly, Secretary of State Frank B. Kellogg did not object when peace activists such as Chicago attorney Salmon O. Levinson and Congregational minister Frederick J. Libby struggled to gain an international renunciation of war as an instrument of national policy. Kellogg transformed proposals for a French-American peace accord into a multinational treaty that international pacifists and women's organizations enthusiastically supported. Sixty-four nations signed the Kellogg-Briand Pact of 1928, which received an 85–1 vote in the United States Senate and earned the secretary of state the Nobel Peace prize. Although few believed that the treaty put an end to war, many Americans felt confident that the diplomats had strengthened the "machinery" for world peace. The Kellogg-Briand Pact confirmed the imprint of the American peace movement upon foreign policy and increased the movement's influence in deterring unilateral military action by American presidents.

LATIN AMERICA AND NONINTERVENTION

While diplomats and business leaders worked aggressively to maintain the Open Door in Europe, the Middle East, and Asia, the United States pursued a closed-door policy in Latin America. Indeed, Latin America emerged as a major outlet for North American capital in the New Era. Loans to cooperative Latin American nations, often tied to the purchase of United States goods or services, totaled $1.6 billion between 1924 and 1929. By the end of the decade, Latin Americans bought nearly half their imports from the United States. In turn, North Americans purchased almost 40 percent of Latin American exports and exploited indigenous resources through multinational mining concerns like the Guggenheim syndicate and agribusinesses like United Fruit.

The United States not only insisted on limiting foreign economic competition in Latin America, but also continued the policy of military intervention to assist friendly governments. American troops withdrew from the Dominican Republic in 1924, but that country remained a financial protectorate until 1941. Three thousand marines left Nicaragua in 1925. Yet they returned the following year, only to face resistance by the nationalist General Cesar August Sandino, whose guerrilla forces harassed American troops until their departure in 1933. By then American power had ensured an orderly transition to a military government trained by the armed forces of the United States. In Honduras, the Marines took control when the State Department feared the

American marines reading comic strips to children during their occupation of Nicaragua in 1927. The military intervention nevertheless produced a bitter legacy among the highly nationalistic Nicaraguans.

development of "a condition of anarchy" in 1924. Meanwhile, Haiti remained under military occupation from 1915 to 1934. During the Pan-American Conference of 1923, Uruguay attempted to make the Monroe Doctrine multilateral by placing enforcement powers on all nations in the hemisphere and by outlawing unilateral intervention into any state's internal matters. But the United States defeated the proposal.

The turning point in American policy in Latin America came with Mexican attempts to nationalize oil fields and mines in the mid 1920s. Although some oil corporations began to talk of a bolshevik threat, both Standard Oil and the Bank of Boston warned that continued American militance in Mexico could "injure American interests." The United States had "advanced from the period of adventure to the period of permanent investment," suggested the director of the Pan American Union. Instead of sending troops, Coolidge appointed Dwight Morrow, an attorney for J. P. Morgan, as ambassador to Mexico and asked Morrow to negotiate the issue of American soil and mine rights in 1927. Meanwhile, Coolidge sent Henry Stimson, another corporate attorney, to work out political differences with Nicaragua.

Coolidge's conciliatory approach received support from President-Elect Hoover's goodwill tour of Latin America in 1928. Hoover talked of the "relation of good neighbors," and hoped to substitute economic and technical cooperation for traditional policies of American arrogance and intervention.

Exhibit 5–19. U.S. Involvement in Central America, 1921–1934.

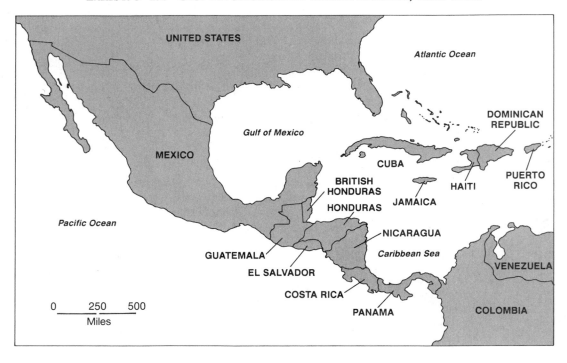

Dominican Republic: Military occupation until 1924. Financial protectorate until 1941.
Haiti: Military occupation until 1934.
Honduras: Military occupation after 1924
Mexico: Negotiated settlement of subsoil rights, 1927.
Nicaragua: Military occupation until 1925 and 1926–1933.

This shift in policy reflected the view that intervention was usually expensive and ineffective. The Hoover administration soon recognized all de facto governments in Latin America, began to withdraw marines from Nicaragua and Haiti, and refused to intervene in the Cuban Revolution of 1929–30. "We cannot slay an idea or an ideology with machine guns," Hoover declared. Instead, he simply insisted that economically underdeveloped nations honor the "sanctity of contracts" and "perform international obligations."

The rejection of military adventurism in Latin America stemmed in part from the effective political organizing of American peace activists and a vocal group of noninterventionists and nationalists in the United States Senate. Led by Republicans Robert LaFollette of Wisconsin, William E. Borah of Idaho, George W. Norris of Nebraska, and Hiram W. Johnson of California, the Senate insurgents spoke for agricultural regions of the West that produced staples for the domestic market. These groups believed that ties to European banking, the military, and diplomatic circles threatened American democracy, nationalism, and independence of action. For this reason, the western "irreconcilables" had worked to defeat United States membership in the League of Nations in 1919–20. Under presidents Harding and Coolidge, the noninterventionist bloc rejected the renegotiations of Allied war debts. The dissenters argued that American taxpayers did not wish to pay for Europe's imperial wars and that suspension of government loans would only protect the private loans made by international bankers.

Noninterventionists were successful in stopping United States membership in the Permanent Court of International Justice, created by the League of Nations in 1922 to resolve civil disputes among nations. President Harding called for membership with reservations in the World Court in 1923. The Senate finally approved his call in 1926, but Senate reservations were so stringent that the court asked the United States to renegotiate its terms of entry. When seven Republican supporters of the court lost their 1926 Senate primary bids, President Coolidge dropped the matter. The United States never joined the international tribunal.

The same distaste for colonialism and militarism provoked congressional pressure to withdraw American marines from Nicaragua between 1927 and 1933. Norris, Senate Foreign Relations Committee chairman Borah, and Burton K. Wheeler, a progressive Democratic senator from Montana, all objected that the United States had assumed the mantle of imperialism in Latin America. Wheeler charged that New York bankers and the State Department had "warshipped" the puppet Nicaraguan dictatorship to power and robbed the country of its sovereignty. As honorary president of the National Citizens' Committee on Relations with Latin America, a Boston-based coalition of reformers that sought to end American intervention in the Western Hemisphere, Norris proclaimed that revolution remained "a sacred right." By 1933, noninterventionists had built up a substantial legacy of skepticism toward the interventionist aspirations of presidential leaders and the military.

THE FARM BLOC

Despite the expanding American economy, small and independent farmers did not share in the prosperity of the New Era. In fact, the agricultural depression of the 1920s brought farm organizations and their political representatives to the brink of despair. The rural depression, an Alabama realtor pleaded with commerce secretary Hoover, "will make bolsheviks of the agriculturalists unless some remedy is provided." North Dakota senator Gerald P. Nye summed up the agraian view in 1927: "I do not believe that we can long prosper as a nation with our basic industry, agriculture, in a state of decay."

Small farmers of the 1920s faced severe disadvantages. Although independent producers remained subservient to the major processors of agricultural commodities, corporate farms retained sufficient capital to withstand fluctuations in the world market and could afford expensive machinery. In contrast, beleaguered independents could not pass their increased mechanization costs, interest rates, and taxes on to consumers. Farm problems deepened when government price supports and patriotism prompted the expansion of

Exhibit 5–20. Agricultural Price Squeeze, 1920–1921
(1910–1914 = 100)

	1920	1921
Prices received for farm products	205	116
Prices farmers paid for commodities bought	206	156
Farm wages paid to hired labor	239	150
Taxes on farm property (1914 = 100)	155	217

Source: *Recent Economic Changes* (1929)

foodstuff and cotton cultivation during World War I. While growers bought Ford tractors, trucks, and expensive machinery, the wartime boom converted the vast expanses of the Great Plains to wheat acreage. With conversion to the peacetime economy, the government abandoned price supports, demand slackened, and farm prices sank. Wheat farmers who received $2.57 a bushel in 1920 earned less than $1.00 a bushel by the end of 1921.

Throughout the 1920s, farm groups and agricultural representatives bitterly attacked the Federal Reserve Board's 1920 decision to raise the *discount* (interest) rate it charged member bankers. Republican Senate critics like Wisconsin's Robert LaFollette and North Dakota's Lynn Frazier and Gerald P. Nye charged that New York bankers had engineered deflation to bring about a contraction of credit and a liquidation of agricultural loans. Because of greedy speculative interests, they thundered, farmers had experienced a disastrous fall in commodity prices, rural banking had collapsed, and investment capital had deserted the countryside for Wall Street. "If you burn a man's house, you are punished," former New Jersey Republican governor Edward C. Stokes observed sympathetically, "but if you destroy the value of his property through control of the money market, you are regarded as a shrewd financier."

Independent producers like farmers fared poorly in a postwar political climate geared to the needs of large corporations. The congressional farm bloc never could accept the Esch-Cummins Transportation Act, which returned the railroads to corporate control after management by the federal government during World War I. Growers complained that the law made shipping costs prohibitive by giving the ICC power to raise intrastate rates to assure the lines a fair return on their investments. As LaFollette asserted, ICC assessments of corporate value were frequently inflated by Wall Street speculation.

Critics like LaFollette, Nye, and Iowa Republican senator Smith W. Brookhart described the Federal Reserve deflation and Esch-Cummins as the "twin crimes" of 1920 and blamed them for the decade's agricultural depression. Bankers and industrialists, in contrast, attacked American farmers for overproduction and inefficiency in the face of foreign competition. The effects of the agricultural collapse could not be denied. The total value of the nation's farm properties declined from $79 billion in 1920 to $46 billion by 1929; farm bankruptcy approached 18 percent in the decade; and total agricultural mortgage debt rose by $2 billion. Unable to hold their land, many small farmers became tenants. By 1930, 42 percent of the agricultural labor force leased farmland as tenants or sharecroppers, and one million farm families had left the land altogether. As agriculture consolidated, large farm operations began to use wage laborers. In the Southwest, for example, one-half million Mexicans legally entered the country and worked as field hands for extremely low pay.

Independent farmers tried to compete with agribusiness through cooperative marketing, an idea spread across the nation by Aaron Sapiro, a young California lawyer. By 1923, one-half million American growers belonged to marketing associations that handled a volume of $400 million. Under Sapiro's system, farmers signed a contract to deliver all salable produce to the association, which then marketed the produce and returned the proceeds to members after deducting costs. Marketing associations were most popular among tobacco, wheat, and cotton growers in the South and West, and among fruit, grain, and dairy producers in the Northwest. By the mid 1920s, however, many marketing associations had overextended themselves through poor management, and the farm cooperative movement waned.

Faced with devastating crop prices and an overriding sense of powerlessness, postwar farmers on the northern plains turned to politics, as they had in the troubled 1890s. Working with groups such as the Nonpartisan League and functioning primarily in the Republican party, the agrarian movement built a significant congressional farm bloc to address its grievances. The bloc worked with western progressives to pass a 1921 law extending federal loans to agricultural marketing associations, as well as the Packers and Stockyards Act, which prohibited meat packers from monopolizing markets, controlling prices, or establishing territorial pools. The Grain Futures Act of 1921 established similar controls over dealers in wheats and grains.

The farm bloc's most important goal surfaced in the McNary-Haugen bill of 1924, the nation's first proposed program of government price supports for basic crops. Buoyed by the Senate election of several western Republican progressives and two Minnesota Farmer-Labor candidates in 1922 and 1923, agrarians called for the creation of a government marketing corporation that would buy surplus commodities at full price and sell them overseas at reduced rates. Government losses would be compensated through a mandatory "equalization fee" levied on each farmer's surplus. Meanwhile, a high tariff would keep out competing agricultural imports.

In the context of falling farm prices and increased agricultural bankruptcy, McNary-Haugen meant to small growers what free silver had signified for the Populists of the 1890s. Yet, despite enthusiasm from Great Plains wheat farmers and the endorsement of Secretary of Agriculture Henry C. Wallace, the bill failed to pass the House of Representatives. And when the farm bloc succeeded in winning congressional approval in 1927 and 1928, President Coolidge twice vetoed the measure, citing the equalization tax as an unconstitutional levy. Farmers did not win any relief until the Agricultural Marketing Act of 1929, a $500 million appropriation for farm cooperative loans that created a Federal Farm Board to supervise marketing associations. By the end of the decade, most rural progressives had come to the conclusion that federal taxing power should be used to subsidize agriculture and provide economic security to the farming community.

ANTI-CORPORATE PROGRESSIVES AND THE ELECTION OF 1928

Although New Era corporate philosophy dominated the politics of the 1920s, the strength of the farm bloc demonstrated the tenacity of rural attitudes and Populist loyalties. Cooperating with "public-interest" reformers such as William Hard of the *Nation,* agrarian interests managed to revitalize a strand of progressivism hostile to corporate methods and practices. Progressive Senate Democrats like Montana's Burton Wheeler and Thomas J. Walsh, worked with Republican dissenters such as LaFollette, Borah, and Brookhart to highlight the Teapot Dome investigation and point to the corrupting influence of monopoly in American government. Nebraska's George Norris, in turn, led a successful fight against President Coolidge's 1925 nomination of Charles B. Warren to succeed newly appointed Supreme Court justice Harlan Fiske Stone as attorney general. A lobbyist for the sugar monopoly and chief solicitor of Republican campaign funds in 1924, Warren faced a bitter confirmation battle that focused on the sugar trust's domination of consumers and midwestern sugar beet growers. The resulting Senate coalition produced a humiliating 41–39 defeat for the president.

Concerns over government coziness with monopolists figured strongly in a progressive triumph over Henry Ford's attempt to make private Muscle Shoals, a group of government nitrate plants on the Tennessee River in Alabama. Norris was incensed at Ford's desire to take a one hundred year lease on the wartime plants and the adjoining Wilson Dam, and mounted a single-handed campaign between 1921 and 1925 to stop the proposal. Using the occasion to campaign for government-owned hydroelectric plants to supply low-cost energy, the Nebraska senator castigated the power trust as "the greatest monopolistic corporation that has been organized for private greed." His proposals for a Tennessee Valley project passed Congress in 1928 and 1929. Despite two presidential vetos, Norris and the progressives managed to save Muscle Shoals for public use and incorporated the facilities into the New Deal's Tennessee Valley Authority (TVA) in 1933 (see chapter 6). Meanwhile, anti-corporate progressives like Norris, Gerald Nye, William Borah, Burton Wheeler, and Robert M. LaFollette, Jr. (son of Robert M. LaFollette), continued to defend individual enterprise by campaigning against the spread of branch banking and the ubiquitous chain store.

Robert LaFollette's 1924 campaign for the presidency constituted the most dramatic example of anti-corporate politics in the New Era. Shying away from Farmer-Labor and socialist alternatives, LaFollette accepted the presidential nomination of the newly created Progressive party in 1924 and chose Senator Burton Wheeler of Montana as his running mate. Unlike Theodore Roosevelt's Progressives of 1912, LaFollette's movement attacked the large corporations. "The great issue before the American people today," declared the party platform, "is control of government and industry by private monopoly." Accordingly, the Progressives condemned the administration's tax program, denounced the protective tariff for manufactured goods, and

Senator George W. Norris, a progressive Republican, who led the fight against Henry Ford's attempt to buy the government facilities at Muscle Shoals on the Tennessee River. Norris saw himself as a champion of the independent farmer, worker, and entrepreneur.

criticized "mercenary" foreign policy. The party also appealed to northern farmers by supporting federal aid to agriculture and criticizing business control of federal regulatory agencies. And it sought the approval of both rural insurgents and urban liberals such as New York representative Fiorello LaGuardia by calling for government ownership of the railroads and water-power resources. Finally, LaFollette and Wheeler appealed to organized labor by demanding the abolition of government labor injunctions while they sought congressional recognition of collective bargaining.

Despite this well-reasoned attempt to build a third-party movement, the Progressives lacked nationwide organization and funds. LaFollette took 16 percent of the national vote in 1924, carrying only his home state of Wisconsin. Yet the ticket finished second in ten states and in sixty-seven industrial counties in the Northeast and Midwest. The obstacles to Progressive success mirrored the contradictions of anti-corporate reform. Activists

ROBERT M. LAFOLLETTE
1855–1925

"There were no silk hats and broad cloth suits," a Senate colleague noted of the mourners at the funeral of Robert M. LaFollette in 1925. At the age of seventy, the nation' leading crusader and progressive had died only months after capturing one-sixth of the popular vote as a third-party candidate in the 1924 presidential election. LaFollette's creed, another colleague told the Senate, was his faith "in the average common sense of the masses." Burton K. Wheeler, the late senator's Progressive party running mate, later proclaimed that LaFollette ranked with Jefferson and Lincoln as the three greatest characters produced by American civilization.

Born in a log cabin, LaFollette graduated from Wisconsin's new state university and went on to defy the Republican machine by winning three congressional elections in the 1880s. The short, stocky, and square-jawed Republican managed to build his own political organization by using university graduates and student volunteers to offset the power of the railroad corporations and timber interests. By 1900, LaFollette had won the Wisconsin governorship. He proceeded to institute the direct primary, civil service and tax reform, and the innovative use of state regulatory commissions.

Sent to the Senate in 1905, LaFollette continued to portray the chasm between the "people" and the "interests." By 1917, he was convinced that New York monied interests had taken over transportation, banking, industry, and commerce and that the nation's growing involvement in Europe was a product of "financial imperialism." LaFollette bitterly resisted the nation's drift to World War I, and then opposed conscription and wartime repression while crusading for war profits taxes and future referendums on military campaigns. He also helped defeat membership in Wilson's League of Nations.

By the time Harding took office in 1921, LaFollette's opposition to involvement in European rivalries had become an article of national faith. He warned that membership in the World Court would serve international bankers hoping to use *(cont.)*

such as Robert LaFollette, Burton Wheeler, George Norris, William Borah, and Hiram Johnson sought to espouse an agrarian social vision in a rapidly urbanizing society. They defended Anglo-Protestant individualism in an emerging corporate order of increasing ethnic diversity. Caught between capital and labor, between government planning and the free market, reformers of the 1920s could not agree on how to combat the institutional clout of organized money without employing institutional power. Described as "sons of the wild jackass" by conservatives in their own party, Republican progressives lacked a political grounding for their agenda. When Iowa's Senator Brookhart told a Senate hearing in 1928 that the country was "headed for the greatest panic in the history of the world," the expert witness, Professor Joseph Stagg Lawrence of Princeton, dismissed his warning as "the curious emissions of a provincial mind."

American wealth and military power to safeguard their tottering European empires. But the irascible senator also organized "people's" lobbies to demand that the government retract the rate increases and tax breaks granted to his old adversary, the railroads. Using the detested Esch-Cummins Transportation Act of 1920 as the basis for a new agenda, LaFollette assembled two national conferences of Progressives in 1922. During the same year he retained his Senate seat by taking unprecedented statewide margins of 3–1 in both the Republican primary and the general election. Buoyed by a fresh confidence and a conviction that the country was returning to its sense, LaFollette helped build a new Progressive party and became its presidential standard-bearer in 1924.

Tired, aging, without a party apparatus, and outspent 20 to 1 by Coolidge Republicans, LaFollette nevertheless mounted a monumental campaign. His supporters formed a coalition of Republican agrarian insurgents, old Populists, urban liberals and socialists, the railroad brotherhoods and trade unionists, and remnants of the independent middle class. Accordingly, LaFollette and Wheeler focused on the broad concerns of the nation's producers by defending private initiative and independent-enterprise and attacking monopoly. Their purpose, the Wisconsinite stated at the climax to the campaign, was "to restore government to the people."

LaFollette was the last significant presidential candidate to crusade against corporate capitalism. Confronted by an increasingly consumerist economy, the fiery orator continued to evoke the producer values of nineteenth-century entrepreneurs and farmers. Nevertheless, LaFollette spoke for a persistent segment of Americans who rejected the dominance of the two major parties by big money.

The Progressive ticket took second place in ten states and sixty-seven industrial counties. More important, the LaFollette legacy, borne by "Fighting Bob's" son and Senate successor Robert M. LaFollette, Jr., continued to draw the connections between the power of corporate capital at home and pressures for increased military presence overseas. To speak of LaFollette was to invoke the spirit of the nation's ordinary people. Even New Era America was compelled to pay homage to a true giant of the Senate. ■

Neither political party provided a serious outlet for reform energies during the 1928 presidential campaign. Seeking support from working-class ethnics in the major cities, the Democrats quickly agreed to nominate New York governor Alfred ("Al") E. Smith. An Irish-Catholic raised through the ranks of lower Manhattan's Tammany Hall political machine, Smith had proven an able campaigner and administrator as four-time chief executive of the Empire State. Although Smith opposed Prohibition, the party chose Arkansas senator Joseph T. Robinson, a Protestant Prohibition supporter, as the vice-presidential nominee to balance the ticket. Like the Progressive platform of 1924, the Democratic plank endorsed collective bargaining for labor, abolition of court injunctions against strikes, federal aid to support farm prices, and government regulation of waterpower. But the party joined Republicans in espousing traditional principles of limited government and acceptance of a self-regulating corporate economy.

FIORELLO LaGUARDIA
1882–1947

Fiorello LaGuardia was a short and stocky man with a loud voice. His mother was Jewish, his father an Italian-American Protestant. LaGuardia spoke six foreign languages. He broke into politics as a Theodore Roosevelt Progressive. To win support for a campaign to Congress, La-Guardia offered free legal services to immigrant pushcart peddlers, icemen, and shopkeepers. He mobilized letter carriers and garment workers and pulled flophouse voters out of bed before Tammany Hall was awake on election day. LaGuardia won the Italian-Jewish district of East Harlem by 257 votes and went to Washington as a Republican in 1916.

LaGuardia was an urban evangelist, the first Italian-American to serve in Congress. Like all successful politicians, he knew his district. Immigrants from southern and eastern Europe had no tradition of rural individualism in their village heritage. Victimized by a dehumanizing industrial system in America, they sought govern-ment assistance. Ten years be-fore the New Deal, LaGuardia agitated for old-age pensions, unemployment insurance, shorter workdays, workmen's compensation, and laws against child labor. The Norris–LaGuardia Act of 1932 banned the use of injunctions to prevent strikes and abolished "yellow-dog" contracts that obligated workers to shun unions. LaGuardia also cam-paigned against high prices levied by corpo-rate middlemen. Rising to speak during a House debate over rising profits in the meat industry, LaGuardia pulled from his pocket a lamb chop, then a steak, then a tiny roast. "What workman's family can afford to pay three dollars for a roast of this size?" he screamed.

The fiery congressman was not a successful Republican or cheerleader for the celebrated New Era. Instead, he displayed a street in-stinct for detecting unwarranted privilege. By 1923, LaGuardia had joined rural progres-sives in denouncing administration *(cont.)*

When President Coolidge dismissed talk of reelection by declaring in 1927 that "I do not choose to run," commerce secretary Hoover emerged as the logical choice for the Republican nomination. Like the popular Henry Ford, Hoover embodied the worlds of both corporate capitalism and traditional American values. Although Hoover had made a fortune in mine engineering and international investment, his early roots lay in the small towns of rural Iowa and Oregon. Raised as a Quaker, he combined humanitarian zeal and organizational skill in widely acclaimed work as wartime food administrator and coordinator of emergency European relief in the Wilson administration. Hoover's well-publicized efforts as secretary of commerce prompted the *Magazine of Business* to call him "the most significant landmark of our age." Yet Republican insurgents from the farm states resented the secretary's opposi-tion to the McNary-Haugen bill and mounted a frantic effort to derail the Hoover candidacy. Once the agrarian progressives lost an early test vote, friendliness toward corporate monopoly and in opposing tax benefits for the wealthy, high tariffs, and instant labor injunctions. LaGuardia led the House attack on Coolidge's plan to sell the Muscle Shoals Dam to Henry Ford, suggesting that "this proposition makes Teapot Dome look like petty larceny." He joined with Senator Norris to campaign for public power, supported Senator Borah's opposition to military occupation of Nicaragua, and demanded the impeachment of treasury secretary Mellon. "I would rather be right than regular," he once explained.

Not surprisingly, the Republican House leadership stripped LaGuardia of all committee assignments in 1924. He attended the Progressive party convention that year, rising to tell the followers of LaFollette that "I speak for Avenue A and 116th Street, instead of Broad and Wall." Denied the Republican nomination in 1924, he sailed back to Congress on Progressive and Socialist ballots.

LaGuardia was the first urban progressive to take his place on Capitol Hill. He worked well with rural insurgents in attacking abuses of power in the Harding and Coolidge administrations. But LaGuardia broke with many in the progressive coalition when he ridiculed federal censorship of the movies and became one of the House's most passionate critics of immigration restriction. He also dramatized ethnic resentment toward Prohibition by manufacturing beer at his Capitol office and defying police to arrest him.

LaGuardia's unique contribution was his understanding that the immigrant working class of the large cities constituted a vital component of a new coalition for reform. The man who munched peanuts on the floor of Congress and whose favorite word was *lousy* instigated the separation of progressive reform from the Purity Crusade of the Protestant elite. By the time LaGuardia became mayor of New York City in 1933, urban ethnics were anticipating a "new deal" in Washington and were beginning to flex their political muscle. LaGuardia, the Republican progressive from East Harlem, had charted the way. ■

however, Hoover took the nomination on the first ballot. In return, the party chose Kansas senator Charles Curtis, a farm bloc leader, as its vice-presidential choice.

The combined effect of Coolidge prosperity, Smith's inability to attract farmer discontent, and cultural discomfort with the streetwise New Yorker (see chapter 4) produced an easy Republican victory. Hoover won over 21.3 million popular votes (58.2 percent) to his opponents's 15.0 million (40.9 percent). The lopsided 444–87 tally in the Electoral College reflected Smith's failure to move much beyond traditional Democratic strength in the Deep South. Yet the Democrats doubled their presidential vote of 1924 and began to emerge as the party of urban America. Four years earlier, the Republican plurality in the nation's twelve largest cities had surpassed 1.25 million. In 1928, the Democrats captured those cities by thirty-eight thousand votes, initiating a political revolution that would ultimately reverse the party's fortunes in presidential contests.

President Herbert Hoover, Henry Ford, Thomas Edison, and Harvey Firestone (l. to r.) on a Florida vacation, 1929. Hoover hoped to employ corporate techniques of planning and cooperation in his new administration.

HOOVER AND THE CRASH OF 1929

"The presidency is more than executive symbol," proclaimed Herbert Hoover during the 1928 election. "It is the inspiring symbol of all that is highest in America's purposes and ideals." Hoover continued to espouse the New Era values that had defined his work in the Department of Commerce. "We in America are nearer to the final triumph over poverty than ever before in the history of any land," he announced. Attempting to balance the machinery of an American system of producers, trade groups, and consumers, Hoover convened a special session of Congress in April 1929 to address the continuing farm depression.

The new president had already responded to rural progressives in his own party by calling agriculture the "most urgent economic problem in our nation today." National Grange lobbyists and the farm bloc campaigned for grower subsidies and increased agricultural tariffs to raise the price of domestic farm commodities. Instead, Congress passed the Agricultural Marketing Act of 1929, which sought to help farmers create the sort of merchandising organi-

Exhibit 5–21. Election 1928.

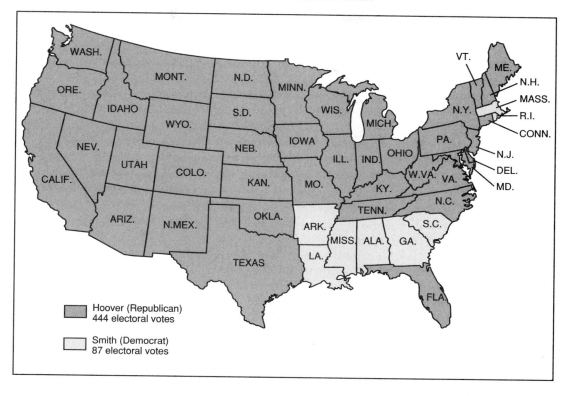

Hoover (Republican)
444 electoral votes

Smith (Democrat)
87 electoral votes

zations that Hoover had supported in the 1920s. The law established a Federal Farm Board authorized to loan $500 million to farm marketing cooperatives and set up stabilization corporations empowered to buy surplus cotton, grain, wool, and other commodities. By interfering directly with agricultural distribution and prices, Hoover's farm bill created the most ambitious government involvement in the history of the nation's peacetime economy.

By 1930, Hoover agreed to seek limited tariff protection for agriculture. Accordingly, he signed the Hawley-Smoot Tariff, which raised the import duties of farm products by 70 percent and increased the rates of industrial goods from 32 percent to 40 percent. More than a thousand economists urged Hoover to veto the bill as detrimental to foreign trade. Nevertheless, farm bloc pressure, Republican partisan interests, and economic nationalism prompted the president to approve the risky tariff.

Hoover had hoped to rely on presidential leadership, instead of extensive legislation, to balance and stabilize the national economy. But events moved beyond his control and severely tested his faith in American institutions and limited government. On Black Tuesday, October 29, 1929, the average price of the fifty leading stocks on the New York exchange fell forty points. By the end of the most devastating day in Wall Street's previous history, securities had dropped $14 billion in value. Two weeks later, losses rose to $25 billion, two-fifths of the value of all stock on the exchange.

Since stock prices often were psychological indicators of investor confidence, the crash of 1929 amounted to a serious setback for the economy. Ironically, the Wall Street collapse stemmed from the same financial practices that had contributed to the speculative boom of the 1920s. Through unregulated margin arrangements, for example, small investors had aggravated market inflation by purchasing stocks at as little as 10 percent of face value. Many then borrowed additional funds by using stock as collateral, inviting disaster should the value of securities fall. In 1927, Wall Street floated nearly $19 billion worth of new stocks with only $3 billion in assets.

Hoover first described the economic decline as a "depression" instead of as a "panic" or "crisis" because he hoped to allay public fears. The president believed that corporate maintenance of employment, production, high wages, and labor peace would sustain the morale necessary for continued prosperity. Within weeks of the crash, he called leading officers of the major corporations to the White House to win promises of cooperation. He also created a host of federal agencies and bureaus such as the Emergency Committee for Employment, the President's Organization for Unemployment Relief, and the Federal Employment Stabilization Board to mitigate the problems caused by the downturn. In addition, Hoover expanded federal outlays for municipal and state public works and asked Congress to appropriate $150 million for federal buildings in 1930. As a result, spending for public works pumped $4 billion into the economy. "I am convinced we have passed the worst," the president assured the Chamber of Commerce in May 1930.

But just as Hoover looked to economic recovery, the Federal Reserve Board sought to discourage stock market speculation and excessive debt by raising interest rates. Accordingly, the amount of money in circulation decreased, industrialists anticipated further drops in consumer demand, and factories, mills, and plants began to lower production and lay off workers. Hoover never succeeded in reversing this disastrous decline. Between 1930 and 1932, tight monetary policies reduced the money supply by one-third. Americans soon lost faith in financial institutions and large investors increasingly withheld capital from the marketplace. "We are going through a period when character and courage are on trial," declared Hoover in February 1931, "where the very faith that is within us is under test."

By 1931, the president remained as concerned with Europe's collapsing credit structure as with developments in the United States. Attention shifted to Europe in the spring of 1931 when France called in German and Austrian loans and Austria's largest bank quickly collapsed. In the ensuring panic, investors withdrew gold from German and Austrian banks. Hoover's one-year moratorium on the collection of German and Austrian debts failed to prevent the spread of the financial crisis to France and Britain. In September 1931, Britain and several European nations repudiated the gold standard and demanded that American banks redeem their $1.5 billion of European investment in gold. Seeking gold to forestall anticipated bank runs in Europe, British and Continental investors quickly sold off securities on the New York Stock Exchange. The resulting withdrawal of capital from American markets injured foreign trade and contributed to the continuing decline of stock prices. Between May and December 1931, the international credit squeeze led to the failure of nearly two thousand American banks. Meanwhile, employment dropped some 12 percent and wages tumbled a demoralizing 30 percent.

Hoover and Failed Recovery

"No president must ever admit he has been wrong," Hoover once told Julius Barnes of the Chamber of Commerce. Despite increasing calls for government action, Hoover continued to favor reduced federal spending and balanced budgets as the road to recovery. In 1931, the president rejected a program of industrial stabilization proposed by General Electric president Gerard Swope. The Swope Plan sought to institutionalize compulsory economic and welfare planning. Under federal supervision, trade associations would have the power to fix prices, control production, and regulate business practices. Swope also argued for federal programs of old-age, life, and unemployment insurance. Hoover objected that such reassertion of wartime government power might encourage a bureaucratic system of syndicates and monopolistic cartels. The president and his advisers preferred to focus on confidence as the key to recovery. "There is more to fear from frozen minds than frozen assets," lectured treasury secretary Ogden L. Mills in late 1931. Business could not "be conducted without credit," he pleaded the next spring, "and credit cannot function without confidence."

Despite philosophic objections, Herbert Hoover became the first president to use the federal government to intervene directly to reverse economic decline. Late in 1931, Hoover called for a massive increase in public works spending, to a proposed $2.25 billion. When Congress responded, the administration undertook the most costly public works program in American history to that time, including construction of the Hoover Dam on the Colorado River. The president also approved the Federal Home Loan Bank Act of 1932. The law created a federal home mortgage board and appropriated $125 million to regional mortgage banks to encourage home ownership and provide loans to distressed banks and mortgage companies. Meanwhile, the Glass-Steagall Act of 1932 expanded the credit supply by permitting the government to use commercial paper as partial backing for Treasury securities. This measure freed about $750 million of gold formerly used as collateral for government bonds and securities.

Pressed to respond to increasing Depression unemployment, Hoover signed the Emergency and Relief Construction Act of 1932, providing $2 billion to local and state governments for public works and $300 million of loans to the states for unemployment and work relief. The president also approved a $500 million appropriation for the Reconstruction Finance Corporation (RFC), a new federal agency empowered to make loans to banks, insurance companies, railroads, and other major institutions. The RFC also received authority to borrow an additional $1.5 billion in tax-free bonds. And in a gesture to organized labor, Hoover signed the Norris–LaGuardia Act of 1932, prohibiting court injunctions against strikes, boycotts, and union picketing.

Exhibit 5–22. Hoover's Recovery Program

1930	agricultural commodity stabilization corporations created by Federal Farm Board
1931	$2.25 billion public works program
1932	Federal Home Loan Bank Act (created Federal Home Mortgage Board)
	Glass-Steagall Banking Act
	Emergency and Relief Construction Act ($2.3b in public works and relief loans to states)
	Reconstruction Finance Corporation (RFC), $2b capitalization
	Norris-LaGuardia Anti-Injunction Act

Despite the president's unprecedented activism, Hoover's political fortunes suffered. After 1930, Democrats controlled the House of Representatives and joined with insurgent Republicans to dominate the Senate. Meanwhile, Hoover's Federal Farm Board lacked the power to limit agricultural production amidst a depressed global market. As a result, the farm board felt compelled to purchase large wheat and cotton surpluses. While crop prices plummeted in a declining market, agricultural income fell by half between 1931 and 1932. By 1932, the Federal Farm Board had lost over $350 million in a futile effort to stabilize American agriculture. That year, a new militant farmers' organization, the Farmers Holiday Association, began to barricade midwestern highways to stop underpriced milk and other produce from going to market.

The Reconstruction Finance Corporation also proved inadequate to the recovery task. Nearly all RFC funds found their way to large corporations, and the agency spent only 10 percent of the monies earmarked for state relief. Despite his dramatic abandonment of laissez-faire and free market economics, Hoover continued to believe that economic recovery would follow the restoration of confidence. Balanced federal budgets, he insisted, provided essential ingredients to fiscal integrity and investor confidence.

Obsessed with curtailing federal spending, the president reluctantly agreed to assist producers such as farmers and industrial corporations. Yet he drew the line at direct help for consumers. Such distinctions left Hoover vulnerable to charges that he willingly lent money to feed farm animals but not farm children. By 1932, the president's dream of a cooperative society lay shattered in the collapse of the national economy.

THE CHALLENGE OF THE DEPRESSION

The stock market crash of 1929 remained a permanent symbol of the worst economic catastrophe in American history. Four years later, one-fourth of the nation's work force lacked jobs. In the same period, wages declined from $53 billion to $31 billion and farm receipts sank from $12 billion to $5 billion. Between 1929 and 1933, both industrial production and national income fell by half, while investment in capital goods decreased 88 percent. At the same

A Depression breadline in New York City. Such demoralizing scenes became symbols of the breakdown of the American economic system after 1929.

time, two major American industries suffered devastating losses: annual sales of passenger cars plummeted from 4.5 million to 1.1 million, and construction spending tumbled from $8.7 billion to $1.4 billion. Between 1930 and 1932, almost six thousand banks with assets of $4 billion failed and more than one-hundred thousand businesses went bankrupt.

The Depression of the 1930s fed on weaknesses in the economy of the previous decade. New England and the agricultural areas of the South, the Midwest, and the mountain states had never shared in 1920s prosperity. Indeed, the postwar economy had experienced substantial declines in coal mining, cotton manufacturing, shipbuilding, shoe and leather production, and the railroad industry, losses aggravated by the contraction of foreign markets that accompanied the period's high tariffs.

Exhibit 5–23. Federal Receipts and Outlays, 1929–1932 (in rounded billions of dollars)

	Receipts	*Outlays*	*Net Balance*
1929	$3.8b	$2.9b	$ + 0.9b
1930	$4.0b	$3.1b	$ + 0.9b
1931	$3.2b	$4.1b	$ − 0.9b
1932	$2.0b	$4.8b	$ − 2.8b

Source: *Historical Statistics of the United States, Colonial Times to 1970* (1975)

Exhibit 5–24. Gross National Product, 1929–1932
(1958 dollars in rounded billions)

1929	$103.1b
1930	$90.4b
1931	$75.8b
1932	$58.0b

Source: *Historical Statistics of the United States, Colonial Times to 1970* (1975)

Other structural weaknesses added to the problem. Because profit gains during the 1920s far exceeded wage increases, the top 1 percent of income holders increased their share of national income from 12 percent in 1919 to nearly 19 percent by 1929. In contrast, the Brookings Institution reported in 1929 that three-fifths of American families earned less than $2000 a year, an income that confined those consumers solely to the purchase of "basic necessities." This limited purchasing power meant that by 1929, investment had surpassed the capacity of sales to return profits. Residential construction, for example, had begun to decline as early as 1927. Moreover, replacement of the automobile could easily be delayed by consumer caution, and by 1929, motor vehicle production and road building had reached saturation levels in an unstable economy.

The Depression made poverty a way of life for some forty million Americans. In single-industry cities such as Akron and Toledo, unemployment skyrocketed to a paralyzing 60 to 80 percent. Landlords evicted two-hundred thousand families from their apartments in New York City during 1931. By 1933, at least one million transients, including two-hundred thousand children, joined the nation's homeless. In Chicago, a journalist described "a crowd of some fifty men fighting over a barrel of garbage which had been set outside the back door of a restaurant." An economist from a New York investment house declared that the economic order threatened to revert to the "feudalism and barter which ensued upon the breakup of the Roman Empire."

The economic crisis created profound insecurity for Americans of all social classes. "I sat in my back office, trying to figure out what to do," newspaper publisher J. David Stern remembered of the crash. "To be explicit, I sat in my

Exhibit 5–25. Income Distribution, 1929
(Percentage of Personal Income Received By Each Fifth of Families and Individuals)

Lowest Fifth	12.5%
Second Fifth	
Third Fifth	13.8%
Fourth Fifth	19.3%
Highest Fifth	54.4%
(Top 5 Percent)	(30.0%)

Source: *Historical Statistics of the United States, Colonial Times to 1970* (1975)

Exhibit 5–26. Imports and Exports of Goods and Services, 1929–1932
(in rounded billions of dollars)

	Imports	Exports	Trade Surplus
1929	$5.9b	$7.0b	$1.1b
1930	$4.4b	$5.4b	$1.0b
1931	$3.1b	$3.6b	$0.5b
1932	$2.1b	$2.5b	$0.4b

Source: *Historical Statistics of the United States, Colonial Times to 1970* (1975)

private bathroom. My bowels were loose from fear." As more than one-hundred thousand Americans lost jobs every week between 1929 and 1932, work no longer appeared to be part of the natural order of life. As a result, noted a writer in the *Atlantic* magazine in 1933, fear had become "the dominant emotion of contemporary America—fear of losing one's job, fear of reduced salary or wages, fear of eventual destitution and want."

Two responses suggested the severity of the economic collapse. One, in 1932, demoralized and jobless graduates of eastern business, engineering, and teaching programs formed the Association of Unemployed College Alumni. Two, as early as 1930, the International Apple Shippers' Association began to sell apples on credit to unemployed men who resold them at five cents apiece. The ubiquitous street corner apple peddlers of the great cities provided a lasting image of the Great Depression.

By 1932, radio commentator Father Charles E. Coughlin customarily referred to bankers as "banksters." As the Depression deepened, public opinion turned bitterly against the New Era business leaders who had promised permanent prosperity. One month after Swedish entrepreneur Ivar Krueger shot himself in Paris in March 1932, auditors discovered that Krueger had forged $100 million of bonds sold to American investment houses. The securities market further deteriorated when the thirty-two state public utility empire of Samuel Insull collapsed shortly thereafter.

With support from Hoover, who wanted to expose the practice of selling short, the Senate authorized a broad investigation of the New York Stock Exchange. As South Dakota progressive Republican Peter Norbeck presided, attorney Ferdinand Pecora led the public questioning of figures such as stock exchange president Richard Whitney and leading bankers Charles Mitchell

Exhibit 5–27. Unemployment, 1929–1932
(percentage of civilian labor force)

1929	3.2%
1930	8.7%
1931	15.9%
1932	23.6%

Source: *Historical Statistics of the United States, Colonial Times to 1970* (1975)

Exhibit 5–28. Consumer Price Index, 1929–1932
(1967 = 100)

1929	51.3
1930	50.0
1931	45.6
1932	40.9

Source: *Historical Statistics of the United States, Colonial Times to 1970* (1975)

and Albert Wiggin. Testimony revealed that Wall Street operators organized stock pools for "insiders," allowed associates to buy securities at special discounts, "pegged" certain stock at artificially high prices, provided lucrative bonuses for themselves, and used improper publicity to induce people to buy questionable stocks. Norbeck told a radio audience that Wall Street "was the worst crap game in the country." Committee investigators soon revealed that Insull's pyramid of utility holding companies had been built on deceit and fraud.

As unemployment, homelessness, and plain hunger increasingly burdened municipal agencies and charities by 1932, recovery programs appeared utterly inadequate. More than one hundred cities had no resources to assist the needy. Yet Hoover consistently opposed all schemes for direct federal relief. Clinging to traditional concepts of Anglo-Protestant personal accountability, the president claimed that federal aid would invite bureaucratic control of private business and bankruptcy of the Treasury. He hoped that Americans could maintain traditions of interclass harmony, voluntarism, and local control. But Hoover's reassurances only compromised his personal credibility. As migrants gathered in shantytowns on the vacant lots of major cities, they bitterly referred to those settlements as "Hoovervilles." Newspapers used to cover sleeping vagrants became "Hoover blankets."

During the summer of 1932, over fifteen thousand World War I veterans gathered in one Hooverville on the Anacostia Flats near Washington D.C. Petitioning Congress for immediate payment of "adjusted compensation" that was legislated as a supplementary veterans' benefit in 1925, the Bonus Expeditionary Force (BEF) reflected the anger and desperation of the nations' unemployed. When the Senate followed Hoover's lead and refused to vote for immediate payment of the full bonus, some five thousand veterans remained at Anacostia Flats after the rest returned home. Following several clashes between the veterans and local police, Hoover ordered the Army to remove the veterans. But Chief of Staff Douglas MacArthur disobeyed the president's orders for restraint and used tanks, tear gas, infantry, cavalry, and machine guns to forcibly eject the veterans from government property, burning their settlement in the process.

The expulsion of the Bonus Army portrayed the unfortunate president as a frightened man who had lost touch with the catastrophic effects of the Depression on the lives of ordinary Americans. Heralded as a visionary Progressive and skilled administrator when he entered the White House in 1929, an unpopular Hoover faced an arduous reelection campaign as the Depression continued to worsen in 1932.

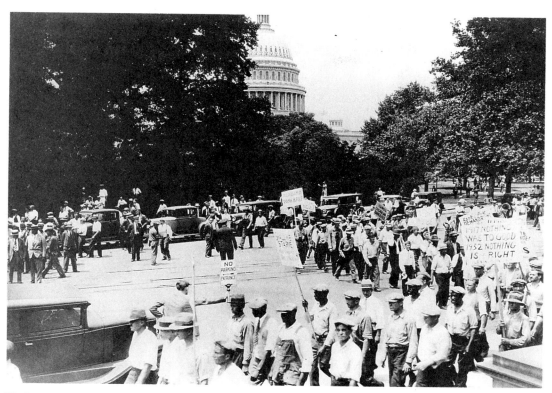

The Bonus Expeditionary Force, dispersed by federal troops in Washington, D.C. in the summer of 1932. The rout of the Bonus Army worked against President Hoover's political fortunes in that year's election campaign.

SUGGESTED READINGS

A useful introduction to the 1920s can be found in Geoffrey Perrett, *America in the Twenties, A History* (1982). A good synthesis of postwar economic history is Ellis W. Hawley, *The Great War and the Search for a Modern Order: A History of the American People and Their Institutions, 1917–1933* (1979). See also Jim Potter, *American Economy between the World Wars* (1975). A detailed view of New Era management is provided in the relevant chapters of Morrell Heald, *The Social Responsibilities of Business: Company and Community, 1900–1960* (1970).

The standard overview of 1920s political history is John D. Hicks, *The Republican Ascendancy, 1921–1933* (1960). Descriptions of the era's presidencies can be found in Eugene Trani and David L. Wilson, *The Presidency of Warren G. Harding* (1977); Robert K. Murray, *The Politics of Normalcy: Governmental Theory and Practice in the Harding-Coolidge Era* (1973); and Murray, *Harding Era: Warren G. Harding and His Administration* (1969). See also Donald B. McCoy, *Calvin Coolidge: The Quiet President* (1967). The period's scandals are described in Burl Noggle, *Teapot Dome: Oil and Politics in the 1920s* (1962).

Herbert Hoover's progressivism is emphasized by both David Burner, *Herbert Hoover: The Public Life* (1978) and Joan Hoff Wilson, *Herbert Hoover: The*

Forgotten Progressive (1975). For a collection of fresh research on Hoover's policies in the cabinet and presidency, see Carl E. Krog and William R. Tanner, eds., *Herbert Hoover and the Republican Era: A Reconsideration* (1984). Robert F. Himmelberg, *The Origins of the National Recovery Administration: Business, Government, and the Trade Association Issue, 1921–1933* (1975) depicts evolving government response to trade associations and corporate consolidation.

The best survey of 1920s foreign policy appears in Warren I. Cohen, *Empire Without Tears: America's Foreign Relations, 1921–1933* (1987). Diplomatic ties with Europe are described by Frank Costigliola, *Awkward Dominion: American Political, Economic, and Cultural Relations with Europe, 1919–1933* (1985). Joan Hoff Wilson, *American Business and Foreign Policy, 1920–1933* (1971) explores economic parameters to overseas policies. The roots of intervention in Nicaragua and Haiti can be found in the relevant sections of Walter LaFeber, *Inevitable Revolutions: The United States in Central America* (1983). For opponents of diplomatic and military expansion, see Thomas N. Guinsburg, *The Pursuit of Isolationism in the United States Senate from Versailles to Pearl Harbor.* (1982).

Conditions of industrial labor and the plight of unions are described in detail by Irving Bernstein, *The Lean Years: A History of the American Worker, 1920–1933* (1960). For the government's response to the union movement, see Robert Zieger, *Republicans and Labor, 1919–1929* (1969). Agrarian discontent is summarized in James H. Shideler, *Farm Crisis, 1919–1923* (1957) and Millard L. Gieske, *Minnesota Farmer-Laborism: The Third Party Alternative* (1979). See also the appropriate chapters of Theodore Saloutos and John D. Hicks, *Twentieth Century Populism: Agricultural Discontent in the Middle West, 1900–1939* (1951). For the dilemmas of 1920s Progressives, see Eugene M. Tobin, *Organize or Perish: America's Independent Progressives, 1913–1933* (1986), and LeRoy Asby, *The Spearless Leader: Senator Borah and the Progressive Movement in the 1920s.* (1972).

The standard account of the 1929 stock market crash is John K. Galbraith, *The Great Crash, 1929* (1961). For an overview of economic history after 1929, see the fifth volume of Joseph Dorfman, *The Economic Mind in American Civilization* (1959) and Jim Potter, *The American Economy between the World Wars* (1975). See also Robert S. McElvaine, *The Great Depression, 1929–1941* (1984).

The Hoover administration is portrayed in Martin L. Fausold, *The Presidency of Herbert C. Hoover* (1985) and in Fausold and George T. Mazuzan, eds., *The Hoover Presidency: A Reappraisal* (1974). For Hoover's anticipation of New Deal policy, see William J. Barber, *From New Era to the New Deal: Herbert Hoover, the Economists, and American Economic Policy, 1921–1933 (1985)* and Elliot A. Rosen, *Hoover, Roosevelt, and the Brains Trust: From Depression to New Deal* (1977). Two critical accounts are Gene Smith, *The Shattered Dream: Herbert Hoover and the Great Depression* (1970) and Albert U. Romasco, *The Poverty of Abundance: Hoover, the Nation, the Depression* (1965). For the social effects of the Depression, see Caroline Bird, *The Invisible Scar* (1966); Robert S. Lynd and Helen M. Lynd, *Middletown in Transition* (1937); and Studs Terkel, *Hard Times* (1970).

6

ROOSEVELT, THE NEW DEAL, AND THE QUEST FOR STABILITY, 1932-1940

If the stock market crash symbolized the Great Depression, Franklin D. Roosevelt embodied the nation's will to achieve recovery. Roosevelt came to personify the state as protector. His New Deal relief and recovery programs brought unprecedented involvement by the federal government in the lives of ordinary Americans. New welfare structures and bureaucratic regulations for the marketplace were two of the more controversial legacies of the Roosevelt era. The president's critics maintained that the New Deal covered up inadequacies with smoke and mirrors and that the expansion of executive and federal power would prove irreversible. Nevertheless, the leading political and cultural concern of the 1930s remained the quest for stability and order in a society desperate to find its bearings.

ROOSEVELT AND
THE ELECTION OF 1932

Sensing victory at the polls, the Democratic party turned to New York's Franklin Delano Roosevelt for the presidential nomination in 1932. A distant cousin of Theodore, Roosevelt graduated from Groton and Harvard, studied law at Columbia, served as assistant secretary of the navy in the Wilson administration, and ran unsuccessfully for the Democratic vice-presidency during the Harding landslide of 1920. The following year, Roosevelt suffered an attack of poliomyelitis, and he remained unable to walk without assistance for the rest of his life. Yet he overcame this disability to participate in party politics, and won two terms as New York's governor in 1928 and 1930.

As a Progressive, Roosevelt sponsored unemployment relief, labor and banking reform, aid to farmers, state hydroelectric power, and conservation measures. Despite Governor Roosevelt's popularity, his presidential nomination faced stiff opposition from former presidential candidate Al Smith and Texan John N. Garner, Speaker of the House. But after three ballots, Garner joined Louisiana populist Huey P. Long and Montana progressive Burton K. Wheeler in providing the New Yorker with the necessary two-thirds plurality. The Democratic platform called for active government aid to the unemployed, but demanded a 25 percent cut in federal spending. To offset the budget deficit, the party proposed to repeal Prohibition and apply revenues from the sale of liquor to finance the difference.

Roosevelt distinguished his quest for the presidency by referring to the "forgotten man at the bottom of the economic pyramid" and the need for "bold persistent experimentation." Breaking precedent, he flew to the Chicago convention site to accept the Democratic nomination personally. "I pledge you," he told the delegates, "I pledge myself, to a new deal for the American people." Always indirect about his political philosophy, Roosevelt described himself as "a Christian and a Democrat." He assured the business community that his administration would address problems of production, underconsumption, and the distribution of wealth and products. The candidate promised relief to the unemployed and an energetic approach to economic recovery. To demonstrate the Progressive belief that the free

Exhibit 6–1. Election of 1932.

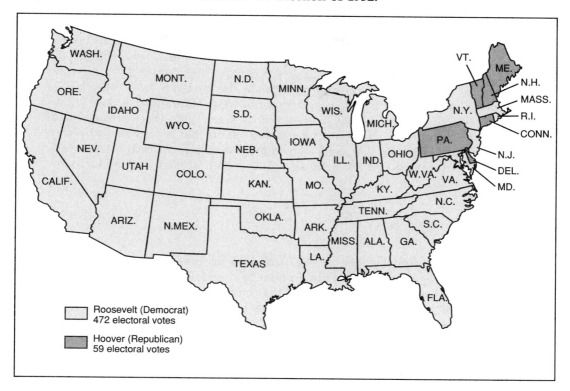

enterprise system needed overall planning by professionals, Roosevelt dramatically invited a "brains trust" of experts from the prestigious eastern universities to join in government planning.

Herbert Hoover responded to the Democratic campaign by warning that his opponent's tariff policies would mean that "the grass will grow in the streets of a hundred cities" and "weeds will over run the fields of a million farms." But, although Roosevelt never presented a clear program to end the Depression and even criticized Hoover's spending policies, voters responded to the New Yorker's warmth, assertiveness, and sense of experiment. Less rebellious than drifting, Americans rejected the apparent impotence of Hoover's leadership and gave Roosevelt and vice-presidential candidate Garner 22.8 million votes (57 percent) to 15.7 million (40 percent) for the Republicans. Hoover and Vice-President Charles Curtis carried only six states for a total of fifty-nine votes in the Electoral College.

By the time Roosevelt took office in March 1933, over five thousand banks with assets of $3.4 billion had closed their doors. In response, twenty-nine states had declared banking moratoriums and placed severe restrictions to prevent mass runs on remaining assets. Federal deposit banks in New York and Chicago even suspended payments. Roosevelt used his inaugural address to win the confidence of the American people. "The only thing we have to fear is fear itself—nameless, unreasoning, unjustified terror," declared the president. He promised to ask for "broad executive power to urge war against the emergency, as great as the power that would be given to me if we were in fact invaded by a foreign foe."

Two days later, the president declared a national bank holiday and called a special session of Congress. Both houses responded immediately by overwhelmingly passing the Emergency Banking Act, which gave the chief executive extraordinary powers to regulate the currency and authorized a reorganization of the banking industry with fresh federal loans. A few days later, as sixty million Americans listened to Roosevelt's first "fireside chat" over the radio, the president assured the nation that it was safe to return savings to the banks. Deposits immediately began to exceed withdrawals. "Capitalism was saved in eight days," Roosevelt advisor Raymond Moley later recalled.

THE NEW DEAL

Seeking to restore balance to the American economy, Roosevelt did not hesitate to use government action to remedy defects in the private market. In April 1933, the president announced that he had taken the United States off the gold standard, thereby fulfilling the historic demand for inflation by western agrarians and Populists. Several weeks later, Roosevelt agreed to a proposal from Oklahoma senator Elmer Thomas that authorized the chief executive to remonetize silver, print greenbacks if necessary, or alter the gold content of the dollar. The Gold Reserve Act of 1934 ultimately set the price of gold at $35 an ounce and gave the president the authority to devalue the dollar over 40 percent from the Hoover era. Through such actions, the White House hoped to restore deflated prices and elevate morale among discouraged producers.

Roosevelt responded to the Pecora investigation by signing legislation to stabilize speculation in stock exchanges and banking. The Securities Act of 1933 required that information on stocks be filed with the Federal Trade Commission and that company directors be liable for improper practices. The next year, Congress created the Securities and Exchange Commission (SEC) to regulate and license stock exchanges. The Glass-Steagall Act of 1933 established a system of federal insurance on bank deposits and stipulated that transactions in investment securities be separated from commercial banking. And the Banking Act of 1935 allowed the Federal Reserve Board to set reserve

Exhibit 6–2. Consumer Price Index, 1933–1936
(1967 = 100)

1933	38.8
1934	40.1
1935	41.1
1936	41.5

Source: *Historical Statistics of the United States, Colonial Times to 1970* (1975)

Exhibit 6–3. Imports and Exports of Goods and Services, 1933–1936
(in rounded billions of dollars)

	Imports	Exports	Trade Surplus
1933	$2.0b	$2.4b	$0.4b
1934	$2.4b	$3.0b	$0.6b
1935	$2.1b	$3.3b	$1.2b
1936	$3.4b	$3.5b	$0.1b

Source: *Historical Statistics of the United States, Colonial Times to 1970* (1975)

requirements and review the interest rates of member banks. Most of these reforms received support from business leaders looking for stability in a period of scandal and decay.

As the banking crisis percolated through the economy, farmers turned to violence and intimidation to prevent mortgage foreclosures at courtroom and auction sites. Several state legislatures in the Midwest declared foreclosure moratoriums early in 1933. Meanwhile, the Farmers Holiday Association scheduled a national strike for May to protest sinking commodity prices. Agrarian leaders such as John A. Simpson of the National Farmers' Union proposed legislation to assure farmers a fixed "cost of production" for their domestically sold crops (the federal government would market the surplus overseas). Simpson's program passed the Senate, but the administration prevailed upon the House to reject it. Instead, Secretary of Agriculture Henry A. Wallace submitted the Agricultural Adjustment Act, which Congress passed one day before the scheduled Farm Holiday Strike.

The new farm law established government price supports to ensure parity for basic commodities, stipulating that farm prices would bear the same ratio to nonfarm prices that they had in the prosperous years between 1909 and 1914. To deal with problems of overproduction, the Agricultural Adjustment Administration (AAA) also awarded subsidies to individual farmers to limit acreage under cultivation. "Kill every third pig or plow every third row under," advised the AAA. In 1933, the agency distributed $100 million in payments in return for the slaughter of six million pigs and the destruction of one-fourth of the national cotton crop. The administration also created the Commodity Credit Corporation in 1933, which enabled farmers to borrow money on crops they agreed to take out of production.

By 1935, basic farm commodity prices had doubled. Agricultural income rose from $2 billion in 1932 to $4.6 billion three years later. Moreover, the Farm Credit Administration (FCA), created in 1933, managed to refinance one-fifth of all farm mortgages and led to a $2 billion reduction of the agricultural debt by 1935. On the other hand, limits on cotton production led to unemployment for over three-hundred thousand poor black and white sharecroppers. Price supports mainly benefited corporate producers and accelerated the historical displacement of the small farmer.

Faced with one thousand home foreclosures a day, the Roosevelt administration asked Congress to create the Home Owners Loan Corporation

Farm Holiday Association activists blocking highways outside of Sioux City, Iowa to restrict the marketing of agricultural goods during the price depression of 1932–33.

(HOLC) in 1933. The new agency issued government bonds to refinance over one million first mortgages, some 10 percent of which it later foreclosed. But Roosevelt's greatest challenge lay with the millions of Americans desperate for immediate relief. The administration responded with a bill to create the Federal Employment Relief Administration (FERA) in May 1933 and provided the agency with $500 million to grant to the states and municipalities. FERA director Harry L. Hopkins eventually spent $4 billion in cash relief and work programs, assisting over twenty million Americans with the federal government's first direct relief program. To weather the winter of 1933–34, Roosevelt also placed Hopkins in charge of a second agency, the Civil Works Administration (CWA), authorizing the direct hiring of unemployed workers. Hopkins quickly spent $1 billion in employing four million people until the following spring.

Two innovative programs, the Civilian Conservation Corps (CCC) and the Tennessee Valley Authority (TVA), gained congressional approval in the first one hundred days of the Roosevelt administration. Both merged public works with administration emphasis on conservation, rational use of resources, and regional planning. The CCC hired young men between the ages of eighteen and twenty-five to work in reforesting, road construction, flood control, land reclamation, range improvement, and soil erosion programs. Organized

Relief administrators Harry Hopkins, Harold Ickes, and Frank Walker, key participants in the emergency bureaucracy created by Franklin Roosevelt's New Deal.

along military lines, the corps provided a total of 2.5 million unemployed youth a mixture of discipline, outdoor experience, and commitment to national service.

The TVA involved an ambitious public power project embracing a seven-state river basin. Promoted by Republican progressive George W. Norris of Nebraska, the massive undertaking coordinated the construction of nine government dams. The dams, in turn, produced inexpensive power for fertilizer and explosive factories and created reservoirs for flood control. An independent public corporation, the TVA used resource experts and social planners to promote soil conservation and reforestation. Although private utility firms opposed the project, the TVA showed that government electric power could stimulate private investment, agricultural development, and market consumption. Indeed, thousands of isolated homesteads became electric appliance consumers under its auspices. The TVA also provided a yardstick for setting reasonable and fair utility rates. The president hoped to

Exhibit 6–4. The Tennessee Valley Authority.

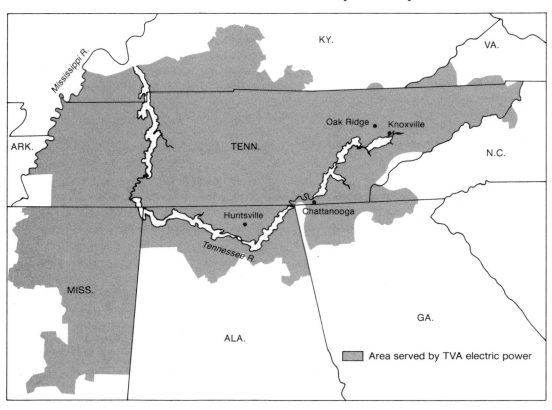

create six more regional agencies in the great river valleys of the nation. But emphasis on economic development and political resistance prevented the establishment of conservation programs outside agriculture.

Roosevelt remained confused about the road to industrial recovery through the spring of 1933. Nevertheless, the president committed himself to action after the Senate passed a radical bill introduced by Alabama Democrat Hugo Black. The Black bill limited the interstate shipment of goods to those produced by employees who worked no more than thirty hours a week. Roosevelt advisors Raymond Moley and General Hugh Johnson responded with the National Industrial Recovery Act (NIRA), an omnibus bill that Congress approved in June 1933. Based on World War I industrial coordination and the 1931 Swope Plan, the new bill freed corporations from antitrust provisions and created a National Recovery Administration (NRA) to supervise the enforcement of self-regulating industrial codes. These agreements allowed competing corporations in over seven hundred industries to curtail production, raise prices, regulate business practices, set minimum wages and maximum working hours, and ban child labor. Section 7(a) of the legislation compelled participating industrialists to accept collective bargaining rights for workers, a concession to urban liberals and union supporters represented by New York senator Robert F. Wagner. Roosevelt soon appointed Wagner to

Exhibit 6–5. First One–Hundred Days of New Deal
(March–June 1933)

- Abandonment of Gold Standard by Executive Action
- Civil Conservation Corps Reforestation Relief Act (created **CCC**)
- Federal Emergency Relief Act (created **FERA**—Federal Emergency Relief Administration)
- Agricultural Adjustment Act (created **AAA**—Agricultural Adjustment Administration)
- Tennessee Valley Authority Act (created **TVA**—Tennessee Valley Authority)
- Federal Securities Act
- Home Owners Refinancing Act (created **HOLC**—Home Owners Loan Corporation)
- Glass-Steagall Banking Act
- Farm Credit Act (created **FCA**—Farm Credit Administration)
- National Industrial Recovery Act (created **NRA**—National Recovery Administration and **PWA**—Public Works Administration)

take a second position as head of the National Labor Board, which Congress created to work out labor code disagreements between management and workers. The NRA labor provisions covered twenty million workers and gave half the nation's industrial work force the forty-hour week.

The NRA also included a Public Works Administration (PWA), funded with an initial appropriation of $3.3 billion. However, Secretary of the Interior Harold L. Ickes, anxious to avoid corruption and poor planning, moved too slowly to generate the purchasing power needed for economic recovery. Worse still, the NRA became bogged down in bitter controversies over code enforcement and agency goals.

Designed to raise prices, end destructive competition, and introduce planning to American industry, the NRA disappointed competing interest groups. Southern Democrats like Virginia's Carter Glass and many business leaders complained of excessive government interference. Consumers objected to high prices. Union representatives argued that corporations evaded the guarantees of Section 7(a). The most frequent criticism focused on charges that corporate-dominated code authorities fixed prices and drove small businesses to bankruptcy.

Roosevelt responded in March 1934 by appointing attorney Clarence Darrow to head the National Recovery Review Board. The Darrow panel confirmed that large corporations dominated the code boards and used their power to stifle competition and reap profits from price fixing. Roosevelt

Exhibit 6–6. The New Deal, 1934

- Gold Reserve Act
- Farm Mortgage Refinancing Act (created **FFMC**—Federal Farm Mortgage Corporation)
- Export-Import Bank
- Securities Exchange Act (created **SEC**—Securities and Exchange Commission)
- Communications Act (created **FCC**—Federal Communications Commission)
- Frazier-Lemke Farm Bankruptcy Act
- National Housing Act (created **FHA**—Federal Housing Administration)

replaced NRA head Hugh Johnson in September 1934, but the controversial agency never stimulated the profits and employment levels sought by its supporters. The NRA did, however, establish the principle of collective bargaining between management and labor and set minimal standards for American working conditions.

THE WELFARE STATE

Supplementing the ambitious industrial recovery program, Roosevelt created a massive government job program in 1935 as an alternative to cash relief for the unemployed. The Works Progress Administration (WPA) initially received an unprecedented $5 billion with authority to hire 3.5 million Americans; eventually, in its seven-year lifetime, it spent $11 billion to employ over seven million people in more than 250,000 projects. State and city governments administered the WPA to minimize charges of federal meddling. The program required applicants to submit to means tests and investigations to determine eligibility, and jobs paid below prevailing wages and excluded positions in the private sector. Despite these limitations, the agency succeeded in rebuilding the infrastructure of American society. In addition to its emphasis on roads, bridges, sewers, airports, and public buildings, the WPA created projects for dramatists, writers, musicians, and artists, providing the first federal sponsorship of the arts. Its National Youth Administration (NYA) also provided jobs and educational subsidies to young people and students.

As the federal government expanded its presence in the American economy, the administration received a stunning blow when the Supreme Court denied the constitutionality of the National Industrial Recovery Act in the *Schechter* case of 1935. The Court ruled unanimously that the NRA constituted an invalid transfer of legislative power from Congress to the president and that the attempt to regulate industry within states involved an improper use of the interstate commerce power. Infuriated, Roosevelt claimed that "we have been relegated to a horse and buggy definition of interstate commerce." Nine months later, the Court overturned the Agricultural Adjustment Act because the AAA processing tax regulated agricultural production outside the commerce clause of the Constitution.

Invalidation of the NIRA increased momentum toward comprehensive labor relations legislation. As a Progressive reformer, Roosevelt remained more concerned about wages and hours regulations than about union representation, but widespread strike activity in 1934 underlined the need for orderly processes of collective bargaining. In May 1935, the Senate approved a bill by Senator Wagner to outlaw "unfair labor practices." When passage in the House appeared certain, Roosevelt called the proposal "must" legislation. Considered the Magna Carta of organized labor, the National Labor Relations Act upheld the right of workers in interstate commerce to join unions and bargain collectively through their own representatives. The law bound employers to collective bargaining and forbade them from firing workers for union activity. It also prohibited company unions, yellow-dog contracts, employer blacklists, and labor spies. The National Labor Relations Board

The WPA in action. The Works Progress Administration employed over seven million Americans between 1935 and 1942 at a cost of $11 billion. Its projects ranged from aid to the arts to the reconstruction of bridges and sewers.

would supervise elections to determine which collective bargaining units workers preferred. The board would also investigate unfair employer practices, could issue cease and desist orders, and could review arbitrary firings. Although the statute did not apply to workers in agriculture, domestic service, public employment, or intrastate commerce, it initiated a historic shift in the relations between management and labor, making the federal government an active force in the recognition of union representation (for union activity in the 1930s, see pp. 253–56).

To satisfy pervasive demands for economic security and to provide for long-run stimulation of purchasing power among older Americans, Roosevelt

Exhibit 6–7. Public Secondary School Enrollment, 1932–1940 (in rounded millions)

1932	5.1m
1940	6.6m

Source: *Historial Statistics of the United States, Colonial Times to 1970* (1975)

Exhibit 6–8. Unemployment, 1933–1936
(percentage of civilian labor force)

1933	24.9%
1934	21.7%
1935	20.1%
1936	16.9%

Source: *Historical Statistics of the United States, Colonial Times to 1970* (1975)

pushed for social security legislation in 1935. The private charity system developed by Anglo-Protestant elites in the nineteenth century had been designed for small cities with homogeneous populations. During the 1920s, older Americans responded to changing conditions by successfully lobbying for pension laws in twenty-nine states. By the 1930s, social work experts and social security activists such as Secretary of Labor Frances Perkins and Dr. Francis E. Townsend challenged the Roosevelt administration to respond to the economic problems of the elderly. These critics argued that declining death rates, a contracting economy, and smaller families had produced an increased need for old-age insurance.

The Social Security Act of 1935 marked the institutionalization of the American welfare state. The law provided those over age sixty-five with monthly federal pensions from a self-supporting Social Security Administration. Unlike social welfare plans in other industrial nations, the American system of old-age insurance depended upon contributions in the form of income tax deductions from employees and payroll taxes on employers. To meet other problems of dependency, the Social Security Act established federal programs of Aid to Dependent Children (ADC), vocational training for the physically disabled, and assistance to homeless and neglected children. The president's Committee on Economic Security also recommended national health insurance, but pressure from the medical profession and fears of congressional resistance eliminated the proposal. Instead, the social security law promoted public health services and provided medical funds for mothers and children in economically distressed areas. Social security also offered federal aid for physically disabled children. The second half of the Social Security Act established the nation's first system of unemployment insurance, funded by federal payroll taxes on employers but administered by the states. The original coverage included only wage and salary workers in commerce and industry, but subsequent amendments eventually protected other Americans as well.

By 1935, insurgent senators such as Huey Long, Burton Wheeler, George Norris, and Robert M. LaFollette, Jr., increasingly pressed Roosevelt for redistribution of wealth and control of corporate power. The president flirted with a proposed personal income tax to "prevent an unjust concentration of wealth and economic power." But when congressional committees weakened the Wealth Tax with loopholes, Roosevelt relegated the bill to a minor revenue measure.

The White House responded more forcefully to attacks on the power industry. In 1935, Roosevelt signed the Public Utility Holding Company Act,

Exhibit 6–9. Changes in Income Distribution, 1929–1936
(percentage of personal income received by each fifth
of families and individuals)

	1929	*1935–1936*
Lowest Fifth	12.5%	4.1%
Second Fifth		9.2%
Third Fifth	13.8%	14.1%
Fourth Fifth	19.3%	20.9%
Highest Fifth	54.4%	51.7%
(Top 5 Percent)	(30.0%)	(26.5%)

Source: *Historical Statistics of the United States, Colonial Times to 1970* (1975)

Exhibit 6–10. The New Deal, 1935

- Emergency Relief Appropriation Act (created **WPA**—Works Progress Administration)
- Soil Conservation Act (created Soil Conservation Service)
- Resettlement Administration (**RA**), created by executive order
- Rural Electrification Administration, (**REA**), created by executive order
- National Youth Administration (**NYA**), created by executive order
- National Labor Relations Act (created **NLRB**—National Labor Relations Board)
- Social Security Act
- Banking Act of 1935 (created Open Market Committee of Federal Reserve System)
- Public Utility Holding Company Act
- Frazier-Lemke Farm-Mortgage Moratorium Act
- Wealth Tax Act

a comprehensive statute that established simplification of the industry's corporate structure and supervision of gas and electric rates. A new agency, the Federal Power Commission (FPC), regulated interstate electric rates and business practices, while the Federal Trade Commission did the same for natural gas. By 1935, the twelve largest utility holding companies controlled almost half the power produced in the United States. The new law empowered the Securities and Exchange Commission to obtain information on the corporate structures of all American holding companies. A death-sentence clause set a term of five years during which each company had to demonstrate that it confined its services to a single area. Utilities that violated these conditions could be dissolved by the SEC. By threatening dissolution of private corporations, the Public Utility Holding Company Act ranked as one of the more radical laws in American history.

THE SECOND TERM

"Who is Ickes? Who is Wallace? Who is Hopkins, and in the name of all that is good and holy, who is Tugwell, and where did he blow from?" This denunciation of lofty New Deal planners, delivered at an American Liberty League banquet in early 1936, came from former Democratic presidential candidate Al Smith. Roosevelt's program of social welfare, taxation, and regulatory controls had provoked creation of the league by conservative Democrats and business allies in 1934. Two years later, when the Republicans selected Governor Alfred Landon of Kansas as their presidential nominee, the minority party focused on similar issues.

Charging that regulated monopoly had replaced free enterprise, the Republican platform characterized New Deal legislation as blatantly unconstitutional. The Republicans demanded a balanced federal budget and the transfer of relief programs to nonpolitical local agencies. By 1936, stories circulated that wealthy Republicans expressed their rage at Roosevelt by refusing to utter his name, often referring to the occupant of the White House as "that man." Conservative Democrats like Smith joined them in charging that the New Deal fostered class animosity and minority-bloc politics. "The trouble with this recognition of class war," complained Wilsonian Newton Baker, "is that it spreads like a grease stain and every group . . . demands the same sort of recognition."

Roosevelt adamantly rejected such attacks. Discarding ideological party labels, the president professed faith in "the capitalist system." "The true conservative," he proclaimed in his acceptance speech at the 1936 Democratic National Convention, "seeks to protect the system of private property and free enterprise by correcting such injustices and inequities as arise from it." The president had a responsibility to save business "from the selfish forces which ruined it," he stated, referring repeatedly to "economic royalists" who hid behind a professed defense of the nation's interest to protect their own power. In a bitter speech in New York's Madison Square Garden, climaxing the 1936 presidential campaign, Roosevelt remarked that the forces of "organized money are unanimous in their hate for me—and I welcome their hatred." If "the forces of selfishness and lust for power" had met their match in his first term, Roosevelt cried, the second term would certainly confront them with "their master."

Two-thirds of the nation's major newspapers endorsed "Alf" Landon and his vice-presidential running mate, Frank Knox of Illinois. The conservative *Literary Digest* even predicted a sweeping Republican victory. But Roosevelt succeeded in conveying the impression that a competent and caring administration had set economic recovery in motion. The results provided the Democrats with a tremendous landslide, giving them every state except

Exhibit 6–11. Federal Receipts and Outlays, 1933–1936 (in rounded billions of dollars)

	Receipts	Outlays	Deficits
1933	$2.1b	$4.7b	$2.6b
1934	$3.1b	$6.5b	$3.4b
1935	$3.8b	$6.3b	$2.5b
1936	$4.2b	$7.6b	$3.4b

Source: *Historical Statistics of the United States, Colonial Times to 1970* (1975)

**Exhibit 6–12. Gross National Product, 1933–1936
(in rounded billions of dollars at current prices)**

1933	$55.6b
1934	$65.1b
1935	$72.2b
1936	$82.5b

Source: *Historical Statistics of the United States, Colonial Times to 1970* (1975)

**Exhibit 6–13. Voter Participation in Presidential Elections, 1932–1936
(percentage of eligible voters)**

1932	56.9%
1936	61.0%

Source: *Historical Statistics of the United States, Colonial Times to 1970* (1975)

Maine and Vermont. As the president gathered 27.7 million votes (61 percent) to Landon's 16.6 million (36.5 percent), the Democrats captured a 76–16 majority in the Senate and took the House by a 331–89 margin. Roosevelt and his party forged an effective coalition that tied farmers and southerners to the urban votes of union workers, white ethnics, blacks, and middle-class liberals. The New Deal coalition also depended upon support from Labor's Non-Partisan League and nearly $800,000 in contributions from industrial unions. Furthermore, black voters began their long association with the Democratic party.

In his second term, Roosevelt extended New Deal reforms to include sharecroppers, tenant farmers, and industrial workers. His 1937 inaugural address set the tone by pointing to "tens of millions" of Americans without the necessities of life. "I see one-third of a nation ill-housed, ill-clad, ill-nourished," declared the president. Promising to eliminate poverty and make every American the subject of government concern, Roosevelt declared that his generation had "a rendezvous with destiny."

The president had already created the Resettlement Administration in 1935, which relocated some tenants and poor farmers in experimental homestead communities and established several government "greenbelt towns" (model suburban communities) for city workers. In 1937, Congress responded to farm union pressure by creating the Farm Security Administration (FSA). In the next four years, the FSA built county health care facilities and sanitary camps for rural migrants. The agency also provided over $500 million in long-term, low-interest loans to tenants, sharecroppers, and farm laborers. However, those loan applications depended upon the approval of committees of local farmers who often sought to preserve the dependency of poor applicants. By 1945, 1.8 million tenants still remained on the land.

Seeking a constitutional formula to aid independent farmers and resume economic planning in agriculture, Roosevelt supported the second Agricultural Adjustment Act in 1938. The new law guaranteed federal support of farm prices but replaced the unconstitutional processing tax with funding from the Treasury. Through the Commodity Credit Corporation, farmers received loans if they took surplus crops off the market. Another agency, the Federal Crop Insurance Corporation, provided "social security" for wheat and cotton farmers by accepting crop payments as insurance premiums against future crop loss. Incentive payments for most farmers averaged less than $100 a year, and 1939 crop prices remained below 1929 levels. Yet farmers received supplementary benefits from New Deal conservation policies. Congress created the Soil Conservation Service in 1935, which sent out government teams to promote contour plowing, rotation of crops, fertilizing, and gully planting. Subsequent legislation provided payments for farmers who grew soil-conserving crops. Another agency, the Federal Surplus Relief Corporation, distributed surplus produce to state relief organizations and inaugurated the food stamp program for needy families in 1939.

With the demise of the NRA, Roosevelt pushed for a federal law to regulate wages and hours in industry. Organized labor balked at government interference with wage negotiations, however, and southerners, citing their region's lower living costs, pressed to conserve the South's lower wage scales. Congress finally overcame the deadlock by passing the Fair Labor Standards Act in 1938. This law gave industrialists two years to implement a forty-cent-per-hour minimum wage and a forty-hour week. Despite the low wage scales and numerous exceptions to its provisions, the Labor Act provided pay increases for over twelve million American workers in interstate commerce and established the principle of national standards for industrial wages. The legislation regulated child labor by prohibiting interstate shipment of most industrial goods produced by minors under age sixteen. The law also banned workers between ages sixteen and eighteen from occupations declared hazardous by the Children's Bureau. These provisions blocked child labor in industrial occupations where it had already declined, although children continued to work in agriculture, retail trades, and small business.

Despite occasional legislative victories, Roosevelt faced an increasingly hostile Congress in his second term. The president's political problems originated in a bitter controversy over the Supreme Court. Stung by crippling Court defeats, Roosevelt introduced a judiciary reorganization bill in 1937. The surprise package authorized the president to appoint an additional

Exhibit 6–14. The New Deal, 1936–1938

1936	• Soil Conservation and Domestic Allotment Act
	• Robinson-Patman Anti-Price Discrimination Act
1937	• Bankhead-Jones Farm Tenant Act (created **FSA**—Farm Security Administration)
	• Miller-Tydings Enabling Act
	• Wagner-Steagall National Housing Act (created **USHA**—United States Housing Authority)
1938	• Agricultural Adjustment Act (created **FCIC**—Federal Crop Insurance Corporation)
	• Fair Labor Standards Act

Supreme Court judge for each justice who did not retire at age seventy. Six Court judges had reached that age at the time, and the administration plan could have increased the tribunal's membership from nine to fifteen.

Fearing that the conservative Court would eventually invalidate the entire New Deal, Roosevelt blindly pushed his bill through hearings of the Senate Judiciary Committee in March and April of 1937. But many Democrats joined Republicans, progressives, and conservatives in opposing the measure as a presidential attempt to ''pack'' the Supreme Court and destroy the balance of power among the three branches of government. Democratic progressive Burton Wheeler assumed leadership of the fight. When Wheeler produced a letter in which Chief Justice Charles Evans Hughes asserted the Court's ability to manage its case load without added help, Roosevelt's prospects for victory dimmed. The impending resignation of Justice Willis Van Devanter, a New Deal adversary, and the Court's increased acceptance of social legislation further weakened the president's position. In July 1937, the Senate quietly ended the acrimonious debate by recommitting the judicial plan to committee in a 70–20 vote.

Charles Evans Hughes, chief justice of the Supreme Court, 1930–1940. Hughes played a major role in the effort to defeat Roosevelt's attempt to restructure the Court in 1937.

By asking Congress for unprecedented powers over another branch of government, Roosevelt lent credence to attacks on his "dictatorial" methods. His single-minded determination to impose the Court bill fed anxieties that a powerful presidential bureaucracy had destroyed traditional American freedoms. Conservatives also criticized White House support for union workers who staged illegal "sit-downs" on the property of industrial corporations (discussed later in this chapter).

These fears figured in congressional defeats for the administration's executive reorganization bills of 1937 and 1938. Recommended by the President's Committee on Administrative Management, the proposals sought to increase government efficiency by regrouping and simplifying federal agencies. But the bitter Court fight helped to destroy the Roosevelt myth of invincibility and gave anti–New Dealers a new lease on life. Newspaper publisher Frank Gannett's National Committee to Uphold Constitutional Government, which was formed to fight Roosevelt's judiciary bill, now portrayed executive reorganization as a dangerous tool of the president's "dictatorial ambitions." Progressives like Burton Wheeler also resented usurpation of congressional power by elite New Deal bureaucrats who were accountable to the White House.

As recovery proceeded, in 1937, Roosevelt became worried about causing inflation and responded by cutting spending by the WPA and PWA. But between August 1937 and March 1938, the most precipitous economic decline in American history sent unemployment soaring from under seven million to over eleven million. The stock market lost two-thirds of the ground it gained during the entire New Deal. After heated debate within the administration, the president agreed to ask Congress to reduce corporate taxes and stimulate purchasing power through government spending. Following the advice of Federal Reserve Board governor Marriner Eccles, Roosevelt also requested an extra $3 billion for government programs such as the WPA. For the first time in American history, a chief executive accepted deficit spending as a tool of economic planning. This use of government expenditures as a substitute for private investment coincided with the ideas of British economist John Maynard Keynes, who argued that government manipulation of capital investment could end depressions forever. Federal spending, which hovered at $2 billion in 1933, leaped to $5.2 billion in 1939.

Inspired into action by the recession and the need for government activism, Roosevelt attempted to mold the Democratic party to his needs.

Exhibit 6–15. Federal Receipts and Outlays, 1936–1939 (in rounded billions of dollars)

	Receipts	Outlays	Deficits
1936	$4.2b	$7.6b	$3.4b
1937	$5.6b	$8.4b	$2.8b
1938	$7.0b	$7.2b	$0.2b
1939	$6.6b	$9.4b	$2.8b

Source: *Historical Statistics of the United States, Colonial Times to 1970* (1975)

Exhibit 6–16. Government Social Welfare Spending, 1929–1939
(rounded billions of dollars)

	Welfare Spending	*Percentage of GNP*
1929	$3.9b	3.9%
1931	$4.2b	5.1%
1933	$4.5b	7.9%
1935	$6.5b	9.5%
1937	$7.9b	9.1%
1939	$9.2b	10.5%

Source: *Historical Statistics of the United States, Colonial Times to 1970* (1975)

Once the president lost the Court fight in 1937, however, an anti–New Deal coalition emerged in Congress. Composed of conservative Republicans and rural Democrats, the powerful bloc reflected nonurban and small business constituencies which did not benefit from New Deal assistance to union workers, ethnics, blacks, and relief recipients. Often holding seniority on major congressional committees, Roosevelt's adversaries attacked the waste of government bureaucracy and pleaded that the emergency measures of the New Deal had gone far enough.

Roosevelt rose to the conservative challenge by campaigning only for administration loyalists in the 1938 Democratic primaries. But the president's attempt to "purge" the party of conservatives backfired when Democratic Senate traditionalists such as Georgia's Walter F. George, South Carolina's "Cotton Ed" Smith, and Maryland's Millard Tydings emerged victorious. In the general election, moreover, the Republicans gained eighty-one seats in the House and eight in the Senate. The new congressional generation of Republican conservatives included John W. Bricker and Robert Taft of Ohio, Thomas E. Dewey of New York, Harold E. Stassen of Minnesota, and Karl E. Mundt of North Dakota, people who would remain on the political landscape into the 1950s.

Roosevelt's political difficulties and the 1937–38 economic recession created a psychology of retreat. Even when sales of military supplies to Britain and France stimulated economic recovery in mid-1938, a large number of Democrats and Republicans remained committed to domestic budget retrenchment, private enterprise, and states' rights. In 1938, Congress revealed

Exhibit 6–17. Unemployment, 1937–1941
(as percentage of civilian labor force)

1937	14.3%
1938	19.0%
1939	17.2%
1940	14.6%
1941	9.9%

Source: *Historical Statistics of the United States, Colonial Times to 1970* (1975)

its impatience with political radicalism by recreating the House Committee on Un-American Activities (HUAC). First established in 1934, the panel had investigated the activities of the German-American Bund, a Nazi group that espoused Adolf Hitler's anti-Semitism and fascist agenda. Congressional liberals such as New York City's Samuel Dickstein hoped to continue monitoring American Nazis in the tense climate of 1938 (see chapter 7). But HUAC chairman Martin Dies of Texas preferred to investigate allegations of communist infiltration of New Deal agencies such as the WPA's Federal Theater Project. The HUAC's insistence on associating domestic reform with international communism created precedents for more damaging inquiries in the next decade.

Congress reacted angrily to charges that WPA office holders interfered politically in the 1938 election, and passed the Hatch Act of 1939. The new law prohibited campaign activity by federal employees and sought to eradicate political influence by New Deal beneficiaries. Congress also scaled down WPA appropriations, reduced agency wage scales, and abolished the Federal Theater Project. As Franklin Roosevelt approached the election year of 1940, both Congress and the country appeared to have turned conservative.

THE MANAGERIAL STATE

Roosevelt's rhetoric about "economic royalists" and selfish business interests bristled conservatives but rarely translated into tangible policy. The New Deal never effectively fought economic concentration, although in 1938, the president asked Congress to participate in an investigation of monopoly practices. The Temporary National Economic Committee (TNEC) Report found monopoly techniques strengthened in the Depression, and called for antitrust prosecution to decentralize corporate resources and activity. Beginning in 1938, Assistant Attorney General Thurman Arnold initiated a flurry of antitrust suits against a few corporate giants, but these remained isolated actions. The Depression, in fact, consolidated the dominance of big business. By 1937, the six leading industrial firms made nearly one-quarter of the profit earned by the one thousand largest companies in the United States.

New Deal reform meant that a federal bureaucracy now regulated and stabilized the nation's economic life through a system of administrative agencies, subsidies, and government transfer payments (social welfare) to individual recipients. But the managerial state did not redistribute income or

**Exhibit 6–18. Gross National Production, 1936–1939
(in rounded billions of dollars at current prices)**

1936	$82.5b
1937	$90.4b
1938	$84.7b
1939	$90.5b

Source: *Historical Statistics of the United States, Colonial Times to 1970* (1975)

Exhibit 6–19. Consumer Price Index, 1936–1940
(1967 = 100)

1936	41.5
1938	42.2
1940	42.0

Source: *Historical Statistics of the United States, Colonial Times to 1970* (1975)

wealth. Indeed, budget deficits forced state governments to resort to regressive measures such as sales and gasoline taxes to supplement less lucrative property and corporate assessments. Furthermore, the New Deal did not bring economic recovery until Britain and France began ordering military supplies from American industry in 1938 (see chapter 7). Yet the Roosevelt presidency involved a tremendous expansion of federal bureaucracy and executive power.

The Supreme Court played a major role in legitimizing this expansion of federal authority. During the debate over Roosevelt's attempt to restructure the Court, the tribunal reversed past practice and began to validate New Deal legislation such as the Wagner Act and the Social Security Act. The "constitutional revolution" of the late 1930s marked the Supreme Court's acceptance of government intervention in the economy. By invoking a broad definition of "stream of commerce," the Court made government economic involvement a political choice rather than a constitutional controversy. Between 1937 and 1939, deaths and retirements allowed Roosevelt to make four appointments to the Court. The new justices included liberals Hugo Black, Felix Frankfurter, and William O. Douglas and extended the New Deal's influence on government into the 1960s.

Roosevelt also expanded the power of the presidency. The White House now became the focus of the federal government, initiating legislation, drafting bills, lobbying Congress, and communicating with the American people. The president delivered sixteen radio "fireside chats" in his first two terms, several to national audiences surpassing sixty million. With passage of the Administrative Reorganization Act of 1939, Roosevelt issued Executive Order 8248, which created the Executive Office of the President and established a White House staff and administrative assistants. Roosevelt also

Exhibit 6–20. Imports and Exports of Goods and Services, 1936–1939
(in rounded billions of dollars)

	Imports	Exports	Trade Surplus
1936	$3.4b	$3.5b	$0.1b
1937	$4.3b	$4.5b	$0.2b
1938	$3.0b	$4.3b	$1.3b
1939	$3.4b	$4.4b	$1.0b

Source:*Historical Statistics of the United States, Colonial Times to 1970* (1975)

moved the Bureau of the Budget from the Treasury to the president's office, setting the precedent for placing agencies directly under the White House. This style of centralized rule by government managers and professionals carried over into World War II, when the demands of national security replaced the mission of economic recovery.

Expansion of the federal bureaucracy also led to increased police powers for executive agencies. The creation of the Federal Deposit Insurance Corporation, for example, inadvertently made most bank robberies federal crimes under the jurisdiction of the Federal Bureau of Investigation (FBI). Highly publicized FBI arrests of Depression bank robbers such as John Dillinger accustomed Americans to the idea of a federal police force. When the son of Charles and Anne Lindbergh was abducted and murdered in 1932, Congress made kidnapping a federal crime. Roosevelt also furthered government police powers when he requested secret investigations of Nazis and Communists for "subversive activities" in the mid 1930s. The Federal Communications Act of 1934 made telephone wiretapping illegal. Yet presidential memos in 1936, 1939, and 1940 permitted the FBI to use electronic eavesdropping, or "bugging," in domestic and foreign security investigations, even without authority from the attorney general.

Depression and
Latin American Relations

New Deal administrators supplemented their recovery programs with an attempt to expand Depression markets in Latin America. In 1934, Congress agreed to the Reciprocal Trade Agreement Act, which gave the president the right to halve tariffs on Latin American goods in return for tariff reductions from other nations. Roosevelt established the Export-Import Bank in the same year. The new agency lent government funds to Latin American republics in exchange for agreements to purchase the products of American corporations. By 1935, the United States sent half its cotton and steel mill exports to Latin America.

In the effort to cement ties to the region, Roosevelt proclaimed the Good Neighbor Policy in 1933. Declaring a hemispheric partnership in which the United States would respect the rights of its neighbors, the president accelerated the military withdrawals initiated by Hoover. Marines left Nicaragua in 1933, and the United States abandoned the interventionist Platt amendment in Cuba. A treaty with Panama consolidated American sovereignty over the Canal Zone, but eliminated American rights of intervention. The Roosevelt administration also withdrew the Marines from Haiti, although it maintained a customs receivership until 1941. To improve its image in the hemisphere, the United States ratified the Buenos Aires Convention at the 1936 Pan-American Conference, obliging Washington to settle inter-American disputes by arbitration. Roosevelt also refused to intervene in Mexico in 1938 when a dispute with American oil corporations resulted in the expropriation of private holdings.

Nicaraguan dictator Anastasio Somoza Garcia (l.) riding with President Roosevelt. The United States supported Latin American strongmen such as Somoza and Cuban dictator Fulgencio Batista because it hoped to promote business interests and stability in the region.

Despite these gestures, the United States continued to employ a heavy hand in Latin American politics. When the Marines left Nicaragua, they handed military power to Anastasio Somoza Garcia, the American-trained commander of the National Guard. Somoza soon ordered the assassination of nationalist guerrila General Cesar Augusto Sandino and had himself elected president in 1936. The ensuing Somoza dictatorship maintained close ties to the Roosevelt administration despite the enmity of the rebel Sandinistas. In Cuba, the United States refused to accept a nationalist revolution in 1933, only to extend recognition to a military government friendly to American interests the following year.

ETHNIC ASSIMILATION AND OPPRESSION

The New Deal helped assimilate ethnic Americans to the national mainstream. As anxieties over the influx of southern and eastern Europeans abated with immigration restriction in the 1920s, many Americans began to accept a pluralist definition of national character. Building on this growing tolerance, and hoping to unify the country behind national recovery programs, the Roosevelt administration carefully cultivated the concepts of multiple "American faiths" and the Judeo-Christian heritage. The president responded to the large Democratic vote among Irish- Americans and eastern Europeans with political appointments. One of every nine Roosevelt positions went to a Catholic or Jew, as opposed to one of every twenty-five Hoover positions. Moreover, Catholics and Jews received 30 percent of the president's nominations for federal judgeships, including the appointments of Supreme Court justice Felix Frankfurter and federal judge Matthew Abruzzo. The administration also cooperated with ethnic political machines in such cities as Boston, Kansas City, and Jersey City.

For ethnic Americans just beginning to grasp the dream of equal opportunity, however, the Depression was a disaster. Immigrant families provided most of the nation's unskilled labor and never recovered from the loss of occupational mobility caused by the economic crisis. Ethnics continued to maintain mutual aid societies and fraternal organizations, first formed in the early years of the century, to promote family, cultural, and religious traditions. But as the Depression deepened, the importance of job security and better wages led many working-class ethnics to join the industrial union movement.

For Mexican-Americans, the Depression brought even worse living conditions. Increased job competition in southwestern agriculture and midwestern industry prompted campaigns to "repatriate" Mexican-Americans south of the border. More than one-half million, half of them American- born, left the United States in the 1930s. In Los Angeles, the largest Mexican community in the nation, police roundups and arrests in 1931 forced inhabitants to flee the country. Colorado used a temporary declaration of martial law to turn away Mexican job seekers at the New Mexico border. In the Midwest, coalitions of civic groups and local authorities encouraged the exodus of nearly half the Mexicans from the area.

Declining wages and increased mechanization led Mexican-American farmworkers in California to form labor unions. By 1934, a confederation of field unions represented fifty locals and five thousand members. Fearing Communist agitation and labor unrest in the perishable citrus and vegetable industry, California growers reacted violently, using a combination of police arrests and vigilante attacks to destroy the farmworker movement. Not until the 1960s would Mexican-Americans succeed in organizing unions in California agriculture.

Over two-hundred thousand Anglo-Protestant refugees from the Great Plains drought fared no better. Immortalized in John Steinbeck's *Grapes of Wrath* (1939), the Okie dust bowl migrants organized farmworker unions only to be attacked by growers as misfits who were dupes for Red agitators.

THE BLACK DILEMMA AND THE INDIAN NEW DEAL

Like poor whites of the Depression South, blacks faced an untenable position in the devastated cotton industry. Both the economic collapse and the use of synthetic fibers sank cotton prices to their lowest levels since the 1890s. As banks and insurance companies foreclosed one-third of southern cotton fields, black farmers found themselves at the mercy of landlords, heavy debt,

Plantation overseer and field hands in the Mississippi delta, 1936. This photograph was taken by Dorothea Lange for the Farm Security Administration.

and high interest rates. The president's Committee on Farm Tenancy described the sharecropper standards of living as "below any level of decency" in 1937. Plagued by mechanization, many black and white sharecroppers and tenants found themselves evicted by landlords who needed to qualify for government farm subsidies by limiting cultivated acreage.

While southern economic conditions worsened, racial segregation continued to confine blacks to a rigid caste system. Public accommodations remained segregated and blacks attended separate schools and churches. Even movie theaters featured a separate black balcony, derisively known as "nigger heaven." Whites in most southern towns addressed blacks only by their first names, regardless of age, and insisted that blacks use the rear door when calling on whites. Southern governments traditionally excluded blacks from jury service, and a rigid arrangement of poll taxes, literacy tests, and white primaries prevented blacks from voting in state and national elections.

Ever since the 1890s, southern racial antagonism had erupted sporadically in orgiastic lynching sprees. White men in the rural South continued to believe that black males constituted a threat to the purity of white women and social decorum. In 1931, Alabama authorities falsely accused nine black teenage hobos of raping two white girls riding the same freight train. The *Scottsboro* case became a major civil liberty cause of the era. Initiated by the Communist party, the campaign to save the black teenagers introduced many white liberals to the racism of southern society. Found guilty in these controversial trials, the defendants saw their convictions reversed by the Supreme Court in 1935.

Communists and socialists also had some success in organizing black tenants and sharecroppers. The biracial Alabama Sharecroppers Union (ASU), initiated by white Communists, claimed twelve thousand members by 1935, and engaged in several violent confrontations with county deputies. In Arkansas, in 1934, the Socialist party helped a group of local blacks and whites organize the Southern Tenant Farmers Union (STFU), which eventually claimed twenty-five thousand members. The STFU not only attacked evictions and low wages, but also demonstrated against racist legacies such as the poll tax, inferior education of blacks, and denial of civil liberties. Since unions like the ASU and STFU threatened local elites, southern conservatives associated civil rights activities with radical Communist agitation.

While southern blacks faced rural poverty and a rigid caste system, migrants to the North and West confronted devastating urban problems. Depression conditions worsened unemployment among northern blacks and trapped others in the most poorly paid service and manual labor positions. Job mobility for northern blacks continued to lag behind that for white ethnics, as black workers frequently found themselves excluded even from semiskilled positions in manufacturing and transportation. Meanwhile, black unemployment rates remained three times higher than those of whites. In the depths of the Depression, about half of all black workers held no jobs. Because employers often believed that no black should hold a position that a white could fill, nearly two-thirds of black jobs fell within agriculture and domestic service.

The New Deal had a mixed impact on northern blacks. With high unemployment rates, the percentage of urban blacks who received Depression relief remained three times that of urban whites. But demoralizing conditions in urban ghettos fostered profound resentment, resulting, for example, in a major riot in Harlem in 1935. The bitterness and incipient violence of northern ghetto life found description in black novelist Richard Wright's *Native Son* (1940).

Although black voters began to support the New Deal with heavy majorities in 1936, the Roosevelt administration failed to offer a civil rights program. Tied to a coalition that included southern Democrats, the president never challenged white supremacy or states' rights on racial matters. Accordingly, when the NAACP drafted a federal anti-lynching bill after a resurgence of vigilante murders of blacks in 1933, Roosevelt refused to support the proposal as "must" legislation. Without the president's help, supporters like Senator Robert Wagner failed to break a filibuster of southern Democrats.

Black leaders also condemned racial discrimination in New Deal work programs. Civil rights organizations such as the NAACP and the Urban

League fought successfully to extend the benefits of the National Youth Administration to blacks, and succeeded in including blacks in the Civil Conservation Corps. Yet the CCC maintained racially segregated camps when local mores so dictated. Black organizations also protested segregation in TVA model towns. Meanwhile, the NAACP continued legal campaigns for black rights in education, voting, and public accommodations. In 1936, a new coalition, the National Negro Congress (NNC), brought together virtually every national black leader to work for "racial progress." Led by union organizer A. Philip Randolph, the NNC encouraged black participation in the labor movement and tied black interests to New Deal liberalism. But a Communist attempt to win control of the organization led Randolph and other black leaders to abandon the NNC.

Although Roosevelt remained cool to civil rights demands, the president's wife was a friendly advocate of black issues. When the Daughters of the American Revolution refused to rent Washington's only concert stage to Marian Anderson, a black opera singer, Eleanor Roosevelt resigned from the organization and arranged for a recital on the steps of the Lincoln Memorial. There, on Easter Sunday 1939, seventy-five thousand people gathered with administration support for the first mass demonstration for civil rights in American history. The previous spring, black heavyweight Joe Louis had defeated German Max Schmeling with a first-round knockout in a boxing match promoted by Hitler as a test of Nazi racial supermen. The Louis victory not only showed that Americans could accept a black man as a fighter, but demonstrated that unlike German power, American strength derived from the pluralism of its culture.

The 1930s also brought a fresh approach to Native American life by the federal government. Spurred by Commissioner of Indian Affairs John Collier, the government acted to preserve Native American culture and resources. Collier's "Indian New Deal" encouraged tribal organization, economic self-sufficiency, and self-management. His Emergency Conservation Work Program, organized in 1933, functioned as an "all-Indian CCC." Collier persuaded Congress to pass the Indian Reorganization Act of 1934, a measure that guaranteed the principle of home rule through tribal constitutions written and ratified by each tribe. The law also provided government financial aid to support college education and promote the study of Native American culture. Its most controversial provision centered on the reversion of land-holdings to tribal title. Since the Dawes Act of 1887, landholding had been individual. By 1934, almost half such property included semiarid or desert lands, and only half the Native Americans in the country owned any land. Average Indian income in 1934 amounted to $48 a year.

Many Native Americans distrusted Collier's reforms, but over two-thirds of the tribes voted to participate. Conservative critics condemned the tribal property arrangement as "sovietization" of reservation life and claimed that the Bureau of Indian Affairs relegated Native Americans to reservation existence. But Collier believed that tribal cooperative and communal experience provided an alternative to the atomization of urban industrialism. Despite reduced appropriations, the New Deal administrator directed the BIA to assist self-governing tribal corporations in using conservation techniques

Exhibit 6–21. Women Workers, 1930–1940
(in rounded millions)

	Female	Male	Total
1930	10.7m	38.1m	48.8m
1940	12.1m	37.5m	49.6m

Source: *Historical Statistics of the United States, Colonial Times to 1970* (1975)

and establishing cooperative businesses. Although federal land policies frequently clashed with tribal traditions, Native Americans won freedom of contract and no longer needed government approval for tribal agreements. Yet, in practice, the BIA continued to deny legal rights to the tribal governments.

WOMEN AND THE RETREAT TO SECURITY

The Depression brought a double message for American women. Family economic pressures pushed women into the labor force, but social conservatism in a period of insecurity emphasized the need for women to stay at home. Women remained in the job force in about the same proportion as in the 1920s, but the percentage of female professionals dropped, and three-quarters of those continued to be teachers or nurses. In industry, female workers still earned between one-half and two-thirds the male wage scale, and tended to concentrate in low-paying textile mills and clothing factories. Nevertheless, Depression economics sometimes worked to their advantage. The willingness of women to perform menial tasks frequently meant that female unemployment ratios dipped below male unemployment ratios. Women often won jobs when corporations replaced old machinery and converted skilled "male" tasks to routine labor. Women also benefited from the ability of light industry and the service sector to recover more rapidly than male-dominated heavy industry from the economic collapse. Furthermore, federal funds brought an expansion of clerical service jobs open to women.

New Deal labor laws and union activity set important precedents for equal treatment in the work force by establishing hour and wage standards for both sexes. But social mores still frowned on female jobholding. During the Depression, psychologists reported alarming rates of sexual impotence among men no longer able to assert the masculine role of breadwinner. A 1936 Gallup poll indicated that 82 percent of the sample believed women should not take jobs if their husbands worked. Secretary of Labor Frances Perkins, the first female cabinet member in history, characterized women who worked "without need" as a menace to society. Twenty-six state legislatures considered bills prohibiting the employment of married women. Federal law stipulated that only one member of a family could work in a civil service job.

The Depression placed great pressure on American families, causing a decline in marriage and birth rates and contributing to a doubling of the divorce ratio. These realities encouraged a romanticizing of motherhood and home. One survey of college women found that three-fifths hoped to marry within a year or two of graduation. Middle-class women received advice to specialize in "feminine" occupations such as home economics or interior decorating, or to stay home. Such attitudes discouraged feminist political activity. While organizations such as the League of Women Voters furthered goals of social feminism, little support emerged for a separate women's agenda. Traditional women's issues such as health care, better working conditions, and the abolition of child labor often merged into broader New Deal and trade union campaigns.

Only in the South, where the Association of Southern Women for the Prevention of Lynching continued the evangelical zeal of Progressive reform, did women organize politically on the basis of gender. Yet the period's outstanding symbol of the socially conscious woman remained Eleanor Roosevelt, who acted as the president's personal advisor on human rights; lobbied for the interests of blacks, the poor, and women; and managed to gain the appointment of unprecedented numbers of women to federal diplomatic positions.

THE TRIUMPH
OF INDUSTRIAL UNIONISM

Many of the Depression gains experienced by blacks, white migrants, ethnics, and women came through increased union activity. By the 1930s, millions of whites and blacks originating from the South had grown accustomed to working with white ethnics in the mass production industries. As a result, ethnic rivalry and regional exclusiveness no longer prevented industrial workers from cooperating to organize labor unions. Despite the economic crisis, or because of it, union membership jumped from 2.7 million in 1933 to twelve million by 1943. By the time the nation entered World War II, nearly one-fourth of workers outside agriculture belonged to unions. Moreover, for the first time in American history, the government supported union recruiting. Section 7(a) of the National Industrial Recovery Act mandated that business codes incorporate collective bargaining procedures. Union leaders could tell workers that the president wanted them to form unions to fight the Depression. By mid-1934, seventeen hundred national and local unions thrived in mass production industries such as automobiles, steel, lumber, rubber, and aluminum.

John L. Lewis of the United Mine Workers (UMW) ranked as one of the most successful union organizers. After bitter struggles in the Pennsylvania mines, Lewis won union recognition under a single NRA code for the entire soft-coal industry. Following passage of the Wagner Act in 1935, he played a major role in forming the Congress of Industrial Organizations (CIO). The CIO organized steel, automobile, rubber, and radio workers on an industry-

FRANCES PERKINS
1880–1965

Government's greatest need is for females "who can be humble . . . and who are willing to begin at the bottom." That is what Secretary of Labor Frances Perkins told a women's conference in the 1930s. Yet the first woman cabinet officer in American history often ignored her own advice. As a Mount Holyoke College student at the turn of the century, the young Perkins found herself electrified by a speech made by Progressive social activist Florence Kelley. The experience rallied her to the crusade against child labor led by the National Consumers' League. A professional social worker who joined Jane Addams at Hull House, Perkins became executive secretary of the New York City Consumers' League in 1910. As the organization's key lobbyist, she worked closely with the legislature in Albany, where she met future patrons of her career such as Alfred E. Smith and Franklin D. Roosevelt.

Perkins soon found herself involved in Progressive crusades to secure workers' rights, negotiate labor-management conflicts, and secure safer working conditions. Until Al Smith assumed the New York State governorship in 1918, she considered her work nonpartisan. But Smith named the dynamic social worker to the State Industrial Commission, and his successor, Franklin Roosevelt, made her chief advisor on labor matters. Perkins played a major role in persuading Roosevelt to act vigorously to combat the economic slump following the stock market crash of 1929. The governor's program of unemployment relief helped launch him toward national office. Elected to the presidency in 1932, Roosevelt named Perkins secretary of labor.

"Many good and intelligent women do dress in ways that are very attractive and pretty," Perkins once commented, (cont.)

wide basis instead of using the AFL's craft divisions. The CIO unions stressed grass roots organization and recruited blue-collar ethnics, southern whites, blacks, and women in all phases of factory and mill work. Sensitive to problems on the mechanized assembly line, the industrial unions responded to grievances with direct and immediate action. Membership in the CIO began with one million workers in 1935 and reached 2.8 million by 1941.

Exhibit 6–22. Labor Union Membership, 1936–1940
(in rounded millions)

1936	4.1m
1938	6.1m
1940	7.3m

Source: *Historical Statistics of the United States, Colonial Times to 1970* (1975)

"but don't particularly invite confidence in their common sense, integrity, or sense of justice." Acutely aware of her pioneering role as the first woman cabinet officer, Perkins intended to be taken seriously. Consequently, she regularly dressed in a plain black dress, a white bow, and a small tricorn hat. Presidential memoranda shared drawer space with needles and thread. An interviewer frustrated by her cautious style denounced her as a "colorless woman who talked as if she had swallowed a press release."

Perkins did not intend to become the special champion of women. She took pride in an often-quoted remark by her fellow cabinet member Harold Ickes: "Frances Perkins is the best man in the cabinet." Despite having her own career, the secretary of labor denounced affluent women who sought employment outside the home. "Any woman capable of supporting herself without a job," she wrote in 1930, "should devote herself to motherhood and the home."

A successful woman skeptical of feminist issues, Perkins was also a labor secretary suspicious of organized labor. A strong advocate of unemployment relief through public works spending, she headed Roosevelt's Committee on Economic Security. In 1934, the panel endorsed a national old-age and survivors insurance plan, a prototype of the Social Security Act. In the tradition of other Progressive Era social workers, Perkins believed that social insurance constituted "a fundamental part of another great forward step in that liberation of humanity which began with the Renaissance." Yet she reacted coolly to the Wagner Act's endorsement of unionization and collective bargaining. In her own words, she "never lifted a finger" for the measure and "had very little sympathy with the bill." Despite such conservatism, Perkins remained an important symbol of the assertive New Deal liberalism that characterized the Roosevelt administration. ■

The industrial union movement provided a major outlet for Depression militancy. Whereas unemployment produced passivity and demoralization, blue-collar workers rose against the arbitrary policies of corporate management. When industrial corporations refused to honor the Wagner Act's provisions for collective bargaining, a series of worker rebellions erupted. In 1936 and 1937, one-half million industrial workers joined CIO sit-downs, in which strikers stopped production by occupying plants and factories. A major turning point in the campaign occurred when President Roosevelt pressured General Motors to negotiate with the United Auto Workers. Shortly thereafter, United States Steel, a bitter opponent of industrial unionism in 1919, settled amicably with the steel workers union.

Unions helped large corporations predict labor costs, provided orderly processes for grievances, and furthered shop discipline. Corporate management resented seniority clauses that interfered with decision making in promotion and hiring, but union bureaucracy prevented costly walkouts and slowdowns. Smaller firms felt more threatened by union wage demands and

Chicago Memorial Day Massacre at Republic Steel, 1937. Labor strife reached violent proportions during the "little steel" strikes of that year. The unrest accompanied the growth of industrial unionism and the use of the controversial "sit-down" by striking workers.

managerial interference. When the CIO's Steel Workers Organizing Committee turned to the lesser steel corporations, for example, it met brutal resistance to industrial unionism. The climax to the emotional Little Steel Strike came when one thousand workers and their families marched on Republic Steel's Chicago plant in May 1937 and were fired upon by city police, who killed ten and injured fifty-eight. The CIO unions abandoned sit-downs after they lost the Little Steel Strike and the Supreme Court declared sit-downs illegal in 1939.

As the industrial economy mobilized for World War II, most CIO unions accepted the restrained "business unionism" of the AFL. Adopting the Progressive consensus that called for a democracy of consumers instead of aproducer's democracy based on worker control, American unions dropped demands to participate in production planning and conformed to managerial imperatives. Through this arrangement, the unions permitted corporations to pass higher labor costs to consumers. As the CIO and AFL grew to impressive proportions during wartime, professional union managers and negotiators began to separate the rank and file from crucial decision making, and worker apathy replaced participation in union affairs.

The union movement of the 1930s won substantive gains for industrial workers. Government and union machinery now required corporations to show cause in disciplining employees, a guarantee against the arbitrary firings that Depression workers feared. Seniority provided job security for older workers frequently victimized by assembly line management. Unions could also set standards of equity and so prod nonunion firms into paying competitive wages. Finally, the union movement gave industrial workers a sense of pride and dignity in an era of social chaos.

Exhibit 6–23. White Collar and Manual Employees, 1930–1940
(in rounded millions)

	White Collar	Manual	All Employees
1930	14.3m	19.3m	48.7m
1940	16.1m	20.6m	51.7m

Source: *Historical Statistics of the United States, Colonial Times to 1970* (1975)

RADICALISM IN THE INTELLIGENTSIA

"There is no longer I, there is WE," exclaimed author Dorothy Parker in the 1930s. "The day of the individual is dead." Amid economic collapse and social insecurity, American intellectuals rejected the self-indulgence of the 1920s and focused on social and political themes. The Depression provided the opportunity to propose a reconstruction of society. Stuart Chase, a widely read economist, argued that a collectivist economy, neither capitalist nor socialist, could best use technology to distribute wealth. Such hopes for a planned cooperative commonwealth found support among progressives like John Dewey, Lincoln Steffens, and economist George Soule. Younger theorists such as philosopher Sidney Hook and theologian Reinhold Niebuhr even borrowed Marxist critiques to suggest that the Depression had outdated liberal approaches to political and economic problems.

Most leading social theorists of the 1930s called for the redistribution of wealth and power in a planned economy directed toward the elimination of poverty and the building of a national community. Socialist Norman Thomas, a Presbyterian minister, garnered 885,000 votes in the 1932 presidential election. In California, socialist writer Upton Sinclair won the 1934 Democratic gubernatorial primary, although business and movie industry leaders helped defeat him in the general election. The obvious failures of corporate capitalism also stimulated a great interest in Marxism and the Communist party. Influenced by such challenges, literary critics Granville Hicks, Edmund Wilson, and *New Masses* editor Michael Gold stressed the need to replace "bourgeois" individualism with collectivist ideas and a commitment to political action.

Literature in the 1930s reflected the political concerns of intellectuals seeking a new order. Writers like Edmund Wilson, Theodore Dreiser, Sherwood Anderson, and John Dos Passos turned to documentary forms to express the problems of ordinary Americans. In a stark photo essay, *Let Us Now Praise Famous Men* (1941), a documentary compiled for the Farm Security Administration, James Agee and Walker Evans portrayed the dignity and perseverance of Alabama sharecroppers. Other middle-class intellectuals including Jack Conroy and Robert Cantwell used literature as a weapon in the class war by writing "proletarian novels" such as *The Disinherited* (1933) and *Land of Plenty* (1934).

The most lasting Depression novels, however, emphasized themes of personal honor and integrity. Ernest Hemingway rooted his concern for individualism in a novel about a strike, entitled *To Have and Have Not* (1937).

In *For Whom the Bell Tolls* (1941), Hemingway introduced discussions of individual will and solidarity within the context of the antifascist campaigns of the Spanish Civil War. A similar concern for endurance and personal survival appeared in Erskine Caldwell's *Tobacco Road* (1932), a popular story about impoverished Georgia sharecroppers. In the *Studs Lonigan* trilogy (1936), James T. Farrell placed the struggle for survival among Irish- Catholics in the slums of Chicago. Two acclaimed works of the period were John Dos Passos's *U.S.A.* trilogy (1930–36) and John Steinbeck's *Grapes of Wrath* (1939). Using a montage of imagery, vernacular language, and historical documentary, Dos Passos depicted the moral disintegration of the American spirit under corporate capitalism. Steinbeck reiterated a traditional belief that when people lost roots in the soil, they lost meaning to their lives.

The Communist party played a major role in the intellectuals' search for a new American community. But the limitations of this approach became clear when threats of international fascism moved the Soviet Union to espouse a "popular front" between national Communist movements and traditional political parties in 1935. The new coalition meant that American Communists accepted New Deal institutions, supported Roosevelt as the people's leader, and viewed social change as an evolutionary process. Fearing the onset of fascism without an alliance with the middle class, communist sympathizers embraced peace, social progress, and democratic values as the leading priorities of their movement. By 1938, the Communist party had recruited fifty-five thousand members. But defeat of the popular front by Fascists in the Spanish Civil War, followed by news of Josef Stalin's purges of fellow revolutionaries in the Soviet Union and announcement of the Nazi-Soviet Nonaggression Pact of 1939, produced profound disillusionment.

By the end of the decade, many American radicals felt sure that capitalism did not face extinction and that human rights received better protection in the United States than in totalitarian regimes overseas. Writers like Dos Passos, Sinclair Lewis, poet Archibald MacLeish, and critic Alfred Kazin looked to the past to establish continuity with a tradition of American vitality and democracy. These intellectuals sought recovery and stability, not revolt, and later welcomed the opportunities of World War II to affirm the core values of American life. Consequently, the political and psychic wounds of the 1930s produced a generation of intellectuals committed to an American consensus. No longer willing to mount criticism against the nation's culture and national institutions, intellectuals increasingly tied their activities to government programs and support of the status quo.

GRASS ROOTS RADICALISM

Violence played a surprisingly small role in Depression radicalism. Moreover, a substantial amount of 1930s dissidence did not originate with the union movement, the writers, or the socialist parties. Instead, the Depression spawned a series of indigenous movements dedicated to private property but suspicious of government and corporate consolidation. As national chain stores continued to spread and replace small shops and groceries, for example, independent merchants organized to fight for survival. Local efforts resulted in four hundred Trade-at-Home campaigns in 1930. Merchants complained of the destruction of personal initiative by the chains and the draining of profits from their communities to Wall Street holding companies. Agitation by chain store opponents resulted in passage of the Robinson-Patman Act of 1936, which outlawed manufacturers' discounts to large distributors, and the Miller-Tydings Act of 1937, which permitted states to pass fair-trade laws controlling chain store price cutting. By 1939, twenty-seven states had singled out chain stores for special regulation or taxation.

Defenders of small business, like Idaho senator William Borah, complained about the inadequacy of New Deal reforms. For example, Borah attacked the NRA for permitting big interests to dominate industrywide agreements with monopoly practices. Small operators could not absorb the increased wage rates negotiated by NRA officials and resented control of pricing by large concerns. Independent farmers experienced similar frustration with New Deal liberalism. In Minnesota, Governor Floyd Olson headed the Farmer-Labor party and persuaded the reluctant legislature to enact relief for farmers facing foreclosures. In neighboring Wisconsin, Philip LaFollette formed a new Progressive party and used the governorship to introduce a series of economic reforms including mortgage relief, property tax reduction, and unemployment insurance.

Elderly Americans provided another source of Depression radicalism. In California, a large retired population saw welfare for the aged as a major issue ignored by the New Deal. Dr. Francis E. Townsend responded by proposing an old-age revolving pension that would grant $200 a month to every American over age sixty, as long as the recipient retired from work and spent the entire monthly sum. The Townsend Plan would be financed by a 2 percent tax on business transactions, but its creator argued that the program would stimulate spending and end joblessness by cutting the labor force. Organizing along evangelical and patriotic lines, Townsend supporters gathered ten to twenty million signatures on nationwide petitions. By 1935, their efforts impelled Roosevelt advisors to push for social security legislation.

Another attack on the New Deal came from Father Charles E. Coughlin, a Michigan Roman Catholic priest with a national radio audience of thirty to forty-five million. An early supporter of Roosevelt, Coughlin began to criticize alleged New Deal connections to both finance capital and communism. Forming the National Union for Social Justice in 1934, the radio priest attracted lower-middle-class support among ethnic Catholics in the urban Northeast and Midwest. His weekly radio commentary denounced conspiratorial bankers and trade unionists while extolling the dignity of working people and small entrepreneurs. Coughlin's picture of a future society of class harmony without bankers remained vague, but his popularity attested to widespread discontent with New Deal liberalism.

Louisiana's Huey Long, "the Kingfish," ranked as the most colorful and effective opponent of the New Deal. Elected to the Senate in 1930 and assuming his seat two years later, Long inaugurated an ambitious "Share Our Wealth" proposal. He focused upon maldistribution of wealth as the key issue before the nation. His economic program called for the liquidation of all

HUEY LONG
1893–1935

Louisiana's Huey Long was the revered leader of the most popular rural insurgency since the Populist crusades of the 1890s. As a folk hero to poor southern farmers and villagers, Long focused on Depression issues to broaden his appeal until he appeared to threaten Roosevelt's re-election to the White House in 1936. His earthy sarcasm and impatience with privilege created nightmares for vested interests from Baton Rouge to Washington.

Long came out of the pine-studded uplands of northern Louisiana, an area of pious Baptists with a long tradition of populism. At the age of twenty-five, he won election as Louisiana's state public service commissioner. Long used his power to lower streetcar and telephone rates and to penalize Standard Oil. He attacked the greed of the oil colossus in an effective campaign for governor in 1924, but the Ku Klux Klan's opposition denied him victory. Four years later, with Klan power diminished, the brash upstart captured the Populist vote and won the governorship.

Long had used an old speech of William Jennings Bryan's to devise a campaign slogan: "Every Man a King." His program consisted of massive highway and hospital construction, and free school textbooks and night classes for poor whites and blacks. To finance these reforms, Long resorted to deficit spending and levied heavy taxes on the oil refineries. Meanwhile, he established an awesome patronage machine.

The Louisiana state house of representatives charged Governor Long with unauthorized use of state funds and impeached him in 1929, but the state senate failed to convict him. Long claimed that Standard Oil had persecuted him and tightened control over the state. By 1934, he had prevailed on the legislature to abolish local government and had taken personal control of police and teaching appointments, the militia, courts, election agencies, and tax-assessing bodies. Critics charged him with running a dictatorial police state that terrorized political enemies.

When Long came to Washington as a senator in 1932, he said he intended to cut the great American fortunes down to *(cont.)*

personal fortunes over $5 million through a capital tax. Long also planned to use the income tax to prohibit families from earning more than $1 million a year. He promised every family a guaranteed annual income, enough for a $5,000 homestead, a car, and a radio. Pensions would be distributed to the elderly, and "worthy youth" would receive free college educations. Long pledged that a massive public works program would combine with a federal minimum wage and a thirty-hour week to bolster purchasing power.

By 1935, twenty-seven thousand Share Our Wealth clubs had sprouted across the country. The senator's mailing list allegedly surpassed seven million. Long won national support with his folksy ridicule of corporate interests and the urbanity of New Deal administrators. Calling "Every Man a King," he planned to run for president in 1936. Democratic party tacticians feared that Long might take three or four million votes from Roosevelt on an independent ticket.

"frying size." An early supporter of Roosevelt, he now turned bitterly against the NRA and called the president "a liar and a faker." Like Borah of Idaho, Long believed that the recovery agency only helped large producers to organize a controlled market. He pointed out that AAA crop reductions compelled rich landlords to force black tenants off the land and attacked farm corporations as the source of agricultural impoverishment. The senator praised Roosevelt's "death sentence" for public utilities, but complained that "we might as well try to regulate a rattlesnake."

Huey Long made redistribution of wealth a focal point of 1930s politics. From the Senate floor, the Kingfish advanced a "Share Our Wealth" program that intended to use tax reform and a guaranteed income to alleviate the inefficient distribution of purchasing power in the Depression. Long savagely attacked plutocrats like the Rockefellers and DuPonts, noting that six hundred American families controlled 90 percent of the nation's wealth. He compared the rich to cannibals and predicted that they would let the country "go slap down to hell" before they surrendered their mastery.

Long's emphasis on stock ownership neglected the corporate structure and ignored capital investment that could not be easily liquidated and redistributed. But concentration of wealth remained an undeniable defect in the American economy. Long spoke to marginal members of the lower-middle class who felt unable to control their own destiny in a world of distant and remote centers of power. Share Our Wealth promised a cooperative solution by using government taxing ability to protect communities from encroaching financial power. Long's followers in the rural South and West assumed that the protective government would not become an intrusive power itself.

In 1935, a secret poll by the Democratic party indicated that Long might take four million votes as a third-party competitor in the coming presidential race. Just a month after he announced his candidacy, however, the Kingfish was assassinated by someone embittered over Long's state patronage manipulations.

Critics condemned Long as an ignorant demagogue and dangerous totalitarian. But as a North Dakota congressman observed, Huey Pierce Long "had more friends among the common people than any man who has lived in this country in the last half century." ∎

But the Kingfish's career ended when he was assassinated by a Louisiana enemy in September 1935. Long supporters joined followers of Townsend and Coughlin to form the Union party in 1936, but its presidential candidate William Lemke amassed less than nine-hundred thousand votes.

TOWARD A NATIONAL CULTURE

Instead of bringing the social reconstruction desired by intellectuals, the Depression seemed to reaffirm conservative traditions in American life. Insecurity brought a new emphasis on material goods and sound family life. Even as New Deal administrators and social workers tried to explain that unemployment remained an impersonal force often beyond the control of its victims, Americans tended to blame themselves, not the economic system. Since traditional Anglo-Protestant values stressed the connection between productivity and personal wealth, unemployment continued to be a sign of individual failure.

The psychology of scarcity produced austere social values in contrast to the middle-class hedonism of the 1920s. Food became an exercise in nutrition, and commentators noted that the tensions of economic insecurity seemed to dampen sexuality. For families unable to make ends meet, children seemed like burdens and pregnancy a disaster. Booming contraceptive sales accompanied the lowest birthrate in American history, and marriage rates dropped dramatically. Social anxiety also surfaced in stricter child-rearing methods. Conservative values received further emphasis in a government campaign against marijuana. Harry J. Anslinger, the first director of the Federal Narcotics Bureau, lobbied successfully for a 1937 Marijuana Tax Act designed to discourage marijuana consumption.

California refugees from the Dust Bowl drought of the mid-1930s. This photograph was taken by Dorothea Lange for the Farm Security Administration. It is an example of the best of the documentary art sponsored by government agencies during the Depression.

The Roosevelt administration hoped to use government programs to sustain Depression morale and bring cultural enrichment to the masses. The WPA spent over $500 million for recreation facilities to democratize sports and further family consumerism. At the same time, the WPA's public murals, community arts centers, traveling exhibits, and free concerts stimulated community participation in the arts and taught Americans how to "consume" culture. The results ranged from the social realism of post office murals to the recovery of lost folklore, handicrafts, and regional art. Through the auspices of government grants, the documentary emerged as a major art form in film, journalism, broadcasting, and the "living newspapers" of the Federal Theater Project. The most compelling Depression documentaries featured the photography of Walker Evans and Dorothea Lange, both of whom collected portraits of ordinary Americans for New Deal agencies.

Perhaps the most significant government influence on 1930s culture came with the repeal of Prohibition. Ratification of the Twenty-first Amendment in 1933 erased an important symbol of Anglo-Protestant cultural dominance. Although eight states chose to remain dry and others adopted local option, the return of alcoholic beverages gave legitimacy to the cosmopolitan culture of the urban middle class. As large nightclubs blossomed in big cities, young people flocked to listen to the mellow, self-effacing vocalists of the big bands led by Benny Goodman, Glenn Miller, and Tommy Dorsey—and to dance to white "swing," a refinement of "hot" black jazz and "boogie-woogie." Meanwhile, blacks in New York, Chicago, and Kansas City crowded huge ballrooms to dance to swing pioneers such as Duke Ellington, Count Basie, and Chick Webb.

Radio provided the most popular form of daily entertainment during the Depression. By 1938, Americans owned forty million radio receivers. Radio news programs familiarized millions of people with national issues. Along with soap operas and other features, they also helped overcome the disintegrating aspects

The Duke Ellington Orchestra, Chicago, 1932. Ellington helped to revolutionize urban popular music with swing rhythms originating in black jazz. Enthusiasm for his music reflected increasing musical sophistication among urbanites of the 1930s.

WALT DISNEY
1901–1966

Two months after President Roosevelt told the nation that "the only thing we have to fear is fear itself," Americans started humming, whistling, and singing a hit tune entitled "Who's Afraid of the Big Bad Wolf." The song came from the sound track of Walt Disney's animated cartoon *The Three Little Pigs* (1933) and served as a metaphor for America's resolve to overcome the Depression. Disney's extraordinary success during this period of crisis reflected his skill in defining popular anxieties—and in resolving them, with Hollywood-style happy endings.

Disney was born in Chicago, but spent several impressionable years on a farm in Missouri. Lonely as a boy, he befriended the barnyard animals and later relied on those childhood experiences for inspiration in his mature cartoon animation. In the 1920s, Disney produced crude animated films in Kansas City, mostly for commercial advertisers,

but could not succeed financially. He moved to Hollywood in 1923 and established an independent production company to make a variety of animated cartoons, including *Oswald the Lucky Rabbit* (1927) and the Mickey Mouse series, which had its debut in 1928.

At a time when American culture was torn between modern values and nostalgia for a rural society, Disney's characters embraced both worlds. The society of domesticated animals, filled with anthropomorphic gestures and human problems, evoked a lost age. Yet the cartoons themselves depended on new sophisticated technologies, including synchronized sound (1928) and color (1932), which distinguished Disney's creations. It was no coincidence that the first Mickey Mouse cartoon, *Plane Crazy* (1928), mirrored America's fascination with the exploits of Charles Lindbergh.

(cont.)

of modern life. By creating national standards of speech, taste, and humor, radio helped homogenize ethnic groups, social classes, and regional identities. Shows such as "Amos 'n Andy," "Fibber McGee and Molly," and "Mollie Goldberg," for example, combined ethnic and racial stereotypes with humor to touch on universal themes. At the same time, radio played recorded popular music, much of it the work of Jewish songwriters such as Irving Berlin, Jerome Kern, and George and Ira Gershwin. Love songs from Tin Pan Alley helped weave fantasy and romanticism into the lives of Depression-weary Americans.

Although radio and popular music had enormous cultural influence, Hollywood remained the nation's primary builder of unifying myths and dreams. By 1939, an estimated 65 percent of the American people went to the movies at least once a week. With the advent of movies with sound in the late 1920s, Hollywood studios began producing provocative and iconoclastic films that questioned sexual propriety, social decorum, and even institutions of law and order. Sensual European actresses such as Greta Garbo and Marlene Dietrich, as well as the American Jean Harlow, spoke frankly of sex in early

The popularity of Disney cartoons in the 1930s illuminated the sublimal anxieties of the economic crisis. In a typical situation, rooms fell apart, houses exploded, or, as in the story of "The Sorcerer's Apprentice," inanimate objects developed a mind of their own, threatening to destroy the natural harmony—only to be restored in the end to the familiar order. Disney fantasies also provided psychological escape. In such movies as *Snow White and the Seven Dwarfs* (1937) or *Fantasia* (1940), Americans found refuge from the sobering world outside the theaters. Yet even films like *Bambi* (1942) hinged on an underlying anxiety about the precariousness of life in the modern world.

During World War II, Disney made propaganda cartoons to support the war effort, and mixed animation and live action in movies for the military. His films of the postwar era blended sentimental fantasy (*Cinderella*, 1950) with a celebration of traditional American mythologies (*Davy Crockett—King of the Wild Frontier*, 1955). Disney entertainment now expanded rapidly into television, collat-

eral brand name products, and the thematic amusement park Disneyland, which opened in 1955. Disney also planned another recreation park in Florida, but did not live to see the opening of Disneyworld. He died in 1966.

Through these various enterprises ran a consistent theme. Disney, a product of white, Anglo-Protestant, midwestern America, remained committed to traditional values and assumptions in the face of rapid social change. His creative work depended on his characters' establishing control over chaos; however irrational the means, reason and order always prevailed in the end. Similarly, Disney's amusement parks, known for their cleanliness and order, offered conservative, prepackaged entertainment with neither surprise nor spontaneity. His sentimental vision of America appealed to a people uncertain about the country's values and worried about its future. Like many of the nation's cultural pioneers, Disney expressed his genius through an uncanny synthesis of modernism and tradition. ■

"talkies," and even portrayed prostitutes. At the same time, the irreverent comedies of W. C. Fields, Mae West, and the Marx Brothers brought lighthearted vulgarity and lechery to the screen in sardonic parodies of middle-class pretensions and social conventions.

As the Depression deepened and cutbacks forced the closing of one-third of the nation's theaters, Hollywood began to reevaluate its product. At the same time, the industry faced a major challenge from the Roman Catholic Church, which created the Legion of Decency in 1933 and announced a campaign to boycott movies considered indecent. Hollywood responded with the self-policing Production Code Administration, built into the machinery of the NRA, which went beyond the guidelines of the 1920s Hays Code by devising specific formulas to keep movie sex and crime within moral bounds. Elements of "good" in film scenarios had to balance "evil"; bad acts had to be followed by punishment or retribution, reform or regeneration. The code also prohibited film portrayals of homosexuality, interracial sex, abortion, incest, drugs, profanity, and vulgar language—including the word *sex*.

The Hollywood code had pervasive implications. Unable to deal frankly with controversial topics, the movie industry turned to escapist fare in what turned out to be the "golden age" of its output. "Screwball comedies" such as *Topper* (1937), *Holiday* (1938), *Bringing Up Baby* (1938), and *The Philadelphia Story* (1940) portrayed the zany antics of the rich, although they celebrated the sanctity of marriage, class distinction, and the domination of women by men. In a similar vein, a series of films starring Shirley Temple romanticized the innocence and playfulness of childhood. Busby Berkeley's musical extravaganzas, and films featuring the dancing partnership of Fred Astaire and Ginger Rogers, further contributed to Hollywood's search for quality entertainment that distracted audiences from the real world.

Other films inspired Americans to overcome the challenges of the Depression. Animated Walt Disney cartoons such as *The Three Little Pigs* (1933) and the Mickey Mouse series suggested how modern heroes might exert control over irrational chaos. Director Frank Capra brilliantly captured this trend with sentimental movies like *Mr. Deeds Goes to Town* (1936) and *Mr. Smith Goes to Washington* (1939), which portrayed comfortable and friendly small towns with close-knit families. Capra's affirmative films suggested that the basic institutions of American life remained sound and that social problems could be solved by ordinary people in a neighborly spirit. Hollywood sagas such as *San Francisco* (1936), *In Old Chicago* (1937), *Gone with the Wind* (1939), and *The Grapes of Wrath* (1940) also conveyed the idea that the American people had rich resources to draw upon in time of trouble.

By the eve of World War II, most American intellectuals, artists, and purveyors of popular culture had arrived at a consensus that stressed a celebration of conformity and an appeal for national unity. This consensus extended across racial, ethnic, and class lines. A whole generation of Americans would never forget the insecurities of the economic collapse and would strive in the postwar years to make sure those insecurities never returned. The dual legacy of the 1930s embraced the expansion of government power and the search for security by a people who felt themselves vulnerable in a world of uncertainties.

SUGGESTED READINGS

For the Depression context of 1930s politics, see Bird, the Lynds, and Terkel, all cited in chapter 5. Useful surveys of New Deal politics include Albert U. Romasco, *The Politics of Recovery: Roosevelt's New Deal* (1983); William E. Leuchtenburg, *Franklin D. Roosevelt and the New Deal* (1963); Paul K. Conkin, *The New Deal* (1967); and George Wolfskill, *Happy Days Are Here Again! A Short Interpretive History of the New Deal* (1974). The most comprehensive account remains Arthur Schlesinger, Jr., *The Age of Roosevelt*, 3 vols. (1957–60). For Roosevelt biographies, see Frank Freidel, *Franklin D. Roosevelt*, 4 vols. (1952–73), which should be supplemented by James M. Burns, *Roosevelt: The Lion and the Fox* (1956). The Roosevelt administration's approach to big business is outlined in Ellis W. Hawley, *The New Deal and the Problem of*

Monopoly: A Study in Economic Ambivalence (1966). See also A. L. Owens,*Conservation under FDR* (1933). Mark Hugh Leff, *The Limits of Symbolic Reform: The New Deal and Taxation, 1933–1939* (1984) describes Roosevelt tax policies.

For an overview of 1930s foreign policy, see the relevant sections of Robert Dallek, *Franklin D. Roosevelt and American Foreign Policy, 1932–1945* (1979). Earl R. Curry, *Hoover's Dominican Diplomacy and the Origins of the Good Neighbor Policy* (1979) uses a case study to establish links between Roosevelt and his predecessor. The constitutional revolution of the late 1930s is depicted in the relevant sections of Arthur S. Miller, *The Modern Corporate State: Private Governments and the American Constitution* (1976). James T. Patterson, *The New Deal and the States: Federalism in Transition* (1969) demonstrates the evolving relationship between the states and the federal government. For a sympathetic portrait of a New Deal activist, see J. Joseph Hutchmacher, *Senator Robert E. Wagner and the Rise of Urban Liberalism* (1971).

For organized labor, see David Milton, *The Politics of United States Labor: From the Great Depression to the New Deal* (1981) and the relevant sections of Robert H. Zieger, *American Workers, American Unions, 1920–1985* (1986), which define the limits to union protest in the 1930s. Communist accomplishments within the labor movement are portrayed by Roger Keeran, *The Communist Party and the Auto Workers Unions* (1980). Lowell K. Dyson, *Red Harvest: The Communist Party and American Farmers* (1982) describes the party's involvement in agricultural cooperatives and farm unions. For agrarian struggles during the 1930s, see Theodore Saloutos, *The American Farmer and the New Deal* (1982). Harvey Klehr, *The Heyday of American Communism: The Depression Decade* (1984) provides a critical account of the Communist party.

The dilemmas of radical intellectuals and writers are treated in Richard Pells, *Radical Visions and American Dreams: Culture and Social Thought in the Depression Years* (1973). See also James Weinstein, *Ambiguous Legacy: The Left in American Politics* (1975) and Theodore Rosenof, *Patterns of Political Economy in America: The Failure to Develop a Democratic Left Synthesis, 1933–1950* (1983).

The conservative response to the New Deal is traced in James T. Patterson, *Congressional Conservatism and the New Deal: The Growth of the Conservative Coalition in Congress, 1933–1939* (1967) and David L. Porter, *Congress and the Waning of the New Deal* (1980). The Supreme Court controversy is described by Leonard Baker, *Back to Back: The Duel between FDR and the Supreme Court* (1967). Dissenting liberals and progressives are treated in Ronald L. Feinman, *Twilight of Progressivism: The Western Republican Senators and the New Deal* (1981); R. Alan Lawson, *The Failure of Independent Liberalism, 1933–1941* (1971); and Ronald A. Mulder, *The Insurgent Progressives in the United States Senate and the New Deal, 1933–1939* (1979). For an excellent portrait of grass roots populism, see Alan Brinkley, *Voices of Protest: Huey Long, Father Coughlin, and the Great Depression* (1982). Leo P. Ribuffo, *The Old Christian Right: The Protestant Far Right from the Great Depression to the Cold War* (1983) presents a balanced account of right wing extremism.

Susan Ware's *Beyond Suffrage: Women in the New Deal* (1981) and *Holding Their Own: American Women in the 1930s* (1982) serve as helpful guides to 1930s women's history in conjunction with the relevant chapters of Sheila Rothman, *Woman's Proper Place: A History of Changing Ideals and Practices, 1870 to the Present* (1978) and Winifred D. Wandersee, *Women's Work and Family Values, 1920–1940* (1981). Black politics and civil rights struggles are described in John B. Kirby *Black Americans in the Roosevelt Era: Liberalism and Race* (1980); Nancy J. Weiss, *Farewell to the Party of Lincoln: Black Politics in the Age of Franklin D. Roosevelt* (1983); and Harvard Sitkoff, *A New Deal for Blacks: The Emergence of Civil Rights as a National Issue* (1978).

Mexican-American repatriation is the focus of Abraham Hoffman, *Unwanted Mexican Americans in the Great Depression: Repatriation Pressures, 1929–1939* (1974), which can be supplemented with the relevant sections of Rodolfo Acuña, *Occupied America: The Chicano's Struggle Toward Liberation* (1981). The government's relationship to Native Americans is described in Lawrence C. Kelly, *The Assault on Assimilation: John Collier and the Origins of Indian Policy Reform* (1983) and Graham D. Taylor, *The New Deal and American Indian Tribalism: The Administration of the Indian Reorganization Act, 1934–1945* (1980).

Relevant sections of Robert Sklar, *Movie-Made America: A Cultural History of American Movies* (1975), portray the conservatism of Hollywood in the 1930s. See also Andrew Bergman, *We're in the Money: Depression America and Its Films* (1971). William Stott, *Documentary Expression and Thirties America* (1973) describes the emphasis on socially conscious art and reporting. For radio, see Hugh G. J. Aitken, *The Continuous Wave: Technology and American Radio, 1900–1932* (1985) and Fred J. MacDonald, *Don't Touch That Dial!: Radio Programming in American Life from 1920 to 1960* (1979). Public art under the WPA receives treatment in Marlene Park and Gerald E. Markowitz, *Democratic Vistas: Post Offices and Public Art in the New Deal* (1984). A cross-disciplinary approach to 1930s culture is Alice G. Marquis, *Hopes and Ashes: The Birth of Modern Times, 1929–1939* (1986), which supplements the more conventional Charles C. Alexander, *Nationalism in American Thought, 1930–1945* (1969).

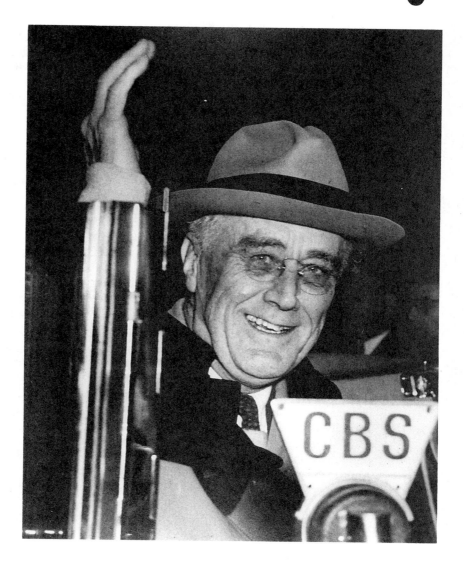

7

THE UNITED STATES IN WORLD WAR II

W orld War II had profound and lasting consequences for American government and society. The magnitude of the war effort involved more private citizens—soldiers, civilian employees, workers, and consumers—in government activities than ever before. Total warfare also justified the federal government's assumption of new powers, including an expanded bureaucracy, executive policy making, and secrecy about important public issues. These changes laid the basis for the postwar national security state, which demanded large military budgets and the creation of a political consensus on the home front. The war effort also required immense costs in dollars, casualties, and the disruption of ordinary lives. Yet ultimate American victory encouraged a belief that military action was not simply a last resort, but the prime means of achieving specific foreign policy goals.

THE OPEN DOOR AND THE ORIGINS OF GLOBAL CONFLICT

Author Claire Booth Luce once observed that each of the major figures of World War II "had his typical gesture—Hitler the upraised arm. Churchill the V sign. Roosevelt? She wet her index finger and held it up." President Franklin D. Roosevelt was a master politician who liked to conceal his intentions, avoid commitments, and allow decisions to drift. Moreover, the president often hesitated to explain his thinking publicly, lest it narrow future options or offend domestic opinion. And he insisted on maintaining personal control over major policy decisions, especially in foreign affairs.

Roosevelt's lack of candor about foreign policy brought a rude awakening. At the outbreak of World War II in Europe in September 1939, the president assured worried Americans that they were the "best informed" in the world. On December 7, 1941, however, the country was stunned by news that Japanese aircraft had executed a devastating attack on the United States naval base at Pearl Harbor, in the territory of Hawaii. "Every single man, woman, and child is a partner in the most tremendous undertaking of our American history," said Roosevelt as he led the nation into war. But one year later, public opinion polls found that one-third of the nation lacked a clear idea of American war aims.

The involvement of the United States in World War II nonetheless resulted from long-standing economic and political commitments. Through the twentieth century, the guiding principle of American policy in Asia was the "Open Door," by which the United States advocated free trade for all nations with equal access to raw materials and foreign markets. Equally important was the American rapprochement with Great Britain and France, which dated to the 1890s and had drawn the United States into the Allied camp during World War I.

These commitments shaped United States foreign policy, even after the Senate rejected the Versailles Treaty and the League of Nations in 1919–1920. At the Washington Arms Conference of 1921–1922, for example, the United States persuaded Japan to accept the principles of the Open Door in the Nine

Power Pact. Japan promised to restore sovereignty to China of the Shantung Peninsula and to remove Japanese troops from southern Siberia. Other Japanese troops would remain in China. Having a limited stake in Asia in the 1920s, the United States raised no further objections to such Japanese presence.

During the Depression, however, American business leaders searched for new markets in underdeveloped areas of the globe—Latin America, the Soviet Union, and Asia—and so gave greater importance to affairs in China. Although American commerce with Japan exceeded the value of trade with China, the vast potential of the China market suggested a permanent solution to recurrent depressions. But Japan followed its own expansionist plans. In 1931, the Japanese easily defeated Chinese armies in Manchuria and converted the province into a Japanese protectorate the next year. Since the Japanese occupation violated international law as well as Open Door principles, Secretary of State Henry Stimson responded with a formal protest. The Stimson Doctrine reaffirmed a commitment to the Open Door and announced that the United States would not recognize the Japanese puppet government in Manchuria. Even this minimal protest outraged noninterventionists in the United States. "The American people," stated the Philadelphia *Record,* "don't give a hoot in a rain barrel who controls North China." When the League of Nations adopted the American policy of nonrecognition in 1933, moreover, Japan simply withdrew from the international organization.

Germany also withdrew from the League in 1933. Under the leadership of Adolf Hitler, who assumed absolute power during that year, German nationalists demanded a revision of the Versailles Treaty to re-establish their nation as a world power. But French rejection of military equality in Europe convinced the Germans to act independently and Hitler announced a rearmament program in 1934. By subsidizing German corporations, Hitler's National Socialism (Nazism) also intensified economic competition with the United States. Meanwhile, Italy, led by the fascist Benito Mussolini, further disrupted peace and international order. Seeking glory and conquest in Ethiopia, Mussolini used a military clash at a desert oasis in 1934 as an excuse to demand an indemnity. When Emperor Haile Selassie refused, Italy prepared for war. As the European arms race escalated in 1935, Japan demanded a revision of the Washington agreement to obtain naval equality. The United States and Britain rejected the request; Japan announced it would increase its navy anyway.

THE POPULARITY OF NONINTERVENTIONISM

Militaristic rumblings abroad reinforced strong traditions of noninterventionism at home. Since the disillusionment of World War I, a majority of Americans believed the country could preserve its unique institutions only by limiting foreign entanglements. Many felt that the United States had been tricked into participation in World War I. In the mid-1930s, Senate investigations, headed by Progressive Republican Gerald P. Nye of North Dakota, revealed huge wartime profiteering by munitions manufacturers and bankers. The public hearings implied a close connection between the arms industry, international financiers, and presidential foreign policy. Walter Millis's best-seller, *Road to War* (1935), popularized the idea that the nation had been lured into the war by a combination of profiteering and Allied propaganda.

Public distrust of bankers and arms interests directly affected American foreign policy. When Roosevelt requested power to stop arms sales to selected aggressor nations, both progressives and conservatives in Congress opposed such increases in executive power. Instead, a noninterventionist Congress passed the Neutrality Act of 1935, which required the president to establish an arms embargo against all warring countries and to notify American citizens that they sailed on belligerent vessels at their own risk. These provisions attempted to shield American citizens from becoming involved, even accidentally, in foreign wars—the very factors many people believed had caused American entry into World War I. The law deliberately narrowed the president's options. In signing the measure, Roosevelt warned that its "inflexible provisions might drag us into war instead of keeping us out."

Five weeks later, Mussolini invaded Ethiopia. Although the League of Nations condemned Italy, Britain and France preferred not to intervene. Roosevelt called for a "moral embargo" on the shipment of oil to Italy, but such gestures were merely symbolic. Mussolini then withdrew from the League of Nations and signed a treaty of alliance with Hitler in 1936. As Europe seemed to move closer to war, Congress attempted to isolate the United States from military involvement. Roosevelt's effort to add a discretionary clause to the neutrality law, allowing the president to apply the embargo more flexibly, raised stiff opposition, forcing the president to accept the 1935 regulations, now buttressed by a ban on loans. Meanwhile, German armies reoccupied the Rhineland in violation of the Versailles Treaty. Caught between a popular wave of noninterventionist sentiment and developing aggression abroad, Roosevelt assured Americans during the 1936 presidential campaign that "We are not isolationists except insofar as we seek to isolate ourselves completely from war."

The principle of noninterventionism shaped Roosevelt's response to the Spanish civil war, which erupted in 1936 when the right wing General Francisco Franco rebelled against the republican government. Although Hitler and Mussolini provided crucial military support for Franco and the Soviet Union and Mexico sent small amounts of aid to the republic, Britain and France adopted a policy of nonintervention. Roosevelt followed their lead. The effect was to deny supplies to the legally-elected republic. In the United States, the Spanish civil war split public opinion. Members of the American left saw Spain as a moral battleground between the forces of democracy and the legions of fascism. Three thousand men formed the Abraham Lincoln Battalion to fight for the republic. Conservatives and Catholics, however, saw Franco as a defender of traditional social order; for them, Franco was a barrier against world revolution and atheism. Though Gallup polls found that republican sentiment greatly exceeded pro-Franco

Exhibit 7–1. Manchuria, 1931.

500 MILES

RAILROAD LINES
+++++++++++++++++

**MANCHURIA AND
ADJACENT AREA, 1931**

support, Roosevelt feared offending the Catholic electorate or supporting a pro-socialist regime. He imposed a "moral" embargo on the shipment of arms to Spain, a policy confirmed by Congress. But American businesses continued to sell war materials to Franco. Neither Congress nor Roosevelt viewed the survival of a Spanish republic as vital to American national interest.

Most Americans believed that neutrality legislation would reduce the likelihood of entering a foreign war. But business leaders realized that the price of neutrality might be the loss of foreign trade, a serious consideration at a time of Depression. Presidential adviser Bernard M. Baruch suggested a revision of the Neutrality Act to protect American interests with the principle of "cash and carry." As enacted by Congress in 1937, cash and carry permitted the sale of nonmilitary products to nations at war, but warring countries had to pay cash (to avoid the debt entanglements associated with American entry into World War I) and goods had to be transported in non-American ships (to avoid the problems of neutral rights on the high seas). Cash and carry favored nations with strong navies and large cash reserves, and Roosevelt understood that Britain and France, not Germany, would benefit by those provisions. The law also required a mandatory embargo on arms sales to all belligerents.

While Congress tried to perfect neutrality legislation, decisions made in other capitals increased the costs of strict neutrality. In 1937, Japan responded to new signs of Chinese unity by attacking the northern provinces of China. Appealing to Asian nationalism, the Japanese promised to create an East Asia Co-Prosperity Sphere that would exclude the European colonial powers from Chinese markets and resources. Such a sphere of influence paralleled Nazi expansion in central Europe, Britain's control of the Commonwealth nations, and United States dominance of Latin America. Yet Roosevelt remained committed to the Open Door in Asia and supported an independent China. The president consequently bypassed the neutrality laws by refusing to acknowledge that a state of war existed between Japan and China. This decision enabled the administration to extend trade credits to Chiang Kai-shek's Nationalists in order to finance the anti- Japanese resistance. Yet such assistance remained small. Despite a rhetorical commitment to a "free" China, American policy makers did not perceive that nation as a vital interest. Moreover, with Europe heading for war, the administration wished to avoid an open break with Japan.

Roosevelt worried nonetheless about the inhibiting effect of noninterventionist sentiment at home. To counteract what he called "isolationism," he spoke out in 1937 against the "epidemic of world lawlessness" and called for a "quarantine" of aggressor nations. Although he offered no particular plan, Roosevelt publicly admitted for the first time that war might become a necessary tool of foreign policy. Internationalist newspapers such as the New York *Herald Tribune* greeted the "quarantine" speech with enthusiasm, but the popularity of noninterventionism prevented the president from seeking any changes of policy. "It's a terrible thing," Roosevelt later said, "to look over your shoulder when you are trying to lead—and to find no one there." When Japanese planes attacked the United States gunboat *Panay* on the Yangtze River in late 1937, the president accepted a Japanese apology and promise of indemnity. Meanwhile, noninterventionists backed the controversial Ludlow amendment to the Constitution. Sponsored by Democratic Representative Louis Ludlow of Indiana, the amendment proposed a public referendum before Congress could declare war. Under extreme pressure from the administration, the House of Representatives voted to table the measure early in 1938 by a 209 to 188 margin.

Americans watched nervously as conditions deteriorated in Europe. Conservatives in Britain and France hoped that Nazi Germany would constitute an effective bulwark against Soviet Communism and feared the social disruption that might accompany another war. As a result the two powers acceded in 1938 to the German takeover of Austria and Czechoslovakia. Roosevelt responded by increasing the size of the American military arsenal, particularly the air forces. Such rearmament, which was haphazard and underfunded, reflected the president's belief that air power would prove a deterrent to Nazi aggression without requiring a large and unpopular conventional army. Roosevelt also realized that the United States might well become a military supplier to France and Britain. But his approach remained ambiguous, partly because he feared that public disclosure of American support of the Allies—for example, American manufacture of French aircraft—would arouse the opposition of noninterventionists in Congress. Potential conflict between the executive and legislative branches thus encouraged presidential secrecy and vacillation. Meanwhile, Germany began to threaten Poland in 1939, prompting the Western Allies to abandon "appeasement." Hitler then signed a nonaggression pact with Soviet leader Josef Stalin in August 1939 to eliminate the danger of a two-front war and invaded Poland on September 1. Two days later, Britain and France declared war on Nazi Germany.

THE FAILURE OF NEUTRALITY, 1939–1941

The outbreak of World War II intensified the contradictions of Roosevelt's foreign policy—his belief that France and Britain must defeat Germany to preserve stability in Europe and his commitment to remain out of war. To reconcile these contradictions, the president emphasized that support of Britain would protect American interests without embroiling the nation in hostilities. Accordingly, Roosevelt called Congress into special session in September 1939 to repeal the arms embargo.

The summons produced a dramatic national debate between interventionists and noninterventionists. "Keep America Out of the Blood Business," read just one of hundreds of thousands of letters that poured into Congress. Senate defenders of the neutrality laws, such as Gerald Nye and Missouri Democrat Bennett Champ Clark, warned that any revisions would bring the United States into the war. But interventionists in both political parties organized well-funded lobbying groups such as the Non-Partisan Committee for Peace through Revision of the Neutrality Laws. Massive press and radio campaigns combined with intense administration lobbying to repeal the arms embargo. The new Neutrality Act of 1939 still prohibited American vessels from entering war zones, but permitted belligerents to purchase military supplies on a cash and carry basis. Because of their maritime strength and

CHARLES A. LINDBERGH
1902–1974

Perhaps the most prominent of the noninterventionist advocates in the years before World War II was aviation pioneer Charles Lindbergh. Since winning international acclaim for his solo flight from New York to Paris in 1927, the flier had been the object of almost unceasing public scrutiny. Always suspicious of both the public and the press, Lindbergh felt those attitudes were confirmed by the spectacle surrounding the kidnap-murder of his son in 1931. He and his wife, writer Anne Morrow Lindbergh, fled to Europe in 1935 where they lived until the eve of World War II. During the 1930s he made five trips to Nazi Germany to inspect the German air industry and came away highly impressed by what he found. "The German aviation development is without parallel," he wrote. By 1938 he considered Germany "probably the strongest air power in Europe, . . . greater than that of all other European countries combined."

With war imminent, the family returned to the United States in mid-1939, where Lindbergh threw himself into the public debate over American involvement in the conflict. The origins of his noninterventionist sentiments were complex. For one thing, his father, a member of the House of Representatives, had strongly opposed American involvement in World War I, and the younger Lindbergh probably inherited some of the midwestern skepticism about European entanglements. Secondly, Lindbergh's conservative leanings and Republican connections made him deeply suspicious of Franklin Roosevelt. Lindbergh regarded Roosevelt as a devious and deceitful man who was exploiting the world crisis to expand his own power.

More troubling, however, was Lindbergh's thinking about the comparative merits of America and Nazi Germany. Clearly he felt considerable resentment toward his native country which, he believed, had given him a celebrity he had never sought and then exploited his family's tragedy. "We Americans are a primitive people," he told *Life* magazine. "We do not have discipline. Our moral standards are low. It shows *(cont.)*

geographical position, Britain and France benefited most by these provisions. The law, in effect, placed the United States in the Allied camp.

Once German armies invaded Scandinavia, the Low Countries, and France in the spring of 1940, the battle between interventionists and isolationists intensified. As Nazi troops blitzed toward Paris, Roosevelt warned against "the illusion that we are remote and isolated." Noninterventionists such as Democratic Senator Burton K. Wheeler of Montana responded by deriding the notion that Germany could ever mount an invasion of the United States. But while Wheeler and nationalists in both parties called for a negotiated peace, the Roosevelt administration won increased defense appropriations from Congress. The president also sought bipartisan support by appointing two leading Republican internationalists to the cabinet: Henry Stimson, as secretary of war, and Frank Knox, the Republican vice presidential candidate up in the private lives of people we know—their drinking and behavior with women. It shows in the newspapers, the morbid curiosity over crimes and murder trials." By contrast, Germany was marked by "a strength and vigor which it is impossible to overlook." And he claimed to have "found the most personal freedom in Germany." Compounding all this was Lindbergh's rabid anti-communism. "An alliance between the United States and Russia should be opposed by every American, every Christian, and by every humanitarian in this country," he declared shortly after Hitler invaded the Soviet Union.

Convinced that the democracies were deteriorating morally and that German technology would dominate the future, Lindbergh first advocated appeasement and then a negotiated peace with Germany. He saw British defeat as imminent and inevitable, a view doubtless influenced by his own confidence that air power would determine the outcome of modern war. Some also saw a tinge of anti-Semitism in his assertion that Jewish groups were working with the British and the Roosevelt administration to push the U.S. into war through their "large own-ership and influence in our motion pictures, our press, our radio, and our government."

The disturbing nature of such statements detracted from some of the significant criticism Lindbergh was offering of interventionist policies. He pointed to the irony of demanding involvement in Europe to defend democratic principles while the Roosevelt administration resorted to subterfuge to advance a policy which public opinion clearly was not yet ready to support. He warned that the delicate balance of power between the executive and legislative branches was being permanently tipped by the undeclared naval war Roosevelt conducted in the North Atlantic without the approval of Congress. Lindbergh also feared that participation would change the character of American life. In order to defeat Germany, the United States must become a "uniformed and regimented nation," possibly for generations to come. Such questions about the legitimate scope of American involvement in conflicts abroad, the use of secrecy in making foreign policy, and the growing militarization of American life would all become significant issues in the decades after World War II. ■

in 1936, as secretary of the navy. The fall of France in June 1940 brought a dramatic rise in pro-British sentiment. But public opinion polls showed that 82 percent of those surveyed still opposed United States intervention in the war. Like Roosevelt, Americans clung to the hope that military assistance would enable the British to defeat Germany without intervention by the United States.

As German planes bombed British cities and German submarines sank Atlantic vessels during the summer of 1940, Prime Minister Winston Churchill pleaded for American naval assistance. Roosevelt responded with an "executive agreement" in which he agreed to trade fifty overage destroyers for British bases in the Western Hemisphere and a promise that Britain would never surrender the fleet. The "destroyers for bases" deal had less military value than symbolic importance, since it dramatized American commitment to the British cause. Eager to show noninterventionists and nationalists that he was strengthening American defenses in the hemisphere, Roosevelt proclaimed that the arrangement was "the most important action in the reinforcement of our national defense since the Louisiana Purchase." But noninterventionists such as the popular aviator Charles Lindbergh and General Robert E. Wood argued that Roosevelt had failed to consult Congress and that aid to Britain weakened the national defense. Lindbergh, Wood, and a bipartisan coalition of congressional noninterventionists insisted that the president was slowly dragging the country into a European war whose outcome was not vital to American national interests. Months earlier, internationalists had set up a Committee to Defend America by Aiding the Allies and prevailed on Kansas journalist William Allen White to serve as chairman. Noninterventionists responded with their own organization in September 1940. Growing out of an earlier student group at Yale University, the America First Committee established headquarters in Chicago and chose General Wood as chairman. The AFC quickly enrolled over eight-hundred thousand Americans, mostly midwesterners, and used Lindbergh, Nye, and others to spread the antiwar message through rallies and radio broadcasts.

Despite the popularity of the noninterventionist position, the brutality of the German war machine and Nazi ideas helped win support for Roosevelt's policies. Twelve days after the creation of the America First Committee, Congress approved the first peacetime draft in American history. The profound sense of national crisis also permitted the president to seek an unprecedented third term in 1940. A bitter fight between internationalists and noninterventionists within the Republican party resulted in the nomination of Wendell Willkie, a Wall Street lawyer who supported both the destroyers-for-bases agreement and the peacetime draft. Willkie campaigned eloquently on a "One World" theme but closed the contest with an appeal to noninterventionist voters that condemned Roosevelt for sacrificing defenses at home. The president, in turn, denounced "appeasors" and pictured the struggle against Nazi aggression, as one of "people versus dictatorship," "freedom versus slavery," and of "religion against godlessness." Yet Roosevelt assured the American people of his intention to keep the United States out of European hostilities. "Your boys," the president reaffirmed on the eve of the election, "are not going to be sent into any foreign wars." One week later, Roosevelt took nearly 55 percent of the popular vote to become the first president to serve more than two terms.

Once reelected, Roosevelt announced that a British victory was essential for the "national security" and that the United States must become "the great arsenal of democracy." In his state of the union address of January 1941, the president continued to lead the nation away from a policy of strict neutrality, condemning the "so-called new order of tyranny which the dictators seek to create with the crash of a bomb." Roosevelt appealed for the defense of "Four Freedoms"—freedom of speech and expression, freedom of religion, freedom from want, and freedom from fear. For most Americans, this rhetoric defined World War II as a conflict of freedom against tyranny, rather than a defense of national interest.

With Britain running out of capital and the United States forbidden by the neutrality laws to extend credit, Roosevelt faced the problem of moving supplies across the Atlantic. The president decided, as he put it, to "eliminate the dollar sign." If your neighbor's house was on fire, Roosevelt explained, it would be prudent to lend him an old garden hose to put out the fire before it spread to your house. Afterward the neighbor would return the hose or, if it was damaged, replace it. Such was the logic of the "Lend-Lease" proposal, which the administration introduced early in 1941. This sweeping package gave the president unprecedented power to sell, transfer, exchange, lend, or lease military equipment and other goods to any nation whose defense he deemed essential to American security. In one of the most bitter debates in American history, noninterventionists insisted that Roosevelt was asking for dictatorial power that would eventually lead the United States into war. Senator Wheeler described the proposal as a dangerous foreign policy that "will plow under every fourth American boy." Wheeler, Nye, Robert M. LaFollette, Jr., and other progressives joined conservative Roosevelt critics in predicting that American participation in the war would end democracy at home. Despite these warnings, however, Congress approved Lend-Lease in March 1941 and authorized $7 billion of supplies for Britain and its allies.

As the critics predicted, Lend-Lease destroyed the fiction of American neutrality. The success of German submarines in sinking Allied vessels, moreover, placed increasing pressure on the United States to assure the delivery of American goods to Britain. Roosevelt now assumed unprecedented presidential powers. In the face of negative public opinion, he would not allow naval convoys to escort Lend-Lease material. Instead he devised a new fiction, the idea of "hemispheric defense," which extended the neutral zone halfway across the Atlantic. He ordered the navy to report the presence of German ships and planes in this area to the British. Roosevelt also signed an executive agreement with the Danish government in exile, allowing the United States to establish bases in Greenland.

Roosevelt's disregard for strict neutrality infuriated his opponents. Criticism escalated when the president extended Lend-Lease to the Soviet Union following Hitler's invasion of that nation in June 1941. Charles Lindbergh announced his preference for an alliance with Germany "with all her faults" rather than one "with the cruelty, Godlessness, and the barbarism that exist in the Soviet Union." Senator Harry S. Truman expressed a third view: "If we see that Germany is winning the war we ought to help Russia," he stated; "if Russia is winning we ought to help Germany and that way let them kill as many as possible."

The controversial alliance with the Soviet Union put strains on the American political system that would reverberate for years. But Roosevelt believed that only a total defeat of Germany could prevent world conquest by Hitler's Third Reich. Thus he advocated unstinted aid to both the Soviets and Britain. As German submarines continued to attack Atlantic shipping (and sank an American vessel in May 1941), the president feared that Britain might lose the war. He resolved to move ahead of public opinion. In July 1941, Roosevelt extended the range of American convoys to Iceland, which brought the United States into direct conflict with German warships. In September,

This anti-interventionist poster of 1941 depicts the crucifixion of Uncle Sam by the internationalist leaders of both political parties who supported Lend-Lease military assistance for Great Britain.

the American destroyer, *Greer*, exchanged fire with a German submarine. The *Greer*, working with a British plane, had tried to sink the submarine. Roosevelt concealed that fact from Congress and the public when he announced a major change of policy: American ships, he ordered, could "shoot on sight" German ships in the so-called neutral zone. "It is time for all Americans," Roosevelt declared, "to stop being deluded by the romantic notion that the Americas can go on living happily and peacefully in a Nazi-dominated world." By concealing all the facts in the *Greer* case, Roosevelt gained wide public support for his undeclared war in the Atlantic. And in the aftermath of the *Greer* incident, German submarines continued to attack American ships. In November, Congress revised the Neutrality Act to permit the arming of merchant ships and allow them to enter the war zone.

These decisions effectively terminated American neutrality. It was now only a matter of time before naval confrontations would create a crisis similar to that of 1917. Equally significant, the arming of merchant ships demonstrated that Roosevelt no longer believed that traditional diplomacy could protect American national interests. Hitler, however, was too involved in the European war and too afraid of American military potential to take up the challenge. But ironically the German invasion of the Soviet Union had altered the military situation in Asia, encouraging Japan to make new threats. Hitler opposed Japanese policies that might draw the United States into the war. But the German dictator no more controlled Japanese foreign policy than did Roosevelt.

To Pearl Harbor

While the United States had protested the Japanese invasion of China in 1937 and had extended credit to Chiang Kai-shek, American businesses continued to trade with Japan. In July 1939, however, Roosevelt moved to increase pressure on Japan by terminating the Japanese-American trade agreement. But the president hesitated to create a crisis. China was not considered important to United States interests, especially in light of the German threat to European stability.

The war in Europe nevertheless had important implications for Asia. German victories in western Europe weakened British, French and Dutch control of their colonial empires in southeast Asia. Japan, seeking to control the natural resources of the region—oil, rubber, and tin—threatened British access to these raw materials. Determined to save Britain, Roosevelt responded in 1940 by placing an embargo on the sale of aviation gasoline and high-grade scrap iron to Japan. As Japan continued to move troops into northern Indochina, the president tightened the economic screws by embargoing all iron and steel, but permitting the export of certain petroleum products. By such gradual means, Roosevelt hoped to stop Japanese expansion. Instead, Japan signed a tripartite military assistance pact with Italy and Germany in 1940.

Economic pressure led Japan to open diplomatic negotiations with the United States in the spring of 1941, but neither nation was prepared to submit to the other's terms. Adhering to the Open Door Policy, Washington insisted that Japan abandon Indochina and China before full trade relations could be restored. Japan's pursuit of the Asian Co-Prosperity Sphere, in contrast, prevented acceptance of such deprivation of crucial resources. Nor were Japanese leaders willing to leave the Asian mainland under American pressure. While negotiations dragged on, the German invasion of the Soviet Union altered the Asian balance, giving Japan a free rein to attack Siberia or to move southward into Malaya and the Dutch East Indies, both areas rich in oil and rubber. The Japanese chose to invade southern Indochina in July 1941. Roosevelt promptly froze Japanese assets in the United States, limiting Japan's ability to purchase supplies.

The Japanese now faced a crucial choice. They could either abandon plans for Asian expansion or attempt to seize oil from the British and Dutch colonies. Given the militaristic values of Japanese leaders, the first alternative was unacceptable. The Japanese also realized—and Roosevelt confirmed this to the British—that the United States would not tolerate an attack on British possessions in Asia. In other words, further Japanese expansion would mean war with the United States. Even by their own estimates, Japanese military leaders realized that they could not win such a war. But they also knew that Roosevelt was committed to a ''Europe-first'' strategy. Faced with the alternative of humiliating surrender in 1941 and an American insistence that withdrawal from China precede any serious negotiations, the Japanese gambled on a German victory.

On Sunday, December 7, 1941, Japan launched an attack on American forces at Pearl Harbor. Catching the base by surprise, the Japanese destroyed or damaged eight battleships, three cruisers, and nearly two hundred planes, and claimed nearly 3500 American casualties, while sustaining minimal losses. The next day, Roosevelt told a joint session of Congress that a state of war existed and promised to lead the country to ''absolute victory.'' Congress, with one dissenting vote by pacifist Jeannette Rankin, promptly voted a formal declaration of war. Three days later, Germany and Italy joined Japan and declared war on the United States, and the same day, December 11, Congress responded in kind.

THE GRAND ALLIANCE

Four months before the United States entered the war, Roosevelt and Churchill signed the Atlantic Charter on a battleship off Canada's Newfoundland coast. Since Hitler's armies had recently invaded the Soviet Union, Roosevelt hoped to forestall any agreement by which Churchill and Stalin might divide Europe into spheres of influence. By the Charter's provisions, the United States and Britain denied any desire for territorial gains and expressed universal principles of self-determination. The 1941 agreement also asserted the right of all nations to ''equal terms to the trade and to the raw materials of the world.'' Roosevelt and Churchill dramatized this commitment to the Open Door Policy by pledging to create a postwar system of collective security to enforce it.

American wartime policy followed similar lines of national interest. Although public opinion polls showed a majority calling for prompt vengeance against Japan for attacking Pearl Harbor, the president insisted that Germany represented the greater threat. But even without such a European-first military strategy, Japanese advances put the United States on a defensive posture in the Pacific. One week after Pearl Harbor, Americans surrendered Guam, and a week after that capitulated at Wake Island. The Japanese moved quickly into the Dutch East Indies, defeated the British naval base at Singapore, and advanced into the Gilbert and Solomon Islands. These setbacks climaxed in the capture of American forces at Corregidor and Bataan in the Philippines—a strategic and psychological blow. The Japanese then compelled American prisoners of war to march fifty-five miles to prison camps, resulting in thousands of deaths. Such atrocities, when confirmed to the public in 1944, intensified American anger against the Japanese and served to justify total warfare against the Japanese people.

Despite the cataclysm at Pearl Harbor, however, the Japanese failed to destroy aircraft carriers and vital shore installations. Within months the American navy assembled a fleet that successfully engaged the Japanese at the Battle of the Coral Sea (May 1942) and at Midway (July 1942), effectively using air power to destroy Japanese aircraft carriers, cruisers, and destroyers. These important naval victories limited the range of Japanese expansion in the Pacific. By 1943, Americans, backed by Australians and New Zealanders, began to reverse Japanese conquests. In a series of bloody island encounters, American troops drove the Japanese from Guadalcanal in the Solomons (January-February 1943), Tarawa in the Gilberts (November 1943), and the Marianas (summer 1944). By February 1945, American troops under General Douglas MacArthur fulfilled his promise of 1942 ("I shall return") and recaptured the Philippines. But military confidence in easily defeating the Japanese abated suddenly after the ferocious combat on the islands of Iwo Jima (over four thousand Americans killed; twenty-one thousand Japanese) and Okinawa (over eleven thousand Americans killed; 110,000 Japanese). Such bloodbaths suggested to Americans that the Japanese might fight to the death to save the home islands.

Each advance brought American aircraft closer to Japan, and Japanese cities became sitting targets for mass bombardments. As early as 1942, General James Doolittle led an air raid on Tokyo, boosting American morale. By mid-1944, American bombers began attacking strategic targets, such as aircraft factories. Weather conditions often prevented great accuracy, and the use of incendiary bombs created dreadful firestorms that brought death to thousands of civilians. Such tactics served both to punish what was perceived as a fanatical enemy and to soften the home islands for an amphibious landing after the projected defeat of Germany.

Meanwhile, in the European theater, political considerations proved more subtle. Within the Grand Alliance, each nation saw its own national interest as paramount. The Soviet Union, reeling under the German advance, desperately needed Allied assistance and urged the opening of a second front in western Europe. Stalin also wanted a postwar settlement that would protect the Soviet Union from future invasions from central Europe. Churchill

Exhibit 7-2. Japanese Expansion, 1937-42.

1. Panay bombed, Dec. 12, 1937
2. Occupied Feb. 10, 1939
3. Occupied N. Indochina Sept. 22, 1940
4. Occupied S. Indochina July 24, 1941
5. Landings Dec. 8, 1941
6. Landings Dec. 10, 1941
7. Landings Dec. 16, 1941
8. Landings Dec. 20, 1941
9. Landings Dec. 24, 1941
10. Hong Kong falls Dec. 25, 1941
11. Singapore falls Feb. 15, 1942

determined to preserve the British colonial empire as well as trade advantages with Commonwealth nations and in the Middle East. Roosevelt, above all, wanted a quick defeat of Germany and Japan with minimal American casualties; politically, he hoped to replace European spheres of influence—whether British or Soviet—with the American Open Door.

These differences had important effects on military strategy. While Stalin pleaded for a second front, American generals advised a concentrated buildup of forces in Europe until an invasion of the continent could be

Exhibit 7–3. The War Against Japan, 1944–45.

SOVIET UNION DECLARES WAR ON JAPAN, AUG 8, 1945

SOVIET UNION

Nikolaevsk

Komosomolsk

Sakhalin

Karafuto

Amur

Hailar

MONGOLIA

Tsitsihar
Changchun

Khabarovsk

CHAHAR

MANCHUKUO

Vladivostok

HOKKAIDO

Hakodate

JEHOL

Mukden

KOREA

⑪ AGREEMENT ON SURRENDER IN KOREA, AUG. 16, 1945

Peking

Dairen

38TH PARALLEL

⑧ FIRST ATOMIC BOMB, AUG. 6, 1945

JAPAN

⑫ JAPAN OFFERS TO SURRENDER, AUG 10, 1945

JAPAN ACCEPTS ALLIED TERMS, AUG. 14, 1945

U.S. OCCUPATION FORCES LAND, AUG. 30, 1945

JAPAN FORMALLY SURRENDERS, SEPT. 2, 1945

Tientsin

Seoul

HONSHU

Tokyo

CHINA

Tsingtdo

Pusan

Hiroshima

① AIR STRIKES FROM CHINA BASES BEGIN, JUNE 15, 1944

⑩ SECOND ATOMIC BOMB, AUG. 9, 1945

Nagasaki

SHIKOKU

Nanking

Kyushu

Shanghai

3½ HOURS

7½ HOURS

FROM CHENGTU 5 HOURS

5 HOURS

Foochow

⑦ OKINAWA OCCUPIED, APR. 1–JUNE 21, 1945

BONIN IS.

Hong Kong

FEINT

⑤ OCCUPIED FEB. 19–MAR. 16, 1945

IWO JIMA

FORMOSA

⑥ AIR STRIKES ON OKINAWA, FORMOSA, CHINA COAST, AND JAPAN PROPER AFTER APRIL, 1945

④ BATTLE OF LUZON, JAN. 9–JUNE 30, 1945

MARIANAS

LUZON

PACIFIC OCEAN

SAIPAN

PHILIPPINE ISLANDS

Manila

③ SUPERFORTRESSES BEGIN AIR STRIKES ON JAPANESE MAINLAND, NOV. 24, 1944

TINIAN

ROTA

② AMERICAN LANDINGS OCT. 20, 1944

GUAM

FROM ENIWETOK

PALAWAN

LEYTE

FROM MANUS AND HOLLANDIA

ALLIED OFFENSIVES
SOVIET OFFENSIVES

THE WAR AGAINST JAPAN: FINAL PHASE, 1944–1945

Beachhead assaults accounted for most American battle casualties in the Pacific theater of the war. These marines discard their lifejackets as they charge from a landing craft to form a secure line.

mounted. But Churchill, anxious for any victory and desiring to protect the Mediterranean, persuaded Roosevelt to support an invasion of North Africa in November 1942. On military grounds, General Dwight Eisenhower negotiated a settlement with French Admiral Jean Darlan, who had earlier collaborated with the Nazis, exchanging an armistice for Darlan's continuation in power. The deal ignored the idealism of the Atlantic Charter and outraged public opinion. But the successful North African campaign eliminated German threats to Middle East oil, protected shipping in the Mediterranean, and provided a base for the invasion of Italy. Soon afterward, Roosevelt and Churchill met at Casablanca in January 1943 and announced a policy of "unconditional surrender." Military advisers criticized the language, fearing it would harden enemy resistance. But Roosevelt wanted to demonstrate his sincerity to Stalin, despite the delay of the second front. The United States hoped for Soviet intervention in the war against Japan.

Anglo-American forces invaded Sicily and Italy in the summer of 1943. Mussolini soon fell from power and was replaced by Marshal Badoglio, who made a conditional surrender in September 1943. In agreeing to negotiate with Badoglio, Anglo-American leaders recognized his importance as an anti-Communist force in postwar Italy. The western Allies also excluded the Soviet Union from the Allied Control Commission, answering Stalin's protests by arguing that the Red Army had not participated in the Italian campaign. This decision became an important precedent for Soviet policy in eastern Europe.

Exhibit 7–4. Western European Theater, 1942–45

1. Allied landings, North Africa, Nov. 8, 1942
2. Surrender Tunisia, May 13, 1943
3. Allied landings Sicily, July 10, 1943
4. Allied landings Italy, Sept. 9, 1943
5. Italian surrender, Malta, Sept. 29, 1943
6. Allied landings Normandy, Jume 6, 1944
7. Allied landings southern France, Aug. 15, 1944
8. Paris liberated, Aug. 25, 1944
9. German surrender, Reims, May 7, 1945

In November 1943, the Big Three—Roosevelt, Churchill, and Stalin—met at Teheren and agreed to open a second front in France in the spring. They also agreed to a temporary division of postwar Germany into zones and to claim reparations for the cost of the war. And Stalin promised to declare war on Japan soon after the German defeat.

As the Allies prepared for the invasion of France, Anglo-American aircraft began strategic bombing of factories and transportation routes on the continent, a policy that caused thousands of civilian deaths. Although postwar studies found that these raids were minimally effective in disrupting German industry, bombing acquired a popular mystique as the ultimate military solution. The air war proved more successful in destroying the German *Luftwaffe*. Air supremacy also facilitated the successful Allied landings on the

AUDIE MURPHY
1924–1971

For Audie Murphy, as for thousands of other young people his age, the formative experiences of his life were the Great Depression of the 1930s and the Great War of the 1940s. One of eleven children born to a family of Texas sharecroppers, Murphy grew up amid tragedy and poverty. As the Dust Bowl destroyed his land, Murphy's father abandoned the family, and his wife, a woman Murphy described as "a sad-eyed, silent woman" who "toiled eternally," died soon after. The family broke up with the younger children going to an orphanage and the sixteen-year-old Murphy drifting through a series of dead-end jobs. A kid with nothing to lose, Murphy saw World War II as his chance to make something of his life, and he tried to enlist on his eighteenth birthday. The Marine Corps and Army Airborne rejected him because he was too small, but he finally got a place in the infantry. The new private assured himself that his assignment was only temporary until he could find a more suitable and more daring role as a glider pilot.

Instead Murphy spent a harrowing two-and-a-half years as a combat infantryman in North Africa, Italy, and France. His most celebrated moment came in February, 1945, when he climbed atop a burning tank and turned its machine guns on an advancing wave of German attackers. Holding the position almost single-handedly, Murphy killed approximately 240 Germans and blunted the assault. His heroics earned him the Medal of Honor and a host of other decorations as well. By the end of the war, Murphy had achieved the rank of second lieutenant and was the most decorated American combat veteran. His brief, sparely-written memoir, *To Hell and Back,* attracted attention in Hollywood and became a movie with the same title. Murphy portrayed himself and launched a career in Grade B films usually playing a cowboy or a soldier.

The young man who had gone to war seeking glory, however, was acutely aware that he had found very little of it. For him, the reality of war was brutal and inescapable. "I see war as it is," he later wrote, "an endless series of problems involving blood and guts." Of his original company of 235 men, only Murphy and one other man escaped the war without injury. As he later affirmed in his GI catechism, "I believe in the force of a hand grenade, the power of artillery, the accuracy of a Garand. I believe in hitting before you get hit, and that dead men do not look noble." His return to civilian life was marked by the stress and disillusionment a later generation tended to think was unique to veterans of the war in Vietnam. The war had "branded" him, Murphy said, and for years afterward he was unable to sleep at night without a pistol under his pillow. The medals he had won were meaningless to him, and he gave most of them away to children as trinkets.

Searing as it was, Murphy's experience was rather atypical for American GIs in World War II. At least in a limited sense, the United States continued through the war years its prewar policy of arming others to do the fighting, thus spending American wealth to conserve American lives. Although sixteen million men and women served in the armed forces, only one in eight saw combat duty. Accordingly, casualties were rather low, and only some 300,000 Americans died in World War II. The other major belligerents suffered much greater losses, most notably the Soviet Union which lost twenty million dead, roughly one-tenth of its population. ■

Normandy beaches on D Day, June 6, 1944. After tough fighting in northern France, the Allies moved eastward, racing to destroy German armies.

As the Allies approached victory in Europe, the Big Three met at Yalta in February 1945 to resolve the political settlement of the peace. At a time when the defeat of Japan seemed both difficult and remote, Stalin repeated his promise to enter the Pacific theater. This move lessened the importance of China in ending the war. No longer worried about Chinese contributions to the war, Roosevelt and Churchill agreed to compensate the Soviets with the Kurile Islands north of Japan as well as economic rights in Manchuria. The Allies also reaffirmed the temporary partition of Germany, including the division of Berlin into occupied zones. But they failed to agree about the amount or the nature of German war reparations.

The main problem at Yalta involved Poland—the country whose defense had triggered World War II in 1939. To protect the Soviet Union's western boundary, Stalin demanded recognition of territory taken from Poland during his alliance with Hitler in 1939–1940. To compensate Poland, Germany would surrender areas of eastern Prussia. Stalin also demanded a friendly Polish government on his vulnerable border, an idea Roosevelt and Churchill reluctantly accepted. But to avoid the appearance of ignoring Polish self-determination, the western Allies convinced Stalin to broaden the Polish government to include some Poles who had established a non-Communist government in exile in London and to permit "free and unfettered elections" as soon as possible. But in Poland, as in Italy, the Allies did not have an equal stake. Roosevelt understood that the Soviet Union would dominate eastern Europe after the war, particularly since the delayed opening of the second front had given the Red Army exclusive control of territory east of Germany.

Though the Big Three made major decisions without consulting all the affected nations, Roosevelt believed that an international organization, the United Nations, was essential for keeping the peace. As a disillusioned disciple of former president Woodrow Wilson, Roosevelt believed that collective security would be meaningless without the participation of the great powers. Where Wilson had envisioned a league of all nations, Roosevelt suggested that Four Policemen—the United States, Soviet Union, Great Britain, and China—would provide greater stability and called for their permanent seating in what would become the United Nations Security Council. Unlike Wilson, the president also worked to gain bipartisan support for the United Nations in Congress. Indeed, it was his hope of winning congressional approval of the United Nations that led Roosevelt to conceal the pro-Soviet Polish settlement, which he knew would be unpopular. And although former noninterventionists feared the loss of national independence in collective security treaties, public opinion strongly supported American leadership in the United Nations. Plans for the United Nations were first drafted at the Dumbarton Oaks Conference in Washington in 1944. The new organization included a Security Council in which each of the Big Four held the power of veto. By assuring no infringement on United States sovereignty, the veto helped win congressional support of the world organization.

At Yalta, the "Big Three"—(left to right) Prime Minister Winston Churchill, President Roosevelt, and Soviet Premier Josef Stalin—search for a consensus on Poland, war reparations, and the U.N., while protecting their separate national interests.

Roosevelt's vision of the postwar world reflected not only the realities of military power, but also his view of American self-interest. As a proponent of free international trade, he opposed returning Indochina to France and expected Britain to move toward decolonization. But the defeat of Japan would create a power vacuum in Asia. To assure stability, Roosevelt envisioned the rise of an independent China, free from European imperialism and strong enough to buffer the Soviet Union. In elevating China to the status of world power, however, Roosevelt exaggerated the role of Chiang Kai-shek as a force of national unity. Numerous American diplomats in China had condemned the ineptitude of Chiang's regime and had stressed the importance of creating a coalition government with Chinese Communists. But Roosevelt distrusted the State Department bureaucracy and rejected its advice. His decision assured the continuation of civil war in China that had raged since the 1920s. Roosevelt's dislike of diplomatic formalities also undermined his plans for decolonization. His unwillingness to issue clear directives about Indochina, for example, gave his subordinates no guidelines for the future. These omissions assumed critical importance when Roosevelt died suddenly on April 12, 1945.

WARTIME MOBILIZATION

Despite a decade of economic depression, the United States entered World War II with a vast industrial potential. Roosevelt had recognized the importance of preparing industry for war as early as 1938. But, typical of his New Deal strategy, he hesitated to commit himself to any one plan or to delegate authority to a single commission. In 1939, he appointed a War Resources Board, but noninterventionist opinion prompted him to ignore its report. Other bureaucracies followed: an Advisory Commission for National Defense, which was later replaced by the Office of Production Management; the Office of Price Administration, which supervised price controls; the Supply Priorities and Allocations Board, which dealt with problems of conversion. These agencies started the economy moving on a wartime basis. During 1941, arms production increased 225 percent. One year after Pearl Harbor, the United States was producing more war material than all its enemies combined.

After Pearl Harbor, Roosevelt created the War Production Board (WPB), but when it proved ineffective he established the Office of War Mobilization. These bodies set production goals and priorities for the allocation of resources. Other administrative decisions involved coordinating supplies for the civilian economy, the military, and Lend-Lease. By the war's end, nearly $50 billion of material was shipped under Lend-Lease (60 percent to Britain; 20 percent to the Soviet Union; the rest to other countries).

In developing a war economy, the government had to convince private business to join the war effort. Many industrialists feared that conversion to war-related manufacturing would cause overproduction, leading to a postwar depression. Others were reluctant to abandon civilian-oriented production that was stimulated by wartime jobs and consumer spending. The administration attempted to restore business confidence by appointing corporate leaders to "dollar a year" positions in government. These administrators adopted policies that helped reduce the risks associated with conversion. For example, the War Production Board, headed by Donald Nelson of Sears Roebuck, offered generous tax advantages and "cost-plus" contracts that guaranteed a fixed profit for war business. Such policies accelerated industrial mobilization. The federal government also began to finance private research and development programs in businesses and universities—over fifty firms and schools received contracts worth $1 million or more—a practice that became a critical ingredient of the postwar economy. To encourage business cooperation, the administration abandoned antitrust actions in war-related fields.

These policies generally favored big businesses over small. Large corporations had greater access to government agencies and more experience with large procurement contracts. Complaints of discrimination against small business led the Senate to create a special committee, headed by Montana Democrat James E. Murray, to investigate the War Production Board's handling of contracts. In response, the administration created a Smaller War Plants Corporation. Yet, as Secretary Stimson suggested of large corporations, "If you . . . go to war . . . in a capitalist country, you have to let business make money out of the process or business won't work." During World War II, industrial production increased by 96 percent and net corporate profits doubled.

The war inevitably demanded tremendous quantities of natural resources, such as petroleum. One armored battalion, for example, used seventeen thousand gallons of gasoline to move one hundred miles; the Fifth Fleet consumed 630 million gallons of oil in less than two months. The American oil industry was prepared to meet these huge demands—at a price: protection from government interference, including immunity from antitrust suits, and a dominant voice in national oil policy making. The petroleum corporations also moved to expand production in the Middle East to lessen the drain on domestic oil reserves. This decision required direct government support, such as Lend-Lease aid to Saudi Arabia, to keep British companies from challenging American expansion. The State Department also backed private efforts to penetrate Anglo-Soviet control of oil in Iran. Such government assistance stimulated the industry to produce six billion barrels of oil during the war. But postwar petroleum policy, including increasing dependence on foreign oil, remained in private hands.

MOBILIZING LABOR

Mobilization of the economy also depended on the recruitment of the work force. Although Congress had been cautious about approving deficit spending to end unemployment during the Depression, the demands of war overcame budgetary scruples, setting a precedent for American economic life. The number of unemployed workers in 1939 was eight million (17 percent of the labor force), but the expanding economy soon provided more than enough jobs. By 1942 other previously unemployable workers—teenagers, the elderly, minorities, and women—also began to find work. The armed services absorbed fifteen million men and women. Another seven million found jobs on the home front. This rapid expansion of the labor force effectively ended the great Depression.

To oversee problems caused by labor shortages and high worker turnovers, Roosevelt created a War Manpower Commission, but the agency lacked enforcement powers. As a result, absenteeism and job mobility remained common. In 1944, the turnover rate in manufacturing industries was 82 percent. As in the Depression, however, losses in the labor force were more than offset by time-saving machinery that increased individual productivity. The Department of Agriculture estimated that farm productivity increased 25 percent per work hour between 1939 and 1945, because of mechanization, land consolidation, and increased use of chemical fertilizers.

The shortage of labor provided opportunities for people who had been underrepresented in the work force. Black agricultural workers, for example, displaced by farm machines or seeking better jobs, moved in great numbers to urban centers. Yet many still confronted racial discrimination in employment, even in government programs and within the armed services. "While we are in complete sympathy with the Negro," declared the president of North American Aviation, in a typical statement, "it is against company policy to employ them as aircraft workers or mechanics . . . regardless of their training. . . . There will be some jobs as janitors for Negroes."

Challenging such discrimination, A. Philip Randolph, president of the Brotherhood of Sleeping Car Porters, called for a protest march on Washington in 1941. The proposal deeply embarrassed the president and forced Roosevelt to issue Executive Order 8802 in June 1941, prohibiting job discrimination in war industries and creating a Fair Employment Practices Commission (FEPC) to investigate complaints. But Roosevelt feared antagonizing conservatives in Congress and in the military and so declined to order the desegregation of the armed services, government departments, or labor unions. Some two million blacks eventually found work in war industries.

Women also succeeded in acquiring new jobs. Though females comprised 25 percent of the prewar work force, middle class opinion disapproved of working women. Even as the nation prepared for war, private contractors often refused to hire women. The shock of Pearl Harbor overcame some of those prejudices. To encourage the employment of women, the Office of War Information supported a domestic propaganda campaign to make women's work appear patriotic. But most women worked because they needed the wages and appreciated the opportunity to enter better paying jobs normally reserved for men. A significant proportion of black women also moved from domestic work into industrial occupations, though they remained at the lowest wage brackets. Between 1941 and 1945, 6.5 million women entered the labor force, a 57 percent increase. By the war's end, 36 percent of all civilian workers were women.

Female workers continued to encounter severe disadvantages. Although women were entitled to the same pay as men for the same work, employers routinely ignored such rules. Most women earned no more than the minimum wage and were usually excluded from management positions. These practices reflected the prevailing belief that war work was temporary—intended not to encourage women's economic independence, but simply to support the men at war. Even though a government survey revealed that 75 percent of women wished to retain their jobs, business and union leaders agreed that women should give way to returning veterans. "Americans may no longer believe that a woman's place is in the home," sociologist Jerome Bruner observed. "But more important, we believe even less that a man's place is on the street without a job."

The wartime labor shortages helped organized labor increase its membership 40 percent between 1941 and 1945. After Pearl Harbor, labor unions pledged a "no strike" policy, but continued to press for higher wages. To deal with labor disputes, Roosevelt created new government agencies which could set wages, hours, and working conditions. The National War Labor Board attempted to control wage inflation by establishing a cost of living standard. But wage limits did not apply to overtime. While hourly wages increased 24 percent during the war, weekly earnings rose 70 percent.

Despite these gains, organized labor opposed government restraints. Numerous unauthorized strikes occurred, even in war industries. A strike of

ASA PHILIP RANDOLPH
1889–1979

A. Philip Randolph, a dignified and soft-spoken man who served as president of a small union of sleeping-car porters, ranked as the nation's single most important black leader of the 1930s and 1940s. By 1941 Randolph's efforts to build a mass movement of black working people elicited the first federal proclamation concerning black Americans since the Civil War.

Born in Jacksonville, Florida, Randolph departed on a steamboat for New York City in 1911. A devout reader of civil rights advocate W.E.B. DuBois, he believed himself to be among the "talented tenth" of black Americans that DuBois had described. Randolph took night classes at City College and gravitated toward socialism. In 1915 he helped to launch the *Messenger*, a radical black magazine that opposed participation in World War I until Americans achieved democracy at home. These efforts resulted in questioning by the Justice Department for violations of the Espionage Act.

Randolph's career took a new direction when black railroad porters asked him to organize a union in 1925. Ever since Eman-cipation, the Pullman Company had hired black men only as porters, believing that subservient and congenial former slaves would accept insults and demands from white passengers. But Pullman was the largest private employer of blacks in the nation, and Randolph hoped to show that his people could build and sustain a movement for their own economic survival without permitting whites to choose their leaders. The Brotherhood of Sleeping Car Porters organized half the Pullman porters and maids within three years, winning higher monthly salaries, respectful treatment, and an end to demeaning tipping.

Randolph's success catapulted him into national black leadership in the 1930s. As president of the National Negro Congress, he called for a "new deal" for America's "submerged tenth" and urged blacks to join the burgeoning union movement. Randolph reasoned that black struggles for social justice paralleled the efforts of white workers and liberal allies. But he also pointed out that "the salvation of the Negro, like the workers, must come from within." *(cont.)*

coal mine workers in 1943 threatened the entire economy and aroused anti-labor sentiment. Congress responded by passing, over Roosevelt's veto, the Smith-Connally Labor Act, which imposed a thirty-day cooling off period before strikes, prohibiting strikes in war industries, and banned union contributions to political parties. This conservative stand toward organized labor would become more common after the war.

THE HOME FRONT

With business booming and with full employment, the administration worked to prevent runaway price inflation. In 1942, the Office of Price (cont.) Accordingly, when the Roosevelt administration failed to heed protests against racial discrimination in government and defense jobs, Randolph prepared to lead a march of 100,000 black working people to the capital in 1941. "Power and pressure," he told the nation's civil rights organizations, "are at the foundation of the march of social justice and reform."

Despite pleas for restraint from white liberals such as Eleanor Roosevelt and New York City mayor Fiorello LaGuardia, Randolph insisted that "there are some things Negroes must do alone." His strategy worked brilliantly. When Roosevelt summoned the black leader to the White House in June 1941, the president asked whether Randolph could actually deliver the 100,000 protestors he promised. Looking the chief executive straight in the eye, Randolph calmly answered that he could assure a huge turnout. The polite and measured confrontation marked one of the few times that the master politician in the White House had ever been out-bluffed. One week before the scheduled demonstration Roosevelt agreed to issue Executive Order 8802, which forbade discrimination in government-related hiring and created a Fair Employment Practices Commission. Randolph appreciated the president's actions as a substantial gain and called off the march.

Black Americans understood the government's desire to maintain racial harmony at home in contrast to Nazi Germany's espousal of Aryan supremacy and other racial ideologies. But although Executive Order 8802 represented the most dramatic gesture that Washington had ever made in behalf of black citizens, enforcement proved to be no easy task at a time of war mobilization and administration dependence on southern political allies. Randolph also faced disappointment when his hopes of structuring the black masses into a permanent March on Washington Movement floundered on disunity and organizational jealousy. Nevertheless, he helped construct the foundations of the postwar civil rights revolution by popularizing the concept of mass demonstrations led and organized by blacks. Twenty-two years later, he saw the fruits of his pioneering when he introduced Martin Luther King, Jr. to a crowd of 250,000 at the celebrated 1963 March on Washington. From DuBois to King, A. Philip Randolph's remarkable career embodied the continuities of black leadership in the twentieth century. ■

Administration froze most consumer prices based on March 1942 levels. But food prices continued to skyrocket. Congress then passed an Anti-Inflation Act in 1942 which regulated agricultural prices and wages. During the last two years of the war, consumer prices increased by less than 2 percent.

The government also instituted a rationing program for scarce materials. These included canned goods (because of tin shortages), rubber, gasoline (because rubber shortages limited tire production), coffee, shoes, sugar, meat, butter, and fuel oil. People with cash could often circumvent these rules in the illegal black market. The government also organized scrap campaigns to collect used goods, such as old tires and tin cans. These drives encouraged civilians to feel part of the war effort. Another mass campaign encouraged the purchase of war bonds. Through payroll deduction plans and bond drives, bond sales reached

$135 billion, $40 billion of which was purchased by small investors. Bond sales also discouraged inflation by absorbing consumer dollars.

During the four years of war, the federal government spent $321 billion, ten times as much as the cost of World War I. Taxation financed over 40 percent of the total bill (and further reduced consumer purchasing power). The Revenue Act of 1942 both increased tax rates and broadened the tax base to include lower income workers for the first time. The measure also increased corporation taxes to 40 percent and raised excess profits taxes to 90 percent, though loopholes and generous legal interpretations frequently lowered these rates in practice. The law also initiated the policy of payroll withholding to keep dollars out of consumer circulation. Taxes on high personal income and excess profits produced a significant, though temporary, redistribution of personal income. The top 5 percent income bracket declined in relative economic worth as its control of disposable income diminished. At the same time, full employment and the increase of two-income families brought greater purchasing power to poorer people. The number of families earning less than $2000 a year was halved, while those making more than $5000 a year increased fourfold.

Commodity shortages and rationing also cut across class lines: people with money could not always find what they wanted to buy. In 1942, for example, the government ordered the automobile industry to stop making cars and light trucks and switch to manufacturing tanks and airplanes. Additional income thus went into personal savings accounts, which would later provide the capital for heavy postwar consumer spending. Wartime advertising also directed attention from shortages to postwar opportunities. "Ordnance Today," boasted the Easy Washing Machine Company, "Washers Tomorrow." The Cessna Aircraft Company predicted that the "Family Car of the Air" would enable weekend golfers to tee off five hundred miles from home after the war."

The shortage of consumer goods led Americans to spend more money on entertainment. Hollywood movie attendance reached eighty million customers a week. The Office of War Information and Hollywood cooperated in making documentary films—such as Frank Capra's *Why We Fight* series—to disseminate an official version of the war effort. *March of Time* newsreels gave American audiences weekly reports on the progress of Allied troops. The political content of fictional movies appeared blatantly patriotic—celebrating American allies, deprecating the enemy and inspiring sacrifices on the home front. Combat films—*Sahara* (1942) and *Lifeboat* (1944), for example—depicted the war effort as a melting pot of nationalities. Popular war novels, such as Harry Brown's *A Walk in the Sun*, released as a movie in 1945, stressed the ethnic diversity of American soldiers. A series of movies—*Mission to Moscow* (1943), *The North Star* (1943), and *Song of Russia* (1944)—praised the heroism of the Soviet people. (During the cold war all three would become political embarrassments, and *The North Star* would be reissued in the 1950s with a new ending as *Armored Attack*.) Hollywood also provided the familiar escapist fare, including a spate of nostalgic musicals (e.g., *Meet Me in St. Louis*, 1944), which depicted a simpler American life.

Popular images of the Axis enemies paralleled the course of the war. In 1942, there were six-hundred thousand Italian Americans who had not become naturalized citizens. Technically they were "enemy aliens." But Roosevelt, aware of the ethnic antagonism of World War I, hoped to reduce racist hysteria against Europeans. He also appreciated the power of the Italian vote in the 1942 congressional elections. On Columbus Day, therefore, the president revoked the enemy alien status of Italians and eased procedures for naturalization. In a similar election situation in 1944, Roosevelt announced both a loan and relief supplies for the defeated Italian enemy, now viewed as an ally against the German occupiers. The desire to differentiate between the Italian people and the fascist government emerged clearly in Hollywood films. In *Sahara*, for example, an Italian prisoner was described contemptuously as a "pot of spaghetti," but the film also suggested that loyal Italian Americans probably had made the steel for the American tank. "Italians are not Germans," the film concluded; the fascist uniform covered only the body, not the soul. Such notions helped prepare the public for the relatively lenient treatment of Italy in 1943.

By contrast, the mass media portrayed Nazis and Japanese as ruthless barbarians. Since the Roosevelt administration played down anti-German feeling, Hollywood also distinguished between Nazis and other Germans. "They despise the world of civilians," said *Life* magazine of the German military. "They wear monocles to train themselves to control their face muscles." Hollywood often used such stereotypes to scoff at Nazi stupidity, a recurring screen phenomenon that encouraged audiences to laugh at the world conquerors. Depictions of the Japanese, however, were utterly humorless. Partly because of the anger aroused by Japanese atrocities and partly because of anti-Asian racism, Americans portrayed this enemy as subhuman. Such racial attitudes would prevent whites from making political distinctions among Japanese Americans.

POLITICS IN WARTIME

While the popular media emphasized the theme of national unity, political disagreements undermined Roosevelt's search for consensus, especially after the 1942 elections increased conservative strength in Congress. Anti-New Dealers now pervaded the Democratic party. As a result, Roosevelt announced at a December 1943 press conference that "Dr. New Deal" had been replaced by "Dr. Win the War."

Despite his difficulties with Congress, the president continued to hope for postwar reform. In January 1944, Roosevelt proposed an economic "bill of rights," arguing that the nation could not "be content if some fraction of our people . . . is ill-fed, ill-clothed, ill-housed and insecure." The president also demanded liberal legislation for veterans' benefits. By 1944, about one million veterans had returned from the armed services, many of them injured or otherwise unable to adjust to civilian life. Congress responded by enacting the GI Bill of Rights, a landmark measure which provided unemployment, social security, and educational benefits to veterans. By providing college

To overcome rumors of his ill-health, Roosevelt launched a vigorous autumn campaign in 1944. Here the president greets a throng of supporters in Poughkeepsie, New York, just before election day.

scholarships, home loans, and life insurance, the GI Bill reintegrated American veterans into the life of the country and by increasing their purchasing power helped stimulate postwar prosperity.

Roosevelt's problems with conservatives dominated the 1944 presidential election. Vice President Henry A. Wallace, an outspoken liberal, had offended regular party bosses as well as conservative southerners. Roosevelt prudently dropped Wallace and chose as his running mate Senator Harry S. Truman of Missouri, who had gained popularity as chairman of the Senate War Investigating Committee, which had exposed government waste and war profiteering. The Republicans passed over the popular conservative, Senator Robert A. Taft of Ohio, to nominate the more moderate Governor Thomas E. Dewey of New York. Dewey endorsed a bipartisan foreign policy, including a postwar United Nations, and accepted such New Deal programs as social security, unemployment benefits, and collective bargaining. The Democrats nonetheless benefited by campaign support from the CIO's Political Action Committee, which brought out the labor vote. This urban electorate provided Roosevelt's margin of victory. Although the president's popular vote slipped below 54 percent of the total, Roosevelt took advantage of the wartime mood of crisis to win an unprecedented fourth term.

BATTLES ON THE HOME FRONT

In seeking to minimize political disturbances, Roosevelt authorized a domestic intelligence program that violated traditional civil liberties and expanded the power of government over private citizens. Concerned initially with the effects of global conflict on domestic peace, the president had requested Federal Bureau of Investigation director J. Edgar Hoover to monitor so-called "subversive activities" by both American fascists and communists in 1936. Hoover defined the mandate broadly. After the outbreak of war in 1939, the FBI's General Intelligence division expanded its investigation of propaganda "opposed to the American way of life" and agitators who aroused "class hatred." Such vague guidelines allowed the FBI to conduct surveillance of the NAACP beginning in 1941. The Army's Counter-Intelligence Corps even bugged Eleanor Roosevelt, the President's wife! Hoover, fearful of antiwar subversion, moved aggressively against communists. Between the signing of the Nazi-Soviet pact in 1939 and the invasion of the Soviet Union in June 1941, the American Communist party had opposed mobilization—"The Yanks are *Not* Coming!" was the slogan—and the Roosevelt administration had encouraged an anti-Communist crusade, which included secret surveillance and legal harrassment. The FBI's Custodial Detention Program of 1940 listed "dangerous" individuals, communists as well as fascists, who should be arrested in time of emergency. (In 1943, the Attorney General ordered the program terminated, but Hoover, in an act of bureaucratic independence, simply perpetuated the list under another name.) After the United States and the Soviet Union became allies, the Communist party became an enthusiastic supporter of the war, but the FBI and military intelligence continued to view communists with suspicion. Ironically, however, the Office of Strategic Services, established to monitor foreign intelligence and conduct guerrilla war behind enemy lines, often welcomed communists because of their political sophistication, personal commitment, and overseas connections.

The administration also ignored constitutional scruples in instituting wiretaps and other forms of surveillance against right wing groups and American fascists. In 1942, for example, Attorney General Francis Biddle invoked the Espionage Act of 1917 to prevent the mailing of Father Charles Coughlin's *Social Justice*, an isolationist, Jew-baiting magazine, and when Coughlin protested, the administration persuaded the Catholic hierarchy to silence the priest. Biddle also indicted twenty-six noninterventionists, including American fascists, such as Lawrence Dennis and William Pelley in a celebrated sedition trial that lasted more than two years before an embarrassed government dropped the charges. Under the Hatch Act of 1939, moreover, the Civil Service Commission instituted loyalty checks to keep subversives from federal employment.

The government also proved intolerant of those who refused to comply with the Selective Service Act on grounds of conscience. Though the law allowed for conscientious objector status, Director Lewis Hershey adopted a narrow definition, ruling that religious conscience implied a belief in divinity. About 35,000 objectors were willing to work at alternative government service, but many draft boards refused to recognize CO status and some pacifists rejected any government work. Over 5500 men, most of them Jehovah's Witnesses, chose prison over compliance with Selective Service. Jail sentences averaged four to five years.

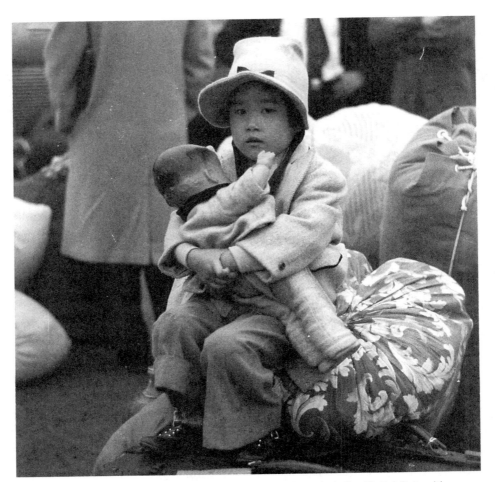

Presidential Executive Order 9066 required all Japanese Americans, including United States citizens such as this little girl, to evacuate their homes and move into concentration camps, where they lived under armed guard.

The administration blatantly ignored the civil rights and cultural differences of 110,000 Japanese Americans, most of whom lived on the West Coast. Alarmed by Pearl Harbor and Japanese victories in the Pacific, white Americans focused their rage on the Japanese-American population. Journalists falsely reported that California Japanese had conspired in the attack on Pearl Harbor and planned further subversion at home. When none occurred, California Attorney General Earl Warren used this demonstrable loyalty as counter proof: "We are just being lulled into a false sense of security," he told a congressional committee, "and the only reason we haven't had disaster in California is because it has been timed for a different date." In this disregard for Japanese rights, racism was no small motive. "It's a question of whether the white man lives on the Pacific or a brown man," admitted one farmer anxious to get rid of Japanese-American competition. The commanding general of the area, John DeWitt, explained the situation more simply: "A Jap's a Jap. . . . It makes no difference if he is an American citizen."

Roosevelt responded to public pressure with Executive Order 9066, which required the internment and relocation of all Japanese. Two thirds of the affected people were American citizens by birth (under the Naturalization Act of 1924, Japanese immigrants were barred from citizenship). Many of these victims, particularly second-generation Nisei, wished to prove their loyalty by complying with the order. Others protested vigorously: "Has the Gestapo come to America? Have we not risen in righteous anger at Hitler's mistreatment of the Jews? Then, is it not incongruous that citizen Americans of Japanese descent should be similarly mistreated and persecuted?' "

Forced to sell their property at short notice—usually to unscrupulous white buyers—the Japanese were herded into detention centers and then relocated into ten concentration camps in remote, often bleak parts of the country. Despite serious constitutional questions, the American Civil Liberties Union hesitated to defend the Japanese. Moreover, government officials conspired to present tainted evidence to the United States Supreme Court, which ruled on the legality of the program. In 1944, the Court upheld the relocation from the West Coast on grounds of military necessity in the *Korematsu* case. But in the *Endo* case, the Court denied that citizens could be detained once their loyalty had been established. By then, the Roosevelt administration understood that incarceration was no longer necessary. But the president delayed closing the concentration camps for five months, lest the release of Japanese prisoners hurt his reelection bid in 1944. Litigation in these areas would continue into the 1980s when surviving Japanese received economic compensation from the federal government.

By contrast to the internment program, the desire for national unity enabled black Americans to challenge traditional race prejudices. Where the theme for blacks in World War I had been W.E.B. DuBois's summons to "close ranks," black leaders in World War II launched a "Double V" campaign: "Declarations of war do not lessen the obligation to preserve and extend civil liberties" at home. Thus Randolph's March on Washington Movement did not disband, but remained as an important all-black, mass-based pressure group. During the war, the NAACP increased its membership ninefold to 450,000. In 1942, the non-violent pacifist James Farmer founded the Congress of Racial Equality (CORE), which used sit-in tactics to desegregate public facilities in Chicago and Washington, D.C. "Not since Reconstruction," concluded Gunnar Myrdal's massive study of racism, *An American Dilemma* (1944), "has there been more reason to anticipate fundamental changes in American race relations.

Changes came slower than Myrdal predicted. In the military, blacks, like Japanese, served in segregated units, while the Red Cross separated "colored" blood from "white." (Ironically, a black physician, Charles Drew, had developed techniques for using plasma.) Military policy, General Hershey explained, "is simply transferring discrimination from everyday life into the Army." Believing that blacks were too docile to make good soldiers, the Army initially assigned them to labor units and denied opportunity for promotion and prestigious duties, such as flying. And despite proven battlefield valor, no blacks were awarded Medals of Honor in World War I or II. To their humiliation, black soldiers discovered that Nazi prisoners of war could use public eating facilities in places where soldiers in uniform were denied service. Such treatment did not go unchallenged in the army. Numerous race riots occurred both on and off base, and in one notorious case, the black athlete Jackie Robinson was court-martialed—and acquitted—for refusing to sit in the back of a bus.

Blacks on the home front also faced racist attitudes. A public opinion poll taken at the beginning of the war found that 18 percent of blacks admitted pro-Japanese feelings; in a similar poll, a large majority of southern white industrialists, when asked to choose between complete racial equality or a German victory, preferred the latter. Such sentiments were equally strong in the North. In Detroit, white crowds rioted in 1942 to prevent blacks from living in a federally funded housing project. Whites also initiated "hate" strikes to protest the introduction of black women in war factories. In 1943, Detroit exploded in a two day riot that left thirty-five dead and over seven hundred wounded. In Philadelphia, trolley car workers went on strike to protest integration, forcing the federal government to send armed troops to break the strike. During the war, major race riots also occurred in Texas, Ohio, Massachusetts, and New York City.

Despite these conflicts, World War II represented an ideological turning point in American race relations. The repudiation of Nazi racism, reinforced at the war's end by the discovery of the infamous death camps, challenged America's own racist assumptions. In 1943, the American Bar Association admitted its first black member. In 1944, the Supreme Court abolished the white primary, which had served to disenfranchise black voters in most southern states. In Hollywood movies, the Sambo stereotypes of the 1930s were replaced by serious depictions of blacks. On Broadway, the black actor and activist Paul Robeson starred in *Othello*. Such changes provided a solid bedrock for the civil rights movement of the postwar era.

The status of Jews also improved. Although Roosevelt appointed many Jews to important positions in government, it was not uncommon before the war for Jews to face discrimination in business, social life, and education. Immigration laws established quotas that discriminated against Jews, even when refugees from Nazi persecution faced death as the only alternative. Not until 1944 did Roosevelt move to facilitate the admission of Jewish refugees from Europe. Yet the horror of Nazi anti-Semitism discredited American anti-Semitism. Although private prejudices remained, the war ended obvious forms of discrimination in such areas as education quotas.

Other forms of ethnic hatred remained. The Spanish-speaking, brown-skinned Mexican Americans of the southwest continued to face overt discrimination: housing segregation, higher unemployment, lower wages. During the war, younger Chicanos formed teenage "pachuco" gangs and dressed in lavish costumes known as "zoot suits." In July 1943, rumors that pachucos had beaten a sailor provoked a four-day race riot in Los Angeles, as white servicemen raided the barrios, attacked zoot suiters, and stripped their clothing. The fiasco showed that Mexican Americans, like the Japanese, lacked the power to defend their communities.

Hostility toward the zoot suiters revealed not only the problem of ethnic antagonism, but also a more general anxiety about American youth. As opportunities in the work force increased, educators noted a simultaneous

Racial tensions between military personnel and Mexican Americans erupted in violence in Los Angeles in June 1943, when sailors attacked these eighteen-year-olds and slashed their "zoot suit" trousers.

rise in teenage runaways, truancy, and high school dropouts. Police reported a dramatic increase in teenage delinquency, particularly in sexual crimes. Such trends paralleled a rise of teenage marriages, the tendency for adolescents to "go steady" at a younger age, and for younger women to become sexually active. Sex researcher Alfred Kinsey found that infidelity increased in only one social group: very young married women. These changes reflected the pressures of wartime—the shortage of young men, opportunities for independence, and fears associated with military service.

The liberalization of sexual behavior, however, reinforced a conservative countertrend—the celebration of the traditional family. After the Depression decade, wartime prosperity encouraged a rise in marriage and birth rates. And although mobilization brought more married women into the work force, women of childbearing age tended to remain at home. Moreover, the appeal for women workers emphasized the temporary nature of wartime employment. "Mother, when will you stay home again?" asks a daughter in one industrial ad campaign; "some jubilant day mother will stay home again, doing the job she likes best—making a home for you and daddy, when he gets back." Thus even when war undermined traditional expectations about women and the family, ideal sexual roles remained unchanged. Here was the ideological basis of the "feminine mystique" of the postwar years.

Most Americans viewed the social changes of wartime as temporary. Where the "doughboys" of World War I were seen as heroic adventurers, the soldiers of World War II appeared as civilians in uniform, eager to resume prewar activities. "Home," wrote the front-line journalist Ernie Pyle, "the one really profound goal that obsesses every one of the Americans marching on foreign shores." Even the fictional heroes were different. The outstanding novel of World War II, Norman Mailer's *The Naked and the Dead* (1948), used the device of flashback to accentuate the temporary nature of soldier status. Such attitudes encouraged the notion that life would revert to prewar conditions after the defeat of the enemy.

World War II nonetheless altered the relationship between government and the American citizen. Bureaucratic controls of the economy, the broadening of the tax base, government-funded advertising campaigns, federal support of technological research and development, the vast expansion of the armed services—these developments did not disappear at the war's end. Equally important, the war inspired a new definition of national security. The defeat of noninterventionism between 1939 and 1941 produced an internationalist consensus that perceived the national interest in a global dimension. In this view, the two oceans no longer protected the American republic; any adverse event in the world could be seen as a threat to the national security. This redefinition, in turn, demanded a strong and vigilant government dominated by an alert executive branch.

TRUMAN AND TRUCE

Truman also inherited the delicate diplomatic responsibility for settling the peace. Though he lacked Roosevelt's experience and skill, Truman determined to obtain concessions from the Soviet Union. Where Roosevelt had pragmatically accepted the vague language of Yalta, the new president insisted that the Soviet Union adopt the American interpretation of the meeting. Truman offended the Allies further when, after the formal German surrender on May 8, 1945 (V-E Day), the United States abruptly halted Lend-Lease, ordering ships in mid-Atlantic to turn around, though British and Soviet protests persuaded the president to reverse the order. Worried about the deterioration of Soviet-American relations, Truman anticipated another summit conference.

Truman's desire to meet with Stalin reflected an important change in the balance of power. As the president learned more about a top-secret military project to build an atomic bomb, he speculated that the weapon might give the United States greater leverage in winning concessions from the Soviets. Truman arranged their meeting at Potsdam for mid-July 1945, the same week the first atom bomb would be tested in New Mexico. As the atom bomb had developed, Roosevelt shared the secrets with the British, who had made important scientific contributions, but he refused to divulge the secret project to Stalin, even though he knew that spies already had passed information to the Soviets. Roosevelt's decision indicated his belief that Britain would be a postwar ally, while the Soviet Union might not. Truman shared that assumption. Within the administration, there was never any doubt that the atom bomb would be used against the enemy. Military and political leaders predicted the new weapon would forestall an invasion of Japan and save one million American lives. They also ignored the moral issues; already fire bombings of Dresden and Tokyo had claimed more victims than would die in atomic bombings.

The Potsdam conference failed to resolve Soviet-American disagreements. With news of the successful atom bomb test, Truman tried to persuade Stalin to alter the political arrangements in eastern Europe, where leftist parties prevailed. Stalin refused to change these governments, viewing Truman's request as a betrayal of the Yalta agreements. At Potsdam, the Big Three did agree to partition Germany, but again failed to resolve the question of reparations. Final treaties were delegated to a later meeting of foreign ministers.

By the summer of 1945, the Japanese cause seemed hopeless. In July, the Japanese premier made overtures through the Soviet Union, indicating a willingness to sue for peace. Truman replied with demands for unconditional surrender and warned that Japan faced imminent destruction. When the Japanese did not accept those terms, the president allowed military decisions to proceed. On August 6, 1945, a single atom bomb incinerated the city of Hiroshima, killing about one-hundred thousand civilians. On August 9, the Soviet Union entered the war. The same day, the United States dropped another atom bomb on Nagasaki. The Japanese now sought immediate peace, agreeing to surrender on August 14 provided only that the emperor be retained. When Truman agreed, World War II was over. "Ours is the supreme position," exulted the New York *Herald Tribune*. "The Great Republic has come into its own; it stands first among the peoples of the earth."

The difficulty in reaching international agreements at Yalta and Potsdam contrasted with Allied unanimity in punishing German war criminals. During World War II, Nazi Germany had violated accepted rules of warfare—indiscriminately killing civilians, instituting reigns of terror in occupied countries, and implementing horrible genocidal policies. The Allies convened an International Military Tribunal at Nuremberg, Germany, in August 1945 to bring Nazi war criminals to trial. The national interests of the judges—Soviet, British, French, and American—precluded a completely fair accounting. But in rendering judgment against twenty two Nazi defendants, the Nuremberg tribunal established the basic principles of modern warfare: aggressive warfare, violations of traditional warfare, and inhuman acts constituted crimes; individuals accused of crimes were entitled to judicial trials; individuals remained accountable for their criminal actions despite their following superior orders. These legal precedents promised to protect civilian populations from military terror. History since then has shown the limitations of the Nuremberg precedent. For the Grand Alliance of World War II did not long outlive the circumstances that had created it.

SUGGESTED READINGS

The most comprehensive treatment of Roosevelt's foreign policy is Robert Dallek, *Franklin D. Roosevelt and American Foreign Policy, 1932–1945* (1979). More critical of Roosevelt is Frederick W. Marks III, *Wind Over Sand: The Diplomacy of Franklin Roosevelt* (1988) as is Arnold A. Offner, *American Appeasement: United States Foreign Policy and Germany, 1933–1938* (1969). American policy is placed in its global context in Arnold A. Offner's *The Origins of the Second World War: American Foreign Policy and World Politics, 1917–1941* (1975).

A brief but thorough introduction to the major issues of foreign policy on the eve of World War II is Robert A. Divine, *The Reluctant Belligerent: American Entry into World War II* (1965). More detailed is a two-volume study by William L. Langer and S. Everett Gleason, *Challenge to Isolation, 1937–1940* (1952) and *The Undeclared War, 1940–1941* (1953). These surveys may be supplemented by John E. Wiltz, *From Isolation to War, 1931–1941* (1968).

The economic assumptions of United States foreign policy are explained in Patrick J. Hearden, *Roosevelt confronts Hitler: America's Entry into World War II* (1987) and in Lloyd C. Gardner, *Economic Aspects of New Deal Diplomacy* (1964). For a thorough account of the politics of non-interventionism, see Wayne S. Cole, *Roosevelt and the Isolationists, 1932–45* (1983), which can be supplemented by two older works: John E. Wiltz, *In Search of Peace: The Senate Munitions Inquiry, 1934–1936* (1963), and Manfred Jonas, *Isolationism in America: 1935–1941* (1966). The implications of non-interventionism emerge in two studies of the United States's response to the Spanish civil war: Allen Guttmann, *The Wound in the Heart* (1962) and Richard P. Traina, *American Diplomacy and the Spanish Civil War* (1968). Roosevelt's perception of the national interest emerges in David Reynolds, *The Creation of the Anglo-American Alliance, 1937–41: A Study in Competitive Co-operation* (1981).

A thorough study of the United States's relations with Japan is Dorothy Borg, *The United States and Far Eastern Crises of 1933–1938* (1964), which should be supplemented by Herbert Feis, *Road to Pearl Harbor* (1950). The ideological nature of the war is emphasized in John W. Dower, *War Without Mercy: Race and Power in the Pacific War* (1986) and Akira Iriye, *Power and Culture: The Japanese-American War, 1941–1945* (1981). Roosevelt's China policy is the subject of Michael Schaller, *The U.S. Crusade in China, 1938–1945* (1979). For the Japanese context, see Robert J. Butow, *Tojo and the Coming of the War* (1961). The attack on Pearl Harbor is examined thoroughly in Gordon W. Prange, *At Dawn We Slept* (1981).

The issues of wartime diplomacy are described in Gaddis Smith, *American Diplomacy During the Second World War, 1941–1945* (1965) and John Snell, *Illusion and Necessity: The Diplomacy of World War II* (1963). An outstanding study of international relations pertaining to Asia is Christopher Thorne, *Allies of a Kind: The United States, Britain and the War Against Japan, 1941–1945* (1978). Gabriel Kolko's *The Politics of War: The World and United States Foreign Policy, 1943–1945* (1968) stresses the inherent contradictions of national interest within the Grand Alliance. The origins of the United Nations is well treated in Robert A. Divine, *Second Chance: The Triumph of Internationalism in America During World War II* (1967). The relationship of oil to foreign and domestic policy is studied in Michael B. Stoff, *Oil, War, and American Security: The Search for a National Policy on Foreign Oil, 1941–1947* (1980). Roosevelt's limited interest in Nazi genocide is documented in David S. Wyman, *The Abandonment of the Jews: America and the Holocaust, 1941–1945* (1984). Wartime diplomacy involving the atom bomb is described in Martin J. Sherwin, *A World Destroyed: The Atomic Bomb and the Grand Alliance* (1975) and Gar Aperovitz, *Atomic Diplomacy: Hiroshima and Potsdam* (1985). For a fascinating analysis of the termination of the war in the Pacific, see Leon V. Sigal, *Fighting to a Finish: The Politics of War Termination in the United States and Japan, 1945* (1988).

The relationship between military and diplomatic affairs is emphasized in A. Russell Buchanan, *The United States and World War II*, 2 vols. (1964). More specific is Raymond G. O'Connor, *Diplomacy for Victory: FDR and Unconditional Surrender* (1971). For U.S. military leadership, see two fine biographies: Stephen E. Ambrose, *Eisenhower*, vol. I (1983) and Forrest C. Pogue, *George C. Marshall*, vols. IV–V (1968, 1973). A brilliant analysis of American air strategy is Michael S. Sherry, *The Rise of American Air Power* (1987). The view of the war from the perspective of the average soldier is presented in Lee Kennett, *G. I.: The American Soldier in World War II (1987)*.

Domestic issues during World War II are best described in Richard Polenberg, *War and Society: The United States, 1941–1945* (1972). A fine study of the Office of War Information is Allan M. Winkler, *The Politics of Progaganda* (1978). For Roosevelt's presidential role, see James MacGregor Burns, *Roosevelt: The Soldier of Freedom* (1970). John Morton Blum's *V Was For Victory: Politics and American Culture During World War II* (1976) explores the cultural context of wartime decision making. It may be supplemented by Geoffrey Perrett, *Days of Sadness, Years of Triumph* (1973), Richard Lingeman, *Don't You Know There's A War On?* (1970), and a compilation of "oral" histories, Studs

Terkel, *The Good War* (1984). For the movie industry, see Clayton R. Koppes and Gregory D. Black, *Hollywood Goes to War: How Politics, Profits, and Propaganda Shaped World War II Movies* (1987); Allen L. Woll, *The Hollywood Musical Goes to War* (1983); and Bernard F. Dick, *The Star-Spangled Screen* (1985).

The impact of the war on American society is summarized in the relevant chapters of Richard Polenberg, *One Nation Divisible: Class, Race, and Ethnicity in the United States* (1980). For the role of organized labor, see Nelson Lichtenstein, *Labor's War at Home: The CIO in World War II* (1983). A good case study is Alan Clive, *State of War: Michigan in World War II* (1979). Broader in scope is Gerald D. Nash, *The American West Transformed: The Impact of the Second World War* (1985). The position of the U.S. Communist party is described in Maurice Isserman, *Which Side Were You On: The American Communist Party During the Second World War* (1982).

The experience of Japanese-Americans is examined by Roger Daniels, *Concentration Camps USA: Japanese-Americans and World War II* (1971), as well as by Edward Spicer et al., *Impounded People: Japanese-Americans in the Relocation Centers* (1969), a report originally written in 1946 for the War Relocation Authority. Critical reappraisals of the internment program are Peter Irons, *Justice at War* (1983) and Richard Drinnon, *Keeper of Concentration Camps: Dillon S. Myer and American Racism* (1987). The administration's treatment of political dissenters emerges in the relevant chapters of Leo P. Ribuffo, *The Old Christian Right: The Protestant Far Right from the Great Depression to the Cold War* (1983). The imprisonment of other victims of the war is the subject of John Christgau, *"Enemies": World War II Alien Internment* (1985). For the government's surveillance programs, see the relevant chapters of Richard Gid Powers, *Secrecy and Power: The Life of J. Edgar Hoover* (1987) and Athan G. Theoharis and John Stuart Cox, *The Boss: J. Edgar Hoover and the Great American Inquisition* (1988).

The experience of blacks emerges in Richard Dalfiume, *Desegregation of the Armed Forces, 1939–1953* (1969). The March on Washington movement is described in the later chapters of Harvard Sitkoff, *A New Deal for Blacks* (1978). Also illuminating are the memoirs of black soldiers compiled by Mary Penick Motley, *The Invisible Soldier* (1975).

The best sources for the impact of the war on women are the relevant chapters of William H. Chafe, *The American Woman* (1972). The intellectual and social implications of women's wartime experiences are explored in Maureen Honey, *Creating Rosie the Riveter: Class, Gender, and Propaganda during World War II* (1984) and Karen Anderson, *Wartime Women: Sex Roles, Family Relations, and the Status of Women During World War II* (1981). A good comparative study is Leila Rupp, *Mobilizing Women for War: German and American Propaganda, 1939–1945* (1978). For the pacifist movement, see Lawrence S. Wittner, *Rebels Against War: The American Peace Movement, 1941–1960* (1969).

For the Nuremberg trials, see Bradley F. Smith, *Reaching Judgment at Nuremberg* (1977) and Telford Taylor, *Nuremberg and Vietnam: An American Tragedy* (1970).

Opposite Page:
Symbolic of "troubled affluence" in the atomic age, Vice-Admiral and Mrs. W.H.P. Blandy cut into a cake shaped like an atomic mushroom cloud, celebrating (with Admiral F.J. Lowery) "Operation Crossroads," the first peacetime atomic bomb testing in 1946.

8

TROUBLED AFFLUENCE: POSTWAR SOCIETY, 1945-1960

"Nobody's job is safe," remarked a woman salesclerk in Hollywood's classic film of 1946, *The Best Years of Our Lives*. With the demobilization of twelve million soldiers and the loss of ten million war-related jobs, Americans in all economic classes feared the return of another Great Depression. Instead, the economy entered an era of unprecedented growth, characterized by a dramatic rise in production and productivity, expanded corporate profits, increased personal income, and soaring consumer spending. By 1955, the 6 percent of the world population that lived in the United States made two-thirds of the world's manufactured goods. In 1956, the annual average American income was 50 percent higher than in 1929 (in constant dollars). But postwar affluence spread unevenly through American society, leaving some social groups to confront old problems of poverty as well as new ones of forced migration. Material abundance also provoked concern about a loss of spiritual values. The tensions between prosperity and its consequences provided the context for the new postwar generation.

REBUILDING A CIVILIAN ECONOMY

Wartime government depended heavily on the expertise of corporate leaders—"dollar-a-year" men—who remained on the payrolls of their private corporations while making economic decisions for the nation. Their primary commitment to big business triggered a bitter debate about the reconversion to a civilian economy. As the demand for war production declined in 1944, Donald Nelson, head of the War Production Board (WPB), recommended that small businesses that were losing war contracts reconvert to peacetime production while larger corporations continue to meet military demands. But corporate leaders vigorously resisted this proposal because they feared that small firms would gain advantages in the transition to civilian production. Military officials, who were unwilling to slacken war manufacturing, also backed the major war contractors. This alliance succeeded in delaying reconversion until 1945, thereby protecting the wartime expansion of big business, but also extending the continued shortage of goods past the end of the war.

Cooperation between the federal government and big business shaped the patterns of the postwar economy. Ignoring the problems of small business, the War Production Board rapidly lifted wartime regulations in 1945. This abrupt end of government control over scarce resources benefitted larger corporations which held most of those materials. Unable to obtain basic resources, many small businesses folded or sold out to bigger corporations. Large corporations also took advantage of Washington's generous reconversion sales and bought government-built plants and resources at a fraction of their cost. Such subsidies assured that the biggest corporations would continue to dominate the economy. The Federal Trade Commission reported in 1947 that 2,450 independent mining and manufacturing firms disappeared since 1940 as a result of mergers and acquisitions. Concentrated economic power, the FTC declared, was "the greatest dramatic challenge to the American theory of competitive enterprise." Organizations such as the National Federation of Small Business pressed Congress to create a permanent Small Business Committee in 1950 and the Small Business Administration three years later.

Exhibit 8–1. Wholesale and Consumer Price Indexes, 1945–60.

(1967 = 100)

The abandonment of government controls also aggravated consumer shortages. Since businesses made greater profits from expensive goods rather than cheaper lines—for example, gowns rather than housedresses—manufacturers tended to produce high-priced goods. The resulting shortage of necessities such as clothing led to skyrocketing prices and an illegal black market. Lifting controls on building materials, for example, stimulated construction of higher-priced industrial plants without alleviating residential housing shortages. Builders and real estate brokers made enormous profits as house prices soared overnight. Rising prices compelled sacrifices on the part of people on fixed incomes, particularly government employees and most of the elderly. But many small producers and merchants found it impossible to meet inflated costs while the OPA regulated selling prices for their goods. As a result, most congressional conservatives opposed extension of wartime controls, but President Harry Truman finally prevailed in continuing some price regulation until mid-1947. Shortages, inflation, and the black market remained important political issues in the 1946 elections, but the consumer price index rose 30 percent between mid-1946 and 1948.

The federal government also cooperated with big business in administering veterans' benefits under the "GI Bill of Rights," which Congress passed in 1944. The law provided for unemployment insurance ($20 a week for one year), life insurance, home mortgage insurance, and educational scholarships. But when only one-fifteenth of the first 1.5 million veterans chose to continue GI life insurance, the military joined with commercial life insurance companies to launch an advertising campaign to reverse the trend. By 1946, one-third of the veterans opted to continue their policies. (Life insurance proved one of the great growth industries of the postwar period. Between 1950 and 1960 sales of individual policies, not counting employee benefit plans, increased by over 200 percent.) The

Typical of postwar overcrowding on college campuses, these former soldiers bunk in double-deckers while enrolling at the University of Maryland. Most had their tuition paid under the G.I. "Bill of Rights."

administration of GI home mortgages also benefited private business. By 1947, over one million veterans obtained government-insured home loans without the usual down payments, enabling most to own their own houses for the first time. But the mortgages had to be approved by the Veterans Administration (VA), which was notoriously lax in appraising houses and protecting quality standards, and veterans had to satisfy the requirements of private bankers.

The availability of government-financed scholarships also offered veterans opportunities for occupational mobility. Between 1945 and 1950, over two million veterans used government money to enroll in colleges and universities. Millions more returned to high schools and vocational training programs. By 1952 the federal government had spent $13.5 billion for these purposes. Postwar surveys found that as many as one-fifth of college-bound veterans would not have returned to school without such aid. The heavy influx of students encouraged colleges to expand facilities, open branch campuses, offer evening instruction, and adjust their curricula to the influx of older and more serious students. By underwriting tuition bills, federal funds boosted the expansion of academia and established a precedent for later support of education.

SCIENCE AND SOCIETY

Wartime engineering and scientific achievement proved the advantages of higher education. The development of radar and jet propulsion, the use of pesticides such as DDT, the effectiveness of "miracle drugs" like penicillin, the emergence of synthetic compounds to substitute for scarce resources like rubber—all testified to the importance of scientific research for social progress. In popular wartime imagery, the scientist and the engineer appeared as heroic figures.

Atomic bombs dwarfed these conventional accomplishments and introduced profound dilemmas about uncontrolled scientific investigation. During the war the government had classified atomic energy research (the "Manhattan Project") top secret, although physicists around the world understood the theoretical basis of the bomb. The Manhattan Project had secretly amassed control of uranium and thorium deposits necessary to manufacture atom bombs, but could not acquire a total monopoly. In 1945 American scientists predicted that other countries could develop similar weapons in three to five years. President Truman, however, preferred the opinion of military leaders who claimed the United States could monopolize atomic bombs for at least twenty years. The president therefore rejected recommendations to share information about atomic bombs with the Soviet Union, a decision supported by public opinion and Congress. The Atomic Energy Act of 1946 established the Atomic Energy Commission (AEC) and placed control of nuclear research and development in civilian hands.

J. Robert Oppenheimer, head of the Los Alamos research team that developed the atom bomb, expressed widely held anxieties about the future of scientific investigation: "In some sense, which no vulgarity, no humor, no overstatement can quite extinguish," he said, "the physicists have known sin; and this is a knowledge which they cannot lose." Such concern appeared on a popular level in postwar science fiction, which enjoyed a remarkable revival. New science fiction writers like Isaac Asimov and Ray Bradbury developed futuristic themes of human beings seeking to avert ultimate catastrophe. In postwar Hollywood films, such as *Cloak and Dagger* (1946), the serious scientist became an ambivalent character, simultaneously capable of bringing salvation or annihilation. "To the average civilized man of 1950," concluded *Scientific American*, "science no longer means primarily the promise of a more abundant life; it means the atomic bomb."

Despite civilian control of atomic energy, nearly all nuclear research and development involved military work. But to counter popular fears, the AEC started a public relations division in 1947 to stress that "atomic energy is already at work for *good.*" Together with private contractors, such as General Electric and Westinghouse, the AEC sponsored public exhibitions and educational programs, which suggested that atomic energy would be used for social betterment. The government also denied the harmful effects of radiation. These deceptions encouraged the expansion of the nuclear arsenal. Although the United States possessed very few atom bombs in the early postwar period—the exact number remains the ultimate military secret—the Truman administration increasingly emphasized a military strategy based on nuclear weapons. After learning of the Soviet Union's first atom bomb test in 1949, Truman ordered the development of the vastly more powerful hydrogen bomb the next year. H-bomb tests in the Pacific and A-bomb tests in the western states often spread radiation on unsuspecting civilians. Such practices probably increased cancer and mortality rates, though the federal government denied responsibility. President Truman also created the Federal Civil Defense Administration to prepare the public for a nuclear holocaust. President Dwight D. Eisenhower continued these policies. In 1953, for example, he advised the AEC to keep the public "confused" about the hazards of radiation. Civil defense programs served less to protect the public than to soothe its fears.

Despite anxieties about atomic research, Americans generally welcomed technological innovations such as the production of synthetic goods. Fibers made of rayon, nylon, and dacron increasingly replaced cotton and wool. In home furnishings, plastics supplanted wood and leather. Artificial flavors, colors, and preservatives became staples of the American diet. Besides changing the quality standards, however, such products interfered adversely with the natural environment. Most synthetics were derivatives of petroleum products. Thus the use of artificial fibers in clothing or vinyl interiors in automobiles drained nonrenewable fossil resources. And artificial waste products remained in the environment to contaminate and even destroy the ecological balance. Only exceptional cases of pollution aroused public attention. For example, scientists disclosed during the 1950s that radioactive strontium 90, a "fallout" of atomic bomb testing, might be poisoning milk.

Scientific technology usually appeared more beneficial. The fluoridation of water, for example, significantly reduced tooth decay, particularly among children. When given the choice of voting for fluoridation, however, nearly all local communities rejected the innovation. But by 1963, fifty million Americans were drinking fluoridated water. During the postwar decade, the United States replaced Europe as the prime manufacturer of precision scientific instruments. New medical technologies included kidney dialysis machines (1945), artificial heart valves (1953), and electronic heart pacemakers (1957). By 1960, American surgeons successfully performed five thousand open heart operations each week. Meanwhile, the introduction of "miracle" antibiotics, such as streptomycin and aureomycin, helped control infectious diseases. Most dramatically, the introduction of Dr. Jonas Salk's poliomyelitis vaccine in 1955 effectively eliminated a dreaded disease that had claimed fifty-five thousand victims each year.

These bold advances reinforced public optimism about the future of technology and the possibility of unlimited progress. Thus when the automobile industry developed high horsepower engines, the petroleum industry introduced appropriate high-octane gasoline. Such innovations ignored the question of ecological limits. "Planned obsolescence" of supposedly durable goods like automobiles exacerbated the waste of natural resources. Some prophetic ecologists, such as William Vogt and Fairfield Osborn, warned about the limits of available supplies. But most Americans accepted corporate assurances that applied science would eventually solve such technological problems.

AN EXPANDING POPULATION

Young adults were among the most enthusiastic postwar optimists. Taking their cue from a popular song of 1945, "Gotta Make Up For Lost Time," ex-servicemen rushed to get married and settle down with their families. In May 1946, nine months after V-J Day, the nation's birth rate began to leap and remained high until 1957. The unprecedented baby boom resulted from couples marrying younger, thereby increasing the years of marital fertility. Yet the number of families with five or more children declined, suggesting a greater willingness to use birth control. As a result of the baby boom, the nation's population grew from 140 million in 1945 to 152 million in 1950 and exceeded 179 million by 1960. Such growth also reflected the slightly declining death rate which resulted from medical advances. Thus between 1950 and 1959 life expectancy for whites rose from 69.1 to 70.5 and for non-whites from 60.8 to 63.5.

The burgeoning population accelerated long-term patterns of mobility. Attracted by industrial expansion during World War II, workers and their families had flocked to the southwestern and western states. In Texas, the growth of the petrochemical industry, stimulated by the increased use of fossil fuels, encouraged a population increase of one-third. In Arizona, Tucson and Phoenix mushroomed into sizable cities, continuing war-induced growth by selling the advantages of a warm, sunny climate. But when asked in 1956 "which city would you most like to live in?" more Americans responded: "Los Angeles." Meanwhile, California, home of numerous war industries, such as aircraft and electronics, attracted over five million people between 1940 and 1960, doubling its size and surpassing New York as the most populous state in 1963. Symbolizing the westward movement were the first new states since 1912—Alaska and Hawaii in 1959.

Exhibit 8–2. Birth Rates, 1940–1960.

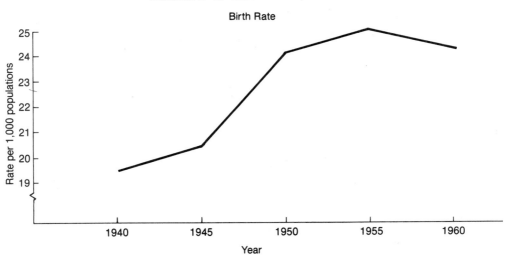

As the center of population shifted to the West, urban populations grew at a faster rate than the national average. By 1960, 70 percent of the American people lived in urban settings. Mechanization of agriculture, particularly in the South, forced twenty-two million rural Americans to migrate into cities between 1940 and 1960. This trend, part of a long historical process, dramatically changed the social composition of metropolitan life. For while black and Hispanic farm workers poured into urban centers, whites increasingly moved out. By 1960, more than half the nation's black population lived in central cities; the outskirts usually remained white.

HOUSING AND SUBURBAN DEVELOPMENT

Military demobilization accentuated the nation's housing shortage, forcing many veterans to live with other families, camp out on public facilities, or accept substandard rooms in converted chicken coops or quonset huts. The postwar baby boom aggravated the problem. This lack of housing reflected the nation's recent economic history. During the Depression and World War II, new residential construction had virtually ended. By 1945, the total value of American housing was worth 7 percent less than in 1929. Postwar shortages of building materials and the inflation of real estate prices perpetuated the shortage. To reduce costs, builders began to construct new dwellings on the suburban fringes of cities. With apartments unavailable, families discovered that it was easier and sometimes cheaper to purchase houses by obtaining a home mortgage backed by the federal government under the Federal Housing Authority (FHA) or VA.

To fill the tremendous demand for residential housing, builder William J. Levitt drew upon his experience as a war contractor and began offering mass-produced, standardized units at affordable prices for the lower-middle class. Using specialized work crews, interchangeable designs, prefabricated materials, and package deals that included interior appliances, landscaping, and legal fees, Levitt produced 4½ room Cape Cod houses for $8,000 in 1949. To keep prices down, he eliminated dining rooms, basements, and attics as well as unnecessary trim. Between 1947 and 1951, Levitt built over seventeen thousand dwellings in Levittown, Long Island, converting a potato field into a community of seventy-five thousand people. Efficient production methods enabled the builder to erect one four-room house every sixteen minutes! "No man who owns his own house and lot can be a Communist," Levitt declared. When critics complained that his structures were monotonously repetitive, Levitt offered different exterior paints, curved streets, and homes placed at slightly different angles. Such housing, imitated by builders around the nation, benefitted by new standardization within the appliance and home furnishing industries.

The growth of suburbia accentuated the mobility of the American people. But as suburban workers commuted to their jobs, housewives and children remained isolated from distant urban life. New housing developments initially lacked community institutions, such as libraries, schools, hospitals, mass transportation, and even common gathering places. To add to the sense of bland uni-

This aerial photograph of Levittown, New York, in the 1950s shows the rapid transformation of rural areas into densely-populated suburbs. Critics lamented the uniformity of such housing and warned about the demoralizing effects of social conformity.

formity pervading the new settlements, few older people were attracted to suburban life.

Suburbanites compensated for this isolation by relying more on automobiles. Where housewives were left behind, second cars became necessary to reach shopping centers and schools. Two-car families contributed to the increase of auto registration from twenty-six million in 1945 to forty million in 1950 to sixty-two million by 1960. Yet the consequences of such mobility proved severe, producing increased national dependence on foreign oil and worsening air pollution at home. In 1947, journalist John Gunther boasted that Los Angeles would use electricity to produce "clean industry" and uncontaminated air. Yet within one decade the city's auto exhausts had created a smog situation that was a serious hazard to public health. Despite such problems, passage of the Interstate Highway Act in 1956 committed the federal government to $26 billion for the development of a continental freeway system, a figure that reached $37 billion five years later.

The novelty of suburban life minimized community attachments. As families grew in size, suburbanites readily moved to larger homes. Residential change often mirrored the interchangeability of jobs in an increasingly white-collar and service economy. By 1960 nearly two-fifths of the American labor force worked for organizations with at least five hundred employees. The proliferation of chain stores reflected this trend. As chains increased their share of total food sales from 29 percent to 44 percent in the ten years after 1948, nearly one hundred thousand independent groceries disappeared. Retail consolidation often meant that management relocated employees at its own convenience. It also destroyed the intimacy between small merchants and their customers. Corporate store managers, Gunther noted, never became "a real ingredient in the life of a community." "Ever since the war," complained TV's fictional Alice Kramden on "The Honeymooners," "the butchers don't treat a woman with respect."

THE URBAN CRISIS

With a rising urban population, new construction in the suburbs did little to relieve metropolitan congestion. Social critics blamed urban slums for encouraging crime, particularly juvenile delinquency. When local governments seemed unable to solve the housing problem, President Truman joined with conservative Senator Robert Taft to persuade Congress to enact the Housing Act of 1949. The law authorized slum clearance and construction of 810,000 units of low-rent housing. But the federal housing program was sidetracked by Korean War expenditures and further undermined by real estate interests and the unsympathetic Eisenhower administration. Federal policy continued to favor private residential housing. In 1962, for example, government housing assistance for the poor amounted to $820 million; that year, tax deductions for private homeowners reached $2.9 billion.

As rural migrants flocked to the cities, however, the suburbanization of middle-class taxpayers shrank the urban tax base, impoverishing municipal services. With increased use of automobiles, mass transit deteriorated for want of funds. In cities such as Los Angeles, St. Louis, Philadelphia, and Salt Lake City municipal officials accepted bribes from General Motors to replace inexpensive electric trolley cars with the company's gas-consuming buses. The resulting traffic congestion could not be eased even by the construction of new freeways that surrounded most major cities. City planners also discovered loopholes in the Housing Act that permitted the destruction of old buildings without constructing low-cost housing. Under the law, over one million residential units faced the wrecking ball while fewer than 350,000 took their place. Thus urban renewal saw old neighborhoods, often with homogeneous ethnic populations, uprooted to make way for convention centers, office buildings, parking lots, and other nonresidential units. Such practices aggravated the problem of homelessness. During the postwar period, every large city had a "skid row" including five to ten thousand homeless people.

CULTURAL DIVERSITY

Urban newcomers, particularly racial minorities, grappled with the problems of congestion. Besides endemic poverty, nonwhites faced a pattern of organized discrimination. Through "restrictive covenants," white property owners frequently adopted legal agreements not to sell or rent dwellings to minorities. The federal government actively supported such policies. "If a neighborhood is to retain stability," advised an FHA underwriting manual, "it is necessary that properties shall continue to be occupied by the same social and racial classes." The FHA also refused to insure non-segregated projects.

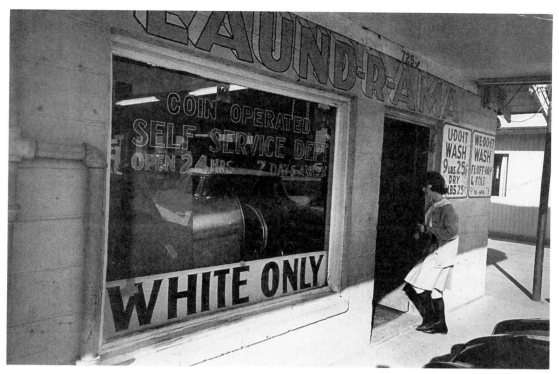

The southern states enforced racial segregation in a variety of public accommodations, including schools, restaurants, toilets, drinking fountains, laundries, and other places where body contact might occur. Such "Jim Crow" laws were not outlawed until 1964.

Residential segregation reflected the principle of "separate, but equal," articulated by the Supreme Court in *Plessy v. Ferguson* in 1896. After World War II, blacks increasingly attacked discrimination in housing. An NAACP-sponsored lawsuit, *Shelley v. Kraemer*, finally persuaded the Supreme Court to deny the legality of government support of restrictive covenants in 1948. In accepting social science testimony that depicted the psychological and sociological damage caused by segregation, the Court laid the basis for later revisions of the *Plessy* doctrine.

Residential segregation nonetheless persisted, affecting not only blacks but also Spanish-speaking and other minorities. Of the nearly one million Puerto Ricans residing in New York in 1960, 40 percent lived in inadequate dwellings. Yet monthly rentals remained high, absorbing as much as one-third of their incomes. In higher income brackets, residential segregation affected such groups as Chinese, Japanese, and Jews, who tended to cluster in homogeneous communities. Levittown did not accept blacks until 1960. The existence of ethnic neighborhoods in cities, however, frequently reflected a positive assertion of cultural identity. Not all minorities wished to be assimilated in the Anglo-Protestant melting pot.

American Indian communities struggled with the issue of assimilation. Prior to World War II, federal policy toward reservation tribes had wavered between detribalization and protection of American Indian tribal rights. In 1946, the Indian Claims Commission Act allowed the tribes to bring legal action against the federal government for violations of previous treaties. But the Bureau of Indian Affairs (BIA) administered the law to speed the termination of government services. For example, when American Indians appealed bureaucratic orders, the BIA refused to allow the use of tribal attorneys. In 1954, Congress embraced detribalization, passing a series of termination laws to dissolve tribal structures, disburse tribal assets, and end federal assistance. Implemented against the Menominee of Wisconsin and the Klamath of Oregon, the policy created severe economic and social problems.

Unemployment rates on reservations appeared staggering: over 70 percent among the Blackfeet of Montana and the Hopi of New Mexico; over 86 percent among the Choctaw of Mississippi. Many job-seekers moved to nearby cities where they lived in poverty conditions. Proximity to white culture. particularly the mass media, undermined Native American customs. Traditional tribal rituals became less important and the number of spoken Native American languages declined. But traditionalists responded to assimilation by mobilizing resistance to white culture. Thus the postwar period also saw a revitalization of Native American religion and identity. Assertions of American Indian pride helped block the termination program in the 1960s.

RURAL AMERICA

Mechanized agriculture increased farm production by 6 percent per year between 1949 and 1959, but the farm population continued its twentieth-century decline and the total number of farms continued to decrease. Benefitting from research and development programs at state agricultural colleges, farmers invested in new equipment and new hybrid crops that could be handled by machines. Farmers also greatly increased the use of chemical fertilizers, pesticides, additives, and antibiotics. While technological agriculture proved extremely profitable, mechanization and chemical farming required large capital expenditures that small farmers could not afford. Modern agriculture thus encouraged the consolidation of farmlands in gigantic holdings and shifted ownership to large agribusiness corporations.

The federal government subsidized this shift to corporate agriculture. In the early postwar years, food shortages in Europe created large markets for American farm surpluses. As those outlets diminished, the Agricultural Acts of 1948 and 1949 authorized government price supports for basic crops. In 1956 Congress began paying farmers not to plant certain crops, while the Soil Bank Act (1956) gave reimbursements for converting crop land into noncommercial conservation acreage. Large acreage farms gained most. "The majority of farm people derive little or no benefit from our agricultural price support legislation," admitted the *Economic Report of the President* in 1959; "those with the higher incomes are the main beneficiaries." Postwar reciprocal trade agreements, moreover, subjected independent dairy and livestock producers to foreign competition that was permitted to sell at prices below American costs of production.

Exhibit 8–3. Price Index, Fresh and Processed Vegetables, 1946–60.

	Fresh	*Processed*
1946	57	69
1948	64	81
1950	62	75
1952	78	83
1954	72	85
1956	77	88
1958	84	92
1960	85	93

Source: *Historical Statistics of the United States, Colonial Times to 1970* (1975)

Technological agriculture also imposed mass produced food on the national diet. Between 1950 and 1959, average per capita consumption of dairy products, fresh fruits, and fresh vegetables declined. Consumers compensated by eating greater quantities of processed and frozen foods. Relying on nutritional additives, artificial flavoring and coloring, and preservatives to maintain a modicum of food value, processed food added as much as 30 percent to the cost of each edible pound. Food processers such as Birdseye dictated which crop strains would be planted, resulting in a decline in the number of available seed and food varieties. Franchise restaurant chains, which also proliferated in this period, preferred standardized menus, creating another vast market for single strains of produce. Similarly, corporate consolidation affected beverage consumption. In the beer industry, the number of breweries dropped from 450 in 1950 to 170 in 1960 to 70 in 1970. Such changes encouraged homogenization of American eating and drinking.

CORPORATE ECONOMY

Many Americans feared that the return of a peacetime economy would reintroduce the Depression. But accumulated wartime savings and a strong consumer desire for durable goods helped resolve those anxieties. Business also benefitted from huge government sponsored exports to war-torn Europe. When the demand for consumer durables finally declined in 1949, causing a significant recession, growing expenditures for residential housing, backed by government mortgage insurance, cushioned the downturn. Later recessions in 1954 and 1958 evoked similar government assistance to the housing industry.

Government spending for military purposes further fueled the postwar boom. Although both Presidents Truman and Eisenhower attempted to trim the military budget, the "Cold War" with the Soviet Union demanded massive military appropriations. In the first year of the Korean War (1950–1951), for example, the military budget leaped from $14 billion to $34 billion and exceeded $50 billion by 1953, the last year of the war. By then military expenditures represented 13.5 percent of the gross national product, while other military-related costs raised the number to 21 percent. Unemployment consequently reached a postwar low of 1.8 percent in October 1953, with slightly more than one million idle workers. Huge military budgets remained a basic element of the postwar economy. Under Eisenhower the government spent more than $350 billion on defense, and 77 percent of every budget dollar went for military-related appropriations.

President Eisenhower warned about the development of a "military-industrial complex" in his farewell address of 1961. "We have been compelled to create a permanent armaments industry of vast proportions," he observed. "We annually spend on military security alone more than the net income of all United States corporations." Government contracts with war-related industries illuminated an inseparable tie between military preparedness and corporate prosperity. Talk of a thaw in the Cold War invariably brought falling prices on Wall Street. Yet Eisenhower offered no solution to the trend, and John F. Kennedy campaigned successfully in 1960 on the false assertion that the Republicans had permitted a "missile gap" in favor of the Soviet Union.

The federal government also supported technological innovation and business expansion by underwriting research and development programs. Between 1950 and 1959, federal expenditures for "R & D" increased threefold to about $12 billion, including support for university research at a rate of $300 million a year. Aircraft manufacturing, one of the largest growth industries of the era, drew 80 percent of its business from military agencies. Employing 1.25 million workers in 1959, the burgeoning aircraft industry boosted the rapid growth of the West Coast economy. Government money also backed expansion in electronics. The transistor, invented in 1948, and the computer, introduced in the marketplace in 1951, stimulated 15 percent annual growth in electronics, making it the fifth largest industry by 1960. Most electronics sales went to the federal government for military equipment.

After the Soviet Union surprised the world by launching the first artificial earth satellite, "Sputnik," in 1957, public pressure demanded greater government support of scientific R & D. Congress created the National Aeronautics and Space Administration in 1958 to coordinate the civilian space program, while the Defense Department worked secretly on military missiles and satellites. Government expenditures for R & D jumped from $6.2 billion in 1955 to $14.3 billion six years later, a 131 percent increase. In 1959 NASA unveiled Project Mercury, a program for manned space flight, and introduced the first seven astronauts to the American public. In the international "space race," however, American rocketry seemed to lag behind the achievements of the Soviet Union.

Exhibit 8–4. Research and Development, 1955–1960.
(current dollars in billions)

	Total	Defense and Space-related
1955	$ 6.2b	$3.0b
1960	$13.5b	$7.4b

Source: *Statistical Abstract of the United States*

The first Mercury astronauts. Left to right: Scott Carpenter, Gordon Cooper, John Glenn, Virgil Grissom, Walter Schirra, Alan Shepard, and Donald Slayton. Following suborbital flights by Shepard and Grissom in 1961. Glenn circled the earth three times the next year.

Early Soviet satellites weighed thousands of pounds and even carried a dog as cargo, whereas the first successful American launch, the Army's Explorer of January 1958, weighed only thirty pounds. Soviet leader Nikita Khrushchev derisively called it a "grapefruit." But in the next decade, electronic miniaturization brought primacy to American space efforts.

Military superiority also justified generous government help for the petroleum industry. Accepting the industry's argument that the national interest depended on preserving domestic reserves while exploiting foreign oil, the federal government waived antitrust regulations to permit profitable development of Middle East oil and devised generous tax credits to subsidize private arrangements with Saudi Arabia. Under the Truman administration's Marshall Plan, the United States refinanced a major shift in western European energy consumption from coal to petroleum—a $384 million subsidy to American oil companies which made the western allies dependent upon imports. In Iran, the Central Intelligence Agency initiated a coup d'etat in 1953 to prevent the nationalization of local oil fields. (See also chapter 4.) In addition, Congress enacted mandatory petroleum import quotas in 1950, which kept cheap foreign oil from lowering prices in the United States. Despite these measures, the large energy corporations continued to cut payments to oil exporting countries, which led as a counter-measure to the formation of OPEC (Organization of Petroleum Exporting Countries) in 1960.

In supporting private business, government agencies continued the World War II practice of awarding contracts to the largest corporations. Only 4 percent of R & D funds reached small businesses. Though convenient for government administrators, this support of big business did not bring reduced costs. Without competitive bidding, federal budgets routinely absorbed business "overruns." There was little irony, therefore, when Eisenhower's secretary of defense Charles E. Wilson, the former president of General Motors, said: "For years I thought what was good for the country was good for General Motors, and vice versa."

CORPORATE CULTURE

Corporate prosperity stimulated tremendous confidence in the economic future. "Not only do the younger people accept the beneficent society as normal," reported sociologist William H. Whyte, Jr.; "they accept *improvement*, considerable and constant, as normal too." Despite economic recessions in 1948–49, 1953–54, and 1957–58, private consumption steadily increased each year. In the immediate postwar years consumers exhausted their savings to buy durable goods such as appliances, automobiles, furniture, and TVs. Then they relied on borrowed money to purchase disposable goods and services such as entertainment and travel. In 1950 Diner's Club introduced the credit card to allow businessmen to charge their meals. By the end of the decade, Carte Blanche, American Express, and Bankamericard extended easy credit to predominantly male members. Installment credit soared from $4 billion in 1954 to $43 billion in 1960. Some of this spending reflected the demands of the baby boom: children's clothing, toys, "family-size" products. In 1956 the airline industry attracted as many passengers as railroads for the first time; two years later, the Boeing 707 brought jet speed to commercial aviation. Consumption often seemed an end in itself. Cars with exaggerated fender "fins" made drivers appear bigger and bolder. Men's clothing styles began imitating women's fashions by undergoing annual changes that made serviceable wardrobes outmoded and brought men into the consumer market.

Advertising, not coincidentally, became one of the major growth industries of the postwar period. "Let's clean up the mess in Washington!" declared General Dwight Eisenhower in the first political advertising to appear on television in 1952. Coached by Hollywood actor Robert Montgomery and inspired by the Batten, Barton, Durstine, and Osborn advertising agency, Eisenhower's campaign proved the political value of the new media. Although popular exposés such as Vance Packard's *The Hidden Persuaders* (1957) explained the psychological techniques of advertising, market research found that consumers remained more responsive to emotional appeals than to product substance. Annual advertising expenditures soared over the $10-billion mark by 1960, mostly touting consumer disposables and luxuries such as tobacco, beverages, drugs, amusements, and extra home furnishings. Postwar advertising relied increasingly on national media, facilitating product recognition for a population that migrated around the country at an increased rate.

The growth of advertising paralleled the expansion of all service industries. Each year consumers spent ever larger sums for insurance, utilities, automobile repairs, medical care, and travel. Expanding service industries also altered the nature of work. As part of a long historical trend, technological innovation increased individual worker productivity, which in turn reduced the number of blue-collar jobs. But the growth of corporations increased the number of managerial jobs for employees who administered the bureaucracies rather than produced commodities. For these "organization men," tasks became increasingly technical, specialized, and separated from any tangible product. In the growing bureaucracies of the corporate economy, expertise and teamwork appeared as prime values. In 1956 the total number of people in service industries exceeded the number of producers for the first time, thus heralding the postindustrial society. Bureaucracies also swelled on all levels of government. Employment in state and local government, for example, rose two million during the 1950s, an increase of 52 percent. By 1960, nearly 8.5 million employees drew government paychecks, largely for white-collar employment.

LABOR UNIONS AND ECONOMIC STABILITY

Despite remarkable economic growth, unemployment remained an endemic problem. Fearing a postwar repeat of the Depression, Congress passed the Employment Act of 1946, an unprecedented measure that committed the federal government to maximize employment by direct intervention in the economy. The law also created a Council of Economic Advisers to help the president formulate policy. But neither Presidents Truman nor Eisenhower accepted the principle of creating government jobs to ease unemployment.

In the immediate postwar years, inflation, rather than depression, seemed the major threat to economic stability. Workers responded to the decline of purchasing power with a series of prolonged strikes, including a bitter railroad walkout that affected the entire economy, and won substantial wage increases as well as "cost-of-living" adjustments to offset inflation. Businesses passed these raises on to consumers, however, thereby feeding the inflationary cycle. Labor unions continued to seek higher wages, better working conditions, and job security packages. But corporations steadfastly rejected efforts by unions to influence management decisions. World War II had restored the prestige business had lost during the Depression, and corporate leaders used the Cold War atmosphere to silence labor activism and radicalism by identifying them with the Soviet enemy. Thus labor leaders preferred to cooperate with business. The expulsion of Communists from AFL and CIO unions protected the conservativism of organized labor. When eleven unions resisted such purges, the CIO expelled them in 1951, thus solidifying labor's support of the Cold War.

Labor-business relations took new forms under the Taft-Hartley Act of 1947. Aimed at protecting the public from labor-management disputes, the law allowed government to seek an injunction against strike action and provided for a sixty-day "cooling-off" period during which federal mediators would try to settle disagreements. Between 1947 and 1959, Presidents Truman and Eisenhower called for strike injunctions seventeen times. Taft-Hartley also prohibited "closed" shops (which forced employers to hire only union members) but permitted "union" shops (in which all employees had to join a union after being hired). Taft-Hartley prohibited secondary boycotts, jurisdictional strikes, and certain "unfair labor practices." The law required union leaders to certify that they were not members of the Communist party or other subversive groups. On the state level, Taft-Hartley encouraged passage of "right-to-work" laws that permitted "open" shops, in which workers did not have to join a union. (For the political context of Taft-Hartley, see chapter 3.)

Organized labor also suffered from its neglect of the unorganized segments of the labor force. During World War II, the NAACP battled with racist unions to win admission for blacks, but often failed to persuade all-white locals to change their policies. Many unions also ignored women workers, who were seen as a threat to male jobs. Instead, rival AFL and CIO unions debated jurisdictional issues and raided each other's membership. And white-collar workers, now a majority of the work force, remained largely non-union. As a result, union membership, which had grown dramatically during the Depression and World War II, increased only slightly from nearly fifteen million in 1945 to eighteen million a decade later, while the proportion of unionized non-agricultural workers declined 14 percent by 1960. Meanwhile, differences between the AFL and CIO had diminished. The AFL accepted the idea of industrial unionism, while the CIO endorsed labor stability. In 1955 the two federations merged into the AFL-CIO and named the AFL's George Meany as president. Yet five years later organized labor accounted for less than one-third of all non-farm workers.

With priorities on industry-wide stability, union leaders often ignored the local problems of rank-and-file workers. "We need the union to insure enforcement of the contract we have signed," acknowledged a business executive, "to settle grievances, to counsel employees in giving a fair day's work..., to help increase productivity." Thus, unauthorized "wildcat" strikes often attacked not only employers, but also an unresponsive labor leadership. Worker participation in union elections declined from 82 percent before World War II to 58 percent in 1958, a trend that continued through the next decades. While critics complained about the labor leaders' "passion for respectability," congressional investigation unearthed widespread corruption in managing union funds. The Landrum-Griffin Act of 1959 required unions to file economic statements with the Department of Labor. By 1960, the militant labor movement of the 1930s had virtually disappeared.

POVERTY AND SOCIAL CLASS

"The saving grace of the American social system," boasted *Life* magazine in 1949, "is...the phenomenon of social 'mobility'—the opportunity to move rapidly upward through the levels of society." In an influential book of 1958, Harvard economist John Kenneth Galbraith described America as "the affluent society," but also warned that private consumption weakened the public sector. Yet even Galbraith minimized the existence of deep poverty. Throughout the prosperous 1950s, unemployment rates remained between 3 and 8 percent, while unemployment insurance reimbursed only 20 percent of lost worker incomes.

Those over sixty-five years of age were among the poorest Americans. A 1960 Senate report found that "at least one-half of the aged—approximately eight million people—cannot afford today decent housing, proper nutrition, adequate medical care, preventive or acute, or necessary recreation." Mandatory retirement programs drove many able-bodied workers into poverty. During the 1950s the number of people entitled to social security benefits increased fivefold to 9.6 million. Yet government assistance provided only a small fraction of their needs. As a result, more than half of the households headed by people over sixty five had incomes below $3,000 a year in 1960.

Nonwhites also suffered disproportionately. As victims of racial as well as economic discrimination, they earned substantially less than whites in all parts of the nation and customarily were barred from better-paying positions. Black women, for example, found themselves mainly confined to unskilled or semi-skilled jobs such as housekeeping, waitressing, and practical nursing. Even when they obtained factory work, black women earned less than white women. The decline of unskilled jobs in urban centers intensified black poverty. Unlike European immigrants of the early twentieth century, black migrants to the cities found the number of blue collar jobs reduced by technological advances, while white collar jobs shifted to the suburbs. In the ten years after 1949 the gap between black and white income increased.

Exhibit 8–5. Distribution of Family Income by Race, 1947–60.

Exhibit 8–6. Unemployment Rates by Race, 1948–1960.

	1948	1951	1954	1957	1960
White	3.5	3.1	5.0	3.8	4.9
Black	5.9	5.3	9.9	7.9	10.2
Total	3.8	3.3	5.5	4.3	5.5

Source: *Historical Statistics of the United States, Colonial Times to 1970* (1975)

On Thanksgiving Day 1960, Edward R. Murrow's TV broadcast, *Harvest of Shame*, stunned the nation by showing the poverty of landless rural workers. In 1959, 1.5 million farmers, five-sixths of them white, had net incomes under $3000. Most lived in the South in dilapidated housing that lacked electricity and plumbing. And migrant farm workers of every nationality had virtually no protection from illegal labor practices that kept them poor and dependent. Minority peoples such as Puerto Ricans, Mexican-Americans, Native Americans, and Asian-Americans earned extremely low incomes in occupations unprotected by minimum wage laws. Eighty percent of New York City's Puerto Rican families earned less than the government's estimated minimum levels for "modest but adequate" living standards. In California the average income of Japanese and Chinese families in 1959 was a lowly $3000 but even that was higher than the income of Spanish-speaking workers. American Indians appeared poorest of all non-whites, living in such squalor that their death rate was three times the national average.

WOMEN AND THE WORK FORCE

Participation in the wartime work force set a precedent for women's postwar employment. Though many women were subsequently replaced by returning veterans, female employment rose sharply in 1947 and returned to World War II levels by 1950. Between 1940 and 1960 the number of female employees doubled, and by 1960, nearly 40 percent of the adult female population was at work. This burgeoning female employment reflected new social patterns. The average age of women employees in 1960 was forty one; and 60 percent of women workers were married. Households in which both husband and wife worked reached the ten-million mark by 1960. These two-income families included a growing number of mothers with young children. Prior to World War II, working wives and mothers usually came from the poorest classes of society. But in the postwar period, an increasing number of middle class women found jobs even when their husbands earned substantial incomes.

Working women emphasized financial necessity as a motive. Widows, unmarried mothers, and women who were divorced, separated, or deserted headed one-twelfth of American households in 1956. Most worked as secretaries, sales help, or in semiskilled trades—occupations that labor unions usually ignored—and earned lower salaries than men for similar work tasks. Female-headed households, then as now, were among the poorest in the nation. Moreover, since real wages remained lower than wartime earnings until 1955, families needed additional incomes to acquire accustomed goods and services. In middle-class households the demand for luxury items or a private home encouraged two-income families. Another inflation of prices at the end of the 1950s again lowered real incomes, providing added impetus for wives to work.

The higher the level of female education, the more likely it was that a woman would enter the labor force. Finding satisfaction in occupational roles rather than in traditional domestic work stimulated a growing awareness of female independence. For the rise of female employment challenged the traditional view that a woman's place was in the home. According to conventional psychological theories, women were naturally passive, unassertive, and therefore ill-equipped to cope with the problems of business. Women who appeared competitive or who ventured into public life were, by definition, unnatural. "I Denied My Sex," a popular magazine story about a woman's career in police work, typified a pulp literature that advocated domesticity. The most popular TV comedy of the 1950s, "I Love Lucy," consistently parodied the housewife's craving for success outside the home. More ominously, even sensitive films like *The Snake Pit* (1949) portrayed rebellion against domesticity as insanity. Middle class magazines like *Good Housekeeping* urged women to accept the satisfaction of raising children while providing moral support for male breadwinners.

FAMILY RELATIONS

TV programs with titles like "The Honeymooners," "Make Room For Daddy," and "Father Knows Best" ostensibly portrayed marital bliss, but the plots usually emphasized intense family conflicts. TV commercials also appealed to an unending battle of the sexes. Troubles at home brought many comfortable middle-class patients into psychiatrists' offices. Indeed, after World War II, the American psychiatric profession shifted its attention from psychotic cases that required institutionalization to cases of neurosis that simply demanded "adjustment" to the strains of modern life. Chemical tranquilizers emerged as standard therapy for frustrated housewives. Psychological depression also provoked more self-destructive behavior, such as alcoholism and shoplifting. Such evidence helps explain why, despite all the propaganda for domesticity, marriage rates steadily declined and divorces increased.

The disintegration of traditional marriages also reflected a conflict between sexual values and sexual behavior. In 1948 Alfred Kinsey of Indiana University published a major research study, *Sexual Behavior in the Human Male*, followed five years later by a similar study of women—both of which became bestsellers. At a time when popular values advocated premarital virginity, the Kinsey report revealed that most of the men and nearly 50 percent of the women interviewed had experienced premarital intercourse. Fully 95% of the study's adult white males had violated at least one law in order to have an orgasm. Half the men and 26 percent of the women interviewed had experienced extramarital sexual relations. Kinsey concluded that two-thirds of the marriages studied had serious sexual tensions and he speculated that sexual incompatibility caused 75 percent of divorces.

The Kinsey report also revealed a surprising amount of homosexual behavior: 37 percent of the men and 13 percent of the women interviewed had at least one post-adolescent homosexual experience. Such figures reflected the growth of homosexual communities in most major cities after World War II. Yet the proliferation of gay lifestyles did not produce greater tolerance for homosexuals. Police raids and blackmail plagued the gay population, and the federal government equated homosexual inclinations with security risks in the Cold War. Thousands of homosexuals lost government jobs during the 1940s and '50s. To protect their communities, homosexuals formed groups, such as the Mattachine Society (1951) and the Daughters of Bilitis (1955). Yet the fear of exposure prevented an effective defense of homosexual rights.

Conservatives blamed working mothers and the collapse of traditional morality for a new national malaise—juvenile delinquency. Newspapers luridly described teenage sex crimes, sex clubs, prostitution, and rape. President Truman joined a chorus of politicians who urged working mothers to end the crime wave by returning to the home. Sociologists, however, argued that poverty caused juvenile crime and advocated slum clearance and social welfare programs as solutions. And Dr. Kinsey said that teenage sexuality appeared normal and healthy and called for greater tolerance from parents and law enforcement authorities.

Kinsey's advice reinforced the message adults received from the most popular pediatrician of the postwar era, Dr. Benjamin Spock, whose book, *Baby and Child Care*, published in 1946, sold over twenty-two million copies. "Trust yourself," Spock told anxious parents. "Don't be overawed by what the experts say. Don't be afraid to trust your common sense." Where earlier government child-rearing pamphlets had recommended strict regimens, Spock called for flexibility. His respect for children led critics to denounce his "permissiveness." Yet Spock advocated firm parental control based on a spirit of love and understanding.

YOUTH CULTURE

"What are you rebelling against?" a teenage waitress asks a motorcycle tough in the Hollywood movie, *The Wild One* (1954). Marlon Brando replies: "What do ya got?" Such movies, including *Rebel Without a Cause* (1955), portrayed dissatisfied youth rejecting the materialistic values of parents. Since adults made the films, however, they also expressed a lack of confidence in their ability to understand and guide the young. "No longer is it thought to be the child's job to understand the adult world as the adult sees it," complained David Reisman in his classic study, *The Lonely Crowd* (1950).

Searching for peer approval and a sense of belonging, many adolescents turned to clubs, cliques, and gangs that experimented with cigarettes, alcohol, and sex. But the prime form of social rebellion among postwar youth came with the discovery of rock and roll music, a derivative of black rhythm and blues introduced to wider audiences by Cleveland disc jockey Allan Freed. Records by 1950s black performers such as Chuck Berry and Little Richard often contained themes which rejected traditional adult authority and assumed knowledge of sexual matters. By 1956 Elvis Presley, a side-burned, white southerner out of the country "rockabilly" tradition, began to achieve cult status by blatantly mixing

Elvis Presley dazzles a crowd of teenagers in Long Beach, California, in 1956. Flaunting sexuality and defiance of adult attitudes, Presley built an enormous following among the nation's youth which dubbed him the "King" of rock 'n roll.

pelvic thrusts with knowing grins and raunchy blues shouts. The introduction of a new dance, "The Twist," popularized by Chubby Checker in 1959, turned suggestive body expression into a national fad and hinted at the social integration of blacks and whites in postwar society.

Clergy and moral authorities professed shock at the frankness of rock and roll and its roots in the working-class cultures of blacks and southerners. In Boston, police banned a live show staged by Freed, claiming that the loud and heavy beat excited teenagers to violence and delinquency. Yet for all its symbolic rebellion, rock and roll served more as a collective ritual for adolescents experiencing the traumas of puberty. Moreover, even "delinquents" in black leather jackets and motorcycle boots emulated the adult world by participating in consumer culture. And when *Blackboard Jungle* (1955) became the first film to use rock and roll in its soundtrack, Hollywood began to tailor its products to the burgeoning youth market. Other youth-oriented commodities included clothing and shoes, jewelry, cosmetics, and even automobiles.

Youth culture reflected the tendency of postwar Americans to seek group identification. Sociologist Riesman referred to an "other-directed" people. "I would like to be able to fly if everybody else did," *The Lonely Crowd* quoted a twelve-year old girl, "but it would be kind of conspicuous." The poet Sylvia Plath put it more succinctly, describing herself suffocating inside a "bell jar" of conformity. "Gary Gray realized he had forgotten how to say I,'" reported *Look* magazine in an uncomfortable comparison of American conformity to communist collectivism. In *The Fountainhead*, a 1949 film based on an earlier work by conservative Ayn Rand, an individualist architect righteously rejected corporate compromise as inimical to personal vision. Despite these critiques, however, a bland concern for conformity and "getting along" dominated college campuses, where a "silent generation" expressed a preference for courses in business administration and education. In such an atmosphere, salaried positions with large corporations became the prime goal of most students.

EDUCATION IN CRISIS

The passivity of campus life mirrored the intellectual consensus that pervaded the social sciences. Sociologist William Whyte observed in 1956 that most social scientists held a "bias against conflict." Such terms as "disharmony, disequilibrium, maladjustment, disorganization," he remarked, were considered "bad things." In sociology and political science, academic scholars stressed the "pluralism" of American society, a belief that a diversity of interest groups competed on an equal basis and adjusted their differences through reason and compromise. Liberal theory held that democracy was unworkable if people maintained loyalties to social class, ethnic groups, or particular ideologies. Indeed, sociologist Daniel Bell declared that ideology was "dead" in America. Historians Louis Hartz, Richard Hofstadter, and Daniel Boorstin, moreover, described the national past in terms of a homogenized culture which succeeded because it avoided major social conflicts. Their well-heralded studies portrayed racism, for example, as an historical aberration peculiar to the ante-bellum South. These interpretations led to the proliferation of American Studies programs that stressed the uniqueness of American culture.

"The best thing about contemporary education," wrote psychologist Paul Woodring in 1952, "is that a great many classroom teachers ignore the gobbledygook and pedagoguese and go right ahead and do a sensible job of teaching." A distorted version of John Dewey's "progressive education," which rejected rote learning and stressed the life experiences of students, dominated public education. Vocational training, social guidance, and "hygiene" formed basic elements of the secondary curriculum. Such subjects emphasized the importance of social adjustment.

The Soviet "Sputnik" launch of 1957 abruptly challenged the pedagogical status quo. Shocked by this Cold War "defeat," educational reformers scurried to improve academic standards. Congress quickly passed the National Defense Education Act of 1958, the first major federal aid to education, to encourage the study of science, mathematics, and foreign lanquages. This government support, which later included such subjects vital to the "national defense" as American history, financed the vast expansion of higher education in the next decade.

Traditional faith in American public education contrasted with a social system that excluded minority students from equal educational opportunities. Under the doctrine of separate but equal, seventeen states required segregated public schools in 1951. Southern states typically spent twice as much to educate white children as black, and whites were four times as likely as blacks to finish high school. Such statistics belied the fiction of separate but equal.

Civil rights groups, led by NAACP lawyer Thurgood Marshall, initiated a series of legal suits to end academic discrimination. Benefiting by postwar criticism of racism, Marshall won legal victories against segregated law schools and graduate schools by arguing that the alternative black institutions were unequal in quality to white schools. Marshall then decided to attack public school segregation by denying the concept of separate but equal. Using psychological evidence demonstrating that "prejudice and segregation have definitely detrimental effects on the personality development of the Negro child," Marshall persuaded the Supreme Court to reconsider the *Plessy* doctrine. In a historic ruling, *Brown v. Board of Education of Topeka*, delivered May 17, 1954, the Supreme Court acknowledged that to segregate children "because of their race generates a feeling of inferiority . . . that may affect their hearts and minds in a way unlikely ever to be undone." In public education, the Court concluded, "'separate, but equal' has no place. Separate educational facilities are inherently unequal."

The *Brown* decision, written by Eisenhower's first appointee to the Supreme Court, Chief Justice Earl Warren, heralded a new era in race relations. Most liberals, including the NAACP attorneys, thought that institutional segregation caused racial prejudice and believed therefore that the new legal principle would establish a society based on racial equality. Other segregated places, such as restaurants, movie theaters, toilets, and transportation, seemed likely to change. To mollify racial conservatives, however, the Supreme Court issued a second decision in 1955, ordering compliance with the *Brown* ruling not immediately, but "with all deliberate speed."

Segregationists remained unappeased. "You are not required to obey any court which passes out such a ruling." advised Mississippi Senator James Eastland. "In fact, you are obligated to defy it." Some opposed any alteration of traditional race relations; others resented the expansion of federal power over states' rights. Southerners launched a program of "massive resistance" to public school integration. Inspired by White Citizens' Councils, some districts simply closed all public schools rather than integrate. Mobs attacked black schoolchildren and resorted to violence to block integration. Such spectacles forced Eisenhower, who personally opposed the *Brown* decision, to send paratroopers to Little Rock, Arkansas, in 1957 to protect nine black students at Central High School. Even with such dramatic efforts, public school integration proceeded very slowly. In 1960 less than 1 percent of black children attended integrated schools in southern states. In the North the Supreme Court decision did not affect a pattern of de facto segregation.

Sports, Entertainment, and Sexuality

Opposition to integration reflected not only racist doctrine, but also an abiding fear of physical contact between the races. In the sports arena, however, black athletes began to challenge such prejudices. Joe Louis, black heavyweight box-

EARL WARREN
1891–1974

Of his eight years in the White House, President Eisenhower later said, the nomination of Earl Warren as Chief Justice of the Supreme Court in 1953 was "the biggest damfool decision I ever made." For the Republican White House, Warren produced a number of constitutional surprises. But in making the choice, Eisenhower had fulfilled a political debt. As the three-term governor of California, Warren represented the liberal wing of the Republican party. He had run for vice president (with Thomas Dewey) in 1948 and remained an important "dark horse" candidate four years later.

Warren's political background had offered few clues to his subsequent career. As a California district attorney and state attorney general, he earned a reputation as a tough law enforcement officer. During World War II he advocated the confinement of all Japanese-Americans, regardless of their political beliefs. His position reflected an undisguised racism that viewed "Orientals" as essentially unassimilable. Elected governor in 1942, Warren supported liberal legislation in such areas as health insurance and prison reform.

Warren's appointment to the Supreme Court, however, led to dramatic reversals of legal precedent. In his first major decision, *Brown v. Board of Education* (1954), the Chief Justice dismantled the doctrine of separate but equal and paved the way for fundamental changes in race relations. Eight years later he carried the principle of democracy further by mandating the reapportionment of all legislative districts according to the principle of one-person, one vote in *Baker v. Carr*. As in the *Brown* ruling, the decision attacked traditional political structures—in this case, state legislatures—that had enabled entrenched elites to ignore numerical majorities of the population.

Warren also emerged as a strong defender of individual civil liberties. In the *Yates* decision (1957), he concurred in reversing the conviction of leading Communists by differentiating between the theory of subversion and its actual practice. This position led to the eventual overthrow of certain loyalty oaths and state laws against Communists. Under the principle of due process of law, he defended the rights of criminals to legal counsel (*Escobedo*, 1964), and fair treatment by police (*Miranda*, 1966). The Warren-led Court tightened the interpretation of obscenity to protect the rights of free speech and the press from censorship. In 1962 the Court supported a rigid separation of church and state in denying prayers and Bible reading in public schools. Such opinions earned Warren the hatred of right-wing groups such as the John Birch Society, which called for his impeachment.

Despite the unpopularity of some of his rulings, Warren was widely respected for personal integrity. President Lyndon Johnson therefore named the Chief Justice to head a commission to investigate the assassination of President John Kennedy. Viewing his task as one of evaluating the evidence rather than gathering it, Warren did not pursue a vigorous investigation. Yet his personal reputation helped persuade political leaders to accept the commission's controversial report in 1964.

The decisions of the Warren Court contributed to the liberal climate of the 1960s, and Warren's retirement in 1969 heralded the end of a liberal era of an "activist" judiciary. In the 1970s the Court would modify its rulings about pornography, criminal rights, and capital punishment. But *Brown* and *Baker v. Carr* had forever changed the constitutional landscape of American politics. ∎

ing champion, struck a blow against white supremacy in 1938 by defeating the German champion, Max Schmeling, symbol of the master race. But in some southern states it remained illegal for white boxers to meet blacks in the ring. Blacks could play football on northern college campuses but were left behind when their teams competed with southern schools. Blacks also were excluded from playing basketball on Big Ten teams. "This is an indoor sport," John Gunther explained, "and taboos are strong...against any contact between half-clad, perspiring bodies, even on the floor of a gym." Jackie Robinson, the first black to play major league baseball, joined the Brooklyn Dodgers in 1947, but even then agreed not to argue with umpires or express aggression toward whites. By 1960, however, professional baseball, basketball, and football had become racially integrated industries, though nonstarring players were usually white.

The acceptance of black athletes coincided with the emergence of mass spectator sports. Rising personal consumption brought larger expenditures for recreation, which jumped from $11.3 billion in 1950 to $18.3 billion in 1959 to $21.6 billion in 1962. In 1958, major league baseball expanded to the West Coast cities of San Francisco and Los Angeles, contributing to the creation of a national sports audience while destroying minor league teams. TV broadcast contracts became increasingly important as a source of sports revenue, and these monies depended on viewer ratings. Black athletes helped increase the size of this spectator base.

Television represented the major innovation in mass entertainment. In 1947 there were ten TV broadcasting stations. TV sets numbered about twenty thousand and manufacturers were producing some seven thousand sets each year. Sales suddenly skyrocketed the next year. By 1957 Americans owned forty million TV sets and could select programs from as many as seven broadcasting channels at a time. Although a new industry, television was controlled by the same corporations that dominated radio. Advertising, rather than the content of programming, determined the broadcast schedule. In 1951 the first coaxial cable linked East Coast and West Coast, enabling all Americans to see the same thing at the same time. That year TV advertising sales surpassed those of radio for the first time. Seeking a common denominator to boost network ratings, TV turned to variety programs, situation comedies, quiz shows, and sports.

Television quickly eclipsed the other popular media—radio, newspapers, magazines, and motion pictures. During the immediate postwar years, Hollywood had examined such controversial subjects as racism (*Home of the Brave*, 1948); anti-Semitism (*Crossfire*, 1947; *Gentleman's Agreement*, 1947); and mental illness (*The Snake Pit*, 1949). But the investigation of Hollywood for Communist subversion in 1947 sent a chill through the industry that discouraged social criticism. Hollywood also suffered from declining attendance. By 1953 ticket sales were a scant half of their 1946 record highs. The postwar baby boom, which tended to keep young adults at home, caused some of the drop in movie popularity. Also influential were rising ticket prices, the closing of neighborhood theaters, and the court-ordered break-up of Hollywood's monopolistic distribution system after 1949. The crowning blow, however, was the fact that by 1953 over 43 percent of American families owned TV sets. As television drained box office attendance, Hollywood introduced production innovations—3-D, wide screens, and more color—that were unavailable on TV. But as movie mogul Sam

Goldwyn predicted in 1949, people were "unwilling to pay to see poor pictures when they can stay at home and see something which is, at least, no worse."

Hollywood's recourse was to concentrate on daring sex. TV's family audiences limited sexual content to vague double-meanings or slapstick transvestite comedy. Milton Berle and Lucille Ball, the two top TV performers, repeatedly dressed in the clothing of the opposite sex. But although the movie industry still adhered to a self-censoring code that prohibited nudity or explicit sexuality, movies exploited the pseudosexuality of symbols like Marilyn Monroe. Women in 1950s films often displayed big bosoms and deep cleavages, licked their lips, and paraded in slips and negligees, but remained remarkably sexless. Movies of the period tended to portray sexual pleasure as a reward of affluence. Actresses like Monroe, Jayne Mansfield, and Anita Eckberg acted as foils for the relaxation of sexual standards among wealthy men. Indeed, the Kinsey Report concluded that erotic images and nudity appealed more to better educated men than the less schooled. The rise of a white-collar managerial class in the 1950s, then, may explain the sexual revolution that began in that decade. With larger discretionary incomes and a rising divorce rate, middle-class men could indulge hedonistic fantasies without being tied to family responsibilities.

These values began to surface in magazines such as *Playboy*, which claimed half a million readers by 1956. *Playboy* combined sexually provocative photographs of young women with advertisements and stories that ridiculed domesticity and idealized the lifestyle of the single male consumer. Meanwhile, Grace Metallious's best-selling novel of 1957, *Peyton Place*, emphasized sexual themes while exposing the hypocrisy of small-town life. The following year Vladimir Nabokov's novel, *Lolita*, aroused further controversy with its artful account of the seduction of a pre-adolescent girl. But public tastes had changed. Ten years earlier, Normal Mailer had to invent the nonword "fug" to get *The Naked and the Dead* past the censors. In 1959 the Supreme Court denied censorship of D.H. Lawrence's *Lady Chatterly's Lover* on grounds of free speech. The decision, though ambiguously enforced, opened the door to other nonconventional sexual literature.

ALTERNATIVE VOICES

Relaxation of urban middle-class sexual standards contrasted with the moral conservatism of most Americans. The postwar era witnessed a resurgence of church membership in all denominations. This interest in spiritual security partly reflected the underlying anxieties of a rootless society and the search for identity in the anonymous suburbs. Appropriately, Congress added the words "under God" to the Pledge of Allegiance in 1954. Yet religious leaders of the 1950s offered less a promise of salvation than a sense of secular reassurance and solace. "Believe in yourself!" the Reverend Norman Vincent Peale proclaimed in the popular tract, *The Power of Positive Thinking* (1952). "Have faith in your abilities! Without a humble but reasonable confidence in your own powers you cannot succeed." Evangelicals like the Baptist Billy Graham also flourished in this religious renaissance, particularly in the urban South and boom towns of the Southwest.

BILLY GRAHAM
1918–

The most famous religious figures of the 1950s were two southerners in the Baptist tradition, Billy Graham and Martin Luther King, Jr. But while King challenged American society with a stinging moral critique in behalf of the dispossessed, Graham won access to the rich and powerful with a message palatable to political and economic elites. Handsome, charismatic, and committed, Graham threw himself into evangelism early in life, honing his skills while traveling the country after World War II for a fledgling fundamentalist group, Youth for Christ. His big break came during the fourth week of a 1949 Los Angeles revival when the powerful newspaper publisher William Randolph Hearst sent a blunt telegram to the editors of his newspapers: "Puff Graham." Attracted to the anti-communist themes of Graham's sermons, Hearst was the first of many powerful figures eager to use the preacher's sincerity and popularity to advance their own agendas. Within a year, Graham had been the subject of major articles in *Time*, *Life* and *Newsweek*, and within a decade, he was the most popular religious figure in America.

Like evangelists before him, Graham blended familiar hymns and an altar call with a dynamic and polished pulpit style. Cutting through the apparent complexities of the "age of anxiety," he called on his listeners to heal their lives through a personal commitment to Jesus. To a nation which had survived depression and war only to find itself in the midst of the Nuclear Age, the simplicity and directness of Graham's message had enormous appeal. While Graham traveled constantly, conducting six major crusades a year, he and his associates soon realized that print, films, radio, and especially television offered enormous opportunities to broaden their ministry even further. His direct mail techniques were so sophisticated that representatives of both political parties visited his headquarters to study them. This pioneering work in marketing and media techniques helped prepare the way for the televangelists of the 1980s.

While Graham has declared himself to be "completely neutral in politics," his fundamentalist, eschatological theology has long made him a particular favorite of conservative Republicans. Called by some a "Gabriel in Gabardine," Graham spent much of his career preaching a gospel which upheld traditional values and confirmed the validity of existing elites while calling for domestic consensus in the face of communist expansion. Although he insisted that his crusade audiences be integrated even before the Supreme Court's Brown decision, Graham typically emphasized other-worldly solutions for both personal and social problems. "My message is so intensely personal," he explained, "that people miss the overwhelming social content." However, as a long-time friend of Richard Nixon, Graham clearly supported Nixon's political career despite the advice of some that he should avoid politics. (His wife once kicked him under the table when he started to give political advice during a White House dinner.) Deeply shocked by the Watergate scandal with its attendant revelations of Nixon's coarse personal manner, Graham subsequently isolated himself more carefully from politics, doing so, ironically, at a time the religious right was just beginning to become major force under the leadership of other religious broadcasters. ■

LENNY BRUCE
1926–1966

A stand-up nightclub performer, Lenny Bruce emerged as the most controversial comedian of the postwar era. Using a jazz soloist's style, Bruce blended plain street talk with Yiddish and black idiom to satirize and demystify social conventions. His most scathing routines focused on religious hypocrisy, the artificiality of traditional sexual relationships,

and racial prejudice. Because of his brutal honesty, the established media labeled Bruce and his ilk "sick" comedians. "I'm not a comedian," Bruce retorted. "And I'm not sick. The world is sick and I'm the doctor. I'm a surgeon with a scalpel for false values. I don't have an act. I just talk." Even the title of his autobiography—*How To Talk Dirty and Influence People*—made fun of the popular homilies for success.

Born Leonard Schneider in New York, he joined the Navy at the age of sixteen and saw active service in the Mediterranean. After the war Bruce hustled as a con-artist for phony charities before drifting into comedy work in sleazy nightclubs and dance halls. By the mid–1950s Bruce's brand of comedy captured national attention. He appeared on network television, made popular records, and captivated audiences at top nightclubs across the country.

Bruce's comic routines illuminated the anxieties and unspoken assumptions of postwar society. While middle-class ethnic groups embraced homogenized suburban values (including, as in Bruce's case, the changing of ethnic names), the comedian's sketches reaffirmed the vitality of ethnic, religious, and racial identity. As middle-class Americans celebrated traditional monogamous marriages, despite a soaring divorce rate, Bruce spoke about alternative premarital, extramarital, and homosexual relationships. He attacked middle-class consumption patterns, raged against bureaucracy and organized religion, and pointed to the absurdity of Christian country waging endless war. "All my humor is based on destruction and despair," he admitted. "If the whole world were tranquil, without disease and violence, I'd be standing on the breadline right in back of J. Edgar Hoover and...Dr. Jonas Salk."

Bruce's insistence on creative freedom led him to attack legal censorship of free speech. "What's wrong with appealing to the prurient interest?" he wanted to know. "We appeal to the *killing* interest." His use of explicit language brought police reprisals, and he faced a series of arrests and court trials in several cities on charges of obscenity. He was also accused of using illegal drugs. The endless litigation drained his energy, and the subject of legal harassment came to dominate his nightclub act. "The halls of justice," quipped Bruce. "That's the only place you see the justice,...in the halls."

As police departments worked with municipal courts to silence the irreverent comedian, Bruce died of an overdose of heroin. His obscenity conviction, however, was overturned posthumously. Bruce's quarrel with the censorship of language provided an important basis for the free speech movements that spread around many college campuses. In merging humor about sex, race, and politics, moreover, Bruce's comedy foreshadowed the radical synthesis of the New Left and the counterculture of the 1960s.

Jack Kerouac (1922-1969), author of a spate of novels, including the classic, On The Road (1957), personified the frenetic energy of young intellectuals searching for spiritual meaning in a society of extravagent materialism.

These conservative tendencies troubled social critics who warned about the stultifying effects of conformity. "The religion that actually prevails among Americans today has lost much of its authentic...content," observed Will Herberg, author of the popular *Protestant Catholic Jew* (1956). The blandness of spirituality reflected a larger problem of alienation. "When white-collar people get jobs," cautioned sociologist C. Wright Mills in *White Collar* (1951), "they sell not only their time and energy but their personalities as well." Similar warnings came from such works as David Riesman's *The Lonely Crowd* (1950), Herbert Marcuse's *Eros and Civilization* (1955), and William H. Whyte's *The Organization Man* (1957). These books attacked the prevalence of social conformity, the decline of individual initiative, and the obsession with security in business and private life. And in a brilliant, prophetic essay, "The White Negro," novelist Norman Mailer predicted an explosion of violent rebellion led by hipster-outlaws against a repressive society.

Alternative voices also emerged in art, music, and comedy. Though most American preferred the representational painting of Thomas Hart Benton, Grant Wood, and Grandma Moses, a new group of "abstract expressionists" turned

New York into an international center of non-representational Action Painting. Jackson Pollock, Willem de Kooning, and Mark Rothko painted with vigororous line and color that compelled viewers to seek their own meaning in the work. Abstract painters also celebrated traditional American subjects: Larry Rivers's tongue-in-cheek version of *Washington Crossing the Delaware* (1953), for example, or Jasper Johns's numerous depictions of the American flag. In music, teenagers danced to rock and roll while their parents worked and shopped to the tune of Muzak. But the "bebop" sound of Charlie Parker and Dizzy Gillespie brought new vitality to jazz, offering hard-driving rhythms and complex harmonies that defied imitation by whites. Nightclubs also featured a new breed of "sick" comedians—Mort Sahl, Lenny Bruce, Dick Gregory—who savagely derided social convention. And college students made the irreverent *Mad* magazine the most popular reading on American campuses.

The strongest voices of protest came from a group of "Beat" poets and writers who congregated in San Francisco. Jack Kerouac, William Burroughs, and Gary Snyder decried the alienating effects of bureaucratic culture and called for a new spiritualism that merged the body and the spirit. Most eloquent was the poet Allen Ginsberg. In *Howl*, published in 1956, he indicted a sterile society that watched "the best minds of my generation destroyed by madness." Strong, rolling cadences condemned "the scholars of war" with their "demonic industries" and "monstrous bombs." Ginsberg pleaded with America to "end the human war." Here in the cultural underground lay the roots of protest and transcendence that would puncture middle-class illusions of stability and security in the 1960s.

Suggested Readings

A detailed social history of the postwar period is Geoffrey Perrett, *A Dream of Greatness: The American People, 1945–1963* (1979), which can be supplemented by Marty Jezer, *The Dark Ages: Life in the United States, 1945–1960* (1982). Also useful are Joseph C. Goulden, *The Best Years: 1945–1950* (1976); Douglas T. Miller and Marion Nowak, *The Fifties: The Way We Really Were* (1977); and Paul A. Carter, *Another Part of the Fifties* (1983). The intellectual context emerges in Richard H. Pells, *The Liberal Mind in a Conservative Age: American Intellectuals in the 1940s and 1950s* (1985).

The relationship between government and the economy is illuminated in the relevant chapters of Gabriel Kolko's *Main Currents in Modern American History* (1976). Government support of science and technology is the major theme of Walter A. McDougall, *The Heavens and the Earth: A Political History of the Space Age* (1985). For the impact of the atom bomb on American society, see Paul Boyer, *By the Bomb's Early Light: American Thought and Culture at the Dawn of the Atomic Age* (1985) and Spencer R. Weart, *Nuclear Fear: A History of Images* (1988). The ordeal of one physicist is described in Peter J. Goodchild, *J. Robert Oppenheimer: Shatterer of Worlds* (1981).

The consequences of the high postwar birthrate are described in Landon Y. Jones, *America and the Baby Boom Generation* (1980). For a good overview of social and economic trends, see William Issel, *Social Change in the United States,*

1945–1983 (1985). More detailed economic analysis appears in Harold G. Vatter, *The U.S. Economy in the 1950's* (1963). For the broader problems of economic class and wealth, see George Lipsitz, *Class and Culture in Cold War America* (1981) and Herman P. Miller, *Rich Man, Poor Man* (1964). Michael Harrington's *The Other America* (1962) remains a valuable study of poverty. For the housing problem in the postwar years, see Richard O. Davies, *Housing Reform During the Truman Administration* (1966). A vast literature examines suburbia in the 1950s. A good starting point is Kenneth T. Jackson, *The Crabgrass Frontier: The Suburbanization of the United States* (1985). Still useful is Robert C. Wood, *Suburbia: Its People and Their Politics* (1959), but it should be supplemented with Scott Donaldson, *The Suburban Myth* (1969).

The best survey of women's history since World War II is Rochelle Gatlin, *American Women Since 1945* (1987). For the status and problems of women in postwar society, see Barbara Ehrenreich, *Hearts of Men: The Flight From Commitment* (1984) and Eugenia Kaledin, et. al., *Mothers and More: American Women in the 1950s* (1984). Women's political activity in the 1950s is described in Leila J. Rupp and Verta Taylor, *Survival in the Doldrums* (1987). For popular images of women in film, see Molly Haskell, *From Reverence to Rape* (1974); Brandon French, *On the Verge of Revolt* (1978); and Michael Wilson, ed., *Salt of the Earth* (1978). The origins of the sexual revolution are treated in the relevant chapters of John D'Emilio and Estelle B. Freedman, *Intimate Matters: A History of Sexuality in America* (1988).

For surveys of the postwar civil rights movement, see Harvard Sitkoff, *The Struggle for Black Equality: 1954-1980* (1981) and Manning Marable, *Race, Reform, and Rebellion: The Second Reconstruction in Black America, 1945–1982* (1984). The legal struggle to end racial discrimination is brilliantly described in Richard Kluger, *Simple Justice: The History of Brown v. Board of Education and Black America's Struggle for Equality* (1976). The legacy of the Brown decision is treated in J. Harrie Wilkinson, III, *From Brown to Bakke* (1979). These titles should be supplemented by Donald R. McCoy and Richard T. Ruetten, *Quest and Response: Minority Rights and the Truman Adminstration* (1973), and Anthony Lewis and the *New York Times's Portrait of a Decade: The Second American Revolution* (1964). An excellent study of the relationship between sports and race is Jules Tygiel, *Baseball's Great Experiment: Jackie Robinson and His Legacy* (1983). See also the relevant titles listed after chapter 4.

Government policy toward American Indians is described in Vine Deloria, Jr., *Custer Died for Your Sins: An Indian Manifesto* (1969) and in the relevant chapters of Richard Drinnon, *Keeper of Concentration Camps: Dillon S. Myer and American Racism* (1987). The emergence of homosexual communities is well-treated in John D'Emilio, *Sexual Politics, Sexual Communities: The Making of a Homosexual Minority in the United States, 1940–1970* (1983).

The problems of youth are described in James Gilbert, *A Cycle of Outrage: America's Reaction to the Juvenile Delinquent in the 1950s* (1986). An imaginative treatment of rock and roll is Greil Marcus, *Mystery Train: Images of America in Rock 'n' Roll* (1975).

Popular culture may be explored through Erik Barnouw, *The Image Empire* (1970), which examines television; Peter Biskind, *Seeing is Believing: How Hollywood Taught Us to Stop Worrying and Love the Fifties* (1983); and James Gunn, *Al-*

ternative Worlds: The Illustrated History of Science Fiction (1975). For the bebop revolt and social attitudes of black musicians, see the relevant chapters of Ben Sidran, *Black Talk* (1981). The fine arts are the subject of two excellent books, Serge Guilbaut, *How New York Stole the Idea of Modern Art: Abstract Expressionism, Freedom, and the Cold War* (1983) and Sidra Stich, *Made in USA: An Americanization in Modern Art, the '50s and '60s* (1987). Postwar novels and novelists are discussed in Josephine Hendin, *Vulnerable People: A View of American Fiction since 1945* (1978). For the Beat writers, see Lawrence Lipton, *The Holy Barbarians* (1959); John Tytell, *Naked Angels* (1976); Dennis McNally, *Desolate Angels* (1979); and Gerald Nicosia, *Memory Babe: A Critical Biography of Jack Kerouac* (1983).

Opposite Page:
President Harry Truman gloats at an erroneous headline on the morning after his upset victory in 1948. Convinced that Truman would lose, pollsters had halted their public opinion surveys prematurely!

9

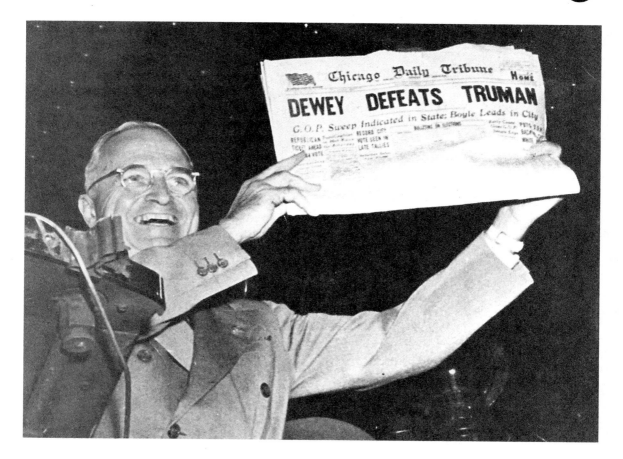

TRUMAN,
THE COLD WAR, AND THE
ANTI-COMMUNIST CRUSADE

Six days after the atomic bombing of Hiroshima, radio commentator Edward R. Murrow observed, "Seldom, if ever, has a war ended leaving the victors with such a sense of uncertainty and fear, with such a realization that the future is obscure and that survival is not assured." For although the United States emerged from World War II virtually undamaged and prepared to assume leadership in world affairs, divisions within the Grand Alliance left numerous unsolved problems to threaten the peace. Within two years of V-J Day, President Harry S. Truman brought the nation into another global war—the "Cold War"—which altered the scope of government activity and inevitably affected political life on the home front.

Problems of Reconversion

"The ultimate duty of government," declared Truman in September 1945, was "to prevent prolonged unemployment." Identifying with Roosevelt's New Deal, the president promptly asked Congress for full-employment legislation as well as a variety of liberal measures, such as a permanent Fair Employment Practices Commission (FEPC), public housing, higher minimum wages, and urban redevelopment. This ambitious program soon collided with a conservative Congress, consisting of southern Democrats and northern Republicans, opposed to government intervention in the economy. "It is just a case of out-New Dealing the New Deal," complained House Republican Leader Joseph Martin. Fearing "creeping socialism," Congress opted for the principle of "maximum" rather than "full" employment and passed the Employment Act of 1946. (See above, Chapter 8.)

Wartime savings buffered the temporary dislocations caused by the shift to a civilian economy. But cuts in overtime work produced a real loss of wages. And consumer demands, which had been thwarted by wartime shortages and rationing, now stimulated a runaway inflation. (For the economic context, see Chapter 8). Soaring prices—and the administration's waffling policies on controls—antagonized consumers. But when Truman requested an extension of wartime controls in 1946, the conservative Congress resisted granting the president additional economic powers. Meanwhile, rising prices impelled workers to seek higher wages. When management balked, a wave of strikes followed in such industries as automobiles, steel, meatpacking, coal, and transportation. Nearly five million strikers participated in over 4500 work stoppages that resulted in the loss of nearly 120 million worker days of labor. Yet economically-motivated unions avoided the violent confrontations of the 1930s. As journalist John Gunther observed about the United Auto Workers strike at General Motors, "There was not one bloody nose." Truman urged business leaders to grant wage increases while maintaining prices. But in the face of their opposition, he could only accept continued inflation.

The president believed, however, that the epidemic of strikes threatened the entire economic structure. When railroad workers walked out in May 1946, Truman assumed unusual executive authority and seized the railroads. He then asked Congress to allow the army to operate the trains, to authorize court injunctions to keep workers on the job, and to permit the drafting of strikers into the military to force them to work. Although the walkout ended before Congress could act, the White House proposal brought wide criticism. "In his angry determination to get the trains running on time again," observed Helen Fuller in *The Nation*. "Truman [took]...a leaf from the book of another man who made railroad history, Benito Mussolini." Congress nonetheless approved the use of court injunctions to stop certain strikes. Truman soon used these powers to end a coal strike by John L. Lewis's United Mine Workers. The union had broken labor's "no strike" pledge during the war. When Lewis called a strike in 1946, Truman seized the mines and ended the walkout by accepting an inflationary settlement. Six months later, in defiance of the government, the UMW again went on strike. Unlike Roosevelt, who in wartime had met Lewis's demands, Truman obtained an injunction and a $3.5 million fine against the union (and another $10,000 against Lewis personally), which forced the UMW to surrender. According to a Gallup poll, the president's stand increased his popularity.

While liberals scorned Truman's failure to maintain price controls and his hostility to unions, Republicans criticized big government, administrative ineptness, and presidential laxity in protecting federal agencies from Communist influence. "The choice which confronts Americans this year," advised the Republican national chairman. "is between Communism and Republicanism." New Republican candidates, such as Joseph R. McCarthy of Wisconsin and Richard M. Nixon of California, openly appealed to a popular fear of communist subversion of "internal security." Their allegations gained credibility by two highly publicized scandals: the discovery of stolen secret documents in the offices of *Amerasia*, a left-wing diplomatic journal, in 1945 and the capture of Soviet spies in Canada the following year. Truman might have defused the issue by admitting that there were no atomic "secrets" to be stolen, but he, too, preferred to believe in the possibility of an American atomic monopoly. Red-baiting, together with resentment of strikes, inflation, and government bureaucracy, gave Republicans ample targets to criticize the administration. With the simple campaign slogan, "Had Enough?" Republicans won a landslide in 1946, obtaining a congressional majority in both houses for the first time since 1928. McCarthy and Nixon stood among the victors.

Once in control of the 80th Congress, Republicans reestablished a working alliance with southern Democrats to thwart civil rights legislation and block other liberal measures, such as public housing, federal aid to education, higher Social Security payments, and certain farm benefits. The conservatives also joined to pass the Taft-Hartley Act of 1947, which limited labor union activities. (For more information on Taft-Hartley, see chapter 8.) Criticizing such "vindictive" legislation, Truman vetoed the bill, but in a show of conservative muscle Congress easily overrode the veto. The president's defense of unions, however, helped return organized labor to the Democratic camp.

POSTWAR FOREIGN POLICY

Although most Americans rejected prewar noninterventionism and accepted United States participation in the United Nations, public demands for rapid demobilization and military budget cuts in 1946 indicated a limited commitment to global involvement. Truman's failure to reach postwar agreements with the Soviet Union contributed to his loss of popularity. But at the same time public suspicion of revolutionary communism enabled the president to develop an increasingly militant and internationalist position.

As the president responded to specific world events, his foreign policy gradually developed. But administration approaches to "national security" revealed a continuation of historic traditions. "Our foreign relations inevitably affect employment in the United States," explained Secretary of State James F. Byrnes in August 1945. "Prosperity and depression in the United States just as inevitably affect our relations with other nations of the world." Such assumptions echoed the concept of the Open Door, first formalized in 1900, which viewed free foreign trade as an alternative to economic stagnation at home. The immense expenditure of natural resources during the war showed the importance of obtaining raw materials. To assure access to markets and resources, postwar leaders advocated a world system of free trade. "Peace, freedom and world trade are indivisible," Truman later remarked. "We must not go through the thirties again."

This economic interpretation of international relations partially reflected the social background of many of the nation's policy makers in the postwar period. Leading State Department officials like Dean Acheson and John Foster Dulles often had personal ties to the nation's largest corporations and held powerful positions as corporate lawyers, financiers, or big-business executives. For example, the names of five of the six secretaries of state between 1945 and 1960, and five of the six secretaries of defense between 1947 and 1960 appeared in the *Social Register*. Such men, appointed by both Democratic and Republican presidents, formulated a foreign policy which expressed and protected the values of the corporate elite. "I am an advocate of business," conceded Secretary of Defense James Forrestal in 1947. "Calvin Coolidge was ridiculed for saying...'The chief business of the United States is business,' but that is a fact."

During World War II American diplomacy had attempted to protect the principles of the Open Door in the postwar world. The International Monetary Fund and the World Bank, both created at the Bretton Woods Conference of 1944, sought to stabilize international currency and trade. Free trade promised distinct advantages for the United States. Recognizing that Europe would require extensive investment to recover from the war, State Department planners hoped to use American economic power to force Great Britain, France, and the Soviet Union to open their trading blocs to American business. When these nations applied for American loans to replace wartime Lend-Lease in 1945, American negotiators delayed action in order to win trading concessions. The following year the United States agreed to lend Britain $3.75 billion only on condition that the British open their empire to American trade. Nearly bankrupted by the war, London had no choice but to accept. The French made similar concessions. But the Soviet Union, though devastated by the war, refused to accept American demands.

Although Soviet leaders continued to advocate the Marxist-Leninist doctrine of world revolution, Josef Stalin primarily sought to rebuild his war-ravaged country with the help of German reparations. Stalin also proceeded to establish "friendly governments" in eastern Europe to prevent another invasion of Russia.

Given historic conflicts between the Soviet Union and antagonistic conservatives in eastern Europe, he refused to consider "free and unfettered elections" in areas occupied by Soviet troops. In Poland, for example, the Red Army enforced the repression of political freedom in favor of a pro-Soviet regime. During the war, Roosevelt had minimized the problem of Soviet expansion in eastern Europe, largely because he could do nothing about it and wanted to preserve the Grand Alliance against Hitler. Although he remained suspicious of Stalin, refusing to share information about the atomic bomb, the president endeavored to treat the Soviet Union as a "normal" state protecting its national interests.

Roosevelt failed, however, to develop public support for his foreign policy. Fearful of a resurgence of "isolationism," he hesitated to move ahead of public opinion. Nor did he challenge the popular view that the United Nations, like the League of Nations, would be based on Wilsonian principles of multinational representation. To be sure, these ideals would be preserved in the General Assembly. But Roosevelt believed that the U.N. could succeed where the League had failed only if the Big Powers dominated international diplomacy. He assumed that the Big Four (Britain, China, the United States, and the Soviet Union) would use their veto power in the Security Council to protect their national interests. At Yalta, for example, Roosevelt and Churchill acknowledged Soviet dominance in eastern Europe, while the British claimed special privileges in the Mediterranean, and the United States maintained power in Latin America. Such spheres of influence contradicted a Wilsonian order as well as the principles of the Open Door. Yet Roosevelt accepted these limitations because of the realities of Soviet power in eastern Europe.

At Roosevelt's death, Truman knew nothing of these foreign policy assumptions. Instead the new president viewed the Soviet presence in eastern Europe as a defiance of the principle of national self-determination and a violation of the Yalta agreements. Determined to prove his strength in the diplomatic arena, Truman clashed angrily with Soviet Foreign Minister V.M. Molotov in April 1945 about the undemocratic character of the Polish government and decided to withhold American economic aid until Stalin relented.

The new administration also shifted American policy toward the European empires, most significantly the French colony of Indochina. Opposed to French imperialism, Roosevelt had insisted that Indochina be placed under international trusteeship until achieving full independence. In 1945 the leader of the Indochinese national liberation movement, Ho Chi Minh, drafted a declaration of independence. Truman soon reversed Roosevelt's policy. Pressured by Churchill, who feared that the liberation of French colonies would set a precedent for the British empire, the president agreed to return Indochina to France. Ho's sympathy to communism had alarmed State Department officials who hoped to preserve an Open Door in southeast Asia, the very area Roosevelt refused to surrender to Japan in 1941. Equally important, Truman wished to retain French support in Europe, where France could join Britain as allies against the Soviet Union. The United States implemented the new policy by providing ships and military assistance to transport French troops to Indochina in 1945. Thereafter, the State Department ignored Ho Chi Minh's appeals for American support.

THE COLD WAR BEGINS

The Big Three met in Potsdam in July 1945 but failed to settle their differences. Stalin, concerned primarily with obtaining German reparations, expressed little interest in reducing Soviet influence in eastern Europe. But Truman, emboldened by the first successful testing of the atomic bomb that month, rejected such a Soviet sphere. He also proposed smaller reparations from Germany, leaving the Soviet Union vulnerable to American economic pressure. Failing to reach agreement, the Big Three postponed these issues to a Foreign Ministers Conference in London in September 1945. Frustrated by Soviet stubbornness, Truman decided to exclude the Soviet Union from participation in the occupation of Japan.

The atomic bombings of Japan in August 1945 reinforced Truman's confidence, but also aroused Soviet suspicions. At the London conference the Soviets offered minor concessions about the imminent elections in Bulgaria and Hungary but the administration demanded western-style contests. Again, the diplomats could reach no agreement. This failure demonstrated the fallacy of atomic bomb diplomacy. When Molotov asked facetiously whether Secretary of State Byrnes had an atom bomb in his pocket, the American replied, "If you don't cut out all this stalling..., I am going to pull an atomic bomb out of my hip pocket and let you have it!" To the surprise of American negotiators, the Soviet Union would not be coerced to accept American demands. Secretary of War Stimson, who had once viewed the bomb as a diplomatic lever, now saw an opportunity to ease tensions by sharing atomic secrets with the Soviet Union. "If we fail to approach them now and merely continue to negotiate with them, having this weapon rather ostentatiously on our hip," he warned, "their suspicions and their distrust...will increase." But after a high-level policy debate, the president chose to maintain the exclusive atomic monopoly.

Despite doubts about further negotiations, Truman permitted Byrnes to meet with Stalin in Moscow in December 1945. The sessions proved remarkably successful, producing tentative agreements about portions of eastern Europe, Korea, and especially a U.N. Atomic Energy Commission. But pressure from congressional conservatives, particularly Senator Arthur Vandenberg of Michigan, forced Truman to adopt a more rigid position, and he abruptly disavowed Byrnes's concessions. "Unless Russia is faced with an iron fist and strong language another war is in the making," he declared. "I'm tired of babying the Soviets."

Truman's stiff position won support within the State Department from George F. Kennan, a prestigious student of Soviet affairs. "We have here," he cabled from Moscow in February 1946, "a political force committed fanatically to the belief that...it is desirable and necessary that the internal harmony of our society be disrupted, our traditional way of life destroyed, the international authority of our state be broken if Soviet power is to be secure." Kennan's "Long Telegram" confirmed the president's belief that there could be no compromise with communist nations. Yet Kennan's message apparently did not reflect public opinion. One month later Truman accompanied Winston Churchill to Fulton, Missouri, where the former prime minister attacked the Soviet Union for drawing an "iron curtain" around eastern Europe. The speech, approved by Truman,

Despite basic disagreements, the Big Three—(left to right) Prime Minister Winston Churchill, President Truman, and Premier Josef Stalin—pose amicably at the Potsdam conference in 1945. Days later, Churchill's defeat at the polls forced his replacement by Clement Atlee.

brought storms of protest. It served nonetheless to publicize the changing of foreign policy.

The United States also challenged the Soviet Union within the U.N. The first major crisis involved Soviet occupation of northern Iran in 1946. Though defined by the United States as a question of territorial integrity, the problem focused on oil. During the war the Soviets, British, and Americans had occupied Iran jointly. But the Soviets hesitated to leave until they received oil concessions similar to those won by the British. Fearing a Soviet attempt to control vital oil resources, the White House supported Iran in the Security Council, where the United States controlled a preponderance of votes. Such diplomatic pressure forced Iran and the Soviet Union to compromise, agreeing to oil concessions and a Soviet withdrawal. Afterward, however, Iran repudiated the oil agreement. Using U.N. institutions, the United States had thwarted Soviet expansion. At the same time, Iran continued its relationship with British oil firms and became part of an American sphere of influence.

The U.N. also sanctioned Truman's decision to keep an American monopoly of atomic weapons. To ease public fears of atomic war, the administration announced the Acheson-Lilienthal plan, providing for the internationalization of atomic energy, in 1946. The United States would relinquish control of atomic weapons in a series of stages. During the transition, it would maintain a monopoly, while other countries would be required to allow international inspection. Truman appointed financier Bernard Baruch to present the program in the U.N.

Exhibit 9–1. Iran, 1946.

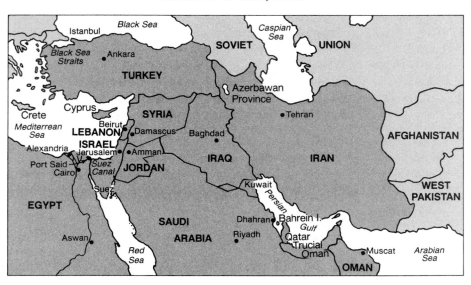

Baruch added other criteria to the plan, including the surrender of the Security Council veto on atomic energy issues and imposition of "condign punishments" against violators by a majority vote (which was controlled by the United States). Unwilling to open its resources to outside inspection and fearful of continued American monopoly, the Soviet Union rejected the Baruch plan. Instead, the Soviets suggested immediate nuclear disarmament and sharing of atomic secrets. Truman, who never intended to surrender the atomic monopoly, considered the Soviet alternative unacceptable.

Truman's inability to appreciate Soviet fears of the atomic monopoly reflected a moral absolutism that dominated Cold War thinking. Defining Soviet communism as "red fascism," American leaders were determined to avoid a repetition of "appeasement" that had allowed Germany to control Europe in the 1930s. Experience with Nazis taught them that totalitarian regimes eventually led their people to war. "The language of military power is the only language which disciples of power politics understand," presidential adviser Clark Clifford assured Truman in 1946. In identifying the Soviet Union with the evils of Nazism, moreover, Truman broadened support of his policy. Under the principle of "bipartisanship," Republicans, led by Senator Vandenberg and foreign policy expert John Foster Dulles, supported administration diplomacy, at least in Europe.

As a Cold War consensus crystalized in 1946, a major critic was Henry A. Wallace, secretary of agriculture in the New Deal, Roosevelt's third-term vice president, and now Truman's secretary of commerce. The president simply ignored Wallace's private protests. But in September 1946, with Truman's approval, Wallace presented a public address at Madison Square Garden, arguing that the United States had "no more business in the *political* affairs of Eastern Europe than Russia had in the *political* affairs of Latin America, Western Europe, and the United States." When other members of the administration protested the speech,

——— ARTHUR H. VANDENBERG ———
——————— 1884–1951 ———————

"The Old Guard dies but never surrenders," wrote journalist Milton S. Mayer of the last-ditch noninterventionists in 1940. "Vandenberg surrenders, but never dies." Michigan Senator Arthur H. Vandenberg stood for many other conservative Americans when he made the transition from prewar anti-interventionism to postwar internationalism. Although staunch Old Guard Republicans, such as Robert Taft of Ohio, refused to compromise their "America-first" principles, Vandenberg believed that national security required a new internationalist commitment. Insisting that the Soviet Union constituted a threat to American interests around the world, he worked with the Truman administration to build a national consensus in support of the Cold War.

Born in Grand Rapids, Michigan, Vandenberg embraced the conservative middle-class midwestern values of his surroundings. As editor of the *Grand Rapids Herald,* he backed Woodrow Wilson's decision to seek intervention in World War I, but opposed American entry into the League of Nations. Appointed to the Senate in 1928, Vandenberg supported Hoover's efforts to end the Depression and later backed early New Deal programs in the interests of bipartisanship. By 1935, however, he rejected Roosevelt's leadership and became an outspoken critic.

Vandenberg also dissented vigorously from Roosevelt's foreign policy. In 1933, for example, he was one of only two senators to oppose American recognition of the Soviet Union. During the 1930s he favored strict neutrality legislation. With other anti-interventionists, he attacked the Lend-Lease plan, arguing that it would hasten American entry into the European war. The trauma of Pearl Harbor changed Vandenberg's position. Embracing internationalism, he appealed to Roosevelt to establish a joint congressional-executive committee to forge a united foreign policy. (Roosevelt, unwilling to share foreign policy with anyone, ignored the plea.) Then, in January 1945 Vandenberg presented a widely hailed speech, announcing his support of a postwar United Nations organization. To win Republican backing of the postwar settlement, Truman chose Vandenberg to attend the first U.N. conference in San Francisco in 1945. Vandenberg succeeded in persuading the delegates to adopt Article 51 of the U.N. charter, providing for regional alliances. Intended to protect United States influence in Latin America, this article later provided the basis for NATO and other regional pacts.

Considered the leading internationalist in the Republican party, Vandenberg demanded a voice in foreign policy in exchange for bipartisan support of the Cold War. Criticizing any sign of "appeasement" of the Soviet Union, he denounced negotiations to internationalize atomic energy in 1946. Yet Vandenberg was personally vain and easily subject to flattery and pressure. Using the principle of bipartisanship, the administration won his support of the Truman Doctrine, Marshall Plan, and NATO. Vandenberg also intervened with Republican leaders to prevent any serious debate of foreign policy in the 1948 presidential election.

Unlike Taft, Vandenberg did not question the high cost of the Cold War or the growth of a national security state. Taft's opposition to the military state prevented him from winning the Republican nomination in 1948 and 1952. Yet Vandenberg, whose foreign policy position seemed more popular, failed to win the respect of his colleagues and never became a party leader. ∎

Truman withdrew his approval and fired Wallace. "The Reds, phonies, and the 'parlor pinks,'" Truman wrote, "seem to be banded together and are becoming a national danger."

Fear of communist influence permeated Washington. Convinced of an imminent attack by the Soviet Union, FBI Director J. Edgar Hoover proceeded with a "Custodial Detention Program" and compiled lists of suspected subversives who would be arrested at the outbreak of war. When the Truman administration attempted to minimize the communist threat, Hoover aligned with more militant anti-communists in Congress. "Communism," Hoover told the House Committee on Un-American Activities (HUAC) "is a way of life—an evil and malignant way of life." Persuaded by such testimony, Congress voted additional funding of FBI investigations of government workers. These political pressures pushed Truman toward a more militant anti-communist position.

The dismissal of Wallace thus revealed the administration's growing intolerance of positions that had seemed acceptable only one year before. After conservative Republican victories in the 1946 elections, some liberals deserted Truman's leadership and formed a coalition group, Progressive Citizens of American (PCA). Complaining that the Democratic party had departed from the tradition of Roosevelt, the PCA urged a return to liberal principles or the creation of a third party. Significantly, the PCA did not discriminate against members of the Communist party. But most liberals bitterly opposed communism and especially resented conservative accusations that liberals were tools of Soviet foreign policy. In January 1947, these non-Communist liberals formed Americans for Democratic Action (ADA). Like the PCA, the ADA endorsed expansion of the New Deal, the U.N., and civil rights. But the ADA explicitly rejected "any association with Communists or sympathizers with communism." And unlike Wallace, the ADA generally supported the Cold War.

THE TRUMAN DOCTRINE

Early in 1947, American intelligence detected a relaxation of Soviet policy, ranging from demobilization of its armies to a willingness to negotiate about Germany. The State Department concluded that such changes were deliberately deceptive. Reinforcing this mistrust was a growing concern about the slow pace of economic recovery in Europe. Economic unrest, the State Department feared, both encouraged communist expansion and undermined American exports. The problem climaxed in February 1947 when Great Britain announced it could no longer provide support for Greece, a client state it had supported since World War II in a civil war against communist guerrillas. Truman welcomed the opportunity to replace Britain in the area. But American intervention required congressional approval at a time when conservatives sought to cut government expenses. And the public appeared to be uninterested in Balkan affairs.

Truman decided to "scare hell out of the American people." In an impassioned speech the president personally presented the "Truman Doctrine" to a special session of Congress in March 1947, requesting $400 million of economic and military assistance to Greece and Turkey. Condemning a communist system based on "terror and oppression, a controlled press and radio, fixed elections and the suppression of political freedoms," Truman depicted an emergency crisis that forced the United States to "support free peoples who are resisting attempted subjugation by armed minorities or by outside pressures."

The Truman Doctrine represented a major turning point in American foreign policy. First, it suggested that the United States must initiate unilateral action without consultation with either the U.N. or the Soviet Union. Second, the Truman Doctrine abandoned the idea of effecting changes within the Soviet sphere of influence and instead stressed the importance of containing further Soviet expansion. In effect, this decision divided the globe into areas of "freedom" and zones of "terror and oppression." Such divisions allowed no room for compromise: all communists appeared evil, all communist threats became equally critical. Third, the Truman Doctrine expanded the definition of "national security" to encompass the entire world. "Wherever aggression, direct or indirect threatened the peace," Truman later explained, "the security of the United States was involved." George Kennan elaborated this idea of containment in an influential article, "The Sources of Soviet Conduct," published anonymously in the journal *Foreign Affairs* in 1947.

Truman's belief that communism represented a monolithic threat now placed the United States on the side of authoritarian governments. Viewing Greek communists as minions of Moscow, Truman supported a conservative monarchy with little popular support. In Turkey, the United States backed a repressive regime that crushed internal dissent and had cooperated with the Germans during World War II. The administration justified these alliances by articulating what later became known as the domino theory: "If Greece and then Turkey succumb," one State Department official advised, "the whole Middle East will be lost. France may then capitulate to the communists. As France goes, all Western Europe and North Africa will go." Such logic alarmed conservatives and liberals alike. Republican Senator Robert Taft of Ohio protested that Truman had adopted fundamental policy choices without adequately consulting Congress. At the other end of the spectrum, Wallace broadcast a scathing critique: "There is no regime too reactionary" to receive American aid, he said, "provided it stands in Russia's expansionist path."

Truman believed that international politics were too complex for average voters, whom he considered overly idealistic. Rather than risk divisive partisan debates, the president preferred to rely on foreign policy experts such as the diplomat W. Averell Harriman and then seek public support. "We are on the right track and we will win," Truman declared, "because God is with us in that enterprise." Conservative Republicans such as Taft objected that Congress and the public were left to ratify Cold War policies instead of formulating them. The administration's ability to coax public opinion proved effective, however, and the announcement of the Truman Doctrine raised the president's approval rating from 49 percent to 60 percent in two months. Yet American aid neither suppressed the Greek rebellion nor made the monarchy less oppressive. "There is no use pretending...that for $400 million we have bought peace," admitted Vandenberg. "It is merely a down payment."

By emphasizing the military threat of communism, the Truman Doctrine diverted attention from the main purposes of the president's foreign policy: the desire to end economic shortages in Europe and stabilize European economies to prevent the spread of communism and to stimulate American trade. Secretary of State George C. Marshall unveiled these plans in a highly publicized speech at the Harvard University commencement in June 1947. Describing severe economic problems in Europe, Marshall called for a massive program of economic aid, offering assistance to all nations, including communist. "Our policy is directed not against any country or doctrine," he stated, "but against hunger, poverty, desperation, and chaos." In inviting Soviet participation, however, Marshall was less than candid, for the plan threatened the independence of each nation's economy. The program seemed to envision a return to prewar conditions that left eastern Europe far less industrialized than the west. Moreover, instead of receiving reparations, the Soviet Union might have to contribute food to other countries. Finally, the plan would revitalize Germany and lead to German integration in the western economy.

The State Department correctly predicted the effect of these objections: the Soviets rejected participation in the Marshall Plan and forced its client states in eastern Europe to do the same. The Soviet Union also moved to tighten political control in that area. This negative response facilitated implementation of the Marshall Plan elsewhere. Sixteen nations drafted a four-year program of economic recovery and gladly accepted $17 billion of American aid. The United States also began to rebuild German industry. Wielding its economic power, Washington persuaded political leaders in Italy and France to drop the Communist party from their coalition governments.

The anti-communist aspects of the Marshall Plan helped create a favorable reception in Congress. But the conservative majority remained suspicious of executive power, foreign aid, and potential benefits to large exporters rather than domestically-oriented small firms. Moreover, as late as November 1947, 40 percent of the public had never heard of the Marshall Plan. The administration then launched a public relations campaign, mustering corporation lawyers, big business executives, organized labor, the ADA, and the Farm Bureau to lobby Congress. "We'll either have to provide a program of interim aid relief until the Marshall program gets going," Truman warned a group of congressional leaders, "or the governments of France and Italy will fall, Austria too, and for all practical purposes Europe will be Communist." By appealing to the dread of communist expansion, such warnings reduced conservative scruples about government spending abroad. Summoning a special session, Truman played down the economic basis of the plan and returned to the militant anti-communist rhetoric of the Truman Doctrine. The strategy worked and Congress passed an interim aid measure. By 1950 the Marshall Plan delivered $130 billion to foreign countries through government grants and loans.

RED SCARE

Anti-communist foreign policy paralleled an anti-communist crusade at home. Responding to Republican election victories in 1946. Truman had attempted to defuse the question of Communist influence by creating a Temporary Commission on Employee Loyalty. Nine days after enunciating the Truman Doctrine, the president created a permanent Federal Employee Loyalty program to elimi-

Exhibit 9–2. Greece, Turkey, and Mediterranean, 1947.

nate subversives from government. The announcement reflected continuing pressures from congressional conservatives as well as anti-communist feelings within the administration. In January 1947, the House Un-American Activities Committee (HUAC) had resumed investigation of communist infiltration of government, Hollywood, education, and labor unions. HUAC's explosive inquiry into the movie industry resulted in contempt charges against the "Hollywood Ten," a group of writers and directors who refused on First Amendment grounds to answer questions about their political activities. After the Supreme Court refused to hear their appeals, the Ten went to prison. Attempting to preempt similar investigations of government, Truman's Executive Order 9835 established loyalty investigations of all federal employees and job applicants. The president also ordered dismissal of any worker for whom there were "reasonable grounds" for suspicion of disloyalty. Truman also instructed Attorney General Tom Clark to publicize a list of "subversive" organizations; there were ninety-one so designated in 1947. "There are many Communists in America," the attorney general declared. "They are everywhere—in factories, offices, butcher shops, on street corners, in private businesses—and each carries with him the germs of death for society." The list stigmatized opponents of government policy, encouraging public and private discrimination against members.

"What," asked a HUAC pamphlet, "is the difference in fact between a Communist and a Fascist? Answer: None worth noticing." In 1947 J. Edgar Hoover published a widely circulated article, "Red Fascism in the United States Today,"

J. EDGAR HOOVER
1895–1972

Without question J. Edgar Hoover was the most successful bureaucrat in American history. A man whose entire life centered on Washington, D.C., he was the son of a bureaucrat, born and raised a few blocks from the Capitol. After graduation from George Washington University, he took a job with the Department of Justice, beginning a half-century career which ended only with his death in 1972. The young Hoover was assigned to the Enemy Alien Registration Section of the Bureau of Investigation and played an important role in investigating and deporting radicals during the "Red Scare" of 1919–1920. He also played a part in federal probes of black activist Marcus Garvey which ultimately led to Garvey's conviction and deportation. During the Harding presidency, the Bureau of Investigation became so corrupt and ineffective that Hoover considered resigning, but after Harding's death, a new attorney general, Harlan F. Stone, offered the twenty-nine-year-old attorney the directorship. Hoover accepted with the stipulation that he be given the authority to professionalize the bureau and to insulate it from politics.

Energetic and capable, Hoover applied modern management techniques to the bureau (it became the Federal Bureau of Investigation in 1935) with remarkable results. He hired agents with backgrounds in law or accounting and schooled them in the application of scientific principles to law enforcement. He supervised the assembling of a huge centralized fingerprint file, the creation of a sophisticated crime laboratory, and the establishment of the National Police Academy to train other law enforcement officers in scientific investigation. Simultaneously Hoover recognized the enormous value of good public relations and steadily built the image of the G-Man through shrewd manipulation of popular culture, an image enhanced by well-publicized and successful manhunts for such celebrated *(cont.)*

expressing the imminent danger of communist subversion. Seeking judicial sanction for his surveillance and detention programs, Hoover pressed the Department of Justice to prosecute leaders of the Communist Party for violating the Smith Act of 1940, which made it a crime to advocate the overthrow of government by force or to belong to a group with such a goal. To Hoover's disappointment, the Justice Department prosecuted only twelve leading Communists in 1948. All were convicted and received stiff prison sentences. Despite headline revelations of communist espionage, however, Truman's Loyalty Program found no government spies.

Communism represented less a domestic threat than an undesirable political philosophy. Polish Americans and other eastern European ethnic groups hated the Soviet Union for invading their homelands and attacking Christian churches. But the core of anti-communism lay in American perceptions of Stalinist Russia. The popular novels of Mickey Spillane, Hollywood films like *The Cold (cont.)* gangsters as John Dillinger and "Machine Gun" Kelly. This concern for image also led him to impose on the bureau a code of conduct rooted in the Victorianism of his upbringing in turn-of-the-century Washington. Special agents should wear dark suits and white shirts; women did not smoke; and FBI employees did not take coffee breaks.

In the years after World War II, Hoover's tenure at the FBI became increasingly controversial. Some critics charged that the FBI focused on sensational but episodic criminal activity while ignoring organized crime and white collar crime. Also the FBI zealously investigated communist subversives, an activity that broadened considerably as first the civil rights and later the anti-war movements stirred the Director's disapproval. In the process of conducting extensive domestic surveillance on these and other dissidents, the FBI collected an extensive set of files on literally millions of Americans, files which Hoover was willing to use ruthlessly. Most notorious was the bureau's attempt to destroy Martin Luther King, Jr. with a tape recording of sexual activity involving the civil rights leader. Although the effort failed, the King incident illustrates the enormous power Hoover derived from domestic surveillance. As a former aide put it, "I'm afraid of him. I can't imagine what he'd do to me, but I'd rather not mess with him."

Even presidents felt the same way. His relationship with John Kennedy was tense, but his position remained secure, perhaps in part because Hoover had a potentially embarrassing tape of a Kennedy sexual liaison during World War II. His disdain for both Kennedy brothers was plain, however. When he telephoned Robert Kennedy with the first word that the president had been killed, Hoover sounded, Kennedy later remembered, "not quite as excited as if he were reporting the fact that he had found a Communist on the faculty at Howard University." Kennedy's successor, Lyndon Johnson, delighted in the bits of scandal which Hoover regularly passed along, and both he and Richard Nixon waived mandatory retirement rules to enable Hoover to remain on the job until his death in May 1972. ■

War (1948), and a spate of magazine articles all portrayed Communism as the epitome of heartless atheism, life-deadening bureaucracy, and ruthless totalitarianism. Given these views, many Americans believed that religion, family, individual liberty, and personal initiative were in jeopardy. "Communism is secularism on the march," J. Edgar Hoover told a Methodist gathering. "It is a moral foe of Christianity."

Ironically, the growth of government bureaucracy, big corporations, and the mobility of American society already threatened traditional American values from within. "Our problem is not outside ourselves," admitted Republican presidential candidate Thomas E. Dewey in 1948. "Our problem is within ourselves." Anti-communist spokesmen such as Joseph McCarthy, J. Edgar Hoover, and Richard Nixon saw themselves defending the traditional American way of life. Their wrath focused not so much on actual Communists as on the sophisticated, cosmopolitan State Department elites who tolerated Communists in govern-

Exhibit 9–3. Gross National Product, 1946–1952.
(current dollars in billions)

1946	$212.4 b
1948	$261.6 b
1950	$288.3 b
1952	$351.6 b

Source: *Economic Report of the President* (1988)

Exhibit 9–4. Federal Budget Deficits, 1940–1950.
(in billions of dollars)

	Receipts	Outlays	Deficit
1940	$ 6.5 b	$ 9.5 b	$ 2.9 b
1945	$45.2 b	$92.7 b	$47.6 b
1950	$39.4 b	$42.6 b	$ 3.1 b

Source: *Economic Report of the President* (1988)

Exhibit 9–5. Government Spending as Percentage of Gross National Product, 1929–1949.

1929	9.9%
1939	19.6%
1949	23.0%

Source: *Historical Statistics of the United States, from Colonial Times to 1970* (1975)

ment and accommodated the Soviet Union. "I look at that fellow," said Senator Hugh Butler of Nebraska about Secretary of State Dean Acheson. "I watch his smart-aleck manner and his British clothes and that New Dealism, everlasting New Dealism in everything he says and does, and I want to shout, 'Get out, Get out. You stand for everything that has been wrong with the United States.'" Thus conservative Republicans like Nixon and McCarthy exploited the anti-communist crusade to attack Democrats and the New Deal tradition. Meanwhile, public distrust of elites who were not accountable to voters—government bureaucrats, intellectuals, scientists, leaders of the media and entertainment industries—encouraged loyalty oaths, public recantations of leftist affiliations, "naming names" of former associates, blacklists, and legal persecution. Spillane's detective novel, *One Lonely Night* (1951), which sold seven million copies, offered one method of policing the communist menace: "Don't arrest them, don't treat them with the dignity of the democratic process of courts of law...do the same thing that they'd do to you! Treat 'em to the inglorious taste of sudden death."

Backed by public opinion and the courts, law enforcement officials and anti-communist activists faced few obstacles in purging "red" elements from American life. Between 1947 and 1954 the FBI processed nearly five million loyalty forms, while its budget increased from $35 million in 1947 to $53 million in 1950

Truman meets with his fourth secretary of state, Dean Acheson, whose connections with the cosmopolitan corporate "Establishment" infuriated Republican conservatives.

to $130 million by 1962. Under Truman over seven thousand federal government employees lost their jobs (thousands more were never hired in the first place); under President Dwight D. Eisenhower the rate of dismissals increased slightly. State and municipal governments adopted similar programs, barring "subversives" from public employment. Workers and management in private industry also cooperated to expel suspected employees. Boston's Little, Brown publishing company, for example, forced the resignation of its editor-in-chief because he published books by left-wing authors. Teachers, union leaders, even factory workers were forced to sign loyalty oaths; the penalty for noncompliance often was dismissal. New York City high school students had to sign loyalty oaths to collect their diplomas, which were often prerequisites for college admission. Meanwhile, the Post Office intercepted and opened mail from certain communist countries. "If ignorant people read it," said one censor, "they might begin to believe it."

Such excesses might have been checked by an independent judiciary. But Truman's appointments to the Supreme Court, including Attorney General Clark, voted against individual civil liberties. In the *Dennis* case (1951), the Court upheld the convictions of eleven leading Communist party members, ruling that "Communist speech" was not protected by constitutional guarantees because communists participated in an international movement. As a result of 141 indictments and other harassment, many Communist leaders went "underground" and the party lost half its membership.

THE MILITARY CRISIS

The sense of national emergency stimulated the reorganization of the military services. The National Security Act of 1947 unified command over the armed services within the new Department of Defense, legalized the Joint Chiefs of Staff, and created an independent Air Force prepared to incorporate the newest advances in technology. The law also established the National Security Council (NSC) and the Central Intelligence Agency (CIA) as confidential bureaus responsible only to the president. The NSC was to coordinate and refine foreign policy for the White House and act as the president's liaison to the security bureaucracy. The CIA was to preside over the gathering of intelligence information. The agency's congressional charter also provided for "such other functions as the Director of Central Intelligence shall, from time to time, deem appropriate." This loophole subsequently allowed the agency to develop major covert action responsibilities abroad. Amendments to the charter in 1949 also exempted the CIA from budgetary accounting requirements, thereby making it an independent agency outside congressional control.

By rationalizing decision-making, the National Security Act consolidated the power of the executive branch. Increasingly important foreign policy decisions became insulated from external scrutiny and confined to a narrowing group of advisers. The shift in power seriously eroded the influence of the State Department.

The new bureaucracy also intensified rivalry between the military branches. In 1948, Truman opted for the "air-atomic" strategy, which made strategic bombing, including nuclear weapons, the primary military force. Yet the previous year, the United States had probably possessed only two atomic bombs and few technicians with the necessary skills to assemble more. To the budget-conscious president, air-atomic technology seemed an inexpensive way to build a viable defense. It had the additional advantage of reducing the need for a huge fighting army. But the decision to rearm faced selected opposition from both conservatives and liberals. Wallace, who announced his presidential candidacy within a new Progressive party, chastised Truman for ignoring the U.N. and provoking the Soviet Union. More powerful opposition came from Republicans like Taft who denounced the swollen federal budget and argued that the war with communism was ultimately a contest of ideas, not military might. When the president requested a large budget for the air-atomic strategy in January 1948, Congress seem uninterested. "The outlook for greatly increased aviation budgets," the trade journal *Aviation Week* lamented early in 1948, "is not bright."

Congress abruptly snapped to attention, however, when communists seized power in Soviet-occupied Czechoslovakia in February 1948. The State Department already treated Czechoslovakia as part of the Soviet bloc, refusing economic aid to the Czechs and ignoring Czech fears of German rearmament. Yet news of the communist coup shocked the public, confirming fears of Soviet aggression through internal subversion. Truman resolved not to repeat the 1938 Munich sellout of Czechoslovakia. When American military leaders in Germany reported a change in Soviet attitudes, the president concluded that war might well erupt. Fearing another Pearl Harbor surprise, he decided to alert Congress and the public of the impending crisis. In this tense atmosphere, Truman told a

Exhibit 9–6. Berlin Blockade, 1948.

joint session of Congress in March 1948 that the Soviet Union had "destroyed the independence and democratic character of a whole series of nations" and so revealed "the clear design" to conquer "the remaining free nations of Europe." "There is some risk involved in action—there always is," he admitted. "But there is far more risk in failure to act." The somber speech persuaded Congress to vote final approval of the Marshall Plan and re-establish the military draft. Conservatives managed to defeat a proposal for universal military training, but Congress allocated $3.5 billion for military purposes, 25 percent more than the administration had requested.

Military confrontation came one step closer when the Soviet Union blockaded Berlin in June 1948. Since the end of the war, the great powers had not signed a final peace settlement. While the United States and the Soviet Union disagreed about German reparations, the former enemy remained divided into occupied zones. When the United States and Britain announced plans to integrate their zones and initiate currency reform, Stalin realized that the western allies were hastening German independence to bring Germany into the western alliance. He responded by blocking access to Berlin through East Germany. Truman feared an immediate war but also opposed capitulation to Stalin. He therefore resolved to support Berlin, ordering a massive airlift of food and supplies that lasted eleven months. Unwilling to go to war, Stalin had to accept American plans for West Germany. Yet the crisis escalated the level of conflict. In July 1948, Truman ordered B-29 bombers to England. These were the only planes capable of dropping atom bombs in Europe, though (unknown to the Soviets) they were not modified for such work until 1949. For the first time, atomic weapons had become an explicit instrument of foreign policy.

The Cold War crisis enabled Congress to reverse administration policy in Asia. The corruption of Chiang Kai-shek's Nationalist regime in China, together with the success of Mao Tse-tung's Communists, had persuaded the president to allow the civil war to run its course. But the Truman Doctrine also suggested that *any* communist expansion threatened American interests. Influenced by a well-funded pressure group, known as the China Lobby, congressional conservatives led by Republican Senator William Knowland of California insisted on a literal interpretation of the Truman Doctrine. Contrary to administration intentions, therefore, Congress appropriated funds for the Chiang regime. Thus the United States became committed to a repressive, but non-communist government in a manner that influenced Asian foreign policy for three decades. Meanwhile, Truman's decision to abandon Chiang accelerated an American accommodation with Japan, which now appeared as a likely non-communist ally. In 1947, the United States extended economic assistance to Japan and strengthened American military forces there.

The United States also solidified its sphere of influence in Latin America. The Rio Pact of 1947 provided for collective self-defense of the Western hemisphere. The following year the Bogota Treaty created the Organization of American States to facilitate consultations, and Washington disavowed intervention in the internal or external affairs of other states. In creating this alliance, the United States avoided economic commitments, preferring to support private development. Yet in a series of bilateral agreements, Washington offered military assistance, including the training of Latin American armies. Such support stabilized military and landed elites throughout Latin America.

THE ELECTION OF 1948

As the nation faced a series of foreign policy crises, political pundits questioned Truman's leadership abilities. A March 1948 Gallup poll showed that Truman would lose the presidential election to a spate of Republican challengers: Dewey, Vandenberg, Minnesota's Harold Stassen, or General Douglas MacArthur. Meanwhile, Henry Wallace asserted, "There is no real fight between a Truman and a Republican. Both stand for a policy which opens the door to war in our lifetime and makes war certain for our children." Yet the military mobilization against Soviet Communism worked to the president's advantage. Following the advice of aide Clark Clifford, Truman moved to isolate Wallace from his liberal supporters. By identifying Wallace with the Soviet threat, the president kept most liberals in the Democratic party. Truman also improved his standing among Jews by promptly recognizing the new state of Israel in 1948.

The Wallace insurgency emboldened Republicans. They bypassed Taft to renominate Dewey, who chose California Governor Earl Warren as his running mate. The Republican platform appeared moderate, if not liberal, calling for federal support of housing, farm payments, abolition of poll taxes, a permanent FEPC, and increases in social security. Confident of an election victory, Republicans deliberately excluded foreign policy issues from debate, which freed Truman from having to defend his positions. The president further undermined the Republicans by calling the 80th Congress into special session and daring the Republican majority to enact their party platform.

Truman also confronted other divisions within the Democratic party. The ADA, led by Minneapolis Mayor Hubert Humphrey, demanded a liberal platform on civil rights. "The time has arrived for the Democratic party to get out of the shadow of states rights," Humphrey told the Democratic National Convention, "and walk forthrightly into the bright sunshine of human rights." Democrats responded by voting a strong civil rights plank. But then angry southern delegates bolted from the convention. Three days later, these Dixiecrats met in Birmingham, Alabama, to form the States Rights party and nominate South Carolina's Strom Thurmond for president. Opposed to civil rights measures, the Dixiecrats objected as much to equal rights for blacks as they did the growing federal bureaucracy.

Supporters of Henry Wallace organized the Progressive party and chose Wallace and Senator Glen Taylor of Idaho as running mates. Though Communists held important positions in the party, the platform primarily reflected liberal principles. Offering a genuine alternative to Truman's Cold War and Dewey's bipartisanship, the Progressives argued that "responsibility for ending the tragic prospect of war is a joint responsibility of the Soviet Union and the United States." But the Progressives could never overcome their association with communism. "Politicians of both major parties have tried to pin the Communist tag on the followers of...Wallace," observed pollster George Gallup. "Apparently their efforts have succeeded." The Wallace campaign encountered systematic harassment, including mob violence and denial of public meeting places.

While Dixiecrats and Progressives attacked Truman, the special session of the 80th Congress convened. If Republicans enacted their platform, Truman would get credit for goading them to action; if not, they would appear hypocritical. After much discussion, Congress adjourned without passing significant legislation. The decision gave Truman campaign ammunition against the "do-nothing" Republicans. While pre-election polls forecast a Republican victory, Truman took to the hustings, launching a whistle-stop campaign that covered over twenty thousand miles. "Give'em hell, Harry!" became a rallying cry, as Truman appealed to anxious farmers about Republican threats to the price support program. He was the first president to campaign for the black vote in Harlem. The results brought a surprise Democratic victory in November when Truman topped Dewey by over two million votes. "The publishers press is a very small part of our population," gloated Truman. "They have debauched [their] responsibility...to the country and the people have shown them just how they like it." In the electoral college, Truman won 304 votes, Dewey 189, Thurmond 34 (all in the South), and Wallace received none. Each third party candidate attracted slightly more than one million votes. But Truman did best in areas of New Deal strength, winning among farmers, organized labor, and blacks.

Exhibit 9–7. 1948 Election.

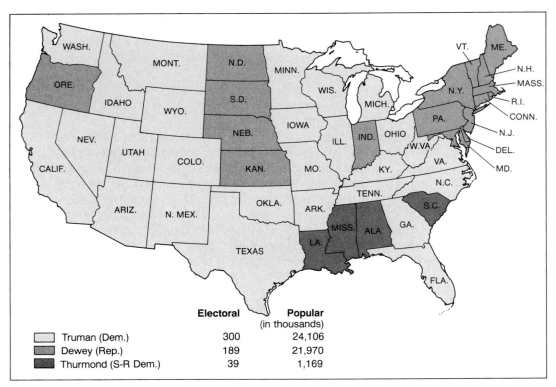

	Electoral	Popular
		(in thousands)
Truman (Dem.)	300	24,106
Dewey (Rep.)	189	21,970
Thurmond (S-R Dem.)	39	1,169

THE FAIR DEAL

"Every segment of our population and every individual," Truman told the 81st Congress, "has a right to expect from our Government a fair deal." Working again with a Democratic majority, the president called for increased social security and minimum wages, civil rights legislation, federal aid to education, national health insurance, and repeal of Taft-Hartley. But White House proposals soon met stiff resistance from the true majority in Congress—a conservative coalition of southern Democrats and midwestern Republicans. By controlling the congressional committee system, these groups prevented serious consideration of Truman's program. Although Congress passed the Housing Act of 1949, providing for slum clearance and federally funded low-income housing, insufficient appropriations limited implementation of the plan. Civil rights legislation languished in committee and Truman chose to avoid a hopeless skirmish.

Support of civil rights within the executive branch also appeared ambiguous. Despite the president's 1948 order desegregating the armed services, the military evaded enforcement. In Truman's inauguration parade of 1949, black soldiers marched with whites, but the army blocked full integration by segregating platoons, a policy that persisted during the Korean war. Truman's Department of Justice supported civil rights suits, but the Federal Housing Authority continued to accept residential segregation, even after the Supreme Court denied restrictive covenants. (For the legal issues, see chapter 2). The president also hesitated to re-establish an FEPC and never gave it enforcement powers to halt discrimination in war industries. Nonetheless, black leaders praised Truman's moral support. "No occupant of the White House since the nation was born," wrote the NAACP's Walter White in 1952, "has taken so frontal or constant a stand against racial discrimination as has Harry S. Truman."

The limitations of Truman's Fair Deal reflected basic changes in liberal thinking. After the defeat of Wallace, liberals repudiated associations with communism and moved away from the left. Arthur M. Schlesinger, Jr.'s book, *The Vital Center* (1949), defended this retreat. Seeking a perfect society, said Schlesinger, appeared naive, self-deceptive, and led to totalitarian excesses. Instead, he called upon Americans to become political "realists," to shun the idealism of perfectionist movements. At a time when many Americans were enjoying personal prosperity, supporting the baby boom, and celebrating conformity, American liberalism understandably supported the status quo.

LIMITING BIPARTISANSHIP

Although political disagreement eventually undermined the foreign policy consensus, a bipartisan spirit prevailed on European issues until 1951. In June 1948 the Senate passed the Vandenberg Resolution, which permitted participation in a peacetime military alliance with the nations of western Europe. The next year, the United States signed the North Atlantic Treaty Organization (NATO) pact

Exhibit 9–8. NATO.

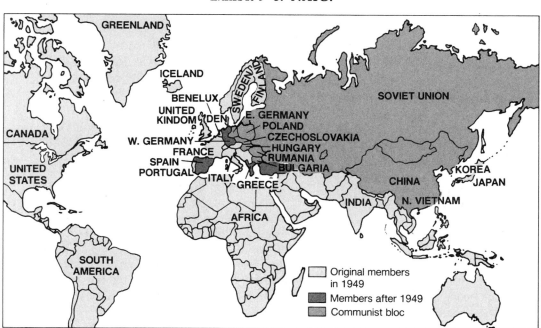

for collective defense. At the same time the United States worked to create a new West German state and in 1949, the Federal Republic joined the western alliance. The NATO pact institutionalized the division of Europe into spheres of influence. Though the treaty obligated the United States to send military assistance to European allies, the purposes of NATO appeared less military than political. First, NATO served as a diplomatic deterrent to Soviet expansion. Second, the alliance assured American dominance of western Europe by obliging its members to adopt a united approach to the Soviet Union and the region's future. "The Atlantic Pact is but the logical extension of the Monroe Doctrine," explained the chairman of the Senate Foreign Relations committee. Third, NATO proposed to reintegrate German industrial and military power with the rest of western Europe without fear of renewing old rivalries. Opposed to permanent military commitments, Taft led the fight against ratification, but could not defeat the president. The House, however, hesitated to allocate funds to implement the treaty provisions, forcing Truman to reduce his arms requests. But then, in September 1949, the president announced that the Soviet Union had exploded an atom bomb. Within a week, the House provided funding for NATO.

Perceiving the Soviet Union as a relentless enemy which now possessed devastating weapons of destruction, Americans felt increasingly vulnerable to "hidden enemies" who might give away the secrets upon which survival rested. Doubts about the competence of communist science led many leaders, including Truman, to question the Soviet achievement. Many believed that spies had given away American "secrets." Allegations that government traitors, including former New Deal and State Department official Alger Hiss, passed secret documents to communist agents supported the climate of suspicion. In any case, policy makers saw no advantage to cooperating on atomic energy with the Soviet Union. Despite unanimous objections by scientists and civilians on the Atomic Energy Commission's General Advisory Council, AEC head Lewis Strauss, backed by physicist Edward Teller, urged the development of a Superbomb—the hydrogen bomb. In January 1950, Truman ended the debate by opting to build the bomb. By the end of the next year, the United States successfully tested the new weapon; within two years the Soviet Union did the same.

Partisan criticism focused on the inadequacy of American assistance to China's Chiang Kai-shek. Despite appropriations of hundreds of millions of dollars to support the Nationalists, Communist armies steadily attacked Chiang's crumbling forces. By August 1949, the State Department saw the inevitability of a communist victory and halted further assistance. "The only alternative open to the United States," asserted a State Department "White Paper," "was full-scale intervention in behalf of a government which had lost the confidence of its own troops and its own people." In December, Communist forces led by Mao Tse-tung swept into power, forcing Chiang to abandon the mainland and flee to the island of Taiwan. Given the logic of containment, the communist victory could be seen only as a devastating defeat of American foreign policy. The China Lobby, including such leading Republicans as former president Herbert Hoover, Taft, and Knowland, attacked the administration for failing to support an anti-communist ally. Such criticism prevented Truman from seeking an accommodation with Chinese communists. Instead, the United States adopted a policy of non-recognition that lasted for more than two decades. Partisan suspicions deepened when Mao signed a mutual assistance pact with the Soviet Union in 1950.

Former State Department official Alger Hiss denied allegations of Communist ties, setting the stage for a dramatic perjury trial. After one hung jury failed to reach a verdict, a second trial convicted Hiss in 1950.

Anxieties over the "loss" of China and the Soviet explosion of an atom bomb escalated in January 1950 when a jury found Alger Hiss guilty of perjury. A debonair member of the liberal foreign policy elite, Hiss had denied passing classified documents in the 1930s to erstwhile Communist Whittaker Chambers. For anti-communists, the sensational case proved an inseparable link between Hiss's New Deal liberalism and Communist influence in government. The case particularly embarrassed the Democratic administration because Truman had labeled HUAC's investigation of Hiss "a red herring" and issued a 1948 executive order barring Congress from access to government loyalty files without presidential approval. Traumatized by the possibility that Hiss may have been "duped" by Communist party spies, liberals henceforth took pains to disassociate themselves from political activities that might prove embarrassing. The Hiss case, together with the arrest of other spies in Britain, also reinforced the image of the Soviet Union as an internal menace. It solidified the Cold War truism that association with the American Communist Party was equivalent to service to the Soviet state. HUAC's Richard Nixon, who had sparked the Hiss investigation, promptly denounced "high officials" for concealing a larger subversive "conspiracy" in American government.

McCarthy and Subversion

One month after the Hiss conviction, Senator Joseph McCarthy captured national attention by announcing proof of a Communist conspiracy in government. "I have in my hands," he told the Women's Republican Club in Wheeling, West Virginia, "a list of 205 [government employees] that were made known to the Secretary of State as being members of the Communist party and who nevertheless are still working and shaping policy in the State Department." In later versions McCarthy changed the number of alleged Communists but he vigorously defended his claim that subversives permeated the Truman administration.

McCarthy's attacks on communism mirrored the national mood. The arrest of Julius and Ethel Rosenberg in June 1950 on charges of transmitting atom bomb secrets to the Soviet Union during World War II underscored the domestic threat. (In a controversial legal case, the couple was convicted and electrocuted in 1953.) Two years earlier, Senator Karl Mundt and Congressman Nixon had unsuccessfully sponsored legislation for controlling the activities of domestic Communists. Revived by Democratic Senator Patrick McCarran of Nevada in 1950, the Internal Security Act authorized the president to declare an "internal security emergency" and to detain suspected dissidents. The legislation banned Communists from defense industries, established a Subversive Activities Control Board, required Communists to register with the attorney general, and excluded Communists from obtaining passports. Truman vetoed the bill, "because any governmental stifling of the free expression of opinion is a long step toward totalitarianism." Congress soon overrode the veto by an overwhelming margin.

McCarthy's accusations concerning Communists in government attracted conservative Republicans, who despite occasional misgivings, supported such attacks on the Truman administration. During 1950, a Senate investigating committee, chaired by Maryland Democrat Millard Tydings, found no evidence to support McCarthy's charges and concluded that the allegations were "a fraud and a hoax." Yet the Senate split along strict party lines in accepting the report. Such party loyalty enabled McCarthy to remain a presence, if not a factor, in the 1950 congressional elections. Reiterating his accusations in Maryland, McCarthy smeared Tydings as a pro-communist and contributed to the senator's defeat. Meanwhile, in California, Richard Nixon defeated Helen Gahagan Douglas, whom he dubbed the "Pink Lady," to win election to the Senate.

Following the 1950 elections, McCarran's Senate Internal Security subcommittee focused on communist influence at the United Nations, while HUAC resumed investigations of Hollywood in 1951. Meanwhile, McCarthy's accusations of Communists in the State Department gained wide public attention. Truman called him a liar. But, significantly, the administration reacted to the charges not by defending the civil liberties of the accused, but by affirming its own anti-communist credentials. In April 1951, Truman issued an executive order introducing a new standard for ferreting out subversives: a federal employee could be fired not when there were "reasonable grounds" but rather when there was "reasonable doubt" about the person's loyalty. The burden of proof thus shifted from the accuser to the accused. In 1952 Truman signed the

McCarran-Walter Immigration Act, providing the president with power to exclude from American borders anyone deemed "detrimental" to the national interest. The law also limited immigration from countries under communist control and facilitated expulsion of undesirable aliens.

THE KOREAN WAR

Crisis conditions led to a reformulation of American foreign policy in 1950. At Truman's request the National Security Council prepared a comprehensive analysis in a document labeled NSC-68. "The Soviet Union, unlike previous aspirants to hegemony," it asserted, "is animated by a new fanatic faith, antithetical to our own, and seeks to impose its absolute authority over the rest of the world." Therefore, the United States must be prepared to halt Soviet expansion and to reimpose pro-American governments throughout the world. Such goals demanded a global defense system that included hydrogen bombs, expansion of conventional military forces, and a network of international alliances. To finance this policy, NSC-68 recommended a quadrupling of the $13 billion national defense budget. This costly plan faced considerable opposition in Congress. Moreover, since 1948 the Soviet Union had avoided any overt action to justify American military intervention.

Suddenly, on June 25, 1950, North Korean troops invaded South Korea. Six months earlier, Acheson had remarked in a speech to the National Press Club that Korea and Taiwan lay beyond the American "defense perimeter" in the Pacific. The statement, challenged by Republican conservatives, justified a reduction of aid to Chiang Kai-shek. But as North Korean armies advanced quickly, Truman ordered American military assistance to South Korea and directed the Seventh Fleet to sail between mainland China and Taiwan to prevent an invasion of the Nationalist-held islands. The next day the United States called an emergency session of the U.N. Security Council, which branded North Korea an aggressor. (The Soviet delegation, boycotting the Security Council on another matter, missed the critical vote.) When South Korean armies continued to collapse, Truman ordered American troops into action. "The attack upon Korea," he declared, "makes it plain beyond all doubt that communism has passed beyond the use of subversion to conquer independent nations." The U.N. subsequently approved Truman's action, giving international sanction to American policy. Sixteen nations eventually participated in the war, but most of the resources came from the United States.

Truman's intervention in Korea stemmed from his conviction that the United States had to "draw the line" against Communist aggression and demonstrate its willingness to fight the Soviets anywhere in the world. But as with his decisions to challenge the Berlin blockade and develop hydrogen bombs, the president bypassed consultation with congressional leaders, thereby setting important precedents for successors. Taft promptly denounced Truman's "complete usurpation...of authority to use the armed forces." But public opinion supported the president's action. Indeed, his subsequent claim to be enforcing U.N. policy won favor among liberals, even though the American military commander, General Douglas MacArthur, took orders directly and exclusively from Washington.

Exhibit 9–9. Korean War.

1. Maximum advance of North Koreans, Sept. 1950
2. Maximum advance of United Nations, Nov. 1950
3. Armistice Zone, July 1953

Yet Truman's failure to build a political consensus with Congress to support the Korean war damaged his relations with the legislature.

American forces arrived in Korea just in time to stop a complete North Korean victory. After hard fighting near the southern port of Pusan, the U.N. allies forced the enemy to retreat. At the start of the war, the United States insisted that fighting was "solely for the purpose of restoring the Republic of Korea to its status prior to the invasion." In September 1950, however, Truman authorized an advance north of the 38th parallel. MacArthur promised victory by Christmas. But 80 percent of America's 142,000 casualties followed from this decision. In October, Truman conferred with MacArthur at Wake Island and agreed to allow American troops to proceed to the Yalu River, which bordered China. Alarmed by American advances, China rushed troops to assist North Korea. The bloodiest fighting of the war forced the U.N. armies into a retreat south of the 38th parallel.

General Douglas MacArthur greets President Truman at Wake Island in the Pacific to discuss Korean War strategy in 1950. It was the only time the two met. Truman fired his general the next year.

Confrontation with China raised the possibility of another world war, including the use of nuclear weapons. Truman, however, exercised his power as commander-in-chief to restrain MacArthur and prevent an attack on Manchuria. By 1951 battle lines again stabilized around the 38th parallel. But MacArthur criticized the limits of American involvement. "There is no substitute for victory," he declared. Unfamiliar with the concept of limited war, public opinion appeared ambivalent, showing both strong support for the use of atomic bombs and a desire to withdraw from the war altogether. When Truman announced a stalemated "cease fire," however, MacArthur, harboring his own presidential ambitions, publicly criticized the president's "no-win" policy. Exasperated by MacArthur's insubordination, Truman fired the general in April 1951. The decision provoked the wrath of conservatives who spoke of impeaching the president and welcomed MacArthur home with parades and a unique address to a joint session of Congress. The general took the opportunity to condemn the idea of limited war. The removal of MacArthur facilitated the opening of truce negotiations that began in 1951 and lasted for two years, while the fighting continued under the command of General Matthew Ridgeway. Truman's refusal to repatriate Communist prisoners-of-war who declined to return to their homelands stalled negotiations. Once again, Truman's failure to consult with Congress intensified criticism from Capitol Hill. The impasse ended only after the inauguration of the next administration in 1953.

The Korean war justified the military buildup envisioned in NSC-68. Wartime appropriations expanded the armed forces and nuclear arsenal and multiplied overseas bases. Funding for aircraft research and development, for example, escalated from $1.8 to $3.1 billion. Furthermore, the CIA augmented its size and scope of operations, consolidating its covert action capacity in the Directorate of Plans and overall personnel from less than five thousand in 1950 to fifteen thousand by 1955. The war led the president to hold regular meetings with the National Security Council, setting a precedent for Truman's successors. To check inflation, Congress gave Truman authority to establish wage, price, and rent controls. In December 1950, the president declared a "national emergency" and implemented those powers, stabilizing the cost of living index for the remainder of the war. The military crisis also emboldened Truman to seize operations of the steel industry to end a strike in 1952, but the Supreme Court ruled the act unconstitutional.

The Korean crisis prompted the administration to proceed with plans to rearm Germany. When France objected, Truman offered the permanent peacetime stationing of American troops in Europe to assure stability. Predictably, congressional conservatives such as Taft and Kenneth Wherry, Republican Senate floor leader, protested against the unprecedented peacetime executive commitments. In the "Great Debate" of 1951 Taft, Wherry, and former president Herbert Hoover led Republicans in severing the bipartisan foreign policy that had characterized American politics since 1947. The Republicans attacked the futility of the poorly executed land war in Korea and expressed frustration that Chiang Kai-shek had not been permitted to enter the fray. But they focused on the unilateral nature of Truman's military decision-making and insisted that Congress had a role to play in the formation of foreign policy. Dramatizing these concerns, Wherry introduced a Senate resolution that blocked American troops from Europe without approval from Congress. Although testimony from NATO's supreme commander, General Dwight D. Eisenhower, blunted some of the criticism, Congress passed a compromise version of the resolution that limited troop deployments to four divisions.

The Korean war also stimulated a more aggressive policy in Asia. Although the administration had been prepared to accept a Chinese invasion of Taiwan in early 1950, the Korean conflict provided an excuse to send the Seventh Fleet to protect the besieged island. Truman also deepened American involvement in Indochina. When Ho Chi Minh, leader of the anti-French liberation movement, accepted support from China and the Soviet Union in early 1950, the United States offered additional aid to France. After the Korean war began, Truman increased this assistance to include military personnel to assist the French. "If Indochina went," explained a State Department official in 1951, "the fall of Burma and the fall of Thailand would be absolutely inevitable." These would be followed by communist victories in Malaya and India. Such assumptions led to increasing commitments in Southeast Asia that culminated in the Vietnam war.

Investment in the French empire contrasted with the lack of support for colonized peoples. In his 1949 inauguration address, Truman introduced the "Point Four" program, asserting that the United States had a responsibility to spread "the benefits of our scientific advances and industrial progress" to the "underdeveloped areas" of the world. But the Point Four foreign aid program offered no alternatives to existing economic relations: "underdeveloped areas" were seen only as suppliers of raw materials and consumers of industrial goods. Rather than a humanitarian program, Point Four funded economic studies to facilitate private business investment. Even so, the administration could not persuade Congress to appropriate more than a token $27 million in 1950. Consequently the government spent more Point Four money in industrialized areas like Canada than in impoverished nations like India.

Such priorities reflected the overwhelming emphasis on using pro-capitalist countries as allies in the Cold War. Thus the United States moved to solidify relations with Japan in a new treaty of 1951. The pact restored Japanese control of the home islands but allowed American occupation of Okinawa and the stationing of American troops on Japanese territory. To overcome objections from Japan's former enemies in the Pacific, the United States promised to protect Australia and New Zealand from attack, an agreement formalized in the ANZUS treaty of 1951. With such alliances, the United States established an anti-communist barrier against Chinese and Soviet expansion in the Pacific.

Alliances with former enemies also promoted support of Italy and Spain. In 1951 the western allies lifted military restrictions imposed on Italy at the end of World War II. At the same time, Truman reversed his opposition to Franco's Spain, culminating in a 1953 treaty that allowed American military bases in Spain in exchange for economic and military assistance. (Meanwhile, within the United States, the attorney general placed the Veterans of the Abraham Lincoln Brigade, whose members had fought against Franco in the Spanish civil war, on a list of subversive organizations.) In supporting Spain, Italy, Germany, and Japan against China and the Soviet Union, Truman had ironically reversed the Grand Alliance of World War II.

By 1952, however, the administration had lost control of its foreign and domestic policies. Truman's commitment to containment had wrecked earlier State Department hopes for an international Open Door. Even worse, containment had bogged down in the "limited" Korean war, which promised neither victory nor an early end. On the home front, the Fair Deal lacked a political base to overcome the opposition of congressional conservatives. Seeking support for his foreign policy, Truman allowed his liberal programs to languish. Meanwhile McCarthy continued his campaign to expose alleged Communists in government. Revelations of corruption by administration officials compounded Truman's difficulties. Republican leaders hoped to reverse these patterns by capturing the White House in 1952.

SUGGESTED READINGS

The major issues of the Truman years are explored in Alonzo L. Hamby, *Beyond the New Deal: Harry S. Truman and American Liberalism* (1973). A conventional and sympathetic account of the Truman presidency is Robert J. Donovan's two volume study *Conflict and Crisis* (1977) and *Tumultuous Years* (1982). A good biography is Roy Jenkins, *Truman* (1986), which may be supplemented by the briefer Robert H. Ferrell, *Harry S. Truman and the Modern American Presidency* (1983). Also useful as an introduction to the period is an anthology, Barton J.

Bernstein, ed., *Politics and Policies of the Truman Administration* (1970). A convenient collection of primary sources is Barton J. Bernstein and Allen Matusow, eds., *The Truman Administration* (1966).

Some of the domestic policies of the Truman administration are examined in the works by McCoy, Ruetten, and Davies listed at the end of chapter 2. On farm policies, see Allen Matusow, *Farm Policies and Politics in the Truman Years* (1967); for labor, see R. Alton Lee, *Truman and Taft-Hartley* (1966). For a landmark case involving the relationship between government and business, see Maeva Marcus, *Truman and the Steel Seizure Case* (1977). The Wallace candidacy is described in Richard J. Walton, *Henry Wallace, Harry Truman, and the Cold War* (1976), which contains many primary sources, and Norman D. Markowitz, *The Rise and Fall of the People's Century: Henry A. Wallace and American Liberalism* (1973). James T. Patterson's *Mr. Republican: A Biography of Robert A. Taft* (1972) examines the career of the leading conservative.

The domestic anti-Communist crusade is described by Francis H. Thompson, *The Frustration of Politics: Truman, Congress, and the Loyalty Drive, 1945–1953* (1979); Athan Theoharis, *Seeds of Repression: Harry S. Truman and the Origins of McCarthyism* (1971); and Alan D. Harper, *The Politics of Loyalty* (1969). The impact of the Red Scare is thoroughly documented in David Caute, *The Great Fear: The Anti-Communist Purge Under Truman and Eisenhower* (1978). The anti-Communist investigations of Hollywood are detailed in Larry Ceplair and Steven Englund, *The Inquisition in Hollywood: Politics in the Film Community, 1930–1960* (1980) and Victor Navasky, *Naming Names* (1980). There are numerous books about the dramatic political trials of the era: Allan Weinstein's *Perjury: The Hiss-Chambers Case* (1978) believes Hiss was guilty, while John Chabot Smith's *Alger Hiss: The True Story* (1977). avers his innocence; Ronald Radosh and Joyce Milton's *The Rosenberg File* (1983) assert the guilt of the Rosenbergs, while their innocence is defended by Walter and Miriam Schneir, *Invitation to an Inquest* (1983). A good background to such trials is Stanley Kutler, *The American Inquisition: Justice and Injustice in the Cold War* (1982). The role of the FBI is detailed in Richard Gid Powers, *Secrecy and Power: The Life of J. Edgar Hoover* (1987) and Athan G. Theoharis and John Stuart Cox, *The Boss: J. Edgar Hoover and the Great American Inquisition* (1988).

For Joseph McCarthy, the best starting point is David M. Oshinsky, *A Conspiracy So Immense: The World of Joe McCarthy* (1983), but also see the titles listed at the end of chapter 4. The close relationship between domestic anti-Communism and foreign policy is presented in Richard M. Freeland, *The Truman Doctrine and the Origins of McCarthyism* (1972). For the split between liberals and radicals, see William O'Neill, *A Better World: The Great Schism: Stalinism and the American Intellectuals* (1983) and Mary Sperling McAuliffe, *Crisis on the Left* (1978).

The literature on the Cold War is vast. A sensible and readable introduction is Walter Lafeber, *America, Russia, and the Cold War* (1985), as is Bernard Weisberger, *Cold War, Cold Peace* (1984). More detailed on the origins of postwar foreign policy is Daniel Yergin, *Shattered Peace: The Origins of the Cold War and the National Security State* (1977). A valuable analysis of foreign policy issues is John Lewis Gaddis, *Strategies of Containment: A Critical Appraisal of Postwar American National Security Policy* (1982). The importance of the atom bomb in foreign policy and military planning is analyzed carefully in Gregg Harken, *The*

Winning Weapon: The Atomic Bomb in the Cold War, 1945–1950 (1980). The role of key personalities in policy making emerges in Robert L. Messer, *The End of an Alliance: James F. Byrnes, Roosevelt, Truman, and the Origins of the Cold War* (1982). The persistence of noninterventionism is the subject of Justus D. Doenecke, *Not to the Swift: The Old Isolationists in the Cold War* (1979). A useful anthology of dissenters from Trumans's policies is Thomas G. Paterson, ed., *Cold War Critics* (1971).

The Cold War in Asia is described in Robert M. Blum, *Drawing the Line: The Origin of the American Containment Policy in East Asia* (1982); William Whitney Stueck, Jr., *The Road to Confrontation: American Policy Toward China and Korea, 1947–1950* (1981); and Nancy Tucker, *Patterns in the Dust: Chinese American Relations and the Recognition Controversy, 1949–1950* (1983). The background of the Korean War is best studied in James Irving Matray, *The Reluctant Crusade: American Foreign Policy in Korea, 1941–1950* (1985), which may be supplemented by Bruce Cumings, *The Origins of the Korean War* (1981) and Rosemary Foot, *The Wrong War: American Policy and the Dimensions of the Korean Conflict, 1950–1953* (1985). Still valuable are David Rees, *Korea* (1964) and Ronald Caridi, *The Korean War and American Politics* (1968).

American policy in the Middle East is presented in Aaron David Miller, *The Search for Security: Saudi Arabian Oil and American Foreign Policy, 1939–1949* (1980); Barry Rubin, *Paved With Good Intentions: American Experience in Iran* (1980); and Zvi Ganin, *Truman, American Jewry, and Israel, 1945–1948* (1979). For international economic affairs, see Fred L. Block, *The Origins of International Economic Disorder* (1977). Also insightful is Ernest R. May, *"Lessons" of the Past: The Use and Misuse of History in American Foreign Policy* (1973).

Opposite Page:
"I Like Ike": Candidate Dwight D. Eisenhower and his wife, Mamie, greet a seven-year-old polio victim during the 1952 cam-paign in Syracuse, New York.

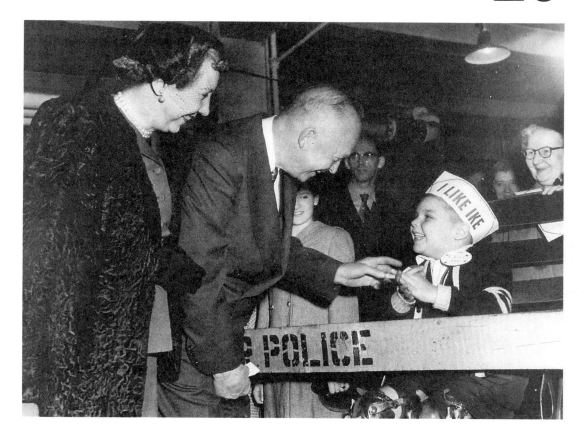

10

THE EISENHOWER CONSENSUS, 1952-1960

Inter-American Conference, declaring that Communist control of "any American State" endangered "the peace of America." Guatemala alone voted against this new interpretation of the Monroe Doctrine. Two months later Arbenz received a shipment of arms from Czechoslovakia, confirming administration fears. The next month a CIA-backed, rebel army and mercenary force invaded and bombed Guatemala and defeated Arbenz. At the same time American military officers in Germany established a blockade of Soviet shipments to Guatemala, in violation of international freedom of the seas. Despite British protests against such interference, administration policy won bipartisan approval at home. "There is no question here of United States interference in the domestic affairs of any American State," insisted Senator Lyndon Johnson.

Claiming to have saved Guatemala from an international conspiracy, the administration arranged to support the regime of Colonel Carlos Castillo-Armas with $90 million of economic and military aid. Armas returned the nationalized land to United Fruit, provided tax benefits for the large corporation, crushed the labor union movement, and took away the vote from illiterate people, who comprised 70 percent of the population. While using force to restore conditions favorable to American investment, the administration had aligned with a reactionary military government in Central America.

CORPORATE COMMONWEALTH

In domestic affairs Eisenhower attempted to steer a middle course between unregulated capitalism and an activist state. The president believed that government should be used to moderate economic conflict and sustain growth without threatening private enterprise or becoming too burdensome. Eisenhower saw the administrative state as a mediator between society's interests and hoped that cooperation and consensus, not coercion, would direct the nation toward social harmony. Instead of prosecuting violations of antitrust laws, for example, the administration preferred negotiated settlements between government and business. The president, moreover, determined to reduce the scope of federal government activities, supporting Secretary of the Treasury George Humphrey's efforts to balance the federal budget by curtailing government expenses. But Eisenhower would not agree to cut basic New Deal programs such as social security and minimum wages. To balance the budget, therefore, the administration reluctantly delayed a tax cut. And despite Humphrey's most frugal efforts and the sharp criticism of conservative Republicans, government expenditures remained a basic prop of the economy.

Although Eisenhower joined "corporate liberals" in retaining New Deal regulations and social welfare nets, he sided with conservative defense of the petroleum industry against federal regulation. The president strongly believed that a prosperous oil industry ranked as an essential ingredient of national defense. For more than a decade, the federal government had contested the claim of several coastal states, particularly Texas, Louisiana, and California, to jurisdiction over tideland oil. Since the major petroleum companies expected beneficial legislation from state governments, they supported the state claims. Conservative Republicans opposed federal control of private business and also supported the

Eisenhower came home in June 1952 to seek the presidential nomination. Benefitting by his immense popularity and some astute convention maneuvering by Lodge, the general captured a first-ballot nomination. As a concession to conservatives, Eisenhower chose as his running mate the conservative Californian, Richard Milhous Nixon.

While Eisenhower grandiosely offered "to lead a great crusade...for freedom," K1C2 dictated the Republican platform. "There are no Communists in the Republican Party," it boasted, whereas Democrats "shielded Traitors...in high places." Denouncing containment as "negative, futile, and immoral," Republicans vowed to bring "genuine independence" to the "captive peoples" of eastern Europe, a promise that appealed to eastern European ethnics who usually voted Democratic. The platform also adopted a conservative position on civil rights insisting that state governments had primary responsibility in that area.

The Democratic spotlight flashed briefly on Tennessee's Senator Estes Kefauver, who won a series of primary contests. But Democratic leaders, including Truman, feared the senator's investigations of organized crime would hurt the party in the cities and turned instead to Governor Adlai Stevenson of Illinois. Stevenson, a cultivated liberal, appeared as a voice of reason, promising simply to "talk sense to the American people." To balance the ticket in the South, the candidate chose as his running mate Senator John Sparkman of Alabama.

Despite the disadvantages of associating with the Truman administration, Stevenson's campaign revealed a continuity of Democratic principles and policies. Defending the Korean war as "a long step toward building a security system in Asia," Stevenson echoed the president's attack on domestic Communism. The candidate took a moderate position on civil rights, emphasizing the importance of state sovereignty. Only after intense criticism form liberals did he endorse a permanent Fair Employment Practices Commission (FEPC). This belated gesture cost Stevenson support among blacks, while alienating southern Democrats. Stevenson further angered Gulf Coast Democrats by opposing state control of offshore oil wells. The candidate's hesitancy to attack the Taft-Hartley labor law also offended a traditional Democratic labor constituency.

Eisenhower, meanwhile, posed as a candidate above parties. After making peace with Taft, he scrupulously avoided antagonizing Old Guard Republicans. Though personally insulted by Senator Joseph McCarthy's attack on General George Marshall, Eisenhower's former superior, the nominee quietly deleted a defense of Marshall when speaking in McCarthy's home state of Wisconsin. Eisenhower also avoided direct attacks on Truman, leaving partisan campaign oratory to Nixon, who denounced "Adlai the appeaser...who got a Ph.D. from Dean Acheson's College of Cowardly Communist Containment."

Nixon's verbal ammunition suddenly exploded when newspapers reported that the vice-presidential candidate had a secret "millionaire's" fund to defray political expenses while serving in the Senate. When Democrats used the issue to reply to Republican accusations about a "mess in Washington," Eisenhower's advisers urged him to drop Nixon from the ticket. But while the presidential nominee delayed, Nixon seized the initiative, buying television time to defend his personal honesty. Emphasizing that his family had not profited from politics, Nixon said his wife still wore a "plain Republican cloth coat" and that despite criticism he would not return a gift his daughter had received, a cocker spaniel named Checkers. The performance seemed sentimental, but proved effective. As public opinion rose in Nixon's favor, Eisenhower decided to keep him on the ticket. The Checkers speech demonstrated the immense political significance of television, highlighting the importance of a candidate's image and suggesting that a politician could effectively appeal over the heads of party leaders to the voters. For Nixon, the speech provided confidence in the medium. In later years he returned to television to win vindication for other aspects of his career, though seldom with the success of the 1952 effort.

Supporting the basic premises of Truman's Cold War, Eisenhower avoided the militant rhetoric of the Republican platform on matters of foreign policy. He approved Truman's intervention in Korea, but also opposed General MacArthur's call for all-out war. When Stevenson argued that the only "answer" to Korea was to "keep it up as long as we have to," Eisenhower hinted at alternative policies. His military experience enabled him to speak with authority. In a late campaign speech in Detroit, Eisenhower suggested that ending the war required his personal presence in Korea. "I shall make that trip," he declared. "I shall go to Korea." Eisenhower's promise touched the hopes of a war-weary nation.

Portraying himself as a nonpartisan soldier, Eisenhower achieved a stunning victory. He captured nearly thirty-four million votes (55 percent) to Stevenson's twenty-seven million (44 percent) and swept the Electoral College 442 to 89. The Republican ticket carried four southern states, breaking the Democrats' "solid

Exhibit 10–1. Election of 1952.

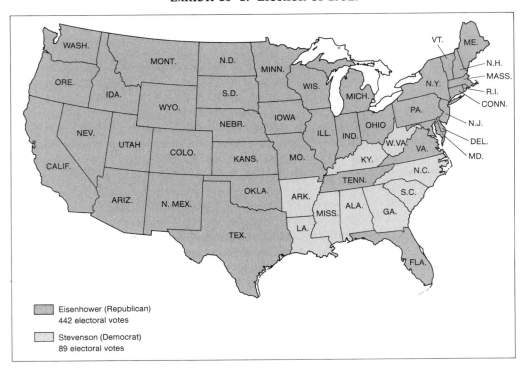

South" for the first time since Al Smith's defeat in 1928. Eisenhower also attracted traditional Democrats in the big cities—blacks, Catholics, and ethnics. And on his coattails, he pulled a Republican majority in both houses of Congress.

Republicans exulted in the destruction of the New Deal coalition. The reelection of conservatives like McCarthy and the defeat of several of his critics seemed to vindicate the anti-Communist crusade. But voting statistics also indicated that Eisenhower ran far ahead of other Republicans, including McCarthy. The election of 1952 was an Eisenhower victory, not a Republican one, and the party controlled the House by only eight seats, the Senate by one. During the 1950s voting behavior generally followed party lines. Voters seemed less interested in political ideology and appeared more sensitive to short-term issues or party affiliation. Eisenhower managed, however, to attract independent voters and Democrats, including a well-funded "Democrats for Eisenhower" organization headed by Hollywood actor Ronald Reagan. The breadth of Eisenhower's support reflected not only his personal popularity but also a political consensus based on internationalism abroad and minimum social welfare at home.

WAGING THE COLD WAR

Eisenhower's success among Democrats reinforced his political philosophy of consensus. As a career military officer the former general represented the new managerial middle class of the twentieth century. In a world dominated by large corporate bureaucracies, he emphasized the importance of voluntary cooperation between government and business. Nearly all his cabinet—including Secretary of State John Foster Dulles, Secretary of Defense Charles E. Wilson, Secretary of the Treasury George M. Humphrey, and Attorney General Herbert Brownell Jr.—came from the highest ranks of corporate management and law. (The exception was Secretary of Labor Martin Durkin, a plumber, who soon resigned and was replaced by a department store personnel manager). To streamline his administration, Eisenhower relied more heavily than Truman on the National Security Council (NSC), but the president frequently overrode the advice of the Joint Chiefs of Staff. Eisenhower distrusted special interests, partisan conflicts, or mass movements. Contrary to the wishes of Old Guard Republicans, he preserved the New Deal and even established a cabinet level Department of Health, Education and Welfare in 1953. But the president initiated no social welfare legislation, believing that enlarged government services would stultify a free capitalist society. "We cannot risk living all our lifetime under emergency measures," he said in cancelling economic controls established by Truman during the Korean war.

Eisenhower envisioned a world order based on free trade and protected by restrained military power. On many occasions, he resisted pressure from military and civilian advisers to increase the Pentagon budget or to rush rashly into war. "I just don't believe you can buy one hundred percent security in every little corner of the world," the president said in 1954. Yet Eisenhower permitted the nuclear arsenal to expand from hundreds to thousands of weapons and ordered the deployment of nuclear weapons overseas. He also relied increasingly on covert

The president looks right, points left: During presidential press conferences Eisenhower demonstrated considerable skill in deflecting questions and keeping reporters from probing too deeply into White House affairs.

operations of the CIA, headed by Allen Dulles, brother of the secretary of state. Always the cold warrior, Eisenhower assumed that the United States should maintain military superiority over Communist nations. "Forces of good and evil are massed and armed and opposed as rarely before in history," the president explained in his inaugural address. "Freedom is pitted against slavery; lightness against the dark....In the final choice, a soldier's pack is not so heavy a burden as a prisoner's chains."

These metaphors of morality and struggle reflected the new administration's approach to foreign policy. Determined to take the initiative in the Cold War, Eisenhower and Secretary of State Dulles replaced the Democratic strategy of containment with a new doctrine of "massive retaliation." Dulles argued that neither the American people nor the nation's economy could sustain a series of limited conventional wars like Korea. Instead, he echoed conservative policy by calling for reliance upon air and naval superiority, a position Eisenhower supported. The nations of the "free world," the president proclaimed, would be prepared "to retaliate instantly" against the ultimate source of evil, the Soviet Union, "by means and at places of our own choosing." Nuclear weapons aimed at the Kremlin—not at some border area—would deter further Communist expansion. A National Security Council memorandum of 1953 spoke of regaining initiative in the Cold War by demonstrating a "capability of inflicting massive retaliatory damage by offensive striking power." In military terms massive retaliation merely reaffirmed the "air-atomic" strategy approved by Truman and updated containment with the doctrine of nuclear deterrence. But although Eisenhower never intended to go to war to overturn Communist control of "captive nations" in eastern Europe, the administration hoped to use its nuclear arsenal as a symbolic weapon in a moral and political crusade of anti-Communist liberation.

Massive retaliation had distinct domestic advantages. Conservative Republicans led by Taft had long dissented from soaring military budgets. Eisenhower shared these sentiments, though he believed that cost cutting should not compromise the nation's strength. The emphasis on air power and nuclear weapons provided a cheaper solution. Eisenhower's "New Look" in military policy enabled the administration to reduce the size of conventional forces, thus cutting $7 billion from Truman's projected budget. Subsequent opinion polls found wide support for these reductions.

Eisenhower's enormous prestige as a military leader as well as his electoral popularity enabled him to accomplish in Korea what Truman had been reluctant to suggest. After fulfilling his campaign promise to go to Korea in December 1952, the new president recognized that a continuation of the ground war would only add to the imbalanced budget. Secretary Dulles joined conservative senators such as Styles Bridges and William Knowland in advocating a war for complete victory. But Eisenhower, primarily concerned with reaching a political settlement, rejected the use of atomic weapons.

The president instead used a show of force to persuade the enemy to negotiate. In his inaugural address Eisenhower announced the removal of the Seventh Fleet from the area separating Taiwan from the Chinese mainland, hinting that he might "unleash" Chiang Kai-shek against the Communist stronghold. The White House also used diplomatic channels to notify China that the United States could resort to nuclear weapons if Korean negotiations failed. The death of Josef Stalin in March 1953 added to China's uncertainties about Soviet support. By then, both China and Eisenhower accepted the limits of the military struggle. The main stumbling point now involved the return of prisoners of war. Hoping to discourage future Communist reliance on loyal troops, the United States refused to require the repatriation of Communist prisoners who did not wish to go home. To force the issue Dulles again threatened war with atomic weapons while the State Department presented a new proposal. Within three weeks the Chinese accepted the idea of voluntary repatriation of POWs. South Korea's dictator, Syngman Rhee, nearly thwarted the truce by suddenly releasing twenty-seven thousand prisoners who promptly disappeared into the countryside. The move violated the armistice agreement. But despite Dulles's advice, Eisenhower ignored Rhee's antics and the United States signed a truce in July 1953. "We have won an armistice on a single battlefield—not peace in the world," Eisenhower reminded the nation. "We may not now relax our guard nor cease our quest."

For most Americans the end of the Korean war brought not a sense of celebration, but plain relief. Thirty-three thousand Americans had died to defend an area that Secretary of State Dean Acheson had acknowledged in 1950 as beyond the nation's strategic defense perimeter. Sensitive to criticism from conservatives about selling out Korea to the Communists, the White House carefully distinguished the truce from any semblance of weakness, threatening massive retaliation against any further aggression. The retention of American military bases in Korea gave muscle to those threats. The United States also adopted a multi-billion dollar program of economic and military assistance to bolster South Korea. The Korean armistice, then, served to formalize the Truman policy of containment in Asia.

Frustrated by the Korean compromise, conservative Republicans criticized Eisenhower's version of containment. In 1951 Republican Senator John Bricker of Ohio had introduced a constitutional amendment requiring congressional approval of all international agreements. A partisan move, Bricker's proposal sought to limit Truman's executive independence, but the measure never came to the Senate floor. The 1952 Republican party platform kept the issue alive, promising to "repudiate all commitments contained in secret understandings such as those of Yalta which aid Communist enslavements." This position reflected strong congressional opposition to presidential independence in foreign policy. But Eisenhower, distrustful of congressional critics, refused to compromise his own presidential powers. Yalta, moreover, provided justification for American presence in West Germany and Berlin. Nevertheless, in 1954 Bricker reintroduced his constitutional amendment. Eisenhower strongly opposed the proposal. But because the president believed in a rigid separation of powers, he exercised minimal leadership in the Senate debates. Democrats, led by Lyndon Johnson of Texas and Walter George of Georgia, saved the president from his own party's conservatives. Though the Bricker amendment won a 60–31 majority, it fell one vote short of the necessary two-thirds required for constitutional amendments. The White House, not Congress, would control subsequent foreign policy.

Eisenhower's policies toward Europe also revealed basic continuities with those of his predecessor. Although the administration spoke about liberating eastern Europe, the principles of massive retaliation appeared too inflexible to respond effectively to minor crises. When East German workers staged anti-Communist protests in June 1953, Dulles could offer only moral encouragement and $15 million of food. Refusing to accept the presence of Soviet power in eastern Europe, however, the administration worked to strengthen American allies in western Europe. Thus when Stalin's successor, Georgi Malenkov, proposed a treaty to neutralize Germany, Eisenhower saw the plan as a ruse to divide the western alliance and promptly rejected the Soviet overture. More concerned with bringing Germany into the West, the administration urged the formation of a European Defense Community. When France objected to rearming Germany, however, the president chose an alternative policy that enabled Germany to rearm under NATO. "These agreements are founded upon the profound yearning for peace which is shared by all the Atlantic peoples," Eisenhower declared. "The agreements endanger no nation." But the entry of Germany into NATO assured the permanent division of central Europe. In 1955 the Soviet Union created the Warsaw Pact, a military alliance that attempted to balance the power of NATO.

SECRET FOREIGN POLICY

While exercising restraint in Korea and Europe, Eisenhower pursued an aggressive, but secret foreign policy beyond the scrutiny of Congress and the public. Under the Central Intelligence Agency Act of 1949, the CIA possessed a multibillion dollar top-secret budget that was exempt from congressional accountability and control. Between 1950 and 1955, the agency tripled in size to fifteen thousand personnel. Besides establishing spy networks around the world, the CIA performed secret operations outside the law that facilitated the formal policy of the State Department. For example, it regularly supported disruptive raids from Taiwan to the Chinese mainland. When such activities were discovered, the United States denied all allegations and used the episodes to denounce its enemies. In 1955 Democratic Senator Mike Mansfield proposed the creation of a congressional intelligence oversight committee, but the Eisenhower administration effectively blocked such interference with foreign policy management by the executive branch.

After futile attempts to penetrate Soviet security in eastern Europe in the early 1950s, the CIA turned its attention to new arenas of the Cold War in the developing ("third") world. In 1953, the United States denied complicity in an American-backed coup d'etat in Iran. Two years earlier, the premier of Iran, Dr. Mohammed Mossadegh, had attempted to end British exploitation by nationalizing the oil wells. The western-owned companies retaliated by instituting a boycott of Iranian oil. Mossadegh appealed to Eisenhower for assistance, but the president rebuffed him, stating "it would not be fair to American taxpayers." Mossadegh soon sought assistance from the Soviet Union. Eisenhower then ordered the CIA to intervene in Iran's internal affairs. In August 1953, American agents provided crucial military support that enabled the hereditary Shah to topple the Mossadegh regime and return to power. In the ensuing negotiations, the nationalized oil wells were replaced by an international consortium, in which American-owned companies held 40 percent interest. The western oil companies then agreed to limit Iranian oil production to maximize their profits at the expense of Iran. By overthrowing Mossadegh, however, the United States not only broke the British oil monopoly, but also placed Iran safely in the non-Communist camp. Continued economic and military aid to the Shah strengthened this realignment. Meanwhile, Eisenhower permitted the private oil companies to conduct American oil diplomacy in the Middle East outside regular diplomatic channels.

The CIA also implemented Eisenhower's foreign policy in Guatemala in 1954. As in Iran, a popular leader, Colonel Jacobo Arbenz, attempted to improve economic conditions by enacting land reform and nationalizing the holdings of the United Fruit Company. Arbenz offered a small compensation for the expropriated property, but United Fruit, backed by the State Department, rejected the sum. The administration then began planning the overthrow of Arbenz with the help of a CIA invasion army trained in Nicaragua and Honduras.

Justifying this new version of dollar diplomacy, the United States described Arbenz as a front for "international communism" which imperiled the entire hemisphere. In March 1954, Washington sponsored a resolution at the Tenth

Inter-American Conference, declaring that Communist control of "any American State" endangered "the peace of America." Guatemala alone voted against this new interpretation of the Monroe Doctrine. Two months later Arbenz received a shipment of arms from Czechoslovakia, confirming administration fears. The next month a CIA-backed, rebel army and mercenary force invaded and bombed Guatemala and defeated Arbenz. At the same time American military officers in Germany established a blockade of Soviet shipments to Guatemala, in violation of international freedom of the seas. Despite British protests against such interference, administration policy won bipartisan approval at home. "There is no question here of United States interference in the domestic affairs of any American State," insisted Senator Lyndon Johnson.

Claiming to have saved Guatemala from an international conspiracy, the administration arranged to support the regime of Colonel Carlos Armas with $90 million of economic and military aid. Armas returned the nationalized land to United Fruit, provided tax benefits for the large corporation, crushed the labor union movement, and took away the vote from illiterate people, who comprised 70 percent of the population. While using force to restore conditions favorable to American investment, the administration had aligned with a reactionary military government in Central America.

CORPORATE COMMONWEALTH

In domestic affairs Eisenhower attempted to steer a middle course between unregulated capitalism and an activist state. The president believed that government should be used to moderate economic conflict and sustain growth without threatening private enterprise or becoming too burdensome. Eisenhower saw the administrative state as a mediator between society's interests and hoped that cooperation and consensus, not coercion, would direct the nation toward social harmony. Instead of prosecuting violations of antitrust laws, for example, the administration preferred negotiated settlements between government and business. The president, moreover, determined to reduce the scope of federal government activities, supporting Secretary of the Treasury George Humphrey's efforts to balance the federal budget by curtailing government expenses. But Eisenhower would not agree to cut basic New Deal programs such as social security and minimum wages. To balance the budget, therefore, the administration reluctantly delayed a tax cut. And despite Humphrey's most frugal efforts and the sharp criticism of conservative Republicans, government expenditures remained a basic prop of the economy.

Although Eisenhower joined "corporate liberals" in retaining New Deal regulations and social welfare nets, he sided with conservative defense of the petroleum industry against federal regulation. The president strongly believed that a prosperous oil industry ranked as an essential ingredient of national defense. For more than a decade, the federal government had contested the claim of several coastal states, particularly Texas, Louisiana, and California, to jurisdiction over tideland oil. Since the major petroleum companies expected beneficial legislation from state governments, they supported the state claims. Conservative Republicans opposed federal control of private business and also supported the states' claims. So did southern Democrats, who saw state control of oil as not only in their economic interests but also as a defense of states rights. In 1946 and again in 1952, Congress passed legislation giving control of offshore oil to the states. Truman vetoed both measures and before leaving office reserved offshore oil for the use of the Navy. But Eisenhower reversed his predecessor's position, and Republicans cooperated with southern Democrats to pass a measure giving control of offshore oil to the states in 1953.

The White House also joined congressional leaders in resisting legislation to alter oil depletion allowances and other tax benefits for the petroleum industry. This alliance reflected the strength of southern Democrats from the oil states, especially Speaker of the House Sam Rayburn and Senate Majority Leader Lyndon Johnson, both of Texas. The coalition worked to end federal control of natural gas. Whereas Truman had vetoed a proposal for industry deregulation, Eisenhower intended to sign such legislation. But when an oil lobbyist tried to bribe a senator during consideration of the bill in 1956, the president felt obliged to veto the measure. Nevertheless, the administration relied on the probusiness Federal Power Commission to protect the natural gas industry from strict regulation. Administration cooperation with the energy industry received another setback when public power advocates exposed collusion between the government and the private Dixon-Yates syndicate, resulting in cancellation of a lucrative contract to provide electricity to customers of the publicly owned Tennessee Valley Authority.

THE ANTI-COMMUNIST CRUSADE

Eisenhower's personal popularity failed to silence conservative criticism of Communist influence in government. Indeed, the president's efforts to stand above the controversy strengthened the most fervent anti-Communists, particularly Joseph McCarthy. Thus the appointment of Scott McLeod, a McCarthy supporter, to head the State Department's personnel program in 1953 accelerated the dismissal of alleged subversives. Soon after taking office, Eisenhower also revised Truman's loyalty program, issuing Executive Order 10450, which established new standards for dismissal. Where Truman required evidence of disloyalty or subversion, Eisenhower authorized dismissal on the grounds that an individual's employment "may not be clearly consistent with the interests of national security." Under the new guidelines, Eisenhower removed twenty-two hundred "security risks" in his first year in office. Few were actually charged with disloyalty.

The administration's definition of security risks revealed other underlying assumptions within the Cold War consensus. Besides obvious cases of negligence, criminality, and insanity, Eisenhower's criteria for dismissal included "notoriously disgraceful conduct, habitual use of intoxicants to excess, drug addiction, or sexual perversion." Persons practicing such acts were risks because they were vulnerable to blackmail, and government loyalty boards frequently dismissed homosexuals. In a single case in 1960, for example, the National Security Agency fired twenty-six employees for sexual deviation. Such cases testified less about political beliefs than about cultural values. During the 1952 campaign,

Republican Senator Joseph R. McCarthy, flanked by his aides captured national attention by claiming to have "proof" of Communist subversion inside the federal government.

Stevenson, who had recently been divorced from his wife, took special care to remain in female company to counter rumors he was a homosexual. *Life* magazine nonetheless criticized the candidate's "Softness Toward Communism," while the anti-Communist *New Leader* praised the political "hards" who were "willing to risk reaction and war...to fight Communism." In a culture that defined courage in terms of hardness and strength, homosexuals symbolized the "soft" side of males.

The loyalty issue coincided with the suppression of political dissent within the federal government. Shortly after moving into the State Department, Dulles fired several career diplomats, including some prestigious China experts such as John Carter Vincent and John Paton Davies who had predicted Mao's victory in 1949. The secretary of state also encouraged the departure of George Kennan, viewed as the architect of containment. To replace Kennan as ambassador to the Soviet Union, the administration supported Charles E. Bohlen. But rigid anti-Communists questioned the nomination, pointing out that Bohlen had acted as presidential translator at Yalta. Eisenhower then permitted two senators to examine Bohlen's confidential FBI file. Their favorable report led to senatorial confirmation. Nonetheless Taft warned the president: "No more Bohlens."

J. Robert Oppenheimer, the celebrated physicist who had directed development of the atomic bomb, also fell victim to the loyalty controversy. (See accompanying biography.) Fearing that Oppenheimer's moral doubts about the hydrogen bomb might influence other scientists, Eisenhower supported the AEC's decision to lift the scientist's security clearance. In yet another controversial case, the president refused clemency to the convicted atomic spies Julius and Ethel Rosenberg, even though the testimony against them appeared ambiguous and the FBI withheld critical evidence. In upholding the sentence federal courts cooperated with government prosecutors to assure that unrepentant Communists would receive ultimate punishment. Eisenhower refused to intervene, charging that atomic spies "may have condemned to death tens of million of innocent people all over the world." In 1953 the Rosenbergs were electrocuted.

"In America," protested the playwright Arthur Miller in *The Crucible,* a 1953 version of the Salem witch trials, "any man who is not reactionary in his views is open to the charge of alliance with the Red hell." Foremost in making such accusations was Senator Joseph McCarthy, a crude, intemperate inquisitor who disregarded formalities in his single-minded search for Communist sympathizers. Even after Eisenhower's inauguration, McCarthy continued to attack Communist influence in government. As chairman of a Senate subcommittee on Government Operations, McCarthy held public hearings in 1953 about the Voice of America, claiming that the State Department's propaganda organ

Ethel and Julius Rosenberg, convicted in a controversial Cold War trial of passing atom bomb "secrets" to the Soviet Union during World War II, were sentenced to death in 1951.

J. ROBERT OPPENHEIMER
1904–1967

The security status of one of the nation's leading atomic physicists provoked a dramatic closed-door clash in 1954 between Cold War loyalty and traditional freedom of scientific inquiry and political association. The ensuing top-secret hearings into the matter of J. Robert Oppenheimer revealed both changing standards of political propriety and a growing concern about "national security" in an age of fundamental insecurity.

A secular Jew who studied quantum mechanics at Harvard, Cambridge, and the University of Göttenburg, Oppenheimer helped to make the University of California at Berkeley the global center of theoretical physics in the 1930s. But the Depression poverty of his students and anti-Semitism in Nazi Germany pushed the affluent bachelor toward social causes. As a "fellow traveler" of the Communist movement popular in intellectual circles, Oppenheimer contributed generous sums to the Communist party because he believed the Communists could effectively mobilize resources to defeat the fascist uprising in Spain. Yet the Roosevelt administration viewed such activity as dangerous "premature anti-fascism."

Both Oppenheimer's socialite wife and brother had Communist affiliations. Once appointed head of the Los Alamos Laboratory in 1942 with responsibility for developing the atomic bomb, however, the scientist cooperated with security investigators by providing the names of program applicants he knew to have Communist backgrounds. Convinced that advancement of the project depended upon keeping Communists out of sensitive positions, the Los Alamos director won a reputation as a man with "unusual discretion with secrets."

As the first nuclear weapon exploded at the Trinity test site in New Mexico in July 1945, Oppenheimer remembered the Sanskrit cry of the Bhagavad-Gita: "I am become Death. The shatterer of worlds." Yet the physicist never regretted his role in the development of the atom bombs which devastated Hiroshima and Nagasaki. Nevertheless, he agreed with most scientists that eventually the Soviet Union would develop a nuclear capacity and recoiled at the unmonitored spread of atomic technology. During 1946 Oppenheimer helped to author politically unpopular proposals for international control of nuclear energy. *(cont.)*

served as a front for Communists. With the tacit consent of Secretary Dulles, McCarthy also meddled in other State Department affairs. Two members of McCarthy's staff, Roy Cohn and G. David Schine, embarked on a chaotic investigation of the United States Information Agency (USIA) in Europe. Their scrutiny of USIA libraries unearthed over thirty thousand "subversive" authors, a category that included Theodore Dreiser, Archibald MacLeish, and Arthur M. Schlesinger, Jr. Facing McCarthy's wrath, the agency removed several thousand volumes from library shelves.

"I will not get into the gutter with that guy," Eisenhower remarked as he avoided direct confrontation with the vitriolic senator. Wishing to prevent a split *(cont.)* As chief advisor to the Atomic Energy Commission, the physicist led efforts to oppose the development of the hydrogen fusion bomb, which he regarded as a "weapon of genocide." Accordingly, Oppenheimer called for the use of tactical nuclear weapons for continental defense instead of the massive strategic bombing preferred by the Air Force. He also insisted that it was technically premature to build nuclear-powered aircraft and opposed construction of atomic-generated submarines.

The AEC cleared Oppenheimer's security status in 1947. But in late 1953 a former congressional staffer sent the FBI a detailed list of accusations against Oppenheimer. The subsequent Bureau report prompted President Eisenhower to demand that a "blank wall" be erected between the physicist and sensitive information. Eisenhower feared that the highly respected scientist might persuade other researchers to abandon the superbomb project. He also wished to head off potentially embarrassing investigations by Joseph McCarthy. Consequently, the president asked the AEC to initiate hearings into Oppenheimer's security clearance.

The agency's Personnel Security Board ruled in a 2–1 vote that as a security risk Oppenheimer should not have access to government secrets. The scientist depicted his associations with "fellow travelers" as naive and apologized for occasional lapses of candor. But physicist Edward Teller testified that although Oppenheimer's loyalty was unquestioned, he lacked the "wisdom and judgment" for a security clearance. Soon the full AEC upheld the security panel's findings. By continuing associations with known Communists and withholding information, the AEC explained, the father of the atom bomb had "consistently placed himself outside the rules that govern others" and "repeatedly exhibited a willful disregard of the normal and proper obligations of society."

By focusing upon Oppenheimer's character, the AEC rejected the view that intellectuals and scientists should be judged differently than military and government personnel. By 1954, many Americans distrusted intellectual cosmopolitans such as Oppenheimer and believed that loyalty to the struggle against Communism was the most important qualification for public service. Without a security clearance, Oppenheimer returned to teaching at Princeton University. In a friendlier political climate, the AEC gave the physicist the prestigious Fermi Award in 1963, but Oppenheimer never again performed government work. ∎

in Republican ranks, the president hoped that by ignoring McCarthy the senator would recede from the limelight. Instead, McCarthy felt emboldened to attack the administration. In September 1953, he launched an investigation of Army security procedures at Fort Monmouth, New Jersey. Concerned about the routine promotion of an army dentist, McCarthy clashed with General Ralph Zwicker, chastising the officer for defending "Communist conspirators." The Army responded by releasing documents showing McCarthy's attempt to obtain special privileges for Cohn's co-worker Private David Schine. McCarthy then ordered a full investigation of the Army, including Eisenhower's Secretary of the Army Robert Stevens.

The president now entered the conflict, refusing to cooperate with the Senate investigation. "In opposing Communism," he told a March 1954 press conference, "we are defeating ourselves if we use methods that do not conform to the American sense of justice." Although Attorney General Herbert Brownell could find no legal precedents for denying subpoenaed documents and personnel, Eisenhower invoked his right of "executive privilege" to block McCarthy's access to his staff. In taking this stand, Eisenhower expressed concern that McCarthy's indiscriminate investigations would uncover the continuing Oppenheimer controversy and disturb scientific work on hydrogen bombs. "We've got to handle this so that all our scientists are not made out to be Reds," Eisenhower remarked. "That goddamn McCarthy is just likely to try such a thing." Such fears reflected the peculiar problems of the modern presidency—the desire for secrecy on matters of nuclear policy, CIA activities, and internal disagreements. To Eisenhower's alarm, McCarthy was threatening to penetrate the secrets of the national security state.

White House resistance to McCarthy coincided with the strategy of Democratic Majority Leader Lyndon Johnson. As McCarthy pursued the investigation of Army security procedures and the Army pressed accusations against McCarthy, Johnson demanded that the public hearings be televised. Beginning in March 1954, all three networks broadcast the much-heralded Army-McCarthy hearings. For thirty-six days the nation witnessed McCarthy's erratic, stormy behavior. While the senator attacked such colleagues as Senator Stuart Symington, threatened witnesses, and ignored legal procedures, his favorable public opinion ratings declined from 50 percent to 34 percent. The hearings climaxed when McCarthy chastised a young Army lawyer for belonging to the National Lawyers Guild, in McCarthy's words, "the legal bulwark of the Communist Party." Chief Army Counsel Joseph Welch used the episode to strike back at the senator from Wisconsin. "Little did I dream you could be so reckless and so cruel," Welch berated McCarthy before the cameras. "Have you no sense of decency, sir, at long last? Have you left no sense of decency?"

When McCarthy added one year to his denunciation of "twenty years of treason," thus implicating Eisenhower in a coverup of Communism, he exceeded his grasp. "Were the junior Senator from Wisconsin in the pay of Communists," Republican Senator Ralph Flanders of Vermont declared, "he could not have done a better job for them." In July 1954, Flanders introduced a resolution to strip McCarthy of his committee chairmanships. But the proposal violated the Senate tradition of seniority on committee matters, and Flanders modified his bill to call for McCarthy's censure by the Senate. In a carefully orchestrated proceeding, a panel of conservative senators, chaired by Republican Arthur Watkins of Utah, recommended censure for conduct that "tended to bring the Senate into dishonor and disrepute." McCarthy continued to rage against his adversaries, accusing the Senate of serving the Communists. But half the Republicans joined the unanimous Democrats in voting his censure by a 67–22 margin. Vice President Nixon, presiding in the Senate, deleted the word *censure* from the final document. It was a formality that made no difference. McCarthy had lost his power. He remained in the Senate, politically ineffective, until his death in 1957.

McCarthy's fall created an illusion that Communist witch hunts had ended. But the attack on Communism extended beyond Congress, revealing the power of systematic political repression. Libraries removed controversial books; school boards and universities fired leftist teachers; industries established blacklists to prevent employment of suspected Communists. Such activities won wide support, even from liberals. Minnesota's liberal Senator Hubert H. Humphrey sponsored the Communist Control Act of 1954, which outlawed the Communist party. "We liberals," added Illinois's Paul Douglas, "must destroy the Communists if this dirty game is to stop."

Encouraged by the anti-Communist consensus, FBI Director J. Edgar Hoover stepped up his attacks on the Communist party. The conviction of leading Communists for violating the Smith Act had been upheld by the Supreme Court in the *Dennis* case of 1951 (See chapter 3). But four years later the Court indicated a willingness to reconsider that decision. In the *Yates* case of 1957, the Court held that violation of the Smith Act required proof not merely of incitement to revolutionary *beliefs*, but incitement to revolutionary *action*. The shift in judicial thinking threatened to derail FBI investigations of Communist party members. Meanwhile, revelations of Stalin's totalitarianism and Soviet aggression in eastern Europe had drastically reduced the party's membership. But since the Communist Control Act stated that the Communist party was "not entitled to any of the rights, privileges, and immunities...[of] legal bodies," Hoover moved to disrupt its remnants with a Counter Intelligence Program (COINTELPRO) introduced in 1956. Using informants, infiltrators, and a variety of "dirty tricks" (forged letters, anonymous telephone calls, police harassment) the FBI doggedly attacked the dwindling Communist movement. Party membership, which had reached eighty thousand during World War II, numbered less than thirty five hundred by the end of 1957. More than half the subscriptions to the party's *Daily Worker* newspaper were held by FBI agents.

AN AGE OF CONSENSUS

Republican leaders expected the anti-Communist crusade to remain an effective campaign weapon in the 1954 congressional elections. Eisenhower, true to his dispassionate style of leadership, avoided the emotionally charged issue. But Nixon, repeating his performance of 1952, attacked the Democrats for tolerating Communists in government. Neither Eisenhower's prestige nor Nixon's rhetoric, however, could overcome the political effects of an economic recession. Although Eisenhower could attract independent voters, other Republicans were linked to traditional party labels. In the end, Democrats won small majorities in both houses of Congress.

Instead of creating partisan conflict between the branches of government, however, the Democratic congressional victories actually encouraged cooperation. Majority Leader Johnson and House Speaker Rayburn, both astute New Dealers from Texas, accepted a political consensus and the balance of power between the parties. Since congressional committee assignments depended on seniority, southerners from the one-party region enjoyed obvious advantages. In 1955, for example, Rayburn proposed a modest tax cut, only to have the president object to this threat to a balanced budget. Republicans joined southern Democrats to defeat the measure. Patterns of congressional representation also strengthened conservative groups. Urban areas, which usually supported liberals, were underrepresented in Congress because state legislatures divided voting districts to suit local needs. The principle of one-person, one vote required a Supreme Court ruling (*Carr v. Baker*) in 1962.

Rejecting conservative laissez-faire attitudes, Eisenhower acknowledged that the federal government "must do its part to advance human welfare and encourage economic growth with constructive actions." Thus the administration continued to subsidize farm prices, even though Secretary of Agriculture Ezra Taft Benson persuaded Congress to lower support levels. While the government guaranteed 90 percent of parity (the earning power of farm prices between 1910–1914) in the Truman era, support for most farm crops dropped to 70 percent under Eisenhower. The president also backed a slight expansion of social security coverage to include self-employed workers and approved modest housing legislation. Using the justification of "national security," Eisenhower signed legislation in 1954 to build the St. Lawrence Seaway to connect the Great Lakes to ocean ports. On the same grounds, the White House endorsed the 1956 Interstate Highway Act. (See chapter 2).

Committed to such "modern Republicanism," Eisenhower presided over a consensus which unified moderates in both political parties through vigorous pursuit of the Cold War. A 1956 survey found no correlation between political opinions on domestic issues and support for a tough stand against international Communism. Democrats and Republicans alike shared a belief in the Communist menace and agreed to seek military superiority. The relationship between military expenditures and economic prosperity also assured minimal resistance to administration requests for large Pentagon budgets.

Foreign Policy in Asia

Democrats nonetheless opposed massive retaliation in the political crisis of Indochina in 1954. Since the Korean war, the United States had supported French attempts to suppress the Viet Minh rebels led by Ho Chi Minh. By 1954 the United States had spent $1.2 billion on military assistance and was financing nearly 80 percent of France's total war costs. These expenses included several hundred "technical" advisers. The administration justified intervention on the grounds that Vietnam provided valuable raw materials such as tin and rubber and remained a vital strategic link in the attempt to halt Communist expansion. The White House also wanted to show support for its French ally in NATO.

Despite American aid, France could not defeat the Viet Minh, who surrounded the French garrison at Dien Bien Phu in 1954. Facing military defeat, France appealed for American assistance, triggering a major debate within the administration. Eisenhower, who saw himself as a crisis manager reducing the levels of Cold War tensions, had no interest in committing the nation to war. Given the doctrine of massive retaliation, American assistance would be limited to air strikes, perhaps with atomic weapons. But this prospect alarmed the British, who feared Soviet retaliation. And congressional Democrats led by Senator Richard Russell of Georgia refused to sanction unilateral intervention.

For Eisenhower, however, Vietnam held the future of Asia. In 1954 a special committee of the NSC called for military victory to "provide tangible evidence of Western strength and determination to defeat Communism." At a press conference that year the president buttressed this directive with the "falling domino" theory: "You have a row of dominos set up, you knock over the first one, and what will happen to the last one is the certainty that it will go over very quickly." The fall of Vietnam would mean that "many human beings pass under a dictatorship that is inimical to the free world." It would interfere with the acquisition of precious resources, and it would imperil Japanese trade, forcing that ally "toward the Communist areas in order to live."

Eisenhower never wavered from this belief that the Viet Minh represented not an anticolonial force but an instrument of world Communism. Consequently, he failed to distinguish between Asian nationalism and an international Communist conspiracy. But Eisenhower had benefited from the experience of Korea. Without support of an ally like Britain and lacking explicit approval from Congress, the president refused to commit large numbers of troops to another land war in Asia. Ironically, Democrat Lyndon Johnson criticized Eisenhower's failure to act when the French surrendered to the Vietnamese in May 1954. "American foreign policy had never in all its history suffered such a stunning reversal," the Senate Majority Leader declared. "We have been caught bluffing by our enemies."

The French defeat made a diplomatic settlement imperative. In July 1954, France signed the Geneva Accords, ending eight years of war by accepting the independence of Vietnam, Laos, and Cambodia. The agreement divided Vietnam militarily at the 17th parallel, but this temporary line did not imply a political separation. To unify the country, national elections, supervised by an international commission, would be held within two years. By acknowledging a Viet Minh government, if only for the northern portions of Vietnam, the Geneva settlement represented a defeat of Eisenhower's anti-Communist foreign policy. The United States announced it would respect the Geneva Accords, but the administration refused to sign the agreement and immediately began to violate its provisions by continuing the secret war against the Viet Minh. As an alternative to Ho Chi Minh, the administration supported Ngo Dinh Diem, an American-educated Catholic seminarian, as premier of the French-controlled portion of the country. The United States also sent a military mission and encouraged acts of sabotage and a propaganda campaign to discredit the Viet Minh in the North.

Besides such covert activities, the United States moved to supplant France's role in Vietnam. Bypassing French administrators, Washington transmitted aid directly to Diem, thus protecting the United States from charges of supporting French colonialism. Such policies led France to withdraw from Vietnam prior to the 1956 election deadline. Quickly stepping into the power vacuum, American advisers began to train a large Vietnamese army "to deter Viet Minh aggression." Acknowledging that Ho Chi Minh would win national elections, the administration worked to forestall national unification under the terms of the Geneva Accords.

Diem made these policies explicit in 1955, announcing his rejection of national elections. Unlike France and Britain, Eisenhower backed Diem and welcomed him in Washington, where the two leaders reaffirmed the struggle

President Eisenhower, determined to block national unification under Ho Chi Minh in Vietnam, personally welcomed South Vietnamese President Ngo Dinh Diem in Washington, D. C., in 1957.

against "continuing Communist subversive capabilities." During the next five years the United States sent over $1 billion of economic and military aid to finance most of Diem's government expenses. Such support enabled the dictator to suppress political rivals as his soldiers made mass arrests of Communists and non-Communists alike. Diem also subverted land reforms begun by the Viet Minh. By 1959 such policies triggered a guerrilla revolt. Although the United States urged Diem to institute political and social reforms, the South Vietnamese leader refused, prompting the American ambassador to suggest "it may become necessary...to begin consideration of alternative courses of actions and leaders." This unresolved predicament passed to President John Kennedy in 1961.

While taking unilateral action in Vietnam, the administration supported collective security to prevent the spread of Communism in other parts of Asia. In 1954, Dulles signed a Southeast Asia Treaty Organization (SEATO) pact with Britain, France, Australia, New Zealand, Thailand, Pakistan, and the Philippines. This treaty provided for mutual defense against armed attack, subversion, or indirect aggression. "An attack on the treaty area would occasion a reaction so united, so strong, and so well placed," Dulles declared, "that the aggressor would lose more than it could hope to gain." But the SEATO agreement had inherent limitations—the refusal of neutral India to participate and the difficulty of implementing massive retaliation against subversion. The Senate ratified the treaty with little dissent, but it was never invoked and the agreement ended in 1977.

Even as Dulles was flying to Manila to negotiate the SEATO pact in 1954, the weaknesses of the treaty became apparent. Chinese shore batteries began to bombard Quemoy, one of the islands (along with Matsu and the Tachens) between China and Taiwan. Presidential military advisers recommended a counterattack, including an atomic bombing of China. Eisenhower recognized that the islands were not crucial to the defense of Taiwan and he rejected the advice. But the president insisted that Chiang remained part of the "backbone" of American security. As war fever rose, Dulles negotiated a mutual defense pact with Taiwan, but made no mention of the disputed islands.

Exhibit 10–2. Taiwan and People's Republic of China.

After the Chinese captured one of the Tachen islands, Eisenhower asked Congress for authority to use armed forces to defend Taiwan and the nearby islands. Approved by nearly unanimous votes of both houses of Congress in 1955, the so-called Formosa Resolution gave the president discretionary power to declare war, a virtual blank check for future presidential foreign policy. And as China continued to bomb the islands, Eisenhower hinted at retaliation. Such threats persuaded China to relax the tension, however, and the crisis passed. In subsequent years, Chiang took the opportunity to strengthen fortifications on the disputed territory. But in 1958, the People's Republic reopened the issue by launching a steady bombardment of Quemoy. The administration again spread the word that it was prepared to use nuclear weapons against China. Both Britain and the Soviet Union promptly advised Eisenhower against military intervention. Such pressure forced the president to concede his preference for negotiations and the crisis again waned. In Asia, therefore, massive retaliation served only to perpetuate the old policy of containment.

EUROPEAN DIPLOMACY

Reluctant to risk his personal prestige, Eisenhower avoided presidential diplomacy during the early years of his administration. While allowing Dulles to conduct negotiations in public, the president preferred to issue broad policy statements. In December 1953, for example, Eisenhower addressed the United Nations General Assembly, presenting a dramatic "atoms for peace" proposal that urged international control of atomic weapons. In offering to join the Soviet Union in pooling nuclear resources for peaceful purposes, the president hoped to overcome the mutual hostility that set the two powers on a deadly course. But Eisenhower also knew, as did the Soviets, that his proposal would preserve American nuclear superiority. When the Soviet Union reacted unfavorably, therefore, the president settled for the propaganda advantages and made no counteroffer.

Two years later Eisenhower again captured international attention with an "open skies" plan designed to prevent surprise attacks. The president had tried to avoid a direct meeting with world leaders, but Democrats urged some gesture toward reconciliation. Eisenhower insisted, however, that the former allies first sign a peace treaty with Austria. When the Soviets agreed in 1955, Eisenhower flew to a summit meeting with British, French, and Soviet leaders in Geneva. The main topics on the agenda—the status of Germany and disarmament—could not be settled. But the open skies proposal was intended to break the stalemate of suspicion and relax global tensions. Yet as with atoms-for-peace, the plan offered more advantages to the less-secretive United States than the closed Soviet Union. The Russians rejected the scheme. Eisenhower proceeded with plans to use a secret spy plane—the U-2—to achieve the goal of open skies. The United States also continued to test better hydrogen bombs and intercontinental missiles. The summit meeting did abate world tensions, however, and Eisenhower asserted in his 1956 State of the Union address that "Communist tactics against the free nations have shifted...from reliance on violence to reliance on division."

The "thaw" in the Cold War had obvious limits. As Poland and then Hungary tried to establish more liberal Communist governments in 1956, the United States hailed the collapse of the Soviet empire. But when Soviet tanks crushed the uprising in Budapest, massive retaliation proved worthless. Although Radio Free Europe broadcast moral support, the president settled for condemnations of Soviet cruelty and allowed twenty thousand Hungarian refugees to enter the country.

CRISES IN THE MIDDLE EAST

The importance of oil in the postwar world underscored the strategic value of the Middle East. Although the United States supported the independence of Israel, both Truman and Eisenhower allowed American oil companies to provide the Arab states with subsidies, which were tacitly repaid by the federal government in the form of tax deductions. Eisenhower also backed British influence in the Middle East to check Soviet expansion and supported a British plan for regional cooperation in the Baghdad Pact of 1955. This alliance alarmed Egyptian leader Gamal Abdel Nasser, who now sought economic and military assistance to strengthen his country. While Nasser negotiated to buy arms from Czechoslovakia, the United States offered to finance the Aswan Dam, a giant hydroelectric project that promised to modernize Egypt. But the scheme found little favor in the United States, particularly after Nasser announced his recognition of the People's Republic of China in 1956.

"Do nations which play both sides get better treatment than nations which are stalwart and work with us?" asked Dulles angrily. Eisenhower promptly withdrew the offer to build a dam. The reversal humiliated Nasser. One week later, the Egyptian leader nationalized the Suez Canal, jeopardizing western Europe's access to oil and Israeli rights of shipping. When Britain and France threatened military reprisal, Eisenhower opposed a reassertion of colonialism. The allies then determined to take independent action along with Israel. In October 1956, the Israelis launched a surprise attack on Egypt, providing Britain and France with an excuse to intervene to protect the Suez Canal. The invasion coincided with the Soviet suppression of the Hungarian uprising. Faced with a double crisis, Eisenhower demanded the withdrawal of troops from Egypt. So did Soviet leader Nikita Khrushchev, who warned the western nations of a retaliatory attack and expressed interest in a Soviet presence in the Middle East. To prevent such Soviet expansion, Eisenhower increased pressure on the allies, halting oil shipments from Latin America. The embargo forced the British and French to remove their forces from the Middle East by the end of the year.

The "Eisenhower Doctrine," presented to Congress in January 1957, attempted to fill the power vacuum in the Middle East. Asking Congress to approve unspecified economic and military assistance, the president also requested a resolution announcing that "overt armed aggression from any nation controlled by international Communism" would be met by American military force. Democratic Senator J. William Fulbright of Arkansas criticized this attempt to manipulate Congress with news leaks and secret meetings "in an atmosphere of suspense and urgency." But after subtle changes of wording, Congress easily

Exhibit 10–3. Middle East, 1956–1958.

Middle East
1956-1958

125 miles

adopted the measure. As with the Formosa resolution of 1955, the president obtained extensive authority for future executive actions.

In confusing Arab nationalism with Communist expansion, the Eisenhower Doctrine served as a convenient excuse for American intervention in the Middle East. In April 1957, for example, Jordan's King Hussein claimed that a pro-Nasser rebellion constituted a Communist attack. Understanding the duplicity of language, Eisenhower nevertheless sent the Sixth Fleet to protect the political status quo. In July 1958, a similar distortion of events led the president to order the Marines into Lebanon. This dramatic gesture served notice to Arab nationalists that the United States was determined to protect access to Middle East oil.

"What makes the Soviet threat unique in history," the president stated in 1958, "is its all-inclusiveness....Trade, economic development, military power, arts, science, education, the whole world of ideas—all are harnessed to the same chariot of expansion." Fear of Soviet influence in economically underdeveloped countries stimulated a reappraisal of American economic foreign policy. As a proponent of international free enterprise, Eisenhower hoped that foreign trade and private investment would assure American influence without adding to

government expenditures. Foreign aid remained largely military and was justified on grounds of national security. By mid-decade, increased Soviet competition persuaded the president to endorse foreign aid as a way of accelerating economic development of other countries and linking their interests to the West. In
1957, Congress established the Development Loan Fund and two years later created the Inter-American Loan Bank for Latin America. But both projects provided relatively small sums and emphasized private investment. And
Eisenhower defined such assistance not as an attempt to alleviate poverty, but
rather as a defense of the national security in the fight against Communism.
Moreover, foreign military aid far exceeded economic assistance and caused a
severe imbalance of international payments that weakened the dollar abroad.
Yet Eisenhower's commitment to foreign economic development provided a
precedent for later administrations.

THE POLITICS OF MODERATION

Surveying the political spectrum in 1956, Adlai Stevenson aptly concluded that
"moderation is the spirit of the times." Although liberals like Hubert Humphrey
and Paul Douglas spoke eloquently about social reform, Democrats worked
closely with Eisenhower's "modern" Republicans to enact minimal welfare legislation. In 1955, for example, Eisenhower proposed a 90 cent-an-hour minimum
wage, 35 cents less than organized labor desired, and extension of coverage to
include certain unorganized workers. But conservatives opposed broadening
coverage to unskilled workers. Congress then enacted a compromise that raised
the minimum wage to $1 an hour, but ignored unorganized workers. Similarly,
Eisenhower requested the construction of 140,000 units of public housing, a
fraction of the needed total, but Congress reduced that number to seventy-five
thousand. And political leaders in both branches of government dismissed proposals for national health insurance as socialized medicine.

To minimize government involvement in the economy, the White House opposed public control of electric power projects. In 1954, for example, Eisenhower
recommended a revision of the Atomic Energy Act to allow private manufacture
and operation of atomic reactors. This legislation led to the first privately run
atomic power plants. The administration's decision to bypass the Tennessee Valley Authority (TVA) in providing electricity for AEC facilities proved more controversial. The idea clashed with the existence of TVA, long a symbol of New
Deal liberalism. Hints of political corruption weakened the president's position,
however, and a compromise measure ended the controversy. The administration did succeed in blocking public power projects in other parts of the country,
such as Hell's Canyon on the Snake River.

Eisenhower, the grandfatherly civilian-soldier, remained extremely popular.
Although the president's heart attack in September 1955 shook public confidence, Eisenhower recovered rapidly and resolved to seek a second term. After
slight hesitation, he agreed to keep Vice President Nixon on the ticket. Democratic chances seemed slim. Stevenson won a first-ballot decision and then, in a
dramatic moment, opened the vice presidential nomination to the floor of the
Democratic National Convention. In the ensuing vote, Estes Kefauver managed

to defeat Senator John F. Kennedy of Massachusetts. The Democrats then adopted a moderate platform. Hoping to regain the South, the party waffled on support of the Supreme Court's school desegregation decision. On foreign policy, Democrats echoed Eisenhower's Cold War principles. Stevenson introduced two controversial proposals into the campaign, calling for the end to the military draft and suggesting a moratorium on hydrogen bomb testing. But both issues played to Eisenhower's strength as an expert on military policy. "The butchers of the Kremlin," said Nixon, "would make mincemeat of Stevenson over a conference table."

Eisenhower's margin of victory exceeded the totals of 1952. Capturing 58 percent of the popular vote, he carried all but seven states. But other Republican candidates fell far behind the president's pace and Democrats strengthened their control of both houses of Congress. This anomalous situation reflected the persistence of party voting habits (there were 50 percent more registered Democrats than Republicans in 1956). Unlike congressional candidates, Eisenhower could attract voters in all parts of the political spectrum because specific issues appeared relatively unimportant.

Domestic Debate and Civil Rights

Emboldened by the congressional elections, Democrats moved to clarify their political position. Eisenhower's success in the black neighborhoods of northern cities goaded congressional liberals into action. "I don't think a party should run on 'trouble,' on economic difficulty," declared Hubert Humphrey. "We must design a new liberal program." Led by Humphrey and Paul Douglas, liberal senators presented a sixteen-point "Democratic Declaration" that advocated civil rights legislation, public housing, unemployment compensation, and other progressive reforms. Meanwhile, Democratic party chairman Paul Butler organized a Democratic Advisory Council, distinct from the congressional leadership of Johnson and Rayburn, to press for a liberal agenda. Such maneuverings assured greater conflict with the Republican administration.

The first controversy erupted when the president presented a $73.3 billion budget request, the highest peacetime appropriations, for fiscal year 1958. Committed to the doctrine of a balanced budget, Treasury secretary George Humphrey blundered by predicting that such expenditures would cause a depression "that will curl your hair." Eisenhower further complicated the situation by inviting Congress to reduce government expenditures. The result was a bitter legislative "battle of the budget" as Congress picked apart the president's entire program. Eisenhower tried to rally public support, but Congress shaved his budget by $4 billion, including $1 billion in foreign aid. For Eisenhower, observed presidential advisor Sherman Adams, the outcome was "a serious and disturbing personal defeat."

Contrary to Secretary Humphrey's predictions, moreover, the reduction of government expenditures, instead of strengthening the economy, slowed economic growth. By mid-1957, industrial production had dropped and unemployment had increased. Eisenhower remained skeptical about the value of government spending to stimulate the economy. Congress had fewer reservations.

Exhibit 10–4. Gross National Product, 1952–1960.
(current dollars in billions)

1952	$351.6 b
1954	$372.5 b
1956	$428.2 b
1958	$456.8 b
1960	$515.3 b

Source: *Economic Report of the President* (1988)

Exhibit 10–5. National Defense and Veterans Outlays, 1955–1960.
(in billions of dollars)

1955	$47.4 b
1960	$53.5 b

Source: *Statistical Abstract of the United States* (1987)

Exhibit 10–6. Government Spending as Percentage of
Gross National Product, 1949–1959

1949	23.0%
1959	26.9%

Source: *Historical Statistics of the United States, from Colonial Times to 1970* (1975)

Increased appropriations, including public works projects, added over $8 billion to the budget, halting the recession. But continued government spending resulted in large budgetary deficits.

While politicians wrangled about the budget, the nation headed toward a major crisis over civil rights. As the issue emerged during the 1950s, Eisenhower, a product of the segregated military and a friend of numerous southern conservatives, showed no leadership. In his first year in office, the president continued Truman's efforts to end segregation in the armed forces, the federal government, and the nation's capital, but otherwise stressed the role of states and cities to resolve these questions. Then, in 1954 the Supreme Court desegregation decision created a new climate of opinion. (See chapter 2).

A grass roots civil rights movement started in the streets of Montgomery, Alabama, in December 1955 when Rosa Parks, a local NAACP worker, refused to obey a law requiring segregated seating on public buses. Her arrest soon blossomed into a citywide bus boycott led by Baptist minister Martin Luther King, Jr. "We have known humiliation, we have known abusive language, we have been plunged into the abyss of oppression," King declared from the pulpit of the Dexter Avenue Baptist Church. "And we decided to rise up only with the weapon of protest. It is one of the greatest glories of America that we have the right to protest." The year-long boycott proved remarkably effective, but it required a Supreme Court decision before municipal officials accepted the desegregation of the buses. Montgomery showed the power of organized black protest and inaugurated the mass actions of the civil rights movement.

⎯⎯ RICHARD B. RUSSELL, JR. ⎯⎯
⎯⎯ 1897–1971 ⎯⎯

One of the great barons of the United States Senate at mid-century was Richard Russell. Styled the "boy wonder" of Georgia politics, he was elected governor in 1930 at the age of 33 (he had already served ten years in the state legislature) and was elected to the Senate two years later where he remained for the rest of his life. A bachelor of spartan habits, Russell devoted himself completely to the Senate and over the years, as his seniority and his shrewdness grew, he became one of its most powerful members. Always mindful of details, he daily read every line of the *Congressional Record* and was an acknowledged master of parliamentary maneuver. Although he rejected an opportunity to become Majority Leader in 1953, Russell functioned as "Dean of the Senate Establishment," presiding over the informal inner club which largely dominated Senate affairs.

Russell's career illustrates both the power and the frustration of ambitious southern politicians in the Segregation Era. The systematic disfranchisement of blacks, poor whites, and urban dwellers produced a political system which generally did not challenge entrenched leadership. Once elected, southern congressmen and senators could expect a long tenure. Consequently, Russell, like many other southerners, steadily accumulated great power in a legislative branch which stressed seniority of membership and the committee system. As seniority made them chairs of major committees, they could channel federal dollars to their constituents, something Russell did extremely well. An advocate of preparedness almost from his earliest days in Congress, he became chairman of the Senate Armed Services Committee in 1951, and by 1960 Georgia had some fifteen military installations employing forty thousand people as well as a major defense contractor in Lockheed Aircraft.

But if the southern political system was an important element in Russell's power, it ultimately served to thwart his broader *(cont.)*

As blacks adopted direct action tactics against racial discrimination, white southerners responded with "massive resistance," which included deliberate noncompliance with the law by government officials, legal harassment of civil rights organizations (the NAACP was outlawed in several states), economic reprisals against black activists, and mob violence inspired by White Citizens Councils and a rejuvenated Ku Klux Klan. At the national level, 101 southern congressmen issued a "Declaration of Constitutional Principles" in 1956 which denied the power of the federal government to order desegregation in the states. Eisenhower, who personally opposed the *Brown* ruling, declared: "The final battle against intolerance is to be fought—not in the chambers of any legislature—but in the hearts of men." The president firmly rebuffed suggestions that he take a stand supporting the desegregation of public schools. He did propose legislation in 1956 to protect the voting rights of blacks, but the measure died in the Senate.

(cont.) ambitions by making him unacceptable to a national Democratic constituency. Russell came to Washington in 1933 as a strong New Dealer, but as New Deal policies began to pose challenges, however limited, to southern elites, Russell grew steadily more conservative. He was a liberal in a depression, he explained, but "I'm a reactionary when times are good." After World War II, he was increasingly uncomfortable in a Democratic party dominated by New Dealers and Fair Dealers, especially as civil rights emerged as a major national issue. In an effort to change the focus of the party, he sought the Democratic presidential nomination in 1952, but was resoundingly defeated. His appeal was limited almost exclusively to the Deep South, and his main influence on the contest was to frustrate the ambitions of his more moderate fellow southerner, Senator Estes Kefauver. A disappointed man, Russell increasingly devoted his energy and talents to opposing civil rights legislation in Congress. Russell's power began to erode after the Civil Rights Act of 1964 was passed over his stalwart opposition, although he remained a major force in the Senate

until his death in 1971.

Richard Russell was the product of political arrangements in the South and in Washington designed to maximize the power of archconservatives like himself. His skills as a legislator enabled him to exploit the potential of that conservative system, but he was unable to reach beyond his heritage to offer constructive leadership in the most pressing issues of his time. His often acute judgment on military affairs was blighted by a chauvinism that was jarringly discordant in the nuclear era. "If we have to start over again with another Adam and Eve," he told the Senate, "then I want them to be Americans and not Russians, and I want them to be on this continent and not in Europe." His unswerving commitment to segregation made him the champion of a demeaning system of economic exploitation and social control. If the integrationists "overwhelm us," he declared, "you will find me in the last ditch." Tragically, both for his region and his own career, too much of his talent and energy went into a misguided defense of what he considered to be "the Southern way of life."■

"Give us the ballot," declared Martin Luther King, "and we will no longer have to worry the federal government about our basic rights." On the third anniversary of the *Brown* ruling in 1957, black leaders organized a "Prayer Pilgrimage" to Washington, attracting over thirty thousand protesters against racial discrimination. That year Eisenhower again requested legislation to protect the right to vote. The proposal won support from Lyndon Johnson, who wished to demonstrate his liberal credentials and so enhance chances for northern support in an anticipated race for the presidency in 1960. Working behind the scenes, Johnson persuaded southern leaders to drop the filibuster in exchange for a mild bill. The new law called for a relatively weak Civil Rights Commission and authorized the attorney general to seek injunctions for violations of voting rights. It was the first significant civil rights legislation since Reconstruction, but in 1960 only 25 percent of eligible blacks could actually exercise their rights.

ESTES KEFAUVER
1903–1963

In an era of political consensus and corporate expansion, Tennessee's Senator Estes Kefauver flourished as a maverick politician and a champion of the ordinary citizen against big business and political corruption. Running for the Senate in 1948, he broke with Tennessee's political machine and adopted a coonskin cap as a symbol of his frontier independence. The folksy style became his political trademark. Kefauver's image as a populist, enhanced by televised broadcasts of his Senate hearings on organized crime in 1950–51, catapulted him to national fame and made the senator a strong Democratic presidential contender. Yet his individualism created a multitude of enemies, who combined to thwart his ambitions. In the end, he was deemed too much a southerner for liberals, too much a liberal for southerners.

Kefauver was born in eastern Tennessee, studied law at Yale, and worked as a corporation lawyer in Chatanooga where he supported the Tennessee Valley Authority. Elected to Congress in 1939, he defended the embattled New Deal, spoke for small business interests against corporate concentration, and advocated congressional reform, coauthoring the book *A Twentieth Century Congress* (1947). Sensitive to civil liberties, he opposed the Taft-Hartley labor law and voted against refunding the House Committee on UnAmerican Activities. Yet as a southern representative, he opposed a federal Fair Employment Practices Commission and antilynching legislation. Unlike most racial opportunists, however, Kefauver urged repeal of poll taxes because they disenfranchised the poor of both races and opposed the use of the filibuster to kill civil rights legislation. Indeed, after the Supreme Court overturned school segregation in 1954, he readily accepted the idea of racial integration.

Kefauver's investigation of organized crime, the first Senate hearings ever televised, created a national sensation in 1950. Exposure of national crime networks and widespread political graft underscored an abiding fear in the Cold War era that secret forces— "government-within-a-government," as Kefauver put it—were threatening Ameri- *(cont.)*

Direct action by blacks, meanwhile, forced the president to support desegregation. In September 1957, Governor Orval Faubus of Arkansas mobilized the National Guard to prevent the integration of Central High School in Little Rock, an action which violated a federal court order. While armed soldiers prevented nine black students from attending the school, Eisenhower remained aloof. But Faubus's defiance of federal authority threatened the constitutional system of government, and Democratic protests aroused Eisenhower to action. "Law cannot be flaunted with impunity by any individual or mob of extremists," he conceded. The president federalized the National Guard and ordered paratroopers to enforce the court decision. Despite continuing mob violence, black students began attending the school under the protection of the federalized Guard. Faubus managed to close the school the next year, but a court order finally ended *(cont.)* can life. For Kefauver, it was crime and corruption, not Communism, that was the prime menace. Significantly, he opposed provisions of the 1954 Communist Control bill that made Communist party membership a felony. Kefauver's crime hearings also showed the political power of television. In his subsequent book, *Crime in America* (1951), Kefauver estimated that twenty to thirty million people watched the hearings; in New York City, the Consolidated Edison electrical company had to install a new generator to handle the demand. As a result, Kefauver suddenly became a nationally-known politician.

Capitalizing on this popularity, Kefauver donned his coonskin cap in 1952 and entered a series of Democratic presidential primaries, the first major candidate to recognize the potential of grassroots support. He surprised the country by defeating President Truman in New Hampshire. But his unorthodox style precluded building a national organization and despite his many victories at the polls, Kefauver controlled few delegates at the Democratic convention. His nonpartisan investigations of organized crime alarmed the Democratic leadership, which feared a loss of party strength in the cities. Meanwhile, Kefauver's spotty record on civil rights weakened his support among liberals, and his opposition to filibusters cut into his southern base. Defeated by Adlai Stevenson in 1952 and 1956, Kefauver staged a dramatic floor rally to win the vice presidential nomination over Massachusetts Senator John F. Kennedy in 1956. Ironically the televised spectacle increased Kennedy's visibility for the next election.

As his presidential ambitions waned, Kefauver focused on problems of corporate capitalism. As chair of the Senate Antitrust and Monopoly subcommittee, he headed investigations of price-fixing and monopolistic practices in the electrical equipment, steel, and drug industries. The Kefauver-Harris Drug Control Act (1962), a landmark consumer measure, provided for product competition and safety requirements in prescription medicine. In the midst of attacking the Kennedy administration's monopolistic Communications Satellite Act, Kefauver collapsed on the Senate floor in 1963. He died two days later of an aneurism. ■

Little Rock school segregation in 1959. Meanwhile, desegregation proceedings provoked bitter debate and occasional mob reprisals throughout the South.

Organizing religious allies, Martin Luther King helped build a coalition of black activists in the Southern Christian Leadership Conference (SCLC) in 1957. Committed to non-violent civil disobedience, such civil rights groups emphasized the spiritual righteousness of their cause and endeavored to touch the conscience of whites. Increasingly a new generation of blacks, educated after World War II, rejected any compromise with racial injustice and demanded the full rights of citizens. The emergence of new nations in black Africa in the late 1950s symbolized the possibility of freedom in America.

"All of Africa will be free," exclaimed black novelist James Baldwin, "before we can get a lousy cup of coffee." Such anger and frustration provoked a series of disciplined non-violent "sit-in" protests by black college students at the lunchcounters of Greensboro, North Carolina in February 1960. The idea spread like wild fire through the South. Instead of waiting for legislative or judicial sanction, young blacks simply violated segregation laws and went to jail for their convictions. These actions won support among white liberals who joined blacks in a national crusade for civil rights, which culminated in mass protests in the next decade.

The astounding news of October 4, 1957 abruptly shifted public attention from Little Rock to the heavens above: the Soviet Union had launched the first artificial satellite. "The Soviets have beaten us at our own game," declared Lyndon Johnson, "—daring scientific advances in the atomic age." Besides the philosophic shockwaves caused by the triumph over the earth's gravitation, the launching suggested that the Soviet Union possessed superior rocket technology. Most Americans assumed that the dreaded Communist enemy had developed the capability of delivering intercontinental ballistic missiles armed with nuclear weapons before the United States held sufficient retaliatory power. This belief in a missile gap fed popular fears of nuclear annihilation. Best-selling books, such as Nevil Shute's *On The Beach* (1957) and Walt Miller's *A Canticle for Leibowitz* (1959) dramatized the imminence of holocaust.

Eisenhower remained calm, however, denying any military deficiences and rejecting a plan to build fallout shelters throughout the country. American technology was actually prepared to match the Soviet achievement. After a few highly publicized failures, the United States lofted its own satellites into orbit in 1958. Moreover, Sputnik put to rest the debate about "open skies," though in the absence of spy satellites Eisenhower continued to rely on the U-2 planes. The President also created a White House Science Advisory Committee, headed by MIT's James Killian. By bringing new scientists into the administration, Eisenhower for the first time had access to authoritative opinions about a range of technological issues. These scientists would later contradict the advice of the Atomic Energy Commission (AEC) and the Pentagon about the feasibility of controlling the nuclear arms race. Democratic leaders nonetheless criticized the president's leadership. In the Senate, Johnson backed legislation to establish a civilian-controlled space agency, the National Aeronautics and Space Administration (NASA) in 1958.

The combination of Sputnik, Little Rock, and the recession brought landslide victories for the Democrats in the elections of 1958 and shifted the political climate in a liberal direction. Democrats controlled the House by seventy votes and the Senate by thirty. Rejecting the president's fiscal austerity, Congress promptly voted to increase the military budget, but Eisenhower succeeded in vetoing a series of public works measures. Congress also enacted the admission of Alaska and Hawaii in 1959, but carefully reversed the administration's priorities by welcoming the Democratic state first. For the first time since 1925, the Senate rejected a White House cabinet nominee, Lewis Strauss, Eisenhower's choice to head the Department of Commerce, because of political disagreements. Despite these disputes, however, the administration worked with Congress to enact the National Defense Education Act of 1958 and the Landrum-Griffin labor law (for details of these measures, see chapter 2) as well as increased support of state unemployment programs and a reorganization of the Pentagon.

PRESIDENTIAL DIPLOMACY

With the death of Secretary of State Dulles in 1959, Eisenhower engaged more openly in personal diplomacy. In 1958 he had sent Nixon on a "goodwill" tour of Latin America, but the vice president had been met by hostile crowds protesting United States economic and political exploitation. The administration dismissed these demonstrations as examples of Communist infiltration of the hemisphere. Democrats disagreed. "It is foolish...to attribute anti-Americanism just to Communist agitation," explained Adlai Stevenson after a trip to Latin America in 1960. Rather, the Eisenhower administration "has been basically concerned with making Latin America safe for American business, not for democracy," especially by supporting "hated dictators."

The issue soon focused on Cuba. After backing dictator Fulgencio Batista since 1952, the administration reacted cautiously to the revolutionary government established by Fidel Castro in 1959. Although the United States offered economic aid, the administration opposed Castro's agrarian reform laws that nationalized some private American holdings. Eisenhower quickly cut aid to Cuba and demanded immediate compensation. As relations between the two nations worsened in 1960, Castro announced the sale of sugar to the Soviet Union in exchange for economic and military assistance.

Eisenhower responded with a two-pronged attack. In 1960, the president ordered the CIA "to organize the training of Cuban exiles, mainly in Guatemala against a possible future day when they might return to their homeland." Meanwhile, the president exerted economic pressure by cutting purchases of Cuban sugar. Castro protested that the reduction of sugar sales was a preparation for an invasion, and Soviet leader Nikita Khrushchev announced that the Soviet Union would protect the Cuban government. Frustrated by Castro's audacity, Eisenhower severed diplomatic relations in January 1961, leaving the problem for his successor.

Eisenhower attempted nonetheless to reduce tension with the Soviet Union without jeopardizing American strength. Since his "atoms for peace" proposal of 1953, the president had emphasized inspection and control as a precondition for disarmament. In 1956 he had sneered at Stevenson's call for a halt in nuclear testing. But a diplomatic conference among Soviet and American scientists in Geneva in 1958 indicated that controls could be implemented. That year the president announced that the United States was ending further nuclear testing. The Soviet Union performed a final series of tests before it too halted such explosions.

Despite such accommodations, Eisenhower vigorously resisted Khrushchev's demands that Allied forces depart from Berlin. "Any sign of Western weakness at this forward position," he declared in 1958, "could be misinterpreted with grievous consequences." Both powers now spoke about World War III. But the next year tensions abated when Khrushchev and Eisenhower agreed to engage in personal diplomacy. The Soviet leader toured the United States and met amicably with the president at Camp David. Though substantive issues remained unresolved, the two powers were close to reaching an agreement about nuclear arms.

The loss of an American spy plane destroyed such hopes. In May 1960, on the eve of a summit conference to discuss arms control, Khrushchev announced that the Soviet Union had shot down an American U-2 spy plane. The administration immediately denied the charge, claiming that a "weather plane" had merely strayed off course. But then, to Eisenhower's embarrassment, Khrushchev produced the CIA pilot, Francis Gary Powers, revealing the lie. While the whole world watched anxiously, Eisenhower proceeded to make a series of diplomatic blunders. First, the State Department acknowledged the U-2 mission, justifying such flights with the "open skies" formula the Soviets had rejected in 1955. Eisenhower still hoped to salvage the summit conference. By claiming ignorance of the U-2 program, the president could escape complicity. But Eisenhower's disavowal of knowledge of the spy mission implied that subordinates were controlling the administration. The situation, especially in an election year, threatened to destroy the president's credibility as a political leader. Reluctantly, Eisenhower acknowledged his involvement. "It is a distasteful but vital necessity," he declared, reminding the public of the lessons of Pearl Harbor. Eisenhower's admission destroyed the summit meeting. At the Paris session, Khrushchev denounced the president and refused to negotiate.

The intensification of the Cold War had a profound effect on public opinion. Democratic politicians criticized the president's clumsy diplomacy. More fundamental, the U-2 affair shocked the American public by revealing the duplicity of its government. Eisenhower, who strove to rise above parties, had lied not only to Khrushchev but also to American citizens. The notion of a credibility gap between the people and their government would haunt American politics for the next two decades.

Suggested Readings

The most thorough account of the Eisenhower administration appears in the second volume of Stephen E. Ambrose's *Eisenhower* (1984). For an astute analysis of the president's political ideology, see an important article, Robert Griffith, "Dwight D. Eisenhower and the Corporate Commonwealth," *American Historical Review*, volume 87 (1982). A traditional view of Eisenhower as a laissez-faire president can be found in Peter Lyon, *Eisenhower: Portrait of a Hero* (1974). But this view has been challenged persuasively in Blanche Wiesen Cook, *The Declassified Eisenhower: A Divided Legacy* (1981) and Fred Greenstein, *The Hidden-Hand Presidency: Eisenhower as Leader* (1982). A detailed collection of primary sources is Robert L. Branyan and Lawrence H. Larsen, *The Eisenhower Administration,* 2 vols. (1971).

Studies of domestic politics remain sparse. For insights into congressional power, see Rowland Evans and Robert Novak, *Lyndon B. Johnson: The Exercise of Power* (1966). The career of Adlai Stevenson is described favorably in Stuart Gerry Brown, *Conscience in Politics* (1961), which includes many original sources, and the more detailed study, John Bartlow Martin's two volume *The Life of Adlai Stevenson* (1976–77). For the vice president's career, see Stephen E. Ambrose's biography, *Nixon: The Education of a Politician* (1987) as well as the superb analysis by Garry Wills, *Nixon Agonistes* (1970). Also helpful on the liberal perspective is Carl Solberg, *Hubert Humphrey: A Biography* (1984). Voting behavior in the 1950s is explained in Norman H. Nie et al., *The Changing American Voter* (1976).

The civil rights movement is surveyed in the books by Sitkoff and Marable listed after chapter 2. More thorough are William Chafe, *Civilities and Civil Rights: Greensboro, North Carolina, and the Black Struggle for Freedom* (1980); Robert F. Burk, *The Eisenhower Administration and Black Civil Rights* (1980); and Juan Williams, *Eyes on the Prize: America's Civil Rights Years, 1954–1965* (1987). A detailed study of southern politics in Jack Bass and Walter DeVries, *The Transformation of Southern Politics: Social Change and Political Consequence Since 1945* (1976). For the Warren Court, see the relevant chapters of Paul L. Murphy, *The Constitution in Crisis Times: 1918–1969* (1972) and two fine biographies: G. Edward White, *Earl Warren: A Public Life* (1982) and Bernard Schwartz, *Super Chief: Earl Warren and His Supreme Court: A Judicial Biography* (1983).

A recent historiographical essay on McCarthyism appears in the revised 1988 edition of Robert Griffith, *The Politics of Fear: Joseph R. McCarthy and the Senate.* Originally published in 1970, that book places McCarthy in the context of his senatorial peers. More thorough studies of the McCarthy phenomenon are David M. Oshinsky, *A Conspiracy So Immense: The World of Joe McCarthy* (1983); Thomas C. Reeves, *The Life and Times of Joe McCarthy* (1981); and Mark Landis, *Joseph McCarthy: The Politics of Chaos* (1987). For the impact of McCarthyism in academia, see Ellen W. Schrecker, *No Ivory Tower: McCarthyism and the Universities* (1986) and also the titles listed at the end of chapter 3. Also helpful on McCarthy's support are Michael Paul Rogin, *The Intellectuals and McCarthy* (1967), and David M. Oshinsky, *Senator Joseph McCarthy and the American Labor Movement* (1976). The role of Senator Pat McCarran is documented in the relevant chapters of Stanley Kutler, *The American Inquisition: Justice and Injustice in Cold War America* (1982).

A good introduction to Eisenhower's foreign policy is Walter Lafeber's *America, Russia, and the Cold War* (1985). A more favorable account is Robert A. Divine, *Eisenhower and the Cold War* (1981). These works should be supplemented by the suggestive articles in Richard A. Melanson and David Mayers, *Reevaluating Eisenhower: American Foreign Policy in the 1950s* (1987). The origin of the "space race" with the Soviet Union is analyzed in Walter A. McDougall, *The Heavens and the Earth: A Political History of the Space Age* (1985). For the disarmament question, see Robert A. Divine, *Blowing on the Wind: The Nuclear Test Ban Debate, 1954–1960* (1978).

Eisenhower's economic foreign policy is the subject of Burton I. Kaufman, *Trade and Aid* (1982). U. S. intervention in Central America is described in R. H. Immerman, *The CIA in Guatemala: The Foreign Policy of Intervention* (1982) and Stephen C. Schlesinger and Stephen Kinzer, *Bitter Fruit: The Untold Story of the American Coup in Guatemala* (1982). The Vietnam issue is described in Melanie Billings-Yun, *Decision Against War: Eisenhower and Dien Bien Phu, 1954* (1988).

11

KENNEDY, JOHNSON, AND THE LIBERAL CONSENSUS, 1960-1968

The 1960s heralded a new era of liberalism. In contrast to the previous Republican administration, Democratic Presidents John F. Kennedy and Lyndon B. Johnson stressed the importance of an active federal government to achieve economic and social progress. Their liberal programs brought increased government benefits to disadvantaged groups, but at the same time accentuated conflicts between competing interests. The assertive foreign policy of the 1960s also intensified disagreements about United States intervention abroad. By the end of the decade, the postwar political consensus had been superseded by bitter strife about the proper uses of American wealth and power and controversy over the very definition of the nation itself.

THE ELECTION OF 1960

"My campaign for the presidency," announced Massachusetts Senator Kennedy, "is founded on a single assumption...that the American people are tired of the drift in our national course, that they are weary of the continued decline in our national prestige...that they are ready to move again." For eight years, President Eisenhower had extolled the warrior virtues of strength and power. But at the age of seventy, then the oldest man to hold the nation's highest office, Eisenhower seemed impotent against Khrushchev's indignation, the eruption of liberation movements in Asia and Africa, and the anti-American protests in Latin America and Japan. Closer to home, voters blamed the administration for the recession of 1957–58. "Wind up the Eisenhower doll," ran a popular joke, "and it does nothing for eight years."

Kennedy, by contrast, was only forty-two when he announced his candidacy. He was youthful in appearance; his daughter was an infant and his glamorous wife, Jacqueline, just thirty-one. And because the candidate concealed his serious illnesses (Addison's Disease of the adrenal glands and chronic back pain, both of which required constant drug therapy), he symbolized strength, vigor, and energy. In the Senate, for example, Kennedy attacked the administration for failing to build enough missiles and creating a "missile gap" between Soviet and American arsenals. "This is not a call of despair," he stated. "It is a call for action."

Kennedy's ambition benefited by great personal wealth, but his Roman Catholic religion loomed as a major handicap. Only one Catholic, Al Smith, had run for president, and he had suffered a devastating defeat in 1928. Kennedy challenged religious prejudices directly, entering a series of primary contests against his major rival, Minnesota Senator Hubert H. Humphrey. But although Kennedy won their first contest in Wisconsin, voting analysis showed that Kennedy carried Catholic districts while Humphrey attracted Protestants. The race moved to West Virginia, an impoverished state with a 95 percent Protestant population. Running an expensive campaign, Kennedy emphasized his commitment to New Deal liberalism. A decisive victory over Humphrey quieted the religious issue and Kennedy went on to win a first-ballot Democratic nomination. To balance the ticket in the South, he chose as his running mate Senate Majority Leader Lyndon Johnson of Texas.

Kennedy's Catholicism remained a controversial issue in the general election against Vice President Richard M. Nixon. To the Houston Ministerial Association, a gathering of Methodist leaders, Kennedy insisted, "I am not a Catholic candidate. I am the Democratic party's candidate...,who happens also to be a Catholic." He vowed to maintain the separation of church and state, expressing disbelief that "forty million Americans lost their chance of being president on the day they were baptized." Despite the rise of liberal values after World War II, religious prejudices prevailed. Thus Kennedy won a high proportion of Catholic supporters, while losing among Protestants. Nevertheless, the candidate managed to overcome the prejudices of black evangelicals by supporting civil rights activist Martin Luther King, Jr., who had been sentenced to prison for trespassing in a segregated restaurant in Georgia. A much-publicized telephone call from Kennedy to King's wife, Coretta, revealed a combination of genuine compassion and astute political calculation in the candidate's mind. By appealing both to blacks and white ethnics, Kennedy restored the New Deal coalition, but subsequent voting analysis suggested that the religious issue probably cost him more votes than he gained.

Religion seemed so important in 1960 because the differences between Kennedy and Nixon remained fairly narrow. Four nationally televised debates, which attracted over one-hundred million viewers, spotlighted their similarities. Both candidates stood as cold warriors, vowing to end further Communist expansion and disagreeing only about whether to defend the islands between mainland China and Taiwan. Both stressed the importance of economic growth. Both used the phrase "new frontiers" to evoke a spirit of opportunity and expansion. "Mr. Nixon says, 'We never had it so good,'" Kennedy stated in a typical remark. "I say we can do better."

Despite these common assumptions, television illuminated not the candidates' words but their manner of presentation. Radio listeners, who were not distracted by visual appearances, reacted favorably to Nixon's speeches. But the television cameras accentuated the vice president's heavy "five o'clock shadow" and dripping makeup. His body movements seemed stiff. Kennedy, by contrast, brought a dramatic flair to the screen and projected self-confidence. Subsequent polls indicated that the debates may have influenced four million voters; of these Kennedy gathered three-quarters.

Such intangible factors had immense significance, for the balloting proved extremely close. With nearly sixty-nine million people voting, Kennedy obtained a popular majority of only 118,000—a margin of one-tenth of 1 percent. The electoral victory was 303-219, but these figures concealed paper-thin majorities and probable fraud in such key states as Illinois and Texas. A switch of only thirty-five thousand votes could have reversed the final decision. Kennedy also trailed behind Democratic congressional candidates. Although the Democrats maintained control of both houses of Congress, a majority of the sixty-three new legislators subsequently voted against the White House on important issues. Republican strength in the South also indicated a revival of two-party competition in that region. Since southern Democrats frequently aligned with Republicans, the administration lacked a working majority in Congress.

Exhibit 11–1. Election of 1960.

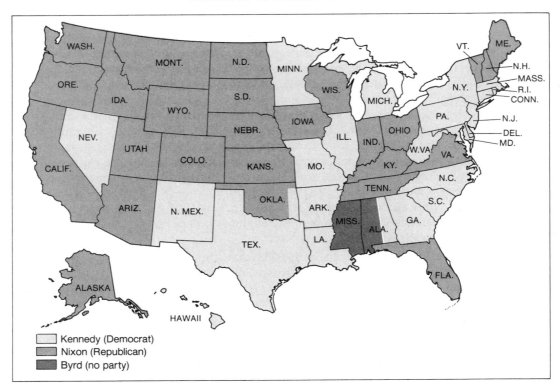

Kennedy (Democrat)
Nixon (Republican)
Byrd (no party)

LAUNCHING THE NEW FRONTIER

With his slender majority, Kennedy hesitated to initiate bold departures of policy. Cabinet appointments such as Treasury Secretary Douglas Dillon and Secretary of State Dean Rusk came from the same corporate elites that had served in previous administrations. But the new president embraced a liberal spirit that demanded dynamic leadership. "Let the word go forth that the torch has been passed to a new generation of Americans," Kennedy declared in his inaugural address. Describing the nation at "its hour of maximum danger," he stressed the "burden" of "relentless struggle" and urged Americans: "Ask not what your country can do for you—ask what you can do for your country."

Denying the importance of emotionalism and ideology, Kennedy's leadership extolled the values of scientific management and cold reason. "Most of the problems...that we now face are technical problems, are administrative problems," he declared in 1962. "They are very sophisticated judgments which do not lend themselves to the great sort of 'passionate movements' which have stirred this country so often in the past." Matters of foreign policy, the president suggested, "are so sophisticated and so technical that people who are not intimately involved week after week, month after month, reach judgments which are based on emotion rather than knowledge of the real alternatives."

This optimism about leadership by experts reflected a growing acceptance of an activist government. Although conservatives condemned the expansion of government services, a large public consensus had become confident that careful management could solve basic social and economic problems. "There is a recurring temptation to feel that some spectacular and costly action could become the miraculous solution to all current difficulties," admitted President Eisenhower. This confidence in public affairs contrasted with older fears about big government. The inclusion of questions about personal income in the census, for example, had aroused bitter controversy in 1940 and 1950, but by 1960 such complaints had evaporated.

Kennedy's Secretary of Defense Robert S. McNamara, former head of the Ford Motor Company, typified the liberal leadership. Taking charge of the Pentagon, McNamara initiated a program of rigorous "cost-benefit" accounting to determine military priorities. In place of Eisenhower's "massive retaliation," the new administration preferred a "flexible response," which included conventional arms for "brushfire" wars and the elite Special Forces (Green Berets) for counterinsurgency and guerrilla warfare.

Having campaigned on the issue of Soviet military superiority, however, Kennedy did not reverse his demand for more nuclear-armed missiles, even when he learned, soon after taking office, that no "missile gap" existed. Viewing military power, rather than traditional diplomacy, as a deterrent to the Soviet Union, the administration launched a major buildup of missiles, warheads, and electronic support systems, including computerized data bases, and orbiting communications and spy satellites. This emphasis on technological developments encouraged, in turn, a managerial revolution within the Pentagon. Under McNamara the defense department centralized all military research and development, created a Defense Intelligence Agency above the intelligence divisions of the separate armed services, and coordinated a variety of military functions—all under civilian command.

Liberal enthusiasm for technical management also defined the administration's space program. Five months after taking office, Kennedy used the continuing Cold War with the Soviet Union to call for the landing of an American on the moon by the end of the decade. "No single space project," he said, "will be more impressive to mankind," and he exhorted "every scientist, every engineer, every technician, contractor, and civil servant [to give] his personal pledge that this nation will move forward, with the full speed of freedom, in the exciting adventure of space." Vice President Johnson, author of the 1958 legislation that established the National Aeronautics and Space Administration (NASA), now served as

Exhibit 11–2. Research and Development, 1960–1968.
(current dollars in billions)

	Total	*Defense and Space-related*
1960	$13.5b	$7.4b
1964	$18.9b	$10.6b
1968	$24.6b	$11.8b

Source: *Statistical Abstract of the United States* (1987)

JOHN GLENN
1921–

"We have stressed the team effort in Project Mercury," said the nation's newest hero three days after becoming the first American to circumnavigate the Earth from outer space on February 20, 1962. "It goes across the board...sort of a crosscut of Americana, of industry and military and civil service, government workers, contractors—a crosscut of American effort in the technical field." At this moment of awesome technological achievement, however, astronaut John Glenn also symbolized the vitality of traditional earth-bound virtues: love of family, religion, and patriotism.

Born and raised in small-town Ohio in the 1920s and '30s, Glenn left home to become a Marine aviator during World War II and remained in the military as a combat flyer in Korea and later as a test pilot of jet aircraft. In 1957 he set the coast-to-coast speed record (three hours twenty-three minutes, eight-point-four seconds) in a Chance Voight F8U-1 Crusader that required three mid-air refuelings with high flying tankers. Such technical proficiency and iron-willed self-discipline qualified Glenn to become one of the seven original astronauts. Yet he deliberately blended his enthusiasm for modern technology with old-fashioned "Manifest Destiny." "I take my religion very seriously," he stated at the first Project Mercury press conference in 1959. "We are placed here with certain talents and capabilities...I think we would be most remiss in our duty if we didn't make the full use of our talents in volunteering for something...as important as this is to our country and to the world in general right now."

Framed by the Cold War with the Soviet Union, the "space race" pitted free-enterprise capitalism against state-supported technological planning. The American astronauts presented the human side of the competition. To the public's dismay, however, the United States appeared to run second. Soviet cosmonaut Yuri Gargarin circumnavigated the globe in April 1961, a month before American Alan Shepard's first sub-orbital flight. Thus despite serious technological malfunctions aboard Glenn's "Friendship 7" space capsule, the mission restored national confidence in *(cont.)*

chairman of the National Aeronautics and Space Council and shared Kennedy's zeal. To Secretary McNamara, moreover, the space program promised to compensate the aerospace industry for major cuts in military contracting demanded by cost-benefit analysis, thus blunting some of the expected unemployment that would result. Concerned about winning support from big business, Kennedy and Johnson also endorsed private ownership of a communications satellite corporation and worked vigorously to overcome a 1962 Senate filibuster, led by Tennessee's Estes Kefauver, to block this federally-supported private monopoly.

A carefully orchestrated public relations program reinforced popular support of space travel. The mass media portrayed the first astronauts as all-American pi-

(cont.) the space program. "This is the new ocean," declared President John Kennedy moments after Glenn splashed down in the Atlantic, "and I believe the United states must sail on it and be...second to none."

The public spontaneously embraced the sunny-faced astronaut. "I still get a hard-to-define feeling inside when the flag goes by," Glenn told a joint session of Congress, which interrupted his patriotic remarks twenty-five times with applause. Four million people—equivalent to half the population of New York City—lined the streets of lower Manhattan to produce the largest ticker tape parade in history. "Freedom, devotion to God and country are not things of the past," the astronaut assured a luncheon audience at New York's Waldorf Astoria. During the next year, Glenn received over half a million letters of encouragement from around the country. He won medals from a variety of organizations. He was named Father of the Year and the Daughters of the American Revolution saluted him "for demonstrating that patriotism is not old-fashioned." Even the many journalists and photographers who covered these events eventually broke ranks to ask for his autograph.

Treated as a prophet of the space age, Glenn felt emboldened to offer opinions on a multitude of subjects, including politics. Spurred by the Kennedy brothers, he ran for the Ohio Democratic senatorial nomination in 1964 but an accidental injury forced his withdrawal. Robert Kennedy's ill-fated campaign of 1968 drew him back to politics. By then, however, the political mood demanded more cogent policy positions and Glenn's homilies failed him. He narrowly lost a Senate bid in 1970. Then, after Watergate, as Americans sought confirmation of traditional virtues, Glenn won election to the Senate by over one million votes. The former astronaut expressed higher ambitions but competed unsuccessfully for the vice presidency in 1976 and for the presidency four years later. His personal fame, obvious sincerity, and diligence on technical issues involving nuclear power and nuclear weapons could not compensate for bland political rhetoric and a penchant for boring detail. The hard-working Glenn kept his seat in the Senate. "I have a very big ego," he admitted. "But for me the glitter, the glamour, the attention mean very little now. I've had it all. I've had the ticker-tape parades." ∎

oneers and heralded John Glenn's 1962 flight around the globe as a psychological victory in the Cold War. As NASA planned Project Mercury (the circumnavigation of earth by single astronauts, 1962); Project Gemini (multimanned flights, rendezvous in space, and spacewalks, 1964–65); and Project Apollo (moon landing, 1969), the space budget leaped fivefold to over $5 billion by 1964. By then, government funded space research and development accounted for 78 percent of all American R&D. But while Kennedy and Johnson emphasized the prestige of space exploration, expenditures for rockets and satellites served basic military functions involving ballistic missiles, communications, and intelligence gathering. For reasons of national security, this aspect of the space program remained secret. And while the Outer Space Treaty, signed by sixty-two nations in 1967, prohibited nuclear weapons in space and declared the moon a demilitarized zone, the defense strategy of both superpowers precluded ending military operations in space. By then, the space program reflected both strategic power and heightened aspirations at home.

KENNEDY ECONOMICS

In the month of Kennedy's inauguration, a Gallup poll found that 42 percent hoped the president would pursue moderate policies; 24 percent hoped he would be conservative; and 23 percent desired a liberal position. This middle-of-the-road climate reinforced the traditional congressional leadership which jealously guarded its power. To assist the new president, House Speaker Sam Rayburn agreed to expand the powerful Rules Committee to weaken the conservative majority. Despite strong opposition from southern conservatives, Rayburn managed to push the measure through on a very narrow vote. But southern legislators, who adhered to states' rights and protection of their region's economic interests, later took revenge by killing or diluting liberal proposals such as higher minimum wages and federal aid to education.

Despite growing public concern about poverty, especially after the publication of Michael Harrington's influential book, *The Other America* in 1962, Congress thwarted significant liberal reform. In 1961, for example, legislators responded favorably to Kennedy's request for an Area Development Agency to stimulate industrial development in depressed areas such as Appalachia by improving public facilities and offering cheap loans to entice business relocations. Yet Congress failed to provide the program with sufficient funds. By 1963, the entire state of West Virginia had gained only 350 jobs. Similarly, although public housing legislation in 1961 permitted the destruction of slum neighborhoods, it failed to mandate adequate replacements. By 1967, some 400,000 buildings had been demolished, resulting in over 1.4 million displaced residents. Kennedy lacked enough political support even to introduce legislation for hospital insurance for the elderly.

Despite these limitations, the president demonstrated bolder leadership in boosting economic expansion. Believing that a healthy capitalist structure could compete effectively against world Communism, Kennedy had criticized his predecessor for failing to stimulate economic growth. He promised to bring the economy to a 5 percent growth rate per year. Such proposals seemed especially relevant because unemployment stood at 7.7 percent in January 1961. Kennedy's economic advisers, particularly the liberal Walter Heller, urged more vigorous federal spending. But the president declined to confront Congress on that issue. Instead, he proposed a tax credit to encourage business to invest in new plant equipment. By stimulating capital investments, the measure would simultaneously attack unemployment and provide for long-term growth. To compensate for the loss of tax revenue, Kennedy also requested tax reforms to close corporate loopholes such as expense accounts and tax-exempt foreign incomes. But these reforms adversely affected influential corporate leaders and Congress delayed action on the tax bill until 1962. Meanwhile, heavy government spending for military defense boosted the sagging economy.

As the recession passed in 1961, the White House struck at the problem of inflation. Early the following year the president's Council of Economic Advisers issued a series of wage-price "guideposts" to limit inflationary increases. These imprecise guideposts linked wage increases to rising worker productivity and remained subject to corporate control. Even so, business leaders objected to government efforts to regulate wages and prices.

The disagreement climaxed in a major clash between the White House and the nation's largest industry—steel—in the spring of 1962. As part of the anti-inflation program, the administration had persuaded the United Steelworkers Union to accept a modest pay increase, assuring workers that the industry would hold the price line. But in April 1962, Roger Blough, president of U. S. Steel, notified Kennedy that his company would raise prices $6 per ton, an amount the White House considered inflationary. Other steel companies said they would follow Blough's lead. "My father once told me that all steelmen were sons of bitches, and I did not realize until now how right he was," Kennedy remarked. He then exerted maximum executive pressure to force the steel industry to retreat. McNamara instructed the defense department to purchase steel only from non-inflationary companies and Attorney General Robert F. Kennedy ordered investigations of industry price-fixing. These pressures led Inland Steel Corporation to reject a price increase, creating a domino effect within the industry. Kennedy had effectively defended his economic strategy.

Despite the fact that lower steel prices reduced costs for manufacturers, many business leaders bitterly resented this show of government economic power. A slumping stock market intensified their anger. In May 1962, Wall Street prices touched the lowest point since the Crash of 1929. The downturn reflected the belated impact of the 1960–61 recession, which had reduced corporate earnings. But the president's stand on steel prices disheartened elements of the business community, which blamed the administration for the slump. Kennedy responded to this crisis of confidence by emphasizing his support of business. At the Yale University commencement in June 1962, the president pleaded for an end to "sterile acrimony." Kennedy also denied the evils of deficit spending. "What is at stake is not some grand warfare of rival ideologies," he declared, "but the practical management of a modern economy."

The administration moved quickly to demonstrate support of corporate prosperity. A lowering of margin requirements stimulated the stock market. The Treasury department liberalized depreciation allowances for business equipment, thus encouraging the replacement of older machinery. Congress finally enacted the proposed tax credit on new investments as well as a diluted tax reform package that maintained specific benefits for business. Kennedy endorsed new legislation for the marketing of drugs that proved favorable to the pharmaceutical industry and lobbied Congress to permit private control of space communications.

The commitment to business culminated in the president's support of foreign trade. Since the late 1950s, the economy had suffered a serious imbalance of foreign payments, largely because of heavy spending for military bases abroad. In 1961, Kennedy created a special position in the Pentagon to encourage sales of American arms to foreign nations. He also continued Eisenhower's policy of trying to persuade the NATO nations to pay a larger share of the common defense.

But when the United States refused to relinquish an absolute veto over the use of nuclear weapons, the allies rejected a plan to create a multilateral nuclear force. Kennedy also persuaded Congress to pass a trade expansion bill in 1962. In addition, the president hoped to negotiate tariff reductions to increase trade with the European allies. But when France vetoed British participation in the Common Market, the prospects of Atlantic economic unity receded.

Kennedy showed greater innovation by scrapping a balanced budget in favor of the "new economics" of John Maynard Keynes. In 1961, the president had rejected the advice of the Council of Economic Advisers to cut taxes to stimulate expansion. By 1962, however, Kennedy accepted the theory that a tax cut would increase consumer spending, lift the "fiscal drag," and thus increase the rate of economic growth. The next year, the president submitted a proposal to Congress that called for a $13.6 billion reduction of taxes, most of it on individual incomes, as well as reforms to shift the tax burden toward the upper brackets.

THE CIVIL RIGHTS CRISIS

Inequities of wealth contributed to a growing awareness of racial discrimination. Recognizing the power of southern Democrats, Kennedy avoided the problems of racial minorities for as long as he could. While appeasing southern patronage demands, awarding federal construction projects to southern states, and raising price supports on cotton, the president declined to introduce civil rights legislation. Instead, he took moderate executive actions, such as the creation of the Commission on Equal Employment Opportunity (CEEO) in 1961. Headed by Vice President Johnson, the CEEO endeavored to end discrimination on work done under government contract. But the commission preferred voluntary compliance and seldom punished violators. And although Kennedy claimed during the 1960 campaign that Eisenhower could eliminate federal support of segregated housing "with the stroke of a pen," the Democratic president became remarkably silent when that power passed into his own hands. Civil rights leaders began sending pens to the White House—to no avail. Hoping to win congressional approval for a Department of Urban Affairs, Kennedy refused to challenge segregated housing. Not until 1962, after Congress defeated his efforts, did the president act to end segregation in federally funded housing. More than previous administrations, however, Kennedy appointed blacks to government positions and allowed them to work in areas other than race relations.

Kennedy's limited support of equal rights for blacks reflected more than a fear of southern power. Like most political leaders, the president believed that changes in race relations could not be forced on the nation. He placed his hopes not on new legislation but on enforcement of the voting rights provisions of the Civil Rights Acts of 1957 and 1960. According to his premises, Attorney General Robert Kennedy would file suits on behalf of black plantiffs, thereby guaranteeing black suffrage and providing the basis for black political power. He believed that other changes would follow from these beginnings. But Kennedy's inertia, after acquiring 70 percent of the black vote in 1960, belied his premises. Moreover, he weakened the possibility of obtaining favorable judicial rulings by appointing segregationist judges to federal courts in the South. One Kennedy appointee openly referred to blacks as "niggers" and "chimpanzees."

Frustrated by the president's indifference, black activists resolved to force legal change by defying segregationist laws. Following the nonviolent, direct action strategy of Martin Luther King and the sit-in demonstrators of 1960, the Congress of Racial Equality (CORE) launched a series of "freedom rides" in 1961 to win southern acceptance of integrated interstate commerce and transportation or force federal intervention. As expected, violent crowds in South Carolina and Alabama viciously attacked the integrated contingent of freedom riders, while law enforcement authorities looked on. The raw violence, coming on the eve of a summit meeting between Kennedy and Khrushchev, embarrassed the White House and compelled Kennedy to act. The president ordered federal marshals into the South and obtained court injunctions against interference with interstate travel. At the same time, Robert Kennedy asked the freedom riders for a "cooling-off period." "We had been cooling off for one hundred years," protested James Farmer, organizer of the freedom rides. "If we got any cooler we'd be in a deep freeze." Meanwhile, the Attorney General petitioned the Interstate Commerce Commission to end segregation in interstate travel. Behind-the-scenes pressure led to the desired ICC ruling in 1961.

Despite Kennedy's desire to remain aloof from the civil rights controversy, black activism and white intransigence continued to force presidential intervention. In 1962, for example, James Meredith, a black Air Force veteran, won a federal court order allowing him to enter the all-white University of Mississippi. But Governor Ross Barnett spoke for the southern leadership when he announced his refusal to comply with the ruling. Following the precedent of Eisenhower in 1957, Kennedy promptly federalized the national guard and sent federal marshals and soldiers into the university town of Oxford. After a night of violence and bloodshed, Meredith gained entry into the university. But Kennedy tried to avoid further antagonism of southern leaders, permitting state officials to maintain their power and making no attempt to punish Barnett for violating the law.

While the administration sought to heal the breaches caused by the civil rights movement, the Student Non-violent Coordinating Committee (SNCC) proceeded with a voter registration campaign among disenfranchised blacks. Such activities threatened the southern power structure, provoking a fierce reign of terror—beatings, bombings, and murders—to deny the exercise of constitutional rights. As in the case of the freedom rides, however, civil rights workers discovered that the federal government did not provide adequate protection on the grounds that it lacked a statutory right to intervene. Government inertia aroused widespread indignation and provoked further protest. To quiet such dissent, Kennedy introduced a civil rights bill in February 1963, calling for prosecution of voting rights violations, federal funds to encourage school desegregation, and extension of the Civil Rights Commission. "We are committed to achieving true equality of opportunity," said Kennedy, "because it is right."

Black leaders rejected Kennedy's modest proposal. In the spring of 1963, King's Southern Christian Leadership Conference (SCLC) carried the civil rights crusade to Birmingham, Alabama, purportedly "the most thoroughly segregated big city" in the nation. The minister's nonviolent strategy aimed at producing so much "creative tension" that segregationist leaders would feel compelled to negotiate a peaceful settlement. The American Gandhi was not mistaken. After several weeks of noisy but relatively peaceful demonstrations, local police chief "Bull" Connor attempted to end the protest by attacking the peaceful demonstrators, including many children, with clubs, fire hoses, and dogs. This brutality steeled the nerves of black protesters and, because of wide television coverage, sent waves of outrage throughout the land.

"We face...a moral crisis as a country and as a people," Kennedy told a television audience in June 1963. "It cannot be met by repressive police action. It cannot be left to increased demonstrations in the streets." The president then introduced a new civil rights bill to prohibit racial discrimination in public accommodations, to authorize the Justice department to initiate suits to desegregate public schools, to improve black employment opportunities, and to protect voting rights. Although black activists questioned loopholes in the proposal, few doubted the clarity of Kennedy's moral position.

While Congress began to consider the civil rights bill, black leaders staged a show of strength by organizing a March on Washington. The president initially discouraged the demonstration, but civil rights activists refused to retreat. On August 28, 1963, 250,000 marchers converged in the nation's capital and heard Martin Luther King proclaim, "I have a dream...that the sons of former slaves and the sons of former slaveowners will be able to sit together at the table of brotherhood." King's passionate language electrified the crowd.

Other voices in Washington, however, indicated deep rifts within the black community and presented an alternative vision of the black future. John Lewis, head of SNCC, attacked the administration for its "immoral compromises" with conservative politicians. "If any radical social, political, and economic changes are to take place in our society," he said, "the people, the masses must bring them about. In the struggle, we must seek more than mere civil rights; we must work for the community of love, peace, and true brotherhood." Three months later, Lewis's words echoed in a speech by black nationalist leader Malcolm X. Recognizing the importance of achieving political power as a precondition for racial progress, Malcolm rejected the limited horizons of racial integration. "A revolutionary," he asserted, "is a black nationalist."

THE COLD WAR ON NEW FRONTIERS

Because of the weakness of his political base and his lifelong interest in world affairs, Kennedy often subordinated domestic issues to matters of foreign policy. Thus he perceived civil rights agitation as a national embarrassment and saw the Birmingham confrontation as a "spectacle which was seriously damaging the reputation of the country abroad." For Kennedy the *image* of the United States served as a crucial weapon in the Cold War against communism. That was why he committed large economic resources to the space race. "If we are to win the battle that is now going on around the world between freedom and tyranny," he explained in 1961, "the dramatic achievements in space...should have made clear to us all...the impact of this adventure on the minds of men everywhere, who are attempting to make a determination on which road they should take." To demonstrate the superiority of American capitalism and technology and to energize youth to national commitment, Kennedy also created the Peace Corps

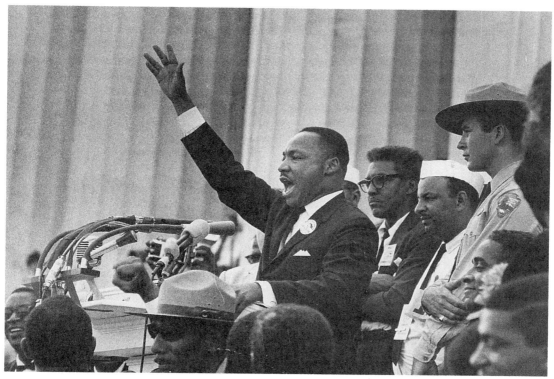

The Reverend Martin Luther King, Jr., addressed 250,000 demonstrators who marched from the Washington Monument to the Lincoln Memorial on August 28, 1963 to demand jobs, civil rights, and racial justice.

in 1961, encouraging citizen volunteers to serve "on a mission of freedom" around the world.

In continuing the global Cold War, Kennedy believed that the nations of Asia, Africa, and Latin America held the key to victory over Communism. He pledged his "best efforts" to assist new nations "to break the bonds of mass misery." The president established a Food for Peace program to send surplus food to poor countries, claiming not to be motivated by international politics. Unlike Eisenhower, Kennedy did not insist that neutral nations take sides in the Cold War. In the former Belgian colony of the Congo, for example, the United States supported a United Nations peace mission to back a neutralist government. But the president expected the U.N. to keep the Soviet Union out of Africa and allowed the CIA to provide secret payments and military aid to friendly Congolese politicians.

In his inaugural address Kennedy called for "a new alliance for progress" in Latin America. Two months later he announced "a vast cooperative effort...to satisfy the basic needs of the American peoples for homes, work and land, health and schools." Promising to bring technical expertise and capital investment, the president envisioned major agrarian reform and public welfare within democratic institutions. At a conference in Punta del Esta, Uruguay, in 1961, the administration pledged $20 billion to alleviate endemic poverty and bring social reform.

Such assistance boosted United States prestige in Latin America, but the White House had no intention of altering political arrangements in the area. Instead, Washington continued to cooperate with conservative landed elites and their military allies. United States corporations appeared equally reluctant to risk additional investment in Latin America. In 1962, Congress approved the Hickenlooper Amendment, which prohibited foreign aid to countries that nationalized or excessively taxed corporate property. The next year, the Foreign Assistance Act established an Investment Guaranty program that required recipients of United States aid to insure investors against losses due to nationalization. But most aid to Latin America went in the form of loans, rather than grants, that had to be repaid with interest and service charges (usually amounting to 50 percent of the face value of the loans). Even these limited funds had to be spent within the United States at prevailing prices. Thus the Alliance for Progress merely protected traditional markets and preserved investment stability for United States corporations.

The Alliance for Progress also promised to blunt the revolutionary appeal of Cuba's Fidel Castro. During his last days in office Eisenhower had broken diplomatic relations with Cuba and ordered the CIA to plan a military coup. As a presidential candidate Kennedy endorsed the overthrow of Castro. Believing that Castro did not represent the Cuban people and could be toppled with sufficient pressure, Kennedy urged business leaders to boycott Cuba and banned the importation of Cuban sugar.

Anti-Castro activities culminated in a military invasion of Cuba at the Bay of Pigs in April 1961 by fourteen-hundred Cuban exiles trained and organized in Guatemala by the CIA. Despite second thoughts, Kennedy approved the scheme, but made no promise of additional military assistance. The CIA planned badly, choosing an indefensible landing position and mismanaging its inital air attacks. Recognizing an imminent disaster, the Kennedy administration refused to provide additional air support, dooming the mission and leaving the invasion force vulnerable to Cuban reprisals. Most serious, the president had underestimated the strength of Castro's political base.

Though American newspapers had received unofficial leaks about the Bay of Pigs operation, the administration persuaded major publications such as the *New York Times* to suppress the story. "There will not be, under any conditions, an intervention in Cuba," the president told a press conference five days, before the futile mission. Secretary of State Dean Rusk also lied blatantly: "The American people are entitled to know whether we are intervening in Cuba or intend to do so in the future," he said on the morning of the invasion. "The answer to that question is no. What happens in Cuba is for the Cuban people to decide." In justifying the invasion, Kennedy saw Castro as a pawn in the Cold War. "We are opposed around the world by a monolithic and ruthless conspiracy," he told the nation's leading news editors, "that relies primarily on covert means for expanding its sphere of influence." This "rising din of Communist voices," said Kennedy, had be matched by strong counterinsurgency. The president then urged the news media to limit reporting of world events. "Every democracy," he claimed, "recognizes the necessary restraints of national security."

In the aftermath of the Bay of Pigs, the president permitted the CIA to conduct illegal military activities against Castro, provided they were "plausibly deniable." Thus the CIA endeavored to disrupt Cuban trade with the Soviet Union, in

President Kennedy's televised press conferences provided a showcase for his personal charisma—spontaneous humor, intelligence, charm, and what the media called "the Kennedy style."

one case contaminating a shipload of sugar with bad-tasting chemicals. Secret CIA operations included support of anti-Castro exiles and underworld gangsters to assassinate the Cuban leader. Kennedy also exerted economic pressure, prohibiting trade with the island. Such destabilizing efforts drew Castro closer to the Soviet orbit.

KENNEDY CONFRONTS KHRUSHCHEV

Having been thwarted in Cuba, Kennedy resolved to prove his toughness on the issue of Germany. While the Soviet Union wanted to formalize the existence of two German states—one linked to the Communist bloc, the other with the West—and so force the Western allies to leave Berlin, Washington still demanded the unification of Germany through free elections (in which the larger population of West Germany would predominate). In his first State of the Union address, Kennedy depicted a monolithic conspiracy aiming at "world domination" and called for increased appropriations for military defense. Two months later, he made the first of three military budget requests, asking Congress for $2.4 billion for missiles. In another two months, the president requested additional appropriations for conventional weapons and counterinsurgency. Knowing that the United States possessed missile superiority, Kennedy hoped to create a preponderance of power that would force the Kremlin to accept American terms about Germany. In this spirit he agreed to meet Khrushchev in Vienna in June 1961.

Kennedy underestimated Soviet resolve. In a blistering encounter, Khrushchev reminded the president that World War II had ended sixteen years earlier and demanded that the western powers sign a final peace treaty that recognized the two German states and terminated the military occupation of Berlin. Kennedy rejected the proposal, insisting that the United States could not abandon its allies in West Berlin. Shaken by Khrushchev's militance, he predicted "a cold winter" ahead. The president returned from Vienna bearing "sober" news for the American people and promptly asked Congress for over $3 billion of military appropriations, increasing the total military package to $6 billion in his first six months of office. Kennedy also increased the size of the armed forces, called up the reserves, and extended the draft. Finally, in a gesture that flashed horror through the land, the president requested increased appropriations for civil defense and bomb shelters. Khrushchev then ordered the erection of a military barrier between East and West Berlin in August 1961, which ended the flood of refugees from East Germany and also symbolized his determination to preserve two German states. Despite an extreme atmosphere of crisis, Kennedy determined to test Soviet strategy by ordering fifteen hundred battle-ready troops to drive from West Germany into West Berlin where they would be met by Vice President Johnson. Khrushchev decided not to aggravate the situation. After American troops entered West Berlin, Khrushchev scrapped his deadline for settling the Berlin question and the crisis passed.

Nevertheless, the Cold War intensified that month when the Russian leader announced an end to the Soviet moratorium on nuclear bomb testing. Within a week, Kennedy declared the United States had "no other choice" but to resume underground testing. Two days later, *Life* magazine published an article, endorsed by Kennedy, asserting (erroneously) that a national program of fallout shelters would assure 97 percent survival rate in case of nuclear war. The news precipitated the first major protests against nuclear testing by peace organizations such as the National Committee for a Sane Nuclear Policy (SANE) and the Student Peace Union (SPU).

As Soviet tests escalated to the fifty-megaton level, the Kennedy administration aggravated the tension by revealing to Khrushchev that United States intelligence knew the extent of Soviet military weakness. This knowledge led the president to propose a resumption of disarmament talks that would preserve the American nuclear advantage. But France, a nuclear power since 1960, refused to participate, and the Soviet Union raised familiar objections to international inspection. Kennedy then ordered a resumption of atmospheric tests in April 1962.

The Cuban Missile Crisis

In admitting the non-existence of a "missile gap," Kennedy may have increased Soviet fears about the imbalance of power. The White House then intensified these concerns by announcing a shift in nuclear strategy in June 1962. Hereafter,

Exhibit 11–3. Cuban Missile Crisis.

American missiles would be aimed not at Soviet cities but at nuclear missile sites. Such targets meant that an American first-strike could obliterate Soviet power to retaliate. This disadvantage may have influenced Khrushchev's decision to place less-expensive short range missiles in Cuba. In the aftermath of Sputnik, the United States had pursued a similar policy by establishing missile bases in Turkey and Italy. During the summer of 1962, the Soviet Union began building sites in Cuba to base missiles with a striking range of two thousand miles, sufficient to reach East Coast cities or the Panama Canal. When U-2 aircraft surveillance confirmed intelligence reports, Kennedy summoned a top-level executive committee in October 1962 to consider appropriate responses. The choices ranged from immediate military attack—a "Pearl Harbor in reverse," objected Robert Kennedy—to diplomatic retreat by closing American missile bases in Turkey if the Soviets removed theirs from Cuba. A consensus eventually emerged that considered armed intervention only a last resort. Yet the administration rejected the possibility of negotiating the removal of the missiles. To Kennedy, Soviet power in the Western Hemisphere was not negotiable.

The president finally accepted a third strategy that did not completely rule out the other two. In a dramatic televised speech, he described Soviet intervention as "deliberately provocative" and demanded the removal of all missiles. "We will not prematurely or unnecessarily risk the cost of worldwide nuclear war in which the fruits of victory would be ashes in our mouth," he promised, "—but neither will we shrink from that risk at any time it must be faced." As the world approached a nuclear holocaust, Kennedy announced the establishment of a "quarantine"—a naval blockade— to exclude offensive weapons from Cuba.

In confronting Khrushchev with public military threats, Kennedy avoided traditional diplomatic channels. The president also rebuffed a U.N. proposal for a three-week moratorium and refused to consult with American allies. Such rigidity exaggerated the crisis. As McNamara observed, nuclear warheads in the Soviet Union could inflict greater damage than the weapons in Cuba. Nor was Castro likely to launch a suicidal strike against the United States. Kennedy's insistence on a rigid deadline probably reflected his desire to settle the crisis before the November 1962 congressional elections.

Khrushchev had not anticipated Kennedy's outraged reaction. In a private letter to the president, the Soviet leader protested the demand for unconditional surrender and refused to recognize the naval blockade. But Khrushchev did not want to start a war that "would not be in our power to stop." In a second, emotional letter, the Russian leader emphasized that Soviet ships in the mid-Atlantic carried nonmilitary goods and that the missiles already had been landed in Cuba. He then offered to remove the weapons, provided the United States ended the blockade and agreed to respect Cuban independence. "Only a madman," Khrushchev wrote, "can believe that armaments are the principal means in the life of a society."

The next day, however, the president received still another message from Khrushchev that stiffened the terms for removal of the missiles. The Soviet leader now demanded the withdrawal of missiles from Turkey in exchange for those in Cuba. Months earlier, Kennedy had ordered the State Department to negotiate the removal of those outmoded weapons. But in the midst of the Cuban crisis, Kennedy refused to negotiate the question, fearing to weaken his public image as a cold warrior or to suggest a wavering of national policy.

Robert Kennedy proposed a solution to this new dilemma. The United States would ignore Khrushchev's last letter and answer only the more conciliatory message that preceded it. Kennedy's reply, therefore, made no mention of the bases in Turkey. Nevertheless, the administration made an informal agreement to remove the missiles from Turkey and Italy. Khrushchev then accepted the arrangement and the crisis passed. Two months later, Kennedy admitted that the Cuban missiles would not have changed the military balance of power. "But it would have politically changed the balance of power. It would have appeared to, and appearances contribute to reality." Although Khrushchev's retreat enhanced the president's reputation, the diplomatic victory obscured Washington's inability to change the government of Cuba. As Castro remained in power the frustrated administration continued its covert program to assassinate the Cuban leader and overthrow the Communist regime.

TOWARD DÉTENTE

The brush with nuclear confrontation convinced Kennedy to seek an end to nuclear testing. As the two superpowers resumed negotiations, the president overcame his doubts about verification by placing his faith in the technology of satellite photographs and distant seismography. In a dramatic speech at American University in June 1963, Kennedy introduced a major reevaluation of the Cold War. Assuring the world that the United States did not seek "a Pax Americana enforced...by American weapons of war," he urged the nation "not to see only a distorted and desperate view of the other side, not to see conflict as inevitable." The United States could not overlook its differences with the Soviet Union, he said. But "we can help make the world safe for diversity."

Kennedy then announced that he was sending a mission to Moscow to negotiate a test ban treaty. In addition, as an act of "good faith," he ordered a halt on nuclear testing. Having set aside the questions of inspection and underground testing, Soviet and American negotiators quickly reached agreement. But the treaty still required approval from Congress, the "military-industrial complex," and public opinion. The administration therefore emphasized that the test-ban constituted an American victory in the Cold War. Since the United States held a clear lead in nuclear technology, the ban on testing would preserve American superiority. Moreover, Kennedy assured the Pentagon that underground tests would continue. These promises were fulfilled after the Senate ratified the treaty in September 1963.

Although Kennedy expressed interest in extending detente with the Soviet Union and approved the sale of surplus wheat in 1963, he rebuffed overtures to open negotiations between NATO and the Warsaw Pact nations of the Soviet bloc. Fearing a weakening of the Western alliance, the president journeyed to Europe in the summer of 1963 and reiterated the polarities first stated by President Truman. "Today, in the world of freedom," he told a cheering throng in West Berlin, "the proudest boast is 'Ich bin ein Berliner'" ("I am a Berliner"). Once again Kennedy reaffirmed the impossibility of compromising with Communism. He never wavered from that belief. In his last undelivered speech, the president defined his sense of historical mission: "We in this country, in this generation, are, by destiny rather than choice, the watchmen on the walls of world freedom."

CONTESTING FOR THE THIRD WORLD

In pursuing a flexible response in the Cold War, Kennedy argued in 1961 that "the great battlefield for the defense and expansion of freedom today is the whole southern half of the globe—Asia, Latin America, Africa, and the Middle East—the lands of the rising peoples." Here the president saw Communism "nibbling away" at the forces of freedom. "The complacent, the self-indulgent, the soft societies are about to be swept away with the debris of history," said Kennedy. "Only the strong, only the industrious, only the determined, only the courageous, only the visionary who determine the real nature of our struggle can possibly survive."

As Eisenhower handed the reins of office to Kennedy, the outgoing president apologized for leaving a "mess" in Laos. "You might have to go in there and fight it out." A political coalition established in 1954 had collapsed, and the Eisenhower administration had then supported an anti-Communist regime. In 1960, Laos erupted in civil war. Kennedy announced his support for an independent country. "We cannot...accept any visible humiliation over Laos," he declared. But since neither the United States nor the Soviet Union intended to fight over Laos, they agreed to allow a neutralist Laos to emerge in 1962. Kennedy, however, continued to seek a pro-American regime. Using the foreign aid program, Washington pressured the neutralist government to exclude Communists, while the CIA provided military assistance to anti-Communist guerrillas in violation of the Geneva agreements. Open warfare exploded in 1963. But the Laotian controversy soon blurred into the larger American commitment to South Vietnam.

Having been humiliated at the Bay of Pigs and cautious about involvement in Laos, Kennedy resolved to act decisively in Vietnam. By 1961, the American-backed regime of Ngo Dinh Diem, an American-educated Catholic, was rapidly losing support to the newly-established Communist Viet Cong as well as to non-Communist dissidents such as Buddhist priests. Responding to Viet Cong pressure, Kennedy increased the number of military advisers and dispatched Green Berets and intelligence agents to engage in covert warfare in 1961. Kennedy's decision reflected the advice of Vice President Johnson, who visited Vietnam for the president in 1961. Failure to help Diem, said Johnson, "would say to the world...that we don't live up to our treaties and don't stand by our friends." Although presidential advisers recommended additional military assistance, Kennedy hesitated to commit conventional forces and risk a repetition of the Korean war. Instead the president viewed Vietnam as an opportunity to prove the value of counterinsurgency. The White House also urged Diem to offer political reforms to broaden his support among Buddhists, but without success.

As American aid poured into Vietnam, the level of violence steadily increased. In 1962, the Viet Cong National Liberation Front indicated a willingness to negotiate a neutralization of South Vietnam, but the White House remained optimistic about military victory and rebuffed the approach. Meanwhile, the United States persuaded Diem to experiment with counterinsurgency based on "strategic hamlets." Assuming that guerrilla armies required a popular base, the scheme proposed the encampment of the peasant population behind barbed wire. Lacking contact with the people, the guerrillas would lose support and disappear. But the hamlets could not provide safety from Viet Cong attack and Vietnamese peasants resented the forced uprooting.

Despite such problems, the administration remained optimistic about final victory. "Every quantitative measurement we have," declared McNamara with his faith in numbers, "shows we're winning this war." In his 1963 State of the Union message, Kennedy boasted that the "spearpoint of aggression has been blunted in Vietnam." The State Department confirmed this optimism, announcing that thirty thousand Viet Cong were killed in 1962. But that figure appeared twice as large as the estimated size of the entire Viet Cong organization at the beginning of the year. Exaggerated administration claims stemmed not only from poor calculations, but also revealed a deliberate effort to deceive Congress and the nation about the nature of the American commitment. While military decisions remained secret, the administration misled the press. When the *New York*

Exhibit 11–4. Indochina.

Times's Saigon reporter David Halberstam, reported failures of American policy, Kennedy personally asked the newspaper to reassign him elsewhere.

By 1963, however, the Viet Cong had taken the military initiative, stepping up terrorist attacks against the Diem regime. Yet Diem refused to make political reforms. Tensions exploded in 1963 when South Vietnamese troops fired on a crowd of protesters, precipitating demonstrations and bloody reprisals. A Buddhist priest dramatically set himself on fire to protest the abuses of power. Such reactions embarrassed the administration, but the president took refuge in the domino theory. "For us to withdraw from that effort," he said, "would mean a collapse not only of South Vietnam, but Southeast Asia. So we are going to stay there." The administration nevertheless began to plan for the removal of Diem and encouraged a military coup. On November 2, 1963, South Vietnamese army officers, encouraged by the CIA took over the presidential palace and murdered Diem.

The assassination shocked Kennedy, but did not clearly alter his policy in Vietnam. By November 1963, the administration had stationed sixteen-thousand troops in South Vietnam. The previous month, Kennedy had announced the withdrawal of one-thousand men by the end of the year and said the United States commitment would end in 1965. But his words may have reflected the same misplaced optimism that characterized American policy toward Vietnam throughout the decade. Yet Kennedy never rescinded the troop withdrawal order. Moreover, a high-level meeting in Honolulu on November 20, 1963 apparently adopted an "accelerated plan" for reducing troop commitments. Such shadowy evidence suggests that with Diem dead, Kennedy was considering a political solution to the war.

ASSASSINATION, CONSENSUS, AND THE GREAT SOCIETY

Kennedy did not live to fulfill his plans. On a political junket to Texas designed to strengthen the Democratic party for the 1964 elections, he was shot and killed by sniper fire in Dallas on November 22, 1963. His alleged assailant, Lee Harvey Oswald, denied complicity in the murder but was killed in police custody by mobster Jack Ruby before he could testify. The mystery surrounding Kennedy's death contributed to the political turmoil of the decade. Although a special presidential commission, headed by Chief Justice Earl Warren, reported in 1964 that Oswald was a "loner" and had acted alone, many Americans believed the murder resulted from some unnamed conspiracy. A 1966 Gallup poll found that a majority of the public doubted the validity of the Warren report and yet a majority also opposed reopening the case.

The assassination shocked the nation—not only at the sudden, inexplicable death of the president, but also at the disruption of normal continuity in public life. To most Americans the events surrounding the assassination appeared as a shared emotional experience. Surveys found that 92 percent of the public learned of the assassination within two hours and that more than half of all Americans watched the same television coverage of the story. (For three days, the networks cancelled all advertising!) Millions watched Jack Ruby shoot Oswald. The mass public mourning inevitably magnified the slain president's stature. Local governments named and renamed public buildings in his honor; Kennedy's grave at Arlington National Cemetery became a national shrine; Kennedy memorabilia—picture books, coins, paintings, and jewelry—proliferated. Ironically, Kennedy created in death what had eluded him in life—a broad affirmation of consensus that transcended the differences of traditional politics.

Kennedy's successor, Lyndon Johnson, understood the power of this consensus. Five days after taking office, he stood before a joint session of Congress and pleaded earnestly, "Let us continue." Determined to preserve the liberal agenda, he retained all of Kennedy's major advisors and called for a "Great Society" to end poverty and racial injustice. Taking advantage of the public grief, he pushed legislation that Kennedy had initiated but failed to pass through Congress. By early 1964, Johnson managed to sign major legislation involving economic development, social welfare, and civil rights. But even such success weakened Johnson's appeal. Where Kennedy appeared quick, witty, and inspired, Johnson emerged a consummate politician, immensely experienced and skilled in political affairs but never quite reliable or sincere. The new president was notorious for bullying subordinates and ignoring political criticism. Failing to charm the public, Johnson eventually personified the duplicity of government and widened the "credibility gap" between the presidency and the people.

In his first legislative triumph, Johnson managed to save Kennedy's tax reform measure. The Revenue Act of 1964 marked the institutionalization of deficit spending and stimulated a 7 percent boost in the gross national product during its first year. To all outward appearances, government management had created unique economic expansion. The new tax laws encouraged productivity while reducing unemployment and inflation and brought booming prosperity for American corporations. Profits jumped 57 percent between 1960 and 1964, as technology continued to stimulate corporate development. Such innovations as pneumatic conveyors, copying machines, piggy-back freight, and containerized shipping increased efficiency and profits. Lucrative military and space contracts, particularly in the "sun belt" states of the South and Southwest, stimulated prosperity and corporate consolidation. By the end of the decade, 71 percent of manufacturing profits went to the four hundred largest firms.

In the reformist climate of the 1960s, however, the scope of corporate enterprise became an issue of public policy. Critics charged that the interaction of private business and public office did not always benefit the nation. Personnel shifted easily between corporate management and federal regulatory boards that set industry standards. Few government officials attempted to protect consumer interests. But Ralph Nader, a private lawyer, worked to publicize the problems of ordinary consumers. His book, *Unsafe at Any Speed* (1965) exposed the problems of General Motors's Corvair. Senate hearings then revealed that the world's largest corporation had investigated Nader's personal life in an effort to discredit his work. With a jury award of $280,000, Nader established research centers to monitor the quality of consumer products as well as investigate mining safety, radiation hazards, pollution, and tax inequities.

Prosperity in the 1960s both reflected and encouraged American enterprise abroad. By the end of the decade investment in western Europe doubled and the total value of American-owned overseas plants and equipment surpassed $100 billion. Standard Oil of New Jersey, for example, sold more oil in Europe than in the United States. While American firms exported $35 billion of goods each year, foreign subsidiaries of American multinationals annually sold another $45 billion. By 1970, the United States controlled nearly three-quarters of the world's oil and produced most of its machinery, electronics, and chemicals.

Amidst prosperity, however, income distribution remained lopsided. For example, the wealthiest fifth of American families received over 45 percent of the nation's personal income in 1966, whereas the lowest fifth took in 3.7 percent. Tax loopholes underlined the problem. Tax-exempt bonds, a refuge for wealthy investors, amounted to nearly $86 billion in 1963. Over 150 persons with incomes exceeding $200,000 paid no taxes in 1968. Corporations benefited from similar loopholes. The percentage of federal revenues coming from corporate income taxes dropped from 20 percent in 1955 to 12 percent in 1970. Yet nearly one-quarter of all Americans still lived in poverty.

Concerned about such inequities, Johnson vowed to make an "unconditional war on poverty" the cornerstone of his administration. Raised in the tradition of southern populism and himself a congressional New Dealer, Johnson believed that medical care, education, job trainings, and racial equality could complete the New Deal by assuring equal opportunity for all citizens. The Economic Opportunity Act of 1964 established training programs for the young and offered loans and grants for self-help projects initiated by local communities. The bill's Community Action program proved especially significant because it called for "participatory democracy" of the poor in shaping government-funded projects. The law also established a Job Corps for youth and VISTA (Volunteers in Service to America), which assigned volunteer workers to assist needy communities. The Office of Economic Opportunity (OEO) created Headstart to provide preschool help for children of the poor.

Johnson's political genius also assured passage of civil rights reforms. Although President Kennedy had lined up support for a civil rights law in 1963, southern senators expected to weaken its provisions. The assassination of the president abruptly changed the political climate. "No memorial or eulogy," Johnson told a stunned joint session of Congress five days after Kennedy's death, "could more eloquently honor Kennedy's memory than the earliest possible passage of the Civil Rights Bill for which he fought so long." Linking the new measure to the martyred president, Johnson refused to compromise its major provisions. With extraordinary legislative skill, he persuaded Republican leaders that civil rights represented "an idea whose time had come."

Backed by northern Republicans, including Minority Leader Everett Dirksen of Illinois, two-thirds of the Senate voted to invoke cloture to end a southern filibuster—the first time the Senate had voted to end discussion of a civil rights measure. The resulting Civil Rights Act of 1964 gave the federal government the power to sue to desegregate public accommodations and schools. The law also prohibited denial of equal job opportunities in all but the smallest businesses and unions and allowed the federal government to monitor state voting records. While blacks and liberals celebrated this landmark step toward equal opportunity, conservatives such as Senator Barry Goldwater of Arizona attacked the law's extension of federal power. Diehard southerners, such as Governor George Wallace of Alabama, detected a communist conspiracy at work.

By the end of 1964, Congress had enacted most of Johnson's social welfare program, including a $1 billion housing program, federal grants for mass transportation, loans for college students, and aid for college construction. The president also expanded a Kennedy pilot project into a food stamp program for the working poor. The rapid passage of these measures dazzled the country, and the media compared Johnson's success favorably with the legislative productivity of the first hundred days of Roosevelt's New Deal. The Kennedy administration had initiated many of these concepts, but it was Johnson's legislative skill that translated liberal intentions into government programs.

THE ELECTION OF 1964

Johnson's legislative triumph aroused opposition among conservatives, particularly in the South and Southwest. Like the followers of Robert Taft in 1952, right-wing Republicans deplored their party's acceptance of New Deal programs and demanded a vigorous purge of "communist" influence in American life. In 1964 Republican conservatives rallied behind Senator Goldwater, author of the best-selling book, *The Conscience of a Conservative* (1960), and defeated the more moderate presidential candidate Nelson D. Rockefeller of New York. "Extremism in the defense of liberty is no vice," declared Goldwater, in his acceptance speech to the stormy Republican National Convention, "...moderation in the pursuit of justice is no virtue." The Republican slogan—"in your heart you know he's right"—provoked a pithy liberal response: "Yes, far right!"

To Goldwater the disintegration of traditional values constituted a source of major concern. His was the first candidacy to embrace the "social issue," the discomfort experienced by many Americans over personally frightening aspects of social change in the 1960s. In his speeches Goldwater lamented crime in the streets, political corruption, aimlessness among youth, anxiety among the elderly, and the loss of spiritual meaning. He blamed social permissiveness for a "growing menace" to "personal safety." Goldwater also opposed the Civil Rights Act of 1964 because it required government to interfere with social and personal relations. "I will give you back your freedom," he promised vaguely.

Echoing these concerns, George Wallace captured national attention by winning one-third of the vote in Democratic primaries in Wisconsin, Indiana, and Maryland. Political commentators described the Wallace vote as a "backlash" against civil rights agitation and integration, but the conservative Democrat aimed most of his criticism at liberal paternalism and big government. "The American people," he said, "are fed up with the continuing trend toward a socialist state which subjects the individual to the dictates of an all-powerful central government." Wallace's surprising success revealed deep dissatisfactions among lower-middle-class whites about liberal support of blacks instead of their own economic and social problems. Recognizing that Wallace threatened his support in the South, Goldwater persuaded the Alabamian to withdraw.

Johnson, himself a southerner, worried more about black activism. In 1964, the Student Non-Violent Coordinating Committee had invited hundreds of white activists to participate in a voter registration campaign in Mississippi. The integrated Mississippi summer project encountered violent repression from vigilantes and local government authorities, which resulted in mass arrests, bombings, burning, beatings, and the murder of civil rights workers. Although only twelve-hundred blacks dared to register to vote during the summer's bloody events, a contingent of SNCC workers and new black voters went to the Democratic National Convention in Atlantic City to demand political representation.

Lyndon Johnson used the politics of consensus to win a 61 percent plurality in the 1964 election. Having signed civil rights legislation that year, he captured over 90 percent of the black vote.

Calling themselves the Mississippi Freedom Democratic party, they argued that the all-white Mississippi delegation should be unseated because blacks could not participate in their selection. But the president feared such reforms would cost white support in the South. In the end, no compromise was acceptable. The regular Mississippi delegates, most of whom backed Goldwater, left the convention, while the unseated blacks remained embittered by the hypocrisy of white liberals. As a gesture of reconciliation, Johnson chose the liberal Hubert Humphrey as his running mate.

Johnson and Humphrey sought a politics of consensus by defending civil rights legislation and promising moderation in Vietnam. "We seek no wider war," the president said, denouncing those who would "supply American boys to do the job that Asian boys should do." In the election, the Johnson-Humphrey ticket scored a record 61 percent plurality, amassing forty-three million votes. Goldwater carried only Arizona and five states in the deep South, while the Democrats won over 90 percent of the black vote. Similar to Roosevelt's victory in 1936, the Johnson landslide provided the president with better than two-to-one majorities in both houses of Congress. The election also inflated Johnson's conception of presidential authority and bolstered his consensus view of the nation. With an overwhelming electoral mandate, Johnson had achieved political independence and a unified nation. He could now attempt to fulfill the promises of the liberal agenda.

The president pressed ahead with Great Society programs. In 1965, Johnson signed an education bill which overcame a controversy about assistance to private schools by basing aid on the number of low-income families in each school district. A Higher Education Act that year provided college scholarships and fellowships. These laws enabled the federal government to influence local political decisions. For example, the Commissioner of Education ruled in 1965 that school districts had to show a "good faith substantial start" toward desegregation or lose federal funds. A year later, the Office of Education issued tighter guidelines, declaring an end to "paper compliance with desegregation orders." As appropriations for education reached $10 billion by the end of the decade, conservatives objected that federal aid was threatening local control over schools. "I'm not fighting the federal government," maintained Governor Wallace in 1966; "I'm fighting the outlaw beatnik crowd in Washington that has just about destroyed the federal government."

Johnson, meanwhile, pushed for health care for the elderly. With the president's approval, congressional leaders accepted a compromise that incorporated Republican demands for voluntary medical insurance to cover doctors' fees and drugs. But the heart of the Medicare package provided for hospital and nursing home care for Americans over sixty-five through payroll taxes administered by Social Security. The law also provided "Medicaid" grants to states that enacted health programs for poor people of all ages. "No longer will older Americans be denied the healing miracles of modern medicine," said Johnson as he signed the bill into law in the presence of former President Truman, who had first proposed national medical insurance in 1948. By 1970, the cost of state health care nearly equaled that of Medicare. But the law did not allow the government to control service fees. Hospital costs, which increased 7 percent in the year before Medicare, average 14 percent more each year for the next decade.

The Great Society peaked in 1965. Johnson signed a $1 billion Appalachia Assistance program, most of which went to road building in the economically depressed region. A portion of the $7.8 billion housing bill included rent supplements to low-income families. Johnson also made the Department of Housing and Urban Development a cabinet-level office, and followed that with approval of the Demonstration Cities and Metropolitan Development Act. The latter appropriated nearly $1 billion for intensive attacks on urban blight. Congress also abolished the national-origins quota system for immigration, designed to show that the United States was not racist. The Immigration Act of 1965 limited admission to 300,000 a year, but favored relatives of American citizens and those with special skills, rather than particular nationalities, and encouraged a significant increase in non-European immigration. (For the new immigrants, see chapter 6.)

The Triumph of Civil Rights

The Twenty-third Amendment to the Constitution, ratified in 1964, outlawed the poll tax, long a barrier to black voting in the South. But when blacks initiated a voter registration drive, including non-violent street demonstrations, in Selma, Alabama in 1965, local officials conspired with white mobs to prevent political change. The violence climaxed on "Bloody Sunday"—March 7, 1965—when police brutally attacked a peaceful march of demonstrators. Filmed and broadcast on national television, the atrocity forced the White House to intervene. Johnson

On "Bloody Sunday," Alabama state troopers used tear gas and clubs to crush a planned protest march from Selma to Montgomery to demand black suffrage. The spectacle outraged public opinion and spurred passage of the Voting Rights Act of 1965.

promptly summoned a joint session of Congress to request federal protection for black voter registrants. Borrowing the language of the civil rights movement itself, the first southern president since Woodrow Wilson declared, "All of us...must overcome the crippling legacy of bigotry and injustice—and we *shall* overcome."

The Voting Rights Act of 1965 abolished literacy tests and empowered the attorney general to assign federal examiners to register voters in states practicing discrimination. Applied to federal, state, and local elections, the law produced a revolution in southern life. The next year, federal examiners registered over 400,000 new black voters. By 1968, one million southern blacks had qualified to vote. And as blacks enlisted on the Democratic rolls, whites increasingly voted Republican, stimulating competition between the two parties in the south.

The Great Society brought other dramatic gains for blacks in national affairs. Robert Weaver, appointed head of the Department of Housing and Urban Development, became the first black cabinet member in history. Thurgood Marshall, former counsel of the NAACP, became the first black to serve on the Supreme Court. In 1966, Massachusetts elected Edward Brooke the first black senator since Reconstruction. Besides these token advances, many blacks made major economic strides as the booming economy percolated through American society. Black median family income increased from under $6000 in 1964 to over $8000 in 1969. At the same time, the ratio between black family income and that of white families narrowed from 54 percent to 61 percent. The percentage of black families living in poverty diminished from 48 percent in 1959 to 28 percent ten years later.

Exhibit 11–5. Unemployment Rates for Whites and Blacks, 1960–1968.
(percent of each group specified of persons
16 years and older in civilian labor force)

	1960	1964	1968
White	4.9	4.6	3.2
Black	10.2	9.6	6.7
Total	5.5	5.2	3.6

Source: *Historical Statistics of the United States, Colonial Times to 1970* (1975)

Despite these political and economic gains, however, moderate black leader-ship found it increasingly difficult to contain the mixture of impatience, rage, and black consciousness that accompanied heightened aspirations and unchanging realities for most black Americans. Passage of the Voting Rights Act marked the last triumph for the nonviolent and integrated civil rights movement. After 1965, national attention shifted to the 53 percent of the black population that lived out-side the South. Northern blacks lived primarily in decaying ghettos in the older industrial cities, where the exodus of manufacturing plants to the suburbs and sunbelt states and the transition to a suburban service economy proved disas-trous for black workers. In 1968, the Department of Labor reported that black unemployment ran three times as high as white rates. Meanwhile, housing, jobs, and welfare were simply inadequate to meet the basic needs of black families. In Chicago, for example, Aid to Dependent Children, the fastest growing welfare program of the decade, gave mothers only 21 cents per meal. Despite federal poverty programs, ghetto life remained depressingly unchanged through the decade.

RACIAL TURMOIL

In 1964, the powder keg exploded. During the next three years, particularly in the summers, over one-hundred riots and rebellions occurred as angry blacks from Harlem in New York City to Watts in Los Angeles seized or destroyed busi-nesses and property in their communities to protest economic exploitation and police harassment. Young blacks chanted "burn, baby, burn," while armed na-tional guardsmen patrolled city streets. Property damage approached $750 mil-lion, while dozens were killed and thousands injured. By 1966, militant black leaders such as SNCC's Stokely Carmichael were predicting another "long hot summer." In Chicago, Martin Luther King's "open city" campaign to alleviate ghetto problems touched off mass rioting, while his open housing marches into the white ethnic neighborhoods provoked violent retaliation. In 1967, Detroit went up in smoke as blacks went on a week-long rampage that provoked vicious suppression by the National Guard. A six-day riot in Newark, New Jersey, left twenty-seven dead. A special report to the governor later blamed police and na-tional guardsmen for "excessive and unjustified force." SNCC leader H. "Rap" Brown expressed the bitter mood of 1967, urging demonstrators in Cambridge, Maryland, to "burn this town down if this town don't turn around and grant the demand of Negroes."

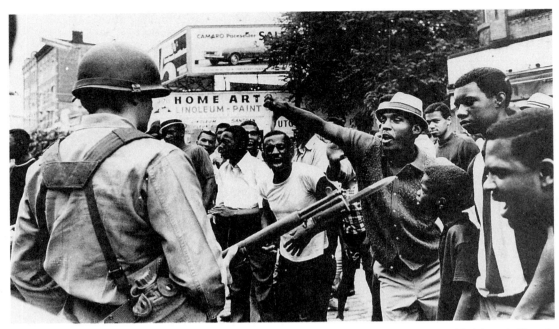

A black demonstrator turned thumbs down at the presence of National Guardsmen sent to suppress racial violence in Newark, New Jersey in 1967. Official reports later blamed police authorities for aggravating the crisis.

Reacting to the violence, Johnson appointed a National Advisory Commission on Civil Disorders, chaired by Illinois Governor Otto Kerner. The 1968 Kerner Report stated that the nation was "moving toward two societies, one black, one white, separate and unequal." Blaming the riots on white racism and white institutional power, the commission urged a massive commitment to housing, education, jobs, and welfare as well as better law enforcement techniques. But by then the White House was preoccupied by matters of foreign policy and remained silent on the Kerner findings.

Mr. Johnson's War

Like his predecessor, Johnson recognized the importance of undeveloped countries in the Cold War and opposed political or economic changes that might destabilize American interests. Thus, for example, Johnson ordered American troops into the Dominican Republic in 1965 when he suspected that Communists controlled a constitutional movement to seize power from the army. Usually, however, the White House preferred clandestine intervention in the Western Hemisphere. Following Kennedy's precedents, Johnson authorized the CIA to build up security forces against subversion in the third world. Techniques included blackmail, bribery, forgery, bombing, sabotage, espionage, propaganda, disinformation (false information), psychological warfare, military training, and paramilitary activities. The CIA also provided financial support to selected individuals, political parties, private organizations, unions, and businesses. Such covert operations were concealed within the enormous military and intelligence bureaucracy.

American military power was awesome. By the end of the 1960s, the United States operated 429 major and 2,972 minor military bases across the globe in thirty countries and had one million military personnel overseas. The nation's arsenal included one-thousand nuclear-armed intercontinental missiles and seventy nuclear-armed and powered submarines. The nuclear storehouse amounted to the equivalent of fifteen tons of TNT for every person in the world. The total tonnage of the Navy exceeded that of all other nations combined. Cost for the military establishment ran to $216 million a day. Between 1945 and 1970, American taxpayers spent $1 trillion for military purposes. Yet the late 1960s brought the United States to the worst military and political disaster in its history.

Among his first presidential acts, Johnson conferred with the American ambassador to South Vietnam, Henry Cabot Lodge, to assess the status of the war. Like his three predecessors in the White House, Johnson believed in the domino theory and the need to maintain American strength as a bulwark against Communist expansion. Now Lodge reported that the Viet Cong had escalated military activity. Obviously insecure in his new position, Johnson replied that he was "not going to be the President who saw Southeast Asia go the way China went." Instead, he canceled Kennedy's order to withdraw troops from South Vietnam and approved a program to accelerate covert attacks against North Vietnam and in Laos. Meanwhile, American destroyers patrolled the Gulf of Tonkin and PT boats occasionally attacked North Vietnamese coastal installations. As military clashes increased, the State Department secretly drafted a congressional resolution for a declaration of war in May 1964.

Two months later South Vietnamese ships, accompanied by American intelligence vessels, began bombarding North Vietnamese territory in the Gulf of Tonkin. When North Vietnamese patrol boats fired on one of the American destroyers, United States fighter planes strafed the attackers. On August 4 the Navy claimed a second attack on American ships, though subsequent reports blamed "freak weather effects, and an overeager sonar man" for that impression. Johnson nevertheless ordered air reprisals on North Vietnamese bases. Just as President Roosevelt had exaggerated the *Greer* incident in 1941, Johnson announced in a televised speech that a "positive reply" was "being given as I speak to you tonight." He insisted the United States sought "no wider war." But the president presented Congress with a reworded version of the secretly prepared May declaration of war, which stated that "Congress approves and supports the determination of the President as commander-in-chief to take all necessary measures to repel any attack against the forces of the United States and to prevent further aggression." The Tonkin Gulf Resolution passed the House unanimously and the Senate with only two dissenters, Wayne Morse of Oregon and Ernest Gruening of Alaska. A Harris poll showed 85 percent approval of the air strikes against North Vietnam. Stopping short of a full declaration of war that might have drawn China and the Soviet Union into the conflict, the president had won a free hand to conduct the war as he chose.

The conflict soon escalated again when the Viet Cong attacked an American base at Pleiku in February 1965. Vowing not to be scared out of Vietnam, Johnson expected to bomb the enemy into submission and ordered a program of retaliatory air strikes against North Vietnam. By March 1965, Operation Rolling Thunder involved full-scale bombing of North Vietnam. Heavy anti-aircraft fire

A B52 bomber drops a 38,000 pound bombload over Vietnam. The original AP caption for this 1966 picture expressed the military's optimism about superior American firepower: "...the B52s have sharply reduced the Communist will to fight, officials in Saigon have concluded...."

and poor accuracy resulted in a high loss of planes and indiscriminate bombing of civilian targets. The air war also required more guard troops to protect American bases, and Johnson ordered an additional one-hundred thousand troops to Vietnam. "We fight because we must fight if we are to live in a world where every country can shape its own destiny," the president explained. "To withdraw from one battlefield means only to prepare for the next." A Gallup poll found that 61 percent approved the increased troop allotments. Johnson hoped to maintain enough force to prevent the Communists from winning, but not enough to precipitate Chinese intervention.

By the summer of 1965, however, the war had again expanded. American ground troops began full-scale combat offensives, engaging in "search and destroy" missions. B-52s flew three-thousand miles from Guam to bomb suspected Viet Cong targets in South Vietnam. By the end of the year, air attacks surpassed seventy-thousand strikes. In December the Air Force attacked industrial areas in the North. But at Christmas, Johnson ordered a bombing moratorium and sent emissaries around the world to explore possibilities for peace. The main stumbling block remained the president's refusal to recognize the Viet Cong National Liberation Front as a political force independent of North Vietnam. Contending that North Vietnam had invaded South Vietnam, the president denied that the United States had become involved in a civil war. When North Vietnamese infiltration continued during the bombing pause, Johnson ordered the resumption of American attacks on the North.

"We do not seek to enlarge this war," the president insisted in May 1966, "but we shall not run out on it." As troop commitments rose to 385,000, dissent surfaced at home. J. William Fulbright, chairman of the Senate Foreign Relations Committee, held open hearings which expressed criticism of administration policy. Nonetheless, in June 1966 Johnson ordered the bombing of Hanoi. "We must continue to raise the price of aggression," he explained. The goal of bombing had changed from breaking the enemy's will to cutting supply lines. But intelligence reports showed that such bombing was militarily ineffective. Johnson promised to end the attacks if North Vietnam pledged to send no more troops south, but Hanoi responded that peace depended on withdrawal of all American troops. Since the president insisted that South Vietnam's independence must be preserved, he rejected Hanoi's demand.

In a surprise visit to a military base in Vietnam, Johnson told American soldiers to "come home with that coonskin on the wall." Yet despite tremendous American firepower, the president's limited war could not defeat the enemy. Military advisers repeatedly made the error of assuming that lessened Viet Cong operations indicated diminished capability rather than changes of strategy. In late 1966, even Secretary McNamara expressed doubts about the course of military operations and commissioned a study, later known as the Pentagon Papers, to evaluate the entire Vietnamese policy. But the bombing continued, and reliable journalists in Vietnam denounced administration claims about the minimal number of civilian casualties.

By 1968, Johnson had ordered half a million Americans to Vietnam. And as ground forces confronted North Vietnamese regulars, casualty figures soared— eventually exceeding fifty-five thousand dead, perhaps one-tenth of Vietnamese casualties. Meanwhile, the Viet Cong controlled the timing and terms of most confrontations. To destroy enemy bases, American planes dropped napalm, defoliants, and herbicides throughout the country. In addition, fragmentation bombs left victims riddled with millions of tiny particles that could not be detected by x-rays. The CIA also launched Operation Phoenix, an assassination program against alleged Viet Cong leaders that claimed at least 20,000 victims.

The futility of the war effort emerged during the Viet Cong's Tet offensive in February 1968. While immense American firepower concentrated on a remote marine outpost at Khe Sanh, Communist forces launched a coordinated attack on every major city in South Vietnam. In Saigon, commandos penetrated the American embassy grounds. In Hue, Communist forces executed police officials and any pro-Americans, while the South Vietnamese retaliated against Buddhists, students, and teachers who appeared as "VC collaborators." An estimated thirty-two thousand insurgents were killed during Tet, while Americans suffered four thousand killed and nearly twenty thousand wounded. But although the offensive greatly depleted Viet Cong strength, Tet demonstrated that the enemy only had to survive in order to prevent the United States from "winning" the war. Tet also revealed the inability of the South Vietnamese armies to defend positions without American assistance. Thus the Tet offensive, a military victory for the United States, actually undermined public support of the war at home.

Exhibit 11–6. South Vietnam.

— WILLIAM CHILDS WESTMORELAND —
1914–

The commander of U.S. military forces in Vietnam from 1964 to 1968, General William Childs Westmoreland embodied the strengths and weaknesses of the American presence in Southeast Asia. He appeared as a picture book soldier, ramrod straight to six feet, jut-jawed, brave, meticulous, self-disciplined, and reverent. In Vietnam he determined to prove that superior technology and organizational skills could defeat a guerrilla army. But like the civilian leadership, he underestimated the passion and power of the enemy, and he failed to appreciate the political dimensions of the war.

Born in Spartanburg, South Carolina, Westmoreland devoted his entire life to the military. He attended West Point, proceeded to become an expert in field artillery, and demonstrated considerable ingenuity in tactical planning. (He wrote one term paper entitled "The Use of Mother's Milk as a Food for Troops in the Field.") During World War II, he fought through North Africa, Sicily, France, and Germany.

In the Korean War, Westmoreland commanded a parachute group and jumped with his men. He then went to the Pentagon's manpower office and took the opportunity to enroll in an advanced management program at the Harvard School of Business. Indistinguishable from the other corporate executives in the seminars, the young general became a proficient administrator and later used former classmates from such companies as General Electric and Union Carbide to increase worker performance and productivity in procurement and manpower allocations. In 1960, President Eisenhower appointed him superintendent of West Point.

Chosen to lead American troops in Vietnam in January 1964, Westmoreland brought along his vast administrative skills. Even to his critics Westmoreland's logistical achievement seemed astounding. Under his command the military constructed six deep water ports, five jet airfields, eighty-four tactical airstrips, and hundreds of helicopter pads; built eleven million square feet of covered storage, five million square yards of open storage, 2.5 million cubic feet of cold storage; laid miles of telephone cable and radio grids; and erected bridges, roads, canals, and seaways. Westmoreland's demand for troops also appeared voracious: from 16,000 in 1964 to 185,000 in 1965 to 385,000 in 1966 to 470,000 in 1967 to 520,000 in 1968.

Such power inflicted immense damage but could not defeat the elusive enemy. Nor could the seemingly unending war justify the tremendous drain on American resources. As political leaders doubted the possibility of achieving victory, President Johnson appointed Westmoreland Chief of Staff of the Army in 1968 and ordered him back to Washington. "We have curtailed the tide of Communist aggression," Westmoreland stated in his final report on the war; "...the enemy has not won a single major victory."

Westmoreland retired in 1972 but his name returned to the headlines ten years later when he sued CBS, Inc. for libel. A documentary program had accused the former general of deceiving the administration about the strength of the enemy. Despite forthright denials, however, Westmoreland dropped the lawsuit without proving his case. "However desirable the American system of civilian control of the military," he argued in his memoirs, "it was a mistake to permit appointive civilian officials lacking military experience and knowledge...to wield undue influence in the decision-making process." ∎

Exhibit 11–7. TET Offensive.

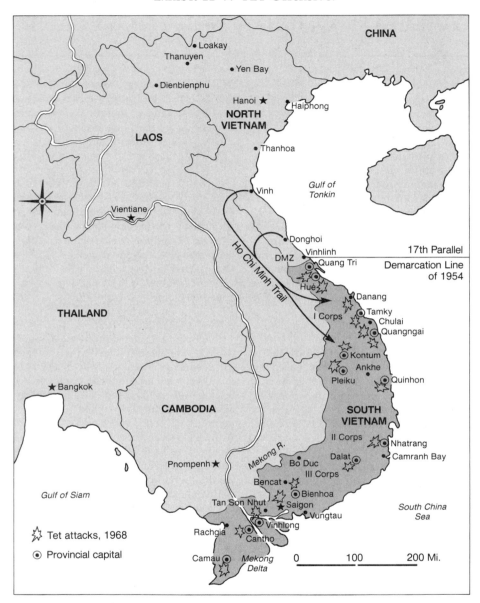

THE WAR AT HOME

As dissent against the war increased (for a discussion of the antiwar movement, see chapter 6), the Johnson administration attempted to impose a domestic consensus on foreign policy. Since the early 1960s, FBI Director J. Edgar Hoover had directed "counterintelligence" efforts against both the Ku Klux Klan and the black civil rights movement. Viewing Martin Luther King as the man responsible for popularizing the "idea that you can violate a law if it is wrong," Hoover soon initiated wiretaps and bugs in an attempt to discredit the black leader. By 1967, however, King had followed SNCC's lead and began criticizing the war in Vietnam. The following year the FBI extended its counterintelligence activities "to expose, disrupt, and otherwise neutralize...the New Left." Other intelligence agencies initiated similar operations. By 1968, the army had compiled one-hundred thousand dossiers on antiwar activists. Johnson also authorized the CIA's Operation Chaos to conduct domestic surveillance, in violation of the agency's charter, against dissidents, demonstrators, and even "suspicious" members of Congress. But when the CIA notified Johnson that domestic dissent appeared to be independent of foreign funding, the president rejected the findings.

Johnson had hoped to finance the war without cutting Great Society funding. Indeed, the president believed that an aggressive anti-Communist foreign policy would increase congressional support of his domestic agenda. But as war costs rose to $2 billion a month in 1966, Johnson admitted the incompatibility of "guns and butter." In a year of record federal spending overseas, Congress abolished the school milk program and cut appropriations for education. While Democrats managed to preserve OEO, the antipoverty agency limped along on half its projected budget. Grassroots protests in the cities and on college campuses offended conservatives and further weakened the liberal position. When Johnson followed King's "open city" campaign in Chicago with submission of an equal housing bill in 1966, two attempts to end a Senate filibuster failed and the administration settled for a modest rat control appropriation.

Congressional uneasiness with domestic programs also reflected the soaring inflation caused by war spending. By 1968, the military budget reached $70 billion. Johnson had persuaded Congress to suspend Kennedy's investment tax credit and accelerated depreciation allowances in 1966, but these minor tax increases proved insufficient to finance the war. The president suffered a severe legislative setback when Congress refused to accept a war tax surcharge, preferring spending cutbacks or tax reform. Johnson eventually gained a small surcharge in 1968. The delay in taxing encouraged inflation. Rising prices, together with war spending, produced a phenomenal rise in the federal deficit, which leaped from $3.8 billion in 1966 to $8.7 billion in 1967 to $25.2 billion in 1968. As a result, the consumer price index rose 5 percent in 1968 alone.

"The bombs in Vietnam explode at home," protested Martin Luther King. "They destroy the hopes and possibilities of a decent America." Angered by both civil rights protests and antiwar demonstrations, American voters supported a

Exhibit 11–8. Gross National Product, 1960–1968.
(current dollars in billions)

1960	$515.3 b
1962	$574.6 b
1964	$649.8 b
1966	$772.0 b
1968	$892.7 b

Source: *Economic Report of the President* (1988)

Exhibit 11–9. Wholesale Price Index, 1960–1968.
(1967-100)
(rounded percentages)

1960	95
1961	94
1962	95
1963	94
1964	95
1965	97
1966	100
1967	100
1968	102

Source: *Historical Statistics of the United States, Colonial Times to 1970* (1975)

Exhibit 11–10. Consumer Price Index, 1960–1968.
(1967-100)
(rounded percentages)

1960	89
1961	90
1962	91
1963	92
1964	93
1965	94
1966	97
1967	100
1968	104

Source: *Historical Statistics of the United States, Colonial Times to 1970* (1975)

Exhibit 11–11. National Defense and Veterans Outlays, 1960–1968.
(in billions of dollars)

1960	$47.4 b
1962	$57.9 b
1964	$60.5 b
1966	$64.0 b
1968	$88.8 b

Source: *Statistical Abstract of the United States* (1987)

Exhibit 11–12. Research and Development, 1960–1968.
(in billions of dollars)
(fiscal years ending in year shown)

	Receipts	Outlays	Deficit
1960	$92.5 b	$92.2	$.3
1964	$112.6 b	$118.5 b	$5.9 b
1968	$153.0 b	$178.1 b	$25.2 b

Source: *Economic Report of the President* (1988)

conservative backlash in the 1966 congressional elections. Stressing crime and the need for "law and order," Republicans made large gains in both houses of Congress. Democrats warned that education, jobs, housing reforms, and an end to discrimination were necessary to end domestic strife, but acknowledged that guns and butter were no longer possible.

The conservative backlash enabled Alabama Governor George Wallace to attract a national following. "A bearded professor...thinks he knows how to settle the Vietnam War," Wallace told one audience, but he "hasn't got enough sense to park his bicycle straight." Articulating deeply held resentments against liberal government programs, ghetto rioting, and student rebellions, Wallace appealed to working people concerned about the rising crime rate and fearful of the loss of traditional values. In 1968, Wallace launched a presidential campaign in the American Independent party, calling for repeal of civil rights laws and a military victory in Vietnam.

Despite Wallace's popularity among northern workers, blue-collar support of the war in 1966 appeared to be only 1 percent higher than the rest of the nation. The next year a national poll found 68 percent disapproval of Johnson's handling of Vietnam. At the same time, however, a majority of Americans believed that peace demonstrations constituted "acts of disloyalty against the boys fighting in Vietnam." To "hawk" and "dove" alike the war had become a volatile political issue. Organized labor, led by AFL-CIO President George Meany remained loyal to the Democratic party and backed the war. In 1967, a New York City march "supporting our men in Vietnam" attracted seventy thousand people.

THE CHAOS OF 1968

The Tet offensive drastically undermined support for Johnson's war policy, provoking one of the most tumultuous years in American political history. As General William Westmoreland requested another two-hundred thousand troops and mobilization of the reserves—proposals that would have added $12 billion to war costs already reaching $30 billion a year—opposition to the conflict increased. Clark Clifford, who had replaced McNamara as defense secretary, found extensive "dove" sentiment within the administration. In March 1968, antiwar Senator Eugene McCarthy of Minnesota astounded the nation by taking 42 percent of the vote in the New Hampshire Democratic primary, a serious political defeat for the president. Four days later, Senator Robert Kennedy announced his candidacy for the presidential nomination. Within a week, Johnson relieved Westmoreland of the Vietnam command and summoned a meeting of senior advisors to reassess the war effort.

The White House conference included twelve of the most prestigious members of the nation's foreign policy, business, and law establishment. Nearly all had approved the escalation of bombing in 1967. But now they concluded that present policy could not achieve its objectives without full citizen support and major budgetary sacrifices, and they warned that the war threatened the position of the American dollar abroad. Johnson agonized about his response. Then, on the evening of March 31, 1968, he presented a dramatic televised speech, announcing a suspension of the bombing of North Vietnam and a willingness to

President Johnson listened somberly to the advice of the administration's "wise men" at a meeting in the Oval Office on March 26, 1968. Five days later, Johnson withdrew from the presidential contest.

negotiate with the Viet Cong National Liberation Front. In a surprising post-script, he also announced his withdrawal from the presidential election.

Four days later, on the day the North Vietnamese agreed to peace talks, a self-proclaimed racist assassinated Martin Luther King in Memphis, Tennessee. The murder provoked a spasm of racial violence. Riots immediately erupted around the country, affecting 168 cities. Goaded by the tragedy, Congress at last passed the long-delayed open housing bill, which banned discrimination in the sale and rental of about four-fifths of the nation's housing. Meanwhile, Johnson's with-drawal emboldened antiwar Democratic candidates, sparking heated campaigns by Senators McCarthy and Kennedy. The president's choice, Vice President Hubert Humphrey, remained on the sidelines. But in June, Kennedy won the California primary, only to be killed minutes after his victory by Sirhan Sirhan, a Palestinian opposed to Kennedy's pro-Israel stand. The Democratic party floundered for want of leadership.

The assassinations of King and Kennedy underscored the political and cul-tural crisis. As it became clear that Humphrey would capture the presidential nomination, several thousand peace activists and young radicals went to Chi-cago to demonstrate at the Democratic convention. Refusing to allow peaceful protests, Mayor Richard Daley met the dissidents with force, permitting what a

——— Robert Francis Kennedy ———
——— 1925–1968 ———

Robert Kennedy's assassination signaled the end of hope in a turbulent era desperately in need of conciliation. Kennedy had served as the New Frontier's principal power broker. He was presidential campaign manager in 1960, attorney general during the stormy civil rights movement, and personal advisor for foreign policy in his brother's presidency. As a tough Irish-American, Kennedy helped to shape counterinsurgency in Vietnam and personally supervised the CIA's covert campaigns in Cuba. Bob Kennedy had the reputation of a cool-handed operator with a streak of ruthlessness.

Dallas changed all that. The heir apparent to the American presidency began a new career in 1964 as junior senator from New York. Deeply affected by his own losses, Kennedy used his prestige to push for greater commitments toward those without privilege or power. He visited Cesar Chavez's grape strikers in California, took testimony on malnutrition in Mississippi, and conducted hearings on the squalor of reservation life in New Mexico. Kennedy warned in 1967 that "We cannot measure national spirit by the Dow-Jones Average, nor national achievement by the gross national product."

The senator was not among the first to question the Vietnam War. But early in 1966 he issued a cautious call for a coalition government in Saigon. A year later, he took the floor to condemn the administration's bombing: "We are all participants...We must also feel as men the anguish of what it is we are doing." In November 1967, Kennedy delivered a spontaneous tirade on national television against American slaughter of the Vietnamese. Commentators began to speculate on his availability for the presidential race, but Kennedy was too much of a professional to risk splitting the Democratic party in a personal vendetta against an incumbent president. Johnson's political fall in 1968 moved the senator to action.

The eighty-five-day campaign of Robert Kennedy stirred an emotional groundswell seldom seen in American politics. Kennedy proposals for a draft lottery, corporate ghetto development, and Vietnam negotiations were modest. But "Bobby" symbolized the lost idealism of the New Frontier, the flickering hope of the 1960s that all classes and races could share in the American Dream. He campaigned on the streets, jacket off, tie loose, and sleeves rolled up. Excited crowds swarmed along the primary trail just to touch his hand.

When Martin Luther King was assassinated in April 1968, Kennedy went directly to a ghetto street gathering in Indianapolis and shared his own feelings of loss by quoting the Greek poet Aeschylus. A nearby graffiti explained his remarkable following among American blacks: "Kennedy white but alright./The one before, he opened the door." But the secret to the Kennedy campaign was the compassion he expressed toward all the nation's working people and dispossessed. Despite his stance against the war, the strict Catholic and father of ten scored heavy primary pluralities in white districts that had previously supported George Wallace.

Robert Kennedy was the only leader of his era who might have united white working people, antiwar students, and the racial minorities in a coalition for change. His assassination by a Palestinian Arab incensed at the candidate's support for Israel was a harsh blow to the national fabric. At the Democratic Convention in Chicago, delegates wept and sang in his memory the "Battle Hymn of the Republic." ■

presidential commission later called a "police riot." While demonstrators chanted "the whole world is watching!" police attacked protesters and passers-by with clubs and mace. Meanwhile, inside the convention, Democrats defeated a dovish platform and proceeded to nominate Humphrey.

With the party split, Humphrey's chances seemed slim. The Republicans nominated Richard Nixon, who cultivated a "new" image of political maturity. Although he did not provide any details, Nixon promised to "end the war and win the peace in the Pacific." In the face of massive civil protest and ghetto violence, the candidate also vowed to "bring the American people together." His vice-presidential running mate, Governor Spiro Agnew of Maryland, had achieved national prominence by attacking civil rights and antiwar demonstrators. "Our objective in the next four years should not be to get more people on welfare rolls—we want to get more people on payrolls," said Nixon. "We're going to build this country up so that no one will dare use the U.S. flag for a doormat again." Such bromides proved effective against the besieged Democratic candidate. But in October, Humphrey separated himself from Johnson's position on the war and rose quickly in the polls. Johnson's last-minute announcement of a cessation of the bombing further narrowed the contest, but Humphrey could never overcome the images of chaos and violence associated with the Chicago convention.

Exhibit 11–13. 1968 Election.

Nixon (Republican)   302 electoral votes
Humphrey (Democrat)   191 electoral votes
Wallace (American Independent)   45 electoral votes

Nixon won the election by less than one percentage point. Wallace's Independent party, which hoped to force the election into the House of Representatives, amassed nearly 14 percent of the vote and claimed forty-five electoral votes in the deep South. In the North, Humphrey managed to preserve the New Deal coalition of labor, blacks, Jews, and Catholics. But Nixon and Wallace carried 57 percent of the national electorate.

The turbulence of 1968 shook faith in the political system. The credibility gap and violent dissent brought widespread alienation from conventional politics. As 1968 ended, the American death toll in Vietnam passed thirty thousand; over half a million soldiers remained in that distant outpost of national aspirations. A weary nation looked to Richard Nixon to restore tranquility at home and a dignified peace abroad.

SUGGESTED READINGS

The political history of the 1960s is best told in Allen J. Matusow, *The Unraveling of America: A History of Liberalism in the 1960s* (1984), which criticizes the liberal consensus. Also valuable is the biographical focus of Milton Viorst, *Fire in the Streets: America in the 1960s* (1979). A balanced discussion of the Kennedy presidency appears in the second volume of Herbert S. Parmet's biography, *JFK: The Presidency of John F. Kennedy* (1983). More critical of Kennedy's policies is Bruce Miroff, *Pragmatic Illusions: The Presidential Politics of John F. Kennedy* (1976). An insightful study of the impact of personality is Garry Wills, *The Kennedy Imprisonment* (1982). Still useful for understanding the political assumptions of American leaders is David Halberstam, *The Best and the Brightest* (1972).

Kennedy's problems with Congress are explored in Tom Wicker, *JFK and LBJ: The Influence of Personality upon Politics* (1968). The space program is well treated in Walter A. McDougall, *The Heavens and the Earth: A Political History of the Space Age* (1985); Clayton R. Koppes, *JPL and the American Space Program: A History of the Jet Propulsion Lab* (1982); and Tom Wolfe's journalistic tour de force, *The Right Stuff* (1979). For astronaut John Glenn, see the relevant chapters in Peter N. Carroll, *Famous In America* (1985). The problems of economic policy are described in Jim F. Heath, *John F. Kennedy and the Business Community* (1969). For the Peace Corps, see Gerard T. Rice, *The Bold Experiment: John F. Kennedy's Peace Corps* (1985).

A critical analysis of Kennedy's foreign policy is Richard J. Walton, *Cold War and Counterrevolution* (1972). For the Bay of Pigs issue, see Trumbull Higgins, *The Perfect Failure: Kennedy, Eisenhower, and the CIA at the Bay of Pigs* (1988). The main issues of the Cuban missile crisis are discussed in an anthology, Robert A. Divine, ed., *The Cuban Missile Crisis* (1971), and David Detzer, *The Brink* (1979). A detailed study of the German question is Curtis Cate, *The Ides of August: The Berlin Wall Crisis, 1961* (1978). Another aspect of Kennedy policy emerges in Richard D. Mahoney, *JFK: Ordeal in Africa* (1983).

For Lyndon Johnson, a good starting point is Vaughn D. Bornet, *The Presidency of Lyndon Johnson* (1983) and Paul Conkin, *Big Daddy From the Pedernales* (1986). Also insightful is Doris Kearns, *Lyndon Johnson and the American Dream* (1976). The internal workings of the administration are covered in Emmette S.

Redford and Richard T. McCulley, *White House Operations: The Johnson Presidency* (1986). See also Carl Solberg's biography of the Vice President, *Hubert Humphrey* (1984).

Johnson's domestic political problems are analyzed by Eric Goldman, *The Tragedy of Lyndon Johnson: A Historian's Personal Interpretation* (1969). The political opposition is described in Richard Rovere, *The Goldwater Caper* (1965); David Halberstam, *The Unfinished Odyssey of Robert Kennedy* (1968); William C. Berman, *William Fulbright and the Vietnam War: The Dissent of a Political Realist* (1988); and Lewis Chester, Geoffrey Hodgson, and Bruce Page, *An American Melodrama: The Presidential Campaign of 1968* (1969). For George Wallace, see Jody Carlson, *George C. Wallace and the Politics of Powerlessness: The Wallace Campaigns for the Presidency* (1981) and the relevant portions of Peter N. Carroll, *Famous in America* (1985).

Two surveys of the civil rights movement are Harvard Sitkoff, *The Struggle for Black Equality: 1954–1980* (1981) and Manning Marable, *Race, Reform, and Rebellion: The Second Reconstruction in Black America, 1945–1982* (1984). The Kennedy administration's relationship to the civil rights movement is analyzed critically in Victor S. Navasky, *Kennedy Justice* (1971), and more favorably in Carl M. Brauer, *John F. Kennedy and the Second Reconstruction* (1977). Two excellent studies of Martin Luther King are Stephen B. Oates *Let the Trumpet Sound: The Life of Martin Luther King, Jr.* (1982) and David J. Garrow, *Bearing the Cross: Martin Luther King, Jr. and the Southern Christian Leadership Conference* (1986). Another facet of government policy emerges in David J. Garrow, *The FBI and Martin Luther King, Jr.* (1981). The role of black students is stressed in Clayborne Carson, *In Struggle: SNCC and the Black Awakening of the 1960s* (1981) and Seth Cagin and Philip Dray, *We Are Not Afraid* (1988). A fine oral history is Howell Raines, *My Soul Is Rested: The Story of the Civil Rights Movement in the Deep South* (1983).

The best overview of the Vietnam War is George L. Herring, *America's Longest War: The United States and Vietnam, 1950–1975* (1986). Also useful are Stanley Karnow, *Vietnam: A History* (1983) and William S. Turley. *The Second Indochina War: A Short Political and Military History* (1986). A critical perspective of U.S. policy appears in George McT. Kahin, *Intervention: How America Became Involved in Vietnam* (1986). More sympathetic to American involvement is R.B. Smith, *An International History of the Vietnam War: The Kennedy Strategy* (1986). Policy toward North Vietnam is described in Wallace J. Thies, *When Governments Collide: Coercion and Diplomacy in the Vietnam Conflict, 1964–1968* (1980). For the military background, see Ronald Spector, *Advice and Support: The Early Years of the U.S. Army in Vietnam, 1941–1960* (1983).

The domestic implications of the Vietnam War are well treated in Herbert G. Schandler, *The Unmaking of a President: Lyndon Johnson and Vietnam* (1977); Loren Baritz, *Backfire: A History of How American Culture Led Us into Vietnam and Made Us Fight the Way We Did* (1985); and Thomas Powers, *Vietnam: The War at Home* (1984). For the 1968 Democratic convention, see David Farber, *Chicago '68* (1988). See also the titles relating to the New Left that appear at the end of chapter 6.

12

THE CRISIS OF
AMERICAN CULTURE,
1960-1980

In the years after Kennedy's election a variety of social groups—middle-class youth, racial and ethnic minorities, feminists, and new immigrants—challenged the consensus of postwar society and endeavored to initiate change on their own terms. As a radical movement emerged in the 1960s and early 1970s, protesters confronted the domination of society by values associated with white, Anglo-Protestant men. Social patterns buttressed this ferment. By 1980, the Census Bureau's "typical" American family of working father, homemaker mother, and two children comprised only 7.7 percent of the population. Although the radical spirit moderated in the mid-1970s and 1980s, cultural conservatives became increasingly insistent upon defending older values and practices. Responding to the earlier assault on basic institutions, white ethnics, evangelical Protestants, and others rallied to support the traditional family, religious orthodoxy, and conventional behavior. By the late 1980s, two Americas—one liberal, the other conservative—competed for political advantage and cultural supremacy but neither could count on the exclusive allegiance of emerging professionals or the young.

THE BABY BOOM AND THE YOUTH MARKET

The postwar population explosion, which lasted until 1958, brought a new generation to maturity in the early 1960s. Twice as numerous as their parents, teen-aged Americans formed a distinctive, self-conscious culture whose sheer numbers exerted tremendous economic and political power. Having grown up in the prosperous 1950s, American youth accepted affluence as part of its birthright and defined its uniqueness through economic consumption. As children, the baby boom generation had constituted an enormous market for diaper services, toys, and toddlers' shoes. The same generation soon created the nation's first "youth market" by consuming vast quantities of records, costume jewelry, and teenage apparel. Purchasing power set the stage for the youth rebellion of the 1960s.

The tremendous popularity of rock and roll music reflected a newly ignited quest for personal independence by young Americans. Teenagers and college students of the 1960s crowded dance floors which reverberated to the "funky" rhythms of "Motown," a hard-driving "soul" music named for the black Detroit record company that produced it. Black performers such as Ray Charles, James Brown, Otis Redding, Aretha Franklin, the Supremes, and the Temptations offered middle-class followers an alternative to sexually repressed music. Soul

Exhibit 12–1. Birth Rate, 1960–1985.
(per 1000 population)

1960	1965	1970	1975	1980	1985
23.7	19.4	18.4	14.6	15.9	15.7

Source: *Statistical Abstract of the United States* (1987)

The long hair of the Beatles revolutionized personal fashion and social attitudes while their use of electric rock helped to pioneer new forms of white popular music.

music also influenced a wave of British "rock" bands such as the Beatles, whose 1964 American tour energized young audiences just months after the Kennedy assassination. And rock songs such as the Rolling Stones's "Let's Spend the Night Together" expressed sexual longing in the most direct terms. Meanwhile, emerging fashions such as long hair, "miniskirts," and blue jeans encouraged liberation of the body and a new confidence in defying social decorum.

These personal and musical styles reflected a changing morality associated with the "sexual revolution." Even before the introduction of the birth control pill in 1960, Americans had begun to engage more frequently in non-marital intercourse. But the trend accelerated and received more attention during the 1960s. "Life was free and so was sex, "novelist Sara Davidson wrote of Berkeley at mid-decade. Reduced risk of pregnancy helped to make sex more attractive. By the 1970s, polls indicated that three-quarters of all Americans approved pre-marital sex for men and women. Furthermore, surveys such as the Kinsey Report of the 1950s, showed that the age of first sexual experience had declined and that the frequency of sexual intercourse within all social classes had increased. Kinsey's findings also suggested that certain "deviant" acts such as oral sex had been widely accepted into heterosexual relations and that the disparity between the sex lives of men and women had narrowed. Such patterns of behavior helped to account for the rise of unwanted pregnancies in the 1960s and an average half-million illegal abortions a year.

The sexual revolution also undermined traditional definitions of obscenity and pornography. In a series of landmark cases in the late-1950s, the Supreme Court denied censorship of such literary classics as *Fanny Hill*, D.H. Lawrence's *Lady Chatterly's Lover*, and Henry Miller's *Tropic of Cancer*. By the mid-1960s, Hollywood had replaced its 1930s production code with a series of graded standards. Taking advantage of the "X" rating that excluded those under eighteen, independent film makers began to market sexually explicit movies for "adults" only. By 1973, *Deep Throat* and *The Devil in Miss Jones*, two examples of this "hard-core" pornography, were among the year's most profitable motion pictures. Traditional morality persisted on widely viewed television. But between the late-1960s and early 1970s, shows like "The Smothers Brothers," "Laugh-In" and "Mary Tyler Moore" broke precedent by joking about non-marital sex, divorce, and "up-tight" behavior.

THE COUNTERCULTURE

For many of the twenty million Americans who turned eighteen between 1964 and 1970, the sexual revolution precipitated a larger assault on adult institutions. As a result of economic prosperity and the service industry's demands for extended education, college enrollment doubled to ten million in the 1960s. Increasingly independent college youth, however, no longer accepted control of their private lives by student deans and other academic officials, who customarily used rigid curfews, sexual segregation, and threats of expulsion to dictate acceptable social behavior. Most campuses abolished the doctrine of *"in loco parentis"* (in place of parents) and its accompanying sexual repression during the 1960s. For example, students won the right to live in coeducational dormitories or to stay out at night. The freedom of personal expression often extended to campus political rights, including the publication of uncensored newspapers and magazines, the recruitment of political support, and public political demonstrations.

Drugs became one of the most controversial routes to youth independence in the 1960s. Whereas earlier generations had consumed alcohol to defy adult morality and discipline, teenagers and college students now learned to smoke marijuana, a hemp-like weed which produced mild euphoria. Sharing marijuana often served as a rite of initiation into youth culture. By 1976 and 1977, surveys would estimate that more than half of the nation's high-school seniors smoked "weed" regularly and that two-thirds of all college students used it at least occasionally. Beyond marijuana, Harvard University psychologists Timothy Leary and Richard Alpert experimented with the government-provided hallucinogenic LSD ("acid") and claimed to discover states of "expanded" consciousness that approached religious ecstasy. When the university fired them for unprofessional conduct in 1963, Leary assumed the role of LSD "guru," advising a generation of Americans to "turn on, tune in, and drop out." Meanwhile, a psychedelic counterculture blossomed from "beat" roots in San Francisco's Haight-Ashbury district. By 1967, Americans had discovered the "hippie."

"I never hold back, man. I'm always on the outer limits of possibility," Haight rock vocalist Janis Joplin declared. Hippies wore their hair defiantly long and dressed in a "free-form" fashion that could include bells, feathers, bandanas, beads, or earrings. Many survived in "crash pads" or in shared housing by pan-handling, making crafts, selling "underground" newspapers, and "dealing" drugs. Some, like the communal Diggers and Hog Farm, set up free kitchens and health clinics. The most important facet of hippie subculture, however, centered on rejection of the mainstream's competitive individualism, materialism, and middle-class pretension. The alternative culture sought honesty, physical pleas-ure, affection, sharing, cooperation, the spirit of experimentation, and absolute inner freedom.

Few college students actually traveled to San Francisco during 1967's "sum-mer of love" and identified themselves as hippies. But many young Americans sensed the counterculture's possibilities of radical change and refashioned their private lives to emulate it. Thousands of middle-class rebels left the cities to form rural communes in northern California, southern Oregon, the desert Southwest, and mountainous Vermont. Others published underground comics and newspa-pers, produced "guerrilla" theater and alternative film documentaries, created color-crazed "pop art" posters, or sought free-form expression in traditional dis-ciplines such as music composition, dance, poetry, and prose. Many more simply shared anti-establishment attitudes, adopted "hip" language, wore informal gear such as blue jeans, and experimented with sexual freedom, marijuana smoking, and rock music.

"Psychedelic" or "acid" rock bands such as the Jefferson Airplane, the Grateful Dead, and Joplin's Big Brother and the Holding Company provided Haight-Ashbury's most direct contact with mainstream society. Using the technology of electric guitars and elaborate light shows, the district's free street bands moved into theaters and dance halls where they developed the piercing "San Francisco" sound. "People now sang songs they wrote themselves," observed music critic Ralph J. Gleason in 1967, "not songs written *for* them by hacks in grimy Tin Pan Alley offices." The introspective and "spaced-out" musical style soon spread to the Beatles and Rolling Stones as well as performers such as the Buffalo Spring-field, Bob Dylan, the Byrds, Jim Morrison, and Jimi Hendrix.

Tom Wolfe humorously captured the irreverent mood of the underground culture in *The Electric Kool-Aid Acid Test* (1968), describing the exploits of writer Ken Kesey, whose Merry Pranksters traveled around the country in a psychedel-ically painted bus while promoting liberation through drugs, sex, and rock music. For the four-hundred thousand people who gathered at "Woodstock," a 1969 rock festival in rural New York, the Kesey fantasy approached materializa-tion. Celebrating love and community amidst marijuana sharing, nudity, and the most heralded rock performers of the era, Woodstock's citizens proclaimed the rise of a "new generation" and the coming of a peace-loving "age of Aquarius."

Counter-cultural explorations such as Herbert Marcuse's *Eros and Civilization* (1955, 1962), Carlos Castaneda's *The Teachings of Don Juan: A Yaqui Way of Knowledge* (1968), and Charles Reich's *The Greening of America* (1970) sought to portray alternative values that cherished the inner spirit and transcended com-petitive ego. Meanwhile, cultural radicals like White Panther John Sinclair called

BOB DYLAN
1941-

Bob Dylan's confrontational style and provocative music made him a major catalyst and symbol of the cultural crisis of the 1960s. Dylan first captured national attention by merging blues and country music with the left-wing political content of the urban folk music scene. Then, in 1965, he dramatically adopted the raucus sounds and electrified twang of rock and roll, which he combined with surreal images and poetic phrasing to attack prevailing assumptions about American values and institutions.

Born Robert Zimmerman and raised in a small town on Minnesota's Iron Range in the 1950s, the young musician had identified with the alienation expressed by actor James Dean and, like the beat writers, concocted fantasies of escape. In 1960, he changed his name to Dylan and took off for New York in search of his hero, folksinger Woody Guthrie, troubadour of radical causes since the 1930s.

Singing in folk clubs in New York's Greenwich Village, Dylan evoked the liberal optimism of the Kennedy era. His 1962 song, "Blowin' in the Wind," denounced the complaisance of middle-class America and quickly became an anthem of liberal dissent. Dylan wrote many songs in support of the civil rights movement ("Oxford Town," "Who Killed Davey Moore?") and performed at the March on Washington of 1963. The Cuban missile crisis inspired "A Hard Rain's Gonna Fall." "Every line of it is actually the start of a whole song," he said. "But when I wrote it, I thought I wouldn't have enough time alive to write all those songs so I put all I could into this one."

Dylan's political optimism eroded further after the Kennedy assassination. Given the Tom Paine Award in December 1963 by the Emergency Civil Liberties Committee at a swank New York hotel, he saw only the "mink and jewels." "It took me a long time to get young," he told the liberal audience, "...and I'm proud of it." For Dylan, the immense success of the first Beatles tour of America the following spring suggested a bridge to reach the mass audience he had always sought. He began to experiment with rock musicians and attached electricity to his guitar to connect a pulsating beat to his lyrical style. The result was 1965's "Like a Rolling Stone," Dylan's first major hit. He had liberated political music from the enclaves of folk, bringing it into the cultural mainstream.

Through the 1960s, Dylan's gravelly voice resonated with the discontents of young America, going beyond social reform to demand a transformation of consciousness. His lyrics became more metaphoric and symbolic: the juxtaposition of familiar Americana with surrealist sequences suggested the absurdity and harsh hypocrisy of contemporary life.

At the peak of his success in 1966, Dylan nearly died in a motorcycle crash and he retreated from public view. When he returned two years later, his music expressed a remarkable withdrawal from hard rock. Such albums as *Nashville Skyline* (1969) and *New Morning* (1970) reflected a more mellow and personal mood of the early 1970s, while later records, *Blood on the Tracks* (1974) and *Slow Train Coming* (1979), emphasized Dylan's growing interest in spiritual values and even "born again" Christianity. He also made movies, experimented with videos, and continued to write songs, although he seemed forever trapped by his first transformation. Yet Dylan's roots in his own generation could not disguise the fact that younger audiences looked to him as a pioneer of the rock form and his occasional concert tours remained commercially successful into the 1980s. ∎

for autonomous economies to sustain these values in the "youth colonies" of university towns and big cities. But Aquarian radicalism could not obscure the stark limitations of the counterculture. Hendrix, Joplin, and Morrison all died of the effects of heavy drug abuse by 1969. Underworld marketing of heroin, amphetamines, dangerous tranquilizers, and impure LSD not only wrecked minds and bodies but helped to destroy the fabric of the emerging culture. As organized crime took hold of the lucrative drug market, violence became endemic. Just months after Woodstock, four people died at a free Rolling Stones concert at the Altamont Speedway in California; one, a black man, stabbed to death by members of the Hell's Angels motorcycle gang acting as the concert security force. Worse still, Charles Manson and a collection of self-styled hippies adopted counterculture rhetoric to justify the brutal murder of seven wealthy people, including movie actress Sharon Tate, in the Hollywood hills in 1969. Meanwhile, rock music developed into a corporate industry capitalized at over $1 billion. The new market included love beads, incense, transistor radios, stereos, blue jeans, waterbeds, granola, "hip" cosmetics and "groovy" hair accessories. Hollywood also earned handsome receipts by portraying youthful rebellion in such movies as *Bonnie and Clyde* (1967), *The Graduate* (1967), and *Easy Rider* (1969).

As the oldest baby boomers moved from college campuses into the job market in the early 1970s, corporate culture readily absorbed their radical expectations. Sexual liberation—"swinging" singles and couples, pornography, birth control, and abortion—became acceptable to Americans in all income brackets; rock melodies filtered into shopping center Muzak; and the riot of psychedelic art and color worked its way into the products of clothing manufacturers and advertisers. Yet on a personal level, the new generation of adults anticipated different satisfactions than their parents had. They remained skeptical about the institution of marriage, choosing more frequently to stay single, live together without marriage (the number of such couples quintupled between 1970 and 1987), or delay their weddings. They had fewer children (the birth rate reached a low point of 1.8 per couple in 1976) or delayed childbirth until their mid- or late-thirties (a second baby boom among parents of this age-bracket commenced around 1980). And they were more likely to accept divorce (the rate doubled in the 1970s and continued to skyrocket through the '80s), second marriages, and new varieties of multi- and step-parenting. As the baby boomers grew older, moreover, so did the average age of the national population. In their middle years the youth of the 1960s would look back nostalgically to a time when radical change seemed imminent.

Exhibit 12–2. Marriages and Divorces, 1970–1983.
(rounded figures)

	1970	1975	1979	1983
Marriages	2.16m	2.15m	2.33m	2.45m
Divorces	708,000	1.04m	1.18m	1.16m
		(m = million)		

Source: *Statistical Abstract of the United States* (1987)

YOUNG RADICALS

"We are people of this generation, bred in at least modest comfort, housed now in universities, looking uncomfortably to the world we inherit." So began the Port Huron Statement of the fledgling Students for a Democratic Society (SDS) in 1962. The cultural rebellion of middle-class youth paralleled and stimulated an emerging political consciousness among a smaller segment of college students known as the "New Left." During the Cold War era, political repression and mass defections from the Communist party had drastically weakened support for both Marxist theory and social activism. But the political challenges of the 1960s stimulated a radical revival among such groups as the Young Peoples Socialist League, the Student Peace Union, and the Student League for Industrial Democracy, which in 1960 changed its name to Students for a Democratic Society.

Student-led civil rights activity in the South galvanized dissent around the country. Following the sit-ins of 1960, veteran activist Ella Baker helped young blacks organize the Student Non-Violent Coordinating Committee (SNCC), which combined a Christian social ethic with a commitment to participatory democracy. The courageous attacks on segregation by SNCC leaders such as John Lewis, Diana Nash, and Robert Moses often inspired liberal white students to political struggle. Equally significant was the young generation's despair at the continuing Cold War and the possibility of nuclear annihilation. The Port Huron Statement, penned by University of Michigan activist Tom Hayden, declared that "we may be the last generation in the experiment with living." Hayden's manifesto attacked the complacent acceptance of poverty, racism, and militarism and called for participatory democracy to overcome the alienation caused by bureaucratic decision-making.

The first massive student protest erupted at the University of California at Berkeley in 1964 when administrators banned political recruiting on campus. Borrowing tactics from the civil rights struggle, the ensuing Free Speech Movement (FSM) organized a sit-in in which eight hundred students submitted to arrest. "There's a time when the operation of the machine becomes so odious," FSM leader Mario Savio told Berkeley students, "that you can't take part...And you've got to put your bodies upon the gears...and you've got to make it stop." Otherwise, FSM warned, American education merely prepared students to take their places in an oppressive corporate order. "You can't trust anybody over thirty," FSM activist Jack Weinberg taunted. A generation once courted by President Kennedy had now selected its own agenda.

Agitation over student rights soon merged with mass protests against the Vietnam War and the draft. Less than a month after President Johnson ordered the full-scale bombing of North Vietnam in 1965 (see chapter 11), twenty thousand protesters showed up in Washington for a demonstration sponsored by SDS. Teach-ins on the war soon spread to major universities. At Berkeley, twelve thousand students and faculty participated in Vietnam Day. As draft calls reached forty thousand a month in 1966, rallies, marches, teach-ins, and draft card burnings multiplied. Young men refused induction orders, thousands deserted the armed forces, and even more fled to Canada and Europe to avoid conscription. Protesters occupied military induction centers and harassed on-

Activist Mario Savio addresses Berkeley's Free Speech Movement in the fall of 1964, the dawn of student protest among white dissidents.

campus job recruiters for the military and the CIA. Representatives for defense contractors such as Dow Chemical, which manufactured napalm, used to kill civilians in Vietnam, and Honeywell, which made anti-personnel fragmentation bombs, also faced militant campus protest.

War opponents viewed the use of technological violence against an economically undeveloped people as tantamount to genocide. Some radicals like SDS's Carl Oglesby pictured the conflict as a laboratory for developing techniques to halt social revolution in the "third world." But most protesters identified with the spirit of Joseph Heller's cult novel, *Catch-22* (1960), an absurdist view of World War II which suggested that escape was the only sane response to war. Escalation by the Johnson administration, nevertheless, convinced antiwar activists that the government would not respond to reasonable criticism and that moral citizens were obligated to act. As folksingers such as Joan Baez and Phil Ochs presided over the largest rallies, antiwar assemblies frequently became instant communities in which outrage merged with political action.

By the fall of 1967, protest had evolved into massive resistance. A "stop the draft" week at the Oakland, California Induction Center resulted in street battles between police and twenty thousand activists. At a demonstration called by the National Mobilization Against the War (MOBE), one-hundred thousand marchers surrounded the Pentagon: Norman Mailer's *Armies of the Night* (1968) described the arrest of 660 protesters, including pediatrician Dr. Benjamin Spock and Mailer himself. Meanwhile, another three-hundred thousand demonstrators gathered in New York City on the same day. Still another phase of the antiwar movement commenced when Father Philip Berrigan led a group of Catholic activists in pouring blood on draft files in Baltimore later the same year. As efforts to destroy draft records spread across the country, a few conscientious objectors in the military refused assignment to Vietnam. Convinced that campuses served as seedbeds for antiwar activity, President Johnson ordered Army Intelligence to join the FBI in putting thousands of students and faculty under surveillance. Nonetheless, by 1968 SDS boasted nearly three hundred chapters and a membership of one-hundred thousand. For many of the nation's increasingly politicized students and peace activists, the Vietnam War had become a symbol of American society's exploitation of the poor and powerless.

BLACK LIBERATION

As young radicals focused on campus issues and the antiwar movement, the biracial non-violent civil rights movement began to unravel. The failure of SNCC to persuade President Johnson to seat a racially integrated delegation from Mississippi at the Democratic National Convention of 1964 (see chapter 5) undermined black confidence in liberal reform. Once activists like Fanny Lou Hamer believed that they had been betrayed by professed allies, they began to see all whites as part of a rigid "establishment." Increasingly, black organizers like Stokely Carmichael identified with other colonized peoples of the "third world," including the peasants fighting the United States in Vietnam. In early 1966, SNCC became the first civil rights group to oppose the war. Aware that blacks suffered disproportionate casualties in combat, Carmichael and other militants coined the slogan "Hell No, We Won't Go!" and urged blacks to resist the draft. The following year, black heavyweight champion Muhammad Ali refused induction on the basis of his status as a Muslim minister and remained defiant when ring authorities stripped him of his crown. "No Viet Cong ever called me nigger," Ali explained.

During 1966, Carmichael asserted leadership of a civil rights march in support of James Meredith, the first black to be enrolled at the University of Mississippi. Meredith had been immediately wounded by a sniper when he attempted to begin a solo trek across the state to encourage black voter registration. When civil rights leaders rushed to continue the march, Carmichael brushed aside talk of non-violence and proclaimed "Black Power!" The words electrified the media and terrified whites, although assertions of black power mainly served to instill feelings of pride and cultural identity among blacks. Nevertheless, SNCC soon moved to purge whites from leadership positions and disassociate itself from a rhetoric of non-violence. "Integration," said Carmichael, was "a subterfuge for the maintenance of white supremacy" and fostered the idea that "white" was better than "black." Meanwhile, SNCC leader H. Rap Brown taunted the media with the quip that "violence is as American as cherry pie."

The magnetism of Black Power testified to widespread frustration within the black community. "To be a Negro in this country, "explained novelist James Baldwin, "is to be in a rage all the time." Eldridge Cleaver, a former convict and

SNCC's Stokely Carmichael, the first black leader to proclaim "Black Power" in 1966, fused black pride with militant and confrontational politics.

emerging leader of the Black Panther party, expressed similar fury in his best-selling *Soul on Ice* (1968). "You're either part of the solution or part of the problem," Cleaver later declared. Black Power also drew on the legacy of the Black Muslim leader, Malcolm X. Born Malcolm Little, he had converted to the Muslim religion while in prison and changed his name to Malcolm X to symbolize independence from white domination. A persuasive, charismatic speaker, he initially opposed interracial political cooperation, arguing that any association with "evil whites" would prevent the attainment of social justice. But after he broke with the Black Muslims in 1964, Malcolm became convinced that capitalism functioned as an oppressive force in the world and that people of all colors must cooperate to achieve a socialist alternative. Assassinated in Harlem in 1965, Malcolm had a profound effect upon black and white radicals through his posthumously published *Autobiography*.

The spirit of Malcolm's teaching continued in the Black Panther party, organized by Bobby Seale and Huey Newton in Oakland in 1966. The Panthers viewed urban riots as self-destructive of black interests and instead fashioned themselves as a community defense league designed to monitor the activities of ghetto police. In order to dramatize the right to bear arms against "occupation" of their communities by white authorities, a group of party members marched into the California legislature with loaded rifles. When police charged Newton with murder after a violent confrontation in Oakland, the Panthers launched a long and insistent "Free Huey" campaign (all counts were dropped after three trials). By 1968, the Black Panther party had devised a ten-point program embracing Marxist concepts of self-determination and opposition to the evil of "welfare colonialism." The Panthers also distributed a national weekly newspaper, established local health clinics, and provided free breakfasts and schools for black children.

Panther rhetoric and militance invoked the wrath of FBI Director J. Edgar Hoover. Fearing the rise of a "black messiah" who might galvanize black anger, Hoover expanded counterintelligence activities in 1967 to "expose, disrupt, misdirect, discredit, or otherwise neutralize the activities of black nationalists." During the next two years police worked with state and federal officials to raid thirty-one Panther headquarters, arrest hundreds of leaders on spurious charges, and disrupt party operations through "disinformation" programs (for Panther trials of early 1970s see chapter 13). In one particularly grisly episode in December 1969, Chicago police and state officers raided the apartment of Panther leaders Fred Hampton and Mark Clark and shot them to death as they woke from sleep. By then both Cleaver and Seale had fled the country, Newton was still in jail, and perhaps forty Panther leaders had been killed in police raids.

As black women like Elaine Brown and Erika Huggins assumed control of the exposed party, Panther organizing spread to the nation's prisons. Several bloody confrontations in California led to the shooting death of Panther prison author George Jackson in 1970. The following year, New York Governor Nelson Rockefeller ordered state troopers to storm Attica prison, where one thousand black, white, and Puerto Rican inmates had rebelled against degrading conditions by taking over the facility. Police bullets killed thirty-three prisoners and ten hostages. By the early 1970s, however, the black liberation movement had abandoned the principles of participatory democracy and lost its following in the urban ghetto.

RADICAL CONFRONTATION

Pressed by the militance of SNCC and the Panthers, the more moderate Martin Luther King, Jr. proposed a merger of the civil rights and antiwar movements in 1967. King shocked liberal followers by calling the United States the "greatest purveyor of violence in the world." That year's "New Politics" convention in Chicago provided an opportunity for biracial political coalition. But although the platform called for "revolutionary change" and "open draft resistance," the gathering could not agree to Panther demands for half its leadership positions. In 1968, the Panthers won white radical support for the Peace and Freedom party, which ran Eldridge Cleaver for president, but the poorly organized effort exerted only a marginal influence on the election.

Cooperation between black activists and SDS briefly surfaced at Columbia University in the spring of 1968 when the two groups separately occupied university buildings to protest campus ties to the war as well as planned expansion into a Harlem community park. But blacks called off their action just before New York City police viciously smashed the SDS occupation. The confrontation, which brought nearly seven hundred arrests, set the tone for clashes at every major American university; over three thousand campus protests occurred during 1968.

As the Democratic party prepared for its national convention, leadership of the antiwar crusade passed to the Youth International Party or Yippies, a loosely-defined, media-conscious group of pranksters who sought to fuse humor, cultural revolution, and political dissent. Led by Abbie Hoffman and Jerry Rubin, the Yippies scheduled a "Festival of Life" to contrast the convention's expected support for the Vietnam War. But Chicago Mayor Richard Daley, a major power in the Democratic party, refused to accommodate any antiwar action and prevented the ten thousand demonstrators from using city parks and thoroughfares. The tension exploded when Chicago police attacked protesters, journalists, and bystanders with clubs, tear gas, and mace. As live television cameras panned on the crowds, angry youth chanted "The whole world is watching!" President Johnson's National Commission on the Causes and Prevention of Violence later described the event as a "police riot" involving "unrestrained and indiscriminate" attacks against people "who had broken no law, disobeyed no order, made no threat." But the confrontation between middle-class youth and working-class police reflected the same class tensions that characterized the bloody Columbia protest and most Americans blamed the demonstrators for the violence.

The tumultuous events of 1968 marked a turning point for the fragile radical coalition. The televised Tet Offensive and the peace candidacies of Eugene McCarthy and Robert Kennedy (see chapter 11) validated antiwar protest and attracted middle-class professionals and liberal politicians to peaceful marches. But Columbia and Chicago taught Movement leaders that only repression and violence awaited efforts to radically restructure American society and values. SDS organizers formed the "Weatherman" faction after Columbia and went underground to escape police detection. Isolated and ideologically committed to alliance with "third world" revolution, secret affinity groups carried out at least fourteen major bombings against government and military installations to show that the war had "come home." The most controversial killed a graduate student at a mathematics research facility at the University of Wisconsin in August 1970. Earlier in the year, three Weatherpeople died in an accidental explosion in a Greenwich Village townhouse used to assemble bombs.

Frustrations over the war and police harassment of students and street people led to a violent riot and the destruction of a Bank of America branch near the University of California at Santa Barbara in late 1968. Similar confrontation erupted at Berkeley the following spring when activists created a "people's park" on a strip of vacant university land. When campus officials directed police to erect a barbed wire fence to prevent unauthorized use of the property, thousands of local residents faced down law enforcement officials. In response, police helicopters indiscriminately dropped tear gas on the city and sheriff's deputies used shotguns to kill one protester and injure one hundred others.

Student activism resurfaced following the 1970 invasion of Cambodia (see chapter 13 for confrontations at Kent and Jackson State). But the violence of both Movement and government forces, as well as the disruptive influence of the FBI and police, discouraged the building of radical coalitions after 1968. So did divisions between blacks and whites, women and men, and cultural rebels and political dissidents. Larger social changes, moreover, contributed to the waning of radical militance. Reduced draft calls lessened the immediacy of the war, while a major economic downturn, begun in the early 1970s, undermined the confidence of middle-class students and placed a higher value on career goals. Students once again showed a decided preference for "practical" courses such as business administration and engineering. Since college students represented a smaller proportion of the American population by the late-1970s and '80s, they displayed less confidence in their ability to bring about social change.

The dissenting spirit of the Vietnam era, however, did not entirely disappear. Protest energy found its way into a variety of causes from ecology to the women's movement. Statewide "fair share" campaigns for lower energy and insurance rates as well as agitation for alternative sources of electric power also assumed new importance in the 1970s and '80s. Furthermore, opposition to presidential foreign policy persisted and took the form of a "post-Vietnam syndrome" in which activists protested United States involvement in the "third world," especially in Central America. The anti-interventionist spirit also encouraged a resurgence of opposition to the nuclear arms race, producing the largest mass demonstrations in American history; over six-hundred thousand dissenters converged in New York's Central Park in 1982. Such pressure pushed Washington towards arms negotiations with the Soviet Union. By the mid-1980s, a new generation of college activists showed greater interest in protesting racial apartheid in South Africa and United States support of "contra" guerrillas in Nicaragua (see chapter 14). Radicals of the Vietnam era participated in many of these causes and sometimes found their way into academic professions where they helped to fashion neo-Marxist interpretations of Amnerican society.

AFRO-AMERICAN CULTURE AND THE URBAN GHETTO

Despite the political limits of Black Power, the ideology incorporated new assertions of racial pride. Contrary to traditional "melting pot" theories which assumed that racial and ethnic minorities would assimilate into white Anglo-Protestant culture, black intellectuals, such as playwright Imamu Baraka (formerly Leroi Jones), insisted on the vitality of a distinctive Afro-American culture that survived the ordeal of slavery and white racism. Motivated by this new pride, black college students at San Francisco State, the University of Minnesota, Cornell, and other campuses organized strikes and building seizures during 1969 to force university administrators to hire more black faculty and create academic programs in Black Studies. Despite the bitterness of these confrontations, white scholars and administrators gradually acknowledged the new interpretation of the black experience. Alex Haley's *Roots* (1976), a personal study of black genealogy, popularized the idea for a mass audience. Over 130 million Americans, more than half the nation, watched one segment of the televised version of the book in 1977. By then most black writers, including the poet Nikki Giovanni and novelists Ishmael Reed, Al Young, and Alice Walker, saw their art as an assertion of cultural independence. Walker drew a direct link with the African legacy in her novel, *The Color Purple* (1982), made into a popular film four years later. Pulitzer prize winning playwright August Wilson used African techniques of storytelling and ensemble performance in *Ma Rainey's Black Bottom* (1984) and *Fences* (1987).

As black musicians, athletes, and entertainers such as Bill Cosby and Eddie Murphy played an increasing role in popular culture, Reverend Jesse Jackson's 1984 and 1988 presidential campaigns (see chapter 14) demonstrated the arrival of black Americans in the political mainstream. The number of elected black officials jumped from 103 in 1964 to over four thousand by 1980. Political acceptance both encouraged and reflected economic success for middle-class blacks, who often benefited from declining discrimination and affirmative action guidelines which set hiring priorities for minorities in federally funded programs. Black women of the 1980s, for example, earned nearly identical wage rates as white women, while the annual income of middle-class black males leaped by half. Top black businesses, moreover, increased their total sales from $600 million in 1973 to over $2 billion ten years later.

Despite these gains, blacks in urban ghettos confronted endemic poverty. Martin Luther King had hoped to draw national attention to the need for jobs and housing with a Poor People's March to Washington in 1968, but the demonstration lost focus without the assassinated leader's direction. By the 1980s, 30 percent of black workers earned less than $10,000 a year compared to 10 percent for whites. Even those figures concealed the depths of black poverty. The mechanization of agriculture after World War II had forced most of the black population to abandon the rural South. Arriving in northern cities at a time when employment for unskilled labor had declined and white collar jobs shifted to the suburbs, black male baby-boomers found few jobs. Teenage unemployment among blacks skyrocketed from 10 percent in the 1950s to 40 percent in the 1960s and remained at that devastating level. When these young men became adults, many ceased looking for jobs. As a result, the employment of adult black men dropped from 75 percent in 1955 to 40 percent in 1985. The inability of black men to support families led large numbers of black women to have babies without marriage. By 1985, 60 percent of black infants were born out of wedlock and more than half of all black children lived with only one parent.

The economic problems of urban blacks produced what sociologists, called an "underclass"—a significant population that was unemployed and unemploya-

Exhibit 12–3. Percent of Families Below Poverty Line, White and Black.

	All families	*Black families*
1959	22.4	55.1
1966	14.7	41.8
1970	12.6	33.5
1975	12.3	31.3
1980	13.0	32.5
1985	14.0	31.3

Source: *Statistical Abstract of the United States* (1987)

Black poverty persisted through the 1980s as one-third of all blacks and 45 percent of black children remained poor.

ble, relying increasingly on hustling and crime to survive. By the late-1980s violent youth street gangs selling "crack," an inexpensive but highly addictive cocaine derivative, terrorized black communities in most major cities. Black leaders such as Chicago's Reverend Jackson stressed self-dignity, discipline, and the rejection of drugs as the first steps out of the morass. But despite creative expressions such as "rap" music and "break-dancing," the black ghetto remained a depressing parody of the American dream of upward mobility. Ghetto rioting during the New York City power black-out of 1977 and in Miami in 1980 underscored the hopelessness of many young blacks. Racial intimidation and violence in such dispersed locations as Forsythe County, Georgia and New York City's Howard Beach also testified to the perpetuation of hardcore bigotry in white society. Black leaders of the 1980s expressed growing concern about nationwide growth of the Ku Klux Klan and other racial hate groups.

NATIVE-AMERICAN MILITANCE AND DEVELOPMENT

Young Native-American radicals used the cultural crisis of the late-1960s to reassert Indian autonomy and peoplehood. During 1969, a group of activists took over San Francisco Bay's vacant Alcatraz Island, formerly a federal prison, and

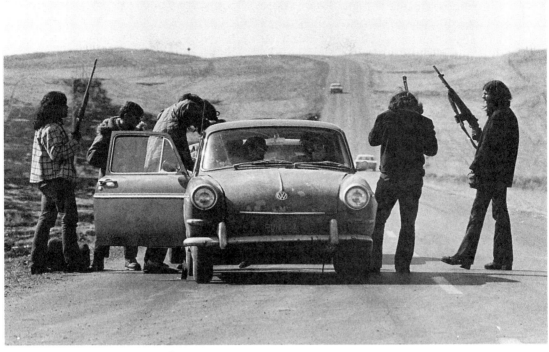

Activists associated with the American Indian Movement (AIM) patrol the road to Wounded Knee, South Dakota, seized in 1973 in protest against government collusion with corrupt tribal leaders.

called for the creation of a self-sufficient Native-American cultural and educational center. The eighteen-month occupation galvanized the American Indian community. Although Native-Americans remained even poorer than blacks, Indian population doubled from five-hundred thousand in 1945 to one million in 1975. Such growth testified to the revitalization of American Indian optimism. In midwestern and western cities, Native-Americans established cultural centers to revive historic traditions of worship, dance, poetry, and healing. Urban activists pressed universities to establish programs in Indian languages and Native-American Studies. But the bitterness of the Indian community took public form when activists organized a "Trail of Broken Treaties" march to Washington in 1972 and occupied the offices of the Bureau of Indian Affairs (BIA) for a week.

During 1973, the militant American Indian Movement (AIM) focused national attention on the Pine Ridge reservation in South Dakota. "We have bet with our lives," AIM leader Russell Means declared, "that we could change the course of...the history of Indian America." Invited by Sioux dissidents to protest against a corrupt tribal government that cooperated with the federal government, hundreds of AIM activists seized the village of Wounded Knee and took hostages. The action provoked a series of fierce clashes with government marshals. After seventy-one days, federal officials agreed to end the siege and consult with traditional tribal leaders. Yet the government refused to reopen disputed treaty negotiations and the Justice Department indicted AIM organizers Means and Dennis Banks, who won acquittal in 1974. Like the black power confrontations of the late-1960s, Wounded Knee symbolized an end to psychological dependence on whites.

Native-Americans like the Sioux focused increasingly on economic issues during the next two decades. Convinced that control of natural resources would provide security and a means of protecting their cultural independence, several tribes went to court to reclaim historical land titles and demand enforcement of old treaties. The Sioux pressed to regain 1.3 million acres of the sacred Black Hills that the federal government had taken under questionable circumstances a century earlier. In Maine the Passamaquoddy and Pebnobscot tribes accepted a $37 million settlement from the federal government in 1978. These legal actions compounded jurisdictional disputes between Native Americans and Washington over land development, water rights, mineral reserves, environmental quality standards, and hunting and fishing prerogatives. By the late-1980s reservation Indians anticipated greater economic self-sufficiency. Yet persistently high suicide rates among young Native-American men led tribal elders to bemoan the loss of traditional values and practices. And rampant poverty, unemployment, and alcoholism still plagued the efforts of Indian leaders in the cities.

THE NEW IMMIGRATION

Young Mexican-Americans embraced a "Chicano" pride in the late-1960s by organizing the Brown Berets and carrying guns to demonstrate their independence from Anglo authorities and police. Like these Los Angeles and Denver militants, rural New Mexican activist Reies Lopez Tijerina armed followers in protests against the loss of nineteenth century land claims. Building on such ethnic pride, Mexican-American students at southwestern universities used confrontation tactics to bring about the establishment of Chicano Studies programs. By the 1970s, the new cultural awakening had produced scholarly journals such as *Aztlan,* the popular magazines *El Grito* and *La Raza,* and moving explorations of Chicano roots by novelists Raymond Barrio, Rudolfo Anaya, and Arturo Islas. The renaissance also generated fresh literary perspectives from feminist poets Lorna Dee Cervantes, Cherrie Moraga, and Angela de Hoyos. Film director Luis Valdez introduced Chicano themes in *Boulevard Nights* (1979), *Zoot Suit* (1981), and *La Bamba* (1987).

Chicano consciousness, however, could not hide the bleak facts of economic existence. Mexican-Americans, who accounted for two-thirds of the nation's Spanish-speaking people by 1980, received only 70 percent the median white (non-Hispanic) income. Fully one-fifth of Mexican-Americans lived below government-defined poverty levels. To aggravate matters, a poverty and population explosion in Mexico pushed between 3.5 and six million illegal immigrants to the United States between 1970 and 1978 alone. These "undocumented aliens" willingly accepted low-paying jobs, mainly in the Southwest, as field hands or service workers without benefit of union contract or government regulation. The predominantly Mexican migrant force comprised 10 percent of California's labor pool (see chapter 14 for the Immigration Act of 1986).

Seeking to improve conditions for field workers, California's Cesar Chavez used Christian nonviolence and product boycotts among liberal supporters to

Cesar Chavez and the United Farm Workers (UFW), a labor movement of Mexican-American field workers that began to demonstrate the possibilities of Chicano power in the late 1960s.

win collective bargaining rights for the small but militant United Farm Workers after 1965. Meanwhile, organizers Corky Gonzáles and José Angel Guitiérrez formed civil rights group in Denver and Texas to mobilize Chicano political power. By the 1970s, a Congress of Mexican American Unity represented two hundred civil and political groups. Mexican-Americans also sent delegates to the National Council of La Raza, a consortium of twenty-six organizations that acted as a Washington lobby for all Hispanics. Constituting one-fourth the Democratic vote in Texas and playing a major role in the Los Angeles area, where they numbered two million strong, Mexican-Americans used political power to fight discrimination, liberalize immigration procedures, and campaign for bilingual education in the public schools.

By the late-1980s, Spanish had become the nation's most frequently spoken foreign tongue and the nearly twenty million Hispanics (8 percent the national population) its second largest minority. High birth rates, illegal immigration, and the liberalizing features of the Immigration Act of 1965 brought the doubling of Hispanic population between 1970 and 1987, a period in which Spanish speakers comprised 37 percent of legal entrants to the United States. Hundreds of thousands of immigrants arrived from the Caribbean nations of Puerto Rico, the Dominican Republic, Haiti, and English-speaking Jamaica. In addition, tens of thousands of Salvadorans and Guatemalans fled poverty, civil war, and military repression in the early 1980s to come to western cities such as San Francisco and Tucson. When the United States denied entrance permits to additional refugees from governments run by its allies in El Salvador and Guatemala, humanitarian activists in over two hundred southwestern churches and synagogues risked imprisonment by extending sanctuary to the illegal immigrants.

Exiles from Nicaragua and Communist Cuba encountered a far warmer response. Between 1959 and 1970, an average of twenty thousand Cubans migrated to the United States each year, most of them skilled professionals or white-collar workers. Their numbers increased until Castro permitted a mass exodus in 1980 of 125,000 predominantly working class men. By the close of the decade, over a million Cuban-Americans comprised one of the most influential Hispanic groups in the United States. Some 750,000 had gathered in Miami, where their capital and entrepreneurial skills helped to make the city the financial and social center of all Latin America. Strictly religious, economically ambitious, and bitterly anti-Communist, the Cuban-Americans succeeded in Florida politics, where they repeatedly won local offices and helped to build a conservative Republican party. Yet the poverty of Miami's Hispanic underclass and its access to Latin America attracted the international narcotics trade. The multibillion-dollar industry brought rising cocaine addiction among all social classes, rampant police corruption, soaring crime and homicide rates, and the occasional complicity of American financial institutions in processing drug money.

With Los Angeles replacing New York as the leading port of entry in the 1970s, over 40 percent of the nation's immigrants were arriving from Asia. Over three million Asians came to the United States after 1970, supplementing the hundreds of thousands of newcomers from China, Taiwan, Hong Kong, and Korea who migrated in the 1960s. Many of these immigrants took advantage of starting capital and American family ties to establish small businesses, particularly in retail food and restaurants. During 1975, airlifts by the American military brought 130,000 Vietnamese to the United States. The refugee laws of 1977 and 1980, moreover, facilitated the arrival of more than 450,000 "boat people" from Cambodia, Laos, and Vietnam—impoverished escapees who received resettlement aid from American relief agencies in Thailand and Malaysia. Once in the United States, the new immigrants won a reputation for hard work and strong bonds of kinship. Asian-Americans, particularly the Japanese and Chinese, sought college education in large numbers and excelled at mathematics and the physical sciences. Several Chinese-Americans won Nobel prizes in these fields in the 1980s.

The political refugee laws also swelled the number of Jews and other exiles from Communist eastern Europe and revolutionary Iran. The sixty thousand Iranians included a large number of technical, medical, and entrepreneurial personnel. As other immigrants from the Middle East increased the American Arab population to two million, an Arab-American-Anti-Discrimination Committee sought to oppose negative stereotypes and bring a fresh perspective to American foreign policy.

By 1980, fourteen million immigrants lived in the United States. The influx of Hispanics, Asians, eastern Europeans, and Middle Easterners lent an enhanced cosmopolitanism to many American towns and cities and heightened the emotional content of debates over international politics. The new immigration also created strains in the American social structure. As demographic statistics suggested that black, red, brown, and yellow Americans would outnumber whites by the middle of the twenty-first century, racial supremacists in groups such as The Order and the Aryan Nation complained of the dilution of national character. In Texas, the Ku Klux Klan accused the Vietnamese of using family labor to take over the gulf shrimp industry. Other Americans objected to "special" treatment for the Indochinese and other political refugees. Meanwhile, poor blacks often resented the presence of Korean and Vietnamese storekeepers in their neighborhoods, while Asian street gangs found themselves competing for turf with entrenched black and Hispanic youth.

Ethnic conflict also carried over into education. Asian-American leaders, for example, charged that some colleges used quotas to limit the admission of academically proficient Asians. Another controversy involved bilingualism. In *Lau v. Nichols* (1974), the Supreme Court ordered public schools to teach children in a language they could understand, thereby supporting the efforts of Hispanic and Asian activists. But California voters overwhelmingly approved a 1986 ballot measure making English the official language of their state. Although most immigrants only desired to preserve their cultural heritages while contributing to an American society they revered, ethnic conflict continued to define the nation's life.

THE NEW FEMINISM

The "new woman," according to Helen Gurley Brown's 1962 bestseller, *Sex and the Single Girl*, "took the pill and lived in an apartment with a double bed. She spent money on herself and men spent attention on her. She was the old feminist ideal of the independent woman with a new twist—she was sexy." Rising female employment in the postwar period, together with the sexual revolution, bolstered a growing sense of female autonomy. By 1960, 40 percent of all women over sixteen held a job outside the home. Yet women workers earned only three-fifths of what men received and seldom held political power. But a combination of feminist agitation and grass roots enthusiasm sparked the first organized women's movement since the 1920s.

Pressed by women in the Democratic party, President Kennedy created a Commission on the Status of Women in 1961 to examine questions of economic equity. Two years later, the panel recommended equal pay laws, child care services, legal reform, and further government action on behalf of women. Similar commissions soon sprouted in every state. Betty Friedan's *The Feminine Mystique*, published in 1963, sharpened the growing debate and brought the question of equal rights for women to a mass audience of readers. The next year, Congress banned gender discrimination in employment in Title VII of the Civil Rights Act. Ironically, southern representatives had extended the bill's job protections to women in order to discredit the entire legislation. But Congress approved the bill anyhow.

Title VII also sanctioned creation of an Equal Employment Opportunity Commission (EEOC), the first federal agency to address the issue of equal hiring rights and wages for women. Yet the commission accomplished so little that Friedan joined twenty-seven other activists to form the National Organization for Women (NOW) in 1966. NOW pledged to "take the actions needed to bring

BETTY FRIEDAN
1924–

At a time when psychologists insisted that the American woman would achieve maximum fulfillment as wife, mother, housewife, and homemaker, author Betty Friedan challenged the cult of domesticity in her best-selling book of 1963, *The Feminine Mystique*. According to Friedan, middle-class women responded to traditional expectations with a bewildered question: "Is that all?" Her book sold three million copies, reached an estimated readership five times as large, and provoked a fundamental reexamination of women's place in American society. Scarcely a single American family was unaffected by its message.

The daughter of immigrant Jewish parents of Peoria, Illinois, Friedan had studied psychology and social science at Smith College and the University of California at Berkeley. "I didn't want to be like my mother" she later recalled. She worked as a journalist during World War II, but lost her job to a returning war veteran. Despite a union contract forbidding such actions, she was fired from another job because of pregnancy. In 1949, she explained, there was no term to describe "sex discrimination."

During the 1950s Friedan lived in the suburbs of New York where she raised three children and continued a free-lance journalist career, writing articles for such magazines as *Harper's*, *Good Housekeeping*, *Redbook*, and *Mademoiselle*. For a piece about her Smith College classmates fifteen years after graduation, she conducted a survey of their attitudes and feelings. It revealed a profound unhappiness among college-educated, middle-class women. But the article contradicted the assumptions of the day. The editors of women's magazines refused to publish it.

Friedan decided to write a book. "Something is very wrong with the way American women are trying to live their lives today", she began. "It is no longer possible to...dismiss the desperation of so many American women." Friedan proceeded to demolish the "happy housewife" syndrome of postwar society, arguing that middle-class women re- *(cont.)*

women into the mainstream of American society...in fully equal partnership with men." The organization pushed for legal abortion, maternity leaves, tax-deductible child care, and an Equal Rights Amendment (ERA) to the Constitution to eradicate sex discrimination from American life. Other feminist groups such as the Women's Equity Action League (WEAL), organized by college faculty in 1968, and the Professional Women's Caucus (PWC), created in 1970, worked to open economic opportunities for middle-class women. In 1970, the Labor Department issued "affirmative action" guidelines to federal contractors which covered women and racial minorities.

The new feminism soon penetrated the political arena. The National Women's Political Caucus, formed in 1971, set out to compel the two major parties to *(cont.)* quired a source of personal fulfillment, a career, to achieve satisfaction.

Having identified a major social problem, Friedan joined other feminists in seeking its resolution. Her philosophy was quintessentially liberal. She demanded that women be given equal opportunities with men to achieve economic and political citizenship. In 1966, Friedan helped found the National Organization for Women (NOW) "to bring women into full participation in the mainstream of American society now" and served as its first president until 1970. Besides demanding employment opportunities and legal rights, NOW advocated child care centers and "the right of women to control their reproductive rights." Working within the liberal consensus, Friedan also helped establish the National Women's Political Caucus in 1971 to pressure the major political parties to accept greater female participation.

Friedan's liberal agenda clashed not only with sexist values, but also with more radical feminism. Viewing politics in traditional terms, she rejected the radical idea that "the personal is political." When, for example, lesbians demanded political recognition within the women's movement, Friedan denounced the "lavender menace" as internally divisive and a needless provocation for a conservative counterattack. Yet during the 1970s, a time of significant, though mixed advances for women in education, employment, and legal rights, Friedan enjoyed considerable stature as a foremother of contemporary feminism.

Never comfortable with radical feminism, Friedan used the backlash against women's rights in the late 1970s and '80s (the defeat of the equal rights amendment, the attack on abortion rights) to address the frustrations of younger women seeking to balance public careers with private needs. In her controversial book of 1981, *The Second Stage*, Friedan denied an antagonism between women's equality and the family. Urging feminists to accept the responsibilities and joys of child-bearing and nurturance, she stressed the greater diversity of contemporary family types, the blurring of traditional gender roles involving work and child care, and the growing equality within American families. "We have to break through our own *feminist* mystique now," she declared, "to come to terms with the new reality of our personal and political experience." ■

promote the participation of women. Democratic congressional representatives Shirley Chisholm and Bella Abzug initiated reforms which increased the percentage of female delegates at national conventions from 10 percent in 1968 to 40 percent in 1972. Meanwhile, the number of female state legislators more than tripled between 1969 and 1981. Altogether, the ranks of elected women officials leaped from less than six thousand in 1975 to more than fourteen thousand by 1981. Yet representation at the top levels of American politics remained rare, although Sandra Day O'Connor won appointment as the first female Supreme Court Justice in 1981 and Representative Geraldine Ferraro became the Democratic vice-presidential candidate in 1984. Congress passed the ERA in 1972, but ratification bogged down in the states. "STOP-ERA" organizer Phyllis Schlafly lobbied against the measure, claiming it would "neuterize" society and relieve men of obligations such as supporting their families. Despite tremendous grass-roots activism and an unprecedented extension to the amendment process, the ERA failed to win ratification in 1982.

Although NOW and the women's professional groups pioneered the new feminism, their reformist approach appeared increasingly limited to more radical women of the late-1960s. Female organizers for SNCC and SDS had learned how to mobilize people on the basis of mutual interests. Yet they frequently faced "second-class" treatment within the radical movement, often confined to menial tasks because male organizers monopolized the decision-making power. Despite SDS's espousal of "participatory democracy," only 6 percent of its 1964 Executive Committee consisted of women. When confronted with similar injustice in SNCC, female civil rights worker Casey Hayden described the implicit code of "male superiority" as oppressive as white racism, but Stokely Carmichael responded to feminist dissent by suggesting that the only proper position for women in SNCC was "prone." In 1967, male leadership of the National Conference for a New Politics ignored demands for equal representation by participating women. As a result, radical women walked out of the convention and vowed to create "a movement for women's liberation."

Radical feminists hoped to change society by reducing exploitation, competition, and "sexism." To attack traditions of female passivity, two hundred supporters of WITCH (Women's International Terrorist Conspiracy from Hell) protested outside the Miss America Pageant of 1968 by tossing "instruments of torture" such as brassieres and high-heeled shoes into a "freedom trash can." Feminists soon began to organize women's "rap groups" and "consciousness-raising" sessions to build self-esteem and begin to confront habits of sexism and deference to men. Inspired by this new spirit, Gloria Steinem and a group of friends launched the feminist *Ms.* magazine in 1971 in which editors shared all tasks without hierarchy. Radical calls for a restructuring of the family and capitalism appeared in numerous provocative books such as Kate Millett's *Sexual Politics* (1969), Shulamith Firestone's *Dialectic of Sex: The Case for Feminist Revolution* (1970), and Robin Morgan's *Sisterhood is Powerful* (1970). These works inspired scholarly research about women and stimulated the expansion of college Women's Studies classes to thirty thousand in 1982.

By 1980, women comprised a majority of the nation's university students and received ten times as many professional degrees as in 1970. The move toward professionalization extended to organized religion. Christian and Jewish feminists fought to obtain rights of ordination and to eliminate sexist language and imagery in scripture and ritual. Feminists also demanded control of their bodies from the male medical establishment, organizing alternative health centers and abortion clinics. The Supreme Court vindicated these efforts, ruling in *Roe v. Wade* (1973) that state laws banning abortion during the first three months of pregnancy intruded unconstitutionally on the client-physician relationship. More than 1.5 million legal abortions were performed each year following the landmark decision.

The ensuing controversy over abortions revealed the profound unrest generated by feminism. Activists like Friedan and Steinem insisted that abortion opponents sought to use the state to deprive women of vital personal choices and

Exhibit 12–4. Legal Abortions, 1972–1982.
(rounded figures)

1972	587,000
1974	899,000
1976	1,179,000
1978	1,410,000
1980	1,554,000
1982	1,574,000

Source: *Statistical Abstract of the United States* (1987)

to limit their social role to motherhood. But conservative clergy and Eagle Forum organizer Phyllis Schlafly replied that fetuses constituted sacred forms of human life and that abortion therefore amounted to legal murder of the unborn. The backlash against abortion, ERA, and affirmative action forced feminist organizations to defend the moderate gains of the 1970s.

Women activists of the 1980s also responded to the persistence of rape, wife-beating, and child abuse by opening crisis centers and shelters. Others worked to strengthen rape laws, recall judges who failed to take the offense seriously, and teach women techniques of self-defense. Feminist attorney Catherine McKinnon claimed that the $4 billion-a-year pornography industry incited male violence and drafted municipal legislation that would treat pornography as an attack on women's civil rights. After heated debates in Minneapolis and Indianapolis, however, her measures failed to pass. Meanwhile, conservative women opposed pornography on moral grounds: But liberal feminists such as Betty Friedan defended the principle of free speech and denounced the entire debate as needlessly divisive. Feminists agreed, nonetheless, on the need to end sexual harassment in the workplace and condemn the objectification of women's bodies and role stereotypes in commercial mass media and advertising. Meanwhile, many working couples strove to correct imbalances in division of childcare and household chores.

Feminists also endeavored to build a grassroots political base for all American women. In 1977, two thousand delegates participated in a federally-funded National Women's Conference in Houston and endorsed proposals for government-financed child day care, shelters for battered women, and protection of legal rights for lesbians. Feminists also organized in the cities and states to enact "comparative worth" programs assuring women equal pay for equal work. But the fiscal conservatism of the subsequent decade defeated congressional attempts to assist single mothers and needy women. In 1980, the Supreme Court upheld the constitutionality of a congressional ban on the use of Medicare funds for abortion for women who could not otherwise afford them.

The "feminization" of poverty became a major social issue of the 1980s. At a time when the number of annual divorces amounted to half the yearly marriages and the number of unwed teenage mothers leaped by 38 percent, single women became the sole support of more than ten million households. Meanwhile, female workers continued to concentrate in poorly paid "pink collar" jobs as clerks, office workers, and retail salespeople and failed to improve their earnings relative to men. The poverty rate for families headed by women in the 1980s was five times greater than that of families supported by husband and wife. In 1984, 28 percent of families presided over by white women, 52 percent of those supported solely by black women, and 54 percent of families headed by Hispanic women, lived in poverty. By federal government definitions, more than two-thirds of the children of those black and Hispanic families were poor. Moreover, women over sixty-five were twice as likely to live in poverty as men their age.

GAY POWER, GRAY POWER, AND THE HEALTH CRISIS

As sexual expressiveness increased in the 1960s, homosexuals identified with mass protest and collective pride. In 1969, New York City police raided the Stonewall Inn, a men's gay bar in Greenwich Village and angry patrons fought back for the first time. Homosexual activists soon announced a national gay power movement. Claiming to represent one-tenth of the American population, gay men and women sought to portray homosexuality as a chosen life-style instead of a disease and demanded civil rights. Each year the anniversary of the Stonewall riot became a time to celebrate gay pride.

Although several cities extended equal protection to homosexuals, a conservative backlash swept the nation in the late-1970s. In 1977, singer Anita Bryant depicted homosexuality as a sin and successfully crusaded to repeal a Miami gay rights ordinance. The following year, similar reversals occurred in St. Paul, Minnesota; Wichita, Kansas; and Eugene, Oregon. But thriving gay populations in California and Seattle, Washington fought off attempts to limit gay occupations and civil rights. By the 1980 elections, the National Gay Task force had become a small but significant factor in the political arena. Numerous public officials such as Massachusetts congressman Barney Frank, publicly announced their homosexual orientation. Yet the Supreme Court refused to extend the right of privacy to homosexual conduct. In a 5–4 vote in *Bowers v. Hardwick* (1986), the Court upheld a Georgia law that made sodomy a crime punishable by up to twenty years in prison. The following year, over two-hundred thousand male and female homosexuals marched on Washington to demonstrate gay pride and demand their rights. Like the new immigrants of the 1970s and '80s, gay men and lesbians sought inclusion in mainstream society without sacrifice of their personal identities.

The rise of homosexual communities focused attention in the 1980s on questions of health and survival. In 1981, American physicians recorded the first deaths from an incurable disease, Acquired Immunity Deficiency Syndrome (AIDS). Transmitted by infected blood or semen, AIDS spread easily through anal intercourse, intravenous injections, and transfusions of contaminated blood. Homosexual men, drug abusers, and hemophiliacs were particularly vulnerable. By mid-1988, AIDS had killed over thirty thousand Americans, including entertainers Liberace and Rock Hudson, and infected another thirty thousand. Health experts warned that without world-wide precautions, the epidemic could become the black plague of modern history. Yet federal health officials

An AIDS-awareness advertisement distributed in the late 1980s by the New York City Department of Public Health.

and a parsimonious government often obscured the severity of the crisis. Gay activists such as author Randy Shilts criticized Washington for delaying AIDS research, documented the lack of precautions in the nation's blood banks, and condemned a prudish media for failing to warn explicitly of dangerous sexual practices.

Within the homosexual community, gays initiated campaigns to close promiscuous bathhouses, limit sexual partners, and promote the use of condoms. But just as spread of the epidemic slowed among male homosexuals, AIDS infections accelerated among young heroin users in poor Hispanic and black neighborhoods. Since anyone who had unprotected sexual intercourse with a carrier was at risk, middle-class heterosexuals became increasingly alarmed about the AIDS threat. The deadly disease dampened the euphoria of the sexual revolution of the 1960s and '70s and stirred public agencies into mass advertising campaigns promoting both sexual abstinence and the rejection of drugs. But AIDS also brought consternation to conservatives such as Senator Jesse Helms of North Carolina, whose strict beliefs in premarital chastity and heterosexual marriage collided with proposals to promote the use of condoms. Black and Hispanic leaders warned that failure to provide realistic sex education could result in near-genocide of their youth. By 1988, Surgeon-General C. Everett Koop, a conservative Christian, called for a national education program that stressed both abstinence and "safe sex" and a presidential task force recommended federal laws to prohibit discrimination against AIDS victims.

Health issues also dominated the concerns of elderly Americans. As their numbers expanded by 20 percent in the 1970s, Americans over the age of sixty-five became the fastest growing segment of the national population. By the 1980s, life expectancy for some twenty-eight million people over the age of sixty-five averaged nearly seventy for white men and over seventy-seven for white women (blacks averaged nearly five years less). New diagnostic techniques, including mammographs (specialized X-rays for early detection of breast cancer), ultra-sound heat testing, tracing by radioactive isotopes (nuclear medicine), and "CAT-scan" computerized images helped to reduce death from cancer, stroke, heart disease, and other killers. So did technological innovations such as organ transplants, artificial heart and bone-joint replacements, laser and microsurgery, open-heart procedures, and kidney dialysis machines. Genetically engineered agents and new forms of chemotherapy (drugs) also helped. Yet the effects on life expectancy for those surviving child birth were surprisingly small. Men who reached the age of forty-five in the 1980s, for example, could anticipate only five more years of life than those who had attained that age in 1900. Medical technology also brought skyrocketing hospital and health insurance costs and contributed to a crisis in malpractice management by raising patient expectations and increasing chances for error. The federal government estimated that $640 billion, over 11 percent of the projected gross national product, would be spent on health care in 1990.

Escalating health costs dramatized potential conflicts between the elderly and the rest of the population. By 1988, older Americans received one-third the federal budget, ten times the amount spent on children. Social Security, Medicare, and private retirement plans such as the I.R.A. helped to halve the poverty rate among the elderly between 1969 and 1986. Yet organizations like the twelve

Exhibit 12–5. National Health Expenditures, 1970–1985.

Billions of dollars

Source: Chart prepared by U.S. Bureau of the Census.

million-strong American Association of Retired People, the largest special interest group in the nation, pressed for continued expansion of government health aid without placing new burdens on its constituents. While AARP lobbied strenuously for government support for terminal health care, it bitterly opposed plans to tax Social Security benefits. Yet analysts predicted that the public retirement plan would be forced to support the 12 percent of the national population that would be over the age of sixty-five by the year 2000. With one-tenth of the nation's payroll already channeled to Social Security, critics sought to tax the benefits of wealthy recipients and use some of the revenue to assist the elderly poor.

Congress responded to such pressures by extending the age of mandatory retirement from sixty-five to seventy in 1978, eliminating it altogether in 1986. Meanwhile, groups such as the Gray Panthers struggled to overcome other forms of age discrimination and to counter popular stereotypes in the media. Florida's octogenarian Representative Claude Pepper complained of "toothless, sexless, humorless, witless, and constipated" parodies of the elderly on television. Older Americans also created support groups to struggle with Alzheimer's disease, a dispiriting malady that destroyed memory and other functions, and sought alternatives to terminal nursing facilities through hospices and publicly funded home care. University graduate programs in gerontology helped to sensitize professionals to the dilemmas of the elderly.

Disabled Americans also organized to gain their rights, pressing for wheelchair access to public facilities as well as legislation against discrimination in employment, housing, schooling, and insurance coverage. Since 1968, the Special Olympics, a program of privately funded sports competition for the developmentally impaired, stressed that "mentally retarded" or "handicapped" people

The fastest growing age segment of the American population of the 1980s, the elderly sought alternatives to institutionalized care and demoralizing nursing homes.

could participate fully in life if not stereotyped as helpless. Sign language translations for the hearing-impaired also accompanied many television and stage lectures. During 1988, students at all-deaf Gallaudet University demonstrated their empowerment by successfully demanding the appointment of a hearing-impaired president.

WHITE ETHNICS AND CONSERVATIVE CRUSADERS

In 1970, the founding rally of the Italian-American Civil Rights League attracted fifty thousand people to New York City's Columbus Circle. The demonstration reflected a new assertion of cultural pride and political power among "white" ethnics descended from European immigrants. As Michael Novak suggested in the influential *The Unmeltable Ethnics* (1971), millions of Poles, Italians, Greeks, and Slavs rejected the homogeneity of media culture and continued to uphold traditional practices in religion, dance, food, music, and humor. A reinvigorated dedication to religious roots and the State of Israel also characterized large numbers of American Jews. Both Catholic and Jewish leaders in the East and Midwest

Mass protests in Washington and across the country reflected the growing strength of the anti-abortion movement and the Christian Right in the 1970s and 1980s.

persuaded major universities to establish programs in Ethnic Studies. Meanwhile, Hollywood films such as *The Godfather, Parts I & II* (1971, 1974), *Rocky* (1976), and *The Deer Hunter* (1978) depicted vital religious and social traditions among the white ethnics.

Assertions of ethnic identity continued to influence urban politics. Both working-class and middle-class Catholics and Jews often opposed mandatory busing as a means of achieving racial integration in the public schools. Ethnics in cities such as Boston, New York, Chicago, and Philadelphia feared that racial integration would bring slums, drug use, and crime to their neighborhoods. In response to black power and other perceived threats they supported "law and order" candidates such as police commissioner Frank Rizzo, who was elected mayor of Philadelphia in 1975 and 1979. In New York's Brooklyn, working-class Jewish youth organized a Jewish Defense League (JDL) to protect synagogues and schoolchildren in a racially tense neighborhood, but black leaders accused them of hooliganism and racial intimidation. Ethnic voters complained about rising welfare costs and taxes, "liberal" judges who appeared to protect the rights of criminals above those of victims, and affirmative action programs which they accused of providing unfair advantages to minorities.

Defense of traditional virtues—patriotism, the work ethic, social obligation— spurred new attacks on political and cultural innovation in the late-1970s and '80s. The conservative Jewish magazine *Commentary*, for example, criticized not only affirmative action and "third world" revolution but complained of a departure from the discipline and moral foundations of Western civilization. Social

REV. JERRY FALWELL
1933–

When Rev. Jerry Falwell resigned from leadership of the Moral Majority in 1987, he was the most influential conservative voice in American life. His Sunday evening cable TV program reached into thirty-four million homes. His enterprises and holdings included television's National Christian Network, Liberty Baptist College, an Israeli-made private jet airliner, and the eighteen thousand-member Thomas Road Baptist Church of Lynchburg, Virginia. Falwell traveled two-hundred thousand air miles each year to raise the annual $100 million needed to sustain these interests. Once described as the "sleeping giant" of American politics, the Virginia preacher was credited with authority over an estimated twenty-one million evangelical voters.

Falwell came from a successful but disreputable Lynchburg family that included bootlegging and a dance hall among its enterprises. A bright student and an accomplished athlete with a flair for rowdiness, he studied mechanical engineering at a local college. One night Falwell attended a Baptist service, fell in love with (and subsequently married) the church pianist, and instantly became a "born again" Christian. Two months later he decided to seek the ministry and transferred to a Baptist Bible college in Missouri.

Upon graduation in 1956, Falwell returned to Lynchburg to found an independent fundamentalist church in an abandoned Donald Duck Bottling facility. He started the Thomas Road Baptist Church with $1000 and thirty-five adults and their families. Falwell immediately arranged to broadcast services over the radio. Six months later his "Old Time Gospel Hour," which merely recorded the service as it occurred, made it to television.

A six-footer with a large waistline and a deep, booming voice, Falwell wore dark suits and always carried a Bible. His upbeat theology conveyed images of success and messages of hope and redemption. At the same time, Falwell never strayed from the fundamentalist belief in the accuracy of the Bible and resistance to anything that conflicted with spiritual command. But in 1977, the Lynchburg preacher reversed a longstanding fundamentalist isolation from social action and politics by affirming a religious leader's right *(cont.)*

critic Allan Bloom used these precepts to assail higher education in *The Closing of the American Mind* (1987). Catholics like Phyllis Schlafly and William F. Buckley, Jr. further maintained that a self-indulgent youth culture had immersed itself in sex, drugs, and the rejection of family duty and religion. Growing numbers of ethnic Americans accepted this critique in the late-1970s and attacked "permissive" schools, the media, and the judicial system. They particularly found fault with Supreme Court decisions that prevented states from banning abortion, restricting the flow of birth control information, and outlawing pornography. Seeking to uphold the sanctity of life at all stages, many joined "right to life" efforts to pass a constitutional amendment that would permit states to eradicate almost all abortions.

(cont.) to disseminate views on abortion, pornography, and homosexuality. During that year, Falwell helped singer Anita Bryant to repeal the Florida county ordinance granting equal rights to homosexuals, whom the minister accused of "perversion and immorality." In 1978 and 1979 he fashioned two "Clean Up America" campaigns to counteract "a tide of permissiveness and moral decay." These efforts climaxed in the founding of the Moral Majority in 1979.

Falwell described the independent Moral Majority as a united front for God and Country. He professed to speak for the vast majority of Americans that subscribed to traditional values in opposition to the "godless minority" that ruled the country. In *Listen America!* (1980), Falwell explained that this "coalition of God-fearing moral Americans" would "reverse the politicalization of immorality" by seeking influence, not control. The enemy was "secular humanism" in government—the attempt to solve problems apart from God. "I believe in the separation of church and state but not in the separation of God and government," Falwell remarked.

The Moral Majority registered four million new voters for the 1980 elections and urged another ten million to vote. With over two million members, Falwell had created a massive political action movement. Yet he rejected party affiliations, choosing to identify himself as "a noisy Baptist" who had a "divine mandate" to fight for laws to save America. Politicalizing the struggle between "good and evil," Falwell warned that a weakened national defense reflected moral impotence. "Jesus was not a pacifist. He was not a sissy," he once proclaimed. The minister's militant anti-communism led him to support conservative governments in Israel, South Korea, and South Africa.

The Moral Majority did not figure substantially in the economics-oriented election of 1984. Falwell even denounced "extremist" views which saw nuclear holocaust as fulfillment of Biblical prophecy. During 1987, the fundamentalist leader assumed the role of conciliator by taking temporary control of Praise the Lord (PTL), a television ministry besieged by sexual and financial scandal. But the effort proved so distracting that a beleaguered Falwell withdrew later in the year. When he left the Moral Majority one month later, the preacher from Lynchburg told journalists that he simply wished to return to his parish church. ■

The conservative backlash found its most dramatic expression in Reverend Jerry Falwell's Moral Majority, founded in 1979. Earlier radio crusaders such as Reverend Carl McIntyre and Reverend Billy James Hargis had combined evangelical enthusiasm with harsh assaults on liberal social programs and world communism. But as "sunbelt" cities grew dramatically in the 1960s and '70s (the Southwest boasted five of the nation's ten largest cities by 1980), fundamentalist and evangelical churches expanded their influence. Between 1965 and 1974, the fundamentalist Southern Baptist Convention gained almost two million followers to reach a total of 12.5 million. Meanwhile, mainstream liberal Protestant denominations lost membership to charismatic sects whose followers believed themselves to possess divinely inspired healing and prophecy powers.

Through his televised pulpit, Reverend Falwell revitalized political involvement and social activism among American fundamentalists. Appealing to a southern and western middle-class constituency, he mobilized conservative Protestants who sought an American Christian republic. This New Christian Right fused anti-communism with a condemnation of "modernist" teachings such as evolution. The movement complained that a liberal "eastern Establishment" had destroyed traditional religion and education by imposing "value-free" standards on churches and schools. And it condemned "secular humanism," a misguided philosophy that placed man above God and was therefore doomed to failure.

Using computerized lists, direct mail, telephone marketing, and audio cassettes, the New Christian Right organized the fifty million Americans it considered "born-again" Christians. During 1980, the Moral Majority induced the Republican party to reverse its support for ERA and endorse a constitutional ban on abortion. The new religious conservatism not only provided support for successful political candidates in the 1980s but fostered a variety of popular television evangelists such as Pat Robertson, who created cable-TV's Christian Broadcasting Network. Robertson used his national television audience as a base in a campaign for the 1988 Republican presidential nomination. Other television preachers such as Jim Bakker, Jimmy Swaggart, and Oral Roberts corporatized their ministries and mobilized conservative Protestants to support opulent charities, seminaries, colleges, foreign missions, and personal life-styles. The fundamentalists preached against "sin" and "moral decadence," attacking abortion, ERA, gay rights, and "satanic" rock music. They also struggled to replace evolutionist teachings with "creationist" doctrines that emphasized literal readings of the Bible. Christian activists on the local level sought election to school boards and organized community campaigns to cleanse school libraries and curricula of books they considered contrary to religious teaching. Others preferred to maintain control over education by instructing their children at home.

When both Bakker and Swaggart were implicated in embarrassing sex scandals in 1988, contributions to television ministries declined. Meanwhile, Robertson's poor showing in the 1988 Republican primaries indicated that enthusiasm from supporters, no matter how intense, did not always translate into political majorities. Yet the Moral Majority and the New Christian Right expressed widely held reservations about the values and behavior associated with youth, feminists, radical minorities, the counter-culture, and the media. White country music, for example, continued to appeal to southerners and westerners by emphasizing the loss of traditional family and community values while lamenting adultery, divorce, drinking, and alienating work. Such concerns mobilized a variety of citizens' groups including Mothers Against Drunk Driving (MADD), the Guardian Angels and neighborhood crime watches, advocates for crime victims, and community drug rehabilitation crusades. As cocaine addiction spread to the middle class and victimized top entertainment and sports figures, some corporations began mandatory testing of job applicants and selected employees. The new emphasis on personal morality also brought increased media surveillance of presidential candidates. As a result, 1988 Democratic candidate Gary Hart left the race following disclosures of adultery while Senator Joseph Biden abandoned his campaign when accused of plagiarism.

The New Right's emphasis on patriotism coincided with the desire of many Americans to transcend the traumas of Vietnam and Watergate and regain national pride and cultural unity. Media-shared rituals such as the 1976 Bicentennial, the 1984 Los Angeles Olympics, and the gala 1986 Statue of Liberty celebration sought to heal the fragmentation of American culture that had occurred since the 1960s. The prideful themes of country music and flag-waving television commercials also attested to the desire to recover positive national roots, as did the popularity of rock star Bruce Springsteen's *Born in the U.S.A.* album and tour.

Integration of the Vietnam experience proved the greatest challenge to the new patriotism. Despite a complete report to the contrary by a House Select Committee in 1976, many of the families of the 2400 servicemen reported missing in Vietnam clung to hopes that their loved ones might still be alive. The accompanying frustration led actor Sylvester Stallone to produce and star in a series of *Rambo* movies, beginning in 1982, which fantasized elaborate rescues of "MIA's" supposedly held in captivity by the Communist government in Hanoi. Such popular films played upon the tendency of male youth to romanticize the Vietnam War. But the dedication of the Washington national monument to Vietnam veterans in 1982 and a Public Broadcasting System television series in 1983 initiated an attempt to portray the conflict in more realistic terms. A new wave of Vietnam films including *Platoon* (1986), *Full Metal Jacket* (1987) and *Hamburger Hill* (1987) explored the stark ethical dilemmas of the war and searched for seeds of humanity amidst the terrible destruction.

YOUNG PROFESSIONALS AND THE NEW AGE

By 1977, service workers comprised two-thirds the American labor force, a development fed by computerized management of information and the creation of jobs in health, government, communications, and corporate finance. New opportunities also abounded in sales, advertising, law, and self-starting businesses in computer technology and specialized services like home-delivered dinners. The "high-tech" environment of the 1970s and '80s flourished in service centers surrounding major cities like Boston; Washington, D.C.; Columbus, Ohio; Minneapolis-St. Paul; Austin, Texas; and San Francisco. Pundits described the highly trained college graduates who administered the new economy as "yuppies"—young, urban professionals. Many, in fact, were baby-boom veterans of the youth culture of the late-1960s and early 1970s. Portrayed as a new breed of "team player," these newly recruited "professionals" brought an increased intensity to "bottom line" profit-making and lucrative "networking."

The new professionals helped to change American consumption patterns. Targeted by corporate advertisers and lured by "high-tech" performance, upwardly mobile men and women spent huge sums on microcircuitry goods such as personal computers and calculators, videocassette cameras and recorders, compact disc players, automobile audio systems, microwave ovens, telephone answering machines, and digital time pieces. They also comprised a prime market for the new products of the publishing and communication industries. These

Sylvester Stallone's <u>Rambo</u> film series addressed the emotional needs of American men who experienced difficulty in adjusting to limitations on the nation's power in the post-Vietnam era.

included national editions of the newspapers *U.S.A. Today* and the *New York Times*, which relied on simultaneous satellite-dispersed laser printing in every major city; *People* magazine, which focused on personal success stories and gossip concerning the rich and famous; and cable television, which cut into network ratings with twenty-four hour news programming and specialized channels. In 1981, Warner Communications inaugurated MTV (Music Television), a twenty-four hour cable outlet devoted exclusively to rock videos, many of them computer synthesized. Meanwhile, network series such as *Hill Street Blues, Miami Vice, St. Elsewhere*, and *L.A. Law* explored the dilemmas of professionals whose work often required the suspension of personal judgment.

Many urban professionals, like Apple Computer co-founder Stephen Jobs, believed that their careers translated countercultural goals of personal growth and social concern into practical life strategies. Their townhouses, condominiums, and specialty shops contributed to the "gentrification" of inner-city neighborhoods, a process which restored vitality to neglected historical districts. Although the high rents that accompanied gentrification often displaced less affluent tenants and shopkeepers, middle-class citizens played an active role in neighborhood associations and campaigns to make cities safe and more livable. Improvement also took on a personal character. Instructional "work-out" materials produced by actress and social activist Jane Fonda, for example, prepared millions for routines of daily exercise and aerobics. Jogging, bicycling, body building, indoor sports, and hot tubs provided convenient outlets for professionals with limited recreational time and available cash or credit for equipment or club fees.

Eating habits also changed. Urban professionals opted for tasty, lower calorie, nutritional meals that did not require extensive preparation. Carry-home specialties and automatic kitchen "food processors" assumed an important role, while natural and organic foods, frozen yogurt desserts, whole-bean coffees, wines, "light" beers, and mineral waters served to complement cosmopolitan needs and tastes. A proliferation of gourmet restaurants included specialists in "California cuisine"—an aesthetically presented menu that replaced salty and fatty foods with fresh fish, poultry, and vegetables prepared with subtle seasoning.

The urban middle class comprised an important clientele for the new medicine. Prenatal tests for birth defects, for example, were particularly important to those women who had delayed childbearing until their late-thirties. Couples unable to have children sometimes considered artificial insemination or invitro-fertilization ("test-tube babies"). Medical reliance on technology nevertheless raised sensitive questions about the "sacredness" of life and parental responsibility. The use of artificial life-support systems, for example, brought disagreement as to when such aid might legally be terminated and on whose authority. After the parents of a comatose patient, Karen Ann Quinlan, sued to disconnect an artificial respirator in 1975, eighteen states followed with laws declaring that legal death was defined by the cessation of brain activity, not heart beat.

The popularity of prenatal exams led some anti-abortion activists to charge that such procedures could encourage parents to terminate pregnancies on arbitrary grounds such as the gender of a fetus. Another controversy erupted over the use of "surrogate" mothers as paid hosts for laboratory fertilized eggs when one such impregnated woman, Mary Beth Whitehead, decided that she wanted to keep the baby. A New Jersey court ruled in 1987 that Whitehead had contractual obligations to surrender custody to the natural father (a physician) and his infertile wife. Some feminists protested that the decision permitted affluent couples to exploit poor women while other critics argued that such arrangements amounted to the "selling" of babies.

Middle-class professionals raised new questions for organized religion. Those in the mainstream Protestant churches helped to dramatize issues of racism, sexism, and the plight of abused children and the homeless. Among Catholics, they initiated sharp debates over divorce, birth control, abortion, euthanasia, homosexuality, interfaith marriage, clerical celibacy, the ordination of women, and papal infallibility. In the Jewish community, controversies over affirmative action, the religious role of women and gays, and Israel's occupation of the West Bank led to creation of the progressive New Jewish Agenda, an organization composed primarily of secular professionals.

The professional middle class also supported the growth of alternative religions. Young cultural dissidents of the 1960s and '70s had experimented with Asian spiritual traditions such as Zen, Tibetan Buddhism, Yoga, I Ching, and the martial arts. These interests led some to involvement in American sects like the Church of Scientology, the Hari Krishnas, and the Reunification Church of Korea's Reverend Sun Myung Moon. But fearing a loss of personal identity among their children, some parents hired "deprogrammers" in the 1970s to reverse alleged brainwashing in former members of these groups. The worst apprehensions of anticultists were confirmed in 1978 when over nine hundred followers of the California-based People's Temple committed suicide in Guyana under orders from their spiritual leader, Reverend Jim Jones. Violent confrontations between black cultists and police erupted in Washington, D.C., Philadelphia, and rural Arizona during the 1980s. Meanwhile, legal prosecution by the federal government and a variety of civil suits damaged the reputation of the sects. In 1986, the government brought immigration charges against the Indian-born Bhagwan Shree Rajneesh, spiritual leader of a thriving "city" of international followers in rural Oregon. When the state prosecuted the Bhagwan's aides for fraud and attempted murder, federal officials quickly deported the venerated guru.

Although some urban professionals embraced the cults, others sought spiritual meaning and social bonds in less-demanding "New Age" philosophies and movements. Scientists of the 1970s and '80s such as Fritjof Capra and David Bohm argued that relativist concepts of quantum physics had destroyed distinctions between spirit and matter. They received support from psychologists like Robert Ornstein and Karl Pribram, who pointed to the mind's ability to influence bodily states such as the pulse and breathing rate. The fusion of these ideas produced a "holistic" synthesis that united spiritual and material realities and signalled what enthusiasts took to be the dawning of a "New Age."

The new spirituality appealed to professional elites because it combined the countercultural spirit with advanced science. This synthesis facilitated the acceptance of holistic approaches involving preventive and natural medicine, balanced nutrition, Chinese acupuncture, meditative techniques, biofeedback, and body exercises such as hydrotherapy and rolfing. Exploring the spiritual and emotional basis to disease and healing, San Francisco psychiatrist Kenneth R. Pelletier encouraged cancer patients to assist their own survival by "visualizing" tumors. By the 1980s, New Age popularizers such as actress Shirley MacLaine were proclaiming that visualization could be used to cleanse the mind of negative thought patterns.

Like the counterculture, the New Age appealed to the consumption habits of its followers. Practitioners led paid self-improvement and inspirational seminars and conducted sessions on the use of body "auras" and "energy fields." Others instructed clients in the more controversial techniques of "channeling" back to past lives, healing disease with the aid of rock crystals, and communicating with varied spirits and "galactic" messengers. Several of MacLaine's books joined other New Age titles on the best-seller lists. In the arts, harpists, flutists, and pianists such as George Winston produced simple, meditative light music for New Age record companies.

Despite its frequent commercialism, however, the diverse New Age movement represented an attempt to overcome the rootlessness and isolation of the modern American city and suburb. Like the counterculture from which it took its roots, the New Age emphasis on "psychic" powers of "extra-sensory" perception illustrated a frank impatience with the pure rationalism of middle-class life. The new spirituality conflicted with church doctrine because it erased distinctions between "good" and "evil" and placed divinity in all things and people. Although its adherents found organized religion either bland or irrelevant to their needs, they nevertheless sought modern answers to the recurring problems of life. By 1987, the turn toward alternative spirituality helped account for the fact that 20 percent of Americans between eighteen and twenty-four (31 percent of the West Coast) identified with a religious commitment other than Protestant, Catholic, or Jewish.

ECOLOGY AND APOCALYPSE

Holistic thinking reinforced a growing belief in the human connection to the physical environment. In 1962, biologist Rachel Carson pointed to the pervasive danger of pesticides in the chilling *The Silent Spring*. "The question is whether any civilization can wage relentless war on life without destroying it," Carson warned. President Kennedy sounded a similar theme in 1963. "We all inhabit this planet. We all breath the same air," he told the students of American University. Space photographs and astronaut Neil Armstrong's visit to the moon in 1969 confirmed that the Earth was a small and frail island of life in an immense universe. Environmentalists such as Barry Commoner emphasized that humans lived within the circle of the Earth's atmosphere and must limit air pollution from manufacturing and automobile sources. Their reports pointed to toxic residues from fossil fuels and petrochemical fertilizers, nonbiodegradable wastes from plastics and detergents, industrial pollutants which turned rivers like Cleveland's Cuyahoga into fire hazards, and damage to the atmosphere's ozone from aerosol sprays and other chemicals. To demonstrate these concerns, activists staged nationwide Earth-Day teach-ins on April 30, 1970.

The implication of the ecological crisis went beyond the need to pick up litter and "beautify" America. The biologist Paul Ehrlich direly warned in *The Population Bomb* (1969) that planetary resources could not support continued population growth. Ecologist Barry Commoner focused on economic expansion, declaring in *The Closing Circle* (1971) that the industrial system interfered with nature's attempts to regenerate the Earth's air, water, and soil. An international study, *The Limits to Growth* (1972), concluded that economic growth threatened to exhaust the planet's resources by the end of the century.

Beginning in 1969, environmentalists succeeded in pressing Congress and state legislatures to control pollution through the creation of environmental protection agencies (see chapter 7). The federal government prohibited the use of the pesticide DDT, banned biological and chemical weapons from its arsenals, and required its agencies to file environmental impact statements before proceeding with their projects. The Endangered Species Act of 1969 also sought to protect animals that faced global extinction. Yet construction of an ecologically destructive eight-hundred-mile oil pipeline across Alaska and the continued shipment of deadly DDT to third world countries pointed to some of the contradictions of enlightened environmental policy.

The central environmental debate of the 1970s and '80s focused on nuclear power. Responding to energy needs dramatized by the Arab oil boycott of 1973–74 (see chapter 13), federal officials pushed nuclear energy as a stimulant to industrial development. "We can't live in a Garden of Eden and still have a technological society," Atomic Energy Commissioner Dixie Lee Ray explained in 1974. But environmentalists like E.F. Schumacher, author of *Small is Beautiful* (1973), insisted that human survival depended upon the development of a harmonious relationship with nature and creation of a livable technology through solar, geothermal, and wind power. Other activists like Norman Solomon concentrated on the inability of the nuclear industry to manage safe radioactive storage facilities.

Anti-nuclear protesters at sites such as Seabrook, New Hampshire revived civil disobedience tactics in the mid-1970s to call attention to the health, safety, and financial problems of atomic fission. But a near "meltdown" of the reactor core at a nuclear facility at Three Mile Island, Pennsylvania shifted attention in 1979 to the credibility of industry management and government regulators. "The history of the nuclear power industry," consumer advocate Ralph Nader told over a hundred thousand demonstrators gathered in Washington the following month, "is replete with cover-ups, deceptions, outright lies, error, negligence, arrogance, greed..." Public confidence slipped further when the graphite core of a reactor in the Soviet Ukraine burned for several days in 1986, spreading radioactive dust across eastern Europe and Scandinavia. Critics noted that the Chernobyl plant contained the same design and safety features as many nuclear facilities deemed safe by American industry and the Nuclear Regulatory Commission. As evidence of the lethal effects of nuclear waste mounted, experts placed cleanup costs for three government disposal sites at $100 billion.

By crossing national boundaries as it circled the Earth, the Chernobyl cloud demonstrated the need for international cooperation in approaching the environment. Similar concerns surfaced over burning of cheap coal by American factories and power plants, a practice that released sulfuric emissions which carried

Planet Earth as viewed from Space. Environmental scientists of the 1970s and 1980s continually warned of the vulnerability of global life forms to ecological disaster and insisted upon the interconnectedness of all living things.

to Canada and fell as "acid rain," thereby defoliating trees and contamination lakes. Environmentalists also asserted that depletion of Amazon rain forests by fast-food cattle interests and other developers soon would pose a threat to world oxygen levels. And the government itself released figures in 1988 that revealed that the Earth's atmosphere had lost 2.3 percent of its ozone layer, an essential protectant from the ultraviolet rays that caused skin cancer and a barrier to excessive heating by the sun.

Nevertheless, Americans remained fascinated by technology. The *Star Wars* and *Star Trek* film series (begun in 1977 and 1978), and *E.T., The Extra-Terrestrial* (1982) thrilled young audiences with exotic creatures, cybernetic robots, and easy galactic travel. Many of the popular films and electronic videogames which swept young America in the 1980s, used computer-generated laser weaponry to update military conflict. But although many adults shared the young's enchantment with high-tech gamesmanship, the dangers of nuclear war continued to feed anxiety. Astronomer Carl Sagan warned in 1983 that radioactive dust clouds from atomic war might block sufficient sunlight to produce a "nuclear winter" for global plant life, thereby condemning the human species to imminent death. That year's network television special, *The Day After*, destroyed precedent by graphically illustrating the potential effects of a nuclear explosion on the typical American town of Lawrence, Kansas. And in a stark reminder of the vulnerability of advanced technology, NASA's Challenger space launch exploded amidst a televised take-off in 1986, killing all seven astronauts and setting back the program for years. Within 1980s youth culture, moreover, images of nuclear apocalypse appeared frequently in rock music videos and cult films such as *Mad Max* (1980), *Road Warrior* (1981), *Blade Runner* (1982), and *The Terminator* (1984). Ironically, these dark visions of the future resembled the dire prophecies of Armageddon recounted by some ministers of the Christian Right.

Suggested Readings

Relevant sections of Landon Y. Jones, *Great Expectations: America and the Baby Boom Generation* (1980) demonstrate the connections between the postwar population increase, the new youth market, and the counterculture of the 1960s and its successors. Changing family life is chronicled by John D'Emilio, *Sexual Politics, Sexual Communities, 1940-1970* (1983). For the sexual revolution see the later segments of D'Emilio and Estelle Freedman, *Intimate Matters: A History of Sexuality in America* (1988) and the analysis of polling data in Daniel Yankelovich, *The New Morality: A Profile of American Youth in the 70s* (1974).

The intellectual pioneers of the counterculture are portrayed in Theordore Roszak, *The Making of the Counter Culture* (1969), while the social and cultural aspects of the movement are discussed in Marvin Harris, *America Now: The Anthropology of a Changing Culture* (1981). Morris Dickstein, *Gates of Eden* (1977), ties together developments in rock music, literature, and social protest. See also John Orman, *Politics of Rock Music* (1984). Sections of Martin A. Lee and Brucke Shlain, *Acid Dreams: The CIA, LSD, and the Sixties Rebellion* (1985) explore the drug scene and alternative consciousness. For the importance of personal fulfilment to both religious and countercultural seekers, see Peter Clecak, *America's Quest for the Ideal Self: Dissent and Fulfillment in the 60s and 70s* (1983).

A useful outline of Vietnam protest is Irwin Unger, *The Movement: A History of the American New Left* (1974), but a more expansive synthesis is provided by Todd Gitlin, *The Sixties: Years of Hope, Days of Rage* (1987). A superb collection of primary materials preceeded by informative discussion is Judith Clavir Albert and Stewart Edward Albert, *The Sixties Papers: Documents of a Rebellious Decade* (1984). Antiwar protest in the Johnson administration can be found in the narrative Thomas Powers, *Vietnam: The War at Home* (1984). A more extensive chronicle is Nancy Zaroulis and Gerald Sullivan, *Who Spoke Up? American Protest Against the War in Vietnam, 1963–1975* (1984).

The politics of confrontation is described by David Farber, *Chicago '68* (1988). Biographical portraits of antiwar and other dissenters are provided in Milton Viorst, *Fire in the Streets: America in the 1960s* (1979). Specific studies of the New Left include Kirkpatrick Sale, *SDS* (1971) and Maurice Isserman, *If I Had a Hammer: The Death of the Old Left and the Birth of the New Left* (1987). Two contrasting views of 1970s activism are Jim Hougan, *Decadence, Radical Nostalgia, Narcissism, and Decline in the Seventies* (1975) and Peter N. Carroll, *It Seemed Like Nothing Happened: The Tragedy and Promise of America in the 1970s* (1982). The political legacy of the Movement is explored in Michael X. Delli Carpini, *Stability and Change in American Politics: The Coming of Age of the Generation of the 1960s* (1986).

The civil rights and black power movements are best outlined in Harvard Sitkoff, *The Struggle for Black Equality, 1954–1980,* (1981) and Manning Marable, *Race, Reform, and Rebellion: The Second Reconstruction in Black America, 1945–1983* (1984). See also Clayborne Carson, *In Struggle: SNCC and the Black Awakening in the 1960s* (1981) and Marable, *Black American Politics: From the Washington Marches to Jesse Jackson* (1988). Two central biographies are David J. Garrow, *Bearing the Cross: Martin Luther King, Jr. and the SCLC* (1986) and Eugene Wolfenstein, *The Victims of Democracy: Malcolm X and the Black Revolution* (1981). For Native-Americans, see Philip Reno, *Mother Earth, Father Sky, and Economic Development* (1981) and the later segments of Francis Paul Prucha, *The Great Father: The United States Government and the American Indians,* Vol. II (1984).

Mexican-American immigration and culture is portrayed in Alfredo Mirandé, *The Chicano Experience* (1985) and the relevant sections of Manuel P. Servin, *An Awakened Minority: The Mexican Americans* (1974) and Matt S. Meier and Feliciano Rivera, *The Chicanos: A History of Mexican Americans* (1972). For the new immigration see David Reimers, *Still the Golden Door: The Third World Comes to America* (1985) and Thomas Kessner and Betty B. Caroli, *Today's Immigrants, Their Stories: A New Look at the Newest Americans* (1981).

An overview of women's history and the new feminism can be found in the relevant sections of Rochelle Gatlin, *American Women Since 1945* (1987). See also William Chafe, *Women and Equality: Changing Patterns in American Culture* (1977). For feminism among radical activists see Sara Evans, *Personal Politics: The Root of Women's Liberation in the Civil Rights Movement and the New Left* (1979). The relationship between feminists and the New Right is portrayed in Myra Marx Ferree and Beth Hess, *Controversy and Coalition: The New Feminist Movement* (1985) and Kristin Luker, *Abortion and the Politics of Womanhood* (1984). See also the relevant sections of Barbara Ehrenreich, *Hearts of Men: The Flight from Commitment* (1984) and Ethel Klein, *Gender Politics: From Consciousness to Mass Politics* (1984). An insightful study is Mary Frances Berry, *Why ERA Failed: Politics, Women's Rights and the Amending Process of the Constitution* (1986). The assertion of homosexual rights is described in Barry D. Adam, *The Rise of a Gay and Lesbian Movement* (1987).

Changes in the status of the elderly are assessed in the relevant segments of Richard B. Calhoun, *In Search of the Old: Redefining Old Age in America, 1945–1970* (1978) and Jill Quadagno, *The Transformation of Old Age Society: Class and Politics in the American Welfare State* (1988). Two contrasting portraits of ethnicity are Peter Schrag, *The Decline of the WASP* (1976) and Richard Krickus, *Pursuing the American Dream: White Ethnics and the New Populism* (1976). A more specific study is Richard D. Alba, *Italian Americans: The Twilight of Ethnicity* (1985). The revival of community activism is described by Harry C. Boyte, *The Backyard Revolution* (1980). For the evolution of suburban life see Kenneth T. Jackson, *Crabgrass Frontier: The Suburbanization of the United States* (1985).

The philosophical roots of the New Right are depicted in Peter Steinfels, *The Neo-Conservatives* (1979) and the relevant segments of George N. Nash, *The Conservative Intellectual Movement in America* (1976). See also Jonathan M. Kolkey, *The New Right, 1960–1968* (1983). Evangelical conservatism is described by Gary Clabaugh, *Thunder on the Right: The New Right and the Politics of Resentment* (1980), and Robert Fowler, *A New Engagement: Evangelical Political Thought, 1966–1976* (1982). The Moral Majority is portrayed in Gillian Peele, *Revival and Reaction: The Right in Contemporary America* (1984) and Dinesh D'Souza, *Falwell Before the Millennium: A Critical Biography* (1986). For the political impact of new religious developments see Margaret M. Poloma, *The Chrismatic Movement: Is There a New Pentecost?* (1982).

A critical view of upwardly mobile professionals is Christopher Lasch, *The Culture of Narcissism: American Life in an Age of Diminishing Expectations* (1979). For a case study of affluent consumerism see Debora Silverman, *Selling Culture: Bloomingdale's Diana Vreeland and the New Aristocracy of Taste in Reagan's America* (1986). The social ethics of professionals are explored in Robert N. Bellah, *et. al.*, *Habits of the Heart: Individualism and Commitment in American Life* (1985). For the spiritual movements of the 1970s see Jacob Needleman and George Baker, eds., *Understanding the New Religions* (1978). Technology's implications in medicine and ethics are explored in Loren R. Graham, *Between Science and Values* (1981) and Basile S. Yanovsky, *Medicine, Science, and Life* (1978). For holistic science and New Age philosophy, see John P. Briggs and F. David Peat, *Looking Glass Universe: The Emerging Science of Wholeness* (1984).

The ecological challenge is described by Frank Graham, *Since Silent Spring* (1970) and Victor Ferkiss, *The Future of Technological Civilization* (1974). Space technology and its implications are explored in the relevant sections of Walter A. McDougall, *...The Heavens and the Earth: A Political History of the Space Age* (1985). The nuclear debate is addressed in Jerome Brian Price, *The Antinuclear Movement* (1982) and Jonathan Schell, *The Fate of the Earth* (1982).

Opposite page:
Antiwar demonstrators in front of the White House during the Peace Moratorium of 1969.

13

LIFE IS SACRED
STOP THE WAR

THE EMBATTLED PRESIDENCY, 1968-1980

R ichard Nixon's 1968 election indicated a reassertion of conservative values. The new president defended traditional precepts of order, discipline, and authority. And his administration sought to counter social disruption and reduce the impact of the federal government at home. It also endeavored to win renewed respect for American power and military strength overseas. But although it ended the participation of the United States in the Vietnam War and established a relationship of détente with Communist rivals, the Nixon presidency disintegrated over the abuse of power at home. The Watergate legacy and a "post-Vietnam" syndrome profoundly affected public trust in government. As successors Gerald Ford and Jimmy Carter attempted to respond to continued global instability and severe economic dislocation, esteem for the presidency sank to new lows. By 1980, the American people appeared to be adrift and searching for new solutions to vexing problems.

NIXONIAN MANAGEMENT

Like his liberal predecessors, Nixon brought techniques of corporate management to national planning. His Office of Management and Budget (OMB) monitored the performance of federal agencies and helped the president set government priorities. A Domestic Council, headed by John Ehrlichman, acted as the president's planning board, while an Urban Affairs Council, led by Harvard's Daniel P. Moynihan, planned administration programs. These agencies continued the centralization of executive power that had begun in the New Deal. And although Nixon had been elected as a budgetary conservative, he embraced the use of government power to maintain social stability. As Great Society programs such as Model Cities and the War on Poverty continued, federal spending as a percentage of Gross National Product actually rose. Aid for Dependent Children (AFDC), a welfare program that covered two million youngsters in 1960, for example, expanded its coverage to twelve million children by 1975. Another thirteen million families received food stamps by that year. For the first time in history, government outlays for income maintenance surpassed defense costs.

The Nixon administration hoped to reduce the cumbersome welfare bureaucracy and channel money directly to the poor. Accordingly, the president introduced a $6 billion Family Assistance Plan in 1969. Although the bill provided a minimum of $1600 a year to every poor family and did not include strict work requirements for recipients, Nixon called his program "workfare." Conservatives still objected, however, and when liberals complained of inadequate support levels, a coalition of the two groups killed the plan in the Senate. Striking out at

Exhibit 13–1. Federal Social Welfare Expenditures, 1965–1976.
(current dollars in billions)

1965	$37.7 b
1970	$77.3 b
1974	$137.2 b
1976	$197.0 b

Source: *Statistical Abstract of the United States* (1987)

the liberals, the president made major cuts in Headstart, the Job Corps, and the poverty program. Nixon hoped to reverse centralization of welfare tasks through a widely proclaimed "revenue sharing" program, but by 1971 the "new federalism" accounted for only 5 percent of state and local funds.

INFLATION AND ENERGY CRISIS

Structural problems in the American economy seriously limited the effectiveness of Nixon's management techniques. Since the late 1950s, military spending, foreign aid, and overseas investment had induced a dramatic flow of dollars from the United States. But the balance of payments deficit, which reached an annual rate of $3 billion by 1970, tripled during the first half of 1971, the first year since 1893 in which the United States had a negative balance of trade. The "dollar drain" also reduced the supply of gold reserves in the United States and contributed to corporate debt, which reached $1.3 trillion by 1974. Corporate debt, in turn, increased the competition for credit and accelerated interest rates and inflation.

By lowering spending power, savings, and "real" wages, inflation disrupted the social stability that Nixon sought. Inflation reduced the number of families who could afford to buy their own home. It also aggravated labor-management relations, precipitating a wildcat Teamsters strike in 1969–1970, an extended autoworkers walkout, and even a brief disruption of mail deliveries in 1970. The president attempted to reduce inflation by cutting spending and encouraging higher interest rates, but these measures only brought "stagflation,"— continuing inflation with rising unemployment. Consequently, Nixon suspended gold payments for dollars in 1971, placed a 10 percent surtax on imports, and proposed further spending cuts. He also declared a ninety-day freeze on wages, prices, and rents, and created a Cost of Living Council to monitor rising costs. The suspension of gold payments effectively ended American participation in the Bretton Woods system of stabilized exchange rates, but by the end of the year Nixon agreed to devalue the dollar and remove the surtax.

Nixon's freeze marked the nation's first peacetime price controls since 1947. But fears of recession led to a relaxation of wage and price guidelines in 1973.

Exhibit 13–2. Imports and Exports, 1968–1976.
(in billions of dollars)

Year	Imports	Exports
1968	$33.2 b	$34.1 b
1969	$36.0 b	$37.3 b
1970	$40.0 b	$42.7 b
1971	$45.6 b	$43.5 b
1972	$55.6 b	$49.2 b
1973	$69.5 b	$70.8 b
1974	$102.6 b	$98.1 b
1975	$98.5 b	$107.7 b
1976	$123.5 b	$115.2 b

Source: *Statistical Abstract of the United States* (1987)

Exhibit 13–3. Gross National Product, 1968–1976.
(current dollars in billions)

1968	$892.7 b
1970	$1015.5 b
1972	$1212.8 b
1974	$1472.8 b
1976	$1782.8 b

Source: *Economic Report of the President* (1988)

The president tried a second freeze, however, when the sale of 8.5 million tons of grain to the Soviet Union led to a 20 percent leap in retail food prices. The administration also raised the dollar price of gold another 10 percent. When these efforts failed to solve the problems of inflation and the balance of payments deficit, Nixon conceded defeat and allowed price controls to expire in 1974. By then, the United States was experiencing 12 percent annual inflation, the highest in twenty-five years.

Inflation stemmed from a revolutionary shift of global power from resource consumers to suppliers. Beginning in 1971, the Arab-dominated Organization of Petroleum Exporting Countries (OPEC) raised the price of crude oil. When the United States airlifted military supplies to Israel during the Yom Kippur War of 1973, OPEC cut off the flow of oil to Japan and the West. The Arab embargo, which lasted from October 1973 to March 1974, dramatically revealed American dependence on foreign energy. By 1974, the people of the United States constituted 6 percent of the world's population but consumed 30 percent of its energy, burning 16.2 million barrels of oil a day. Since multinational corporations had developed more profitable foreign oil sources in preference to domestic production, the United States found itself in the position of importing 38 percent of its petroleum in 1974. The quadrupling of the price of crude oil early that year brought increased operating costs for essential petroleum products such as gasoline, diesel, heating oil, plastics, fertilizers, and synthetic fibers.

Seeking alternatives to foreign oil dependence, Nixon had created an Energy Policy Office and allotted $100 million for research in 1973. But the embargo brought a major domestic crisis when prices at the gas pump doubled and long lines of motorists sought dwindling supplies of fuel. The president ordered that government thermostats be lowered to sixty-eight degrees, cut air travel by 10 percent, requested the relaxation of environmental regulations affecting energy consumption, and lowered the speed limit on interstate highways from 70 mph

Exhibit 13–4. Consumer Price Index, 1968–1976.
(1967-100)

1968	104.2
1970	116.3
1972	125.3
1974	147.7
1976	170.5

Source: *Economic Report of the President* (1988)

to 55 mph. Nixon also created a Federal Energy Administration and announced plans to make the nation energy self-reliant through a "Project Independence." Yet estimates placed the costs of the plan, which relied on the development of nuclear reactors and the burning of coal, at $1 trillion.

Nixon effectively focused on the "energy crisis" but refused to consider rationing to cut expensive gasoline consumption. He also vetoed a 1974 bill to tax booming oil profits that critics claimed to be the result of the hoarding of supplies by energy corporations. Deepening public mistrust led half the sample in a Gallup poll to blame either the president or the oil companies for the fuel shortages. Confronting rising costs in the deepening recession of 1974, both workers and farmers agitated for increased benefits. The Agricultural and Consumer Protection Act of 1973 had replaced the New Deal system of acreage restrictions and government price supports with a program of government payments when market prices fell below established levels. But such efforts failed to protect farmers from increased expenses brought by the energy squeeze. Meanwhile, the administration's Environmental Protection Agency (EPA), created in 1970, consolidated government antipollution programs and sought controls over private resources. But when Congress overrode a Nixon veto to pass a massive water pollution bill in 1972, the president impounded the funds in order to cut back federal spending. As "stagflation" worsened, the president's fiscal conservatism prevented him from playing a creative role in the management of inflation and the energy crisis.

CONSERVATIVE SOCIAL AGENDA

As the cost-conscious Nixon administration faced rising unemployment and poverty levels, it searched for alternatives to government social welfare. Blacks constituted 11 percent of the labor force but nearly one-fifth of all unemployed, while 40 percent of black teenagers lacked jobs. Yet the administration insisted that "black capitalism," not government activism, would lead to equal opportunity and shared prosperity. Following a policy that Domestic Advisor Moynihan described as "benign neglect," the White House discouraged the use of federal power to insure racial integration in the work force and schools. Nixon characterized minority job quotas as "a dangerous detour away from the traditional value of measuring a person on the basis of ability." Accordingly, the Labor Department announced that "proportional representation" was a goal, not a requirement, of federal contract compliance. The federal government nevertheless began to withhold money from certain northern communities and ordered hearings on racial discrimination in Boston schools. When the Supreme Court unanimously approved school integration through busing, however, Nixon reaffirmed his personal distaste for the practice and proposed a busing moratorium. Although civil rights groups attacked the administration, actual school desegregation proceeded at an increased pace since the Johnson years.

Nixon also tried to reverse the "permissiveness" of the Supreme Court, which in the 1960s had abolished compulsory prayer in public schools and required procedural protections for criminal suspects. When Chief Justice Earl Warren retired in 1969, Nixon chose moderate Warren E. Burger to replace him. But when a second vacancy occurred that year, the president nominated South Carolina Judge Clement F. Haynsworth. When the Senate questioned a conflict of interest in Haynsworth's judicial record, however, he became the first Supreme Court nominee in forty years to be rejected. Nixon responded by nominating another southerner, G. Harrold Carswell, a Florida appeals court judge whose ratings as a jurist were as mediocre as Haynsworth's. But Carswell failed to win Senate confirmation after inquiries revealed that he had made white supremacist statements earlier in his career. Infuriated, Nixon denounced "regional discrimination" and claimed that his power of appointment had been abrogated by liberals hostile to a strict interpretation of the Constitution. Yet the president eased the tension by selecting another Minnesota moderate of impeccable credentials, Harry Blackmun, whom the Senate confirmed without difficulty.

The Court fight demonstrated Nixon's determination to attack liberal institutions with conservative principles. By the end of his first term, additional vacancies gave the president the opportunity to appoint conservatives Lewis Powell and William H. Rehnquist to the increasingly cautious Supreme Court. Although the Burger Court outlawed domestic "national security" wiretaps without judicial permission and prohibited states from interfering with most abortions, it generally followed Nixonian lines of social conservatism. Court decisions limited the immunity of witnesses from prosecution, allowed non-unanimous jury verdicts in criminal cases in certain states, and compelled news reporters to testify before grand juries. The Court found capital punishment unconstitutional in 1972 but reversed itself four years later to approve state death penalty laws if worded carefully and applied without discrimination. The tribunal further pleased conservatives by opening the door to "local option" on obscenity and pornography censorship in 1975.

Détente and Coup

The opening of friendly relations with the People's Republic of China provided the Nixon presidency with its most creative and important legacy. Ever since the Communist revolution of 1949, the United States had refused to recognize China. Cold warriors, including Nixon himself, continually warned that recognition would entail abandoning the Nationalist government on Taiwan (Formosa) and would legitimize Communist subversion against established regimes. But when the Chinese made diplomatic overtures in 1969, Nixon reasoned that he could win concessions from both China and the Soviet Union if he took advantage of the deepening rift between the two rivals.

Accordingly, the president eased restrictions on American travel to the mainland and in 1971 announced the end of a twenty-one year embargo on Chinese trade. The United States also accepted China's admission to the United Nations. This proved to be a controversial step since China claimed the seat that Nationalist Taiwan had held with American support since 1949. Nixon formalized China détente when he toured the Communist nation in 1972. The president and Chinese Premier Chou En-lai released a joint communiqué that pledged the two nations to "peaceful mutuality," but the most important part of the negotiations involved an American promise to withdraw military forces from Taiwan.

President Nixon at the Great Wall of China, 1972. Detente with China, a dramatic reversal of policy for Nixon, remained a prime achievement of his presidency.

Nixon followed the agreement with China by traveling to Moscow to negotiate an arms treaty with the Soviet Union. The Strategic Arms Limitation Treaty (SALT I) of 1972 limited the construction of antiballistic missile sites and nuclear delivery systems. Although the treaty did not rule out the development of new weapons, it established the Cold War's first regulation of existing arsenals, the biggest step toward nuclear disarmament since the partial test ban treaty of 1963. The Nixon-Brezhnev talks also produced agreements on the status quo in divided Berlin and a trade pact which resulted in sales of $750 million worth of grain to the Soviets, about one-fourth the American crop. When Brezhnev visited Washington in 1973, the two leaders signed additional pacts covering nuclear arms, cultural exchanges, and peaceful uses of atomic energy.

Détente with China and the Soviet Union reaffirmed Nixon's conviction that the United States must maintain its image of global strength. American hegemony in the Western Hemisphere was a particularly important symbol of such credibility and strength. Thus the White House reacted harshly to the election of Salvador Allende, a Marxist, to the presidency of Chile in 1970, ordering the CIA to organize a Chilean military coup. Government and private lending agencies refused credit to Chile, creating severe economic shortages, while the CIA provided funds to opposing politicians, friendly media, and anti-Communist unions. Between 1970 and 1973, the United States spent $8 million in the covert effort to turn Chile against its elected president. Finally, Allende was assassinated in a bloody coup in 1973, and a military regime abolished Chilean democracy.

Exhibit 13–5. National Defense and Veterans Outlays, 1968–1976.
(in billions of dollars)

1968	$88.8 b
1970	$90.4 b
1972	$89.9 b
1974	$92.7 b
1976	$108.0 b

Source: *Statistical Abstract of the United States* (1987)

Exhibit 13–6. National Defense as Percent of Total Federal Outlays,
1968–1976.

1968	46.0
1970	41.8
1972	34.3
1974	29.5
1976	24.1

Source: *Statistical Abstract of the United States* (1987)

PEACE IN VIETNAM

Nixon hoped that détente with Moscow and Peking would also bring pressure on North Vietnam to conclude a workable settlement of the war in Southeast Asia. But the president's desire to end the war was not as great as his fear of surrender. "Precipitate withdrawal" would be a "popular and easy course," he said in 1969, but warned that defeat and humiliation would bring the "collapse of confidence in American leadership." As another four years of war took a devastating toll in Southeast Asia, the president searched for a means of extricating the United States from Indochina without admitting defeat.

Despite Nixon's refusal to accept a Communist victory in Vietnam, he understood how massive commitments of fighting men had destroyed the Johnson presidency. As disaffection mounted among soldiers and the public, the president announced a Nixon Doctrine in 1969 by which ground troops would be withdrawn while the United States escalated the air war and provided economic and military aid to South Vietnam. Amid massive antiwar demonstrations in the fall of 1969, Nixon told a television audience that "we are Vietnamizing the search for peace," and began to move toward an all-volunteer Army. By the spring of 1970, the president had withdrawn 110,000 troops and announced a "Vietnamization" program to train the South Vietnamese Army to assume the burden of the fighting. But Nixon simultaneously increased the air war. By 1973, the administration had unleashed four million tons of bombs on Indochina: twice the tonnage ordered by Johnson and 1.5 times the total dropped on Europe and Asia in both World War II and the Korean War.

In order to protect withdrawing American troops, defend Saigon, and preserve a bargaining position with the North Vietnamese, Nixon continued to expand the war. But fearing public opinion, the president ordered a highly secret

Exhibit 13–7. Thrust Into Cambodia, 1970.

bombing of Communist forces in Cambodia during March 1969. Nixon ended the covert stage of the campaign in 1970 when he told a stunned nation that twenty-five thousand American and South Vietnamese troops had entered Cambodia in an "incursion" designed to "shorten the war." The object of the invasion, the commander-in-chief explained, was "cleaning out major North Vietnamese and Vietcong occupied territories," and destroying the "main headquarters for the entire Communist military operation in South Vietnam." The president also hoped to bolster the anti-Communist military regime that recently had taken control of the Cambodian capital.

For Nixon, Cambodia was a test crisis to demonstrate American resolve. Proclaiming that the United States could not act "like a pitiful, helpless giant," the chief executive confided that he would rather be a one-term president than see the nation become a "second-rate power." The president also underscored American determination by resuming "protective-reaction" air strikes against the North.

Failing to find Communist insurgents, American troops withdrew from Cambodia two months later on the day that Congress prohibited their continued presence. But in February 1971, the president announced an invasion of Laos, where American bombing had persisted since the early 1960s. Neither of these campaigns, however, affected the march of North Vietnamese regulars into South Vietnam's central highlands or the chaotic retreat of Saigon's army from the northern provinces. Faced with the failure of Vietnamization, Nixon announced the mining of North Vietnamese ports. Three months after his triumphant visit to China, the president described the government in Hanoi as "international outlaws" and ordered the bombing of railroad lines leading to the People's Republic from North Vietnam. He also instructed the Air Force to hit industrial targets in the populated North and sent American B-52s to attack the Vietnamese dike system.

Weeks before the 1972 presidential election, National Security Advisor Henry Kissinger and North Vietnamese negotiators secretly agreed to a military cease-fire. Under Soviet influence, North Vietnam decided to postpone a political settlement while keeping its military units in the South. In turn, the Nixon administration agreed to stop bombing of the North. When South Vietnamese allies rejected the truce, however, Kissinger abruptly announced the suspension of negotiations and resumption of the air war. In the "Christmas Bombing" of 1972, the most intensive air attack in military history, B-52s attacked populated areas, resulting in the destruction of a children's hospital at Bach Mai. The campaign demonstrated the administration's repeated contention that brute force would push Hanoi toward peace. Nixon and Kissinger also hoped to create fears of American retaliation should North Vietnam overwhelm the South.

Nixon finally announced a Vietnam peace agreement that would "end the war and bring peace with honor" in January 1973. But there was little in the accord that could not have been negotiated when he assumed office four years before. The settlement provided for the withdrawal of the twenty-five thousand remaining American troops in exchange for the repatriation of 587 American prisoners of war. But the peace agreement also provided official recognition of the National Liberation Front (Viet Cong) by the United States and resolved the nineteen-year controversy over the two Vietnams by declaring the 17th parallel a provisional boundary instead of a political or territorial dividing line.

Military involvement in Vietnam ended with withdrawal of the last troops and a televised homecoming for the POWs in March 1973. Three months later, the president accepted a congressional deadline on funding for combat activities in Indochina, a measure designed to end the bombing of Cambodia. Congress also overrode a Nixon veto in 1973 to pass the War Powers Act, which stipulated that the president had to inform Congress of the deployment of overseas military forces within forty-eight hours and provided a sixty-day limit on the commitment of troops without congressional consent. Although no president has acknowledged the constitutionality of the statute, the War Powers Act provided the most important limit on presidential military action since 1951. Altogether, the Vietnam War left over fifty-six thousand Americans dead, more than three-hundred thousand wounded, over 1.5 million Vietnamese killed, and ten million homeless. But the injury to national cohesion went far beyond the awesome destruction and the $150 billion in war costs.

Secretary of State Henry Kissinger conducts negotiations with the North Vietnamese shortly before the two sides signed a peace treaty early in 1973.

POLARIZED AMERICA

The Vietnam War demonstrated the high costs of interfering in foreign affairs when the vital interests of the United States were not directly threatened. Americans had assumed that President Johnson's turn to negotiations in 1968 signified a major reversal of Vietnam policy. But Nixon's inability to end the war undermined prospects for social peace at home. By the fall of 1969, 57 percent of the country favored a specified deadline for complete disengagement. As the antiwar movement broadened, massive rallies attracted Americans who had never before demonstrated. On October 15, 1969, Vietnam Moratorium Day, over two-hundred thousand protesters marched in Boston, New York, and Washington, D.C. A second moratorium in November brought 250,000 protesters parading to the Washington Monument. When ten thousand demonstrators were teargassed near the Justice Department, Attorney General John Mitchell remarked that "it looked like the Russian Revolution."

The invasion of Cambodia in 1970 brought new militance to campus protest. As students around the country demonstrated against the war, Ohio Governor James Rhodes bitterly condemned outside agitators and ordered the National Guard to several college campuses. At Kent State, rioting students trashed the town business district and burned the headquarters of the university Reserve Officers' Training Corps. The next day, May 4, 1970, protesters failed to respond to a dispersal order at a noon campus rally and threw rocks and bottles at guards-men setting off tear gas. Finding themselves surrounded, several of the tense troops wheeled around and fired rifle shots into the crowd, wounding nine and killing four, including two students leaving their classes. The Kent State deaths electrified a nation already shocked by news of the Cambodian invasion. University presidents had warned Nixon that there was no hope of restoring peace on American campuses without ending the war. But Vice President Spiro T. Agnew responded to the killings by blaming "elitist" permissiveness toward "psychotic and criminal elements" for the "traitors and thieves and perverts...in our midst."

Responding to the Kent shootings, student strikes closed 350 universities and colleges. At Jackson State in Mississippi, two black students were killed when police inexplicably fired on a dormitory. In a period in which draft calls were de-clining and students faced a deteriorating job market, the campus shootings served to intimidate further demonstrations. Yet students remained committed to the antiwar movement. During May 1971, thirty thousand activists arrived in Washington to protest the invasion of Laos by blocking traffic and employing civil disobedience to disrupt the capital. Monitored by a joint command of the CIA and local police, twelve thousand people were swept off the streets in the largest mass arrest in American history. Such police activity involved wide-spread suspension of legal procedures, however, and federal courts later ruled the arrests unconstitutional.

Reacting to dissent against the Vietnam War, the Johnson administration had prosecuted numerous prominent protesters, including pediatrician Benjamin Spock and Yale chaplain William Sloane Coffin, for aiding draft evasion. They were later acquitted. Under Nixon, federal grand juries continued to collect in-formation on radicals and antiwar groups but prosecution frequently faltered in court. In 1969, the government indicted eight leaders of the 1968 Chicago dem-onstrations for conspiracy to violate the antiriot provisions of the Civil Rights Act of 1968. The explosive trial of the Chicago Eight became a showplace for rad-ical protest and revolutionary culture. Yippies Jerry Rubin and Abbie Hoffman wore long hair, talked back to the judge, and introduced songs as evidence. When Black Panther Bobby Seale objected to proceedings without his bedridden attorney, Judge Julius Hoffman ordered Seale gagged and chained. Although the jury rejected most of the charges, Judge Hoffman cited defendants and their law-yers for 175 acts of contempt during the five-month trial. Charges against Seale, who won a separate trial, were dropped. Meanwhile, a grand jury indicted Cath-olic radicals, led by the Berrigan brothers, for conspiracy to kidnap Henry Kissinger. But another jury failed to convict them when the prime evidence turned out to be a whimsical letter delivered to Philip Berrigan through an FBI informer. Thirteen Black Panthers also were acquitted of conspiracy to bomb New York City department stores in 1971, while a New Haven jury failed to agree on a verdict in a case that charged Seale and other Panthers with conspir-acy to murder an alleged police informant.

The Nixon administration mounted an intense public relations campaign against antiwar activism and radical violence. Labeling demonstrators a "vocal minority" in contrast to the nation's "silent majority," the president pitted his own prestige against antiwar protesters in the 1970 congressional elections.

Vice President Spiro T. Agnew carried on the Nixon administration's rhetorical campaign against antiwar dissenters and other critics.

Convinced that liberal-dominated institutions such as the Supreme Court, universities, and mass media were preventing the White House from reaching the silent majority, Vice President Agnew described antiwar activists as an "effete corps of impudent snobs who characterized themselves as intellectuals" and complained that a "tiny enclosed fraternity of privileged men" in TV journalism distorted the president's peace efforts through the "instant analysis" that followed televised speeches. The implications of the vice president's criticism were crystalized when the newly confirmed chairman of the Federal Communications Commission requested transcripts of network commentaries and the White House communications director threatened government intervention if the media did not correct their bias.

Agnew also criticized the print media for concentrating on bad news instead of good. But the day following the November moratorium, newspapers published the first reports of the recently uncovered My Lai massacre, in which 347 South Vietnamese peasants had been massacred by troops under the command of Lieutenant William Calley. The highly publicized affair resulted in a military trial for Calley and his 1971 murder conviction. But the case brought an emotional burst of support for the defendant from Americans who insisted that Calley had only performed his military duty. Another segment of opinion held that he had been made a scapegoat for American brutality in Vietnam. Intervening in the volatile proceeding, Nixon promised to review the final sentence. Military and civilian court assessments reduced the lietuenant's sentence to ten years and he won parole with an honorable discharge in 1974.

Attempting to fuse consensus over Vietnam, the Nixon administration began employing covert tactics normally used by the CIA. When the liberal *New York Times* publicized the secret bombing of Cambodia in 1969, the White House ordered "national security" wiretaps on the telephones of four newsmen and thirteen of its own aides. To stop further leaks, Nixon officials prevailed upon the president's personal attorney to tap surplus 1968 campaign funds to hire two former police agents as private investigators. The team arranged for a wiretap on the telephone of columnist Joseph Kraft. But the "national security" operation directed most of its attention to partisan political purposes, including the surveillance of Democratic Senator Edward M. Kennedy, a potential candidate for the 1972 presidential election. Kennedy had driven his car off a bridge in a late-night accident, at Chappaquiddick, Massachusetts in the summer of 1969, drowning a female former campaign aide. Questions concerning the senator's relationship with his companion, in addition to a delay in reporting the accident, made Kennedy a logical subject of interest to the White House.

By 1970, Nixon pressed for a more formalized program of domestic intelligence to counter the threat of internal dissent. Following the Cambodian invasion, presidential aide Tom Huston drafted a proposal for an interagency intelligence unit composed of the FBI, CIA, National Security Agency (NSA), and the Pentagon intelligence agencies. The illegal Huston Plan called for burglary, wiretapping, mail openings, campus informants, and monitoring of international communications, but the presidentially approved program functioned for only five days before FBI Director Hoover squelched it. Hoover feared disclosure of the unlawful procedures and hoped to maintain FBI control of domestic security. Despite the demise of the Huston Plan, however, each of the agencies continued their ongoing secret and illegal monitoring of domestic dissenters. The Internal Revenue Service, moreover, began using tax audits to harass individuals and organizations with "extremist views and philosophies." In late 1970, the White House created an Intelligence Evaluation Committee to coordinate the surveillance of radical dissenters.

When the *New York Times* began to publish the secret Pentagon Papers in 1971, the Nixon White House faced another crisis. Commissioned by former Defense Secretary Robert S. McNamara, the Papers focused on the continuity of government duplicity during the Kennedy and Johnson administrations' conduct of the Vietnam War. But National Security Adviser Kissinger feared that future leaks might threaten Soviet and Chinese confidence in the American ability to conduct secret negotiations. Shortly after federal courts refused to permit the government to stop publication of the Pentagon study, Nixon authorized creation of a Special Investigations Unit (the "Plumbers"). When Daniel Ellsberg, a former Defense Department planner, confessed that he had released the papers to expose government lying and help end the war, the Plumbers burglarized the office of Ellsberg's psychiatrist to gain information that could be used to discredit the former Pentagon aide. The Justice Department indicted Ellsberg and Anthony Russo for espionage and conspiracy in 1971 but was forced to drop the charges when it refused to produce wiretap logs that contained conversations involving the defendants. Instead, presidential assistants John Ehrlichman and Charles Colson faced conviction three years later for authorizing the illegal attempt to obtain Ellsberg's medical records. A federal court ruled in 1974 that a president had no constitutional right to authorize a break-in, even if it targeted foreign intelligence operatives and threats to national security.

RE-ELECTION OF THE PRESIDENT

Polarization of public opinion over the Vietnam War led to the emergence of South Dakota's George McGovern as the Democratic candidate in the 1972 presidential election. The climate for McGovern's candidacy had been prepared by New Left critiques of the war, black and radical demands for social justice, and the counter-culture of middle-class youth. Senator McGovern, a World War II bomber pilot, had also been instrumental in obtaining party reforms which assured that delegates would be chosen not by party bosses, but in primaries, caucuses, and other ballots. The new rules also required equitable representation for women and minorities. The candidate called for a "politics of conscience" embracing tax reform and a shift of spending from defense to social needs. Citing ties to big business, he castigated the Nixon administration as "the most corrupt in history."

McGovern hoped to take advantage of the Twenty-sixth Amendment to the Constitution, which in 1971 awarded the vote to eighteen-year olds. But the broadest youth movement centered on George Wallace, whose opposition to busing brought him the largest vote in the Democratic primaries before he was paralyzed by an assassin's bullet in May 1972. Wallace supporters and many mainstream Democrats associated the McGovern candidacy with draft card burning, campus destruction, street riots, and disrespect for national values. These fears crystalized when the Democratic Convention openly debated culturally abrasive issues such as abortion, the legalization of marijuana, and gay rights. Over one hundred delegates used the occasion to publicly acknowledge themselves as homosexuals. McGovern also suffered when a carelessly presented plan for a guaranteed income conveyed confusion about economics. The fatal blow came when newspaper reports indicated that vice-presidential candidate Thomas Eagleton had been hospitalized several time for emotional depression. McGovern first gave Senator Eagleton a "1,000 percent" public endorsement, then asked for his resignation, thereby creating an image of indecisiveness and hypocrisy.

DANIEL ELLSBERG
1931–

When Daniel Ellsberg was arrested in 1985 for blockading a CIA office in protest of United States policy in Nicaragua, he added one more chapter to a public career immersed in the contradictions of the Cold War. Born in Depression Chicago and raised in Detroit, Ellsberg attended an exclusive prep school on full scholarship before getting an economics degree at Harvard. Yet he abandoned the academic life in 1954 by volunteering for the Marines and becoming an infantry sharpshooter. Two years later, Ellsberg resumed his studies at Harvard and Cambridge. His Ph.D thesis in economics focused on strategic military planning.

A tall, lean man with a sharp-featured, narrow face, Ellsberg followed Cold War passions by advising Senator John Kennedy on foreign policy. In 1959, he signed on with the Rand corporation, a California consultant to the Defense Department, as a strategic analyst whose specialty was nuclear warfare. But by 1964, the effusive Ellsberg had become convinced that the future of democracy hinged on the war in Vietnam. First he served as special international security aide to the assistant secretary of defense. Still not satisfied, Ellsberg volunteered to become State Department liaison with the counterinsurgency effort in the Vietnamese countryside. By 1967, he was special assistant to the deputy ambassador.

With a Boys Scout enthusiasm for containing Communist aggression and preventing World War III, Ellsberg often donned military gear to accompany Vietnam counterinsurgency teams on "clearing operations." But by 1966, he began to note the failure of pacification campaigns, the rising number of civilian casualties, widespread corruption in the South Vietnamese government and military, and repeated reports of the torturing of Viet Cong prisoners. Ellsberg informed defense secretary McNamara that the war was stalemated at increasing levels of violence and that official reporting was not telling deci- *(cont.)*

Nixon professed to place himself above politics and simply derided the capture of the Democratic party by a radical clique. "Let us reject," the president proclaimed, "the policies of those who whine and whimper about our frustrations and call on us to turn inward." Nixon's campaign followed the strategy outlined in Kevin Phillips's *The Emerging Republican Majority* (1969), which sought to form a new coalition of Wallace voters, white southerners, urban supporters in the Southwest, working-class Catholics, suburbanites, and rural Americans. These voters had not benefited from costly welfare programs erected after World War II, and many depended on military defense spending for their livelihood. The president also pointed to Kissinger's negotiations to end the Vietnam War.

(cont.) sion-makers what they needed to know. Upon leaving Saigon in 1967, he proposed a high-level study of American policy in Vietnam. When McNamara later ordered such a history, Ellsberg had returned to Rand and became one of thirty-six researchers to work on the project.

The Pentagon study convinced Ellsberg that the war involved a sordid history of American aggression perpetuated by several presidents. Each had chosen stalemate as a substitute for failure. Seeing no justification for American policy and feeling guilt over his complicity in the pacification program, Ellsberg made copies of the secret study in 1969 and resigned from Rand the next year. Once convinced that the Nixon administration was about to repeat the mistakes and deceptions of its predecessors, he released portions of the Pentagon Papers to the *New York Times* in 1971.

The first instalment of the classified study revealed that the Johnson administration had misled Americans with public statements of peace while moving toward war. After a temporary injunction halted further publication in the *Times*, the Supreme Court overruled any prior restraint in the matter. Meanwhile, Ellsberg was indicted for conspiracy, theft, and violation of the espionage laws. He responded by pointing to the "Vietnamization" of America. In order to discredit the disaffected strategist, the White House assigned his case to a newly formed Special Investigations Unit. Memoranda concerning its covert operations were later destroyed by Nixon counsel John Dean during the early Watergate coverup. In September 1971, the "plumbers" broke into the Los Angeles office of Ellsberg's psychiatrist. Such government misconduct resulted in dismissal of all charges against the man who had leaked the Pentagon Papers.

Once Ellsberg had punctured the mystique of the presidency, he threw himself into the 1970s antiwar movement with the brilliant intensity that marked his Vietnam activity. He attended peace conferences, testified before congressional committees, and appeared at the trials of draft resisters. Ever the strategic analyst, Daniel Ellsberg failed to see why a rational foreign policy could not serve the national interest and remain just and humane. ■

The results of this strategy were spectacularly successful. The president received 61 percent of the popular vote, nearly equaling Johnson's landslide of 1964, and carried every state in the Electoral College except Massachusetts and the District of Columbia. While McGovern took only 29 percent of the southern vote, Nixon reversed Democratic domination of the white ethnics by winning a majority of Catholics, Irish-Americans, and Italian-Americans. The election thereby demonstrated that the Democratic New Deal coalition of the 1930s had lost much of its cohesion. But in a show of widespread political apathy, less than 55 percent of eligible voters cast ballots in the 1972 election, and thirty-nine million qualified Americans did not even register to vote.

JOHN SIRICA
1904–

Beneath the dark judicial robes sat the oldest son of a poor Italian immigrant barber, and although in 1973 he was presiding as chief judge of the federal district court in Washington, D.C., John Sirica never forgot his humble beginnings. "I came up rough-and-tough," he liked to say. "If it had not been for the Republican party, I might never have done much better than my father." Standing before him, four of the seven defendants were members of the Spanish-speaking Cuban exile community of Miami. They triggered an instinctive sympathy. If it had not been for the Republican party, the judge suspected, they might not be here either.

Sirica had barely worked his way through law school. Poorly educated and with little success as a lawyer, he managed to get a job as an assistant government attorney in the Hoover administration. With the arrival of the New Deal, he returned to an unprofitable private practice, but served as chief counsel for a congressional committee investigating corruption in the Federal Communications Commission in 1944. To his annoyance, Democratic politicians squashed the case.

After the war, Sirica strengthened his position in Republican circles by campaigning actively for Eisenhower. He was also a close friend of Senator Joseph R. McCarthy. For his political loyalty, Eisenhower appointed Sirica to the federal court in 1957. The judge soon gained a reputation for brusqueness and impatience with abstruse legal argument. The severity of his sentences earned him the nickname "Maximum John," but many of his decisions were overturned on appeal.

By 1973, Sirica's seniority made him chief judge of the Washington, D.C. district court. As a loyal Republican, he felt a special obligation to assure a fair trial for the seven *(cont.)*

WATERGATE AND NIXON'S FALL

Nixon's awesome victory involved more than clever strategy. In 1971, Nixon associates organized a Committee to Re-Elect the President (CRP) and created four hundred "dummy" corporations to channel secret contributions to the campaign. Altogether, CRP collected $55 million from corporate donors seeking preferential treatment from the government. The committee also directed intelligence operations against strong Democratic contenders like Edmund Muskie and worked covertly to support weak candidates like McGovern. A "dirty tricks" operation issued false and misleading literature "signed" by Democratic candidates and engaged in other pranks to embarrass the Democrats. In the spring of 1972, CRP Director John Mitchell approved a covert entry into Democratic headquarters at the Watergate apartment and hotel complex in Washington. When an *(cont.)* men accused of breaking into the Democratic party headquarters at the Watergate complex in June 1972. For Sirica, the defendants divided into two social classes: E. Howard Hunt, James McCord, and G. Gordon Liddy— all privileged associates of the Nixon administration; and four Cuban exiles who apparently did the dirty work. When in an effort to establish a conspiracy of silence they all pleaded guilty, Sirica replied: "I don't think we should sit up here like nincompoops." Exercising his authority as a federal judge, he broke into the courtroom examinations and asked specific questions about payments, which brought to light additional incriminating evidence. Then, after a jury convicted the burglars, he reserved sentencing to pressure the defendants to talk. To his delight, McCord took the bait, and Sirica eventually presided over the trials of many high-level co-conspirators.

Meanwhile, congressional investigators had issued a subpoena for tape-recorded evidence to President Richard Nixon, but the White House had rejected the request on grounds of "executive privilege." The constitutional dispute came to Sirica's docket. "Beyond all the legal debate, one question kept nagging at me," he recalled. "If Nixon himself were not involved why would he stand on such an abstract principle...when by voluntarily turning over the tapes he could prove himself innocent and put the Watergate case behind him?" Sirica ordered the release of the subpoenaed material.

Nixon's compliance merely intensified the judge's outrage, for in listening to presidential tapes he discovered that the man he had supported in 1972 was vulgar, devious, and dishonest. On the day before his seventieth birthday, in his last act as chief judge, Sirica ordered the release of grand jury files to the House of Representatives, which was debating Nixon's impeachment. This material contained explosive and incriminating evidence, forcing Nixon to resign the presidency in August 1974. "I was often described as an 'obscure federal judge' and that was true," Sirica observed, "but I was not a damn fool." ■

electronic listening device malfunctioned, five CRP operatives returned for a second entry on June 17 and were arrested for burglary.

Although presidential press secretary Ron Ziegler dismissed the crime as a "third-rate burglary," money and an address book notation found on the burglars enabled police to link the team to White House "Plumbers" G. Gordon Liddy and E. Howard Hunt. CRP and White House aides began an immediate coverup, destroying revealing campaign records, lying to the FBI and grand jury, removing incriminating evidence from a White House safe, and pressuring law-enforcement agencies for "cooperation." Americans would not discover the fact for two years, but Nixon conducted the preliminary steps in the Watergate coverup, personally ordering aides to request the CIA to stop an FBI inquiry into the source of Watergate funds.

Former White House Counsel John Dean offered detailed testimony about presidential conversations before the Senate Select Committee on Watergate, 1973.

By the time the trial of the Watergate burglars opened in early 1973, two of the men had received promises of executive clemency in return for continued silence. In March, White House counselor John Dean brought new demands to Nixon at an Oval Office meeting in which he outlined a "cancer on the presidency" and estimated that eventual hush-money payments could reach $1 million. The next day, Nixon ordered Mitchell to continue the cover-up. Despite these precautions, however, news reports soon linked top White House and campaign aides to the Watergate affair. Attempting to place responsibility on Dean, Nixon fired the White House counsel and asked for the resignation of his two key assistants, John Ehrlichman and H. R. Haldeman. The president also acceded to the appointment of a special Watergate prosecutor.

As a Senate Select Committee, chaired by Democrat Sam Ervin, began dramatic televised hearings into the scandal in May 1973, Dean testified about the president's continuing knowledge of the coverup. He also produced evidence of the Plumbers unit, the illegal Huston Plan, and an administration "enemies list" submitted to the IRS for possible audits. Even more astounding, White House aide Alexander Butterfield revealed that Nixon had installed secret tape-recording devices in the Oval Office. Although Nixon's attorneys claimed that the separation of powers and executive privilege gave him the right to preserve the confidentiality of conversations with advisors, a federal court ruled in October 1973 that nine tapes be turned over to the courts. But when Special Prosecutor Archibald Cox rejected the president's demand that no further subpoenas be issued, and announced Nixon's "noncompliance" with court orders, the president stunned the nation by ordering Attorney General Elliot Richardson to fire Cox and abolish the Special Prosecutor's office. Richardson refused and resigned in protest. When Deputy Attorney General William Ruckelshaus objected to the presidential order, Nixon fired him before securing the compliance of Solicitor General Robert F. Bork. After a "fire storm" of protest over the "Saturday Night Massacre," however, the president relinquished the tapes and appointed a new special prosecutor, Leon Jaworski, a prominent Houston attorney. Yet three of the tapes proved to be missing, and evidence revealed that extended blank spots on the others had been caused by manual erasures.

By the fall of 1973 both the president and Vice President Agnew faced income tax problems. Agnew had been under investigation for participation in a "kickback" scheme with Maryland contractors. In October the vice president pleaded "no contest" to tax evasion and promptly resigned. Adhering to the succession provisions of the Twenty-fifth Amendment, ratified in 1967, Nixon nominated House Republican leader Gerald R. Ford for the vice presidency and Congress quickly confirmed him. When the IRS announced that it was re-examining Nixon's back taxes to investigate deductions for the donation of his vice-presidential papers, he told a televised meeting of newspaper editors that "I'm not a crook." The agency subsequently reported that the president of the United States owed $450,000 in back taxes and interest penalties. Meanwhile, a grand jury indicted Haldeman, Ehrlichman, Mitchell, Colson, and three others in March 1974 for perjury and hush-money payments, and named the president himself as an unindicted co-conspirator. As Special Prosecutor Jaworski prepared his case, the House of Representatives voted 406-4 to authorize the the Judiciary Committee to investigate whether sufficient grounds existed for the impeachment of the president.

The turning point in the Watergate drama came when the Burger Court unanimously decided to compel the president to surrender all subpoenaed tapes in July 1974. "When the claim of privilege is based only on a generalized interest in confidentiality," the Court ruled, "it cannot prevail over the fundamental demands of due process of law in the fair administration of justice." At the same time the Judiciary Committee voted three bills of impeachment against the president, charging him with obstruction of justice, abuse of power, and unconstitutional defiance of committee subpoenas. A few weeks later, the White House released excerpts from subpoenaed tapes which showed that the president had played a key role in the early days of the coverup. On August 9, 1974, Nixon became the first president in American history to resign from office. "Our long national nightmare is over," newly inaugurated President Ford told the nation. "Our constitution works. Our great republic is a government of laws and not of men."

FORD VS. CONGRESS

President Ford, the first chief executive not to be elected to either the presidency or the vice presidency, faced a nation shaken by the traumas of Vietnam and Watergate. But government credibility suffered another blow when the president announced that he was pardoning Richard Nixon "for all offenses against the United States." The Judiciary Committee quickly initiated hearings to discover whether Ford had made assurances to Nixon before the resignation. But

President Nixon chose House Minority Leader Gerald Ford to succeed Vice President Agnew in 1973. Less than one year later, Nixon himself resigned.

the new president insisted that the pardon was designed simply to remove the disruptive Watergate issue from the national spotlight. Ford also offered "clemency" to Vietnam draft law violators and deserters, but only 6 percent of the eligible 350,000 applied. The majority of Americans believed that Nixon should go to jail for his crimes, and despite an amiable personality, the new president never recovered his initial popularity.

Ford successfully nominated former New York Governor Nelson D. Rockefeller to fill the vice-presidential vacancy. But Rockefeller, whose family fortune exceeded $1 billion, faced hostile questions about loans and gifts to state officials and the financing of a vicious biography of a former political opponent. In the post-Watergate atmosphere, such ethical issues received careful congressional scrutiny. Congress also passed a campaign reform law which provided the first use of public money to finance presidential elections and limited private contributions and candidate spending.

With Henry Kissinger acting as both national security advisor and secretary of state, Ford continued Nixon's balance of power strategy. Late in 1974, the president went to Vladivostok to discuss arms limitations with the Soviets and signed

Chief Justice Warren Burger administers the oath of office to Gerald Ford as thirty-eighth president of the United States, August 9, 1974.

an accord that set negotiating guidelines. The following year, Ford met Brezhnev and other European leaders in Helsinki and agreed to a declaration on European security that implicitly recognized Soviet annexations and the Communist regimes in eastern Europe since 1945. The Helsinki Accords also promoted peaceful cooperation between European nations and recognition of basic human rights. Meanwhile, Kissinger continued his peace mission in the Middle East, where American energy needs dictated the stabilization of hostilities in the oil-rich area. Through his efforts, Egypt and Israel concluded an interim peace agreement in 1975.

Despite Kissinger's successes, Congress resisted administration efforts to conduct a unilateral foreign policy in the post-Vietnam era. Thus, for example, Congress undercut Kissinger by denying the Soviet Union most-favored-nation status in trade until it relaxed restrictions on emigration, particularly for Soviet Jews and other dissenters. Congress also defeated administration requests for increased military aid to South Vietnam. Without American support, South Vietnam could not stop Communist advances. On April 30, 1975, an emergency helicopter evacuation completed the removal of one thousand Americans and fifty-three thousand Vietnamese dependents from Saigon. A few hours later, the Communists geographically re-unified the country and the Vietnam War was over.

The Vietnam War showed the limits of power in an age of international diversity and nuclear stalemate, but the Ford administration saw it as a failure of national determination and credibility. In May 1975, one month after the fall of Saigon, Ford sent troops to recapture an American merchant ship held by Cambodian patrol boats. Just as the *Mayaguez* was being released, the United States conducted a massive aerial bombing. The action led to the inadvertent loss of fifteen marines and the death of twenty-three others in a helicopter crash in Thailand. The incident indicated Ford's reluctance to accept both the American loss of pride in Southeast Asia and the tarnished image of the United States as a guarantor of world order.

The administration also experienced frustration in Africa, where it confronted Soviet and Cuban support for the MPLA, a nationalist movement struggling to gain supremacy in newly independent Angola. Defining the struggle in Cold War terms, Ford authorized $53 million for covert CIA operations to sustain a pro-Western faction in the ongoing civil war. But the chief executive faced an increasingly restive Congress. During 1974, legislators had passed the Hughes-Ryan Amendment, which compelled the president to certify that covert actions served the national interest and report them to Congress "in a timely fashion." Briefed on the Angolan operation in his role as chairman of the Senate Foreign Relations Subcommittee on Africa, Iowa Democrat Dick Clark introduced a resolution to cut off CIA aid to the insurgents sponsored by the agency. By early 1976, both houses had approved the Clark Amendment and the MPLA assumed control of the Angolan government.

"Stagflation's" lethal combination of inflation and unemployment continued to plague Gerald Ford. During Nixon's last months during 1974 Congress had acted to combat the recession by passing the first housing bill since 1968, appropriating $3.8 billion for public school assistance, and reviving the war on poverty. The legislators also provided nearly $12 billion for a six-year program of urban mass transit designed to reduce dependence on the automobile for com-

Exhibit 13–8. Government Spending as Percentage of Gross National Product, 1969–1976.

1969	30.5%
1976	33.9%

Source: *Historical Statistics of the United States, from Colonial Times to 1970* (1975)
Economic Report of the President (1977)

Exhibit 13–9. Federal Budget Deficits, 1968–1976.
(in billions of dollars)
(fiscal years ending in year shown)

	Receipts	Outlays	Deficit
1968	$153.0 b	$178.1 b	$25.2 b
1972	$207.3 b	$230.7 b	$23.4 b
1976	$298.1 b	$371.8 b	$73.7 b

Source: *Economic Report of the President* (1988)

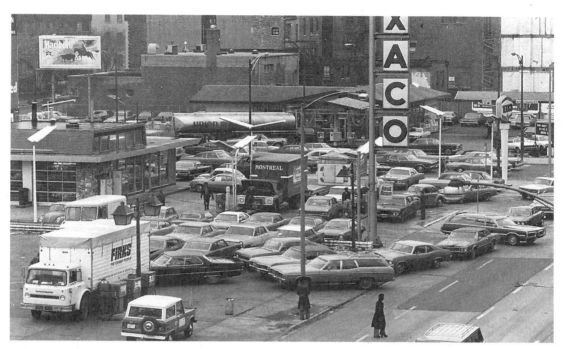

Gas station traffic jams, such as this one in Chicago, were a common sight in 1974. An OPEC oil embargo and a subsequent price hike caused many service station operators to impose quotas or close early in order to conserve their dwindling fuel supplies.

muting. Like Nixon, however, Ford objected to continued spending and castigated Congress for feeding inflation. When the legislators rejected a 5 percent surcharge on corporations and middle-income taxpayers and overrode a Ford veto to extend education benefits to Vietnam veterans, the president took his antispending crusade to the voters. But Watergate and the Nixon pardon worked against the Republicans, and the Democrats used the 1974 elections to win a two-thirds majority in the House and added strength in the Senate.

Buoyed by their increased power, the Democratic Congress scaled down a Ford tax cut, ended depletion allowances for large oil corporations, and curbed investment tax shelters. Ford reluctantly agreed to a Comprehensive Employment and Training Act (CETA) late in 1974, which created temporary jobs in state and local governments and became the administration's most important anti-recession weapon. Nevertheless, the president forced Congress to compromise on an administration energy bill that combined continued oil price controls with a schedule of gradual price increases. Ford and Congress also consented to a $2.3 billion loan to welfare-burdened and financially pressed New York City in 1975.

JIMMY CARTER

Public bitterness over Vietnam and Watergate made personal trust a key issue in the 1976 presidential campaign. Emerging from a wide field of Democratic candidates, former Georgia Governor James ("Jimmy") Earl Carter, Jr. overcame

Promising to restore public trust to government following Vietnam and Watergate, newcomer Jimmy Carter refashioned the Democratic party's electoral coalition in 1976.

near-anonymity to sweep the early primaries. As chairman of the 1974 Democratic campaign committee, Carter had plugged the party's nominees in sixty congressional races. But except for his service in the Navy, the candidate had never worked for the federal government. Neither was he a lawyer, a distinct advantage in the post-Watergate climate. Carter played upon his role as outsider, attacking a "confused and overlapping and wasteful federal bureaucracy" and promised to restore trust and openness in government. The Georgian also called for tax reform, a national health program, and a comprehensive energy policy.

Supported by Atlanta black leaders such as Representative Andrew Young, Carter also sought to capture the votes of white southerners who had deserted the Democrats in the previous two presidential elections. The candidate's "born-again" Christian credentials helped to defeat George Wallace in the southern primaries and demonstrate his broad appeal. Carter, moreover, took pride in his experiences as a nuclear engineer and member of the Trilateral Commission, an international symposium of corporate-minded leaders who engaged in long-run planning and problem solving. To further unify the party, the nominee chose Minnesota liberal Senator Walter F. Mondale as his vice-presidential candidate. Speaking to the public mood in his acceptance speech, Carter proclaimed "a time for healing. We want to have faith again. We want to be proud again." But the candidate also assumed a populist anger toward political and economic elites.

Exhibit 13–10. 1976 Election.

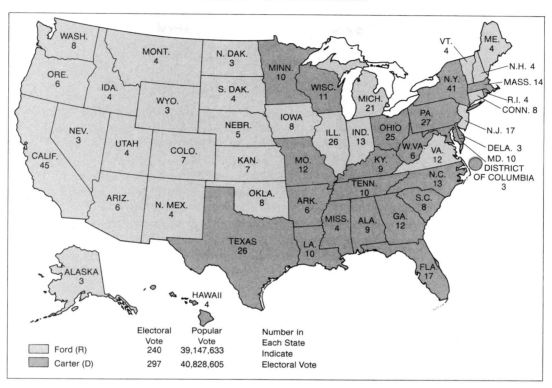

	Electoral Vote	Popular Vote	Number In
Ford (R)	240	39,147,633	Each State Indicate
Carter (D)	297	40,828,605	Electoral Vote

"It's time for the people to run the government," he stated softly, "and not the other way around."

Despite a strong run by California conservative Ronald W. Reagan, Ford won the Republican nomination in a close vote. The president and running mate Senator Robert Dole of Kansas campaigned strenuously on the need to curb federal spending but faced a thirty-three percent deficit in public opinion polls following the harmonious Democratic Convention. When Carter accused Ford of trying to "hide in the Rose Garden," therefore, the president agreed to hold three televised debates with the challenger, the first such exercises since 1960. The newcomer Carter benefited from the exposure and went on to win the nation's first publicly financed presidential race by a scant two percentage points and two million popular votes. The Electoral College tally of 291 to 241 comprised the closest margin of victory since President Woodrow Wilson's re-election in 1916.

Although Ford carried the entire West except Hawaii, Carter rode the strength of Mexican-American votes in Texas and strong black support to sweep the entire South. Moved by regional pride and an affinity with Carter's roots in evangelical Protestantism, black and white southerners provided the candidate with 90 percent of his national plurality. By uniting the South, the industrial Northeast, organized labor, minorities, and middle-class liberals, Carter succeeded in restoring the New Deal coalition. Yet national voter participation remained below 55 percent.

When Jimmy Carter assumed the presidency, he soon learned that anti-recession spending brought rising inflation, huge federal deficits, and large increases in the national debt. Like Nixon and Ford, the Democratic president leaned toward conservative fiscal and monetary policies. Yet political pressures for high-level employment and economic growth narrowed Carter's options. The president signed the Humphrey-Hawkins Act in 1978, which proposed a 3 percent ceiling on inflation, but called for the reduction of unemployment rates to 4 percent and made the federal government the employer of last resort. Similar pressures pushed Carter into requesting a $28 billion tax cut in 1980, although he asked that the measure not be implemented until 1981. As the administration responded to demands for lower unemployment and increased wages, the inflation rate tripled to an annual 14 percent by 1980, the highest since 1947. To worsen matters, foreign investors reacted to burgeoning federal deficits and government borrowing by selling off dollars in international currency exchanges.

Although the decline of American productivity rates, down one-third from the 1960s, contributed to inflation in the Carter years, a more direct source lay in the 50 percent oil price hike by OPEC in 1979. By then, petroleum accounted for nearly half of all energy consumed in the United States. The administration moved to counter these inflationary trends by encouraging the Federal Reserve to raise interest rates to 15 percent in 1979, by establishing voluntary guidelines for wage and price increases, and by promising cuts in federal spending. Carter felt compelled to respond to a national taxpayers revolt which now had spread to Congress. Nevertheless, the administration's monetary restraint and program cuts worsened the ongoing recession, sent unemployment rates up to 7.6 percent in mid-1980, and traumatized many low- and middle-income Americans.

Accepting the conservative doctrine that deregulation increased economic performance and lowered costs, Carter rescinded government control over much of the airline, transportation, communications, and securities industries. But when Chrysler, the nation's tenth largest corporation, faced bankruptcy in 1979, the president approved $1.5 billion in government loans to the automaker. Carter also responded to pressure by large wheat producers in 1977 by placing massive reserves under grower control through a price-support system which operated under surplus conditions. As a result, farmers sold grains only when market prices met their demands. Despite the fact that the United States had emerged as the world's bread basket by the 1970s, the legislation was not able to save small farmers squeezed by escalating production costs. By 1977, the number of American farmers had decreased by more than half since the mid-1930s. Carter's efforts to establish a consumer protection agency and a hospital cost-control plan failed to pass in Congress. But the president was successful in establishing a Department of Education. Carter also supported legislation to control strip mining, to establish a chemical contamination cleanup fund, and to restrict the development of federal lands in Alaska.

The energy crisis presented Jimmy Carter with his most compelling opportunity. As Americans faced fuel shortages and soaring prices, Carter depicted the emergency as the "moral equivalent of war." In a major televised speech in 1977, the president pleaded with Americans to conserve electricity and fuel, and called for limits on oil imports and for subsidies to develop alternative energy. Carter's

Exhibit 13–11. Unemployment Rates, 1976–1980.

1976	7.5%
1977	9.0%
1978	6.0%
1979	5.8%
1980	7.0%

Source: *Economic Report of the President* (1988)

Exhibit 13–12. Federal Social Welfare Expenditures, 1976–1980. (rounded billions of dollars)

1976	$197.0 b
1978	$239.7 b
1980	$302.6 b

Source: *Statistical Abstract of the United States* (1987)

Exhibit 13–13. Gross National Product, 1976–1980. (current dollars in billions)

1976	$1782.8 b
1978	$2243.7 b
1980	$2732.0 b

Source: *Economic Report of the President* (1988)

Exhibit 13–14. Imports & Exports, 1976–1980. (in billions of dollars)

	Imports	*Exports*
1976	$123.5 b	$115.2 b
1978	$174.8 b	$143.7 b
1980	$244.9 b	$220.6 b

Source: *Statistical Abstract of the United States* (1987)

comprehensive energy program included a plan to tax excess consumption and a contingency scheme for rationing gas. But when Congress insisted on cutting consumption by deregulating energy prices, the president responded that increased prices must be offset by a windfall profits tax on the oil corporations. A 1980 compromise provided for gradual deregulation and decontrol of the domestic energy industry and a limit on the president's power to implement rationing. Meanwhile, Carter got his windfall tax, a Department of Energy, and a federally funded synthetic fuels program. The Carter energy program lacked the comprehensiveness the president sought, but per capita use of energy fell 20 percent between 1978 and 1981 through the additional use of home insulation, fuel-efficient cars, and increased conservation measures.

Exhibit 13–15. Consumer Price Index, 1977–1980.
(1967-100)

1977	181.5
1978	195.4
1979	217.4
1980	246.8

Source: *Economic Report of the President* (1988)

Exhibit 13–16. Consumer Credit Outstanding, 1970–1980.
(rounded billions of dollars)

1970	$141 b
1974	$211 b
1977	$279 b
1980	$369 b

Source: *Economic Report of the President* (1988)

Carter's approach to the energy crisis reflected his strengths and weaknesses. The president sought issues like energy and nuclear proliferation that crossed ideological lines. Yet once he made his television appeals, Carter's unfamiliarity with Washington politics impeded his effectiveness. Billing himself as an outsider, the president chose advisors who lacked experience in congressional politics. Carter's failure to win the confidence of congressional leaders was aggravated by a suspicion that the president was more image than substance. The chief executive attributed some of his legislative failure to narrow economic interests and single-issue lobbyists, and spoke of a general American "malaise" in an era still affected by Vietnam and Watergate. But the American people saw their leader as hesitant, evasive, and impotent. By 1980, Carter's approval rating had plummeted from a high of 75 percent upon taking office to less than 25 percent.

THE LIMITS OF POWER

Carter campaigned on the promise to cut defense spending and bring a fresh approach to foreign policy. Proclaiming that the United States was at last free "of the inordinate fear of communism...the fear that led to the moral poverty of Vietnam," Carter cancelled production of the B-1 Bomber, which Air Force leaders wanted as a replacement for the aging B-52. The president also deferred preparation of the neutron bomb, and proposed withdrawal of ground troops from South Korea. Following the foundations laid by Nixon and Ford, Carter moved to stabilize relations with the Soviet Union by signing a Strategic Arms Limitation Treaty (SALT II) in 1979. The new accord set limits on the number of long-range missiles, bombers, and nuclear warheads to be held by the super powers. Washington also exchanged ambassadors with China on New Year's Day, 1979, and agreed to sever diplomatic ties with Taiwan within the year.

Exhibit 13–17. Middle East.

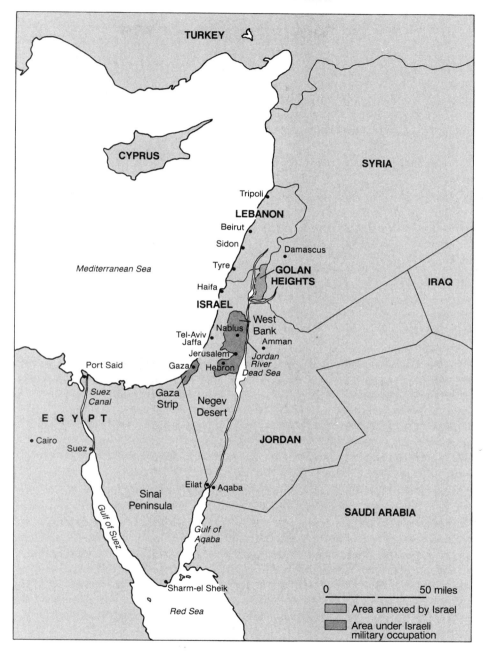

The search for political stability in the volatile Middle East led Carter to promote a peace agreement between Egypt and Israel. Following a dramatic visit to Jerusalem by Egypt's Anwar Sadat in late 1977, Carter brought Sadat and Israeli Premier Menachem Begin to Camp David for a personal summit. When further negotiations stalled early in 1979, the president flew to the Middle East to continue his low-key diplomacy. Egypt and Israel finally signed a peace treaty in Washington in 1979. The most controversial stumbling block to Mideast stability, however, continued to be the fate of Palestinians living in Israeli-occupied territories. To their dismay, the 1979 treaty failed to give Palestinian Arabs a role in negotiating their own status.

The Carter administration had greater success in linking American foreign policy to the aspirations of "third world" people in Africa and Latin America. Stressing the importance of human rights as a foundation of global strategy, Carter became the first president to visit black Africa. Andrew Young, the administration's black ambassador to the United Nations, denounced apartheid in white-dominated South Africa and defended the president's refusal to recognize the government of Rhodesia (Zimbabwe) until the white minority permitted political participation of black organizations. Carter also continued negotiations begun by Nixon and Ford to return the Panama Canal to Panama by the year 2000. Despite strong opposition by Republican conservatives and a lengthy Senate debate, the president signed the Panamanian treaty in 1978, although the United States reserved the right to intervene to preserve the neutrality of the Canal Zone. The agreement also awarded Panama $1 billion in compensation. By negotiating American sovereignty over the canal, the Carter administration removed the most obvious symbol of American military aggressiveness in the hemisphere. In a similar vein, Congress approved $75 million in emergency aid for Nicaragua when a 1979 revolution by Sandinista nationalists overthrew a brutal military dictatorship.

By 1980, however, Carter's foreign policy focused on the Cold War. Angered by the Soviet invasion of Afghanistan in 1979, the president called the action "the most severe threat to world peace since the Second World War." Carter promptly suspended grain sales to the Soviet Union and ordered an American boycott of the 1980 Olympic Games in Moscow. The president also asked the Senate to shelve ratification of SALT II. Defense-minded senators from both parties had denounced the treaty for restricting development of cruise missiles while allowing the Soviets to improve their backfire bombers and other missiles. But the main objection to SALT II centered on difficulties in verifying compliance. Fearing Soviet expansion in Africa and the Middle East, the White House issued a Carter Doctrine which stated that any attempt by an outside force to gain control of the Persian Gulf would be regarded as an assault on American interests. Carter also escalated verbal attacks on Soviet treatment of dissidents,

Exhibit 13–18. National Defense and Veterans Outlays, 1976–1980. (in billions of dollars)

1976	$108.0 b
1978	$123.5 b
1980	$155.2 b

Source: *Statistical Abstract of the United States* (1987)

A substantial triumph for Carter, Israeli Prime Minister Begin and Egyptian President Sadat prepare to exchange "land for peace" at Camp David, September, 1978.

and persuaded Congress to resume military draft registration, but not conscription itself. Most important, however, the president reversed his defense policy by requesting a 25 percent growth in military appropriations over the next five years, a plea fueled in part by Pentagon assertions that American forces had badly deteriorated because of the diversion of military funds to the Vietnam War. Defense outlays leaped from $108 billion in 1977 to $155 billion in 1980 and Carter called for further increases. The administration also supported Pentagon plans for the deployment of Trident submarines to carry mobile nuclear missiles.

Carter's most vexing foreign policy issue arose with the overthrow of pro-American Shah Mohammed Reza Pahlavi in Iran during 1979. Led by the Moslem cleric Ayatollah Ruhollah Khomeini, Shiite revolutionaries demanded a religious state that would withdraw from military and economic cooperation with the United States and eliminate western secularism and materialism. The Iranians remained embittered over the CIA coup which had restored the shah to

Exhibit 13–19. Research & Development, 1968–1980.
(current dollars in billions)

	Total	Defense and Space-related
1968	$24.6b	$11.8b
1972	$28.5b	$11.7b
1976	$39.0b	$13.3b
1980	$62.6b	$18.2b

Source: *Statistical Abstract of the United States* (1987)

Exhibit 13–20. Federal Budget Deficits, 1976–1980.
(in billions of dollars)
(fiscal years ending in year shown)

	Receipts	Outlays	Deficit
1976	$298.1 b	$371.8 b	$73.7 b
1978	$399.6 b	$458.7 b	$59.2 b
1980	$517.1 b	$590.9 b	$73.8 b

Source: *Economic Report of the President* (1988)

power in 1953. Like Nixon and Kissinger, Carter recognized Iran's importance as an oil-rich nation which bordered the Soviet Union and functioned as a reliable client state. The president first supported the shah but then watched helplessly as the dictator's repressive regime crumbled. Forced into exile, the deposed leader sought medical treatment in the United States. When Kissinger and the Rockefeller family convinced Carter to grant the request, outraged Iranian militants seized the United States embassy in Tehran and demanded repatriation of the shah and his fortune.

After the United States refused to comply, the Iranian government assumed control of the embassy hostages. Carter responded by freezing Iranian assets, severing diplomatic relations, and ordering trade sanctions. The White House portrayed the president as singularly committed to the release of the hostages and helped to dramatize their plight. Under pressure to break the deadlock, Carter ordered a military rescue operation in 1980, but two of the American helicopters necessary for the commando raid malfunctioned in a desert sand storm, killing eight servicemen and terminating the mission. Protesting the decision to

Exhibit 13–21. Location of Hostage Rescue Effort in Iran.

resolve the crisis through military means, Cyrus R. Vance became the first secretary of state to resign over a matter of policy since William Jennings Bryan in 1915. After complex negotiations with intermediaries over Iranian assets held by American banks, however, Tehran agreed to release the fifty-two remaining hostages—but only after Jimmy Carter left office. Hours after the inauguration of a new president on January 20, 1981, the American captives ended 444 days of incarceration. The Iranian hostage crisis remained a bitter symbol of the diminished capacity of the United States as a world power in the post-Vietnam era. It also helped to produce a major power shift in Washington.

SUGGESTED READINGS

The Nixon years are outlined with insight by Jonathan Schell, *The Time of Illusion: An Historical and Reflective Account of the Nixon Era* (1975). See also A. James Reichley, *Conservatives in an Age of Change: The Nixon and Ford Administrations* (1981). For foreign policy see Robert S. Litwak, *Détente and the Nixon Doctrine: American Foreign Policy and the Pursuit of Stability* (1984), and Robert Hargreaves, *Superpower: A Portrait of America in the 1970s* (1973). Critical accounts of approaches to the developing world include Mel Gurtov, *The Roots of Failure: United States Policy in the Third World* (1984), and John Stockwell, *In Search of Enemies: A CIA Story* (1978). See also Victor Marchetti and John D. Marks, *The CIA and the Cult of Intelligence* (1974).

The relevant sections of Herring, Karnow, and Turley, listed at the end of chapter 5, describe the last stages of the Vietnam War. See also Harry G. Summers Jr., *On Strategy: The Vietnam War in Context* (1981). These works can be supplemented by the policy assessments of Allan E. Goodman, *The Lost Peace: America's Search for a Negotiated Settlement of the Vietnam War* (1978), and Michael P. Sullivan, *The Vietnam War: A Study in the Making of American Policy* (1985). Norman Podhoretz, *Why We Were in Vietnam* (1982), provides a conservative defense of the Vietnam effort while Leslie H. Gelb and Richard K. Betts, *The Irony of Vietnam: The System Worked* (1979), defend the role of national security advisors. These assessments can be compared to the highly critical Gabriel Kolko, *Anatomy of a War: Vietnam, the United States, and the Modern Historical Experience* (1986), and William Shawcross, *Sideshow: Kissinger, Nixon, and the Destruction of Cambodia* (1979). Kissinger is treated to unflattering journalistic portraits in Tad Szulc, *The Illusion of Peace: Foreign Policy in the Nixon Years* (1978), and Seymour M. Hersh, *The Price of Power: Kissinger in the Nixon White House* (1983).

The relationship between the Vietnam War and political ferment at home is graphically described in Alexander Kendrick, *The Wound Within: America in the Vietnam Years, 1945–1974* (1974). For domestic protest see Todd Gitlin, *The Whole World is Watching: Mass Media in the Making and Unmaking of the New Left* (1980); the last segment of Gitlin, *The Sixties: Years of Hope, Days of Rage* (1987); and Nancy Zaroulis and Gerald Sullivan, *Who Spoke Up?: American Protest Against the War in Vietnam, 1963–1975* (1984). Nixonian social management is outlined in the last chapter of Otis L. Graham, Jr., *Toward a Planned Society: From*

Roosevelt to Nixon (1976), while economic policies are analyzed in Richard Barnet, *The Lean Years: Politics in the Age of Society* (1980). The best summation of Watergate remains Anthony Lukas, *Nightmare: The Underside of the Nixon Years* (1976). For psychological portraits of Nixon see Garry Wills, *Nixon Agonistes: The Crisis of the Self-Made Man* (1971), and Fawn Brodie, *Richard Nixon: The Shaping of His Character* (1981).

The Ford presidency is treated by Robert T. Hartmann, *Palace Politics: An Inside Account of the Ford Years* (1980), and James L. Sundquist, *The Decline and Resurgence of Congress* (1981). For the Carter administration see Haynes Johnson, *In the Absence of Power: Governing America* (1980), and Charles O. Jones, *The Trusteeship Presidency: Jimmy Carter and the United States Congress* (1988). The president's foreign policy is outlined in Gaddis Smith, *Morality, Reason, and Power: American Diplomacy in the Carter Years* (1986). Carter's 1980 defeat is analyzed by journalist Theodore H. White in the concluding segment of *America in Search of Itself: The Making of the President, 1956–1980* (1982).

Opposite Page:
Former President Gerald Ford, Ronald Reagan, and George Bush campaign for the 1980 election. Reagan successfully unified Republicans behind a conservative agenda.

14

THE REAGAN
REVOLUTION,
1980-1988

R onald Reagan introduced the most dramatic changes to the management of government since the New Deal. Sensing frustration with economic stagnation at home and declining world influence, Reagan sought to mobilize the American people for a new beginning. His two-term presidency succeeded in winning the support of a new coalition of conservatives, aspiring entrepreneurs, and professionals by implementing an ambitious program of government deregulation, lower taxes, reduced social welfare, and increased military spending. Yet Reaganomics failed to compensate for structural weaknesses in the American economy. As trade imbalances and budget deficits mounted in the 1980s, congressional Democrats played an increasingly large role in moderating the popular president's policies. By 1988, the Reagan program had come under careful scrutiny and intense debate.

REAGANOMICS

Jimmy Carter used the powers of incumbency in the 1980 Democratic primaries to turn back a challenge from Senator Edward M. Kennedy, who represented traditional Democratic constituencies associated with labor, civil rights, and social reform. But the president faced a more effective opponent when Ronald Reagan defeated George Bush in the Republican primaries and won the nomination for the top slot on the ticket. A minor star in 1940s film dramas and comedies, Reagan had forged anti-communist credentials as president of the Screen Actors Guild during the Hollywood Red Scare. As his movie career declined in the early 1950s, the actor hosted a weekly television western and then became national spokesman for General Electric. Moving into politics, Reagan espoused fiscal conservatism and traditional values. In 1966, he won the governorship of California, where he attracted attention as a militant opponent of student activism and a proponent of the Vietnam War. By 1980, Reagan had become the nation's leading conservative voice, questioning détente with the Soviets, demanding strong defense, and attacking government bureaucracy and inflationary spending on social welfare. Reagan claimed that federal regulation constituted the major problem of the economy and promised to cut "waste, extravagance, abuse, and outright fraud."

The Republican candidate also identified with values promoting family, religion, and traditional education. By doing so, Reagan attracted many southern Democrats and conservative Protestants to his party, particularly the Moral Majority followers of Reverend Jerry Falwell, a Southern Baptist minister. Like Falwell, the candidate hoped to redeem the nation from moral permissiveness and collectivist values. Following the prepared remarks in his acceptance speech at the 1980 Republican Convention, Reagan asked delegates to join his "crusade" to "recapture our destiny" with a moment of silent prayer. "God bless America!" he intoned as the moment passed. The nominee's heartfelt performance complemented his often repeated remark that the United States was an "island of freedom."

Reagan's campaign won the support of corporate leaders concerned with declining American influence in the world economy. But he also appealed to blue-collar and middle-class voters who hoped his economic policies would prove more successful than Carter's. In addition, Reagan attracted upscale professionals and entrepreneurs by refusing to acknowledge limits to the nation's power to solve economic problems. "We do not have to go on sharing scarcity," the candidate proclaimed in direct response to Carter's notion of economic and ecological limits. Promising that he would "take the government off the backs of people" and restore the nation's global power, Reagan announced that it was "morning in America." The message appealed to taxpayers concerned with inflation, government spending, and the erosion of overseas strength.

In an unusual reversal, Democrats stressed issues of war and peace while Republicans emphasized economics in the 1980 election. But Carter's allusions to Reagan as a right-wing threat to world peace backfired when the challenger appeared relaxed and amiable in a televised debate with the president. As Carter and Mondale waited in vain for settlement of the Iran hostage crisis, Reagan and vice-presidential candidate George Bush took 51 percent of the popular vote (nearly forty-four million) to the Democrats' 41 percent (less than thirty-six million). Representative John B. Anderson, a liberal Republican from Illinois, received less than 7 percent of the popular tally (below six million) as an independent candidate, but scored well with Jews dissatisfied with Carter's lukewarm approach to Israel. In the Electoral College, Reagan swamped the president by an overwhelming 489–49 margin. Meanwhile, Republicans captured control of

Exhibit 14–1. 1980 Election.

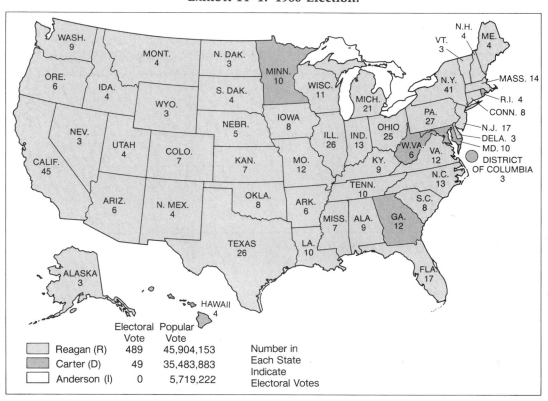

	Electoral Vote	Popular Vote	
Reagan (R)	489	45,904,153	Number in
Carter (D)	49	35,483,883	Each State Indicate
Anderson (I)	0	5,719,222	Electoral Votes

the Senate for the first time since 1952. As low Democratic turnout, particularly in the East, contributed to a less than 53 percent participation rate for eligible voters, Jimmy Carter became the second consecutive presidential incumbent to suffer defeat.

George Bush had accused Reagan of espousing "voodoo economics" during the Republican primaries. But Reagan insisted that he could reduce government spending while increasing outlays for defense, lower taxes while balancing the federal budget, and simultaneously restore economic prosperity. The president borrowed his reasoning from "supply-side" economists like Professor Arthur Laffer of the University of Southern California, who maintained that government regulations and high taxes held back production and pushed up prices. Supply-side policy called for generous tax cuts and government deregulation to increase employment and reduce inflation. Reagan insisted that the anticipation of improvements from his economic program would spur the market on to recovery. Popularizing proposals previously advanced by Republican congressional leaders Jack Kemp and William Roth, the president asked for the largest tax cut in history. In order to placate skeptical critics, the administration sent David Stockman, director of the Office of Management and Budget, to Congress with figures that purported to show that tax decreases would produce a balanced bud-

Exhibit 14–2. Gross National Product, 1981–1987.
(current dollars in billions)

1981	$3052.6 b
1983	$3405.7 b
1985	$4010.3 b
1987	$4486.2 b

Source: *Economic Report of the President* (1988)

Exhibit 14–3. Consumer Price Index, 1981–1987.
(1967-100)

1981	272.4
1983	298.4
1985	322.2
1987	340.4

Source: *Economic Report of the President* (1988)

Exhibit 14–4. National Defense & Veterans Outlays, 1980–1986.
(in billions of dollars)

1980	$155.2 b
1982	$209.3 b
1984	$253.0 b
1986 est	$292.4 b

Source: *Statistical Abstract of the United States* (1987)

get by 1984, even if offset by leaps in military spending. Despite Stockman's off-hand admission that the reductions served to ease taxes on high-income supporters of the president, conservative southern Democrats worked with House Republicans to pass the Reagan bill. Reagan had translated his impressive electoral victory into a working majority in Congress.

The Economic Recovery Act of 1981 enacted a three-year cumulative tax reduction of 23 percent on individual incomes. It also stipulated that tax rates would be indexed to inflation in order to eliminate "bracket creep," a pattern by which people moved into higher tax brackets without increased real income. The tax bill provided incentives for individual retirement accounts, reduced profit assessments on small corporations, and increased investment allowances. Total tax decreases came to $38 billion by 1984. "Reaganomics" led to a $150 billion tax reduction for corporations between 1981 and 1986.

Yet as unemployment surged to 10.8 percent in 1982 and budget deficits continued to soar, the Democratic congressional majority vowed to combat the deepening recession with new tax legislation. By closing loopholes and enacting stricter tax compliance, Congress restored nearly $100 billion in cut revenues over the next three years. The legislators also revoked about one-third of the 1981 corporate tax cuts. A 1982 provision requiring withholding of interest and dividend taxes, however, brought a massive protest organized by banks and financial institutions and congressional repeal the following year. Congress completed Reagan's tax program, nevertheless, when it passed comprehensive reforms in 1986 which dramatically reduced rates for corporations and wealthy individuals but eliminated or curtailed many lucrative deductions. The president's tax overhaul reduced the number of individual income brackets to three and shifted $120 billion over five years from individuals to corporations. Despite such changes, 1980s tax relief reduced the corporate share of total obligations and sharply increased the percentage of wealth controlled by the affluent.

Exhibit 14–5. National Defense as Percent of Total Federal Outlays, 1975–1986.

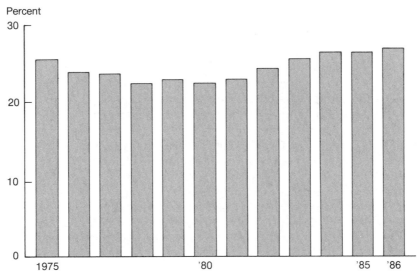

Exhibit 14–6. Unemployment Rates, 1981–1987.

	Total	Black
1981	7.5%	14.3%
1983	9.5%	15.6%
1985	7.1%	15.1%
1987	6.1%	13.0%

Source: *Economic Report of the President* (1988)

Exhibit 14–7. Corporate Profits & Dividends After Taxes, 1981–1987* (in billions of dollars)

1981	$106.8 b
1983	$136.5 b
1985	$180.9 b
1987	$167.8 b

Source: *Economic Report of the President* (1988)

* includes inventory valuation and capital consumption adjustments

Although the economy recovered from the recession of 1981–1982, huge deficits in the federal budget continued to trouble economic planners. But the president refused to go along with a congressional preference for tax increases and slower defense buildups. Facing a $200 billion budget deficit in 1985, Congress passed the Gramm-Rudman-Hollings Act, which mandated steady decreases in the deficit until the budget could be balanced in 1991. If deficit targets were not met, the bill required automatic, across-the-board spending cuts. Despite this dramatic attempt to control appropriations, Congress failed to agree on budget reductions, and the Supreme Court declared the automatic cuts unconstitutional in 1986. By fiscal 1987, the budget of the United States Government had risen to $576 billion and Congress agreed to massive spending cuts.

Despite its pledge to redeem the American economy, Reaganomics had difficulty in arresting enormous foreign trade deficits, which mushroomed to $161 billion in 1987. Part of the problem stemmed from budget deficits which compelled the government to borrow money in international exchanges. The resulting shortage of dollars raised the price of American exports. Foreign-based manufacture by American multinational corporations and international competition also contributed to rising trade deficits, resulting in the loss of thousands of American industrial jobs. Congressional representatives from beleaguered textile, shoe, and copper producing regions succeeded in passing legislation that curbed imports in 1985, but Reagan vetoed the measure as protectionist. After Japanese manufacturers dumped low-priced computer chips in the United States in 1987, however, the president agreed to place retaliatory tariffs on their electronics products. By then, the American trade deficit with Japan had surpassed $50 billion. Congress passed a second trade bill in 1988 that gave the president broad power to retaliate against unfair foreign trade practices and provided over

Exhibit 14–8. Federal Budget Deficits, 1980–1988.
(in billions of dollars)
(fiscal years ending in year shown)

	Receipts	*Outlays*	*Deficit*
1980	$517.1 b	$590.9 b	$73.8 b
1982	$617.8 b	$745.7 b	$127.9 b
1984	$666.5 b	$851.8 b	$185.3 b
1986	$769.1 b	$990.3 b	$221.2 b
1988 est	$909.2 b	$1055.9 b	$146.7 b

Source: *Economic Report of the President* (1988)

Exhibit 14–9. Exports & Imports, 1981–1985.
(in billions of dollars)

	Imports	*Exports*
1981	$261.0 b	$233.7 b
1983	$258.0 b	$200.5 b
1985	$343.3 b	$213.1 b

Source: *Statistical Abstract of the United States* (1987)

Exhibit 14–10. Research & Development, 1980–1986.
(current dollars in billions)

	Total	*Defense and Space-related*
1980	$62.6b	$18.2b
1983	$87.1b	$29.6b
1986 est.	$118.6b	$43.9b

Source: *Statistical Abstract of the United States* (1987)

$3 billion in aid to American industries and workers facing overseas competition. But Reagan vetoed the package because one provision required manufactures to give workers sixty days notice of plant closings and major layoffs. When a defiant Congress easily passed a new plant closing bill, the president allowed it to become law without his signature. Congress then approved much of the original trade bill and Reagan agreed to sign it.

New jobs in computer assembly and retail and food service chains contributed to low unemployment rates in states such as Massachusetts and California. But although they replaced many of the blue-collar jobs lost to foreign competition, the new positions usually came in non-union industries offering low wage scales and little chance for advancement. More than half the nine million jobs created between 1981 and 1986, for example, paid less than $7000 a year, many of them attracting older Americans unable to get by on social security and pensions.

Similar paradoxes prevailed in the stock market, where soaring prices created billions of dollars of profits for traders in the mid-1980s. Yet analysts conceded

Exhibit 14–11. Consumer Credit Outstanding, 1980–1987.
(rounded in billions as of December of each year)

1980	$369 b
1981	$390 b
1983	$468 b
1985	$657 b
1987	$756 b

Source: *Economic Report of the President* (1988)

that foreign investment, projected to reach $700 billion by 1990, accounted for much of the boom and that Americans would be paying an annual $60 billion in interest for these obligations by the end of the decade. Meanwhile, Wall Street feared that Mexico, Brazil, and Argentina would default on $250 billion of loans and interest owed to American banks. In 1985, the United States became a debtor nation for the first time since 1914, and the center of international capital shifted from New York to Tokyo. Two years later, foreign investors reacted to the bloated federal budget and continuing trade deficits by abandoning the stock market. On October 19, 1987, the New York Stock Exchange suffered its worst day in history with a calamitous one-day drop of 508 points on the Dow Jones Average. In eight terrifying days, the stock market lost one-third of its value. By the time the crash ended, the New York exchange assessed total investor loss at $1 trillion. Fearful of future assaults on the declining dollar, foreign speculators sold off American currency. By the end of the month, the exchange rate between the dollar and the Japanese yen had tumbled to its lowest point since the late-1940s. Although the market recovered from its shock in 1988, economic analysts remained nervous about the $2.4 trillion consumer debt and persistent trade and budget deficits. Economic indices promised continuing prosperity, but Americans seemed no closer to controlling their unpredictable and debt-ridden economy than they were when Reagan first took office.

REAGAN DEREGULATION

Supply-side economists saw excessive government interference as a major constraint on private initiative. Influenced by conservative planners in "think tanks" such as the Heritage Foundation and the American Enterprise Institute, Reagan quickly abolished Carter's wage-pricing guidelines. Yet the new administration also welcomed the deregulation begun in the Carter years. Following an antimonopoly suit filed against American Telephone and Telegraph (AT&T) in 1978, the corporation agreed to divest itself of local telephone service. The 1982 divestiture created twenty-three independent companies and permitted AT&T and other subsidiaries to compete on an unregulated basis in the lucrative computer processing and information service business. Similar results stemmed from Carter's Monetary Control Act of 1980. The law brought nearly all financial institutions under Federal Reserve protection and regulation, but encouraged greater competition by permitting all banks to offer interest-bearing checking accounts and full consumer services. A Banking Act of 1982 also gave new investment and lending authority to saving institutions. When the airlines industry completed the deregulation also initiated by Carter, Reagan officials pointed to increased competition, lower fares, and more flexible schedules. The president also accelerated Carter's deregulation of domestic oil prices and pipeline routes, asked Congress to reduce the windfall profits tax, and cut funding for research on alternative fuel sources. In this spirit, Reagan approved a congressional plan to allow states to raise the speed limit on interstate freeways to 65 mph in 1987.

As OPEC prices declined by 1982, many Americans welcomed the return to a deregulated market. But there were unforeseen consequences to the Carter-Reagan policies. When the Republican president reduced the authority of the Occupational Safety and Health Administration (OSHA) in 1981, union representatives complained that the administration had abandoned American workers to excessive noise levels and lethal chemical exposure. Deregulation of banking encouraged the offering of loan and investment services by unqualified providers and resulted in the bankruptcy of vulnerable savings and loan institutions. By 1987, cut-throat competition in the airlines industry had brought a wave of bankruptcies and mergers, while the absence of coordinated scheduling had produced flight delays and overcrowded skies at peak periods. Beleaguered air traffic controllers complained that the Federal Aviation Administration (FAA) had not allocated sufficent personnel and technology to deal with the increase in domestic flights. Meanwhile, the restructuring of the telephone industry encouraged the lowering of long-distance rates for the affluent at the expense of increased costs for local service.

Despite Reagan's concern for free-market economics, the government continued agricultural price supports and the president authorized the purchase of $2 billion of surplus milk products. Reagan also signed a 1985 farm bill appropriating nearly $170 billion in income subsidies, price supports, and food stamps for the next five years. Rampant mortgage foreclosures and bankruptcies among farmers, which reached their highest level since 1946, played a role in prompting such spending by a cost-conscious Congress and a conservative president when farmers descended upon Washington in several protests. The administration's greatest problem in curtailing federal controls, however, came with its policy of eliminating "unnecessary" environmental safeguards. Secretary of the Interior James G. Watt, an enterprising Wyoming attorney, pursued pro-development policies by leasing off-shore oil drilling rights and proposing timber sales in national park lands. Under intense criticism from environmentalists and liberals, Watt resigned in 1983.

The Reagan administration's coziness with developers and industrialists surfaced in a major scandal when Anne M. Burford, the administrator of the Environmental Protection Agency (EPA), resigned amid congressional investigations

Exhibit 14–12. Government Spending as Percentage of Gross National Product, 1976–1986

1976	33.9%
1986	22.8%

Source: *Economic Report of the President* (1977)
Economic Report of the President (1988)

into charges of unethical conduct in 1983. Congress accused Burford of promoting "sweetheart" deals between the EPA and some of the industries it regulated, but Reagan ordered the administrator not to provide materials sought by a House subcommittee. When the full House cited Burford for contempt, the Reagan Justice Department refused to prosecute. Nevertheless, a jury convicted Rita M. Lavelle, former head of a "superfund" program to clean up toxic waste dumps, of perjury and obstruction of a congressional investigation. In response to abuses at the EPA, Congress strengthened the laws regarding the handling of hazardous wastes, prohibiting the land disposal of liquid and some solid materials. Reagan, moreover, agreed to an $8.5 billion superfund for a five-year cleanup of toxic dumps in 1986, although he refused to pursue controls on industrial emissions until scientists completed more research on the effects of "acid rain."

Buoyed by a cooperative Congress and supportive electorate, Reagan cut domestic programs by $35 billion and introduced welfare reform in 1981. Confining benefits to the "truly needy," the president reduced allowable deductions and tax breaks. Despite Reagan's conviction that welfare sapped initiative and trapped recipients in impoverishment, poverty remained a reflection of complex national economic forces. By 1981, thirty-two million Americans, or one-seventh the nation, had cash incomes lower than minimal standards established by the federal government. Thirty-eight percent of these people were children, while two-thirds of poor adults were women. Eight million Americans, moreover, found themselves forced into poverty between the energy crisis of 1979 and the end of the 1981–1982 recession. Political and economic pressures pushed the administration to address the problems of economic deprivation. During the 1982 recession, the president signed a gas tax and highway jobs measure appropriating $71 billion in transportation projects for the next four years. Reagan also referred the deteriorating social security situation to a presidential commission, and in 1983 supported a plan to revitalize the troubled system. By increasing payroll taxes on both employers and employees, social security expanded its outlays from $138 billion in 1981 to $200 billion in 1986. Medicare spending, which amounted to $41 billion in 1981, leaped to $74 billion in 1986. The president also persuaded Congress to appropriate $1.7 billion for a drug enforcement and education program in 1986.

Although Reagan had won surprising support among organized labor in 1980, he reacted strongly to a walkout of government air traffic controllers during his first year in office. Firing the twelve thousand striking technicians and

Exhibit 14–13. Federal Social Welfare Expenditures, 1980–1984.
(rounded billions of dollars)

1980	$302.6 b
1982	$367.7 b
1984 prel	$419.3 b

Source: *Statistical Abstract of the United States* (1987)

dissolving their union, the president ordered the FAA to use military controllers in their place. The strategy worked and appeared to symbolize management's harsh approach to labor in the Reagan economy. The president, however, left the more complex question of illegal alien labor to Congress. After years of squabbling, the legislators fashioned a compromise in the Immigration Act of 1986. The law fined employers who knowingly hired illegal aliens, but created an amnesty program for millions of illegal immigrants (mainly Mexican-Americans) who could prove their entry to the United States before 1982. By 1988, two million of the nation's estimated six million illegal aliens had applied for amnesty under terms of the legislation.

Reagan did not win approval for his entire political agenda. When the president asked for a "new federalism" in his State of the Union message of 1982, Congress refused to shift programs to the poorly funded states. Neither did the legislators respond to the president's proposal for tuition tax credits for private school education, which liberals saw as a means of undermining racial integration. Nor did Congress approve abolition of the departments of Energy and Education. Furthermore, Congress failed to pass constitutional amendments requiring a balanced budget, barring abortion, or permitting school prayer. Yet the conservative administration won substantial victories. During 1978, the Burger Court had limited preferential treatment of minorities in education in the Bakke case by prohibiting rigid admission quotas. The Reagan Justice Department happily responded by reducing affirmative action and school desegregation suits. The president also expressed pleasure when the Equal Rights Amendment (ERA) fell three states short of ratification in late 1982, and when the House came six votes shy of reviving the measure early the next year.

Despite Reagan's open conflict with feminists on such issues as the ERA, legalized abortion, and subsidized day care, the administration sought out conservative women such as Elizabeth Dole (Secretary of Transportation), Margaret Heckler (Secretary of Health and Human Services), and Jeane J. Kirkpatrick (Ambassador to the United Nations). In his most dramatic move, Reagan appointed conservative Judge Sandra Day O'Connor in 1981 to become the first woman to sit on the Supreme Court. Since O'Connor's record included qualified support for a woman's right to abortion, conservatives such as Reverend Falwell criticized the nomination. Yet Reagan moved further toward establishing a conservative majority on the Court when Chief Justice Warren Burger retired in 1986. The president not only chose Antonin Scalia, a conservative academic legalist, to fill the vacancy, but elevated William Rehnquist, the Court's most conservative member, to the presiding chair. Reagan anticipated further influence on the Court when he selected appeals court judge and constitutional scholar Robert H. Bork to fill a third vacancy in 1987. But a grass-roots campaign of liberals, feminists, and civil rights activists convinced the Senate that Bork's strict interpretation of constitutional rights appeared "extremist" and potentially disruptive of political stability. Forced to abandon the nominee, Reagan ultimately settled on a less abrasive conservative, Judge Anthony M. Kennedy of California.

Sandra Day O'Connor became the first woman to serve on the Supreme Court in 1981. Reagan's three appointments moved the Court to the right.

RE-ELECTION AND THE REAGAN DOCTRINE

By 1984, a sharp drop in oil prices had eased inflation and accelerated the economic recovery begun two years earlier. Voters who since the 1930s had identified the Democrats as the party of prosperity, now looked to the Republicans. "We Brought America Back," the White House proclaimed. Meanwhile, Democrats chose among three finalists in the presidential race. Reverend Jesse Jackson's "rainbow coalition" attempted to link those outside the Reagan constituency: feminists, racial minorities, the poor, and peace activists. Senator Gary Hart of Colorado appealed to young urban professionals and focused upon the technological nature of the new service economy. But it was former Vice President Mondale who carried the Democrats' traditional constituencies in labor, education, and the big cities, and faced Reagan in the 1984 election. Mondale's running mate was Representative Geraldine A. Ferraro of New York, the first woman to be nominated for national office by a major party.

Exhibit 14–14. Percent of Voting Age Population Participating in Presidential Elections, 1960–1984.

1960	62.8
1964	61.9
1968	60.9
1972	55.2
1976	53.5
1980	52.6
1984	53.1

Source: *Statistical Abstract of the United States* (1987)

Mondale and Ferraro found themselves caught in the growing polarization between the affluent and poor. By the 1980s, the richest fifth of Americans continued to absorb over 41 percent of national income while the lowest fifth subsisted on 5 percent. Fearful of offending middle-class voters, Mondale barely challenged Reagan's huge military budget or social program cuts. The candidate tried to preserve the alliance of selected corporations, unions, and big government that had defined the Democratic party since World War II. Yet corporate leadership had abandoned these ties, and union membership and bargaining power had suffered in an economy decreasingly dependent on manufacturing. In contrast, Republican campaign committees outspent the Democrats 4–1 and used capital-intensive techniques of campaigning such as media advertising and sophisticated polling. Furthermore, Reagan's informality and lack of pretension made him a believable communicator despite a difficulty with nuance and detail.

The result proved to be a stunning Republican victory. With 59 percent of the popular vote, the president captured majorities in every state but Mondale's Minnesota and the District of Columbia. The Democrats tallied 90 percent among blacks, 65 percent among Hispanics, and 53 percent among those earning under $12,500 a year. In contrast, Republicans scored 80 percent among evangelical Christians, 72 percent among southern whites, and 68 percent among those earning over $50,000 a year. Most disturbing to the Democrats, however, was Reagan's majority among voters between the ages of eighteen and twenty-five. For these Americans, Reagan and the Republicans represented new economic opportunity, and Mondale and the Democrats stood for a tired status-quo. Eligible voter participation in the election increased slightly to just over 53 percent.

Reagan campaigned on a revitalized sense of national pride, contrasting American moral superiority to the "evil empire" of the Soviet Union. In his second inaugural, the president called the United States the "blessed land" of a "chosen people" and predicted there were no limits to growth and progress. Jimmy Carter had translated this moral imperative into a demand that American allies like Chile and El Salvador adhere to higher standards of human rights. But United Nations Ambassador Kirkpatrick, a foreign affairs specialist from Georgetown University, rejected this policy as naive and insisted in 1983 that "authoritarian" dictatorships of the right were susceptible to democratic change while "totalitarian" regimes of the left were not. The Reagan administration held Soviet adventurism in the developing nations responsible for "world terrorism"

JEANE J. KIRKPATRICK
1926–

Like her boss, Ronald Reagan, Jeane Kirkpatrick became a prominent Republican after years of loyalty to the Democratic party. Born into a staunchly Democratic family, Kirkpatrick went to Barnard and Columbia, but delayed her career to care for family responsibilities. She returned to academic life in the early 1960s and joined the faculty of Georgetown University in 1967, completing her Ph.D. in political science at Columbia University the following year. Quickly establishing herself as a prolific and respected scholar, Kirkpatrick produced significant work on American politics and foreign policy.

Kirkpatrick played an active role in the Democratic party in the 1960s and early 1970s, but grew steadily estranged from liberal politics after 1968. Controversies over the Vietnam War seemed to change the party in ways she found extremely disturbing. Kirkpatrick particularly objected to the influx of Democratic dissidents she described as "antiwar, antigrowth, antibusiness, antilabor..." She found, moreover, that Democrats now expressed a reluctance to wield military power to defend American interests. Kirkpatrick preferred an older version of liberalism best articulated in the 1970s by Senators Henry Jackson of Washington and Hubert Humphrey of Minnesota. Characterizing herself as a "welfare conservative," she defended the "noble tradition of caring in domestic affairs, of...providing minimum standards of well-being" while simultaneously "being deeply persuaded of the legitimacy and success of American society and the failure and tyranny of Communist societies."

In 1972, Kirkpatrick helped to organize the Coalition for a Democratic Majority to limit the influence of George McGovern's wing of the Democratic party. These neo-conservatives opposed the values of the counterculture and explicitly rejected the view that America was a sick society dominated by materialism and technology. They saw the McGovern campaign as dangerously radical and predicated on unrealistic, utopian reform impulses. And coalition members believed that *(cont.)*

and most global conflict. Consequently, by 1985 national security planners adhered to an unofficial "Reagan Doctrine" in which the CIA rebuilt its covert action capacity by assisting anti-communist insurgencies across the world. During that year, the president persuaded Congress to lift the 1976 restrictions on CIA activity in Angola, and personally designated the UNITA recipients of an $11 million military aid program for anti-government subversion, thereby allying the United States with a similar South African effort. The administration also supplied rebel armies in Afghanistan, Cambodia, Ethiopia, and Nicaragua.

Despite its insistence that communism contributed to the worst human rights abuses, the Reagan administration faced intense pressure from Congress when the white minority government of South Africa used violence against black demonstrators in 1984. Protests against racial apartheid spread around the United *(cont.)* the Democratic nominee lacked sensitivity to the threat that communism and the Soviet Union posed to American interests.

The issue of foreign policy finally prompted Kirkpatrick's break with the party during the Carter administration. She insisted that the Democratic president reflected the guilt-ridden and irresolute approach to world affairs that pervaded the leadership of his party. Kirkpatrick voiced these concerns in a biting article for the conservative journal *Commentary*. Entitled "Dictatorships and Double Standards," her polemic attacked the failure of Carter's foreign policy as "clear to everyone except its architects." Kirkpatrick particularly scored the administration for opposing pro-American right-wing authoritarians while tolerating leftist or revolutionary regimes unfriendly to the United States. She found the source of this double standard in liberal guilt over America's alleged role as a defender of an exploitative *status quo* in the third world. Kirkpatrick further argued that for all their faults, right-wing authoritarians more easily accepted democratic reforms than left-wing totalitarians. Consequently, support of rightist dictatorships served both American interests and ideas. "Liberal idealism," she concluded, "need not be identical with masochism, and need not be incompatible with the defense of freedom and the national interest."

Deeply impressed by the *Commentary* piece, Ronald Reagan appointed Kirkpatrick as Ambassador to the United Nations shortly after his election in 1980. During her five years at the United Nations, she acquired a reputation as a combative and forthright advocate of American policy, but her role as United Nations ambassador increasingly frustrated her. Kirkpatrick called the body a "dismal show" where conflicts never were resolved. When Reagan did not appoint her to a high-level policy-making position, she resigned in 1985 and returned to Georgetown. Almost simultaneously, she joined the Republican party. One of the few prominent women to serve in the Reagan administration, Kirkpatrick often received press consideration as a possible candidate for elective office or a future political appointment. Adored by conservatives and vilified by liberals, Jeane Kirkpatrick remained an outspoken beacon of plain talk and provocative viewpoints. ■

States. As American civil rights leaders led daily demonstrations against apartheid at the South African embassy, conservative Republicans embraced the campaign to improve the party's image in the area of race relations. The administration responded with a policy of "constructive engagement" which called for peaceful persuasion of an anti-communist ally rich in strategic materials. But congressional Republicans saw this as implicit support for the repressive South African regime. Only when the House passed legislation to impose sanctions in 1985 did the president ban the sale of South African gold coins and prohibit new bank loans and computer sales to Pretoria. The following year, Congress banned imports of several South African goods, suspended direct air travel, and promised stricter sanctions if apartheid continued. In a dramatic foreign policy defeat, Reagan's veto of the measure was easily overridden in both houses.

The administration faced another challenge to its support of anti-communist allies when the dictatorship of Ferdinand E. Marcos of the Philippines fell in early 1986. Under pressure from the United States, Marcos had called for popular elections to be monitored by American observers. Reagan first backed Marcos, but Senator Richard Lugar, Republican Foreign Relations Committee Chairman, persuaded the president to honor commitments to democracy by abandoning his personal friend. Following the vote, the international election commission accused Marcos of widespread fraud, and opposition candidate Corazon Aquino declared herself president. When Aquino won support from dissident military leaders and millions of Filipinos demonstrating in the streets, Marcos fled to Hawaii. Not long after, the United States escorted another ally, Haiti's Jean-Claude Duvalier, to safety in Europe after rioting broke out on Duvalier's improverished Caribbean island. As relations with military dictatorships in Chile and Paraguay cooled by 1986, Reagan announced that the United States would encourage democratic movements among right-wing allies. The following year, South Korean students led massive street protests to accelerate a timetable for national elections and the Reagan administration successfully prevailed upon the dictatorship in Seoul to agree. The State Department opposed another dictator in 1988 when federal prosecutors in Miami and Tampa indicted Panamanian strong man General Manuel Antonio Noriega for international drug trafficking. But Noriega, a former CIA asset and administration ally, resisted Washington's attempts to use an embargo and other pressures to force him from power.

THE MIDEAST QUAGMIRE

Challenges to American power in the strategic Middle East proved even more frustrating for Reagan. During 1982, Israel invaded Lebanon and bombed West Beirut to destroy the bases of Palestinian resistance fighters. Meanwhile, a Christian militia sponsored by the Israelis entered two Palestinian refugee camps and massacred hundreds of unarmed civilians. Although the United States supported the Israeli move into Lebanon, it condemned the massacres and sent 1200 Marines to participate in a four-nation peacekeeping force. But the Americans soon clashed with Syrian troops and Moslem militiamen allied with Iran, resulting in two truck bomb attacks in Beirut which killed 241 American servicemen. Amidst Pentagon objections that the Marines had been deployed for diplomatic purposes instead of military, Congress invoked the War Powers Act for the first time. Although Reagan stipulated that he did not recognize the constitutionality of the law, he agreed to withdraw all troops from Lebanon in eighteen months. With the consensus over Middle East policy split for the first time in the Cold War, the president removed the last forces by 1984. By then, peace in the Lebanese civil war appeared more remote than ever and American goals unclear.

The Reagan administration's Middle East policy centered on the protection of regional oil fields and shipping lanes, support for "moderate" Arab leaders, and a steady commitment to Israel's security. But while the United States spent $4.5 billion a year on military and economic aid to the Israelis, it failed to forcefully address the issue of peace between Israel and the Arabs. Like his predecessors,

Exhibit 14–15. Lebanon.

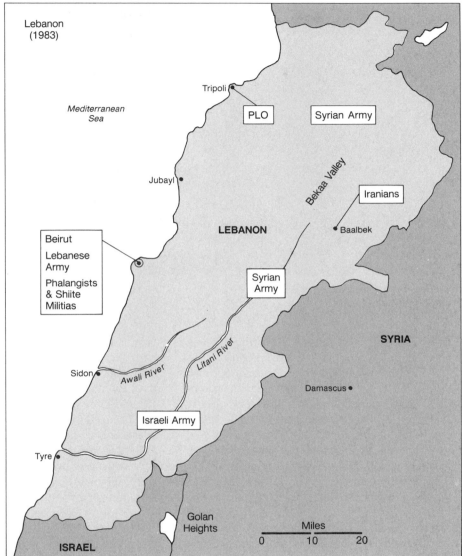

Reagan seriously underestimated the importance of Arab nationalism and Islamic fundamentalism. When Palestinian youth organized an unarmed uprising against Israeli occupation of the West Bank and Gaza territories in 1988, Secretary of State George P. Shultz attempted to start negotiations by proposing an international peace conference. But the conservative Israeli government rejected talks with "terrorists" and the Palestine Liberation Organization (PLO) condemned Shultz's refusal to meet with their leaders. Despite the rebuke, the secretary refused to consider the use of economic pressure to bring Israel to the bargaining table.

Military personnel sift through the wreckage of the American Marine barracks in Beirut following a devastating bombing by Moslem fighters allied with Iran in 1982.

Arab nationalists perceived the United States as a protector of Israeli expansion and as an imperialist force in the Middle East. As a result, Americans found themselves the targets of violent attacks, kidnappings, and hijackings. After an elderly American was shot and tossed overboard from an Italian cruise ship in 1985, Reagan ordered Air Force fighters to force the landing of the Egyptian civil airliner carrying the accused terrorists. The president soon accused radical Libya of supporting Middle East terrorism and ordered a trade embargo against that nation. Early in 1986, Reagan deployed massive air and naval forces to challenge Tripoli's assertion of sovereignty over the Gulf of Sidra, a large inlet on Libya's Mediterranean coast. When the United States claimed intelligence linking the Libyans to the bombing of a West German discothèque frequented by American military personnel, Reagan ordered an air attack on Libya, killing forty people and destroying the family quarters of Libyan leader Moammar Gadhafi. This show of force expressed American frustration toward the spread of terrorism but alienated allies on the European continent and in the Moslem Middle East. Nonetheless, in order to further traumatize Gadhafi, the White House conducted a "disinformation" campaign in the American press which suggested that the United States planned further attacks.

While the Reagan administration publicly depicted Gadhafi as a major source of terrorism, it privately held revolutionary Iran responsible. Tying Tehran to the capture of several American hostages in Lebanon by Shiite Moslem extremists, the United States embargoed military shipments to Iran and urged European allies to do the same. Later, however, concern over potential Soviet influence in the region and hopes for renewed ties with Tehran led the administration to re-evaluate its relationship with Iran. The president, moreover, felt political pres-

Exhibit 14–16. Libya & Gulf of Sidra.

sure to win the freedom of the hostages, while CIA Director William J. Casey desperately sought the release of kidnapped Beirut station chief William Francis Buckley, the agency's top expert on counter-terrorism. Using Israeli intermediaries and private arms dealers, National Security Council operatives began to arrange an exchange of American arms for the hostages in Lebanon in 1985. The complex arrangement centered on the sale and transfer of two thousand anti-tank missiles for Iran's use in its war against Iraq. American officials even accompanied one arms shipment in an unpublicized visit to Tehran. The covert and risky arms deal violated Reagan's public pledge to never negotiate with terrorists. But even news that a tortured and emaciated Buckley had died in captivity failed to deter the president from his efforts to free the remaining hostages. Release of several Americans taken in the hijacking of a TWA airliner in 1985 and subsequent freedom for three of the Beirut captives convinced the administration it was on the right track.

Once a Beirut newspaper leaked details of the bizarre exchange in November 1986, however, the Reagan administration denounced the trading of arms for hostages and resumed its hard-line policy toward Tehran. As the "tanker war" between Iran and Iraq escalated in 1987, the United States became increasingly concerned with assuring Western and Japanese access to Middle Eastern oil. When Iran refused to accept a United Nations Security Council resolution for a cease-fire, Washington pressed the Soviet Union to support an arms embargo. Not satisfied with the response, and fearing increased Soviet influence in the Persian Gulf, Reagan invoked the Carter Doctrine to deploy a Navy task force of ultimately forty ships to the strategic waterway. The president initially instructed the Navy to escort eleven Kuwaiti oil tankers which the United States had "re-flagged" as American ships.

The risks of a naval presence in the gulf became clear in May 1987 when bombers belonging to Iraq, Iran's opponent, attacked the frigate *U.S.S. Stark*, killing twenty-eight American sailors. As Iranian mines continued to damage com-

Exhibit 14–17. Persian Gulf Shipping Lanes.

mercial shipping, moreover, Reagan sent eight minesweepers and a fleet of attack helicopters to the gulf. Between late 1987 and mid-1988, the United States responded to Tehran's naval provocations by destroying strategic Iranian oil platforms and several of its war vessels. Although Iran bitterly denounced the American presence in its neighboring waters, Reagan repeatedly defended the mission as one befitting a world power responsible for the maintenance of peaceful navigation. Yet the president's ill-defined policy came under fire in July 1988 when the Navy inadvertently shot down an Iranian airliner flying over the gulf during a minor confrontation involving warships of the two nations. The disaster killed 290 civilians and raised questions about the Navy's ability to carry out sensitive policing operations in an area such as the well-travelled Persian Gulf. One week later, however, Iran announced its desire to seek a negotiated end to the war with Iraq and peace talks soon commenced.

CRUSADE IN CENTRAL AMERICA

The Reagan administration put particular stress on anti-communism in Central America and the Caribbean. During 1980, Cuba's Fidel Castro had permitted 125,000 exiles to go to the United States, but American officials charged that many of the refugees were criminals, mental patients, and social undesirables. As relations between Havana and Washington deteriorated, Castro consolidated ties with the Marxist government of the tiny Caribbean island of Grenada. But when dissident Marxists murdered that nation's prime minister and ruling leaders in 1983, Reagan used the pretext of civil strife to mount an invasion against the Cuban client state. Labeling the operation a "rescue mission" to protect one thousand American medical students, the president sent 4600 marines, rangers, and paratroopers to take control of the island in a matter of days. Polls revealed public endorsement of the nation's first military victory in the post-Vietnam era.

In Central America's impoverished El Salvador, the administration faced a more complex challenge. A 1980 military coup had precipitated a guerrilla movement with strong ties to trade union and democratic elements. But while President Carter pushed for a centrist government that adhered to moderate reforms, he encouraged military and para-military units to defeat the guerrilla insurgency. The result was a bloody civil war in which government security forces and vigilante "death squads" accounted for an estimated thirty thousand civilian killings between 1980 and 1983. The Reagan administration, fearing a communist revolution, stepped up the Carter program of military aid, although Congress attached riders requiring the president to certify human rights progress and democratic reforms. When centrist leader José Napoleón Duarte won a 1984 election boycotted by the left but supervised by international observers, Congress approved nearly $200 million in military aid to defeat the guerrillas who dominated much of the countryside. The flow of American money enabled the Salvadoran government to conduct brutal bombings of peasant villages that reminded critics of the Vietnam War. But by 1987, the conflict had so devastated the Salvadoran economy that Duarte sought to incorporate the rebels into the country's political structure. Nevertheless, the right-wing ARENA party won control of the National Assembly the following year and vowed to crush the widespread insurgency by force.

The Reagan administration directed its greatest vigilance against Nicaragua. Directly upon assuming office in 1981, the president suspended economic aid, claiming that the Sandinista government of Daniel Ortega wanted to establish a Marxist state under the influence of Cuba and the Soviet Union. Reagan authorized the CIA to support a rebel army to force the overthrow of the Nicaraguan

Exhibit 14–18. Central America and Caribbean.

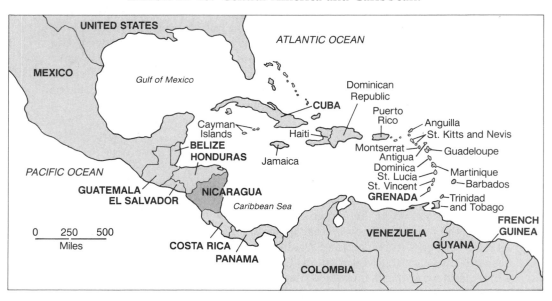

government. When news reports in 1982 described a CIA manual which advocated the kidnapping and killing of Nicaraguan officials, Congress passed the first Boland Amendment to prohibit direct agency activity in overthrowing the Sandinistas. Two years later, the legislators learned that the CIA had mined Nicaraguan harbors. In response, angry House members adopted a second Boland Amendment and handed Reagan a major defeat. The 1984 measure stipulated that no funds of any military or intelligence agency be used to support military or paramilitary operations in Nicaragua.

When Managua protested the mining of its ports to the World Court, the United States boycotted the proceedings. In 1986, the Court ruled that Washington had violated international law by mining and attacking Nicaraguan ports and by aiding the "contra" rebels. The House rejected assistance to the insurgents in 1985, but provided $27 million in "humanitarian" aid when Sandinista leader Daniel Ortega flew to Moscow seeking financing. Reagan also announced a trade embargo against Nicaragua. With election fears of appeasing communism and deserting the president's "freedom fighters," Congress awarded $100 million in military and economic aid to the contras in 1986 and lifted restrictions on CIA activity.

Like all Cold War presidents, Reagan viewed legislative restrictions on his actions as unwarranted intrusions into his constitutional powers. As a result, he sought to bypass Boland Amendment prohibitions on aid to the contras by encouraging financial contributions of $36.7 million for that purpose from both wealthy Americans and conservative allies such as Saudi Arabia and Taiwan. Meanwhile, CIA Director William Casey, National Security Advisor Rear Admiral John M. Poindexter, and NSC aide Lieutenant Colonel Oliver North coordinated a scheme to divert profits from the $38 million Iranian arms sales to the "freedom fighters" in Central America. Following orders from Casey, North used

CIA Director William Casey, named by NSC aide Oliver North as the mastermind of the scheme to divert funds (from the sale of arms to Iran) to the Nicaraguan contras.

the president's name and illegal logistical and tactical support from the CIA to establish a private network of men, equipment, corporations, and Swiss bank accounts designed to channel military supplies to the contras. The Reagan administration also pressured the governments of Honduras and Costa Rica to permit rebel bases to operate from their territory.

Disclosure of the Iran-Contra diversion in late 1986 created the greatest crisis of Reagan's presidency. Having weathered an assassin's bullet in 1981, the chief executive had forged a reputation as a survivor, a "teflon" president to whom no blame stuck. But after first denying the arms sale to Iran and then insisting that missiles were not traded for hostages, Reagan had to face questions about his own involvement in the illegal transfer of funds to the contras. A presidential commission led by former Senator John Tower concluded in 1987 that the commander-in-chief had mismanaged his staff, but that he had no personal knowledge of the diversion. Televised hearings conducted by the House and Senate Committees investigating the Iran-Contra affair later supported this conclusion. Yet Reagan felt compelled to fire North, accept Poindexter's resignation, and support Attorney General Edwin Meese III's request that Lawrence Walsh, a former president of the American Bar Association, be appointed special prosecutor in the case. Walsh indicted North, Poindexter, and two private arms dealers in 1988 for conspiring to defraud the government and for various coverup charges, including the destruction of official documents. But Reagan reiterated

Lt. Colonel Oliver North's televised testimony before the Joint Select Committee on Iran-Contra revealed deep divisions among the American people over the fundamentals of foreign policy.

his belief that "Ollie" North was "an American hero" for assisting the contras and refused to rule out eventual pardons for Poindexter and the former NSC marine.

Despite North's sincere and compelling performance in the televised hearings of the summer of 1987, moderate Republicans joined Democrats on the investigation committees to issue a harsh assessment of the Reagan administration's involvement in the Iran-Contra scandal. In a year's-end report that summarized the most thoroughly and highly publicized investigation since Watergate, panel participants complained of "pervasive dishonesty and inordinate secrecy" and "disarray at the highest levels of government." In particular, they cited the administration for failing to comply with the Boland Amendment and the Intelligence Oversight Act of 1980, which required the president to inform two congressional watchdog committees of CIA covert operations "in a timely fashion." Blaming Reagan for failing to live up to the constitutional mandate that "'the laws be faithfully executed,'" the report charged that a "cabal of the zealots" had taken control of the administration's foreign policy in key areas. Reagan officials failed to report the Iranian arms sales to Congress as required by law, the committees concluded. But the panels placed greater emphasis on the administration's attempt to pursue foreign policy goals already rejected by Congress, and concluded that Ronald Reagan bore "ultimate responsibility" for policies managed by aides.

Exhibit 14–19. U.S. Troops in Honduras, 1988.

Following the Iran-Contra hearings, Costa Rican President Oscar Arias Sanchez induced Guatemala, El Salvador, Honduras, and Nicaragua to agree to a five-nation Central American peace settlement. The 1987 accord, which won Arias the Nobel Peace Prize, required participants to increase political freedoms and lift states of siege, provide amnesty for political prisoners, prohibit use of territory for insurgencies against neighbors, and work toward negotiated cease-fires in El Salvador and Nicaragua. Perceiving the regional settlement as a means of reducing American influence in Central America, Nicaragua sought to implement the accord by permitting the reopening of opposition newspapers and radio stations. Congress responded to the Arias plan by refusing an administration request for continued military aid to the contras. The peace process quickened in early 1988 when the Sandinista government reversed a long-standing policy by agreeing to negotiate directly with the rebels over terms of a cease-fire. In turn, the House of Representatives rejected another administration military package by a 219–211 vote, although it approved $48 million for contra food, clothing, and medical supplies.

Stymied by Nicaraguan cooperation with the Arias plan and congressional refusal to fund the contras, Reagan reacted to a minor border clash between Sandinista regulars and Honduran-based contra rebels by sending 3200 troops to southern Honduras. Yet the soldiers stayed for only ten days and served merely as a symbolic show of American force. In April 1988, the Nicaraguan government and the contras agreed to a cease-fire which obliged both sides to negotiate the release of 3300 Sandinista-held political prisoners and the extension of political freedom to those contras willing to lay down arms and return home. Having spent over $200 million in aid to a failed insurgency since 1981, the Reagan administration now faced the final collapse of its Central American policy. Once again, American policymakers had allowed a narrowly focused Cold War vision to distract them from the realities of third world poverty and nationalism.

COLD WAR CATHARSIS

Reagan's presidency restored the Cold War militance of Truman and Kennedy. But changing conditions and an increasingly critical Congress seriously hampered the president's agenda in dealing with the Soviet Union. Following dissolution of the Solidarity labor movement and the 1981 declaration of martial law in Poland, Reagan expressed American outrage by banning the export of construction equipment destined for a gas pipeline linking Siberia to western Europe. But when these sanctions met disapproval from European allies, the president withdrew them. At the same time, he delayed negotiations over a new wheat deal with Moscow. Reagan had responded to farmer complaints by ending Carter's embargo on grain sales to the Soviets, but despite discomfort with the Polish situation, he completed a five-year wheat pact with the Russians in 1983.

Although the president vacillated on economic ties with the Soviet Union, he refused to retreat from campaign promises for revitalization of national defense. In the largest peacetime military buildup in American history, Congress approved an $18 billion increase in defense spending in 1981. The new budget included construction of neutron bombs, production of the B-1 bomber that Carter had cancelled, and creation of a rapid deployment force. By 1982, however, administration defense policy faced grass-roots opposition from the nationwide nuclear freeze movement. Reagan believed that both political parties had placed too much faith in arms control as a response to Soviet military increases, and that the Russians would surrender their advantages only if faced with the prospect of escalation. But critics like former defense secretary Robert McNamara contended that Soviet and American nuclear arsenals were equivalent and that further modernization of American weaponry would only provoke a corresponding Soviet buildup. Nuclear freeze advocates particularly objected to the president's casual remarks about "limited" nuclear war and the possibility of confining nuclear devastation to Europe. Working to pass resolutions and ballot measures in scores of towns, cities, and states, and amassing hundreds of thousands of demonstrators, activists brought the issue to Congress in 1982. The freeze campaign called for the president to propose a mutual and verifiable moratorium on the testing, deployment, and production of all nuclear weapons to the Soviets. Reagan pleaded that the resolutions would undermine SALT negotiations by weakening the bargaining position of the United States. Nevertheless, the House barely defeated freeze resolutions in a 204–202 vote.

By 1983, the Reagan administration moved toward a more flexible position on arms control, acknowledging for the first time that nuclear war should be deterred at all costs. The president also reversed himself by promising to refrain from undercutting the still-unratified SALT II treaty. The compromise continued when Congress voted funding for MX missiles in 1985 but limited deployment to half the one hundred missiles that Reagan requested. Meanwhile, the Democratic House placed severe restrictions on the president's military budget, limiting increases to a figure just above inflation in 1984 and below it in 1985. Just as Congress began to assert control over the administration's defense program, the president proposed a new anti-missile system in 1983. Based on the possible use of space satellites armed with laser weapons, the Strategic Defense Initiative (SDI), dubbed "Star Wars," intended to fend off Soviet missile attacks before

Soviet Secretary Gorbachev and President Reagan at the Geneva Summit of 1985, the first of four such meetings between the two superpower leaders.

they could penetrate American air space. Prominent scientists argued that research costs and labor would be astronomical and minimized the chances of developing the necessary technologies in the near future. Other critics noted that SDI could never act as a fool-proof shield and that true security lay in reducing the arms race, not introducing it to outer space. Congress responded cautiously to Reagan's proposals, appropriating no more than 20 percent of the first instalment in 1984. While doing so, the legislators permitted only three tests of anti-satellite missiles before prohibiting them altogether and trimming one-third of the SDI budget in 1986.

The Reagan administration increased military spending from $157 billion in 1981 to $233 billion in 1986. Yet Americans felt no greater sense of security in a tumultuous world endangered by the spread of nuclear weapons. Pressed by the anti-nuclear movement, Democratic congressional leaders, and Republican moderates, Reagan met with new Soviet leader Mikhail Gorbachev in Geneva during 1985, the first summit since 1979. Gorbachev expressed a desire for *"glasnost"* (openness) in both Soviet society and in relations between Moscow and Washington. Democratic reforms in Communist party governance, liberalization of censorship rules, and new freedoms for political dissenters and emigration applicants boosted Gorbachev's image in the Western press. Seeking to modernize the Soviet economy by redirecting defense spending to computers and consumer goods, the Russian leader persuaded Reagan to agree in principle to a 50 percent cut in nuclear weapons. The following year, the two leaders met at Reykjavik, Iceland, where they came close to a pact on the reduction of offensive nuclear weapons.

REV. JESSE L. JACKSON
1941

"God hasn't finished with me yet," Baptist minister Jesse L. Jackson told the 1984 Democratic National Convention after finishing third in the party's presidential sweepstakes. Four years later, Jackson stomped the country in a fiery campaign that compelled Democrats to seriously consider the nomination of a black for president. By 1988, Jackson's biracial reform agenda earned him the right to speak as the conscience of the Democratic party and as undisputed leader of American blacks and other minorities.

Jackson was the illegitimate son of a teenage domestic from the cotton mill town of Greenville, South Carolina. Raised in a three-room house with an open toilet on the back porch, he shined shoes, waited on tables, and caddied at the golf club before becoming quarterback on the state high school championship football team. Jackson won an athletic scholarship to the University of Illinois, but transferred to the predominately black North Carolina Agricultural and Technical College in Greensboro after Illinois placed him on academic probation in his first year. Arriving in Greensboro months after students initiated the 1960 lunch-counter sit-ins, he became star quarterback, student body president, and leader of the non-violent demonstrations that ultimately integrated downtown businesses.

Chosen for a Rockefeller Foundation grant, Jackson attended the Chicago Theological Seminary, but left one semester short of graduation to work with Martin Luther King's Southern Christian Leadership Conference. King made the young activist head of Operation Breadbasket—an SCLC campaign that used boycotts and mass picketing to win jobs and contracts for black workers and businesses. But the ambitious and individualistic Jackson received criticism for heavy-handed tactics in intimidating businesses and came into frequent conflict with King and his associates. In 1971, the SCLC suspended the young minister who wore his hair in a "natural" Afro and liked to appear in African dashiki robes, citing Jackson's lack of organizational loyalty and discipline. Jackson seized the opportunity to create his own Operation PUSH (People United to Save Humanity).

Chicago-based PUSH sought to build a national campaign to restore black pride. "I am somebody," Jackson chanted with the black youngsters he addressed; "I may be poor, but I am somebody." Jackson brought his self-help motivational programs into the public schools, where he crusaded against drug abuse, teenage pregnancy, truancy, and high drop-out rates. Between 1971 and 1983, PUSH attracted $17 million in government grants and private donations, although critics pointed to the organization's chaotic financing and poor management. "I'm a tree-shaker, not a jelly-maker," Jackson later explained.

During 1979, the Chicago leader took his message to South Africa and the Middle East. In Israel he preached acceptance of the Palestine Liberation Organization. But he *(cont.)*

(cont.) counseled Arabs to adopt non-violence, calling for a "freeze" in the armed struggle for Palestinian nationhood and recognition of Israel's right to exist. Nevertheless, a photograph of Jackson embracing PLO leader Yasser Arafat enraged American Jews, as did revelations that the Arab League had donated $200,000 to PUSH.

An influential supporter of Jimmy Carter in 1976 and 1980, Jackson left PUSH to mount voter registration drives in 1983. Following that year's election of Chicago black reform mayor Harold Washington, Jackson announced his candidacy for the presidency. Party leaders, he proclaimed, were "too silent and too passive" about Ronald Reagan's policies. Jackson promised to represent "the poor and dispossessed of this nation" and forge a "rainbow coalition" for those who were "rejected and...despised." Yet his campaign faltered when a black reporter revealed that the candidate had privately referred to Jews as "Hymies" and New York City as "Hymietown." Jackson apologized, but never managed to repair the estrangement with the Jewish community. Relations worsened when he was slow to disavow the support of Louis Farrakhan, a Nation of Islam black minister given to anti-Semitic rhetoric.

Seeking to broaden his agenda of human rights, Jackson met with Soviet leader Mikhail Gorbachev during the 1985 summit to plead for Soviet Jewry. The following year, he launched the National Rainbow Coalition, a diverse amalgam of peace activists, labor, environmentalists, farmers, liberals, and minorities. Having prevailed upon the Democratic party to adopt proportional representation in the primaries, Jackson announced his second candidacy for the presidency in late 1987. This time he combined traditional values of self-respect and hard work with a populist program of economic justice. Jackson proposed to tax corporate mergers and enact protections against plant closings and farm foreclosures. He spoke of "economic violence" against those "locked out of the system" and castigated multinational corporations for exploiting cheap overseas labor at the expense of thirty-eight million American jobs since 1973. Jackson proposed to invest 10 percent of all public employee pension funds in housing, mass transit, and the nation's infrastructure. And he promised to pay for essential education and health care by cutting defense spending and taxing corporate and individual wealth.

"If I can win, you can win. We the people can win!" Jackson told Americans in the 1988 primaries. Astounding political professionals, the candidate captured five southern primaries, several state caucuses, and finished a strong second in the overall delegate count. As a result, he played a major role at the Democratic Convention. Jackson succeeded in redefining the political debate by tying liberal programs to structural changes in the world economy. His 90 percent pluralities among black Democrats also brought the party in touch with an important constituency. "Even when we're not sure what Jesse is," a civil rights colleague from the 1960s observed, "we see ourselves in him." ■

Although the Iceland summit floundered on Reagan's refusal to abandon SDI research on space defense, the two leaders agreed to talk again. By December 1987, when Reagan and Gorbachev met for a third summit in Washington, the American president faced widespread criticism of his leadership during the Iran-Contra affair and sought to complete an arms deal as a legacy of his administration. The Senate, in which Democrats won a 55–45 majority in the 1986 elections, also pressed Reagan for progress on disarmament. As a result, the president signed an intermediate nuclear force (INF) treaty with Gorbachev. The pact called for the dismantling of 2611 Soviet and American medium and short-range missiles based in Europe, and provided for hundreds of inspectors to visit each side's installations—the most extensive system of weapons surveillance ever negotiated by the two nations.

One month before Reagan prepared to go to Moscow for a fourth summit in May 1988, the Soviets announced the scheduled withdrawal of 115,000 troops from Afghanistan. Signing on as a co-guarantor of the ensuing Geneva accords, the United States nevertheless extracted an agreement from Moscow that acknowledged Washington's right to arm Afghan Moslem rebels if the Soviets continued to supply the Marxist government in Kabul. The following month, the Senate ratified the INF treaty. Meanwhile, a report by a panel of distinguished Soviet officials and former American defense and intelligence officers urged the two superpowers to gradually demilitarize by cutting back forces and agreeing to an immediate comprehensive nuclear test ban. But despite the relaxation of Cold War tensions, Reagan's commitment to SDI minimized the chances for dramatic progress on nuclear disarmament.

As the Reagan administration drew to a close, presidential campaigners evaluated its eight year tenure with predictable results. Vice President George Bush, the Republican nominee, pointed to continued prosperity and economic opportunity, lower taxes, and a consistent foreign policy that brought the Soviets to the bargaining table without sacrificing American interests. Bush and his running mate, Indiana Senator James Danforth "Dan" Quayle III, reminded Americans that Ronald Reagan and the Republicans had sought to restore the nation's sense of greatness and destiny and had succeeded. In contrast, Democratic leaders such as Jesse Jackson and Massachusetts Governor Michael Dukakis attacked "Reaganomics" for its inflated military spending and federal budget deficits, as well as persistent trade imbalances and accompanying plant closures. Pressure from Bush and Republican officeholders led to the resignation of Attorney General Meese following an unfavorable ethics report by a government special counsel. Meanwhile, Dukakis and Texas Senator Lloyd Bentsen sought to unify the Democratic party by stressing that a competent administration could strengthen defense and the economy while providing equal opportunity and social services. But Dukakis's message faded as Bush repeatedly condemned "liberal" views on defense, patriotism, crime, and abortion. In their fifth victory in the last six presidential elections, the Republicans took 54 percent of the popular vote and a 426-112 margin in the Electoral College to take an easy victory in the 1988 contest.

As the United States moved toward the last decade of the century, its leaders continued to picture the nation as poised on the edge of greatness. Yet after nearly a century of frenzied economic development, vast political change, and intense global involvement, Americans found themselves part of a troubled and complex world in which uncertainty and confusion, not destiny, prevailed. Many sensed that they were on the edge of cataclysmic changes that not even their leaders could fathom. But whether their visions encompassed technological utopia, spiritual renaissance, or nuclear terror, most Americans realized that their future remained intricately connected to the frightening but fascinating planet they shared.

SUGGESTED READINGS

Ronald Reagan's political success is the subject of Hedrick Smith, *Reagan: The Man, the President* (1981); Robert Dallek, *Ronald Reagan: The Politics of Symbolism* (1984); and Michael P. Rogin, *Ronald Reagan the Movie, and Other Episodes in Political Demonology* (1987). See also William E. Leuchtenburg, *In The Shadow of FDR: From Harry Truman to Ronald Reagan* (1985) and Garry Wills, *Reagan's America: Innocents at Home* (1987). A less sympathetic view is Paul D. Erickson, *Reagan Speaks: The Making of an American Myth* (1985).

For the changing economic basis of American politics, see Kirkpatrick Sale, *Power Shift: The Rise of The Southern Rim and Its Challenge to the Eastern Establishment* (1975). Reagan's economic policies are critiqued in Thomas Byrne Edsall, *The New Politics of Inequality: How Political Power Shapes Economic Policy* (1984), and Greg J. Duncan, *Years of Poverty, Years of Plenty: The Changing Economic Fortunes of American Workers and Families* (1984). The last segments of Richard H. K. Vietor, *Energy Policy in America Since 1945: A Study of Business-Government Relations* (1984), contrast Carter and Reagan approaches toward energy.

Political conservatism in the 1980s is portrayed in the last sections of David W. Reinhard, *The Republican Right Since 1945* (1983), and in Kevin J. Phillips, *Post-Conservative America: People, Politics, and Ideology in a Time of Crisis* (1982). For an innovative view of 1980s conservatism, see Michael X. Carpini, *Stability and Change in American Politics: The Coming of Age of the Generation of the 1960s* (1986). An example of the new political mobilization of conservatives is Richard A. Viguerie, *The New Right: We're Ready to Lead* (1981). For a critical approach to emerging conservatism, see Thomas Ferguson and Joel Rogers, *Right Turn: The Decline of the Democrats and the Future of American Politics* (1987). See also Michael Nelson, *The Election of 1984* (1985).

The best synthesis of Reagan's relations with Moscow is provided in the relevant segments of Raymond L. Garthoff, *Détente and Confrontation: American-Soviet Relations from Nixon to Reagan* (1985). For the roots of the disarmament question, see Strobe Talbott, *Deadly Gambits: The Reagan Administration and the Stalemate in Nuclear Arms Control* (1984). Critical accounts of policy in Central America may be found in Raymond Bonner, *Weakness and Deceit: United States Polity and El Salvador* (1984), and Walter LaFeber, *Inevitable Revolutions: The United States in Central America* (1983). See also Jay Peterzell, *Reagan's Secret Wars* (1984).

INDEX